BOB DAVIS

Inside Windows NT Server

Drew Heywood

New Riders

New Riders Publishing, Indianapolis, Indiana

Inside Windows NT Server

By Drew Heywood

Published by:
New Riders Publishing
201 West 103rd Street
Indianapolis, IN 46290 USA

Printed in the United States of America 1 2 3 4 5 6 7 8 9 0

Heywood, Drew
Inside Windows NT Server / Drew Heywood
p. cm.
Includes index
ISBN 1-56205-472-4
1. Operating systems (Computers) 2. Microsoft Windows NT
I. Title.
TK5105.7.D85 1995
005.7'1369—dc20 95-23986
CIP

Warning and Disclaimer

This book is designed to provide information about the Windows NT Server computer program. Every effort has been made to make this book as complete and as accurate as possible, but no warranty or fitness is implied.

The information is provided on an "as is" basis. The author and New Riders Publishing shall have neither liability nor responsibility to any person or entity with respect to any loss or damages arising from the information contained in this book or from the use of the disks or programs that may accompany it.

Publisher *Don Fowley*
Associate Publisher *Tim Huddleston*
Marketing Manager *Ray Robinson*
Acquisitions Manager *Jim LeValley*
Managing Editor *Tad Ringo*

Acquisitions Editor
Alicia Buckley

Production Editor
Cliff Shubs

Copy Editors
Stacia Mellinger
Fran Blauw
Laura Frey
Anne Owen
Lisa Wilson

Technical Editors
John Flynn Matthew

Assistant Marketing Manager
Tamara Apple

Acquisitions Coordinator
Tracy Turgeson

Publisher's Assistant
Karen Opal

Cover Designer
Sandra Schroeder

Book Designer
Sandra Schroeder

Manufacturing Coordinator
Paul Gilchrist

Production Manager
Kelly Dobbs

Production Team Supervisor
Laurie Casey

Graphics Image Specialists
Dennis Clay Hager
Clint Lahnen
Dennis Sheehan

Production Analysts
Angela Bannan
Bobbi Satterfield

Production Team
Angela Calvert
Kimberly Cofer
David Garratt
Aren Howell
Aleata Howard
Shawn MacDonald
Beth Rago
Erich J. Richter
Regina Rexrode
Christine Tyner
Karen Walsh

Indexer
Bront Davis

About the Author

Drew Heywood has been involved in the microcomputer industry since he purchased an Apple IIe in 1979. For the past nine years, he has focused on networking. From 1991 through Februrary 1995, Drew was a product line manager at NRP, where he launched NRP's network book line and expanded the line to include some of the most successful book titles in the industry. Drew and his wife, Blythe, have most recently founded InfoWorks, Inc. to support his dual interests as a computer book author and a consultant. Drew was the author of NRP's *Inside NetWare, Fourth Edition,* and has contributed to several NRP books, including *Networking Technologies* and *CNE Short Course,* both of which are members of NRP's CNE Training Guide series.

Trademark Acknowledgments

Dedication

For Blythe.

Acknowledgments

No person or project succeeds on the efforts of one person. Although the words in this book are mine, the sources of these words are many and varied, for they could not have come about without the support of others.

My wife, Blythe, herself a seasoned professional in the computer business, understands the effort that is required to accomplish a major project such as this book. Without her support, there would be no book for these acknowledgments to accompany.

Karanjit Siyan and I have collaborated on a half dozen books, he as author, and I as project manager, all of which give me great pride. For over three years, he has been a source of encouragement and inspiration to me, and working with him was a major factor in preparing me for my new career as an independent author and consultant.

I learned something from every author I worked with at New Riders. Let me single out a few for special mention: Dorothy Cady, Deb Niedermiller, Brian Chaffin, Doug Bierer, Blaine Homer, and Larry Morris.

Many thanks are due to Microsoft. Without good products to write about and good support, I would be out of business. Windows NT Server is an excellent product, and I consider myself fortunate to have the opportunity to write about it. And Microsoft's support for publishers has provided me with ready access to the betas and the actual products that made this book possible. Special thanks are owed Tracy Van Hoof at Microsoft for all her supporting efforts.

Finally, my heartfelt thanks to the staff at New Riders Publishing for their support in the past and for giving me the opportunity to do this book. Everyone at NRP has been helpful to me, but there are some terrific debts I need to pay. Special thanks are due to Rob Tidrow for helping me make the transition as an independent author. Don Fowley was kind enough to offer me a great project to kick off my new career. During our year working together, Emmett Dulaney has been the source of much useful advice from which I continue to benefit. And, on my first project as an independent author, it was good to know that an editor as capable as Cliff Shubs would be leading the editorial team. Thank you NRP, one and all.

Contents at a Glance

Table of Contents

Part II: The Basics

New Riders Publishing

The staff of New Riders Publishing is committed to bringing you the very best in computer reference material. Each New Riders book is the result of months of work by authors and staff who research and refine the information contained within its covers.

As part of this commitment to you, the NRP reader, New Riders invites your input. Please let us know if you enjoy this book, if you have trouble with the information and examples presented, or if you have a suggestion for the next edition.

Please note, though: New Riders staff cannot serve as a technical resource for Windows NT Server or for related questions about software- or hardware-related problems. Please refer to the documentation that accompanies Windows NT Server or to the applications' Help systems.

If you have a question or comment about any New Riders book, there are several ways to contact New Riders Publishing. We will respond to as many readers as we can. Your name, address, or phone number will never become part of a mailing list or be used for any purpose other than to help us continue to bring you the best books possible. You can write us at the following address:

New Riders Publishing
Attn: Associate Publisher
201 W. 103rd Street
Indianapolis, IN 46290

If you prefer, you can fax New Riders Publishing at (317) 581-4670.

You can send electronic mail to New Riders at the following Internet address:

dheywood@iquest.net

NRP is an imprint of Macmillan Computer Publishing. To obtain a catalog or information, or to purchase any Macmillan Computer Publishing book, call (800)428-5331.

Thank you for selecting *Inside Windows NT Server*!

I

Introduction

No one can say that Microsoft is not persistent. In the mid 1980s, when I bought version 1.0 of Windows, nothing in the product indicated that two generations and nearly ten years later, Windows would become the dominant personal computer operating system with over 60 million copies in use by 1995. Microsoft might not succeed with a product the first or even the second time, but more often than not, they eventually produce a winning version that the market takes seriously.

Dominance in networking has consistently eluded Microsoft. Several generations of Microsoft network products have sought but failed to win the network marketing battle, but Windows NT Server version 3.5 has significantly altered the user community's feelings about networking with Microsoft products. After many attempts, Microsoft has produced a product with the performance, features, and reliability that organizations demand for their most critical networks.

Windows NT is an eclectic grab bag of good ideas from lots of products. It looks like Windows and is used like Windows, so lots of people already know quite a bit about using it, but underneath, Windows NT is completely new. Windows NT works a lot like Unix, and its design will satisfy most critical administrators, but most will find it a lot friendlier than Unix. Finally, Windows NT incorporates some of the best reliability features available, such as a roll-back capability that practically bulletproofs the Registry that is used to store configuration data for the server.

In many ways, however, Windows has burst the bounds of previous products, and Windows NT Server builds in features that are often add-ons. Among features that leap to mind are the ability to automatically replicate directories among servers and the ability to configure RAID level 5 drives using only conventional hardware and software built into the Windows NT operating system.

Because Windows NT can be a desktop platform, a network file server, and an application server, many organizations regard Windows NT as an opportunity to consolidate their networks around a single operating system that is friendly, versatile, and powerful.

Who Should Read This Book

This book targets two groups of readers:

- New network administrators. If Windows NT Server is your first encounter with network software, you will find all the help you need, both to get started and to succeed.
- Experienced administrators who are making the transition to Windows NT Server. If you are already comfortable with networks, the organization of this book will help you become productive efficiently.

I assume that readers come to this book with some working familiarity with Windows. With 60 million copies of Windows in use, that seems like a safe bet. Consequently, I do not spent any time teaching you how to use a mouse, control Windows, or use tools such as Notepad. If you are completely new to Windows, please consult a beginners book to become comfortable with the user interface.

Beyond that, however, I have supplied everything you should need. For beginners, I've included some background information in the early chapters, along with some theory about networking. The book is organized in a logical sequence that takes you from equipment and software in boxes, to a working network.

Experienced network administrators might want to skip or skim the introductory material and cut to the chase. You should still find the chapter sequence helpful, but I've carefully concentrated related material into chapters that focus on specific topics. This approach is designed to make the book a useful reference that enables you to locate answers to your questions efficiently.

How This Book Is Organized

When I was planning the outline for this book, I noticed that the Microsoft manuals, as well as other Windows NT books, were organized around the utilities. You will see a chapter that tells you everything about the User Manager for Domains, for example. The problem with this approach, however, is that most of the Windows NT Server utilities perform a wide variety of tasks. Yes, User Manager for Domains is responsible for managing user accounts, but it is also used to establish domain trust relationships, which logically belong in a separate chapter from user accounts. A simple utility for managing server properties is responsible for tasks as diverse as monitoring user sessions, maintaining shares, replicating directories, and handling alerts.

As a result, I chose to organize this book around topics and tasks. If a utility performs tasks in several areas, a given chapter focuses on features of the utility that are related to the chapter's focus. You might see material on a given utility, such as Server Manager, in several chapters, but I think the topic focus will make it much easier for you to learn about Windows NT Server, to get your network up and running, and to answer your questions as they arise.

Unless you have some experience with Windows NT Server, I recommend that you approach the chapters in this book in sequence. In general, the chapters follow each other logically, and you will often need some understanding of previous chapters to comprehend the current chapter.

You need, for example, a good understanding of domains and groups before you can understand how privileges are assigned to users. So don't skip the chapters on domains with the intent of quickly adding some user accounts so that users are up and running. If you stick to the chapter outline, you will build your knowledge of Windows NT Server on a firm foundation.

After you have gained some experience, however, you should be able to skip around the book as required to isolate the specific information you need.

Finally, a word about what I had to leave out. Windows NT Server is a really big product. Microsoft's documentation exceeds 4,000 pages, so it wasn't possible for me to cover everything there is to know about Windows NT Server. In fact, I doubt that any one book could exhaust the topic. This book is intended to be a first book on Windows NT Server for new and experienced network administrators. My focus is to give you the information you need most and to make the information as accessible as possible.

For some readers, however, there can never be enough detail. If you finish this book and still crave more information about the nuts and bolts of Windows NT Server, look for NRP's *Windows NT Server: The Professional Reference* in late 1995. Written by Karanjit Siyan, this book will provide the same detailed coverage of Windows NT Server that NetWare administrators have come to expect from his *NetWare: The Professional Reference,* which is now in its fourth edition and sets the standard for NetWare references.

Keep In Touch

No book is perfect. I am sure that I have missed topics readers want to know about, and I haven't seen a computer book yet that hasn't had an error or two. So I would like to hear from you, whether your words are blessings or curses. What questions have I left unanswered? What tips have I left unmentioned? How can I make the next edition of this book better? Please let me know.

You can send e-mail to me on CompuServe at 76415,140 or on the Internet at dheywood@iquest.net. Also, feel free to send letters to me care of NRP. Schedules and deadlines might prevent me from replying as promptly as you would like, but I will respond as quickly as possible.

Thank you for buying my book. Thank you for reading it. And thank you in advance for letting me know what you think.

Part I

Background Information

New Riders Publishing
INSIDE
SERIES

CHAPTER 1

Understanding Networks

If you have never managed a network before, this chapter is written especially for you. Don't skip it, however, just because you have some experience. Although nothing in this chapter is essential to understanding the rest of the book, it does serve a purpose—to get you in the right frame of mind. Local area network (LAN) administration is a challenging profession, and the right mindset will help you succeed.

Every experienced LAN administrator has been exposed to the highs and lows of a crazy business. One day you can be a hero for helping a critical project meet its deadline; the next you're a goat because someone lost an important file. Never mind whether or not it's the network's fault; you'll be blamed. I know of an organization that typically operates with better than 99.5 percent uptime—7 days a week, 24 hours a day—with users who complain vehemently that the LAN isn't reliable enough. In other words, the pressure on a LAN administrator can be severe.

This book's goal is to make you a hero, but it takes some effort to win your LAN hero medal. The goal of this book is to help you succeed in each of the following areas:

- Know everything you can about your LAN
- Design your LAN for reliability
- Make your LAN easy to use
- Anticipate problems before they become serious
- Fix problems promptly when they occur
- Have a disaster plan

Task-by-task, section-by-section, *Inside Windows NT Server* shows you how to succeed as a LAN administrator.

This chapter starts with a general discussion of LANs to give you an understanding of the technologies you will encounter as an administrator of a Windows NT Server LAN. Armed with this information, you will be better prepared to learn the many job skills that are presented in later chapters.

What Is a Network?

A network consists of hardware (servers, workstations, cables, printers, and so forth) and software (such as operating systems and applications). Following chapters tackle these hardware and software components. Before digging in to the details, however, you should look at networking in more general terms.

Even if you have never used a PC on a network, you have experience with networking. Every time you make a telephone call, you use a network with some amazing properties. By pressing a few buttons, you can connect your telephone to virtually any other telephone in the world. This remarkable capability is so invisible for us, we usually take it for granted. Do you ever think about the steps required to place a long-distance call between California and New York?

It seems simple, but the process is quite complicated. Automated systems at a central office in California must connect the wire from your phone to a long-distance service, which routes your call to the correct central office in New York through a combination of cables, microwave links, or communication satellites. In New York, the central office must connect the call to the wires running to the telephone you are calling. Each of these steps must happen quickly, reliably, and invisibly millions of times a day.

We telephone users are fortunate because teams of highly trained communication technicians and engineers keep the entire process running smoothly. If you were responsible for running the public telephone network, you would need to know a great deal about media, signaling, switching hardware, and so forth. As users, however, we do not see these details.

As a LAN administrator, however, you will become responsible for just this sort of thing. You will be managing the cabling system that enables your LAN to communicate. You will probably be required to install the hardware that enables your users' PCs to connect to the network. Your servers will require frequent attention. Like it or not, you will need to learn the skills of network engineering.

Fortunately, a LAN isn't as complicated as a worldwide telephone network. In fact, network administration has become progressively easier over the years. Windows NT Server makes it possible to build powerful networks that are easy to administer.

Chapter 3, "Understanding Network Administration," provides a job description of a LAN administrator. Before rushing into the actual tasks of running a LAN, however, you should be familiar with basic LAN theory.

What Are the Components of a Network?

All networks—even the most complicated—contain the same three basic types of building blocks.

- Devices that provide network services
- Devices that use network services
- Something that enables the devices to communicate

You will now look at each item with regard to the public telephone network. A good example of a telephone service is the time and temperature service. Another example is the service provided by many banks that enables you to call in and obtain your account balances by keying in the account number and a pass code. Whenever you call one of these services, you become a service user.

To enable you, a service user, to communicate with a service provider, the telephone company provides a network of cables and switches. These cables and switches connect your telephone to the service and carry information between the two.

The remainder of this section examines these network components in the context of a computer network. In the process, the section explores the types of devices that function as service providers, service users, and communications facilitators.

Servers Provide Services

For a long time, the most common types of service providers on networks were called *file servers*, although they typically provide at least the following two basic types of service:

- Sharing access to files
- Sharing access to networked printers

Historically, these services were the first to attract users to LANs. Even low-end printers were expensive, and users felt a strong incentive to share them. Although various types of printer-sharing devices are available, a network server remains the most effective means of sharing printers. Network servers have many advantages; Chapter 12, "Managing Printing Services," discusses these advantages in greater detail.

File services were also significant incentives for setting up LANs. Until LANs became affordable, sharing files meant swapping media. A few files could be exchanged on floppy disks. Large numbers of files required the use of tape data cartridges. *Sneakernet*, my favorite network pseudo-technical term, describes the process of literally running around to exchange files on floppy disks. File services enable computers on the networks to share their files with other computers, transferring them through the network media.

File and print services can be provided by running special software on users' PCs. This software enables users to share files on their hard drives, as well as any printers attached to their PCs. This approach is called *peer-to-peer networking* because all PCs on the LAN are basically equal.

A contrasting approach uses a special centralized server to provide file and print services. The centralized server is usually called a *dedicated server* because it is devoted entirely to providing file and print services.

Centralized servers generally are based on fairly powerful hardware—high-end Intel PCs or RISC systems are commonly used. These systems have to be fast because they must service the needs of many users. Dedicated servers typically have a great deal of memory and hard drive capacity (often tens of gigabytes).

Dedicated servers usually have features that improve their reliability. Fault-tolerant features enable the server to continue functioning even when a component fails. Extra hard disks that mirror primary disks are common fault-tolerant features. When the primary disk fails, the mirror disk takes over without interruption of service.

Figure 1.1 illustrates a typical centralized server. Starting with this figure, you can begin to build a picture of a complete LAN.

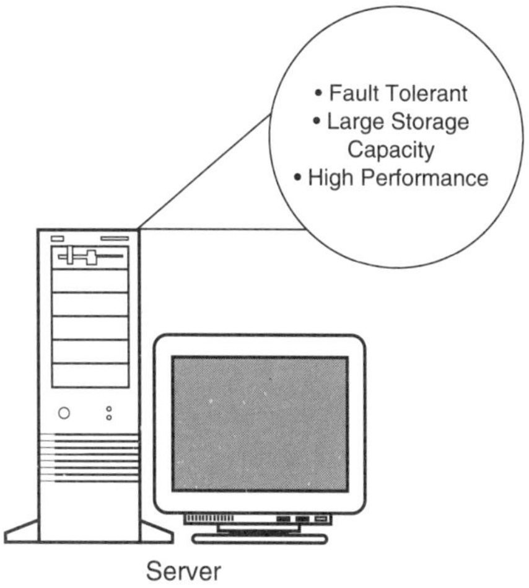

Figure 1.1

A network starts with a server.

Clients Use Services

A *client* is anything on a network that uses the services that a server provides. The term client comes from a metaphor based on servers in restaurants. The servers provide food services that are consumed by the restaurant clients. Because so much networking is based on service providers and clients, this model of networking is typically called *client/server* computing.

The most common clients are user workstations, and virtually any PC can be turned into a network client. Many PCs are now factory-equipped with network interface boards. All Macintosh computers are network-ready, as are virtually all Unix workstations. Manufacturers have made it increasingly easy to network computers because the majority of computers now being purchased end up attached to a network.

It is important to understand the difference between client/server computing and the older terminal/host computing, which is typically employed with mainframe computers. A terminal is a dumb device with no computing capability. In a terminal/host environment, the terminal accepts user input and displays data to users, but all computing is performed by the central mainframe.

In client/server computing, the client is a powerful computer in its own right. The client may request data from the server, but most of the actual computing is performed in the client computer. Although the client uses the network to share files, printers, and other resources, it can perform most functions quite well without the network.

This book introduces several types of clients. In Microsoft networking environments, the most common clients probably run some version of Microsoft Windows; this book, therefore, focuses on Windows clients. DOS clients, however, are also supported and are covered in another chapter.

Clients are typically highly individualized, configured for the needs of diverse users. Figure 1.2 illustrates the network you are constructing, which now consists of a server and a client.

Figure 1.2

Network with a server and client.

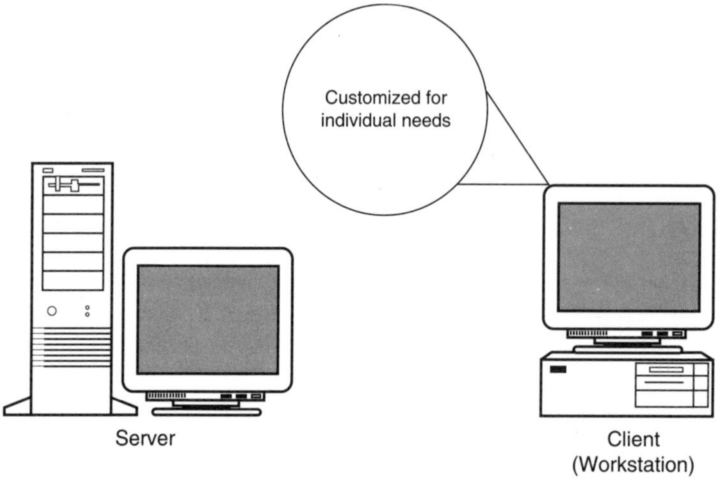

Note The distinction between peer-to-peer networks and centralized server networks is significant. Both network types are supported by Microsoft products, and you want to choose the correct approach for the needs of your organization.

Centralized server networks are based on specialization. The server is often over-designed to provide fast, reliable service. Critical data stored in a centralized location can be easily protected. Security is easier to maintain if the operating system (OS) is designed with tight security in mind, and it is easier to administer security if data has been stored in one place. Many desktop operating systems have no provisions for security. Others provide some security but not enough for critical data.

Peer-to-peer networks enable every PC on the network to function as both a server and a client. This type of network eliminates the need for an expensive server but does have several drawbacks. Files are spread out over many workstations, making it difficult to back them up. Security is difficult to maintain. Desktop PCs are seldom as reliable as a centralized server. Do you have an uninterruptible power supply on your desktop PC so that you won't lose data during a power outage?

Peer-to-peer networks can be cumbersome to administer as well. When users share files on their PCs, they must maintain a list of who in the organization can access the files. Each PC has its own access control list. When staff changes occur, each user must update the access control list on his or her PC (could add up to a great many changes).

For informal sharing of files and services, a peer-to-peer approach might work fine. When networking is a mission-critical activity for your organization, however, opt for a centralized server.

Communications Media Interconnect Servers and Clients

Something must be present to enable servers and clients to communicate. That something is called the network *medium.* The range of available media is extremely broad. Copper cable, fiber-optic cable, and microwave links represent just a few examples. Leave the more exotic media—such as satellite microwave links—to the experts. On the other hand, you probably will become very familiar with the cables and other media located within the walls of your organization. Because different media are associated with different types of networks, this section marks a good place to discuss network types.

Local area networks (LANs) typically are confined to a single building or suite of buildings, although LANs can grow to a size of several square miles. Because LANs typically include large numbers of computers, media are often selected for low cost. The most common media used with LANs are copper cables, which offer excellent performance at moderate cost. Fiber-optic cabling can be used on LANs, particularly for longer cable runs or for high-speed connections. Fiber-optic cable costs considerably more than copper, however, and few organizations choose to run fiber to users' workstations.

The most important characteristics of LANs for you to remember are high performance and low cost. Local area networks tend to be inherently reliable, so little extra emphasis is placed on reliability.

When networks grow larger than a few square miles, they typically are called wide area networks (WANs). A WAN can cover a city, a country, or even the world. The media used for WANs are generally quite different from the media used for LANs.

WANs must cope with the problems of communicating across public streets and crossing international borders; only large organizations with deep pockets can create private wide area networks. For most of us, wide area networking involves purchasing communication services from a service provider. Options include leasing a dedicated circuit from a public telephone service, renting communication capability on a satellite link, or subscribing to a public data network. Figure 1.3 illustrates a network that incorporates several types of LAN and WAN media.

Figure 1.3

A network with LAN and WAN components.

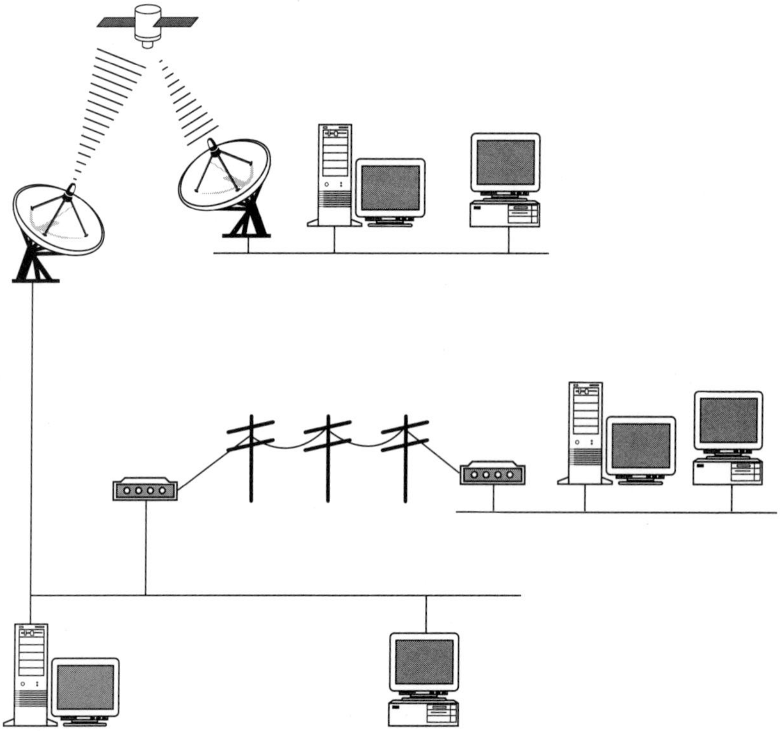

Compared to LANs, WANs are quite costly. You generally pay based on the data-carrying capacity your organization requires. Most services require you to reserve a specific capacity, which you pay for whether you use it or not. Services are emerging, however, that enable you to pay a basic rate and access higher levels of service as needed.

With WANs, you don't have to worry about the actual media being used. The service provider supplies it. However, a wide variety of service types is available. If you are setting up a WAN, familiarize yourself with the options so that you can choose the most cost-effective service for your organization's needs.

Compared to LANs, WANs tend to offer lower performance and to cost much more. The costs of running a WAN directly relate to the amount of network traffic the WAN must support. Long-distance networks tend to be less reliable than LANs, and special effort goes into ensuring network reliability.

Chapter 4, "Planning and Installing Network Media," expands on this basic discussion of media.

Network Operating Systems Run Servers

A computer is nothing without an operating system (OS). The OS is the software that gives the computer its basic capability to communicate, store data, and run programs. You are almost certainly experienced at using one or more workstation operating systems, such as DOS, Windows, Windows NT, or Unix.

Because it must potentially service the needs of tens or hundreds of users, a file/print server typically is a fairly heavy-duty computer. A server, therefore, requires a heavy-duty operating system. A network operating system (NOS) must be powerful enough to service many users simultaneously. A NOS also must be reliable because those users are dependent on it to perform their work. You probably have to reboot your PC occasionally when it hangs up. Would you be as comfortable rebooting a network server supporting hundreds of users?

Microsoft Windows NT Server is the NOS considered in this book. Windows NT Server is actually the fourth generation of Microsoft network operating systems. The evolution is as follows:

- **MS-NET.** Microsoft developed and licensed it to other vendors but never distributed directly.
- **LAN Manager.** A NOS based on OS/2 version 1.3.
- **Windows NT Advanced Server.** Based in Windows NT version 3.1
- **Windows NT Server.** The current product, which derives from the latest version of Windows NT, version 3.5.

With each generation, Microsoft has improved performance and reliability. Windows NT Server is a world-class NOS that competes effectively in the network marketplace with other products, such as Novell NetWare, IBM LAN Server, and Banyan VINES.

In addition to providing file, print, and other services, a NOS must be capable of maintaining network security. Businesses appreciate LANs because they offer dependable and inexpensive computing services. Business managers, however, need to know that critical information cannot be accessed by competitors or unauthorized staff. (The majority of computer crimes are inside jobs, regardless of all the media coverage of hackers breaking into computers.) Windows NT Server is capable of establishing a high level of network security. Maintaining security is one of the network administrator's most critical jobs. Several chapters in this book explore security concerns, including Chapter 9, "Managing Domains and Trust Relationships," and Chapter 10, "Managing Users and Groups."

Figure 1.4 adds the Windows NT Server NOS to the file server.

Figure 1.4

The network server requires a network operating system.

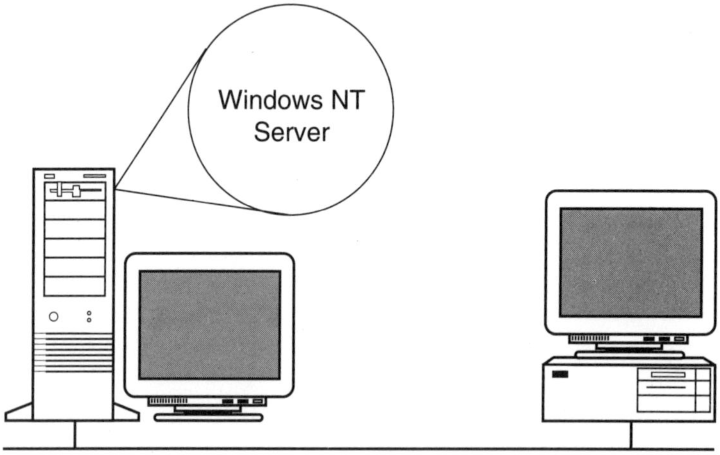

Workstation Operating Systems Run Workstations

Network workstations, or *clients*, also require operating systems. The needs for a workstation OS are less stringent than for a network OS. Operating systems have become increasingly sophisticated, however, and some offer capabilities that make then nearly as powerful as a NOS.

Although DOS has long been the dominant desktop operating system, it is gradually diminishing in popularity. Some users have come to appreciate graphical user environments. Others require higher levels of reliability than DOS provides. Still others need operating systems that can support large amounts of memory or that can multitask. The latest generations of workstation operating systems offer each of these advantages over good old DOS. A modern networking strategy must be capable of supporting most, if not all, of these more advanced operating systems.

As workstation OSes have evolved, they have taken on many of the features of network OSes. You can, in fact, create complete networks using nothing but Windows for Workgroups, Windows NT Workstation, Macintoshes, or Unix. In most cases, however, these networks are based on peer-to-peer resource sharing, and the need for a dedicated network operating system remains.

Figure 1.5 illustrates a network supporting several different types of client workstations.

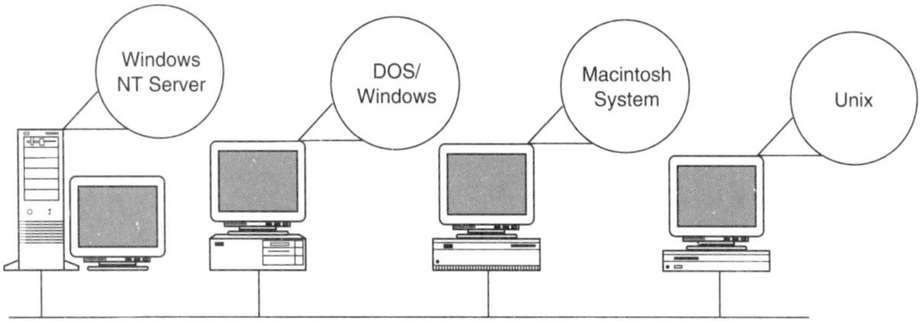

Figure 1.5
A server supporting several types of clients.

Other Servers Enhance Network Services

File and print services aren't the only kinds of services a network can provide. There are many types of communication servers, for example:

- **Mail servers.** Enable users to exchange electronic mail with users in the same building or in offices throughout the world.
- **Modem servers.** Enable users to share a pool of modems for dialing in to or out of the network. Having a separate modem for each person in your office is not necessary.
- **Fax servers.** Enable users to send and receive faxes through the network. Users can send faxes electronically without having to print copies. Incoming faxes can be routed to users much like e-mail, without a single paper document.
- **Gateways.** Enable users to communicate with mainframe or minicomputers, or with outside networks such as the Internet.

Figure 1.6 illustrates some of the possibilities a network has in offering users a wide variety of services.

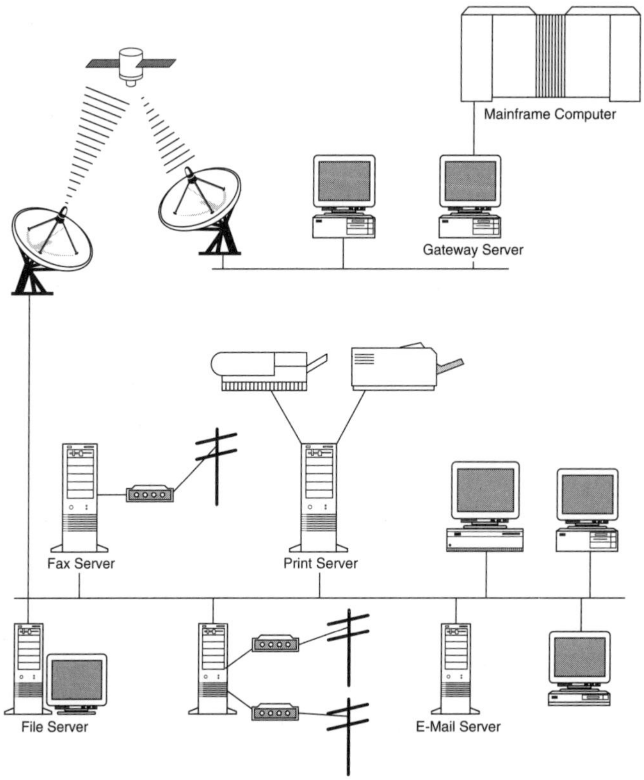

Figure 1.6
A modern LAN offers a wide variety of services.

So, How Hard Is This Stuff?

Fortunately, LANs are built from relatively small building blocks. You can begin networking with little more than a server and a couple workstations. You then can expand your understanding by adding other types of workstations and by providing more types of services.

Windows NT Server is one of the easiest ways yet invented to build a powerful network; it's easy to install and to administer. If you have used Windows, you are already familiar with much you need to know about networking with Windows NT Server.

If you are new to networking, Chapter 3, "Understanding Network Administration," should be your next step. Chapter 3 examines your job description as a LAN administrator. It explains that the challenge you face isn't so much in terms of difficulty as it is in number (of challenges). You need to learn about hardware, software, servers, workstations, printers, utilities, and operating systems. You must learn a great deal, but this book will help you.

Chapter 4, "Planning and Installing Network Media," marks the beginning of this book's gradual approach to teaching you networking. It teaches one area of networking pretty thoroughly and then moves on to the next. In my mind, that's a key to learning—take on one challenge at a time, master it, and move on. If you try to understand the entire process at once, it will overwhelm you. Remember, "Yard-by-yard, it's hard; but inch-by-inch, it's a cinch."

A Formal Approach to Defining a Network

Up to this point, this book has described network concepts in pretty general terms. As you work through it, however, a more formal set of definitions that can be used to organize your knowledge becomes necessary.

Because the Open Systems Integration (OSI) reference model provides a common framework for depicting the organization of network components, practically every book about networking discusses it. The OSI reference model was originally intended to serve as a blueprint for a complete set of network protocols. The protocols have not taken root, but the reference model has.

The OSI reference model works on the premise that a complex task is most easily performed by breaking that task down into subtasks. If you were an engineer designing a car, would you take on the entire challenge at once—body, engine, chassis, suspension, electronics, and so on? Or would you start with one part, the body style, for example, and then design the other systems to work with the body you have selected? Some designers start one place, some others, but few start by trying to plan every nut and bolt at once.

When the task of network communication is broken down into subtasks, solutions for the subtasks are easier to design. This building-block concept offers another benefit as well—if properly implemented, the various subtask solutions can be treated as building blocks so that different large communication problems can be solved by choosing different building blocks.

The following is an example of a communication process in everyday life: mailing a letter. This process requires several steps:

1. You print the letter at your computer.

2. You insert the letter in an envelope and address the envelope according to a standard address format that includes the recipient's company mail stop code. You also might indicate whether the letter is to be routed by standard mail or overnight.

3. You drop the letter in a pickup box.

4. A mail clerk picks up your letter and puts it in a clearly marked box for pickup by the desired carrier.

5. The appropriate carrier picks up the box, which contains dozens of letters, and transports the box to the carrier's depot.

6. At the depot, machines and people sort the items into containers to be sent to the desired destination. The carrier probably has evolved elaborate procedures to ensure that this process happens efficiently and reliably.

7. Another mail carrier picks up the box and transports it to the recipient's office.

8. A mail clerk sorts the items and delivers each one to the appropriate recipient.

9. The recipient retrieves the envelope, opens it, and receives your message.

I'm not telling you this because I don't think you know how mail is delivered. But I do want to emphasize that even the everyday process of delivering mail is, in fact, quite complex.

If you had to reinvent the entire process each time you sent a letter, would you try? Or, imagine if each letter you sent had to include complete instructions on what would happen to it every step of the way. Would you bother sending much mail? Fortunately, because each subprocess has clearly established procedures, one simple address is all your letter needs to get through the system and to the correct receiver.

The key to making the mail system work is a layered approach. Each layer in the process concentrates on its relationship with adjacent layers, and does not worry about the entire process. The postal service does not need to understand your company's internal mail distribution system and can ignore your internal zip code. Each layer focuses on its specific job and assumes that other layers do the same.

Also of note, some of the steps in the process can change without affecting others. If the mail clerk wants to send the letter by overnight express rather than the postal service, a simple modification to step 4 can redirect the letter and substitute a different service in steps 5, 6, and 7. None of these changes has any significant effect on the procedures in steps 1, 2, 3, 8, or 9.

The OSI Reference Model

Figure 1.7 illustrates the layered approach taken by the OSI reference model. The process of network communication is divided into seven layers. You will work more closely with some of these layers than with others. This section examines each of the layers so that you can understand the relevance of the model to your activities as a LAN administrator.

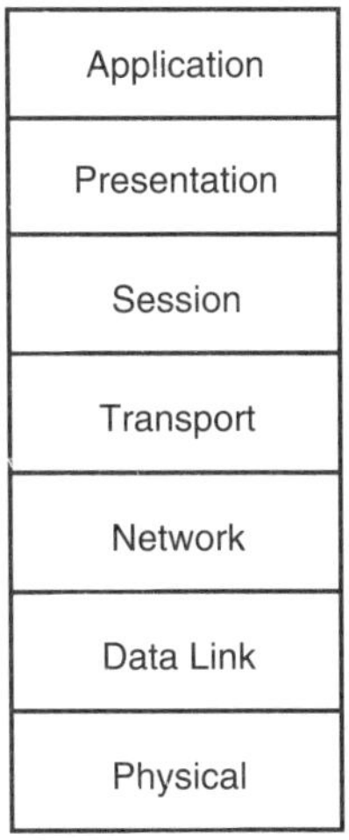

Figure 1.7
The seven layers of the OSI reference model.

Note You never know when you and your fellow LAN administrators will want to sit around and recite the layers of the OSI model while seeking cosmic truth in an infinite universe. It's kind of a LAN administrator's mantra that shows you've arrived at a higher level of understanding. To help you on the path of enlightenment, here's a catch phrase that lists the first letters of the layer names in order:

All

People

Seem

To

Need

Data

Processing

It's an easy phrase to remember, and helps LAN administrators feel indispensable.

The Physical Layer

The *physical layer* is concerned with the way data signals are transmitted on the network medium. At this level, the network transmits and receives individual bits. Higher layers break messages into bits prior to transmission and then reassemble these bits into messages as they are received.

The OSI physical layer does not define the medium itself, just the signaling methods to be used. Designers of physical layer protocols, however, must be aware of the characteristics of the signaling medium to some degree.

Note The OSI reference model ignores media; it is concerned with *protocols* (the rules that govern network communication).

The data communication industry borrowed the term *protocol* from the process of diplomatic communication. Government ambassadors obey complex protocols to ensure that communications are clear and inoffensive.

Each layer of the model is associated with one or more protocols, which are carefully defined standards for carrying out the functions assigned to that layer. Physical layer protocols define the way signals are to be transmitted and received, but they do not describe the cabling or other media.

Although the OSI model ignores media, we as LAN administrators cannot. Occasionally, media is described as an unofficial "layer zero" of the OSI reference model.

The Data Link Layer

The *data link layer* performs the following tasks:

- Fragments messages into bits for transmission by the physical layer.
- Reassembles bits received by the physical layer into messages.
- Establishes node-to-node communication and manages the flow of data between nodes. (Every device that communicates on the network is a *node*.) This process is called logical link control (LLC).
- It checks for errors in transmission. This is also a logical link control function.
- Controls access to the communication medium. Most networks can support only one transmission at a time. The data link layer implements media access control (MAC) protocols to ensure that nodes have the opportunity to transmit but do not conflict.
- Assigns a *node address* to each device on the network and uses the node addresses to enable devices to receive messages that are intended for them.

The data link layer is typically divided into two sublayers: LLC and MAC (see fig. 1.8). The MAC sublayer works very closely with the physical layer. The MAC and physical layers, in fact, are frequently defined by the same standards. Ethernet (IEEE 802.3) and token ring (IEEE 802.5) are standards that define MAC and physical layer functions. Chapter 4, "Planning and Installing Network Media," discusses both of these standards.

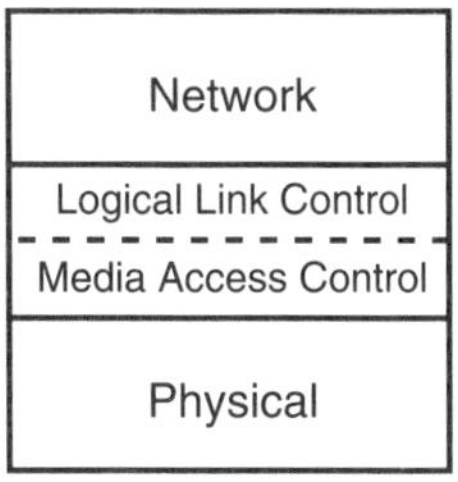

Figure 1.8
The data link layer consists of two sublayers: MAC and LLC.

Note Together, the physical and MAC layers work much like an old-time telegraph operator and a telegraph line. The sending telegraph operator is given a message to be transmitted in the form of words and phrases. He converts the text into a series of dots and dashes. The receiving operator must reverse the process and reassemble the dots and dashes into letters, words, and finally phrases.

Computer networks use encoding schemes that are similar in many ways to the Morse dot-and-dash code. Data are converted into strings of ones and zeroes for transmission on the network medium and are reassembled into data frames at the receiving node. A common code for converting character data to bits is ASCII, which assigns a number to each letter and symbol. The capital letter A has an ASCII value of 65, which can be represented by the binary number 01000001.

The messaging unit at the data link layer is usually called a *frame*. Each frame consists of a string of bits that are grouped into fields. Figure 1.9 illustrates the fields in a generic MAC frame. The fields are as follows:

- Two address fields identify the physical addresses of the source and destination nodes of the frame. Physical addresses—also called MAC addresses because they are used at the MAC layer—are typically programmed into network cards when they are manufactured and provide a unique means of identifying each node on the network.
- A data field includes all data that has been sent down from the upper layers.
- An error control field enables the receiving node to determine whether errors occurred in transmission of the frame.

Figure 1.9

The structure of a generic data link frame.

Destination Address	Source Address	Data	Error Control

The Network Layer

The *data link layer* performs communication in a fairly simplistic manner, by transmitting a frame on the media. Each node on the network examines all frames that are transmitted and receives only those frames that identify that node in the frame destination address.

This approach to communication works fine on simple networks, but networks seldom remain simple. Consider the network in figure 1.10. If every message were transmitted through every possible path, the network would quickly become saturated with redundant message units. The *network layer* routes messages efficiently and reliably through a complex network.

Note Complex networks such as the one shown in figure 1.10 are frequently called *internetworks* to distinguish them from simple networks.

Figure 1.10

The network layer routes messages through complex networks.

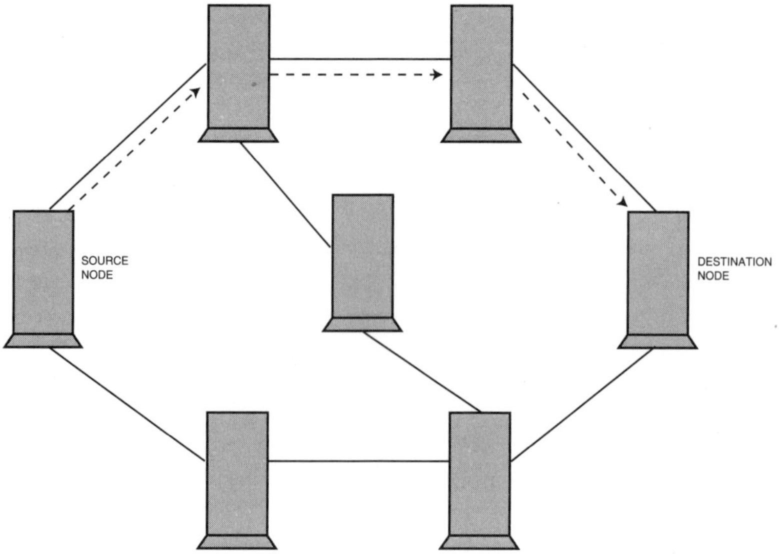

The unit of information at the network layer is the *packet*, and it is the network layer's responsibility to transmit packets through the internetwork. The process of delivering packets through an internetwork is called *routing*.

Windows NT Server supports two primary network protocols: IPX, the standard protocol for NetWare; and IP, a protocol in the TCP/IP protocol suite. Since TCP/IP is the most widely used network protocol, you probably will internetwork your Windows NT Servers with IP, which is discussed in Chapter 15, "Using TCP/IP."

Windows NT Server also supports the NetBEUI protocol, the *NetBIOS Extended User Interface*. NetBEUI is a protocol that was designed to support networking on small, simple networks, and performs very well in that role. NetBEUI, however, cannot be routed through an internetwork, and Microsoft is de-emphasizing NetBEUI as support for IPX and TCP/IP are improved.

Other protocols supported by Windows NT Server are Data Link Control and AppleTalk. Data Link Control (DLC) is a protocol used to communicate with printers that attach directly to the network. AppleTalk is the protocol used by Macintosh computers, and is supported by the Windows NT Server Services for Macintosh.

The Transport Layer

The network layer does not check for errors. It transmits a packet and assumes that the packet will arrive at the chosen destination. Because LANs are generally highly reliable, this assumption can be a fairly safe. In many cases, however, errors cannot be tolerated. Suppose you transfer $5,000 from your savings to your checking account. Would you be satisfied if a network error enabled the withdrawal but prevented the deposit?

Service as provided by the network layer is called *unreliable service*. The word unreliable doesn't mean that errors occur frequently, only that errors are not detected.

The *transport layer* adds *reliable service* to the network. Reliable service detects errors and, when detected, retransmits messages.

To provide reliable service, Windows NT Server supports two transport protocols. One is SPX, which is a companion protocol to IPX in the NetWare protocol suite. Also supported is the TCP protocol in the TCP/IP protocol suite. TCP is an extremely robust protocol that can cope with a wide variety of network difficulties.

The Session Layer

The layers discussed thus far are concerned with the delivery of single messages. The *session layer* deals with dialogs between nodes and adds a lot of new rules to the basic rules established by the network layer.

When two nodes begin a dialog, they are establishing a *session*. They negotiate to establish the rules of communication and the protocols to be used. They might go through a security procedure where the nodes establish their identities and grant each other access. In the process, the nodes establish what each is permitted to do. When a user establishes a session with a file server, for example, the server probably restricts the user's access to specific server resources.

When a workstation connects to a Windows NT Server, it undergoes a login process in which the user's identity is verified and a session is established. Once the user is recognized by the security procedures, the workstation is permitted to become a network client and to access server resources.

The Presentation Layer

The *presentation layer* is frequently defined incorrectly, in part because the name is somewhat confusing. The presentation layer presents data from the session layer to the application layer. In doing so, the presentation layer might need to convert data from one format to a format required by the application layer.

The presentation layer does not present data to the user and has nothing to do with displaying information on the computer screen.

Several types of data format conversion can be performed at the presentation layer, including data encryption, data compression, and format conversion.

The Application Layer

The *application layer* is also often a source of confusion. This layer does not correspond to end-user applications such as word processors. Rather, the application layer enables user applications to interface smoothly with the network.

The following is a list of some of the functions performed at the application layer:

- Remote file access
- File transfer
- Remote program access
- Directory services that catalog network resources
- Remote job execution

Often, the application layer functions are performed by workstation and server operating systems, and Windows NT Server can be regarded as providing application layer services.

Comments on the OSI Reference Model

Although the OSI reference model is a useful tool for understanding network protocols, none of the protocols you will encounter exactly fit the model. This discrepancy is particularly true of the TCP/IP protocol suite, which was developed prior to the OSI reference model and consists of four layers.

The lack of an exact fit, however, does not diminish the usefulness of the reference model. It is a useful tool for organizing your knowledge as you dig deeper into the details of networking.

CHAPTER 2

Introducing Windows NT Server

Windows NT Server version 3.5 is the latest in a long line of Microsoft networking products. In Windows NT Server you can see echoes of numerous products, coming together in a robust, feature-rich network operating system.

The most obvious influence is Microsoft's line of Windows products, particularly Windows for Workgroups 3.11. Windows is the most popular graphical user interface in the personal computer market, and Microsoft has carried that interface over to Windows NT with few changes. As a result, the significantly enhanced power of Windows NT is given a familiar face that makes it easy for most experienced Windows users to adapt to.

The networking model for Windows NT Server evolved out of two product lines: LAN Manager and Windows for Workgroups. From LAN Manager came the approach of administering multi-server networks in domains, making it unnecessary to manage each server independently. From Windows for Workgroups came an intuitive approach of sharing network resources that users browse for and connect with. Any user who has shared a printer with Windows for Workgroups will find it easy to work on a Windows NT network.

The robust character of Windows NT arises from lots of experience at designing operating systems. Some of this experience was internal. Microsoft had, after all, developed the XENIX implementation of Unix during the 1980s. And they had worked with IBM on the first two generations of OS/2. When it came time to design a full-featured, multitasking OS, however, Microsoft went one step further and hired David Cutler, who had gained considerable experience with multi-user operating systems while at Digital. These influences came together into an OS that many feel rivals Unix for power and features while retaining the ease of use of Microsoft Windows.

This chapter serves as a brief tour of the features of Windows NT. Here you will gain an understanding of the architecture of Windows NT, which will help you to understand the capabilities of the product. Many of the features will receive chapter-length treatment later in the book.

Windows NT Workstation and Server

Windows NT is available in two versions: Windows NT Workstation version 3.5 and Windows NT Server version 3.5. The server version is essentially the same as the workstation with the addition of features that enable it to perform as a versatile network operating system.

Microsoft's approach has significant advantages. With Windows NT you can buy workstation and server products that are managed nearly identically, run the same programs, and take the same software drivers. You buy only the capability you need for a given computer. The prices are quite reasonable. Windows NT Server lists for $699, and Windows NT Workstation lists for $319. While the closest comparable operating system, Unix, typically sells for about $1,500 per computer, Windows NT stacks up as a bargain.

Another advantage of Windows NT Server is that network clients are packaged separately at a per-client price of $39. With some network servers, if you want two servers, both of which will be used by the same 100 users, you need to purchase two 100-client server licenses. With Windows NT Server, you buy the client licenses once and use them with as many servers as you require.

The workstation and server products are highly synergistic. In fact, Windows NT Workstation serves a number of networking roles. For example, any Windows NT computer can function as a network print server, and any Windows NT computer can serve as a TCP/IP router.

Windows NT computers also make the best clients for Windows NT Server. The first time you print to a network printer from Windows NT, you might not believe how easy it was to set up network printing. If you are familiar with Windows for

Workgroups, you know that you need to install printer drivers on each computer. A single copy of the printer driver on a Windows NT print server is enough to take care of all Windows NT clients; they just connect to the shared printer and print.

All Windows NT computers can take advantage of *profiles,* files that store detailed information about a user's working environment from session-to-session.

Windows NT Operating System Features

Windows NT has many features that place it in the upper ranks of operating systems for microcomputers and workstations. Many of these features are highly desirable on a workstation and essential on a network server.

Portability

The majority of operating systems are written for a specific hardware platform. MS-DOS, for example, was written for the Intel 8086/8088 series of microprocessors. To this day, MS-DOS applications are limited by the features of microprocessors you can no longer buy. The 8086 and 8088 could address but one megabyte of memory, and that limitation affects DOS applications over a decade after the birth of MS-DOS.

If you are planning the computing strategy for an organization, having operating systems and applications tied to specific hardware should remind you of the bad old days of proprietary mainframe computers. Once you bought a mainframe, you were locked into that vendor's hardware, software, and support. Suppose that a new computer architecture offers more bang for the buck. Wouldn't you like to have the freedom of changing out your hardware without the need to upgrade your operating systems and applications?

Windows NT might be the most portable OS on the market thanks to two design decisions. First, the operating system was written in C, a language that enables programs to be ported easily to other hardware. Second, all of the parts of Windows NT that must be written for specific hardware were isolated in an area called the Hardware Abstraction Layer (HAL). To move Windows NT to hardware, developers need do little more than recompile the C code for the new hardware and create a new HAL.

As a result, you can select the hardware platform that provides you with the cost and performance features you select. Windows NT is already available for several platforms with more on the way. The standard product includes installation files for the following:

- Intel x86 computers
- MIPS RISC architecture computers
- Digital Alpha AXP RISC architecture computers

Multi-processor computers are available for all of these hardware platforms.

Large Storage Capacity

Windows NT was designed to take full advantage of 80386 and later Intel processors. As a result, Windows NT can support as much as 4 gigabytes of RAM.

Multitasking and Multithreading

Multitasking is computer slight of hand. The computer's central processing unit (CPU) isn't really performing several things at once, since it can only do one thing at a time. Instead, the operating system quickly switches several tasks in and out of the CPU, doing a bit of task A, a bit of task B, a bit of C, and then a bit of A again. Properly executed on a sufficiently fast system, multitasking presents the illusion that A, B, and C are running at the same time.

Multitasking can be a blessing or a curse. Implemented well, multitasking enables an operating system to perform several tasks, more or less at the same time, almost as though each task were running on its own processor. The quality of a multitasking system depends on how well the designers have isolated the various tasks.

It is possible, for example, to implement a sort of multitasking with MS-DOS, which is not by nature a multitasking OS. But add-ons such as Windows can expand the capabilities of MS-DOS to embrace a sort of multitasking. The problem is that the tasks aren't isolated, and one hung task can screw up everything.

Windows NT doesn't have that problem. Tasks are well-isolated and can't hurt each other. Moreover, if a given task hangs, you can kill it without the need to reboot the entire computer.

Multitasking is the illusion of doing several things at once. Multithreading actually does it. Multithreading takes advantage of the capabilities of some processors of executing two or more tasks—called *threads*—in separate areas of the CPU. Many RISC processors support multithreading as does the Pentium processor from Intel.

Windows NT makes it possible for applications to start their own threads. A complex task might spawn several subtasks that would execute simultaneously and come together to produce a result. Multithreaded applications can take care of more business simultaneously than is possible with simple multitasking.

Multi-Processor Support

When an OS supports multithreading, it has the potential to use more than one processor. The quality this brings to a computer is called *scalability*. If you buy a multi-processor network server, you might get along for awhile with a single CPU. As your network grows, however, the server might start to choke on the extra work. When that happens, you can scale the server up by installing additional CPUs.

The two styles of multiprocessing are the following:

- *Asymmetrical* multiprocessing assigns different types of tasks to different processors. This approach is relatively easy to implement, but can result in some processors being busier than others.

- *Symmetrical* multiprocessing has the capability of running any task on any processor. It's a lot more difficult to design an OS for symmetrical multiprocessing, but the payoff is that you are sure of using each processor more fully.

Unfortunately, doubling processors doesn't double processing capability. Some overhead is required to manage the process of assigning tasks to processors and coordinating the results of various tasks. As a result, you will encounter diminishing returns as you add processors.

Standard versions of Windows NT Server 3.5 support symmetrical multiprocessing with up to four processors, while Windows NT Workstation 3.5 supports two processors.

NT File System

Windows NT introduced the new NTFS file system that improves network performance, reliability, and security. The FAT file system used with MS-DOS and the HPFS file system developed for OS/2 are not well-suited to network servers. They cannot dynamically compensate for disk flaws and cannot secure files against intruders who have access to the server.

NTFS compensates for disk flaws by using a hot-fix feature that automatically redirects data in a bad disk sector to a substitute sector.

NTFS also builds security into the file system. A user cannot gain access to an NTFS file volume by rebooting the computer from a floppy disk. To access the files, the user must have a suitable user account and password.

Note Windows NT file systems are discussed in detail in Chapter 16, "Managing Disk Storage."

RAID Support

RAID (redundant arrays of inexpensive disks) is a technology for improving the performance and fault tolerance of hard drives. Ordinarily, to have the benefits of RAID, you need to purchase special RAID hardware. Windows NT enables you to configure RAID drives using only standard drives and SCSI hardware.

Security

Windows NT can be configured to maintain a very high level of security. Using the proper procedures, it is possible to configure a network using Windows NT computers for Class C2 security, defined by the U.S. Department of Defense as providing "discretionary (need-to-know) protection and, through the inclusion of audit capabilities, for accountability of subjects and the actions they initiate."

Windows NT Workstation security is based on securing shared network directories. Entire directory structures are assigned the same set of access restrictions.

Security on Windows NT Server is much more detailed. Administrators of Windows NT Server determine who will access the network and what resources they are permitted to access, right down to the file level.

Windows NT Server includes several security classes that solve old LAN administrator headaches. Consider the problem of the nightly tape backup. To be any good, the backup should include every file on the server. Ordinarily that requires full administrator privileges, something you really don't want to give to nighttime operators who will probably be performing the backups. Windows NT Server provides a special set of user privileges that enable tape backup operators to archive files without having the run of the network.

Windows NT design incorporates some clever security features. You will notice, for example, that you log on to a Windows NT computer by typing Ctrl+Alt+Del. This is a protection against programs that attempt to intercept passwords by substituting themselves for the normal login program. The Ctrl+Alt+Del sequence always directly invokes the login routine in the Windows NT program, an area of Windows NT that cannot be modified by users or intruders.

Another aspect of Windows NT security is that computers as well as users must be permitted access to the network. Even though a user has a valid user account, he or she can't log on from any old Windows NT computer. The computer itself must have been added to the network. If the network consists only of Windows NT computers, it can be made very secure indeed.

Compatibility

Windows NT supports a wide variety of programs, including programs written for the following operating system standards:

- MS-DOS
- 16-bit Windows applications
- 32-bit Windows applications
- OS/2 (limited support)
- POSIX, a Unix-style interface that enables applications to be easily ported among systems

Ease of Administration

Over 90 percent of Windows NT administration tasks are performed with graphic utilities. As a result, the user interface is consistent and there are few commands to remember. But the GUI interface is not the only feature that makes an administrator's life easier.

Centralized User Profiles

Windows NT computers can utilize profiles that describe a user's working environment in great detail. Profiles fall into the following two categories:

- User profiles can be modified by individual users. An advantage of a centralized user profile is that users can access their profiles from any Windows NT computer on the network, effectively making their working environment portable.
- Mandatory profiles cannot be modified by users. They enable an administrator to define a fixed environment for use by individuals or by large groups. A mandatory profile is a great means of ensuring that all users in a particular area have a common working environment. Support is greatly simplified.

Domain-Based Administration

Without some form of enterprise-based server administration, multi-server LANs are hell for an administrator. In some LAN environments, when you create a user account on one server, you need to create an identical account on every other server on the LAN. Two accounts are more than double the work because you need to cross-check everything and problems inevitably arise.

Windows NT Server supports an administration approach that organizes multiple servers into commonly managed groups called *domains.* Users are not given logon privileges for an individual computer. Their account gives them permission to log on to the domain and gain access to all computers in the domain based on their security permissions. Domain-based administration significantly reduces the effort required to manage user accounts.

Domains also work fine in conjunction with workgroups, so Windows NT Workstation and Windows for Workgroups users can continue to use peer-to-peer resource sharing even as they access central resources on Windows NT Servers.

Directory Replication

If you ever want to distribute files to several servers, you will appreciate the directory replication feature of Windows NT Server. Directory replication enables you to designate an export directory on one server and import directories on other servers. The directory replication service takes responsibility for ensuring that any changes made to files in the export directory are copied to all import directories, without any further intervention from the administrator. Directory replication is a great way to distribute newsletters, phone lists, and commonly used files.

Task Scheduling

You will almost certainly have a need to schedule tasks to happen at particular times. The most common example of a timed task is kicking off the nightly tape backup job, which usually happens in the wee hours of the morning when your users have gone home. Windows NT has a built-in task scheduler that can execute batch and EXE files at any time you designate, on a daily, weekly, or monthly basis.

Remote Administration

All network management functions can be performed remotely, enabling you to manage all of your network servers from a central location.

Auditing

The more critical your LAN becomes, the more you will want to keep track of who is using and abusing it. Windows NT Server has a powerful, but easy-to-use auditing feature that can track all sorts of file access and printing activities. This data can be exported in formats that can be used by spreadsheet and database programs, enabling you to track events and statistics on your network.

API Support

Application program interfaces (APIs) are the commands programmers use to enable their applications to access services provided by operating systems and other applications. In the world of Windows applications, two major APIs are commonly employed, NetBIOS and Windows Sockets, both of which are supported on Windows NT.

NetBIOS

The Network Basic Input Output System (NetBIOS) has long been the standard API for Microsoft network products. Windows applications access the network through the NetBIOS interface. With Windows NT version 3.5, Microsoft has ensured that NetBIOS applications can network with all three of the transport protocols that are included. NetBIOS applications can participate in a wide area network using the NetBIOS over TCP/IP feature of Windows NT Server 3.5, for example.

Windows Sockets

Windows Sockets is a Windows-based implementation of the sockets API that is commonly used with Unix. Windows applications written to the Windows Sockets API are ready to network over TCP/IP.

Transport Protocol Support

As you learned in Chapter 1, "Understanding Networks," protocols are the languages that enable computers to communicate. The computer industry has failed to gravitate toward a single protocol, although TCP/IP is winning many hearts and minds. Fortunately, Windows NT includes support for the three most common protocol suites on LANs: NetBEUI, Novell's IPX/SPX, and TCP/IP.

Figure 2.1 shows how NDIS supports multiple protocol stacks. It also shows another layer that enhances the versatility and simplicity of Windows NT. The Transport Driver Interface (TDI) layer insulates upper-layer applications from protocols, and technically resides between the OSI session and transport layers.

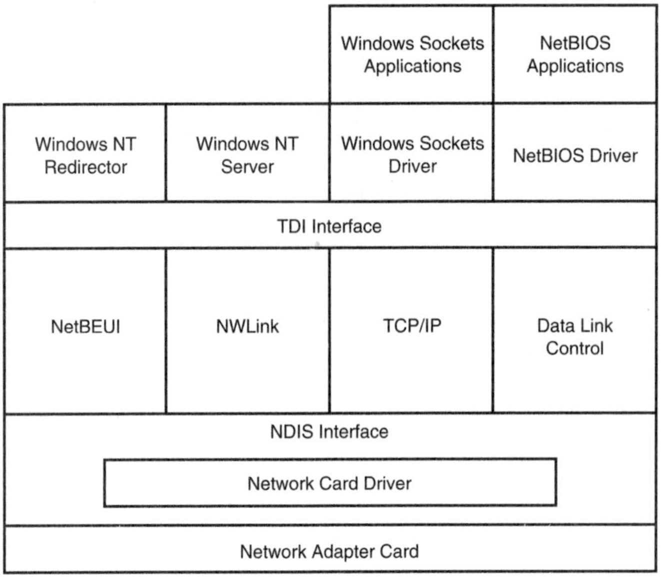

Figure 2.1
Protocol support on Windows NT.

The Network Driver Interface Specification (NDIS) is a key component in Windows protocol support. NDIS enables a computer to run multiple protocol stacks over the same network adapter card. NDIS effectively enables a computer to speak three network protocol languages at the same time.

NetBEUI

NetBIOS extended user interface (NetBEUI) was designed for running NetBIOS applications on local area networks. NetBEUI is a simple, efficient protocol that provides high performance on small networks. Prior to Windows NT 3.5, NetBEUI was the standard protocol for Microsoft networking products. NetBEUI is a great fit for Windows networking because it is essentially a plug-and-play protocol that requires no configuration other than a simple installation procedure. NetBEUI is, therefore, well-suited to networks, such as Windows for Workgroups, that will be administered by end-users.

NetBEUI has a significant problem in that NetBEUI cannot be routed and cannot, therefore, be used as the transport protocol on larger, multi-segment networks. As a result, Windows NT 3.5 now uses NWLink as its standard protocol. NWLink also is a plug-and-play protocol that can function on a routed network.

NWLink

NWLink is an NDIS-compliant transport that is network-compatible with Novell's IPX/SPX protocols. The IPX/SPX protocols offer high-performance and good functionality on wide area networks while requiring little setup. NWLink conforms to TDI and can support applications written to the NetBEUI and Windows Sockets APIs.

Another benefit of NWLink is that it simplifies the interface between Windows NT and NetWare networks. Windows NT includes NetWare client software and a NetWare gateway, both of which enable Windows network users to access resources on NetWare LANs.

By default, Windows NT installs the NetBEUI and NWLink protocols.

TCP/IP

TCP/IP is named after the two primary protocols in the suite: Transmission Control Protocol (TCP) and Internet Protocol (IP). TCP/IP is a robust, versatile protocol suite that is the most widely used protocol suite in terms of the number of devices networked and the variety of supported computers. TCP/IP is particularly well-suited to wide area networks where reliable delivery is essential.

The downside of TCP/IP is that considerable and expert work is required to install and maintain TCP/IP networks. There is no such thing as a plug-and-play TCP/IP network.

That said, Microsoft has made great strides in simplifying TCP/IP installation and support. Administrators are burdened with relatively little manual editing of configuration files, a significant consumer of labor on TCP/IP networks. The Domain Host Configuration Protocol (DHCP) can be used to assign addresses dynamically to network computers. And the Windows Internet Naming Service (WINS) adds a relatively low-effort naming service to Windows NT networks using TCP/IP.

You will want to install TCP/IP on a network in several situations:

- Your network needs to interface with a TCP/IP network, such as the Internet.
- TCP/IP is your corporate standard.
- TCP/IP is required to connect some devices on your network.
- Your network includes two or more network segments, possibly in a wide area network, and you require a protocol that can be routed among the segments.

Note TCP/IP is discussed in detail in Chapter 15, "Using TCP/IP."

DLC

Data Link Control (DLC) is used in two situations: connecting to IBM mainframes and printing to a DLC-compliant printer. DLC printers can attach directly to the network, eliminating the need for print servers.

Note DLC is discussed in Chapter 12, "Managing Printing Services."

NetWare Interoperability

NetWare dominates the local area network world. Something like 66 percent of all network computers are networked with NetWare. It is highly desirable for other LAN products to enable users to access resources on NetWare LANs.

Windows NT Server 3.5 provides the following two means of connecting users to NetWare servers:

- Client software that can access bindery-based NetWare servers such as NetWare 3.12
- A NetWare gateway that enables users to access NetWare services as though they resided on the Windows network

Both of these features are discussed in Chapter 22, "Windows NT Server and NetWare."

Remote Access Services

Users rely on their LANs, and most LAN administrators have received requests from users who want to log on to the LAN from their homes or while they are traveling. Remote Access Services (RAS) is built into Windows NT and Windows for Workgroups. A Windows NT RAS server provides an inexpensive, easy to manage capability that enables users to dial into a LAN. As an added benefit, a RAS server can provide local users with a pool of shared modems, enabling local users who do not own modems to dial out to remote services.

RAS supports modem connections and enables you to configure modem pools. RAS also enables you to connect to a wide area network using X.25 or to access high-speed digital services with ISDN. See Chapter 20, "Using the Remote Access Server," for more information.

Note Before I leave the topic of Windows NT features, let me mention some resources you really should have if you plan to work with Windows NT Workstation or Server.

The *Windows NT Resource Kit* is the official reference on Windows NT. It consists of four fat volumes, and, although there is some overlap with the product manuals, the *Resource Kit* contains material that is unavailable anywhere else. It also contains a CD-ROM and several floppy disks of programs and data, some of which I make reference to in this book.

Another important resource is Microsoft's *TechNet*. A subscription to *TechNet* costs only $295 a year, a profound bargain in the computer support industry. Each month you receive two CDs containing product and troubleshooting databases, program patches, and information about Microsoft programs.

CHAPTER 3

Understanding Network Administration

LAN administration can be one of the most challenging careers you can imagine. Getting the LAN up and running might be the easy part because after your users' PCs are connected to the LAN, every problem they have suddenly will be the fault of the LAN. Be prepared for many calls, such as "I never had any problems until you hooked me up to the LAN!" or "Your LAN's losing my files." You will need all your technical and interpersonal skills to do a good job.

Okay, so being a LAN administrator "looks like a job for Superman," right? Well, relax. The perfect LAN administrator doesn't exist. Although dozens of job skills appear on a LAN administrator's job description, each person fills the job in different ways. As a rule, the best technicians are weak on people skills, whereas the staff psychologist who is an expert at soothing shattered nerves probably will not know his way around a TCP/IP router. You probably will find your niche somewhere between Thomas Edison and Sigmund Freud.

Because the job is so complex, the best way to run a LAN is with a team of complementary personalities. If you must do the job alone, however, read on. This chapter introduces you to the various skills you will need on the job, and gives you some tips on how to succeed in each job that you will perform.

Installing and Managing Servers

Your server probably will be the most complex piece of computing equipment you will have on your LAN. On early LANs, servers were little more than well-equipped PCs, and many LANs continue to function well with PC-class servers. The increasingly critical nature of LANs in business operations, however, has lead to the purchase of more sophisticated hardware for network servers.

Windows NT Server can function on Intel PCs based on the IBM PC architecture (PC compatibles). Many vendors have improved the capabilities of the Intel PC architecture until their server products bear little resemblance to standard desktop PCs. The most powerful of these systems often are classified as *superservers.* Here are some of the features found in more powerful LAN servers:

- **Support for massive amounts of memory.** 256 MB and greater system RAM capacities are becoming increasingly common, and gigabyte capabilities exist. Most desktop PC architectures are limited to 64 MB or 128 MB.
- **Large hard drive subsystems.** These often are based on Redundant Arrays of Inexpensive Disks (RAID) technology and are designed for large capacity, high performance, and reliability. *See Chapter 16, "Managing Disk Storage," for a full discussion of how Windows NT Server supports RAID.*
- **Support for multiple processors.** Windows NT Server is capable of utilizing multiple processors by employing a feature called *symmetric multiprocessing* (this term is explained in Chapter 2, "Introducing Windows NT Server"). Multiprocessing can increase server performance.
- **Fault tolerance.** A server's resistance to hardware failures can be improved in many ways. Several of the techniques are too expensive to be practical with most desktop PCs. Some of the possibilities follow:

  Uninterruptible power supplies.

  Fault-tolerant disk subsystems that prevent a single hard drive failure from causing data or service loss.

  Error-correcting memory (ECM) that can detect and correct damaged data in memory. When an ordinary PC detects a memory error, it simply shuts down. ECM enables a system to continue functioning despite an occasional memory error.

- **Management.** When server operation is critical, it is desirable to know when problems are developing. The best servers can generate network-management alerts that can anticipate problems before they cause a server failure.

Many of the servers used with Windows NT Server will not be based on the Intel PC architecture at all. Many high-performance servers are based on Reduced Instruction Set Computing (RISC) processors such as the MIPS and the Digital Alpha AXP.

If you will be a network administrator, you should become as familiar as possible with your servers. After all, you are the person on the scene. Even if you have purchased technical support from a vendor, that support might be hours away, and hours of downtime are costly. Many organizations that use LANs to support critical systems invest in hardware training for their LAN support staff to ensure a large pool of on-site expertise.

Although you should become familiar with your server, don't feel that you must install and configure it. When dealing with more sophisticated servers, you often will be wise to pay your vendor to set it up for you. Just be sure to ask a great deal of questions during the process.

Managing the Server

After the server is up and running, it is your responsibility to manage it on a daily basis. One of your goals is to develop a feel for how the server is operating. Make notes of the performance statistics you observe under normal operations so that you have a sense of the standard performance of the server. Statistics gathered under normal operation describe the baseline operation of your network. These statistics have several values:

- If a statistic changes gradually or suddenly, it will tip you off on a trend, which may be a change in usage patterns or an impending problem.
- When problems arise, you can compare current statistics to your baseline. Doing so often tips you off to the cause of the problem, or at least to the area in which you should look first.
- Statistics supply you with ammunition when the time comes to upgrade your server or network.

That last point illuminates one of your ongoing problems as a LAN administrator: User demand for services always increases faster than you planned. Gigabytes of hard drive space can be filled in days, and you won't believe how quickly a server can outgrow 32 MB of memory. Frequent monitoring of disk storage and memory gives you time to control usage or to order more hardware before your server runs out of a critical resource.

You will be in a constant battle to use your current hardware to the best of its capabilities. Before you tell your boss that you need to upgrade to a multiprocessor RISC superduperserver, be sure that you have done the best job possible with your current hardware. And be sure when you request an upgrade that it will serve for a reasonable period of time. There are few things managers have less patience with than LAN administrators who frequently request additional server capacity.

Installing and Managing the Network

Networks can be simple or incredibly complicated. The level of complexity has much to do with your involvement in installing the cabling and network hardware. As with the server, the rule is this: The more you know, the better. You are responsible for monitoring the network on a day-to-day basis, and you are the person on-site when a problem arises.

Small networks are easy to install. Premade cables eliminate the need to buy expensive tools. If your network requires cables to pass through walls or over ceilings, however, you often are better off hiring a cable installer. The installer knows the wiring codes and can ensure that you are within the law. The installer also has the equipment and expertise to do the job efficiently and correctly. High-performance cables, such as fiber-optic cable and Level 5 UTP, never should be installed except by trained personnel (see Chapter 4, "Planning and Installing Network Media"). Few organizations can justify the costs of training in-house staff for these jobs. Pay for the expertise of a professional LAN installer so that the job is done right the first time.

Your network will change, and it is your job to know it intimately, to make minor changes, and to hire contractors when the modifications become major. Therefore, you should work with your installer to ensure that the system will be easy to reconfigure. You also should be involved in the cabling of your network so you know how it is configured, and so you can make maintenance changes.

Maintaining Network Security

PC users tend to have a cavalier attitude toward security. DOS (or OS/2 or Macintoshes, for that matter) cannot be secured to any great degree, except with sophisticated and tricky security software that few organizations want. Many companies have suffered critical data losses simply because of the amount of unsecured data that is sitting around on users' desktop PCs.

After users start sharing data on a LAN, the need for security can no longer be ignored. Allowing free-and-easy access by everyone to everything is a recipe for disaster, especially when your LAN is equipped with dial-in capabilities or attachments to outside networks such as the Internet.

Windows NT Server can be made very secure, but be prepared to work hard to achieve a proper security level. Also, be prepared to take some heat from users who don't understand the need for security and complain every time they are forced to change their passwords.

Security is a sensitive topic because it inconveniences users. Part of your job is to coordinate with management to establish security policies for your organization. Explain to management the risks of not defining and enforcing a solid policy, assist them in creating a policy, and get management to buy in on enforcing the policy. There is nothing more frustrating than trying to enforce security without a partnership with management.

Protecting Data

I'm feeling repetitious, but I'll say it again: The data on your LAN is important. Besides ensuring that proper access security is maintained, you need to ensure against disasters that could jeopardize your data.

Your most important duty in this area is to back up data on a regular basis. If you do nothing else in a day, make sure that last night's backup ran properly and that tonight's will run. Make periodic checks to ensure that the files you are backing up actually can be restored.

Unfortunately, performing backups is only a rewarding activity when disaster strikes. If everything goes well, your safeguards are invisible, and this can make it difficult to sell management on the necessity of backups and to justify equipment that is up to the job. Remember, users and management are viewing the situation from the perspective of desktop PCs, which seldom experience hard drive failures. Because they have only one hard drive, and that hard drive isn't working all that hard, users seldom experience hard drive failures. Although LAN hard drives are extremely reliable, they do fail, and many users lose their data. More important, critical shared data is present on the LAN. Loss of some of this data could cost your company thousands or millions of dollars.

Make your backup plans carefully and do your duty daily. Eventually, you will be rewarded. A user will "accidentally" erase a critical file, and your ability to restore the file from yesterday's backup tape will make you a hero. After this happens a few times, the invisible activity of file backup will have much more visibility and respect in your organization.

Viruses have become a significant threat to computer data, and LANs enable viruses to reproduce like rabbits. Make it a point to identify and obtain antivirus software for your network. Such software is expensive, and management often is reluctant to make the purchase. But a virus on a LAN can mean days of downtime, and once bitten, few organizations will hesitate any further.

Documenting the Network

If you're like most computer specialists, you carry a great deal of information in your head that isn't written down. Even if you are the only person in your organization who needs that information, failure to document your LAN is a recipe for disaster.

Considerable time might elapse between when you first do something and when you need to do it again or fix it when it is broken, for example. There are few small problems on a LAN, and when something breaks, you will be under pressure to fix it NOW! Proper documentation can compensate for a memory that has gone flat in the heat of the moment.

Also, you will not be your organization's LAN administrator forever, and you should plan for the time you move on or you get some help. Documentation produced during an event is much more useful than documentation produced during a hurried, training, hands-off period.

Few organizations have a good handle on their computer-equipment inventories. As LAN administrator, you might get involved in determining what equipment and software is on hand, as well as any changes that might occur. Fortunately, several commercial LAN inventory-software packages are available to help you perform this task.

Supporting Network Applications

Installing an application on a network can be much more involved than installing an application on a stand-alone PC. By now, most vendors have made installation of stand-alone applications as simple as typing **A:SETUP**. Installation of a networked application, on the other hand, can take hours or even days to plan and complete.

When you select an application for network installation, you need to check for its compatibility with your type of network server. You also need to confirm that it will work with the various workstation configurations that are present on your network. If workstation upgrades or changes are required, the equipment and labor costs should be part of your planning.

Whenever you install software on a network, you need to be aware of licensing issues. Some software packages incorporate licensing mechanisms. Others require you to use a separate usage-metering system to ensure that your network is operating within license restrictions.

Networks introduce new considerations into running applications. When many users are sharing an application, you need to take special steps to ensure that the users' application setup files remain separate. This can mean that some application files are located on the network, while others are located on the users' workstations—certainly more complicated than the normal situation in which all files are on the users' local hard drives. When users need to share certain files, you might need to spend extra time ensuring that the files are available but that users cannot interfere with each other's files.

Supporting Users' Workstations

It all starts when you stuff a network board into a user's PC and show the user how to log in and use the network. The minute a workstation is attached to the LAN, it becomes the LAN administrator's problem. Users who "never had any trouble until this PC went on the LAN" come out of the woodwork. Your LAN suddenly is the cause of everything from lost files to global warming.

Add to this the fact that users' PCs always are changing. The evolution of software requires that older computers be upgraded or discarded. The computers might be getting more memory, a bigger hard drive, a processor upgrade, or new peripherals. As the LAN administrator, you are regarded as the resident PC expert and you are called for everything PC-related.

Accept it: As a LAN administrator, you probably know more about computers than anyone else in your organization. Expect to get many more phone calls.

Planning the User Environment

By the time you finish this book, you will be pretty comfortable with Windows NT Server and LANs in general. But don't expect your users to read this book or invest the time you spend to become LAN-literate. Your users will want the LAN to be as invisible as possible.

One of your jobs is to make the LAN as easy to use as a local PC, and that takes much more work than simply hooking up your users. This might involve using menus, standardizing Windows interfaces, or providing documentation and training for your users.

Training Users

Even after the LAN is as easy to use as you can make it, something will be left over that your users will not understand. If a LAN is new to your users, or if they simply are being introduced to new services, your users probably will require some training.

Training is an ongoing activity in any organization with a LAN. Users need training on LAN-related topics such as logging on, printing to the LAN, sharing files, or sending electronic mail. But they also are likely to call you with their questions about WordPerfect or 1-2-3. Remember, you're the expert!

Training is often the LAN skill in which the top technicians are the weakest. If you're lucky, you will be part of a team that includes an ace technician and an ace trainer. If you fall into one category and have any influence on hiring your teammate, lobby for a coworker who complements your skills. Technicians often don't appreciate trainers, but training is at least as tough a job as running a LAN, and not all people are up to the job. Although a good trainer should be a skilled technician, a trainer's patience and psychology skills might be more important than technical competence.

Solving Problems

LANs will always have problems. Frankly, ordinary server problems might not be the worst you will encounter. User problems often are more troublesome because they always occur when the user is on deadline, and it always seems to be your LAN's fault for causing the project to fail! Make it your goal to solve the user's problem as efficiently and sympathetically as possible. Even though it's not the fault of your LAN, even though you have a dozen alligators waiting for a piece of you, bail your user out as calmly as possible. You're going to find that users approach LANs with a high level of anxiety that can backfire on you if you lose your cool.

Remember, many users are nervous around PCs and especially around LANs. Your behavior can calm or enhance that nervousness, and much of your performance is gauged on the impact you have on users' comfort levels. In the end, it matters less how well your LAN is running than how your users *perceive* the LAN and you. A LAN that runs perfectly will not win you any points if users hate your guts!

There are some things you can do to improve your problem-solving skills:

- **Learn, learn, learn.** LAN administration is an extremely challenging job. Devote some time each day to improving your skills.
- **Know how LANs work.** Don't just know *how* to do something. Know *why* you are doing it. Good technicians possess a solid mix of theoretical and practical knowledge.
- **Know your LAN.** Get a feel for how your LAN is running. Then, like an auto mechanic who can tell you when an engine is misfiring, you will know when your LAN isn't working up to its normal level.
- **Develop a rapport with your users.** Make their concerns your concerns. Let them have a voice in LAN policy. Get them involved in training. Make it their LAN.
- **Plan for success.** Document your LAN and keep the documentation up-to-date. Record the problems you encounter and the solutions you find. Whenever you plan a change, overplan to ensure a smooth transition.
- **Expect problems.** Files are going to be lost, so be sure that your backups happen. Equipment is going to break, so have spares or have a way to get replacements quickly.
- **Change things gradually.** Make one change at a time and test it thoroughly. Then it's easy to determine the cause of a new problem.

CHAPTER 4

Planning and Installing Network Media

The network media marketplace traditionally has been a free-for-all of technologies competing for your equipment-purchasing dollars. You readily can find a wide variety of products ranging from tried-and-true to flaky to leading-edge (typically called *bleeding edge* by those who have been wounded by adopting a new technology too early).

This chapter introduces you to various network media that you might encounter, and emphasizes technologies that are well-accepted and work well.

Characteristics of Media

You can make more intelligent media selections if you are aware of a few general media characteristics. No single medium excels in all the characteristics you will examine, and your decisions always will be based on the medium that makes the best compromise for your requirements.

EMI Sensitivity

Electrical signals and magnetic waves are inextricably linked. Changing electrical signals in wires create magnetic fields around the wires, and changing magnetic fields around wires create electrical signals in the wires. As a result, any source of changing magnetic fields can produce electrical noise in your LAN cables. And your LAN cables can create magnetic fields that can interfere with nearby electrical devices and with signals in nearby wires.

The noise produced in cables by magnetic fields is called electro-magnetic interference (EMI). Sources of EMI include radio transmissions, electric motors, fluorescent lights, and environmental phenomena such as lightning. You probably have heard EMI on the telephone or in AM radio broadcasts.

Most of the buildings LANs run in are filled with EMI noise sources. If your LAN includes cables that are pulled across ceilings, the cables probably are running near fluorescent lights. All copper cables are sensitive to EMI, and you should be sure that your cable installer is aware of the need to run cables properly to avoid noise sources.

Cables that are sensitive to EMI have another problem: They all produce electromagnetic fields that broadcast radio signals. These radio signals are a potential security risk because electronic eavesdropping equipment can receive the signals and intercept the network transmissions. If your network is carrying highly critical information, you have two choices: use fiber-optic cable, which is not electrical and cannot broadcast electrical signals; or encrypt the signals on your LAN. Few organizations need to be this concerned about security, but you should evaluate the risk for your organization.

Bandwidth

Bandwidth is a measure of the data rates that a given medium can support. The cables used in LANs typically can support data rates up to about 20 megabits-per-second (Mbps). This rate limit is adequate for many LANs, but some newer LAN-based services are demanding higher performance.

Increasingly, LANs are being used to deliver high volumes of data—including large files and graphic, audio, and video data. These applications are extremely demanding, and 20 Mbps of bandwidth is insufficient when it is shared among several users on a LAN. Network designers are expending considerable effort to bring down the cost of high-bandwidth LANs, and several media choices now can provide 100-Mbps bandwidths at reasonable costs.

Bandwidth in a medium can be used in two ways. When the entire bandwidth is devoted to a single data signal, the cable is operating in *baseband* mode. Most LANs use baseband signaling modes.

When the bandwidth of a medium is used to carry several independent signals, the medium is operating in *broadband* mode. You are familiar with one example of broadband signaling. The cable that brings television signals into your home is carrying several dozen independent television channels. You select a particular channel by setting the tuner on your TV. Network media can operate in much the same way, enabling a high-bandwidth medium to carry multiple lower bandwidth signals.

Cost

Cost is always relative. At present, the cost of connecting a computer to a network can range from less than $100 to more than $1,000. If your network needs the best performance available, $1,000 per computer might be the only way to go. Remember that a low-cost solution you quickly outgrow is not a bargain.

There are many strategies for improving the performance of a basic network—each with advantages and disadvantages. In this chapter, you will examine high-speed networks, along with other strategies such as switching hubs and full-duplex connections that might provide you with the added performance you might require at a lower cost.

Performance is not the only factor to consider when examining cost. Particularly with larger LANs, you should be willing to pay for features that make your LAN more reliable and manageable. Managed network components are more costly than basic components, but the extra cost can be justified if just one major network failure is prevented.

Cable Media

The vast majority of LANs utilize media consisting of copper or fiber-optic cable. Copper is inexpensive and an excellent conductor of electricity, and copper cable is by far the more popular LAN media choice. The performance potential of copper cable has been pushed up year by year until it has edged into applications that once were reserved for fiber-optic cable.

However, the cost of fiber-optic cable has edged downward, and many organizations that have long avoided fiber now are selecting it for its virtually unlimited performance potential. Although the performance of copper cable has improved steadily, fiber-optic cable always will be the medium of choice for the highest performing networks.

This section examines four broad categories of cable:

- Coaxial
- Shielded twisted-pair (STP)
- Unshielded twisted-pair (UTP)
- Fiber-optic

The goal in this section is to introduce you to the most common cables used in LANs and to enable you to choose appropriate cables for specific circumstances.

Coaxial Cable

If you examine the structure of a coaxial cable, you can see that the name *coaxial* comes about because the two conductors—the center conductor and the outer shield conductor—share a common axis (see fig. 4.1).

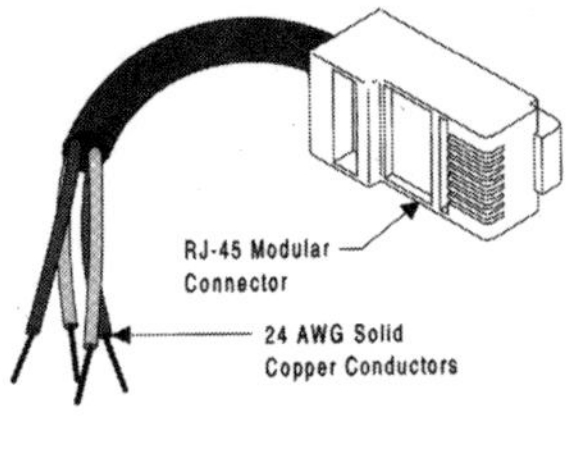

Figure 4.1
The structure of coaxial cable.

The components of coaxial cable follow:

- **Center conductor.** In most coaxial cables, the center conductor is a fairly thick solid-copper wire. Stranded center conductors can be used when cables need to be flexible, but stranded conductors reduce the cable lengths that can be used. Solid conductors are preferable for permanent installations.
- **Insulation layer.** This layer serves two purposes. It electrically insulates the center conductor from the shield conductor, and it ensures that the center conductor remains centered. A precise physical relationship between the center conductor and the shield is required for peak performance.

- **Shield.** The shield is a conductor that completely surrounds the center conductor. The shield serves as the second conductor of the cable, and it protects the center conductor from outside EMI. The shield also reduces electro-magnetic signals that otherwise might radiate from the cable. For many years, shields were required for LAN cables.

- **Jacket.** A plastic or Teflon coating protects the outside of the cable. The jacket insulates the shield electrically from the outside and protects it from abrasion and other damage.

Figure 4.1 also shows a common connector used with coaxial cable. This connector is called a BNC connector (for BayoNet Connector) because you install it by twisting angled slots in one connector over pins in the matching connector.

Coaxial cable was used in the first LANs and has many characteristics that make it ideal for high-performance data transmission. Coax can support very high bandwidths, but this capability has not been exploited in most LAN implementations.

The performance of coax is closely related to the diameter of the cable and the thickness of the conductors. To improve the distance characteristics of coax LANs, early designers used thick coax that was expensive, bulky, and difficult to work with. More recent designs have resorted to thinner cable.

Coax cable types are not interchangeable. Besides the diameter of the cable and the nature of the conductors, another important characteristic of a coaxial cable is *impedance.* The impedance of a cable is a measure of the cable's resistance to the flow of alternating current such as data signals; impedance is measured in *ohms.* The following network types require cable with a specific impedance:

- RG-8 and RG-11 are 50-ohm coaxial cables with a diameter of approximately one-half inch. These cables are used with the oldest form of Ethernet, commonly called thick Ethernet or simply thicknet. Because these cables are stiff and difficult to work with, you sometimes hear them called "frozen, yellow garden hose."

- RG-58 is a thinner 50-ohm cable used with an Ethernet type commonly called thin Ethernet or thinnet. RG-58 is approximately one-quarter inch in diameter and is much easier to work with than RG-8 and RG-11. The thicker cables can carry signals much farther, however, and often are used when longer cable runs are required.

- RG-59 is a 75-ohm cable; it is the same cable that is used to wire cable television networks. RG-59 is inexpensive and is used to implement a broadband version of Ethernet.

Coaxial cable has several advantages:

- The shielding makes coax highly resistant to EMI.
- Networks that use coax have been in use for a considerable time (20 years, in the case of Ethernet) and are well understood, inexpensive, and reliable.
- The cables are durable.

However, coax has some disadvantages you should consider:

- Coaxial cable is not totally invulnerable to EMI, and it should be avoided in electrically noisy environments.
- Coax can be fairly expensive—particularly the thicker types, which can approach fiber-optic cable in cost.
- Coax cable is bulky—particularly the thicker varieties.

Shielded Twisted-Pair

After coax, the next cable type to be used in LANs was shielded twisted-pair (STP), as shown in figure 4.2. A twisted-pair consists of two insulated wires that are twisted together. The twists do much more than simply hold the wires together. They cause the wires to alternate positions, causing EMI noises in the wires to cancel out. The twists also reduce the tendency of the cable to radiate electrical signals. Without the twists, the cable would tend to function as an antenna, readily absorbing signals from the environment and emitting its own signals to cause interference in other devices.

Figure 4.2
Shielded twisted-pair cable.

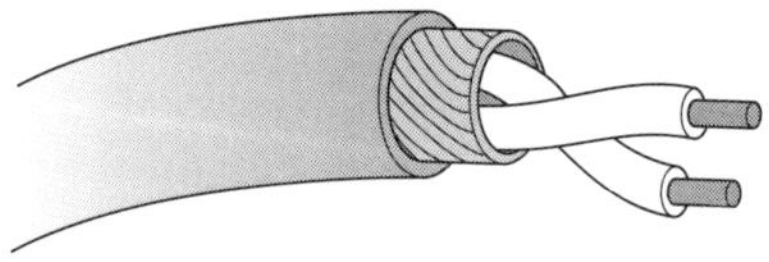

The cable shown in Figure 4.2 uses a shield to further improve the cable's noise characteristics. Like the shield in coaxial cable, this shield absorbs outside signals that could cause interference and also absorbs signals that would otherwise be radiated from the wires.

In most implementations, STP cables include more than one pair of twisted wires. Figure 4.3 illustrates a common twisted-pair cable configuration that is used in token ring networks. IBM created the specifications for the cables that generally are used to wire a token ring, and figure 4.3 shows a cable type that is designated as IBM Type 1. This cable consists of two twisted-pair wire pairs enclosed in a common shield.

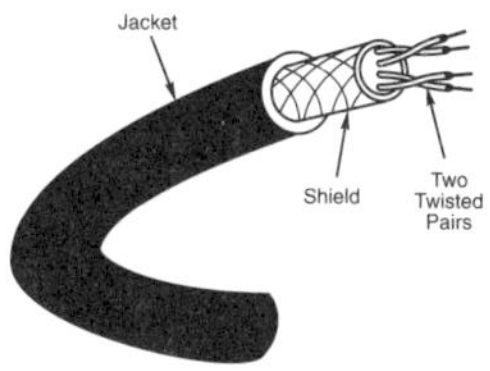

Figure 4.3
IBM Type 1 cable.

Shielded twisted-pair cables are comparable to coaxial cables in many ways. Costs are similar, as are bandwidths and cable diameters. Both perform well for the networks designed around them.

Some advantages of shielded twisted-pair cable follow:

- **EMI resistance.** STP is highly insensitive to electromagnetic interference.
- **High bandwidth.** Until recently, shields were required to achieve high bandwidths with twisted-pair cables. Bandwidths as high as 16 Mbps were achieved in the 1980s.
- **Durability.** STP cables generally include large-gauge conductors and are built for sturdiness.

STP cables have some significant disadvantages as well:

- STP cable is not totally invulnerable to EMI, and it should be avoided in electrically noisy environments.
- The cost of STP is comparable to thin coax, although less in general than fiber-optic cable.
- STP cable can be particularly bulky.

STP cable remains in use but, like coax, it has grown less popular. Shielded cables have fallen into disfavor due to their fairly high costs and their bulk, which often fills up wiring paths far too quickly. The emphasis these days is on unshielded twisted-pair cable.

Unshielded Twisted-Pair

Unshielded twisted-pair (UTP) uses twisted pairs of wire, but it does not incorporate a shield. Removal of the shield reduces the cost and bulk of the cable, but makes it more sensitive to EMI and more likely to emit electronic noise. The bulk of UTP cable is reduced even more, because most UTP cables use relatively small wire gauges—significantly smaller than gauges commonly used with coax and STP. Figure

4.4 shows an example of a two-pair UTP cable along with the RJ-45 connector that typically is used. UTP cable was used first for telephone systems, and many of the connecting devices used on UTP LANs are borrowed from telephone technology.

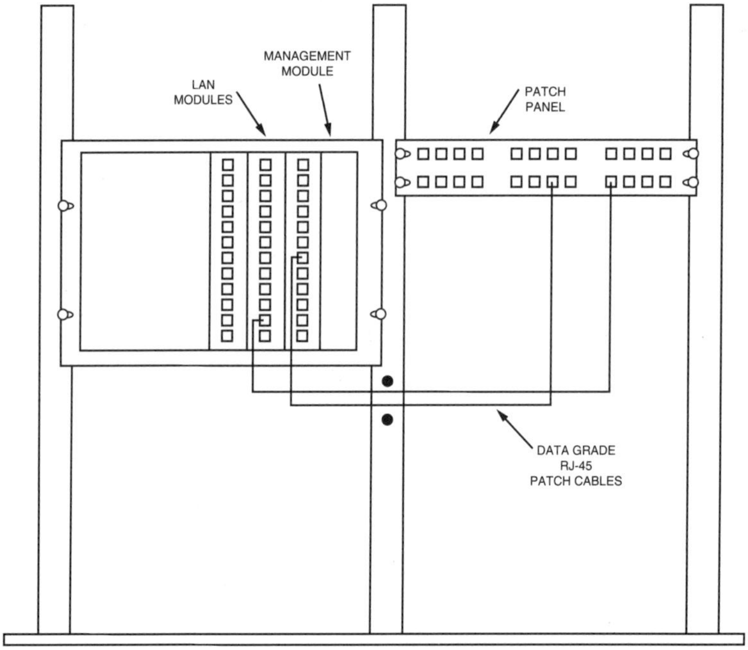

Figure 4.4
UTP cable with an RJ-45 connector.

UTP cable has been used for many years for the premise wiring for telephone systems, and many organizations are wired with extra pairs of voice-grade wires. Consequently, customers have long sought to use their leftover telephone pairs to support LAN traffic. However, telephone voice cable is designed only for audio frequencies, and voice-grade cable cannot be adapted easily to data requirements. Businesses have come to expect more from telephone cabling than voice-grade service, and it is now universal practice to cable new commercial properties with data-grade UTP. Many business desktop phones are digital and require data-grade cable.

In the 1980s, work started on adapting higher grade UTP cable for data. Several LAN designs were introduced, but they were restricted by fairly low data rates. IBM's original specification for their token ring network restricted the use of UTP cable to 4-Mbps data rates, while STP was sanctioned for 16-Mbps rates. At higher data rates, cables have a greater tendency to radiate electrical noise that can interfere with nearby cables or electrical devices.

Note You will see the terms *token ring* and *Token-Ring* in this chapter. *Token-Ring* originated as an IBM technology, and IBM capitalizes *Token-Ring* and includes a hyphen in the name. Since Token-Ring is an IBM trademark, other vendors generally use lower case and omit the hyphen. This book will use lower case unless it is specifically referring to the IBM brand of Token-Ring.

Customer demand for higher data rates over UTP has driven vendors to push the limits upward, and several types of networks now can use UTP cable at data rates as high as 100 Mbps. To achieve these data rates, however, it has been necessary to define higher grades of UTP cable. Here are the five grades or categories of UTP cable:

- **Category 1.** Voice grade only. Not usable for data.
- **Category 2.** Low-speed data transmissions such as PBX and alarm systems. Not usable at LAN data rates.
- **Category 3.** Usable for data transmissions at rates up to 16 Mbps. Used for UTP Ethernet and token ring.
- **Category 4.** Usable for data transmissions at rates up to 20 Mbps. Generally used in the same situations as Category 3.
- **Category 5.** Usable for data transmissions at rates up to 100 Mbps. Most of the newer 100-Mbps network designs are based on Category 5 cable.

Amazing progress has been made at raising the performance levels possible with UTP. Customers want UTP, which is perceived as being more cost-effective than shielded cables or fiber-optic cables. "Cat 5" cable does indeed deliver on the promise of high LAN speeds, but it is a mixed blessing.

Proper installation of Category 5 cable is considerably more costly than is installation of lower grades of UTP. When pulling Category 5 cable, the standard specifies that a maximum force of 25 Newton meters should be applied. Don't ask me how much 25 Newton meters is. Suffice it to say that most cable installations consist of pulling cable through openings, over ceilings, and through walls; and pulling as hard as it takes to get the cable moving. Cable installers do not use force gauges to ensure that cables are not stretched. Keep in mind that stretching Cat 5 cable does lower its performance potential, however.

UTP data cables frequently are installed using connection devices similar to those used with telephone cables. UTP connectors resemble the RJ-45 connectors used with telephones, and cable interconnections often are made with punchdown blocks. A *punchdown block* is a plastic block that is studded with metal fingers. Wires are pushed between these fingers to make electrical connections between two cables.

In order for a network to perform at Category 5 levels, all components in the network must be designed to Category 5 specifications. Prior to about 1992, however, Category 5 punchdown blocks were unavailable, so many networks cabled with Category 5 cable prior to that time cannot be expected to perform at top speeds.

Installers need to be more careful in other ways when installing Category 5 cable. With lower grades of UTP, it is common to untwist two or three inches of wire prior to attaching the wires to a punchdown block. The Category 5 specification states that no more than one-half inch of the twisted pair should be untwisted prior to punching it down.

Therefore, installation of Category 5 cable systems is costly in several areas:

- The cable itself is more costly.
- The connection devices cost extra.
- Installers require more training.
- The procedure is slower.

As a result, properly installed Category 5 cable is not always a bargain. One vendor estimates that the cost difference between Category 5 cable and fiber-optic cable is only about $50 per station. (However, the electronic components required for fiber-optic cable are considerably more expensive than the components used with UTP.) In summary, select Category 5 cable for solid technical reasons—not because you are looking for a bargain.

Some advantages of unshielded twisted-pair cable follow:

- UTP is the most inexpensive of all cable types.
- UTP has a low bulk. Because many pairs can be enclosed in a single cable jacket, a given cable path can accommodate more UTP pairs than STP or coax cables.
- Installation methods are similar to those used with telephone cabling. The required skills are easy to obtain.

Care should be taken when selecting UTP, however, due to some significant disadvantages:

- UTP is potentially very vulnerable to EMI.
- At present, 100 Mbps is about the limit of bandwidth for UTP. It's risky to predict, but 100 Mbps might be about the most that UTP can support.
- Thin-gauge cables are more vulnerable to damage.

Fiber-Optic Cable

Fiber-optic cable is a nearly perfect medium for the transmission of data signals. Maximum data rates exceed 1,000 gigabits-per-second, and new cable types promise to extend signal ranges to several thousand kilometers. Unfortunately, the performance of fiber-optic cable comes at a high cost, and few organizations choose to use 100-percent fiber-optic cable.

Fiber-optic cable consists of a glass or plastic core that carries data signals in the form of light pulses. Figure 4.5 shows an example of a fiber-optic cable, along with a typical connector.

The components of the cable follow:

- **Core.** Silicon glass generally is used, due to its high transparency, but some cables with plastic cores have been tried. Glass cables can carry signals for several kilometers without a need to refresh the signals, but the range of plastic cables is limited to about 100 meters.
- **Cladding.** A glass coating surrounds the core. The characteristics of the cladding are chosen carefully so that light will be reflected back into the cable, reducing signal loss.
- **Sheath.** A tough covering, usually made of Kevlar, protects the cable. Multiple fibers can be bound together in the same sheath.

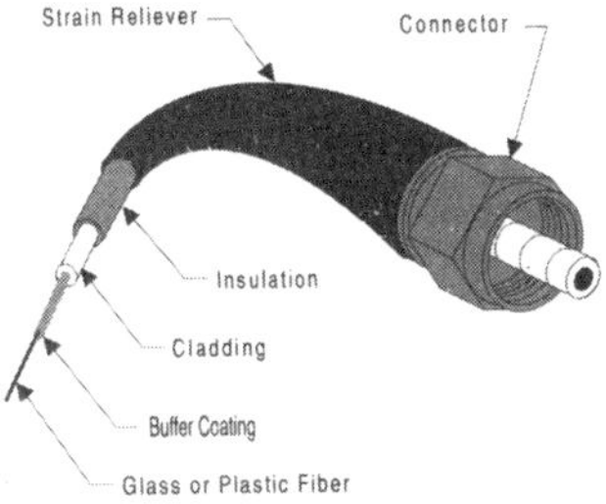

Figure 4.5

Fiber-optic cable and a typical connector.

The light source for fiber-optic cable is generally a solid-state laser called an injection laser diode (ILD). The laser light produced by ILDs has several desirable characteristics. It is monochromatic, consisting entirely of a single light wavelength. Laser light also is *coherent*, meaning that all light waves are traveling in the same direction.

Although fiber-optic cable is only slightly more costly than copper cable, the transmitter and receiver devices required are considerably more expensive than comparable devices used with copper cable. Although the cost of a fiber-optic connection gradually has fallen below the $1,000 mark, a 100-Mbps, fiber-optic connection costs several times as much as a 100-Mbps connection based on Category 5 UTP.

The advantage of installing fiber-optic cable is that it has virtually unlimited performance potential. Many organizations already are forced to contemplate the day when 100-Mbps bandwidths are insufficient. Although miracles have been performed in pushing the bandwidth of UTP upward, 100 Mbps might represent a performance limit for UTP cable. Although copper cable is running out of steam at 100 Mbps, fiber-optic cable is just getting started. Using fiber-optic cabling therefore is an excellent long-term investment.

Fiber-optic cable is superior to copper cable in several ways:

- The fibers are small, and large numbers of fibers can be bundled to fit through the same space as a single copper cable.
- Because light is used for signaling, fiber-optic cable is immune to EMI and cannot radiate electrical noise. Therefore, fiber-optic cable is the only LAN medium that is virtually immune to electronic eavesdropping.
- Fiber-optic cables are durable. Glass cannot corrode and connections seldom go bad.
- The bandwidth of fiber-optic cable is for all intents and purposes unlimited. Your organization can outgrow copper, but fiber is forever.

The cost of installing fiber-optic cable has crept downward as improved installation methods have been devised. You can install fiber with a few hundred dollars worth of tools and a couple of days training. Fiber-optic cable's reputation for being expensive to install therefore is somewhat outmoded.

Summary of Cable Characteristics

Table 4.1 compares the virtues and liabilities of several types of cable.

TABLE 4.1
Characteristics of Cable Types

Cable Type	Bandwidth	EMI Sensitivity	Cable Cost	Installation Cost
Coax	High	Low	Medium	Medium
STP	Medium	Low	Medium	Medium
UTP	5–100 Mbps	Highest	Lowest	Low to Medium
Fiber-optic	Highest	None	Highest	Highest

Wireless Media

Many people think that LANs shouldn't be cabled at all. Cables clutter up the office and make it difficult to move equipment. Even if you have no objection to cables, you might find occasions when it is impossible to install them. Consequently, a variety of network media vendors have attempted to market practical, wireless media.

Here are some situations when cable might be undesirable:

- If you are installing a LAN in an old building, it can be difficult to identify cable paths without incurring high costs. In historic buildings, you might be prohibited from running cables. A church, for example, might not want you drilling holes in its marble walls to run network cables.
- When LAN signals must cross a public street, you have two choices: lease a line from a telephone provider (expensive) or use wireless media.
- If users move frequently, wireless media gives them greater mobility.
- If an organization frequently modernizes and remodels, wireless media might be less expensive than the cost of periodically recabling.
- Now that most executives have portable PCs, you might simply have a boss who wants, and has the authority to demand, the capability to move PCs anywhere without changing cables.

Two types of wireless media are available: optical and radio frequency.

Optical LAN media use a technology similar to a modern television remote control. Pulses of infrared light are transmitted between devices. Optical LANs operate primarily within buildings, but some types can transmit several hundred yards between buildings.

Radio LAN media use a wide variety of radio techniques. Some use low-power transmissions and a technology similar to cellular telephone networks. Others use high-power and can transmit signals for considerable distances. Because installing high-power, long-distance radio transmissions such as microwave requires skilled and licensed specialists, this chapter focuses on the shorter-range solutions.

Optical LANs

Optical LANs can be implemented in two ways:

- By broadcasting signals to several receivers
- By relaying signals from node to node using point-to-point transmissions

Figure 4.6 illustrates a network that broadcasts infrared signals throughout a room. Signals are transmitted toward a reflective surface on the ceiling that disperses the signals to all receivers in the room. This method does not require careful alignment of transmission and receivers, as does the point-to-point approach. However, receivers must be capable of functioning with fairly weak light signals. This system therefore can be sensitive to excess ambient light.

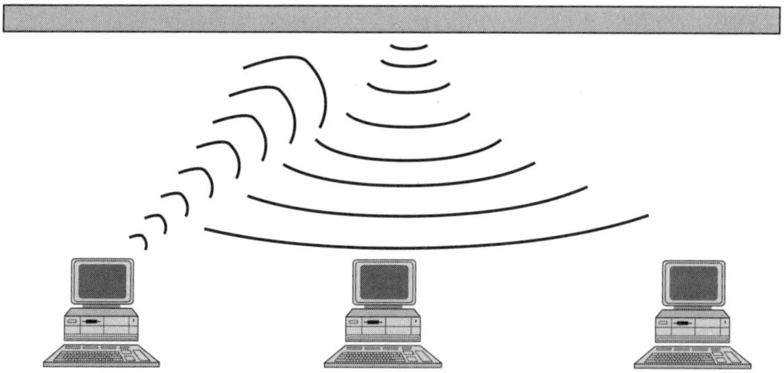

Figure 4.6
Operation of a broadcast optical LAN.

The point-to-point approach is shown in figure 4.7. Because a tight beam is used, receivers can depend on working with a fairly strong light signal. Of course, the transmitters and receivers must be situated so that they will not be obstructed as people walk through the office. That can be a significant challenge that can work against the theoretical advantage of wireless media: that they should be easy to install.

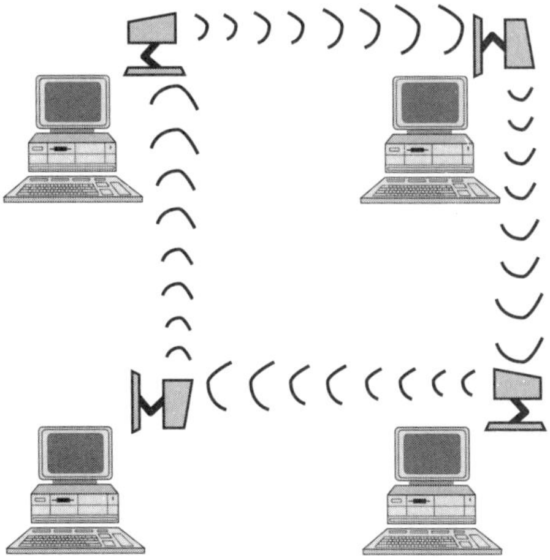

Figure 4.7

A point-to-point optical LAN.

Point-to-point optical LANs are not limited to short-range operation. If you need to connect two buildings that are separated by a few hundred yards, you might consider an optical connection that is based on laser transmitters. Gas lasers can generate very high signal levels that can travel reliably for a considerable distance. Of course, rain or fog can disrupt all such optical communication links.

Although infrared light has the potential for supporting high bandwidths, current infrared LAN technologies typically support bandwidths below 5 Mbps.

Radio Frequency LANs

The majority of wireless LANs use radio frequencies. Two LAN technologies are available:

- **Spread spectrum.** This is based on a technology developed by the military to transmit secure signals that are highly resistant to noise.
- **18 GHz LANs.** These use a low-power radio technology similar to cellular telephone networks.

Spread Spectrum

Spread spectrum transmissions use several frequencies to transmit a given message. In one scheme, the transmitter hops among the various frequencies, depending on which channel has the least noise at a given time. The transmitter informs the receiver which frequencies it will use so that transmitter and receiver can remain synchronized.

Another scheme divides the message into parts, transmitting different parts over different frequencies. To make the data more secure, dummy data can be transmitted over a separate channel. The intended receiver knows which frequencies carry legitimate data, but eavesdroppers will have difficulty isolating the original message from the many possible frequency channels.

Spread spectrum LAN designers rely primarily on unlicensed frequencies—frequencies that can be used without acquiring a permit from the Federal Communications Commission (FCC). Three unlicensed frequency ranges that can be used for radio LANs are 902–928 MHz, 2.4–2.483 GHz, and 5.725–5.85 GHz. (*Hz* or *Hertz* is a measure of radio frequencies in cycles per second.)

Unlicensed frequencies can be used freely with few limitations. This sounds convenient, but you might find yourself sharing a frequency with a radio-controlled model airplane enthusiast or an alarm system. Without the added reliability provided by spread spectrum technology, use of unlicensed frequencies would be impractical.

Spread spectrum transmissions can be powerful enough to penetrate many types of walls. Therefore, spread spectrum is a media option in older construction areas where cables cannot be installed.

Note Spread spectrum is the way to go if your users want to operate free of cables. One vendor even provides a radio transceiver that installs in the PCMCIA slot of a laptop portable. Although this product has extremely short range, it does make it easy for users of portable computers to hook into the network or move around the office.

18 GHz

The engineers at Motorola have capitalized on their experience with cellular telephones to build a LAN product that operates on similar lines. The key to cellular networks is to use low-power radio transmissions that cover a very limited area called a *cell.*

Devices within a cell communicate with a hub that functions as a transmitter/receiver for the cell. When a message is directed to another device in the same cell as the message's originator, the hub retransmits the message to the cell. When a message is directed to a device in another cell, the hub forwards the message through a cable to the appropriate hub. The organization of a Motorola 18-GHz network is shown in figure 4.8.

18 GHz is a licensed frequency. To simplify licensing, Motorola has obtained licenses in all major metropolitan areas. Motorola handles all the licensing requirements for the customer.

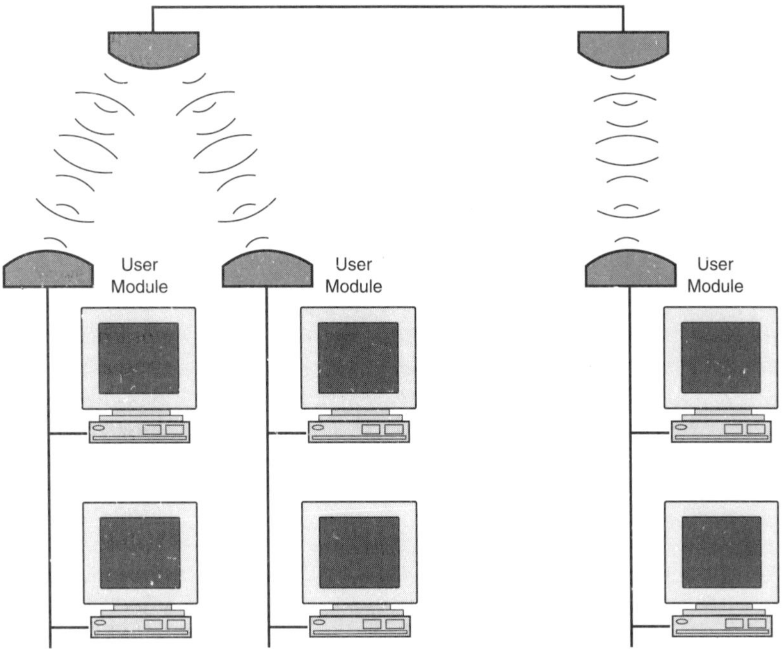

Figure 4.8

An example of a Motorola 18-GHz network.

Notice that the Motorola technology is not completely wireless. Computers communicate with hubs through user modules, which are connected by cables. Also, most hub-to-hub connections are cabled.

Note This discussion might have you wondering about the possibility of networking through the cellular telephone network. Using modems, this is possible to some degree when devices aren't moving. When a device crosses a cellular boundary, however, the process of handing off the signal from one cell to the next almost always interrupts data flow.

Observations on Wireless LANs

Vendors of wireless LANs are fond of quoting high estimates for the costs of moving PCs within an organization. Estimated costs of $500 to $1,000 per move are not uncommon. The claim is that the added cost of a wireless LAN is recovered quickly by money saved in moving computers.

It is difficult to see how these high costs can be justified in real life. With a modern structured cabling system (described later in this chapter), it is common to install cable in every place a computer is likely to be needed. Moving a computer is a simple matter of unplugging it from one location, moving the hardware, and plugging it into a new LAN outlet. Most of the labor is in moving the PC. Recabling the system is a matter of a few minutes.

As you saw in figure 4.8, many wireless LANs are not really wireless. Cables are needed to interconnect hubs or to enable devices to share LAN interface modules. Reorganizing the cabling of a "wireless" LAN could be a significant undertaking.

18-GHz radio and optical LANs cannot penetrate walls. Once again, you are faced with the need to use cables to interconnect different sections of the LAN. Few wireless LANs truly are wireless.

Wireless LANs are significantly outperformed by even low-end cabled LANs. Ethernet delivers a bandwidth of 10 Mbps. Wireless LANs seldom approach even half that level, and 1–2 Mbps of bandwidth are common. If your organization is moving into network-intensive applications such as graphics or multimedia, it is unlikely that you will find a wireless LAN technology that fills your needs. LAN technologies such as 100-Mbps Ethernet or the emerging 455-Mbps ATM are unlikely to be supported by wireless media.

You probably should consider wireless LANs only when cabling is not an option. Some buildings do not structurally permit you to run cables, and some organizations require that workers be mobile with their PCs. Other than these two requirements, it is difficult to imagine applications where wireless LANs would be the technology of choice.

Topologies

Devices can communicate on networks in two ways, and all network configurations are variations on these two methods:

- The bus
- The point-to-point link

Bus Networks

Ethernet, the earliest LAN technology, was based on a bus configuration. A example of a bus is shown in figure 4.9. Notice that all the devices are connected to the same wire. Computer B is transmitting, and its signal travels down the wire in both directions. Every device on the network "hears" the signal. That is the distinguishing characteristic of a bus: If every device on the network can intercept every signal, the network is functioning as a bus.

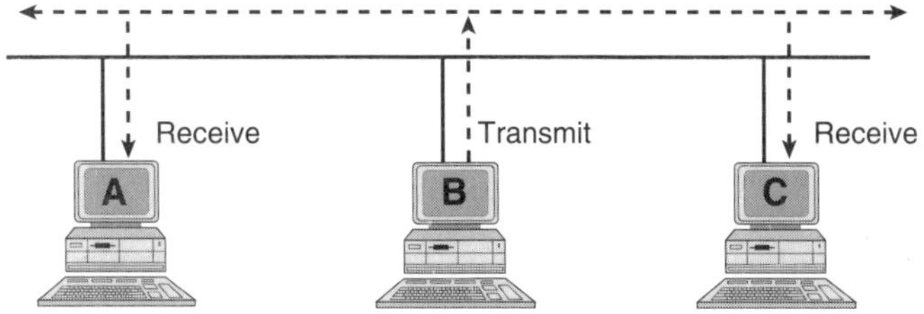

Figure 4.9

A bus-topology network.

A bus operates much like human conversation in a room—everyone can hear everything that is said by everyone else. Just like computers on a bus, humans in a room are sharing the same communication channel.

Point-to-Point Connections

The majority of networks are based on point-to-point (P-P) connections. Basic P-P links are illustrated in figure 4.10. A one-way link is established by connecting the transmitter of one device to the receiver of another. Two-way communication can be accomplished in a variety of ways.

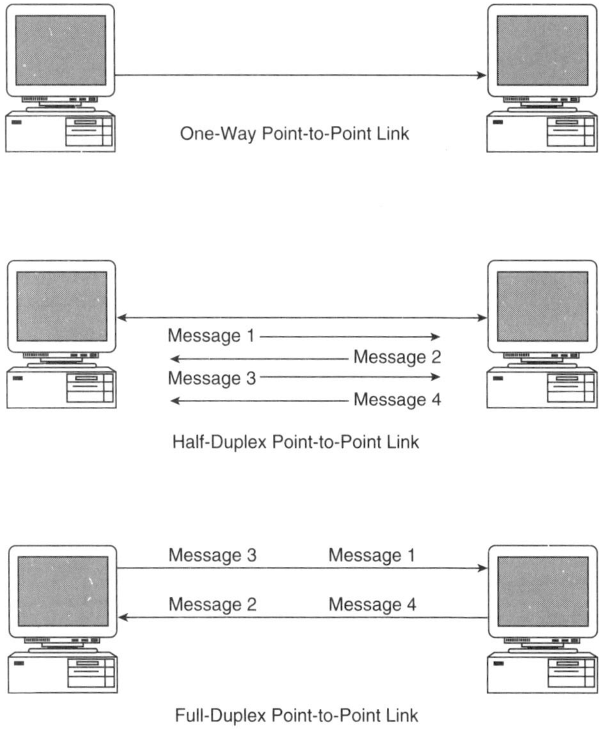

Figure 4.10

Types of point-to-point connections.

Two-way communication often is referred to as *duplex* mode. If only one communication channel exists, the devices must take turns transmitting; this is called *half-duplex* mode. In half-duplex mode, the devices take turns using a single wire. When one device is finished transmitting, it must "turn over" the communication channel so that the other device knows that it is permitted to transmit.

If both devices can transmit at the same time, the operation is called *full-duplex.* Full duplex operation requires two communication channels. On LANs, full-duplex channels usually are created by adding a second pair of wires.

Building Complex Networks

Bus networks grow simply by extending the bus and adding devices. At some point, the bus will not be able to accommodate additional devices. At that point, additional buses can be connected together—usually with devices called *bridges.* A two-bus network is shown in figure 4.11. Ethernet is the most common network design based on a bus. You examine the rules for extending Ethernet LANs later in this chapter.

Figure 4.11

Extending a bus network with a bridge.

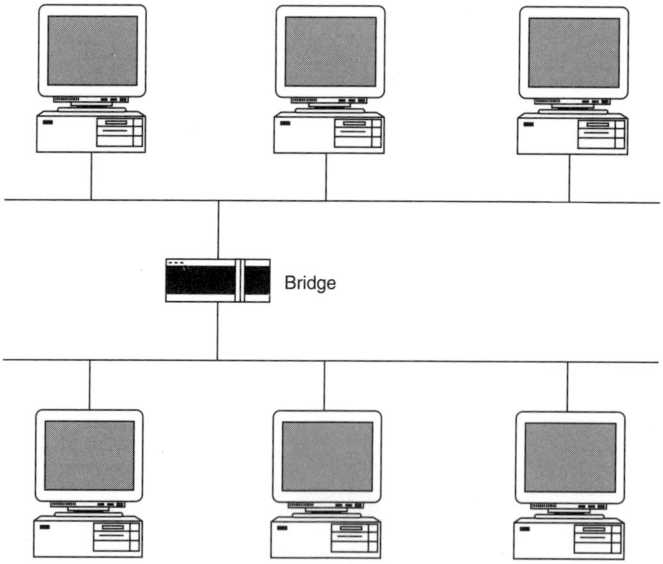

When P-P links are used, devices can be added simply by adding more P-P connections. Several multi-device networks are shown in figure 4.12. When each device is connected to every other device, the network design is called a *mesh.* You will notice that the number of P-P links in a mesh network rises rapidly as the number of devices increases. A three-device network requires three P-P links, but a four-device network requires six links. Obviously, this is not a practical way to network large numbers of devices.

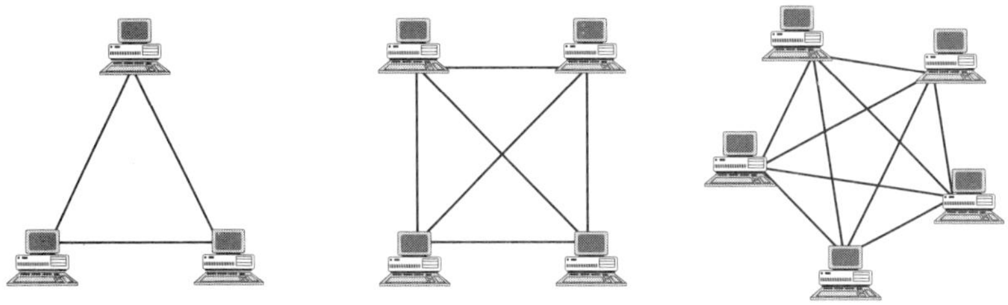

Figure 4.12
Mesh networks.

Mesh networks have several significant advantages. Each device has a dedicated communication link with every other device and has access to the full bandwidth available for that link. Devices on buses must share the bandwidth available on the bus medium. Another advantage of a mesh is that multiple paths exist between devices. If a direct path between devices goes down, messages can be routed through other devices.

Many large networks are constructed using a variation on the mesh design. The *hybrid mesh* approach shown in figure 4.13 uses extra links to establish redundant paths, but does not build in enough links to create a complete mesh. When the network links stretch for long distances, as in a countrywide or worldwide network, the redundancy of a hybrid mesh network can provide an important improvement in reliability.

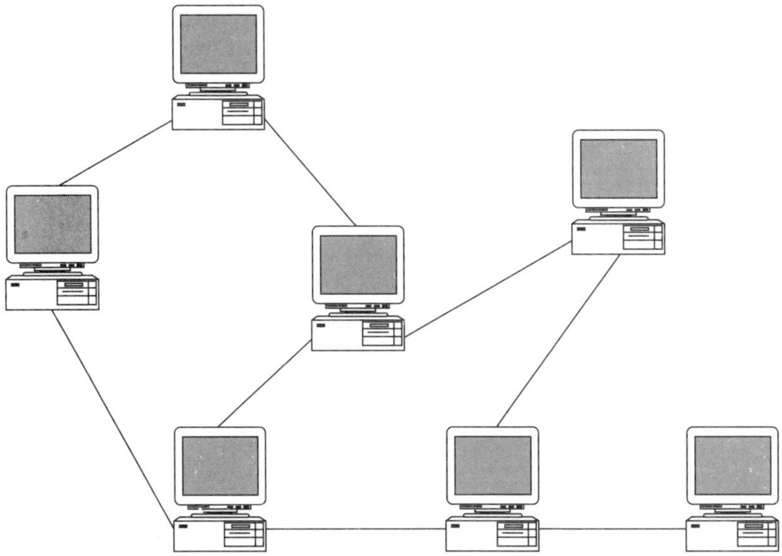

Figure 4.13
A hybrid mesh network.

LANs generally are presumed to be reliable, and they seldom are configured as meshes. Meshes seldom are used to build LANs. The approaches most commonly used to build LANs with P-P links are rings and stars.

Figure 4.14 shows a *ring* network design. In this approach, the transmitter of one device is connected to the receiver of the next device in the ring. In this way, messages are forwarded around the ring until they are examined by each device on the network.

Figure 4.14

A ring network.

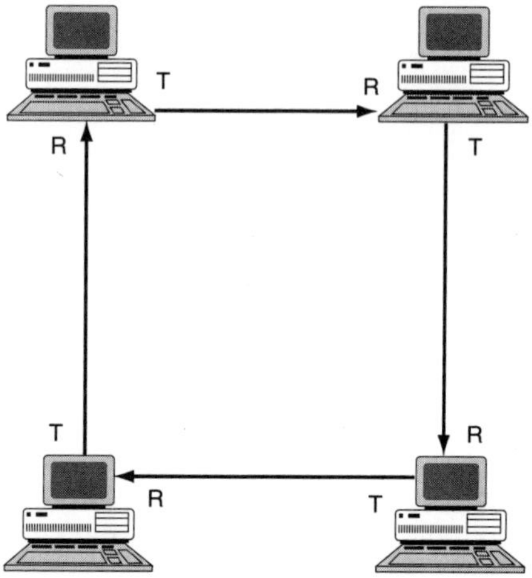

Another common approach is the *star*, shown in Figure 4.15. Star networks concentrate all network connections in wiring hubs. Each device connects to the network through a P-P link with the wiring hub.

Figure 4.15

A star network.

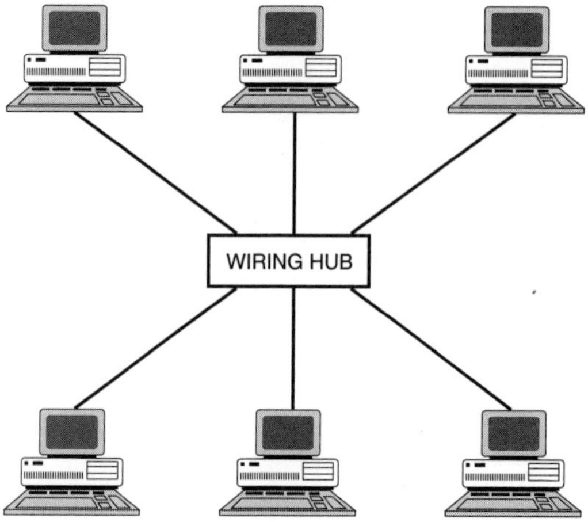

Physical and Logical Topologies

The *topology* of a LAN is a description of the network's shape. The topologies you have seen to this point are called *physical topologies* because they describe how the cabling of the network is physically laid out.

In addition to having a physical topology, every network design has a *logical topology*, which describes how the network looks from the perspective of the signals traveling through it. A given network design can have different physical and logical topologies. In other words, the way a network is cabled does not necessarily reflect the way in which signals flow through it.

Note Here is another way to distinguish physical topology from logical topology:

- If you can see and touch it, it is physical.
- If you cannot see or touch it, it is logical.

Figure 4.16 is an example of a physical star network that functions logically as a ring. Each computer is connected to a central network hub with a cable that includes separate wires for receiving and transmitting signals. If you trace the cables through the figure, you will discover that the signal path is logically the same as that shown in figure 4.13. The network is wired in a star, but it functions as a ring as far as the network signals are concerned.

Figure 4.17 shows a star-wired network that functions as a logical bus. In this case, the hub mixes the signals from all the attached devices. All messages are retransmitted to all devices attached to the hub. Recall that this is a defining characteristic of a bus: all devices hear all signals on the network. The network is a physical star because each device connects to the hub through an individual cable, but the network functions as a bus.

Most new LAN standards are based on star physical topologies. Star networks have several advantages. If each device is connected with its own cable, it is easy to move computers and reconfigure the network. This is, in fact, the basic principle behind structured wiring, a concept that is explained later in this chapter.

Star wiring also makes it easy to isolate malfunctioning devices. If a computer goes bad and starts corrupting data, it is easy to disconnect the faulty device by disconnecting its cable or by turning off its connection electronically at the hub.

When all devices connect to hubs, the hubs become central points from which to manage the network. It is increasingly common to build diagnostic capabilities into hubs, enabling them to detect problems and to notify network managers.

Figure 4.16

A network that is wired as a star but functions logically as a ring.

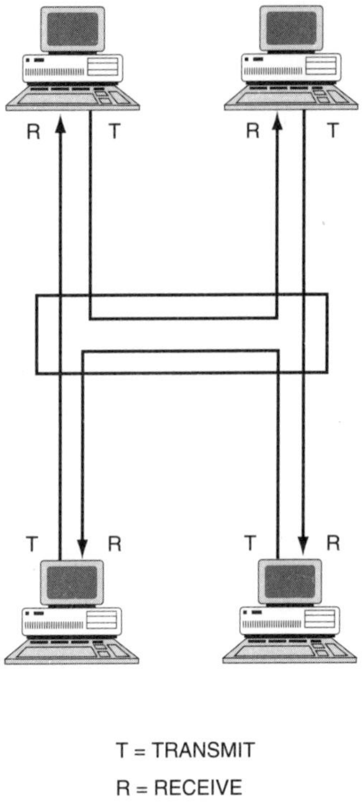

Figure 4.17

A network that is wired as a star but functions as a bus.

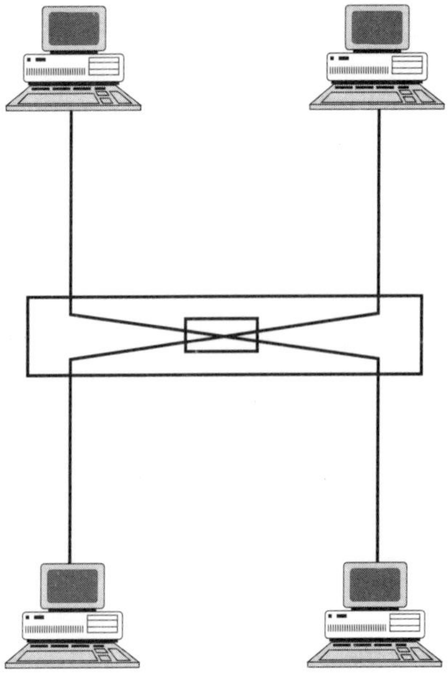

Hubs

Star-wired networks are based on hubs, and you should know something about the types of hubs that are available. Broadly speaking, there are two hub varieties: passive and active.

Passive hubs do not incorporate any powered electronic components. As a result, the only function of passive hubs is to provide a central point for connecting cables. Passive hubs cannot provide network management or improve the quality of network signals. You encounter only one type of passive hub in this chapter: the IBM model 8228, a relay-based hub that was developed for IBM's Token-Ring network.

The majority of hubs are *active*, meaning that they include electronic components that can process signals. Active hubs can include several interesting capabilities:

- Amplification of weakened signals
- Reshaping and retiming of distorted waveforms
- Detection of network problems
- Sending performance and error reports to management
- Remote management, enabling network administrators to control hubs that are located a considerable distance away

An interesting and fairly new category of active hub is the *switching hub* (see fig. 4.18). A switching hub can quickly switch signals between any two attached devices. Each device attached to the hub enjoys a private connection and has access to the full bandwidth capabilities available from its connection. Switching hubs improve network performance by freeing devices from the need to share the bandwidth of a common cable segment.

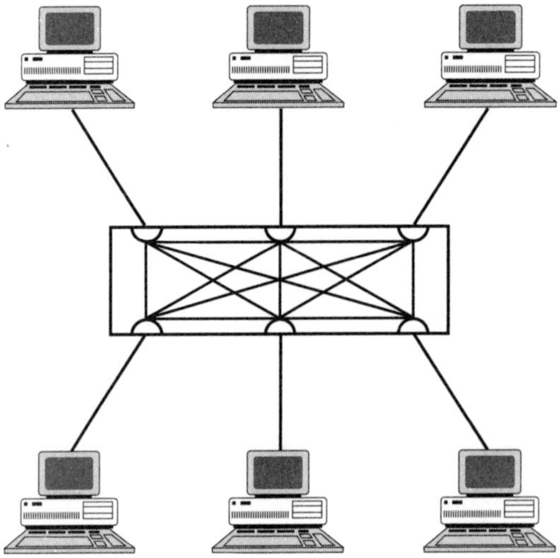

Figure 4.18
An example of a switching hub.

LAN Cabling Standards

The vast majority of local area networks are based on two standards: Ethernet and token ring. Both of these network types have been standardized by the International Electrical and Electronics Engineers (IEEE) organization, the largest professional organization in the world. The IEEE has a well-established standardization process that is open to a broad range of input. As a result, standards developed by the IEEE generally receive universal industry support.

IEEE LAN standards are grouped under the heading 802. A wide variety of 802 standards have been or are in the process of being defined. Some of those standards follow:

- **802.2.** Defines a network layer called the logical link control (LLC) layer.
- **802.3.** Defines the IEEE version of Ethernet.
- **802.5.** Defines the IEEE version of token ring.

Figure 4.19 illustrates the relationship of these standards to the OSI model. Notice that the 802.2 standard describes the upper half of the data link layer. Both the 802.3 and the 802.5 standards describe the physical layer, along with the lower half of the data link layer. All the lower-level 802.*x* standards are designed to work with the same LLC layer as defined by standard 802.2.

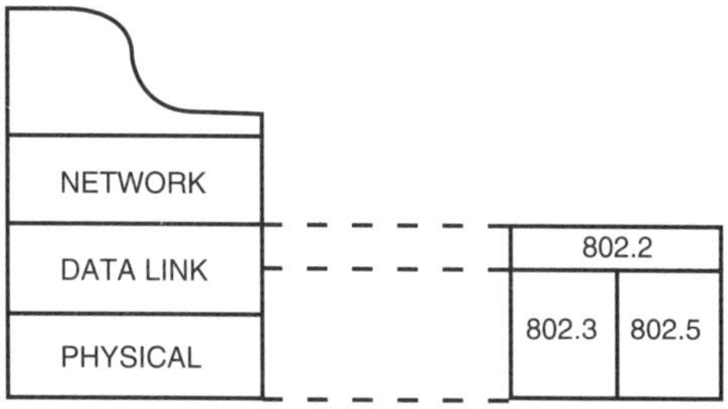

Figure 4.19
The relationship of several IEEE standards to the OSI reference model.

The 802.3 and 802.5 standards cover the OSI physical layer. They also cover the lower half of the data link layer—a sublayer called the medium access control (MAC) sublayer. The *MAC sublayer* defines the way in which devices on the network share the network medium.

By defining a common LLC protocol for all LAN standards, the IEEE approach makes it unnecessary for the upper layer protocols to be aware of the type of network on which they are operating. In fact, a network device can be moved from one network cabling system to another simply by changing the physical layer protocols.

You do not need to know a great deal about the 802.2 layer. However, you should be at least somewhat familiar with the characteristics of the physical layer that is used on your LAN. The Ethernet (802.3) and token ring (802.5) standards are discussed in the following sections.

The Fiber Distributed Data Interface (FDDI) is another network that Windows NT Server supports out of the box. FDDI is a standard for a fiber-based network that was developed by the X3T9.5 committee of the American National Standards Institute (ANSI). The ISO has adopted FDDI as standard 9314. FDDI was developed for wide-area networks (WANs), but has been used in MANs and LANs as well. FDDI is designed around fiber-optic media and has a data bandwidth of 100 Mbps, but it has been adapted to copper media as well. FDDI also is discussed later in this chapter.

Ethernet

Ethernet is the oldest LAN cabling system in current use—it dates back to the early 1970s. It developed originally out of research at the Xerox Palo Alto Research Center (Xerox PARC), and was refined through the joint efforts of Xerox, Intel, and Digital Equipment. Ethernet was submitted to the IEEE for standardization and, with some modification, became the IEEE 802.3 standard.

The original Digital/Intel/Xerox (DIX) Ethernet differs from the 802.3 standard. The most recent version of DIX Ethernet commonly is referred to as Ethernet II or Ethernet version 2. Ethernet II remains in common use on TCP/IP networks and on Digital's DECnet networks. The IEEE 802.3 standard is the dominant Ethernet version on most other network types.

Xerox has surrendered the Ethernet trademark to the public domain, and there is considerable controversy whether the DIX or the IEEE standard has the strongest claim to be called Ethernet. For what it's worth, the opinion of Robert Metcalf, credited as the inventor of Ethernet, is that the Ethernet label should be assigned to the latest standard, which is IEEE 802.3.

This book is not the place to settle the argument. The Ethernet variants are quite similar and are based on a medium access control method called CSMA/CD. Consequently, the term *Ethernet* is used in this book to describe features of both CSMA/CD networks. When it is important to make a distinction, the terms *Ethernet II* and *Ethernet 802.3* will be used.

How CSMA/CD Works

Ethernet is based on a bus, and you have learned that all devices on a bus share the same network medium. Because multiple frames on the same cable would interfere with each other, only one frame can be permitted on the network at a given time. CSMA/CD is the mechanism that enables devices to share the medium without excessively interfering with each other. This behavior sometimes is described as *listen before talking.*

CSMA/CD is an abbreviation for *Carrier Sense Multiple Access with Collision Detection.* That's a mouthful, but it's easy to understand if you take the name apart.

Carrier sensing describes the behavior of a device that wants to transmit on the network. When a device needs to access the network, it first listens to determine whether the network is busy. If the network is busy, the device waits for a bit and tries again. If the network is quiet, the device begins to transmit its frame. This behavior is quite similar to your behavior when you want to speak at a meeting. To avoid interrupting anyone, you listen for a lull in the conversation before you talk.

Multiple access means that many devices can share the network medium.

Collision detection describes the behavior of devices when they determine that two computers have sent frames at the same time. As a device is transmitting, it continues to listen to the network. If another frame appears on the network, it collides with the frame that the device is transmitting. Devices know collisions have occurred because they cause a higher than normal voltage to appear on the network.

When it detects a collision, a device stops sending its data and transmits a *jamming signal* that notifies all devices on the network of the collision. After the jamming signal is transmitted, each device waits for a random amount of time before attempting to retransmit. The random delay is important. If each device waited the same amount of time before retransmitting, another collision would occur. If devices wait for different lengths of time, collisions become less likely.

Collisions are a fact of life on CSMA/CD networks. This is because signals do not travel instantly down the entire length of the cable. Signals on cables travel somewhat slower than the speed of light. As Figure 4.20 shows, when a device transmits, other devices will still sense a quiet network for a small period of time. A second device might, therefore, choose to transmit even though a signal from the first device was already on its way. Somewhere in the middle, the two signals will collide.

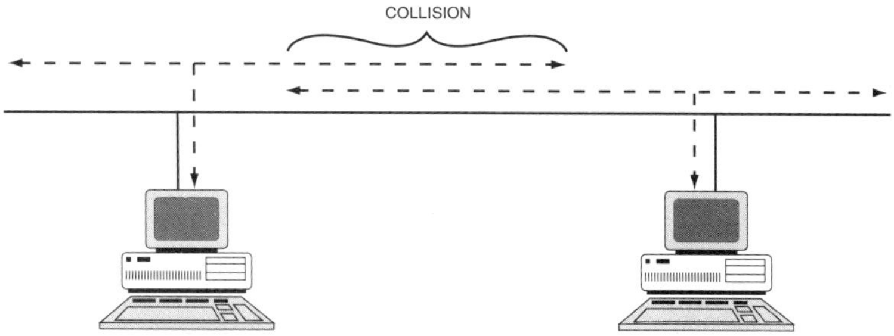

Figure 4.20

How Ethernet collisions occur.

You might correctly conclude that collisions are undesirable and that they detract from network performance. However, unless an Ethernet is overloaded with traffic, collisions remain at a reasonable level and performance is excellent. An Ethernet frame can consist of no more that 1,518 bytes, and an Ethernet has a bandwidth of 10 million bits per second (1.25 million bytes). Unless the network is loaded heavily, collisions should occur with only a small percentage of frames transmitted.

At low LAN traffic levels, CSMA/CD is actually an extremely effective protocol. Little housekeeping is required to keep the network running, so the majority of the network's bandwidth is devoted to useful traffic.

When a CSMA/CD network is loaded too heavily, however, it is possible for collisions to become so frequent that little useful traffic can find its way onto the network. Under such circumstances, a device might find it impossible to transmit.

Ethernets tend to function very smoothly until some critical threshold is exceeded. At some point, traffic increases result in much more frequent collisions and network performance degrades, often catastrophically. You should make it a habit to monitor your LAN to determine whether usage levels are increasing to a potentially troublesome level. A good rule of thumb is that Ethernets work fine with constant traffic loads of 30 percent of capacity and traffic bursts of about 60 percent of capacity. If your LAN is exceeding these levels, you should take steps to divide your Ethernet into additional segments to reduce the number of stations that are sharing a given segment's bandwidth.

CSMA/CD is a *probabilistic* access control method, meaning that a given device probably will have a chance to transmit at roughly the time it needs to, but that the opportunity to transmit is not guaranteed. On most LANs, probabilistic access control works fine. In some applications, however, it might be necessary to be more certain that devices can transmit. Suppose that the network is controlling a manufacturing process and that things must happen at precise times. The possibility that a device might not gain access to the network at a critical time is unacceptable. This state of affairs is one reason why IBM invented the Token-Ring network.

Ethernet Cabling

Until recently, all Ethernets were cabled with thick or thin coaxial cable. Customers demanded a UTP configuration, however, and the IEEE responded with the 10BASE-T standard. This section reviews the three most common Ethernet cabling standards.

Thick Ethernet (10BASE5)

The original Ethernet cabling used a thick, half-inch diameter coaxial cable and is referred to as thick Ethernet or thicknet. As with most varieties of Ethernet, thick Ethernet operates in baseband mode with a bandwidth of 10 Mbps. The maximum cable length of a segment is 500 meters. The IEEE label 10BASE5 summarizes these characteristics: 10 Mbps bandwidth, baseband operation, and 500 meter segments.

Figure 4.21 illustrates the components of a thick Ethernet. Workstations do not connect directly to the thick coaxial cable. Instead, they attach by way of multistation access units (MAUs). An MAU can be installed on the cable by cutting the cable and installing N-type connectors. The more common practice is to use MAUs that clamp onto the cable. Pins in the clamp-on MAU penetrate the cable to make contact with the shield and center conductor. MAUs that attach in this way are called *vampire taps.* For best performance, MAUs should be attached to the thick coaxial cable at intervals that are even multiples of 2.5 meters.

Both MAUs and device network interfaces are equipped with a special 15-pin connector called an attachment unit interface (AUI) connector. A multiconductor AUI cable of up to 50 meters can be used to connect the device to the MAU.

Figure 4.21 shows a common feature of networks based on coaxial cable. The ends of an Ethernet bus must be equipped with *terminators*—connectors that incorporate a 50-ohm resistor that matches the impedance characteristics of the cable. The terminator absorbs any signals that reach them and prevents the signals from being reflected back into the cable as noise. One of the terminators must be connected to an electrical ground. Without the grounded connection, the cable's shield might not do an effective job of protecting against EMI. Only one terminator should be grounded. Grounding both connectors can produce electrical problems in the cable. A common source of an electrical ground is the screw in the center of an electrical wallplate. You should have your outlets tested to ensure that a good ground is present.

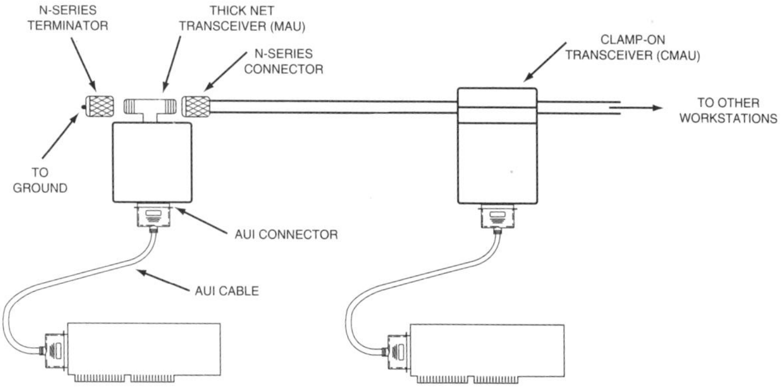

Figure 4.21
Components of a thick Ethernet.

Two sets of terminology are used with thick Ethernet. The IEEE 802.3 standard refers to the connectors as *attachment unit interface connectors.* Practitioners of the older Ethernet II standard, however, refer to these connectors as *DIX (Digital-Intel-Xerox) connectors.* Also, although the IEEE 802.3 standard refers to the cable interface as a *medium attachment unit,* it more commonly is called a *transceiver* when used in an Ethernet II environment. You often will find these terms used interchangeably.

Apart from naming conventions, cabling is identical for Ethernet II and IEEE Ethernet 802.3. In fact, messages from both standards can coexist on the same cable segment.

An Ethernet *segment* consists of the coaxial cable between two terminators. The maximum length of a thick Ethernet segment is 500 meters, and each segment can support a maximum of 100 connections. When it is necessary to construct larger networks, segments can be connected by using repeaters, as shown in figure 4.22. Repeaters serve several purposes: they electrically isolate the coaxial segments, they amplify signals that pass between segments, and they reshape waveforms to correct distortions that arise as signals travel through cables.

A repeater segment is called a *link segment.* At most, an Ethernet can include three coaxial cable segments and two link segments. Repeaters connect to coax segments using AUI cables, which are limited to 50 meters. The maximum length of a link segment therefore is 100 meters. If longer link segments are required, fiber-optic cable can be used to create a fiber-optic repeater link (FIORL) segment. FIORL segments can be up to 1 kilometer.

Thickwire Ethernet is seldom used in new LAN installations. The cable is expensive and bulky. Network components are also expensive, and are difficult to install.

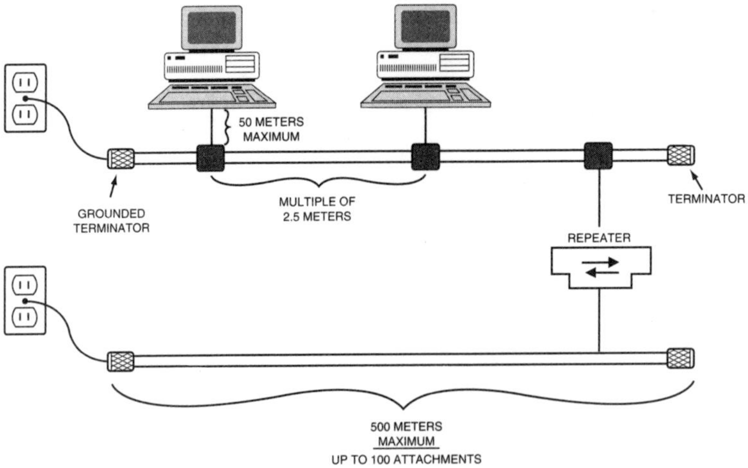

Figure 4.22
Extending a thick Ethernet with a link segment.

Thin Ethernet (10BASE2)

The IEEE 10BASE2 specification describes a CSMA/CD network with these features: 10 Mbps bandwidth, baseband operation, and segment lengths of approximately 200 meters. (The precise limit is 185 meters.) The coaxial cable used with 10BASE2 is considerably thinner than thicknet coax. Consequently, this Ethernet cabling system often is called thin Ethernet, thinnet, or just Cheapernet.

You can examine the connectors used in thin Ethernet in figure 4.23. The connector used is a BNC (bayonet connector), which attaches and locks by twisting into place. NICs attach to the network by means of T connectors, which attach directly to the NIC. Although it is possible to use MAUs and AUI cables with thinnet, this seldom is done due to the high cost of components.

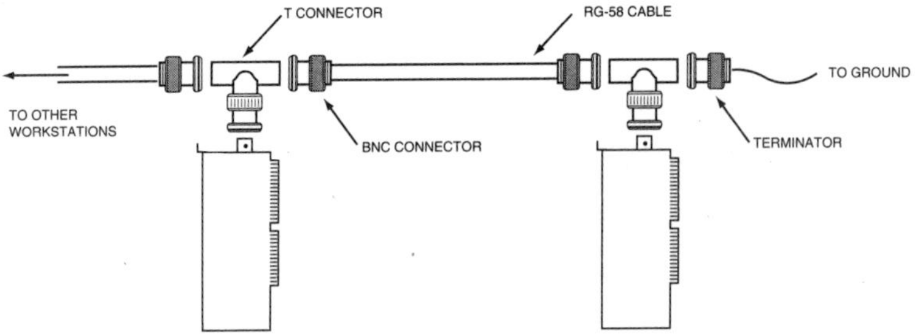

Figure 4.23
Components of a thin Ethernet.

As shown in figure 4.23, thinnet coaxial cable segments must have a terminator at each end. One of the terminators should be grounded (not both terminators).

A thin Ethernet segment should not exceed 185 meters or include more than 30 attached devices. For best performance, devices should be spaced along the cable at even multiples of one-half meter.

BNC connectors are easy to install with a few simple tools, or you can buy premade cables. Manufactured cables have two advantages: the connectors are securely installed, and cable lengths conform in length to the rule of one-half meter multiples. Thin Ethernet is easy to install in most situations.

Like thick Ethernet, thinnet networks can be extended using repeater links. A thin Ethernet that includes two coax segments is shown in figure 4.24.

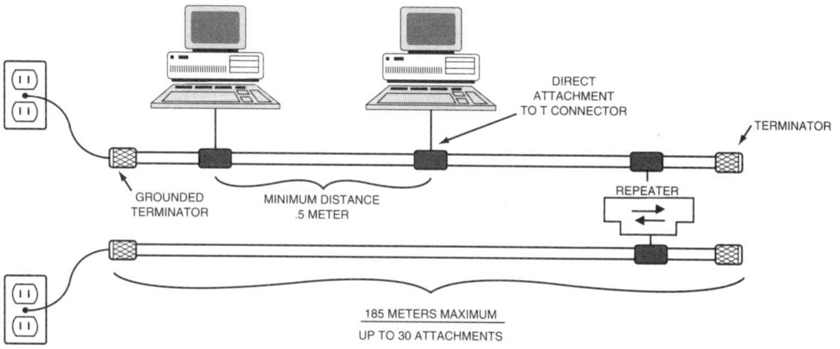

Figure 4.24

A thin Ethernet that includes a repeater link segment.

Each workstation connection involves three separate BNC connectors; these are the cause of most problems with thin Ethernets. It is quite common for users to accidentally dislodge connectors or to pull the cable out of a connector—perhaps when moving the PC. Any break in the coaxial segment can disrupt network communication for the entire segment.

Although thinnet gradually is being replaced by a preference for UTP networks, it remains an excellent choice—especially for small networks. The cost of a connection for thin Ethernet is the lowest of any network cabling system—easily less than $100 per device. No hubs are required, which can raise the cost of a network connection by $20 to more than $100 per device. Thinnet cannot be surpassed as an inexpensive medium for networking small organizations in a fairly restricted area.

One problem with thin Ethernet networks is that they can be difficult to reconfigure. Adding a device requires you to add a T connector to the coax, which cannot be done without cutting the cable. As a result, you can add users only when the network is shut down.

For large networks or networks that must be reconfigured frequently, it is a good idea to choose a star-wired network that includes intelligent hubs. These networks are easy to reconfigure and manage. The next section describes the IEEE 10BASE-T standard, which describes a hub-based version of Ethernet that uses UTP cable.

The features of 10BASE5 and 10BASE2 networks are summarized in table 4.2.

Table 4.2
Features of 10BASE5 and 10BASE2 Networks

Feature	10BASE5	10BASE2
Bandwidth	10 Mbps	10 Mbps
Maximum segment length	500 meters	185 meters
Maximum number of devices	100	30
Maximum link segments	2	2
Optimum device spacing	2.5 meters	.5 meter

Twisted-Pair Ethernet (10BASE-T)

The IEEE has developed an Ethernet standard called 10BASE-T, which describes 10 Mbps Ethernet that uses unshielded twisted-pair cable. Unlike coax Ethernet, 10BASE-T uses a star wiring topology based on hubs. The length of the cable that connects a device to the hub is limited to 100 meters. A simple 10BASE-T network is shown in figure 4.25.

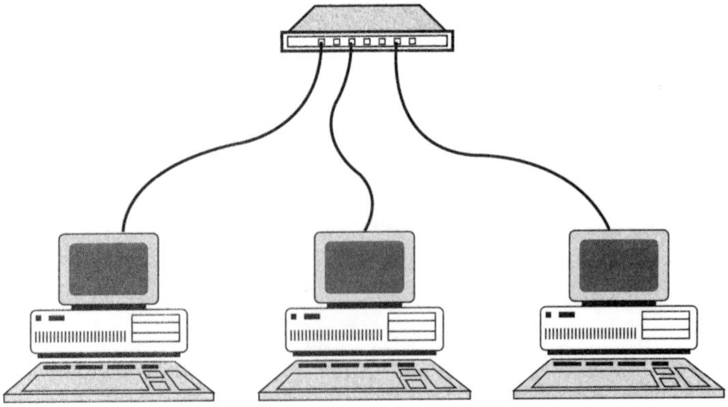

Figure 4.25
Crossing over twisted pairs in a 10BASE-T network.

The cables used with 10BASE-T include two twisted pairs. These cables must be configured so that the transmitter of the device at one cable end connects to the receiver of the device at the other end. Figure 4.26 shows that this configuration can be accomplished in two ways:

- By crossing over the pairs of wires in the cable itself.
- By reversing the connections at one of the devices. The device in which connections are reversed is marked with an X by the manufacturer. This is a common approach with 10BASE-T hubs.

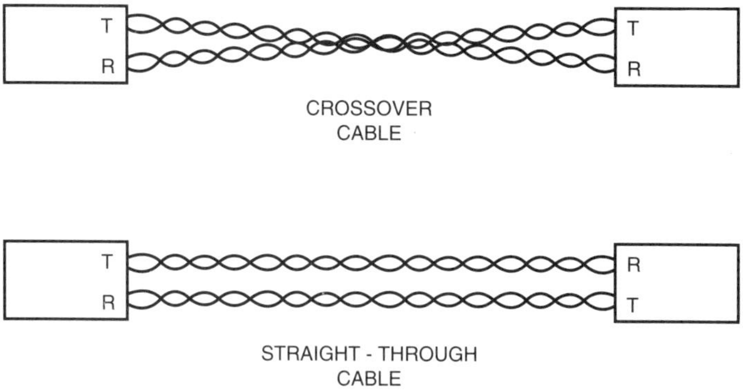

Figure 4.26
Methods of crossing pairs in 10BASE-T connections.

10BASE-T networks require at least Category 3 UTP cable connected with RJ-45 connectors. Never be tempted to use installed telephone wiring without determining whether it meets Category 3 specifications. And never use telephone-grade patch cables for connecting devices to hubs. Pairs of wires are not twisted in the flat satin cables that normally are used to attach telephones to the wall. Also, flat-satin cables are designed for voice-grade service, and they cannot support LAN data rates.

It is important for you to understand that the star physical topology of a 10BASE-T network does not alter the logical topology of Ethernet. A 10BASE-T network remains a logical bus. All devices on the network share the 10-Mbps bandwidth of the network, and only one device is permitted to access the network at a given time.

Your primary reason for choosing 10BASE-T should not be the goal of saving money with UTP cable. Instead, you should focus on the advantages a star network offers in terms of reconfiguration and management.

How 802.3 Ethernet Compares to Ethernet II

Although IEEE 802.3 Ethernet and Ethernet II networks can operate with the same cabling components, one significant difference exists between the two standards. This difference is illustrated by figure 4.27, which compares the frame formats defined for the two standards.

Figure 4.27

Frame formats for 802.3 Ethernet and Ethernet II.

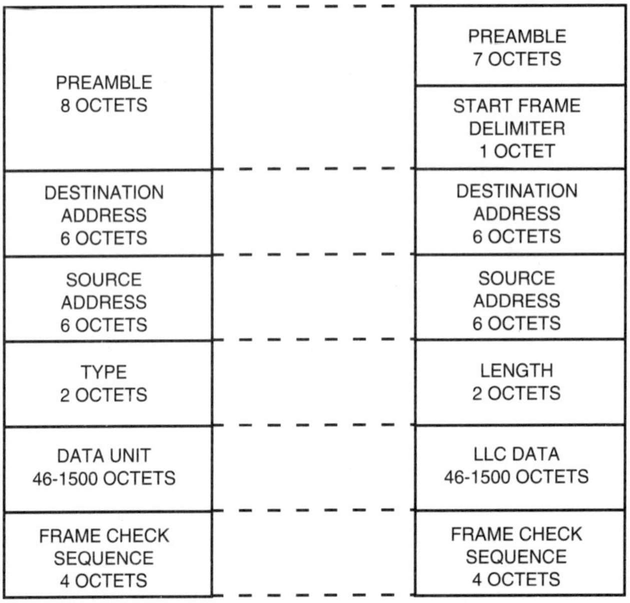

As shown in figure 4.27, data frames are organized into fields. In most cases, the fields used in 802.3 Ethernet and Ethernet II have the same formats, although the names often are different. Incidentally, the term for an 8-bit unit in an Ethernet frame is *octet.* This list summarizes the similarities and differences between the two frame formats:

- An Ethernet II frame starts with an 8-octet Preamble, which has the same format as the Preamble and the Start Frame Delimiter of the IEEE 802.3 frame.

- Ethernet II uses 6-octet source and destination address fields. 802.3 Ethernet can operate with 2- or 6-octet addresses, although 6 octets are used most commonly. Manufacturers are granted blocks of addresses by an Ethernet address registry, and a unique 6-octet address is burned into each Ethernet NIC during manufacture. This hardware address typically is used in the address fields.

- Ethernet II uses a Type field, using values that are defined by the IEEE. The 802.3 specification replaces the Type field with a Length field that describes the length in bytes of the LLC Data field. Because the LLC Data field has a maximum length of 1,500 octets, it is easy to distinguish an 802.3 frame from an Ethernet II frame by examining the value of the Type/Length field. If the value is 1501 or greater, the frame is an Ethernet II frame.
- The data fields have different names but otherwise are identical. The 802.3 standard calls the field the LLC Data field, because it contains data that is passed down from the Logical Length Control sublayer. Data fields have a minimum length of 46 octets and are padded with extra data if they fall short of the minimum. The maximum length of an Ethernet data field is 1,500 octets.
- The Frame Check Sequence field contains a value that is used to detect transmission errors. Before it transmits a frame, a device calculates a mathematical value called a cyclic redundancy check (CRC) that summarizes all the data in the frame. The receiving device recalculates the CRC. If the calculated CRC matches the value in the Frame Check Sequence field, it can be assumed that the frame was transmitted without error.

Ethernet Frame Types

Several types of Ethernet frames are in common use. If you network only with Microsoft products, you are likely to encounter only two types of frames: IEEE 802.3 Ethernet and Ethernet II. When you configure Windows NT Server, the correct frame formats are selected for you. Windows NT Server is engineered to work smoothly with Novell networking products, however, and you frequently will see another frame type mentioned.

Novell began networking with Ethernet before the IEEE 802 standards were fully defined. The original Ethernet frame format used by Novell did not include information associated with the IEEE 802.2 LLC standard. This frame format, which Novell now calls Ethernet_802.3, is incompatible with non-Novell network implementations. It is supported by Windows NT Server when it is required for interfacing with a Novell LAN, however.

Novell has begun to use the full IEEE 802.3 frame format. Because the format includes IEEE 802.2 data, Novell calls the frame format Ethernet_802.2. This is now the standard Novell Ethernet frame format and it also is supported by Windows NT Server.

In most cases, Windows NT Server can detect the frame format that is being used on a Novell network, and no special configuration effort is required.

High-Speed Ethernets

10-Mbps Ethernet performs well in many traditional LAN settings, but it is running out of steam with modern applications such as graphics imaging, voice data, and video. Users of Ethernet appreciate its simplicity and would like to see the standard scaled up to support higher data rates.

The Fast Ethernet Alliance has proposed a 100-Mbps Ethernet that is similar to 10-Mbps Ethernet. To achieve the higher data rate with normal Ethernet frames, it is necessary to reduce the maximum network size to 250 meters. This might sound restrictive, but studies have shown that 90 percent of desktops are within 100 meters of a wiring hub. To support Fast Ethernet, however, a suitable physical layer definition is required. Several have been proposed.

The IEEE 802.3 committee is working on the 100BASE-TX specification, which supports 100-Mbps operation using two pairs of Category 5 UTP cable.

Many organizations have Category 3 cable in place and do not want to upgrade their cabling systems. The Fast Ethernet Alliance has put forth a proposal called 4T+ that supports 100-Mbps operation over four pairs of Category 3 cable. This network specification has been designated as 100BASE-T4 by the IEEE 802.3 committee.

A separate 802.12 committee is developing a proposal based on technology refined by Hewlett-Packard. The network described in this standard commonly is called 100BASE-VG. The access method used is called Demand Based Priority Access, and it operates on completely different principles than Ethernet. However 100BASE-VG supports Ethernet frames and can be used with standard Ethernet networks. The Hewlett-Packard 100BASE-VG adapters are among the network adapters that are supported by Windows NT.

Hardware for 100-Mbps Ethernet now is available, but the standards remain somewhat unsettled. If you choose to install a high-speed Ethernet, you run some risk that your equipment will become outmoded as the standards battle is sorted out.

Ethernet Switches

The life of 10-Mbps Ethernet has been extended considerably by the use of switching hubs. These versatile devices enable you to configure an Ethernet in several interesting ways. Several options are shown in figure 4.28.

Each port on an Ethernet switch supports a full 10-Mbps bandwidth. Within the switch, frames are routed at high speeds, and the switch is capable of switching all the traffic that can be generated by the attached networks without causing performance bottlenecks.

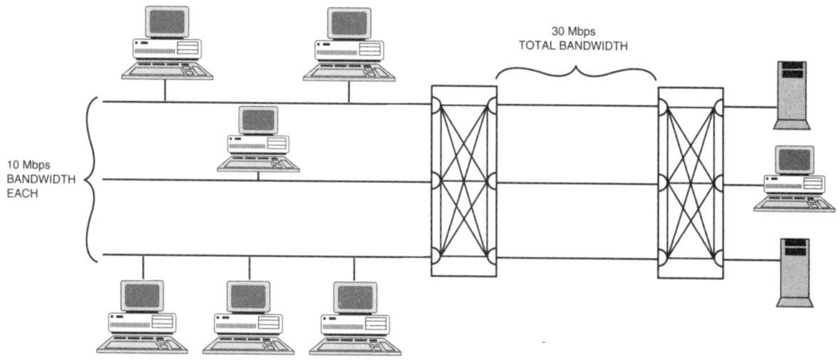

Figure 4.28

An Ethernet network using switching hubs.

Switching enables you to allocate bandwidth as required for various devices. The servers at the right end of figure 4.28 are each assigned an individual 10-Mbps segment. By eliminating the need to share a segment, each server experiences a significant increase in network performance.

Figure 4.28 also shows an interesting approach that can be taken with some switching hubs. In the middle, two hubs are connected using three ports each. This enables the switches to route traffic through any of the three network segments and results in an effective bandwidth between the switches of 30 Mbps.

10 Mbps is really quite a bit of bandwidth, capable of supporting many data-intensive applications. Switching is not an inexpensive technology, but it does represent a practical way of extending the life of existing Ethernet networks.

Note Switching hubs have become quite popular for Ethernet and now are being introduced for token ring as well.

Vendors have been introducing support for full-duplex communication along with switching hubs. Normally, when a device is connected to a switch, both the device and the switch send messages on the same cable. Full-duplex capability introduces two data paths between the device and the switch. The device has a dedicated Ethernet cable that it uses to send data to the switch, and the switch uses a separate cable to send data back to the device.

Full-duplex connections eliminate Ethernet collisions entirely and give each device a monopoly on the entire bandwidth available on the cable. Understandably, full-duplex communication is more expensive, because additional cables are required and hardware must be more elaborate. However, if you follow the advice in this chapter on installing new cable, you will be installing extra cables in your buildings anyway, so the extra cabling requirements might not be a problem. Full-duplex operation is yet another technology for extending the life of proven technologies such as Ethernet and token ring.

Token Ring

Token ring is the major competitor to Ethernet in the LAN arena. Ethernet has been so successful that even IBM, the originator of token ring technology, now markets Ethernet hardware. Although Ethernet has increasingly dominated the LAN market, token ring has some unique advantages that recommend it in many situations.

IBM originally developed the Token-Ring network technology, which was submitted to the IEEE to be considered as a standard. The IEEE 802.5 token ring is derived from IBM's Token-Ring network design.

Ethernet has been winning the LAN war for several reasons:

- The cost per device for Ethernet is considerably lower than the cost for token ring. Token ring NICs cost from $300 to $600, compared to less than $100 for some Ethernet cards.
- Even though token ring is an IEEE standard, it is viewed by many as an IBM-proprietary technology. Many customers and vendors have shied away from token ring for this reason.
- Token ring is more complex, and management of it requires more technical knowledge. However, much of the added complexity comes from the management tools that make it easier to diagnose and correct faults in a token ring network than in an Ethernet.

You might want to choose token ring instead of Ethernet for the following reasons:

- Close integration with IBM technologies is required.
- The random nature of Ethernet medium access is unacceptable. In many applications, each device must be guaranteed an opportunity to transmit at regular intervals. Ethernet cannot guarantee this, but token ring can.

Token Ring Access Control

All networks must provide a medium access control method that controls how devices can use the shared network medium. The method used by token ring is called *token access.* You can examine how token access control works in figure 4.29.

Token ring operates as a logical ring. The transmitter of each device is connected to the receiver of the next device in the ring. This enables the devices to pass messages around the ring.

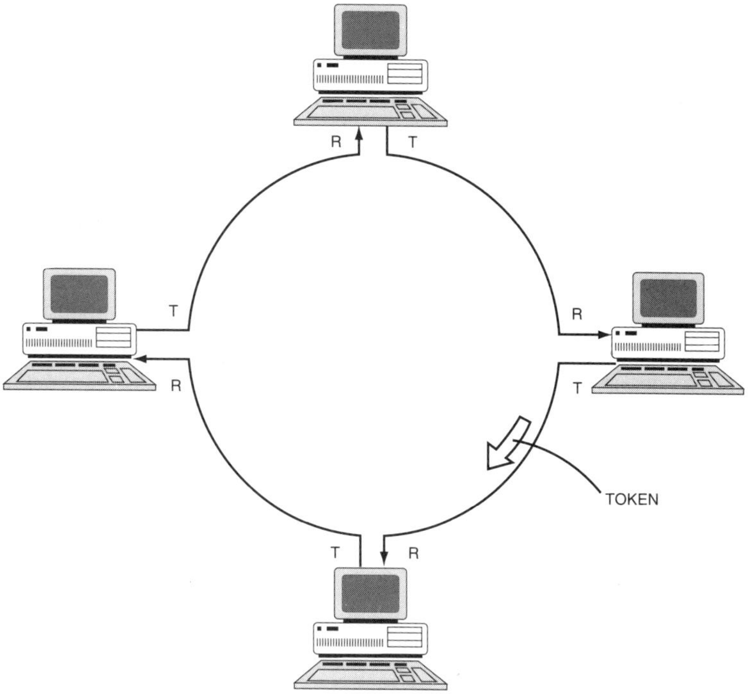

Figure 4.29

The token access control method.

A *token* is a special type of data frame that circulates around the ring. A device can transmit only when it is in possession of the token, and it must wait until the token arrives to transmit data. After a data frame is transmitted, the device releases the token to the network so that other devices can transmit.

The apparent simplicity of the token-passing method hides some complexities that had to be accounted for by the network designers, as these examples show:

- Like any network data, tokens can be lost. How is a lost token to be detected and how is a new token to be created?
- What steps should a station take if it stops receiving data?
- What if a station that was to receive a frame goes off the network? How is the network to identify frames that have circulated the network too many times?

To handle these and other potential problems, one device on a token ring is designated as a ring error monitor (REM). The REM can regenerate lost tokens and remove bad frames from the network. Additionally, each device is capable of signaling certain network problems by transmitting a beacon signal that notifies network management of the problem. The error-detection and diagnostic tools available on a token ring are quite extensive. By contrast, no such tools are built into Ethernet networks.

For these and other reasons, the development of token ring was a complex process. The mechanisms that control a token ring network are much more involved than the mechanisms required for Ethernet. That is one reason that token ring hardware costs more than Ethernet.

Token ring is preferred over Ethernet when a *deterministic* access method is required. Ethernet is probabilistic, and does not guarantee devices opportunities to transmit. On a token ring, however, every device is guaranteed a chance to transmit each time the token circulates the ring.

The IBM Cabling System

Unlike the IEEE 802.3 standard, the 802.5 token ring standard does not specify a cabling technology. Therefore, it is common practice for vendors to base their equipment designs on the IBM cabling system.

IBM has specified a wide variety of cables for its Token-Ring network. The most common cable types follow:

- **Type 1.** Includes two data-grade, twisted-pairs consisting of solid copper conductors. Both pairs are enclosed by a single shield.
- **Type 2.** Includes two solid-conductor, data-grade, twisted pairs enclosed by the same shield. In addition, the cable incorporates two voice-grade cables, enabling the same cable to be used for voice and data.
- **Type 3.** An unshielded twisted-pair cable similar to Category 3 UTP. IBM specifications originally limited use of Type 3 cable to 4 Mbps token ring.
- **Type 6.** Includes two data-grade twisted pairs constructed with stranded wires. The stranded wires make Type 6 cables more flexible and, therefore, better suited for cables that frequently are moved. Stranded cables cannot carry signals as far as cables with solid conductors, however.

Cable Types 1, 2, and 6 are fairly thick and use a special IBM data connector (see fig. 4.30). The connector is fairly bulky but has several interesting features. When disconnected, it shorts pairs of conductors together, enabling you to disconnect devices from the network without introducing a break into the ring wiring.

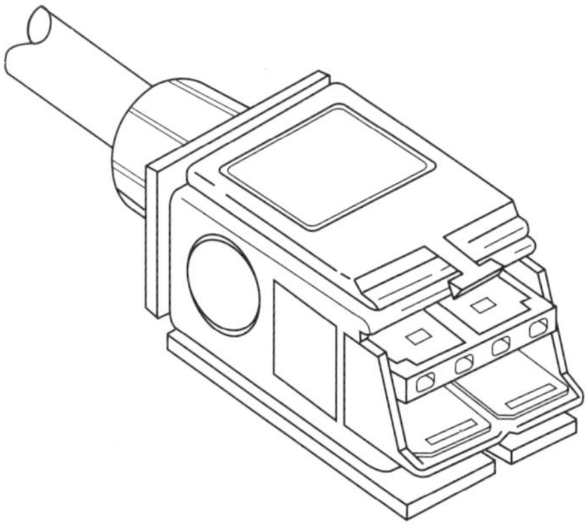

Figure 4.30

An IBM data connector.

IBM's Token-Ring cabling uses a type of hub called a Multistation Access Unit (MSAU). The original IBM MSAU was called the 8228. It was a passive hub that used relays (electro-mechanical switches) to control network signal flow.

Although the 8228 still is available, more recent MSAU designs invariably use active designs with electronic switches replacing the relays. Active hubs are desirable because they enable hubs to correct signal distortion, to detect errors, and to be managed from a network-management console.

Figure 4.31 shows how MSAUs are used to build a network. The 8228 has eight ports, but modern MSAUs often have 16 or more ports to which devices can be connected. Each MSAU has two special ports called Ring In (RI) and Ring Out (RO). A ring network is created by connecting the Ring Out port of each MSAU to the Ring In port of the next MSAU in the ring.

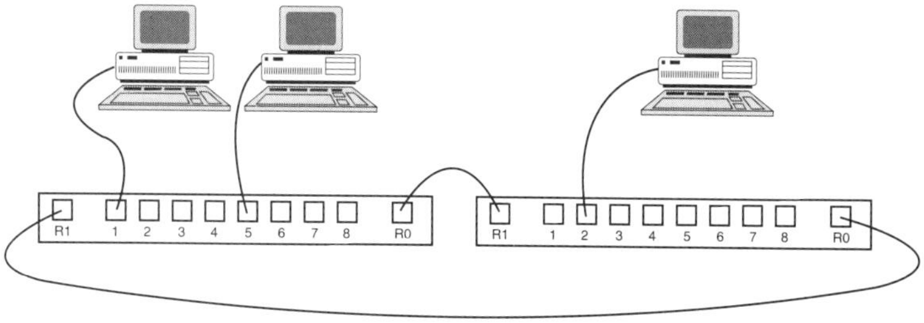

Figure 4.31

How devices and MSAUs are connected to build a token ring network.

Token ring networks have a ring logical topology, but they are wired as physical stars. For this reason, the token ring topology frequently is described as a star-wired ring.

Each device on the network is connected to a MSAU by an individual cable. Figure 4.32 shows how the relays in an MSAU operate to configure the network as a logical ring. Relays in the MSAU normally are closed, permitting signals to flow around the ring. When a device connects to the network, the relay for that station opens, forcing signals to flow out to the device. The device returns the signal to the MSAU and the signal continues around the logical ring.

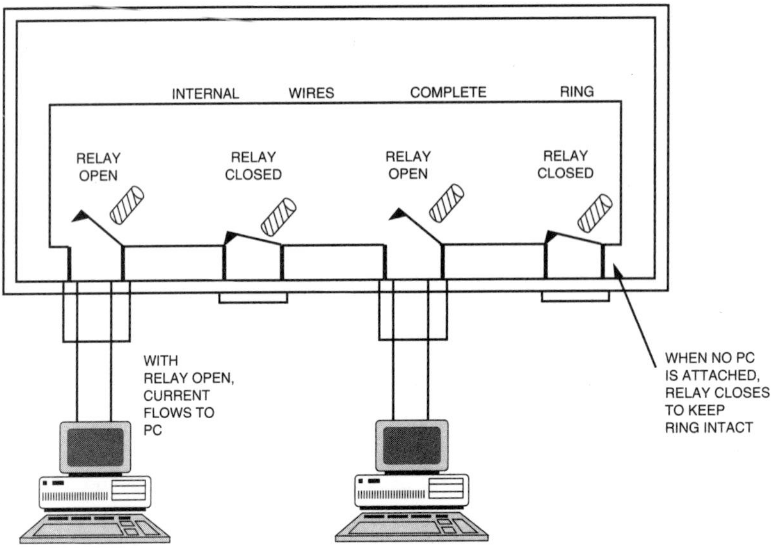

Figure 4.32
Operation of an 8228 MSAU.

STP Token Ring

Originally, IBM sanctioned two speeds for Token-Ring operation. IBM specified 4-Mbps data rates for use with STP and UTP cable. STP cable was required for 16-Mbps data rates. Type 1 and Type 2 cables commonly are used for running cables to workstations. These cables are called *lobe cables* in IBM token-speak. In general, lobe cables are limited to 100 meters.

Up to 260 devices and up to 33 8228 MSAUs can be attached to a ring. Repeaters can be used to extend the physical size of a ring, and they count as ring devices.

The actual number of devices a ring can accommodate depends on the ring size, the number of MSAUs, and the length of the longest lobe cable. Figuring out the capacities of a token ring is a fairly involved process. One IBM Token-Ring network planning guide devotes 22 pages to the subject of ring capacities and dimensions.

Most networks now are cabled with active MSAUs. IBM's active Token-Ring hubs are called controlled access units (CAUs). Active hubs and heavy use of UTP cable have rendered many of the old guidelines obsolete. The manufacturer's specifications of your network's token ring components will be a better guide to the capacities you can expect on your network.

UTP Token Ring

Originally, IBM blessed UTP cable only for 4-Mbps data rates. In the 1980s, numerous IBM engineers expressed the opinion that 16-Mbps data rates over UTP cable would never be practical.

Other vendors, however, did not listen to that theory and did not wait for IBM to develop a 16-Mbps UTP specification. Vendors such as Proteon delivered MSAUs that could support 16-Mbps token ring networks with UTP a couple of years before IBM announced comparable products. In fact, IBM, the inventor of Token-Ring, was among the last manufacturers to develop a 16-Mbps Token-Ring network that satisfied customer demands for UTP. UTP now has wide support for use at both 4-Mbps and 16-Mbps data rates. RJ-45 connectors are used with UTP cable.

In order to control noise on the network, token ring devices must be connected to the UTP cable by a media filter. On older token ring NICs, the media filter was often an extra item. Most currently manufactured NICs include the media filter on the network board and provide an RJ-45 connector for a network connection.

Because most token ring NICs and MSAUs now support both 4-Mbps and 16-Mbps data rates, there is no cost advantage to opting for 4-Mbps operation. 16-Mbps token ring has been widely available for about five years and now can be regarded as a mature technology.

FDDI

Drivers for FDDI, the Fiber Distributed Data Interface, are included with Windows NT Server, and a brief discussion of the capabilities of FDDI are in order.

FDDI is a 100-Mbps network that functions much like token ring. FDDI networks are based on a ring topology and use token access control. Figure 4.33 illustrates several features of an FDDI network.

One feature of note is the manner in which FDDI networks can incorporate two rings that are configured to route signals in opposite directions. Devices that attach to both rings are called *dual-attached stations.* Devices that attach to only one ring are *single-attached stations.*

Because of the way in which FDDI rings are configured, the network can recover from a cable break between any two dual-attached stations. The right side of figure 4.33 shows what happens when a link is broken. The two stations next to the break rework their connections so the two counter-rotating rings are reconfigured into a single ring.

Figure 4.33

Operation of an FDDI network.

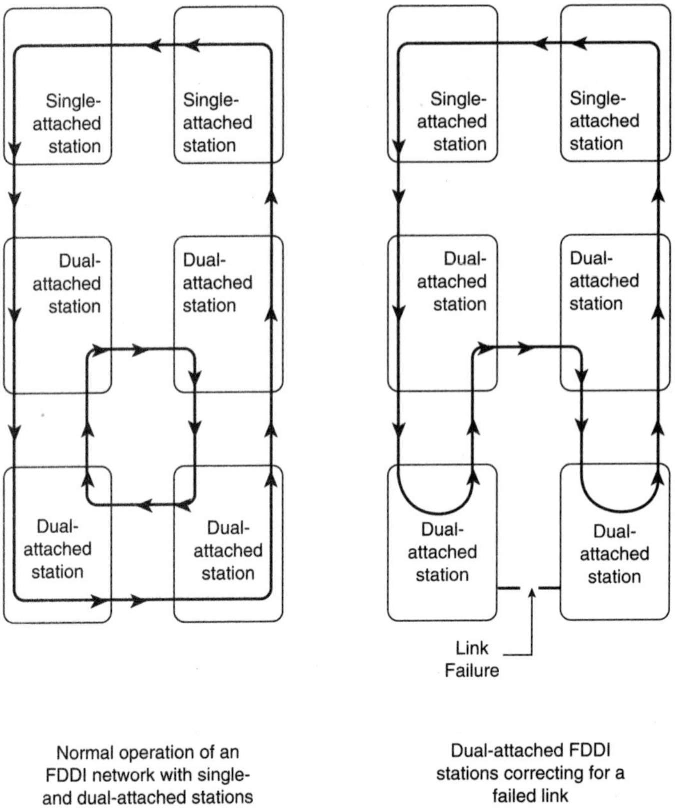

FDDI is not well-suited to workstations because it does not expect devices to be turned on and off. Also, only the fastest PCs can keep pace with FDDI networks due to the limitations of most PC I/O bus designs.

However, FDDI makes an excellent high-speed backbone. Also, because dual-attached FDDI rings can extend to 100 kilometers in diameter, they can be adapted for use as a campus or metropolitan area network.

Acceptance of FDDI has been slow, however, due to the high cost of network hardware. Costs have been reduced somewhat by the introduction of standards for running FDDI protocols over copper cable, the so-called Copper Data Distributed Interface (CDDI).

High-speed Ethernet designs have more momentum than FDDI due to the lower cost of hardware based on Ethernet technologies. Nevertheless, FDDI is superior to Fast Ethernet in much the same way that token ring is superior to standard Ethernet. If your organization needs a deterministic, high-speed network that is fault-tolerant and highly manageable, FDDI is worth considering.

Network Components: Hubs, Concentrators, and Structured Cabling Systems

Proper planning of your LAN's cabling system can pay big dividends. A well-designed LAN can be more reliable and easier to troubleshoot when problems occur. The LAN also can be easier and less costly to reconfigure. If you ever hear estimates indicating that it costs several hundred dollars to relocate a networked PC, you can bet that the cabling system is to blame. The key is to use a structured cabling system along with a judicious selection of modern hubs and concentrators.

Structured Cabling Systems

If you are involved in planning a new LAN or upgrading an existing one, you should examine the merits of structured cabling systems. Although the equipment and installation of a structured cabling system represents a high up-front cost, network-maintenance costs are reduced considerably.

Structured cabling systems rely heavily on star wiring. Cabling from all devices converges in centralized wiring closets. Centralizing the distribution of all network cables is the key to making the system easy to configure.

Typically, network designers identify all the places where networked devices could be located and prewire those locations. Each location is equipped with a jack panel consisting of one or more RJ-45 jacks. A typical four-jack panel is shown in figure 4.34. These four jacks can be used for telephone or data purposes.

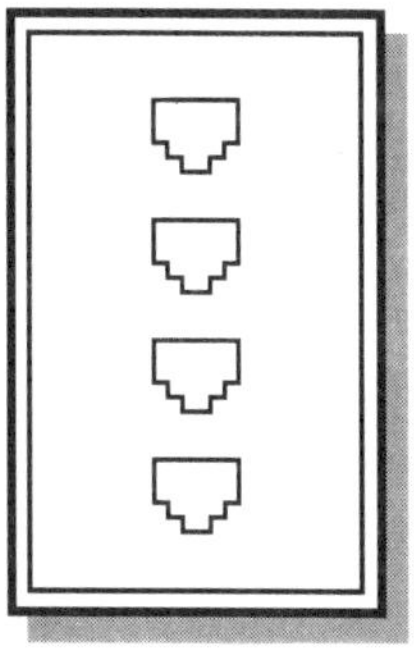

Figure 4.34
A typical workstation jack panel.

Each of the connectors in the jack panel corresponds to a matching connector in a patch panel in the wiring closet. Figure 4.35 shows a greatly simplified example of an equipment rack that includes a network concentrator and a patch panel. The patch panel enables network managers to connect any jack at the desktop to any resource on the patch panel quickly and inexpensively. Most network hubs already are equipped with RJ-45 connectors and are designed for convenient use with a patch panel.

Most types of equipment are available in configurations that can be rack mounted. Although they represent an additional up-front cost, racks are a great way to exercise control over the cabling room, which quickly becomes an incredible mess unless the system is designed carefully.

In summary, the characteristics of a structured cabling system follow:

- A design based on star wiring that converges on centralized wiring closets
- Use of patch panels to make reconfiguration easier
- Prewiring anticipated locations with some extra cable thrown in for unanticipated needs
- Selection of hubs and concentrators that contribute to the goal of easy reconfiguration

A structured cabling system is a long-term investment in a network that is easy to manage and reconfigure. A properly installed cabling system, although costly, can be an ongoing asset. The workstations might change, your LAN servers might be upgraded, or you might completely change your network's physical layer (upgrading from standard to Fast Ethernet, for example); a structured cabling system can roll with the punches.

Hubs and Concentrators

This chapter has emphasized the tendency of the network industry to move toward network designs that are based on star wiring and centralized network hubs. These hubs can be basic, such as the IBM 8228, or they can be part of elaborate systems.

Basic passive and active hubs do not incorporate any management capabilities. If your LAN is of any size at all, you should pay serious attention to hubs that incorporate management features.

A few years ago, when manufacturers such as Synoptics and Cabletron were beginning to build components for structured networks, the cost of management capability was quite high, and designers attempted to spread that cost over as many devices as possible. This lead to the design of wiring concentrators, similar to the one shown in figure 4.35.

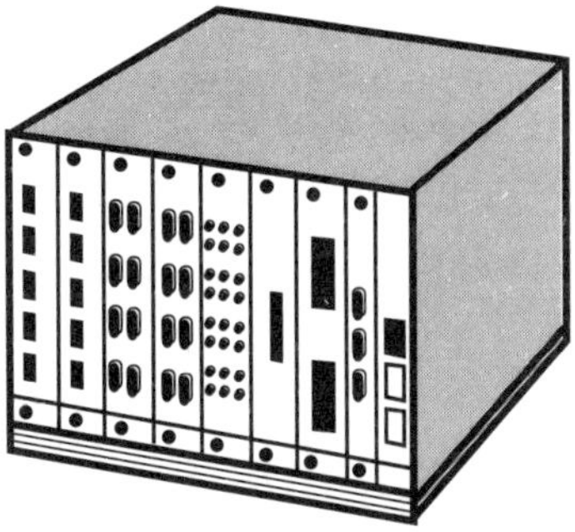

Figure 4.35

A typical wiring concentrator.

A *concentrator* is an enclosure with slots that accept slide-in modules. The concentrator supplies power to the modules and provides a means for the modules to communicate with one another. Network implementors can mix or match the modules to suit the requirements of their network. It is possible, for example, to install 10BASE2, 10BASE-T, and token ring modules at the same time in some concentrator designs. Most concentrators can be equipped with a management module that adds management capabilities for all the options in the concentrator.

Wiring concentrators represent the high end of network cabling systems. These concentrators can include advanced features such as redundant power supplies or other fault-tolerant options. Other concentrators enable you to configure several separate networks within the same concentrator, enabling you to move devices from one network to another, and so on, to balance network loading. Some concentrators even enable you to install server modules that can provide network services without the need for a separate PC.

Aside from high cost, the big disadvantage of concentrators is that they must be expanded in fairly large increments. If your concentrator accommodates 192 10BASE-T devices and you need to add device number 193, you will incur the cost of a new concentrator in addition to the 10BASE-T module that is required to support the new device.

For this reason, many LAN designers prefer the modularity of stand-alone hubs. Most hubs supports about 12 to 24 stations, and stack easily on shelves or in racks. If you need to add one more station, a single hub is less costly than a complete new concentrator.

New hub designs known as *stackable hubs* are designed for easy, incremental expansion. The hubs include connectors that enable you to easily add another hub to the stack. Some simply snap together.

The great thing about many modern hubs is that they include network-management capabilities. Now it is no longer necessary to invest in a concentrator-based system to have hubs that can be managed. With some stackable hub systems, the cost for managed Ethernet has dipped to less than $100 per port. If you don't need the more advanced features available in concentrators, stackable hubs can be an effective approach for your LAN.

Installing Network Cabling Systems

Installation of a structured cabling system is a job for experts. They will be adept at planning the network and installing the network components. They also will be able to muster the technicians required to install the network. Make no mistake about it: Installing a structured cabling system is a great deal of work.

The best time to install a new cabling system is when a building is under construction. Cables can be run in finished buildings, and most modern buildings are designed with the installation of cables in mind, but the process is more difficult.

You need to check building codes before you begin to install cable. If you will be pulling cables in the crawl spaces above suspended ceilings (the *plenum*), you need to select fire-resistant cables. Plenum-rated cables are coated with Teflon instead of plastic so that they will have a reduced tendency to burn and produce toxic gases.

Getting the right installer is especially important, because many LAN problems can be traced to failures in the cable system. This is true particularly if your network will be based on Category 5 UTP. Many installers are not trained to respect the more stringent requirements of Cat 5.

Small networks, however, easily can be installed by do-it-yourselfers. You can simplify things by using premade cables that even eliminate the need for special tools. The easiest networks to install yourself use thin coax or Category 3 or 4 UTP.

If your network uses coaxial cable, the best connectors after factory installed are crimp-on connectors. Screw-on connectors are available but were not designed for LAN data rates. Be sure to obtain the right connectors and tools for the cable you will be using. A poorly installed crimped connector will pull right out of the cable. Expect to spend about $200 for the right tools, which include a cable stripper and a good crimper.

Don't look for bargains on coax connectors. The key to a reliable Ethernet is quality connectors that are installed properly. A good crimp-on BNC connector costs about $3.

If you are using UTP, don't buy your RJ-45 connectors from a telephone supply counter. Be sure that you are obtaining data-grade connectors that match or exceed the specifications of the cable you are installing. Expect to pay about $1 per connector. A good crimping tool costs from $40 to $150.

Ideally, you should invest in a cable tester for your type of cable. Unfortunately, prices for data cable test devices start at $2,000.

Small organizations always should hire an installer for fiber-optic cable. The tools are too expensive to be cost effective unless they will be used extensively. In fact, few organizations will find do-it-yourself fiber installation cost effective. After your long cable runs are in place, your primary need will be for patch cords, which can be purchased preassembled. Organizations determined to bring fiber-optic cabling capability in-house will not find the cost prohibitive, however. The primary difficulty of fiber-optic cable installation is the installation of connectors. Although termination of cables was once a complex task that required a variety of specialized tools such as a curing oven, new approaches have simplified the procedure. A kit for field-terminating fiber-optic cable costs about $1,000. Unfortunately, equipment to test fiber-optic cable is extremely expensive and seldom can be justified unless it will be used frequently.

Installing cable in existing construction often calls for ingenuity and patience. You might need to obtain specialized items to "fish" cables through walls. Fish tapes and long drill bits are available from electrical supply outlets.

If you cannot run cables through walls, you might want to install cable raceways. These consist of snap-together components that are attached to walls. After cables are installed, they can be covered, protecting the cables and making the installation more attractive. Figure 4.36 illustrates an example of a cable raceway installation.

You might have difficulty finding quality cable, tools, and connectors where you live, so here are a few sources:

The Black Box catalog is an excellent source of nearly any LAN components, and a copy should be on your bookshelf. In addition, Black Box offers excellent telephone technical support. For a catalog, contact Black Box at the following address:

> Attention: Vice President of Direct Marketing
> Black Box Corporation
> P.O. Box 12800
> Pittsburgh, PA 15241
> (800)552-6816

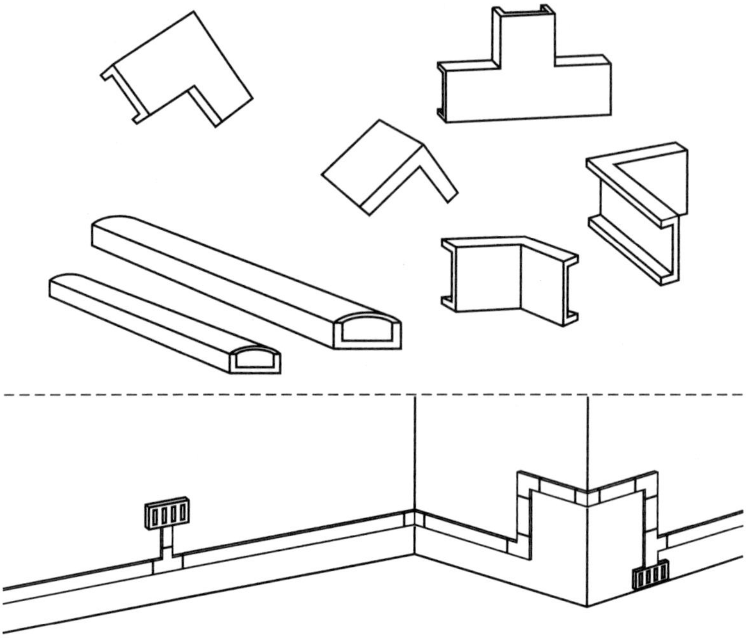

Figure 4.36

Installation of a plastic raceway.

Another source of LAN components is South Hills Datacomm:

South Hills Datacomm
760 Beechnut Drive
Pittsburgh, PA 15205
(800)245-6215

Finally, if you need tools, there is no better source than Specialized Products Company. Their catalog includes more than 300 pages of every imaginable tool, all of the highest quality. The address follows:

Specialized Products Company
3131 Premier Drive
Irving, TX 75063
(800)866-5353

CHAPTER 5

Understanding Server and Workstation Hardware

From the beginning, one of the design goals for Windows NT was to make it easily portable to different hardware platforms. Windows NT version 3.5 already supports systems based on three distinct hardware architectures:

- Intel x86
- MIPS RISC
- Digital Alpha AXP RISC

Because Windows NT is easily portable, you can expect it to show up on other hardware platforms as well.

Of course, Windows NT Server supports workstation OSes that are based on other processors as well. Macintoshes traditionally have used microprocessors from the Motorola 68000 series, but a new line of Power Macintoshes is using the Power PC processor jointly developed by IBM, Apple, and Motorola. Additionally, a wide variety of system architectures is used on Unix workstations.

There are too many system types to discuss in one chapter or even in a book, so this chapter focuses on one narrow area of the workstation/server hardware market.

Given the popularity of Intel-based PCs, it seems likely that the majority of servers and workstations on your network will be based on Intel processors. Current systems trace their basic architecture back to the IBM Advanced Technology (AT) computer introduced in 1985. Although new features abound, the basic design of Intel-based PCs continues to reflect design decisions made 10 years ago.

You will not learn everything there is to know about Intel-based PCs in this chapter. Several more extensive PC hardware books are available if you would like more information. These books often do not address the issues that are related most closely to server performance, however, so this chapter focuses on those issues.

Note Some of the information in this chapter is based on data published in a white paper published by IBM. It makes interesting reading, and you should be able to get a copy by requesting the *IBM Server Systems Performance* white paper at the following address:

> IBM LAN Systems Performance
> IBM Boca Raton Laboratory
> 1000 N.W. 51st Street
> Internal Zip 1214
> Boca Raton, FL 33467

Performance curves similar to the one shown in figure 5.1 make it easy to illustrate the impacts of certain system changes on the performance of a server. Be sure to note the following features in figure 5.1:

- Under light loads, throughput increases smoothly to accommodate demand.
- At some point, throughput peaks. This is the greatest throughput that the server hardware configuration can support.
- The peak reflects the server's capability to service requests from memory. At some point, demand outstrips available memory and throughput begins to diminish as increasing numbers of requests must be fulfilled from disk.
- Throughput levels off at a point that is determined by the performance of the hard disks. At this point, most data requests are being serviced from disk rather than from memory cache.

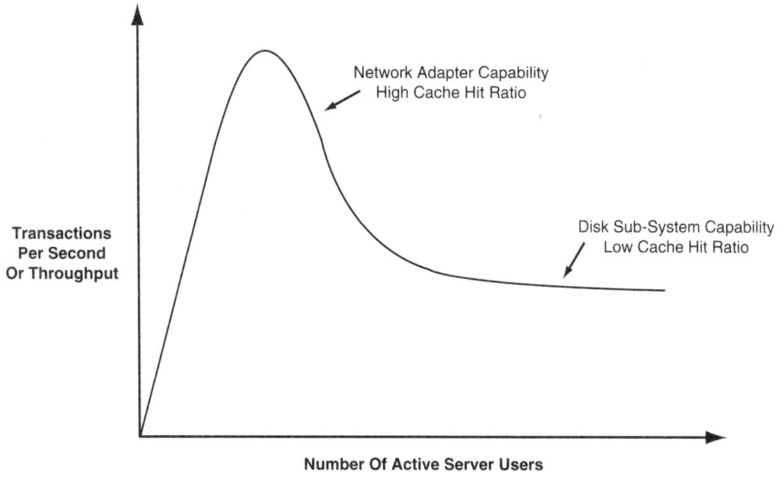

Figure 5.1
Server performance characteristics as discussed in the IBM white paper.

Features of Intel Microprocessors

The central component of a microcomputer is, of course, the microprocessor. This section takes an opinionated look at the Intel microprocessor family to point out the best choices for servers and workstations.

The classes of Intel processors are summarized in table 5.1. Frankly, everything older than the 80486 is pretty much a dinosaur, and you would be hard-pressed to buy new hardware based on 80386 or earlier chips. The 80386 laid the groundwork for all Intel processors to follow, however, so this discussion begins with that model.

Table 5.1
Characteristics of Intel Microprocessors

	8086	8088	80286	80386DX	80386SX	80486DX	80486SX	Pentium
Register size	16 bit	16 bit	16 bit	32 bit	32 bit	32 bit	32 bit	64 bit
Data bus size	16 bit	8 bit	16 bit	32 bit	16 bit	32 bit	32 bit	64 bit
Address size	20 bit	20 bit	24 bit	32 bit	32 bit	32 bit	32 bit	32 bit
Max. memory	1 MB	1 MB	16 MB	4 GB	4 GB	4 GB	4 GB	4 GB
Virtual memory	No	No	1 GB	32 TB	32 TB	32 TB	32 TB	32 TB
Speed in MHz	4.77–10	4.77–10	6–20	16–33	16–20	25–33	20–25	60–100

continues

Table 5.1, Continued
Characteristics of Intel Microprocessors

	8086	8088	80286	80386DX	80386SX	80486DX	80486SX	Pentium
Math coprocessor	Extra	Extra	Extra	Extra	Extra	Built-in	Extra	Built-in
Real mode	Yes	Yes	Yes	Yes	Yes	Yes	Yes	Yes
Protected mode	No	No	Yes	Yes	Yes	Yes	Yes	Yes
Virtual real mode	No	No	No	Yes	Yes	Yes	Yes	Yes

Here are brief definitions of the features discussed in table 5.1:

- **Register size.** The number of bits the microprocessor can process at one time.
- **Data bus size.** The number of bits the microprocessor can input and output in a single operation.
- **Address size.** The maximum number of bits in memory addresses determines how many bytes of memory the processor can manage.
- **Maximum memory.** Determined by the address size. The larger the memory address, the greater amount of memory the processor can utilize.
- **Virtual memory.** Some models can use hard drives to simulate memory. Performance suffers, but the system does not run out of memory so readily. Intel processors starting with the 80286 have this feature.
- **Speed.** A clock determines how rapidly the processor performs operations. Until recently, microprocessors that operated faster than 33 MHz were forced to interface with outside components at 33-MHz speeds.
- **Math coprocessor.** Performs complex mathematical operations such as floating-point arithmetic more efficiently than a program running in a standard microprocessor. Originally purchased as an add-on item, coprocessors are included in newer Intel models. This feature is more important to workstations than to servers.
- **Real mode.** Enables the processor to simulate an original 8086 processor. Some programs such as DOS still require compatibility with the 8086. Real mode is limited to working with 1 MB of memory.
- **Protected mode.** Enables processors to directly utilize memory above 1 MB. Required for Windows NT and for all non-DOS operating systems.
- **Virtual real mode.** Enables processors to simulate multiple, real-mode processors. This feature was important to early versions of Microsoft Windows, but now seldom is used.

Virtually all operating systems except DOS require at least an 80386 processor. The following discussion examines the 80386, 80486, and Pentium processors.

The 80386 Processor

The 80386 processor laid the groundwork for all later Intel processors. The 80386 introduced several features to the Intel line:

- 32-bit registers and data bus, making this the first Intel 32-bit processor.
- 32-bit address bus, enabling the 80386 to address 4 GB of memory.
- 32 TB of virtual memory. Virtual memory is an important performance enhancement because running out of RAM is a serious bottleneck to computer performance.

Earlier Intel processors were obsolete almost from the time they were introduced. Their limited capabilities were accepted due to the high cost of memory and 32-bit components. The 80386 architecture, however, left considerable room for growth.

No 32-bit bus architectures were available to match the 32-bit bus of the 80386 when it was introduced. The prevailing buses in the IBM PC world were the 8-bit and 16-bit versions of the ISA design (discussed later in this chapter). The first versions of the IBM Micro Channel Architecture (MCA) bus were limited to 16 bits.

Because the 32-bit capability of the 80386 often was not supported by external hardware, Intel introduced the 80386SX. Inside the 80386SX was a 32-bit 80386 processor. The standard version now is called the 80386DX. Outside, the 80386SX had a 16-bit bus, matching it to the most popular hardware of the period.

The 80386 processors could operate in *real* mode, enabling them to run software that expected to run on "real" 8086 or 8088 processors. Real mode is severely limited. Most significantly, it is limited by its compatibility with the 20-bit addressing used by DOS, preventing real-mode programs from accessing memory above the 1-MB line.

Also available in the 80386 was *virtual real mode*, which enabled the processor to simulate multiple 8086 processors. Virtual real mode seldom was taken advantage of and was really only important for running DOS programs. Microsoft Windows 3.*x* was probably the most significant program to make use of virtual real mode.

Of greater significance was protected mode, which enabled the 80386 to work with memory above 1 MB as if it were a continuous memory range. Protected mode was introduced with the 80286, but seldom was exploited. The 80386 could work with 4 GB of protected mode memory—a capability that is taken advantage of by Windows NT and other 32-bit operating systems.

The 80486 Processor

The 80486 processor combines three sets of features:

- ◆ The architecture of the 80386
- ◆ A built-in math coprocessor
- ◆ A high-speed memory controller that significantly improves performance

The 80486 did not introduce any new features and is a compatible upgrade of the 80386. Performance was enhanced considerably, however.

The most important enhancement is a *cache controller*, which improves the speed with which the processor can access memory. The cache controller stores recently read data and reads data in anticipation of future needs. Performance is improved because the processor can access memory in the cache controller more rapidly than memory on the motherboard.

A math coprocessor can perform advanced mathematical operations by operating directly on decimal numbers without the need to convert them into their decimal equivalents. Many applications take advantage of math coprocessors, which were extra-cost items prior to the 80486. Examples include CAD, spreadsheets, and financial and engineering software.

Many users do not run applications that require a coprocessor, however, so Intel introduced an 80486SX version that was identical to the 80486 except that the math coprocessor had been disabled. The version with a coprocessor now is called an 80486DX. You will notice that the SX and DX labels have different meanings for the 80386 and 80486 processor lines. Could Intel have made things any more confusing?

Intel persistently has pushed up the clock speeds of the 80486 processors. First they introduced a clock-doubled series called the DX2 series that operated at 50 MHz and 66 MHz. More recently, they introduced the clock-tripled DX4 series, operating at 75 MHz and 100 MHz. In many cases, owners of 25-MHz and 33-MHz versions can purchase an Overdrive module that doubles the clock speed of the original processor.

The Pentium

Intel found out that it could not copyright a numbered name for a processor, so it named the successor to the 80486 the Pentium, which is currently at the top of the Intel processor lineup.

The Pentium adheres to the 80386 external architecture with one exception: It incorporates a 64-bit data bus. The Pentium therefore can move data twice as rapidly as the 80486.

Pentiums also incorporate two 8-bit caches (the 80486 had one) improving the processor's capability to move data to and from memory.

Pentium processors have been introduced with 60-, 66-, 90-, and 100-MHz clock speeds. The earlier 60-MHz and 66-MHz versions were based on a 5-volt design. System designers had considerable trouble with the heat produced by the 5-volt Pentiums, so Intel changed to a 3.5-volt design for the 90-MHz and 100-MHz versions. Both heat and power consumption are reduced greatly in the 3.5-volt chips.

Some of the features of the Pentium were new to the Intel processor line. The Pentium incorporates two data pipelines, enabling it to execute two instructions at one time.

Multiple data pipelines enable an operating system to perform *multithreading*, which involves running two separate tasks at one time. Multithreading differs from multitasking, which is possible on any CPU. *Multitasking* is performed when the CPU turns its attention to several tasks in rapid succession. Only one task is being performed at any given instant in time, but if the processor is fast enough, the outside observer has the illusion that several tasks are performed at once. A multithreading CPU, on the other had, can genuinely perform two or more tasks at the same time. The Pentium functions almost as if it were two processors.

Software must be rewritten to take advantage of this multithreading capability. Windows NT is one of the few operating systems that can take advantage of multithreaded processing.

Selecting Processors for Windows NT Servers

Windows NT loves powerful CPUs and will benefit from all the processing power you throw at it. If you are purchasing a new server, your choice almost certainly should be a 90-MHz to 100-MHz Pentium system. It also is a good idea to ignore the bargains that are available on 60-MHz and 66-MHz Pentiums. These versions use more power and produce considerably more heat than the 90-MHz and 100-MHz versions.

You will not save much by buying an 80486 system, and you will give up a great deal of performance. One thing you give up is multithreading in the CPU. Windows NT supports Pentium multithreading if it is available. However, if you have a 66-MHz or better 80486 server, it should give you good service on a smaller LAN.

Later in the chapter, you will read about buses and discover that the current favorite for server buses is the Intel PCI bus. PCI was designed for the Pentium and is available only on Pentium systems—another reason for choosing a Pentium server.

Windows NT has the capability to perform asymmetrical multiprocessing, meaning that it will take advantage of a second processor if one is available. This is an important capability that enables servers to be scaled up in processing power. You might want to consider a multiprocessor server for your LAN.

Selecting Processors for Workstations

About the only users who will be happy with an 80386 are those who still are using DOS. If you have moved to a graphics environment, working on an 80386 is sheer torture. For Windows, Windows NT, and other graphics 32-bit operating systems, a clock-doubled 80486 should be considered entry level.

I am writing this chapter about nine months after I first moved from a 50-MHz 80486 to a 90-MHz Pentium. The experience has convinced me that even for mundane tasks such as word processing, it is difficult to have too much processing power. Tasks that used to inspire me to take coffee breaks now are performed almost instantaneously.

Because time is money, processing power is a good investment. Has anyone ever estimated how many person-hours are wasted waiting for slow PCs to save files, print, perform spell checks, and so on? The estimate probably would surprise most managers who insist on economizing by buying the cheapest hardware available.

If you have an older PC, processor upgrades probably are not the way to go. The technologies built into 80386 PCs are hopelessly out of date. Most 80386s use older hard drive controller technologies, and all rely on video technologies that just cannot keep up with modern graphics-intensive environments. Upgrading your processor cannot improve the performance of your other systems.

For any modern operating system such as Windows 3.1 or Windows NT, it is a good idea to have the following features:

- At least an 80486 66-MHz processor
- A VESA local bus video for an 80486, and a PCI bus for a Pentium (buses are discussed in the next section)
- An IDE or SCSI hard drive controller

If your system lacks the last two features, upgrading the processor will not buy you much.

Microcomputer Buses

The expansion bus is the primary means of adding hardware to a PC. It is made available in the form of expansion slots, which usually are mounted on the motherboard (system board) of the computer. In some cases, expansion slots are mounted on daughter boards that plug in to special slots on the motherboard.

Several bus designs have been used on Intel PCs. The connectors for these buses are shown in figure 5.2. Each connector is discussed in this section. The features of each bus are summarized in table 5.2.

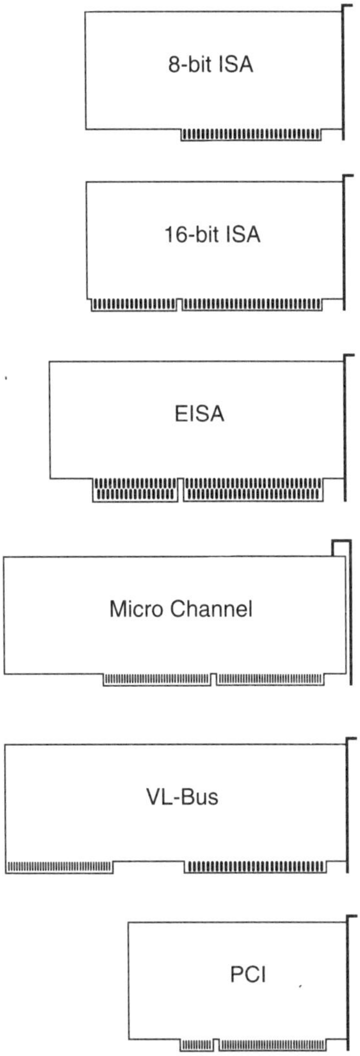

Figure 5.2

Buses used in Intel-architecture PCs.

Table 5.2
Characteristics of Expansion Buses

	ISA	EISA	Micro Channel	VLB	PCI
Data bus (bits)	8/16	16/31	8/16/32	32	32/64
Data rates MB/Second	10	32	10–160	132	132–264
Available Connectors	8	12	8	2	3
DMA channels	7	7	15	N/A	System dependent
Data/Address Parity	No	No	Yes	No	Yes
Card ID	No	Yes	Yes	No	Yes
Auto Configuration	No	Yes	Yes	No	Yes

Before examining the buses in detail, look at some of the characteristics that distinguish the bus designs:

- **Data bus.** The data bus of a bus serves the same function as the data bus of a microprocessor: moving data in and out of expansion devices. The wider the data bus, the more data can be moved in a given operation.
- **Data rate.** The amount of data a bus can move in a second is a function of both its data bus width and its clock rate measured in megahertz (MHz). A 16-bit bus can move 16 bits per operation and would move twice the data at the same clock rate as an 8-bit bus.
- **Maximum connectors.** Each bus design supports a maximum number of expansion slots.
- **DMA channels.** Direct memory access (DMA) enables expansion devices to directly manipulate memory without tying up the CPU. Some systems need additional DMA channels.
- **Data/address parity.** Parity is a basic means of checking for I/O errors.
- **Card ID.** If a bus supports a card ID, system-configuration software can determine the hardware that is in the bus, and it can configure the system accordingly.

- **Automatic configuration.** This option configures hardware options such as interrupts and memory by running a software-configuration program rather than setting jumpers. EISA and Micro Channel require you to run a special program to set up the system. PCI supports Plug and Play, which enables some operating systems to automatically identify and configure option cards.

The ISA Bus

The expansion bus IBM developed for the original PC was based on an 8-bit I/O bus that matched the capabilities of the 8088 microprocessor. When the Advanced Technology PC was introduced, a 16-bit version of the bus was introduced to support the 16-bit data bus of the 80286. This bus design has been adopted widely in almost all PCs based on the IBM/Intel architecture and has come to be called the ISA (Industry Standard Architecture) bus.

Performance of the ISA bus begins to run out of steam with VGA 640×480 video. The ISA bus is limited to a clock rate of 8 MHz, which is quite inadequate for 80386 and later microprocessors. ISA remains viable for options such as printer and com ports and mouse controllers, but is far too slow to support modern hard drives or video adapters.

Micro Channel Architecture

When IBM introduced the Micro Channel Architecture bus in 1987, it did so with the limitations of the ISA bus in mind. Micro Channel could be implemented with 16-bit and 32-bit data buses and theoretically could operate at clock rates of 100 MHz, although that speed has not been made available in an Intel-based IBM PC. Micro Channel supported a feature called *bus mastering*, which enabled controllers on expansion cards to take control of the bus. Bus mastering permitted bus operations to take place without requiring the CPU to control the process. Bus mastering is an important feature on a server that performs large amounts of I/O with the outside world.

IBM made several tactical errors with the Micro Channel Architecture. Most significantly, IBM treated it as a proprietary technology and expected vendors to license it. Because the ISA bus was free, almost no vendor chose to pay the license fees. Also, systems equipped with Micro Channel buses did not support older ISA cards, forcing customers to discard their investments in expansion cards. For some functions, ISA cards offered adequate performance, and many organizations were reluctant to make the hardware investment required to change over to Micro Channel Architecture.

The EISA Bus

Industry wanted the features of the Micro Channel; it just didn't want to pay for it. So a consortium of nine vendors developed the Extended Industry Standard Architecture (EISA) bus. EISA could do almost everything Micro Channel could do. It offered 32-bit I/O and bus mastering, for example. This was accomplished without sacrificing support for 8-bit and 16-bit ISA cards by designing a unique two-level connector. The top row of the connector was identical to the 16-bit ISA bus. The bottom row supported the new EISA features. ISA cards still could be used, because they would contact only the top row of contacts. EISA cards would insert fully into the connector and use both rows.

The main problem EISA could not solve was the 8-MHz clock-rate limit, which is inherent in the design of the ISA connector. That was the main reason that IBM chose to abandon the ISA connector for the newer Micro Channel design. EISA has achieved some popularity in servers, but could not support the high speeds needed for advanced video.

The VESA Local Bus

A superior video bus was required, and one was developed by the Video Electronics Standards Association (VESA). The VESA design uses a *local bus* technology that connects the expansion bus directly to the microprocessor. By eliminating intervening components and limiting the number of connectors the VESA bus would support, significant speed improvements became possible. The VESA Local Bus (VLB) can perform 32-bit data transfers at rates of 132 MB per second.

VLB connectors are installed in-line with ISA slots on the motherboard, as shown in figure 5.3. Only two VLB expansion slots are permitted.

Figure 5.3

Location of VESA Local Bus slots on the motherboard.

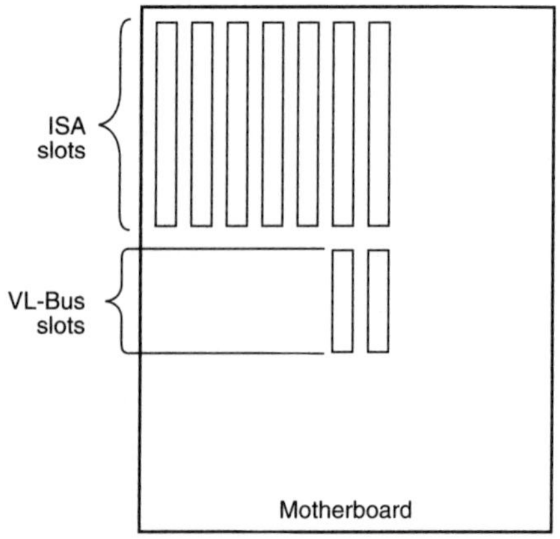

The VESA Local Bus was the first nonproprietary bus to significantly surpass the limits of the ISA design. Consequently, many vendors attempted to design nonvideo cards for the bus. Network interface cards and disk controllers have been introduced in VLB versions. VESA Local Bus, however, was designed for video, and other technologies are a forced fit.

VLB has some significant constraints. First, it is limited to two expansion slots, making VLB less than ideal for servers that often must support more than two high-performance expansion options. The local bus approach is temperamental, because the design must closely match a specific microprocessor. This drawback made it difficult to adapt VLB to the newer Pentium processor.

VESA began to run out of steam when the Pentium processor became popular. Pentiums require a 64-bit I/O bus. Although a 64-bit VESA II bus has been introduced, it arrived after PCI was well established and has received little support.

The PCI Bus

PCI is a high-performance bus that avoids many of the problems of a local bus by using a mezzanine approach, where an interface layer is sandwiched between the microprocessor and the bus, much like a mezzanine floor is found between the first and second floors of a building. Special circuitry buffers the microprocessor from the PCI bus itself. Unlike previous nonlocal buses, the design used with PCI exacts a very small performance toll while greatly simplifying design.

Pentiums require a 64-bit bus, and PCI was the first design to deliver. PCI supports bus mastering and operates at clock rates of 33 MHz and 66 MHz, enabling it to support data-transfer rates of 132 MB to 264 MB per second.

PCI connectors generally replace ISA connectors on the motherboard, as shown in figure 5.4. A common implementation includes three PCI slots and five ISA slots. One PCI slot generally is paired with an ISA slot; one slot can be used, but not both.

Early PCI designs were limited to three PCI slots. This might be acceptable for workstations, but servers generally need more high-speed slots. Recently, Intel has been demonstrating a technology that enables it to support multiple three-slot PCI buses on a system. Intel recently demonstrated a dual-PCI server that could deliver sustained data transfers in excess of 300 MB per second.

Almost any type of expansion option now is available for PCI. Interestingly, the PCI design enables designers to work with reduced numbers of chips. Consequently, PCI expansion cards often have comparable costs to ISA cards.

Figure 5.4
Location of PCI slots on the motherboard.

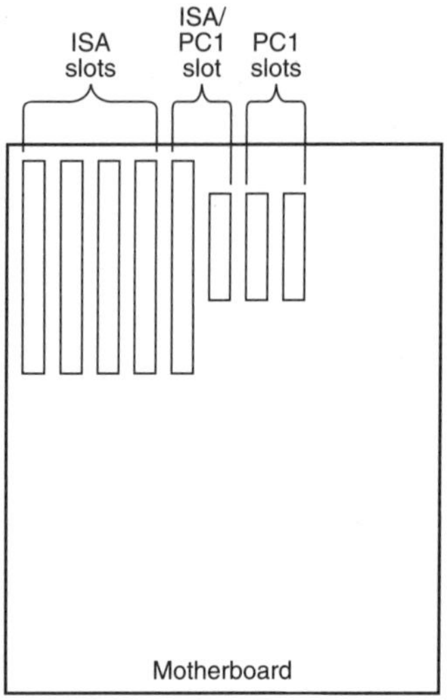

One last feature of PCI is that it offers a new Plug-and-Play capability that will be supported by future operating systems such as Windows 95. Plug-and-Play enables operating systems to detect installed hardware and to set parameters such as interrupts, DMA channels, and address automatically, without the need for manual configuration.

Selecting Buses for Servers

It now appears that the Intel-designed Peripheral Component Interconnect (PCI) bus will become the dominant bus in high-performance Intel-architecture PCs. At this writing, all but one large server manufacturer has announced support for the PCI bus. PCI probably will replace EISA as the most common bus for network servers. Don't rush out to replace your old server for one with a PCI bus, however, unless you have some pretty demanding requirements.

Disk and network I/O are the most intensive tasks that a server bus must perform. Memory performance suffers too much when memory is installed on standard buses, although some manufacturers have designed proprietary buses to support memory expansion.

Unless you are supporting a 100-Mbps network, EISA or Micro Channel buses should be able to keep up with your network. An EISA bus can handle data rates as high as 33 Mbps, which should adequately handle three or four Ethernet segments.

Your hard drive subsystem might be another question, however. If you are using multiple, high-performance RAID (Redundant Arrays of Inexpensive Disks) hard drive systems, you might need to move to a faster bus.

One of the most significant improvements you can make in your hard drive subsystem is to use a bus-mastering network interface card. A bus-mastering controller can improve server performance by raising the peak transactions-per-second level, as shown in figure 5.5.

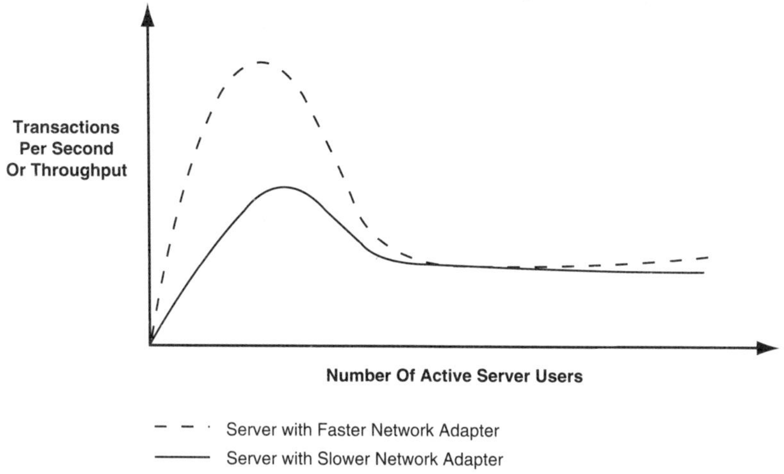

Figure 5.5
Performance improvement of a bus-mastering network interface card.

Selecting Buses for Workstations

Most I/O on workstations is related to video and hard drives, although that will change as LANs become vehicles for delivering graphics, video, and voice data to the desktop. In organizations that are examining these technologies, the days of the ISA bus are numbered. Don't even consider putting a PC on a 100-Mbps network if it has a 16-Mbps ISA bus.

In many cases, however, 16-bit buses provide adequate support for LAN I/O. Unless a PC is attached to a dedicated, full-duplex Ethernet channel, you are unlikely to exceed the performance of a 16-bit ISA. An 8-bit ISA is another story, however, and you should avoid using 8-bit ISA cards or PCs equipped with 8-bit buses. Your LAN is expensive. When a PC is transmitting, it is using all the LAN's capacity and you don't want slow NICs tying up your network.

At present, the choice of bus is fairly simple. 80486 systems generally are equipped with a combination of VESA and ISA slots. Pentium systems usually include PCI and ISA slots, although a very few include VESA II support.

Memory

PCs have become increasingly memory-hungry in recent years, and the minimum desirable memory seems to go up year by year. Now, 8 MB of memory is no longer a large amount; it is the minimum required in most situations. In this section, you examine the types of memory that are available.

Types of Memory

You probably know the types of memory well, but a review of them follows:

- **ROM (read-only memory).** Permanent memory that cannot be reprogrammed easily (or cannot be reprogrammed at all), and that retains its contents when the system is turned off. The basic input/output system software (BIOS) for a PC is installed in ROM.
- **DRAM (dynamic random-access memory).** Used for the main system memory in a PC. RAM is memory that can be modified easily by the computer. Each memory location in DRAM functions like a little battery that is charged and discharged to store data. The charges in DRAM fade with time, and a memory-refresh operation is required to maintain data in memory. DRAM is not as fast as SRAM, but it is considerably less expensive and generally is used for system memory for that reason.
- **SRAM (static random-access memory).** A type of RAM that does not require a refresh operation. Memory locations in SRAM work like switches that retain their settings as long as power is applied. SRAM is faster than DRAM but is used sparingly because SRAM costs considerably more. High-performance systems often use SRAM caches to buffer I/O to slower DRAM memory. Much of the performance of a high-speed system relates to the way in which the designers have used SRAM.

When you add memory, it is important to obtain memory that matches the speed requirements of your system. All memory types have a speed rating that is specified in nanoseconds (ns). Speeds range from 40ns (fastest and most expensive) to about 100ns (much too slow for most new PCs). Most memory you encounter will have a speed rating in the range of 70ns. Your system will not run faster if you buy memory that is faster than it requires. However, you might want to purchase memory that is slightly faster than the minimum. Memory performance varies, and some manufacturers hold tighter tolerances than others. Buying faster memory ensures that the memory you buy will meet or exceed your system's requirements.

Starting with the 80386, most CPUs have the capability of outrunning most DRAM, and system designers have used a number of techniques to slow down memory access.

An early approach was to use *wait states*—"do-nothing" operations that slowed down processing to a speed that the memory could cope with. Wait states are a serious drag on system performance and you should avoid systems that require them.

Most modern designs make use of an SRAM cache. SRAM operates much faster than DRAM. An SRAM cache between the CPU and memory buffers memory access. The CPU can write data very quickly to the SRAM, from which the data can be written to DRAM at DRAM speeds. SRAM cache is vital to the performance of top-performing PCs, particularly Pentium systems.

Memory Expansion

The discussion about buses makes the point that most expansion buses operate at much slower speeds than faster CPUs can support. A Pentium processor can perform burst data transfers at rates as high as 528 Mbps and is capable of outrunning even a PCI bus. For that reason, it is not practical to install memory on expansion cards with most bus types.

With the exception of some proprietary memory-expansion designs, it has become common to install all memory directly on the motherboard, where it can be more directly serviced by the microprocessor. A special memory bus on the motherboard operates at CPU speeds.

Most memory sold today is packaged in single in-line memory modules (SIMMs), which consist of memory chips that are preinstalled on small circuit boards. When you obtain SIMMs, you need to be aware of several characteristics:

- SIMMs for Intel PCs come in 9-bit and 36-bit widths. Examples of both widths are shown in figure 5.6. Macintoshes use 32-bit SIMMs.
- SIMM memory capacities typically range from 256 K bits to 8 M bits.
- SIMMs can be used individually. In many cases, however, SIMMs are used in banks of two or four SIMMs. You must review your system specifications to see what you need.

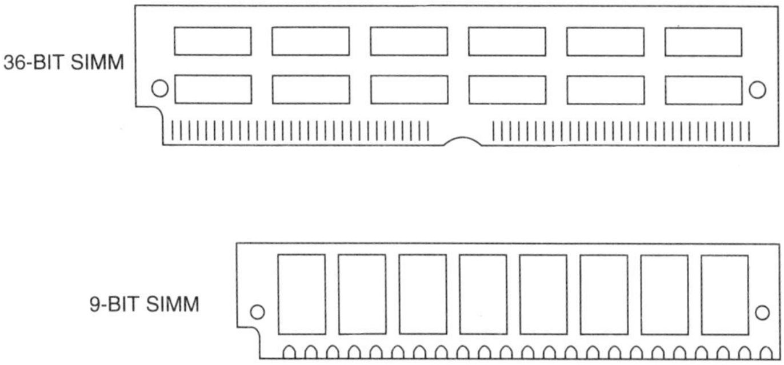

Figure 5.6

9-bit and 36-bit SIMMs.

All SIMMs have a bit width that is expressed in multiples of nine for Intel PCs. This number comes about because IBM designed PCs to use a ninth bit for parity checking of each byte of data. *Parity checking* is an elementary method for detecting memory errors.

Figure 5.7 shows how memory was arranged when individual chips were used. A byte of data is represented by one bit in each of eight chips. A ninth bit is used for parity. (Macintoshes do not check parity and use eight bits for each byte of data.)

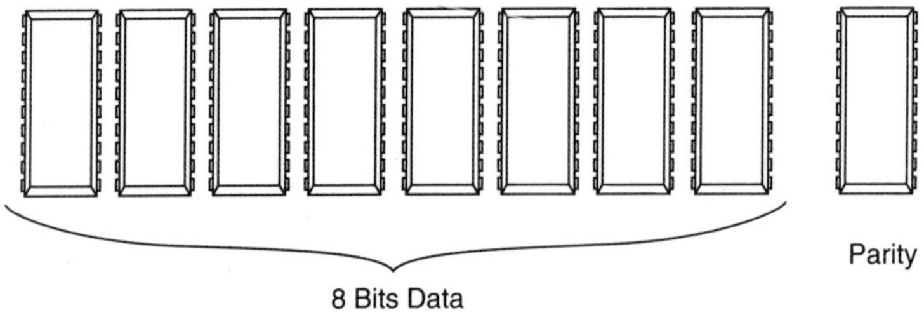

Figure 5.7
The organization of chips to represent data with parity.

A SIMM with a 1-MB capacity would be configured as a 1×9 SIMM, meaning that its size is 1 M bits by 9 bits.

Most currently manufactured PCs use 36-bit SIMMs. A 1×36 SIMM contains 4 MB of memory because it has a width of 4 bytes.

Remember that it is very important to match SIMMs to your system's specifications. Also, if your system uses multiple SIMMs in banks, try not to mix brands or even different production runs in a bank. SIMMs can be arranged in banks so that a performance technique known as *paging* can be used. Paging distributes data for a byte across several chips, which might be in different SIMMs in the bank. Unless the SIMMs closely match each other's characteristics, bit read errors or parity errors might occur.

Memory and Windows NT Server

Windows NT Server, like most servers, is designed to take full advantage of any memory that is available. So that it is not dependent on the performance limits of hard disks, often the slowest things on a server, a network operating system makes heavy use of memory in order to cache data. This is one of the most important techniques for improving server OS performance.

Because Windows NT Server will run with 16 Mbps of RAM, you probably will be rewarded if you add extra memory. Figure 5.8 shows how adding memory can extend the peak of the performance curve, extending the time data can be serviced out of cache rather than disk.

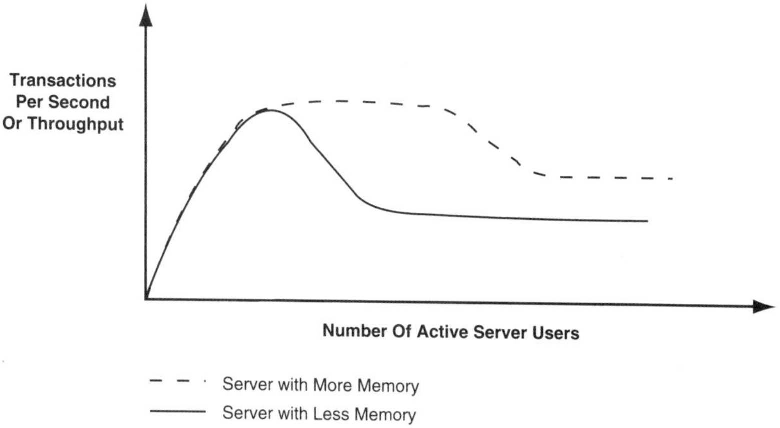

Figure 5.8
The effect of increasing memory in a server.

Workstation Memory Requirements

The memory required for a workstation depends on the operating system. Software vendors will state minimum requirements for marketing purposes, but you usually will be rewarded by adding memory. As with servers, extra RAM enables workstations to reduce reliance on hard drives to store data during processing.

Here are some suggestions for memory with various operating systems:

- **Microsoft Windows 3.1.** Although it will run with 4 MB of RAM, Windows will spend an exorbitant amount of time swapping data to disk unless you have a minimum of 8 MB.
- **Windows NT Workstation.** The specifications say 12 MB, but more will improve performance. Besides, it's easier to configure most systems with 16 MB of memory, so go for the extra 4 MB.
- **IBM OS/2.** Again, ignore the stated minimum of 4 MB and install at least 8 MB.
- **UnixWare and other Unix versions.** Install 16 MB or more.

DOS cannot directly access more than 1 MB of memory, but it can use expanded memory to increase the memory available to applications. *Expanded memory* consists of extra memory, installed outside the DOS range, that is swapped into DOS memory in 4-KB to 16-KB chunks by a memory manager. An application can access one memory chunk and then request another. That method is not as good as directly accessing several megabytes of memory, but it's better than being stuck with a 1-MB limit.

PCs equipped with 80386 and later processors can simulate expanded memory without the need for special expanded memory hardware. This is accomplished by using an extended memory manager to make memory above 1 MB available to an expanded memory manager, which then performs the memory swaps.

Hard Drives

Two major classes of hard drives are used on IBM-compatible PCs:

- Drives that owe their heritage to the original ISA-based drives used by IBM in the IBM XT. This family includes the currently popular IDE drives.
- Drives based on the Small Computer Systems Interface (SCSI).

Each of these classes meets a specific set of hard drive performance and cost needs. One class is ideal for workstations, and the other serves the more demanding needs of network servers admirably.

ISA, ESDI, and IDE Hard Drives

IBM designed the disk systems for the IBM XT computer around the ST506/412 interface developed by Shugart. This interface requires two cables to support a hard drive:

- **A control cable.** This cable supports two drives. The cable is daisy chained from one drive to the next and easily is distinguished by a twist in some of the wires in the otherwise flat cable.
- **A data cable.** Each drive was serviced by an individual data cable.

The IBM XT design could support two controller cards, each of which could support two hard drives for a total of four drives in a system. By today's standards, the ST506/412 interface was outrageously slow, but with average seek times of 80 milliseconds, hard drives weren't very fast themselves. Data was transferred serially at a 5-MHz rate.

Data first were encoded on these drives using a method called modified frequency modulation (MFM), but MFM gradually was replaced by run length limited (RLL) encoding, which increased drive capacity by 50 percent. RLL required better performing drives and more precisely manufactured drives, but it was an inexpensive way to increase hard drive capacity.

IBM introduced the Enhanced Small Device Interface (ESDI) with the PC AT. ESDI was essentially a better performing version of ST506/412. ESDI used the same cables as the older system, but it was not interchangeable with older devices. ESDI was too little too late and quickly fell behind the performance needs of PCs. Both ST506/412 and ESDI hardware are difficult to locate these days.

In 1986, Compaq started work to integrate Western Digital controller technology with Control Data Corporation hard drives. The eventual result was the Integrated Drive Electronics (IDE) design, which had several advantages. Besides a power cable, only a single cable was required. More important, however, close integration of controller and hard drive has resulted in dramatic performance improvements, even while drive costs have been plummeting. IDE drives now offer outstanding performance at costs of less than 40 cents per megabyte.

IDE drives do not require an elaborate controller on the motherboard. A simple, inexpensive interface is all that is required. Most new motherboards have built-in IDE controllers, but inexpensive IDE expansion boards also are available.

As with the older ISA technologies, a PC can support two IDE controllers, each of which can support two drives. A PC therefore can support four IDE drives.

When operating in pairs, one IDE drive is configured as master and the other as slave. The master drive controller manages all operations on both drives. One problem with this approach is that a failure of the master drive deactivates both drives.

IDE drives are excellent for workstations, but are poor choices for servers. The four-drive limit is an important disadvantage where servers are concerned. More important is the fact that only one drive in a master/slave set can be active at one time. This behavior is not well-suited to servers that must freely access all drives in the system. This characteristic also makes IDE drives poor candidates for *disk mirroring*—an important fault-tolerance capability that is built into Windows NT Server.

Note Standard IDE drives allow for only 512 MB of disk space to be accessed without special drivers. This is due to a 1,024 cylinder limit in the original IDE specification. EIDE allows newer systems to access sizes above 512 MB on one drive, up to 2 GB.

Many new drives advertised as being greater than 512 MB are of the EIDE type. Make sure your system board and controller can support these types of drives and their entire capacity.

SCSI Subsystems

Most high-performance disk subsystems are based on the Small Computer Systems Interface (SCSI). A SCSI host bus adapter (HBA) can support up to seven peripherals—including hard drives, CD-ROMs, tape drives, scanners, and other types of devices.

Hard drive access on IBM PCs always has been managed by the BIOS, which directly controls hard drives in terms of tracks, sectors, and heads. SCSI, however, is a block-level interface. The application simply requests a block of data, and it is up to the SCSI subsystem to perform the disk-hardware operations that will retrieve the data. The physical structure of a SCSI hard drive is invisible to applications running on the computer. In order to adapt SCSI to PCs, hardware designers had to develop procedures that translated BIOS operations into SCSI terms so that the PC would view the SCSI subsystem as a conventional hard drive organized in tracks and sectors. Surprisingly, this approach works quite well, and SCSI has become a viable option on IBM-compatible PCs.

SCSI has been enhanced several times. The original SCSI-1 standard had the following features:

- An 8-bit data bus
- Data transfers at 5 MB per second
- Seven devices per host bus adapter
- One command at a time per device

The newer SCSI-2 standard is backward-compatible with the SCSI-1 command set, but adds several features:

- Parity checking identifies errors and requests retransmission.
- The bus disconnect feature enables a disk to service a request while it is disconnected from the host bus adapter. This frees the HBA to service another device. Bus disconnect makes SCSI-2 a multitasking interface that is ideally suited to the needs of a server.

For servers, you should look for SCSI adapters that include the following extensions to SCSI-2:

- Fast SCSI, which doubles the bus clock speed to 10 MB per second
- Wide SCSI, which doubles the bus width from 8 bits to 16 bits

Another feature to look for in a SCSI-2 HBA is Tag Command Queueing (TCQ). This feature enables the bus to queue up several commands for a given device.

SCSI is practically required to implement RAID technologies, which are designed to improve the performance and fault-tolerance of hard drive subsystems. Windows NT Server provides excellent support for RAID, as you will learn in Chapter 16, "Managing Disk Storage."

Table 5.3 summarizes the features of various SCSI standards.

TABLE 5.3
Features of SCSI Standards

	SCSI-1	SCSI-2	Fast SCSI-2	Wide SCSI-2	Fast/Wide SCSI-2
Bandwidth	8 bits	8 bits	8 bits	16 bits	16 bits
Data transfer rate (MB/sec)	5	5	10	20	40

Selecting Disk Subsystems for Servers

Figure 5.9 shows how server performance is improved by enhancements in the hard drive subsystem. A faster disk system raises and extends the peak of the maximum transactions curve and improves the cache hit rate because data can be written from cache to the hard drives more expediently. Finally, faster hard drives raise the plateau at the high-demand end of the curve.

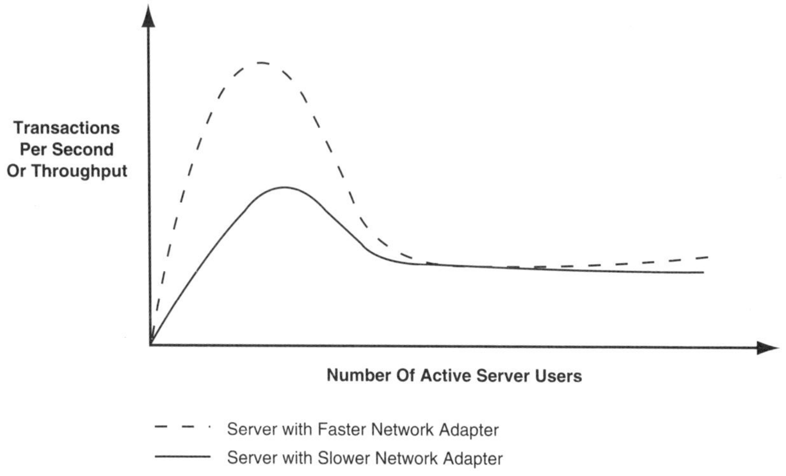

Figure 5.9

Effects on server performance of an improved hard drive subsystem.

IDE drives are not well suited to the requirements of servers. Only one drive in a pair can be active at a given time. Consequently, a single IDE drive might perform as well as a single SCSI drive, but multiple SCSI drives always will outperform multiple IDE drives.

Although Windows NT Server will put IDE drives into RAID configurations, the fact that drives cannot function simultaneously prevents the RAID system from performing well.

SCSI is nearly ideal for use on servers. The many performance enhancements that are available for SCSI-2 make SCSI the only choice for top performance.

Selecting Disk Subsystems for Workstations

Workstations, on the other hand, can prosper with IDE drives. IDE is supported by nearly all operating systems, and single IDE drives perform comparably to SCSI drives at about half the cost. Currently, 1-GB IDE drives are available for less than $400.

If your organization has PCs that still are using older ST506/412 or ESDI hard drives, a drive upgrade is a great way to improve performance at a low cost. An IDE expansion board costs about $30, and drives are available for less than $250.

At present, IDE hard drives are limited to 1 GB in capacity. If you will require larger hard drives, SCSI is the way to go. Costs of SCSI drives have been coming down as well, and now hover around 60 cents per megabyte. A good SCSI host bus adapter can cost more than $300, however, so the startup cost for SCSI is somewhat higher than for IDE.

If you will be running a SCSI-based CD-ROM or tape backup unit on a workstation, however, much of the cost of a SCSI subsystem already will be paid for. Adding a SCSI adapter to a workstation is a worthwhile investment because it can service a wide variety of peripherals. SCSI can be surprisingly inexpensive. Adaptec produces a one-chip SCSI upgrade that can be built into computer motherboards for a cost of $50. Don't be surprised if one day SCSI replaces IDE as the standard hard drive controller on PC motherboards.

Part II

The Basics

CHAPTER 6

Planning and Installing Server and Workstation Hardware

Every LAN administrator needs to know something about the hardware on his or her LAN. Emergencies always happen when your contract support people are unavailable (in fact, they write into their contracts that support can be called only when support is unavailable). Hardware vendors will attempt to sell you more hardware than you need, or they will push their favorite products rather than the products you really need. Ignorance is not bliss as far as network hardware is concerned.

You need to arm yourself with two things: basic knowledge and patience. Most installation and troubleshooting procedures are not outrageously difficult, but they can take a great deal of time. So keep your confidence and your cool. Most of the hardware problems on your LAN can be taken care of by you.

Using the Proper Tools

A basic PC tool kit doesn't need to be expensive. You can buy one at just about any PC dealer for about $30. If you want to get unusual tools or tools of exceptional quality, a good source is Specialized Products Company. Its address is included at the end of Chapter 4, "Planning and Installing Network Media."

Your basic took kit will include the following:

- Large and small slotted screwdrivers
- Large and small Phillips screwdrivers
- Size 10 and 12 Torx drivers. You will probably get one driver with a reversible tip. A Torx driver is required for Compaq computers and used by some others. The Torx driver is the one with the funny tip that looks like a flower.
- 1/4-inch and 3/16-inch hex drivers
- A chip puller and a chip-insertion tool. These tools were more useful in the days when chips were installed in sockets. Now that most chips are surface mounted and soldered, you seldom will need these tools.
- A pickup tool for retrieving the parts you will be dropping into the guts of your PC.
- A parts container so that you will only lose half of your loose parts.

Other useful tools include the following:

- A wire cutter/stripper.
- A wrist grounding strap. Use this to ground yourself when you are installing static-sensitive components, which include almost anything you can put into a PC.
- Some good needle-nosed pliers.
- An inexpensive volt/ohm meter.
- A variety of plastic wire ties. Have several sizes on hand. These little wonders have a hundred uses, from tidying up cable to attaching equipment labels, to securing connectors so that they can't slip loose.
- A portable case that includes all the disks you need for troubleshooting the PCs in your office. As you use a new utility, add it to a disk in your tool kit. Start out with at least the following:

Disks for installing the standard version of DOS used in your office.

A bootable DOS disk with utilities such as FDISK and FORMAT.

Configuration software for any expansion cards used in your office.

Any configuration programs required for PCs in your office. Most PCs build the configuration program into the BIOS, but older PCs and PCs based on EISA and Micro Channel buses require configuration disks.

At least one diagnostic program.

Several good diagnostic programs are available. Microsoft Windows includes a basic program named MSD. Good commercial programs include CheckIt and QA Plus.

A favorite of mine is Micro-Scope from Micro 2000. A unique feature of this product is that it boots up under its own operating system, enabling it to test even the memory areas that normally are occupied by DOS. Programs that run under DOS cannot test some memory areas. Micro-Scope includes several other unique features as well. Contact Micro 2000 for information:

Micro 2000, Inc.
1100 E. Broadway 3rd Floor
Glendale, CA 91205
(818) 547-0125

Binary and Hexadecimal Numbers

Computers don't work directly with the decimal numbers with which you are familiar. The heart of a computer consists of memory locations that are either on or off. These on and off states are used to represent 1s and 0s, from which all other numbers in computers are derived. Numbers in 1s and 0s are referred to as *binary* numbers. Another numbering system called *hexadecimal* makes large binary numbers easier to manage.

A single 1 or 0 in the computer numbering system is a *bit*. Numbers that can have only two values are called *binary*, and *bit* is an abbreviation for the phrase *binary digit*.

Patterns of bits can represent data much like the dots and dashes of Morse code represent letters. Bits are strung together to build larger codes. The most common code is ASCII, which uses strings of 8 bits to represent characters. The capital letter A, for example, is represented by the binary pattern 01000001.

Unfortunately, to humans, 01000001 looks a lot like 01000010, so most people like to convert long binary numbers into forms with which they are more familiar. To convert binary numbers to decimal, you need to have an understanding of how decimal and binary numbering systems work.

Decimal numbers are based on powers of 10. The digits in the decimal number 5,432 have the following meanings:

5 represents 5×10^3, which is $5\times10\times10\times10$ or 5,000

4 represents 4×10^2, which is $4\times10\times10$ or 400

3 represents 3×10^1, which is 3×10 or 30

2 represents 2×10^0, which is 2×1 or 2

The same principle applies to binary numbers. Consider the binary number 1010, for example. The digits have the following meanings:

1 represents 1×2^3, which is $1\times2\times2\times2$ or 1×8

0 represents 0×2^2, which is $0\times2\times2$ or 0

1 represents 1×2^1, which is 1×2 or 2

0 represents 0×2^0, which is 0×1 or 0

As you can see, 1010 is the binary equivalent of the decimal number 10.

Here is a summary of the powers of 2:

$2^0=1$

$2^1=2$

$2^2=4$

$2^3=8$

$2^4=16$

$2^5=32$

$2^6=64$

$2^7=128$

$2^8=256$

A byte consists of 8 characters. The highest possible value of a byte is 11111111. If you convert this to decimal form by adding the values 2^0 through 2^7 you will see that a byte can represent values of 0 through 255.

When large binary numbers are encountered, it is common to convert them to *hexadecimal* (hex), which is a numbering system based on powers of 16. The easiest way to convert binary numbers is to organize them in blocks of four bits, which easily convert to hex equivalents. Table 6.1 lists hexadecimal, binary, and decimal equivalents for the numbers 0 through 15.

Table 6.1.
Hexadecimal, Binary, and Decimal Equivalents

Binary	Decimal	Hexadecimal
0000	0	0
0001	1	1
0010	2	2
0011	3	3
0100	4	4
0101	5	5
0110	6	6
0111	7	7
1000	8	8
1001	9	9
1010	10	A
1011	11	B
1100	12	C
1101	13	D
1110	14	E
1111	15	F

Hexadecimal uses the letters A through F to represent digits ranging from 10 through 15 decimal. Hexadecimal numbers often are distinguished from decimal by adding an h to the number—for example, 3135h is a hex number. You also will encounter the C programming convention of attaching 0x to the beginning of a number, such as 0x5A29.

To convert a binary number to hexadecimal, just substitute the corresponding hexadecimal digit for each four-bit chunk:

0100	1010	0111	1110
4	A	7	E

You often run into some odd decimal numbers in association with computer characteristics. These apparently random choices make more sense when you remember that the numbers are based on binary equivalents. Here are some common values you will encounter:

Value	Decimal	Binary	Hexadecimal
1 KB	1024	0100 0000 0000	400h
640 KB	655360	1010 0000 0000 0000 0000	A0000h
1 MB	1048576	0001 0000 0000 0000 0000 0000	100000h

Note The Calculator utility that is included with Windows can perform number base conversions. Just select View, Scientific to put the calculator into scientific mode.

Parameters Used to Configure Microcomputers

As you add devices to microcomputers, you need to ensure that they don't step on each others' toes. Each device needs to obtain access to certain system resources to get attention or exchange data. To enable devices to cooperate without conflicting, you need to attend to four system settings:

- Interrupts
- I/O addresses
- Shared memory addresses
- DMA channels

Interrupts

Computers are multitasking machines. When they are busy printing, saving files, or performing other operations, they need to be alert for key presses, messages from networks, or other systems that need attention. A couple of methods are available for meeting this requirement.

The CPU periodically can check each resource to see whether it needs attention; this process is called *polling*. Most of the time, though, this is a waste of the CPU's energy.

Or, the CPU can recognize a mechanism by which systems can signal for attention on their own. That mechanism is based on *interrupts* (or *IRQ* for *Interrupt ReQuest*). Each device that might need attention is assigned an interrupt. When it wants to signal the CPU, the device *asserts* the interrupt. This interrupt signals the CPU to stop what it is doing and to come to the aid of the device.

If two devices are configured with the same interrupt, considerable confusion can arise. An important step in system configuration is ensuring that each device in the system has a unique interrupt. Unfortunately, that can be more difficult than you might think.

All Intel PCs now being made inherit their basic interrupt mechanisms from the 16-bit ISA bus of the 1985 IBM AT. Table 6.2 lists the interrupts as defined by the AT architecture (interrupts 0 and 1 are not listed because they are reserved for the system).

Table 6.2
Interrupts Used in IBM PC Compatibles

IRQ	Use
2	Cascade to IRQ 9
3	COM2 and COM4
4	COM1 and COM3
5	LPT2
6	Floppy disk controller
7	LPT1
8	Real-time clock
9	Cascade from IRQ2
10	Available
11	Available
12	PS/2 and Inport mice (if present)
13	Math coprocessor
14	Hard disk controller
15	Available

Lower numbered interrupts have higher priorities. That's why interrupts 0 and 1 were reserved for the system clock and keyboard. You can free up some of the low interrupts by disabling I/O ports. If your system doesn't support a directly attached printer, disable the LPT ports. Some ports are deactivated by removing jumpers on I/O cards. Newer systems usually enable you to disable ports from the BIOS setup program.

Interrupts 2 and 9 are special interrupts. To understand why, you need to understand how IBM implemented interrupts on the IBM AT. The 8259 interrupt controller chip used by IBM supports eight interrupts. When IBM designed the model AT, it elected to add eight new interrupts to the eight that had been supported by the IBM PC design. To do this, it added a second 8259 chip.

IBM chose to control the new 8259 by connecting IRQ 2 of the first 8259 controller to IRQ 9 of the new controller. IRQ 2 is called a *cascade interrupt* because it enables interrupts 8 through 15 to cascade down through IRQ 2 to get system attention.

When interrupts 8 through 15 fire, IRQ 9 is asserted, which cascades to IRQ 2. When the system is interrupted by IRQ 2, it knows that the real interrupt comes from the second 8259. It then checks to determine which of interrupts 8 through 15 actually was asserted.

Because of this cascade mechanism, interrupts 2 and 9 are really not available because they are responsible for performing interrupt cascades. If you can avoid it, don't configure option cards for these interrupts. They might work, but you might get a flaky system if you try.

Because IRQ 2 has a high system priority, interrupts 8 through 15 inherit that priority. If possible, put your most critical option cards such as NICs in these interrupts. SCSI adapters generally use IRQs 10 or 11.

Note

COM ports can be scarce resources on a Windows NT Server. You will need one COM port for the interface cable to your uninterruptible power supply. If you need to configure remote access, you will need a COM port for a modem. And most mice interface with COM ports.

Even though PCs officially can support four COM ports, notice that interrupts are shared by COM1 and COM3 and by COM2 and COM4. It can be chancy to use two devices on the same interrupt at the same time, so you should avoid COM3 and COM4 on a server.

The solution to the dilemma is to use a PS/2-style mouse, possibly with a Microsoft Inport adapter. This option uses IRQ 12 and will not conflict with other uses for COM1 and COM2.

I/O Addresses

After an expansion card has the CPU's attention, it needs to be able to communicate data. This is done by assigning memory blocks that can be used to exchange data. Two types of memory assignments can be made:

- I/O addresses or ports—small addresses that are located in lower system memory.
- Shared memory addresses that enable expansion cards to use larger amounts of system RAM.

I/O addresses (also called *ports*) are found in the memory range 100h through 3FFh. Typically, a port will be 8 bytes to 32 bytes. Unfortunately, the documentation for many option cards doesn't tell you how big a port the card requires. In general, assume that an 8-bit card requires 8 bits and that a 16-bit card requires 16 bits. If two cards overlap I/O address ranges, some very strange things can happen, so always suspect I/O address conflicts when two cards have neighboring addresses.

Table 6.3 lists some common I/O ports.

TABLE 6.3
Common I/O Port Assignments

Base Address	Device	Typical Address Range
200	Game port (joystick)	200–20F
260	LPT2	260–27F
2E8	COM4	2E8–2EF
2F8	COM2	2F8–2FF
300	Common factory setting for many network cards	300–31F
330	Adaptec and other SCSI adapters	330–33F
360	LPT1	360–37F
3CD	EGA video display	3C0–3CF
3D0	CGA video display	3D0–3DF
3E8	COM3	3E8–3EF
3F8	COM1	3F8–3FF

Shared memory addresses are found in memory above the DOS 640-KB line. Actually, not much memory is available in that range, as shown in figure 6.1. A0000-BFFFFh are used by video systems and F0000-FFFFFh are used by the system's ROM BIOS.

Consequently, shared memory addresses generally need to fit in the range of C0000h through EFFFFh. As with I/O ports, it is essential that shared memory addresses don't overlap. Table 6.4 lists some common shared memory addresses.

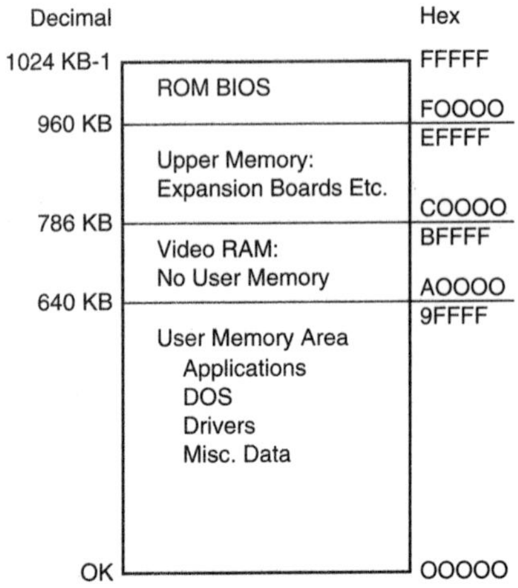

Figure 6.1
DOS memory usage.

Table 6.4
Common Shared Memory Addresses

Device	Memory Range
Mono Video	B0000–B1000
CGA	B8000–C0000
EGA	A0000–C0
VGA	A0000–C4000
BIOS	F0000–FFFFF

DOS PCs that use expanded memory also require that an area above 640 KB be set aside as a page frame for swapping memory in and out of expanded memory. The location of this memory is declared as a parameter of the EMM386.EXE memory manager. Be sure that this page frame does not conflict with memory used by your expansion cards.

Windows NT provides automatic emulation of expanded memory as required by applications.

Note You also should exclude expansion card shared memory from the extended memory used by your system. This is achieved by including the X= parameter when EMM386.EXE is run in CONFIG.SYS. Consult a DOS manual for more complete instructions.

DMA Channels

DMA channels enable peripherals to communicate with memory directly without bothering the CPU. Eight DMA channels are available, numbered 0 through 7. Lower numbered channels have the highest priorities.

The DMA address 0 is reserved for DRAM memory refresh.

Installing Expansion Cards

Modern PCs generally include many options that were rare not too long ago. The majority of PCs purchased today have CD-ROM drives and sound cards, for example. As a result, interrupts and memory addresses represent some pretty precious real estate in many PCs. When buying an expansion option, it makes sense to obtain cards that support as many interrupt and address options as possible.

Cards that are designed to the limitations of 8-bit ISA are a definite liability. At one time, I was trying to add a Novell/Eagle NE2000 card to a system. Although it is a 16-bit card, it supports only 8-bit interrupts and is limited to IRQ settings of 2, 3, 4, and 5. The PC in question had no interrupts available in that range, and I couldn't find any way to reconfigure the existing options to free up an interrupt. Consequently, I had to dig up another, more versatile, card.

Things to look for when buying an expansion card include support for IRQ 8 through 15 and easy setup procedures.

Note Most of the components you can install in a PC are extremely sensitive to static electricity and can be damaged even by static charges you would not notice. For this reason, it is important that you ground yourself before installing most hardware.

You probably will be advised to unplug the PC. Doing so, however, removes the ground connection from the PC—a great invitation for static electricity. Instead, leave the PC plugged in, but make sure that it is turned off.

continues

Use a grounding strap to ensure that you don't build up a static charge. A *grounding strap* is a bracelet that you wear on your wrist. The bracelet connects to a wire that is attached to a ground, such as the metal chassis of your PC. Only after you are grounded properly should you remove a component from its anti-static bag.

It's also a good idea to work on an anti-static mat—a surface that also is grounded. Grounding straps and portable anti-static mats can be obtained from Specialized Products Company. A field service kit with both components costs about $50. See the end of Chapter 4 for this company's address.

Configuring Cards with Jumpers and Switches

Many cards still configure with jumpers and switches. Figure 6.2 illustrates both options. Setting jumpers and switches is usually the pits. Many vendors don't provide clear instructions, and the pins and switches usually are not labeled in any sensible way. You might be told to add a jumper to pins 14 and 15 to set a memory address of 360h. (Now who could possibly forget that?) So, unless you work with a particular card every day, you need to consult the manual each time you need to set one up. Don't lose the manual or you're sunk.

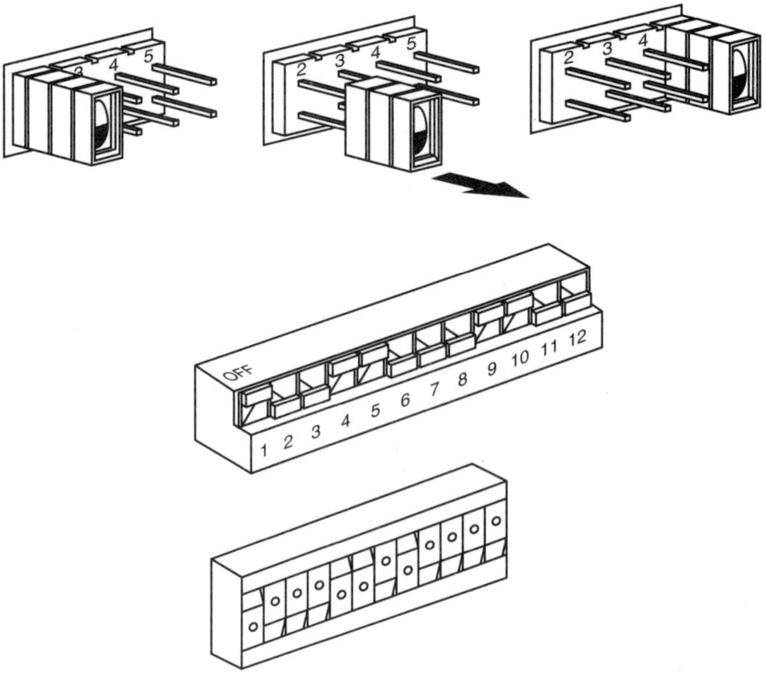

Figure 6.2

Examples of jumpers and switches for setting expansion options.

When you need to disable a jumper setting, don't completely remove the jumper. You might need it later when you reconfigure the card. Instead, place the jumper over one pin of the pair to keep the jumper with the card. Never throw a jumper away! Put it in your junk drawer. You will need it some day. And there are at least two sizes of jumpers, so be alert to the difference and save some of both sizes.

Switches are easier to set and cannot be lost. They are called DIP switches because they are packaged in *dual-inline pin* assemblies, not because the guy who designed them was a dip.

Before you start reconfiguring a card, write down its settings so that you can restore them easily if things don't work. There is a lot of trial and error involved in configuring a PC, and proper documentation can save you a great deal of hassle.

Software Configurable Cards

Most cards are available in configurations that have replaced switches and jumpers with nonvolatile memory that is configured with a setup program. Many setup programs have the capability of examining systems to determine a configuration that will not conflict with existing options.

Configuring ROM BIOS

Some options are configured from the ROM BIOS. Most new motherboards include many features that once were located on expansion cards, including COM and LPT ports and disk controllers. In most cases, the ROM BIOS routine has an option for disabling or reconfiguring the settings for some or all of these features.

Configuring EISA and Micro Channel PCs

Option cards for EISA and Micro Channel buses do not have jumpers or switches. They incorporate a manufacturer's ID, which enables a setup program to determine which cards are installed in the expansion bus. When you run the configuration program, it generally does a pretty good job of configuring cards with nonconflicting settings.

The catch with EISA is that most EISA systems include non-EISA cards, which cannot be configured or read by the setup program. You will have to keep these settings in mind as you run the EISA setup. Micro Channel PCs don't accept non-Micro Channel cards, and cannot have this problem.

Some EISA PCs don't enable you to set all system options from the EISA setup program. You still have to run a CMOS setup program to configure settings such as the system clock, hard drive configurations, and so on.

The setup programs for EISA and Micro Channel run from a disk which must be booted on the system. When you add a hardware option to the PC, you need to copy some configuration files to the setup program. These setup disks are among your most precious possessions. Store several copies that include all the setup files required by the systems in your organization.

Note After you configure the options in a system, be sure to record the settings you used. There is nothing more frustrating than having to remove every card and determine its settings before you can add a new board.

You should record settings in one of the following ways:

- **On a page in a configuration log.** The problem with this approach is that you are at the user's PC and the log is back at your desk.
- **On a tag that you attach to the PC.** One good choice is a *cable tag*, which is a self-adhesive label intended for use on cabling systems. They are durable and do not come off easily. Add one to the PC's monitor cable and record the settings. Get them from Black Box Corporation, whose address is at the end of Chapter 4.
- **Record the settings in a text file which you store in the PC's DOS directory.** Flag the file as System files, making them read-only and hidden, so that users cannot easily erase them.

Installing Memory

Some guidelines for selecting memory were covered in Chapter 5, "Understanding Server and Workstation Hardware." There are a few more considerations, however.

Take care when installing SIMMs in their sockets. There is no guaranteed way to repair a broken SIMM socket other than replacing the motherboard. Even with great patience, removing the old socket and soldering in a new one probably will not work.

Many cheap SIMM sockets secure the SIMM with plastic fingers that break off easily. When you buy a new PC, always look for metal fingers in the SIMM sockets. Plastic fingers are a good tip-off that your vendor likes to use cheap components.

SIMMs will have cutouts and alignment holes that prevent the SIMM from being installed in the wrong position. If you have to force the SIMM, it isn't oriented in the right direction.

Memory size is set by the PC's CMOS configuration program. Always reconfigure CMOS after you change memory.

Some EISA systems automatically recognize changes in memory, but some do not and require you to run the setup program to register changes in memory.

Micro Channel systems always require you to run the setup program to register changes in memory.

Installing Hard Drives

Only IDE and SCSI drives will be considered here. If you have older drives, you probably cannot buy replacement controllers or drives. Besides, the performance improvements of IDE and SCSI more than justify the cost of upgrading.

Installation Considerations

This section gives you some general guidelines that will be of interest when you are installing any type of hard drive.

Drive Bays

Desktop PCs are including fewer and fewer drive bays these days. If you will be adding many options to a desktop system, look for a minitower case.

Servers always should have full-tower cases with as many drive bays as possible. Be sure, however, that the case design provides proper ventilation. Large hard drives put out considerable heat and you want to ensure that they will have good air circulation. It often is best to mount hard drives in individual, external drive cabinets. Then each drive has its own power supply and ventilation fan.

Some cases require drive rails in order to mount drives, but the best approach is to select a tower case that does not require drive rails. You then will have more options for where you can install equipment. Drive rails don't really simplify much. You still have to screw something to the drive to hold it in place.

Be sure that your server cabinet provides plenty of ventilation. A second fan is a useful precaution. Also, with Pentium processors, it is a good idea to mount a cooling fan on the processor itself. Such a fan generally is included on better Pentium systems.

Power and Power Connectors

A server generally should be equipped with a power supply that has at least a 300-watt capacity. The power supply should be fitted with a large number of power connectors.

PCs use two power connectors (both are shown in fig. 6.3). The larger connector is more common, but you will encounter the smaller connector on devices that are designed with a 3 1/2-inch form factor.

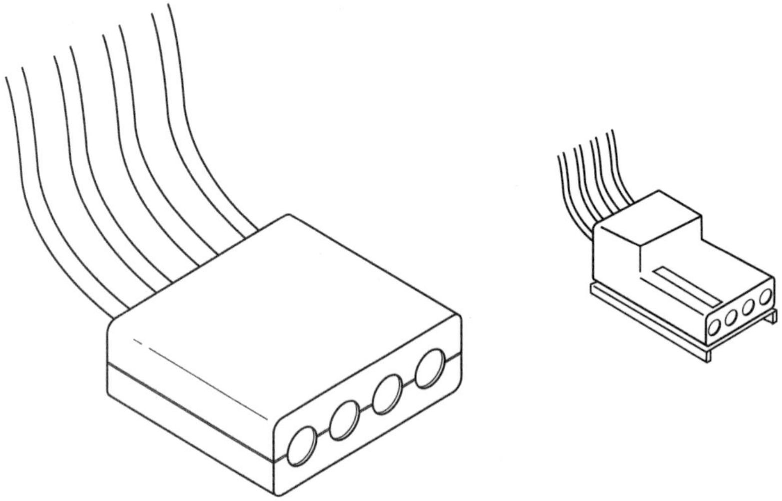

Figure 6.3
Power connectors used in PCs.

IDE Drives

IDE drives couldn't be much easier to install. Most new PC motherboards are equipped with an IDE connector.

If your system includes only one IDE controller, the addresses are preset and standard. The I/O address for the first controller is always 1FE hex, and the interrupt is always 14.

If you need more than two IDE drives, you can include a second IDE controller. IDE controllers are available for ISA, VESA, and PCI slots. The address for the second controller is usually 170 hex. You will need to determine an available interrupt.

Each IDE drive must be configured as a master or a slave, usually by setting jumpers. The first drive always is configured as a master and is seen by your system as drive C. If you add a second drive, set its jumpers to the slave setting.

A single ribbon cable with two drive connectors supports both the master and slave drive. Drives can be connected to the cable in any order. Be sure that line 1 of the ribbon cable attaches to pin 1 of the drive connector. Line 1 usually is identified by a stripe along one edge of the cable.

SCSI Adapters and Drives

You have to work a bit harder to install a SCSI subsystem. There are a fair number of rules, but they are pretty easy to follow:

- SCSI is configured as a bus, and each device on the bus must be assigned a unique address in the range of 0 through 7.
- The SCSI adapter always will be assigned address 7, which is the factory default.
- Most SCSI adapters expect device 0 to be the hard drive that boots the system. Adapters also might expect drive 1 to be a hard drive. If that is the case, don't assign address 0 or 1 to other types of devices.
- Lower numbered SCSI addresses have higher priorities. If your server has hard drives and a CD-ROM, assign the hard drives lower addresses.
- A system can support up to four SCSI adapters, for a total of 28 SCSI devices. You must, of course, ensure that each adapter is assigned unique settings.
- Most SCSI adapters are equipped with floppy drive connectors. If your floppy drives are attached to other controllers, be sure to disable floppy drive support on the SCSI adapter.
- Devices are added to the SCSI bus by daisy chaining cables from device to device.
- The first and last devices in the SCSI daisy chain must be terminated.
- Devices in the middle of the daisy chain must not be terminated.
- External SCSI devices must be separated by at least .3 meters of cable.
- The total length of the SCSI cable daisy chain cannot exceed 6 meters.

SCSI Addressing

SCSI is an attractive technology, because one controller can manage seven devices. The only device setting you need to be concerned about is the SCSI address. Several precautions were mentioned in the preceding list.

A PC can support four SCSI buses, and devices on separate buses can share the same address.

The addresses on internal devices usually are set with jumpers. Many external devices are equipped with switches that make it easy to set the addresses.

Connecting SCSI Devices

Internal SCSI devices connect to a 50-pin ribbon cable. The cable simply is daisy chained from one device to the next. Be sure that line 1 of the ribbon cable attaches to pin 1 of the SCSI connector. Line 1 usually is identified by a stripe along one edge of the cable. If you're lucky, when you reverse a cable, the attached device will only complain. If you're unlucky, it will die.

Figure 6.4 illustrates three common connectors:

- The top connector is a 25-pin D connector.
- The middle connector resembles a Centronics printer connector but has 50 contacts.
- The bottom connector is a miniaturized connector with 50 pins. This connector sometimes is called a SCSI-2 connector.

Figure 6.4

Connectors used with external SCSI devices.

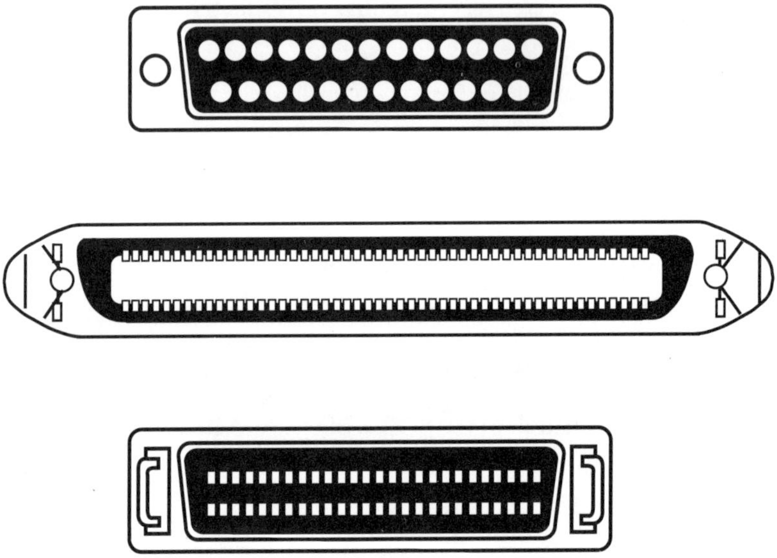

If you are using wide SCSI-2, you will encounter a connector much like the bottom connector in figure 6.4, but equipped with more pins.

External devices generally are equipped with two connectors, which are used to daisy chain cables between devices. You can use either of the connectors in any order. There is no "in" or "out." Just connect a cable to one connector and use the other connector to daisy chain to the next device.

Each connector will have some mechanism for securing it, which can consist of clips or screws. Be sure that the connector is secured properly. Most problems with external SCSI devices can be traced to loose connectors. If one connector lets go, the entire bus shuts down.

Figure 6.5 shows a complete installation with internal and external devices.

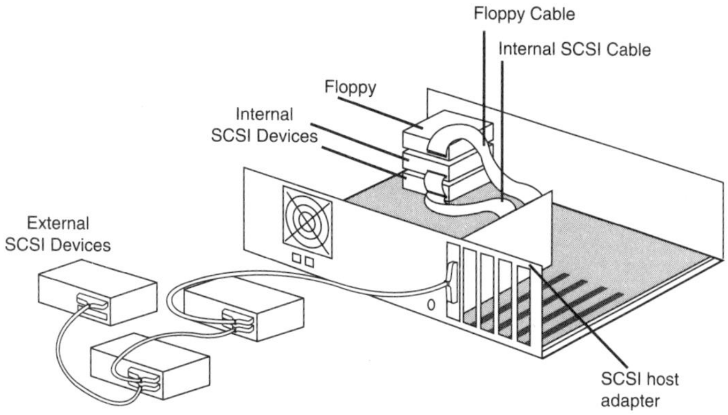

Figure 6.5
A SCSI system with internal and external devices.

Terminating the SCSI Bus

SCSI devices are terminated in several ways:

- Some SCSI devices, particularly internal devices, incorporate *resistor packs*. These are little in-line packages that plug into connectors on the device. You will find three resistor packs on most devices, but some will have two. Resistor packs are delicate and nearly impossible to replace. Be careful when you remove or install them, and don't lose the ones you remove. It is a good idea to tape resistor packs to the drive from which they were removed.

- Banks of switches or jumpers can be used. Some devices use a single switch to control termination.

- External devices can use *external terminators*—special connectors that include the termination resistors. A terminator is just plugged into the open connector of the last device in a daisy chain.

- Some all-too-rare devices know where they are in the daisy chain and set their termination characteristics automatically.

- Adapters that are at the ends of daisy chains also must be terminated. Some use resistor packs, but most newer adapters enable you to use a setup program to enable or disable termination.

SCSI buses can be configured in three ways:

- If external devices only are used, as shown in figure 6.6, the SCSI adapter is terminated, as is the last device in the daisy chain.

- If internal devices only are used, as shown in figure 6.7, the SCSI adapter is terminated, as is the last internal device in the daisy chain.
- If both external and internal devices are used, as shown in figure 6.8, the SCSI adapter is not terminated. The last external device is terminated, as well as the last internal device.

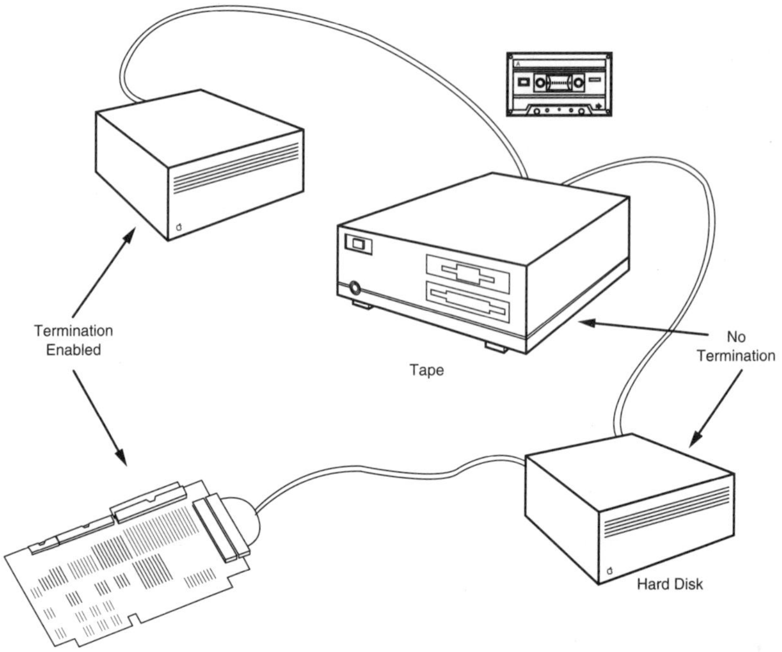

Figure 6.6
SCSI termination with external devices only.

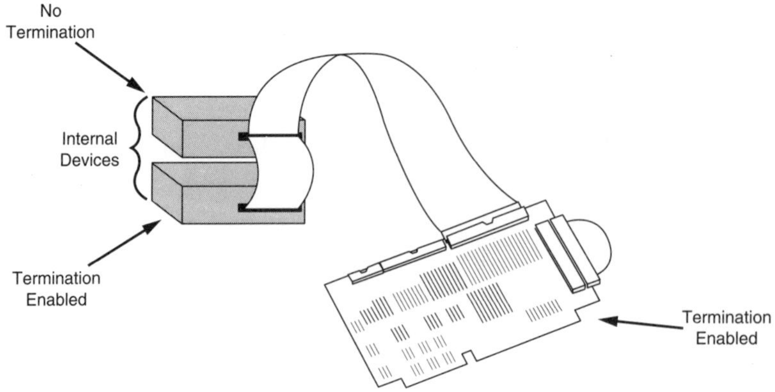

Figure 6.7
SCSI termination with internal devices only.

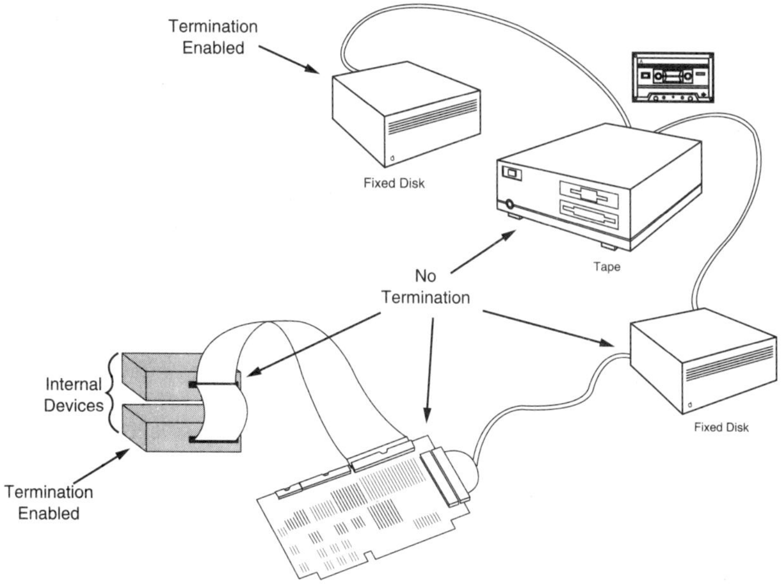

Figure 6.8
SCSI termination with internal and external devices.

CHAPTER 7

Installing Windows NT Server

Microsoft has put considerable thought into the installation procedures for Windows NT. The Setup program is highly automated and works with incredibly few flaws. It is sophisticated in its capability to identify computer hardware and select the proper drivers and driver settings. Most of what you as a user have to contribute during installation involves entering personal information such as your name, the license number, and so forth.

This chapter walks you through the complete installation procedure. I'm assuming that your hardware has been installed and configured using the information covered in the previous two chapters.

This chapter first covers planning, then the actual installation. It follows with a look at some miscellaneous procedures related to installation, reconfiguration, and starting and stopping the server.

Planning for Installation

Before charging into installation, you need to do some planning and preparation. This section discusses the plans you need to make.

Planning Disk Partitions

During system setup, you are required to designate a primary partition on the first hard drive for Windows NT to use as a system partition, the partition from which Windows NT boots. *Chapter 16, "Managing Disk Storage," covers partitions in detail.*

In general, designate the entire first drive as the system partition. This partition becomes drive C after it is formatted. This configuration is done for you if you elect to perform an express setup.

The following is a list of some guidelines for setting up partitions:

- The system partition must have a capacity of at least 90 MB for Intel x86 systems.
- The system partition for a RISC computer must be configured with the FAT file system. The system partition must have a capacity of at least 90 MB for x86 systems and 110 MB for RISC systems. Alternatively, a 2 MB FAT partition can be used to boot the RISC computer, after which all software can be run from an NTFS partition.
- The system partition cannot be configured as a volume set or a stripe set (see Chapter 16).
- Partitions on a RISC computer are configured following procedures described in the system documentation. Windows NT Setup cannot configure partitions on RISC computers.
- Windows NT cannot be installed in an existing partition if the partition is compressed.
- If you want to configure the computer to dual-boot under both MS-DOS and Windows NT, the boot partition must use the FAT file system.

Note The system partition can always be referenced by the Windows NT system variable %SystemRoot%. Although the system partition is virtually always drive C, the %SystemRoot% variable enables Windows NT (and you) to identify the system partition without knowing which drive letter was assigned.

Selecting File Systems

Windows NT supports the following three file systems:

- **FAT (file allocation tables).** The file system used by DOS.
- **HPFS (high-performance file system).** The file system developed and still used for OS/2.
- **NTFS (NT file system).** A file system developed for Windows NT.

NTFS has the following advantages (which are particularly significant for network servers):

- Complete support for Windows NT security. NTFS is the file system of choice for Windows NT Server because it is the only one that provides security at the server computer. Unauthorized users cannot bypass security on an NTFS volume by booting the server from a floppy.
- Long file names—up to 256 characters—with support for mixed-case letters. OS/2 users can access long file names; MS-DOS users see shortened versions of the long file names.
- Disk activities can be logged to enable activities to be rolled back in the event of a system failure. Corrupt files due to hardware or power failures are much less common with NTFS.

Although only Windows NT computers can directly use NTFS files, network users can access files on Windows NT servers quite normally whether they are using MS-DOS, OS/2, Unix, or Macintosh computers. Windows NT presents the files to non-NT computers in a form that the computers can accept.

With Intel x86 servers, the only reason not to use NTFS is that you need to dual-boot the computer using DOS or OS/2. Frankly, for servers, that's not an advantage. You want servers to be locked up tightly, and you most certainly don't want users to be able to boot the computer under DOS and attack your files.

With Advanced RISC computers, the system partition must be formatted with the FAT file system to enable the computer to boot. All other partitions can be formatted with NTFS.

In summary, all Windows NT computers should use NTFS whenever possible (with the sole exception of the system partition on a RISC-based server).

Choosing Network Protocols

Network protocols—as covered in Chapter 1, "Understanding Networks"—are the languages that enable computers to carry on conversations on the network. Windows NT supports the following three transport protocols:

- **NetBEUI** (the protocol used in all earlier Microsoft network environments). NetBEUI is well-suited for small networks. Its primary disadvantage is that it cannot be forwarded through routers and is, therefore, unsuitable for large networks. NetBEUI is required if you need to communicate with other computers that are configured to use only NetBEUI.

- **NWLink** (a Microsoft-developed protocol that is compatible with Novell's IPX/SPX protocols). The Novell protocols are particularly notable for their plug-and-play nature—very little configuration is required. IPX/SPX is routeable and can be used on large networks, providing solid performance. Network routing, long a weak spot with IPX/SPX, has improved greatly with a new routing protocol named NLSP, which is now available on most third-party network routers. Unfortunately, relatively few systems outside of the Novell network arena support IPX/SPX.

- **TCP/IP** (the most widely used network protocols in the computer industry). Virtually every combination of computer and operating system can be configured to support TCP/IP. TCP/IP provides outstanding reliability and performance. The primary disadvantage to TCP/IP is that it requires considerable configuration and management, and a fair amount of knowledge concerning how the TCP/IP protocols function.

As described in Chapter 6, "Planning and Installing Server and Workstation Hardware," NDIS enables a Windows NT computer to load all three protocol stacks at the same time if required.

Because NetBEUI and NWLink require essentially no configuration, both are installed by default. TCP/IP is optional and, because TCP/IP configuration is fairly involved, installation is not covered in this chapter. Chapter 15, "Using TCP/IP," however, does examine TCP/IP concepts and installation.

Planning the Computer's Security Role

Windows NT computers are organized in *domains*, groups of computers that share a common administrative database. User accounts in a domain are all managed together, even though the domain may have many computers. Administration is considerably simpler than maintaining separate user accounts on each server. Domains and their relationships to servers are discussed in Chapter 8, "Understanding User Accounts, Groups, Domains, and Trust Relationships."

Windows NT computers can perform three security roles in a domain:

- **Primary Domain Controller (PDC).** The Windows NT Server computer that maintains the primary copy of the domain account database.
- **Backup Domain Controller (BDC).** Additional Windows NT Server computers that keep backup copies of the domain account database.
- **Server.** Windows NT Server computers that do not store copies of the domain database.

A computer can only be configured as a PDC during installation. Creating a PDC automatically creates its associated domain since the domain essentially consists of the domain database that is created on the primary domain controller. The first Windows NT Server computer in the domain must be a primary domain controller. Additional Windows NT Server computers can be backup DCs or servers.

When you add a backup domain controller or a server to a domain, you must designate the domain to which the computer will be added. If a PDC has not been created for that domain, the domain doesn't exist, and you cannot add a computer to the domain.

When you add a BDC to a domain, you must have a user name and password that has administrative access to the domain. Administrative privileges are required to add the new BDC to the domain database. (There is a way to add the BDC to the domain before it is installed. See Chapter 9, "Managing Domains and Trust Relationships," for the technique.)

To create a primary domain controller, the only real requisite is a working network. Setup examines the network to ensure that you are not duplicating an existing domain. If a network is not available, setup of a domain controller cannot succeed.

To set up a backup domain controller you must have the following:

- A working network that enables the BDC to communicate with its intended PDC.
- A working domain. You can't create a BDC without accessing a domain that is run by an active primary domain controller.
- An administrative user name and password for the domain.

Starting Installation

CD-ROM installation is the preferred method for installing Windows NT Server. It is far less labor-intensive than installing from floppies, and requires less setup than a network shared drive installation. Further, with a CD-ROM, you need to duplicate only three floppies to have a working copy of the software. Are you really going to copy all those floppies from a floppy disk version?

At the time of this writing, a SCSI CD-ROM drive can now be purchased for little more than $200. Considering this, do yourself a favor and make the investment. Once the CD-ROM drive is installed on the server, there is the added benefit that it can be easily shared with the network.

Installation from a shared network drive makes a lot of sense if you need to install large numbers of servers on an established network or if some networked servers are not equipped with CD-ROM drives. You can use the same procedure to install from a non-SCSI CD-ROM.

Starting Installation from a SCSI CD-ROM

You will need the following to install Windows NT Server from a SCSI CD-ROM:

- Three setup floppy disks matched to your A drive. These should be copies of the setup floppies, not the originals!
- One high-density floppy disk, matching your A drive, that can be overwritten to prepare an emergency repair disk. Label this disk "Emergency Repair Disk."
- The Windows NT Server CD-ROM, installed in a properly connected CD-ROM drive. Don't worry about setting up drivers. Setup will select and install SCSI and CD-ROM drivers for you if you are using supported hardware.

To begin a CD-ROM installation do the following:

1. Insert the Setup Boot Disk in Drive A: and turn on or reboot the computer.
2. Insert Setup Disk 2 when prompted. Setup Disk 2 begins to load a large number of drivers.
3. When you see the message `Welcome to Setup` proceed to the section "Installing Windows NT Server."

Starting Installation from Floppy Disks

You will need the following to install Windows NT Server from floppy disks:

- Three setup floppy disks matched to your A drive. These should be copies of the setup floppies, not the originals!
- All of the floppies from your copy of Windows NT. You should be working from copies of these as well.
- One high-density floppy disk, matching your A drive, that can be overwritten to prepare an emergency repair disk. Label this disk "Emergency Repair Disk."

To install from floppy disks do the following:

1. Insert the Setup Boot Disk in Drive A and turn on or reboot the computer.
2. Insert Setup Disk 2 when prompted. Setup Disk 2 begins to load a large number of drivers.
3. When you see the message `Welcome to Setup` proceed to the section "Installing Windows NT Server."
4. Change floppy disks when prompted.

Starting Installation from a Shared Drive or an Unsupported CD-ROM

This approach has advantages. You don't need a CD-ROM during installation, and you can install by reading files from another computer through the network. This method, however, has the disadvantage of requiring the most preparation.

You will need the following:

- Three freshly formatted high-density floppy disks matched to your A drive. Label the disks Setup Boot Disk, Setup Disk 2, and Setup Disk 3.
- One high-density floppy disk, matching your A drive, that can be overwritten to prepare an emergency repair disk. Label this disk "Emergency Repair Disk."
- The Windows NT master CD-ROM.

Preparing to Install from a Master Server

To install from a master server, you must have already built a working network. Therefore, this is probably not the first setup method you will try. Network installation requires the most knowledge about Windows NT Server networks.

Copying Master Files to a Server

Before installing from a network server, you must copy master files from the CD-ROM to the source server. The files are stored in the \I386, \MIPS, and \ALPHA directories on the master CD-ROM. You need only copy the files that are required for your network servers.

The master server must have access to a CD-ROM drive, which can be directly attached to the server or a shared drive that is connected through the network. To copy the master files do the following:

1. Create a master file directory. This procedure assumes the directory will be named \NTMASTER.

2. Use the XCOPY command or File Manager to copy the appropriate subdirectory (or subdirectories if you have more than one type of server) from the CD-ROM to the \NTMASTER directory.

3. Share the master directory (see Chapter 9). Only the Administrator group needs Read permissions to this share.

Starting Installation of Windows NT from a Network Server to a DOS Computer

The following procedure is performed from DOS:

1. Use FDISK to create a FAT partition in which Windows NT will be installed.

2. Format the partition with the /S option to make it bootable.

3. Using procedures described in Chapter 13, "Using Windows and DOS Clients," install and activate DOS client software.

4. Log on to the master server using an account that can access the shared master installation directory.

5. Connect a network drive to the shared master directory.

6. Change to the installation directory, for example, enter the command CD \NTMASTER\I386.

7. Type **WINNT** at the command prompt.

8. When prompted, enter the logical drive letter and directory path where the master files are located.

9. Supply disks as requested.

10. Follow the instructions to complete Setup. After the three setup disks are created, the procedures will closely follow the Setup walk through in this chapter. Read the section "Installing Windows NT Server."

Starting Installation of Windows NT from a Network Server to a Windows NT Computer

To install to a computer that is running Windows NT, do the following:

1. Log on to the server that contains the Master files.

2. In File Manager, connect a drive to the shared master directory.

3. Change to the directory that contains the master files for your hardware version (I386, MIPS, or ALPHA).

4. Execute the command WINNT32.

5. When prompted, enter the logical drive letter and directory path where the master files are located.

6. Supply disks as requested.

7. Follow the instructions to complete Setup. After the three setup disks are created, the procedures will closely follow the Setup walk through in this chapter. Read the section "Installing Windows NT Server."

Starting Installation of Windows NT from a Non-SCSI CD-ROM to a DOS Computer

The following procedure is performed from DOS:

1. Use FDISK to create a FAT partition in which Windows NT will be installed.

2. Format the partition with the /S option to make it bootable.

3. Install the appropriate drivers for your CD-ROM drive.

4. Reboot the computer to activate the CD-ROM drivers.

5. Insert the Windows NT CD-ROM in the CD-ROM drive.

6. Change the default drive to the CD-ROM.
7. Change to the directory that contains the desired software version, for example, enter the command CD \I386.
8. Type **WINNT** at the command prompt.
9. When prompted, enter the logical drive letter and directory path where the master files are located.
10. Follow the instructions to complete Setup. After the three setup disks are created, the procedures will closely follow the Setup walk through in this chapter. Read the section "Installing Windows NT Server."

Installing Windows NT Server

A remarkable amount of Windows NT Server setup is automatic, and your actions will in most places be limited to a few key decisions. You might not even need to read this blow-by-blow description, but here it is just in case.

1. Choosing Installation or Repair

The `Welcome to Setup` screen branches in two directions:

- Press Enter to continue. This is what you'll do in this section.
- Press **R** to repair the server. Later in the setup procedures you will create an Emergency Repair Disk, which enables you to use this repair option if crucial server files are damaged and the server cannot be started. Repair procedures are described later in this chapter.

Note In most steps, press Enter to take Microsoft's preferred path through the setup procedure.

Throughout Setup, you have these options:

- Press F1 for Help tailored to the step you are executing.
- Press F3 to exit the Setup procedure.

2. Choosing Express or Custom Setup

After you press Enter on the Welcome to Setup screen, select the type of setup you want to perform. Two choices are available:

- Press Enter to begin an Express Setup
- Press **C** to begin a Custom Setup

An Express Setup uses default settings wherever possible.

Although Microsoft recommends Express Setup, Custom Setup is not very involved and will teach you a bit more about how the server is set up. The following sections assume that a Custom Setup is being performed.

3. Selecting Disk Controller Drivers

Next, Setup must select a disk controller driver. You can do the following:

- Press Enter to have Setup examine your hardware to detect mass storage devices and identify required drivers. I recommend having Setup scan for devices unless you have unsupported hardware.
- Press **S** to skip detection and select a driver from a list.

If your disk controller is on the supported hardware list, it is easy to permit Setup to detect your hardware and select the driver for you. The only disadvantage is that detection takes a few minutes because Setup loads every available driver and tries it to see if your hardware responds. All of the available drivers are tried even after a match is found because you might have two or more disk controllers of different brands or models.

Choose to skip detection if either of the following is true:

- You know which driver(s) you need, and it would be faster to choose the driver(s) from a list.
- You are using unsupported hardware and need to supply drivers on a disk.

3a. Detecting Mass Storage Devices

While Setup is scanning for mass storage devices, you are prompted to insert Setup Disk 3.

Setup can detect a wide variety of SCSI adapters. If Setup identifies more than one mass storage system, you will be presented with a list that you can accept or reject. Devices like IDE and ESDI hard drives don't appear in the list; these drivers are installed in a later step. You have a choice of the following:

- Pressing Enter to accept the list and continue.
- Pressing **S** to specify additional devices. If you choose this option, you will go through the manual driver selection procedure.

3b. Selecting Drivers Manually

If you press S to specify additional devices, Setup presents a scrolling list containing a wide variety of drivers for SCSI host bus adapters. To load a driver, use the following steps:

1. Scroll through the list by pressing the up and down arrow keys.
2. If the required driver is in the list, highlight it by pressing Enter.
3. If the required driver is not in the list and you have the driver on disk, select the bottom choice, Other.

   You are prompted, `Please insert the disk labeled manufacturer-supplied hardware support disk into drive A:`. Do so and press Enter to load the driver.
4. The driver you selected will be added to the mass storage devices list. You may add other drivers by pressing S.
5. When all required drivers appear in the list, press Enter to continue installation.

4. Loading More Device Drivers

Setup now test loads every driver under the sun, including IDE, ESDI, and CD-ROM. By the end of this process, Setup will know almost everything about all of your mass storage devices unless you have something really unusual.

5. Choosing CD-ROM or Floppy Installation

If Setup finds a CD-ROM drive, you have a choice of installing from the CD or from the A drive.

- Press Enter to install from the CD-ROM drive.
- Press **A** to install from Drive A.

6. Identifying Computer Hardware

Next, Setup examines your system to determine its basic hardware configuration. The following characteristics are typical for Intel x86 servers:

```
        Computer:  Standard PC
         Display:  VGA or Compatible
        Keyboard:  XT, AT, or Enhanced Keyboard 83-102 keys)
 Keyboard Layout:  US
 Pointing Device:  Microsoft Serial Mouse
```

Setup will probably be right about all this information, but you can change any item by using the up and down arrow keys to select an item and pressing Enter. A list of options will be presented.

If you are not located in the United States, for example, you might want to select a different international standard for the keyboard layout. A considerable number of nationalized keyboard layouts can be selected from a list.

When this list is correct, select `The above list matches my computer` and press Enter.

7. Partitioning the Hard Drive

Next Setup shows a list of the hard drives on your server, along with the partitions on each drive. The first partition on the first drive (Drive 0) is highlighted. This is the default partition for installing Windows NT. You must designate or create a primary partition on this drive to be used as the system (startup) partition for Windows NT.

7a. Deleting Existing Partitions

You might want to delete an existing partition by highlighting the partition entry and typing **D**. This enables you to create new partitions if required. You will be asked to confirm your request to delete the partition.

7b. Creating a Partition

To create a partition, use the following steps:

1. Select any area labeled `Unpartitioned space`. When you do so, a new option, `C=Create Partition`, appears at the bottom of the screen.
2. Enter **C** to create a partition.
3. A new screen is presented that declares the minimum size for the new partition (1 MB) and the maximum size (the full capacity of the unpartitioned space).

In the box labeled `Create partition of size (in MB):` enter a size for the partition that is in the minimum-to-maximum range.

4. Press Enter.

When you return to the partition list after creating a partition, you will see an entry similar to the following:

```
C:  New (Unformatted)                  1016 MB
```

7c. Selecting a System Partition

You can select either of the following as a Windows NT Server system partitions:

- ◆ A New (Unformatted) partition
- ◆ An existing primary partition on the first drive. Windows NT can be installed over existing software in a FAT, HPFS, or NTFS partition provided the partition is of sufficient size. (RISC-based servers must start from a FAT partition.)

Select a partition from the partition list and press Enter

8. Formatting the System Partition

The options you see next depend on whether you have designated a New (Unformatted) partition or a partition that was previously formatted.

8a. Formatting a New (Unformatted) Partition

If you selected a New (Unformatted) partition, you have two choices on the next screen:

- ◆ Format the partition using the FAT file system
- ◆ Format the partition using the NTFS file system

Select one of these options and press Enter.

Note NTFS partitions are first formatted with the FAT file system. The first time the server starts after setup has been completed, the FAT partition will be converted to NTFS.

Partitions can also be converted to NTFS at a later time. *See Chapter 16 for the procedure.*

8b. Formatting an Existing Partition

If an existing, formatted partition was selected in step 7, you will see the following four options:

- Format the partition using the FAT file system
- Format the partition using the NTFS file system
- Convert the partition to NTFS
- Leave the current file system intact (no changes)

Choose the last option if files exist on the partition that you want to retain. This is, of course, the option to use if you are upgrading or re-installing Windows NT Server.

9. Selecting a Directory for Windows NT

After the partition is selected and formatted, files can be installed. You will be asked to specify a directory for Windows NT. The default directory is \WINNT35. Files will be installed on the system partition that you designated in step 7.

If an existing Windows NT installation is found on the system drive, you have the option of installing in the same directory or designating a separate directory for installation.

Note If you retain the existing Windows NT installation and install in a new directory, both versions will be entered into the boot menu, enabling you to boot the old OS as well as Windows NT.

10. Examining the Hard Disks

Next Setup gives you the option of performing an exhaustive secondary examination of your hard disks. For first-time installations in particular, this test should always be performed, even though it can take quite awhile on systems equipped with large hard drives.

- Press Enter to have Setup examine your hard disks
- Press Esc to skip disk examination

11. Copying Files

After the hard disks have been examined, Setup copies files to the system partition.

If you are installing from floppy disks, you will be prompted to change disks as needed.

12. Restarting the Computer

When files have been copied, the computer must be restarted. Remove any floppy disk from Drive A and press Enter.

13. Entering Identification Information

After the system restarts, a Windows dialog box appears requesting the following information:

- Name (required)
- Company (optional)

Complete these free-form text entries and click Continue. Then confirm the entries by choosing Continue again.

14. Entering the Product ID

The next dialog box prompts you for a Product ID number, which you will find printed inside the back cover of your *Windows NT Installation Guide.* This information is optional, but will be useful to have if you need to contact Microsoft for support. You can recover the number after installation by examining the About option in the Help menu of the Program Manager.

Click Continue to accept the entry and Continue again to confirm.

15. Selecting a Server Security Role

Windows NT Server can be configured with two network security roles. You specify one of the following options in the next dialog box:

- Domain Controller (Primary or Backup)
- Server

Choose one of these options and click Continue. (The rest of this example will assume that Domain Controller was chosen.)

16. Specifying a Computer Name

Each computer on a Windows network must be assigned a unique name. This can be the name of the primary user of the computer, a designation of the computer's function, or some other meaningful name.

Enter a name in the Computer Name box and choose Continue. Choose Continue to confirm.

17. Selecting a Language Setting

Windows NT can adapt to a wide variety of language requirements. The next box enables you to select a language or locale setting. The setting you select determines how currency, numeric, date, and time values are displayed.

If you do not want to use the English (American) default setting, pull down the list by clicking the arrow and select a locale setting from the list. Press Enter to choose the highlighted option.

Choose Continue to accept the selected option.

18. Choosing Setup Actions

The next box enables you to specify which of the following setup actions will be performed:

- **Set Up Only Windows Components You Select.** This option gives you control over which files will be copied. If this option is not checked, all Windows application, screen saver, wallpaper, and other such files will be installed (see step 19).
- **Set Up Network.** This option is required (and cannot be unchecked) if the computer will be configured as a primary or backup domain controller, which must be on the network. Otherwise, you can uncheck this option to postpone network setup until later.
- **Set Up Printers.** If printers will be attached directly to this computer, select this option. Do not check this option if users of this computer will share printers on another computer, since Windows NT computers that share printers on other Windows NT computers do not require local print drivers.

- **Set Up Applications on the Hard Disk(s).** If you are installing over an existing partition, this option instructs Setup to scan for existing applications and create program items (icons) for them in the Program Manager desktop.

The following discussion assumes that all actions have been checked.

19. Choosing Optional Windows Components

If you checked `Set Up Only Windows Components You Select` in step 18, the next screen enables you to specify which of the following will be installed:

- **Readme Files.** I suggest you install these on one server only.
- **Accessories.** Altogether, these files use up over 2 MB of valuable disk storage. Lots of the accessories, such as the CD Player, are inappropriate for a file server and can be removed.
- **Games.** Uncheck this option to save a third of a megabyte.
- **Screen Savers.** You only need one. (3D Objects is a lot of fun. There's also a Logon Screen Saver that secures the computer until a password is entered.) It is suggested that you remove the rest.
- **Wallpaper, Misc.** This option contains various wallpaper and sound files that you almost certainly don't need on a server.

For each category, you can perform a detailed file selection. To select specific files, follow these steps:

1. Click the Files button for a category. A Customize Files dialog box is displayed for that category. The files that are listed in the `Install these files on the hard disk` list will be installed.
2. To install a file, select the file in the `Do not install these files` list. Then choose Add.
3. To not install a file, select the file in the `Install these files on the hard disk` list and choose Remove.
4. Choose Add All to install all files in the `Do not install these files` list.
5. Choose OK to accept your choices.

When you have specified all files to be installed, click Continue in the Optional Windows Components box.

20. Setting Up a Local Printer

If you checked `Set Up Printers` in step 18, the next window you see will be labeled Set up Local Printer. To set up a printer, use these steps:

1. Choose Cancel if you want to postpone or cancel printer installation.

2. Enter a name by which the printer will be known in the Printer Name box. A name is required.

3. Click the arrow by the Model box to select a printer model from a list. If your model isn't shown, see Chapter 12, "Managing Printing Services," for suggestions on compatible print drivers. If you can't find a drive to match your model, you will need to install the printer later using procedures described in Chapter 12.

4. Click the arrow by the Print to box to specify the port to which the printer is attached (LPT1-3:, COM1-4:, or FILE:).

5. Choose Continue to accept your selections.

21. Selecting Network Cards

A domain controller must have a network card because it must attach to the network before its domain security role can be established. Servers do not require network cards during setup, but you will need to install one later to enable network communication.

Setup has a sophisticated capability to scan your computer, identify network cards, and determine their settings. You can take advantage of this capability at the dialog box named Network Adapter Card Detection.

It is recommended that you choose Continue to use automatic card detection, which is described in step 21a.

Choose Do Not Detect to skip card detection and go to Step 21b, or to skip card selection altogether.

21a. Using Automatic Card Detection

If Setup is able to identify your adapter card, a box names the card that was found.

- Choose Continue to accept the entry.

- Choose Find Next to find another card if more than one is installed. (If your cards all use the same drivers, you do not need to do Find Next.) You can, however, activate only one card at this stage in Setup. In step 23 additional cards can be installed.

- Choose Do Not Detect to cancel automatic card detection.

21b. Selecting Network Adapters Manually

If you choose Do Not Detect in step 21, you can use the Add Network Adapter box to select a driver from the Network Adapter Card list. In addition to drivers for supported hardware you can choose:

- **Other.** Requires disk from manufacturer. You are asked to supply a driver on a floppy disk.
- **None.** Network interface to be chosen later. You can always add network adapters using the Network utility in the Control panel. However, you cannot set up a domain controller unless a network adapter is successfully selected during Setup.

After you select a network adapter, choose Continue.

22. Setting Up the Network Adapter

After you select a network adapter, Setup loads the drivers. Depending on the driver and hardware, different setup parameters must be verified. A Network Card Setup dialog box lists settings such as IRQ Level and I/O Port Address.

The settings displayed will probably be correct, but should be carefully verified and corrected if necessary. Choose OK to continue.

If you have two or more cards that use the selected driver, you can select one of them as your first adapter by entering that card's settings at this time.

23. Selecting Protocols

Next, Setup presents a dialog box with check boxes for three protocols:

- NWLink IPX/SPX Compatible Transport (checked by default)
- TCP/IP Transport (not checked by default)
- NetBEUI Transport (checked by default)

Select the desired protocols and choose Continue.

Configuration of the TCP/IP protocols is discussed in Chapter 15 and will not be covered here. No setup is required for NWLink or NetBEUI.

24. Choosing Network Settings

The Network Settings box is shown next. It enables you to add and remove network adapters, add and remove software for adapters, and examine protocol bindings. A later section in this chapter explains the procedures. If you need to add or reconfigure an adapter, examine this section at that time.

Choose OK when Network Settings are correct. Network software will be installed.

25. Configuring the NWLink Protocol

NWLink supports several frame types. If you have a specific preferred frame type, you can choose it in the NWLink IPX/SPX Configuration box. You can probably accept the default setting of Auto Frame Type Detection. Details of this configuration procedure are described later in this chapter in the section "Managing Network Adapters."

Choose OK to continue.

Note Setup should be able to connect to all segments of your network to enable it to identify existing domain controllers. Otherwise, you might configure a domain controller that conflicts with one on a segment that is not currently reachable.

Before you proceed, you should ensure that:

- All network adapters in the server have been properly configured, as discussed later in this chapter.
- All primary domain controllers are active and reachable through the network.

26. Establishing the Domain Security Role

After at least one network adapter is established, Setup will load the network software and connect to the network. This enables Setup to identify any existing domain controllers on the network.

The Domain Settings dialog box enables you to configure the server as a primary (PDC) or backup domain controller (BDC).

If this is the first Windows NT Server on your network, follow the steps in step 26a.

26a. Creating a Primary Domain Controller

If the server is the first one on the network, it will be a PDC. It can also be installed as the first PDC of a new domain. To configure a PDC:

1. Select the **P**rimary Domain Controller option.
2. Enter a domain name in the dialog box. Domain names cannot contain spaces. The name you enter must not match the name of any domain that is currently running on the network.
3. Choose OK.

Setup will search the network for a domain that matches the name you entered. If no matching domain is found, you will be permitted to proceed. This search might take awhile.

26b. Creating a Backup Domain Controller

To add a BDC to an existing domain:

1. Select the **B**ackup Domain Controller option.
2. Enter the name of the domain that this BDC will join. The PDC for the domain you name must be running.
3. Enter an **A**dministrator Name and Administrator Pass**w**ord for the domain to be joined. This name and password will be used to gain access to the domain and add the BDC to the domain.
4. Choose OK.

Setup will search the network for a domain that matches the name you entered. If a matching domain is found, you will be permitted to proceed.

27. Building the Desktop

After the domain security role is established, Setup builds the desktop. No action is required on your part.

28. Creating the Administrator Account Password

Each Windows NT domain has an Administrator account, and you will need to create the account if you are creating a primary domain controller. By default, this account is placed in the Administrators global group, which in turn is placed in the Domain

Admins local group. These group memberships give the Administrator user account administrative privileges for the entire domain. The Administrator Account Setup dialog box requests two entries:

- Password
- Confirm Password

These entries must match.

The password is optional, and you can get away without entering one, which is fine while you are experimenting with Windows NT Server. (Because Setup regards no password as a questionable choice, you will be asked to confirm your decision.) You should be sure to enter a password for any in-service server, however, because the Administrator account has full control over all resources on the server.

Because domains have a global account database, installing a backup domain controller does not require you to create an Administrator account. The Administrator account for the domain is used.

If you are creating a stand-alone server (the computer is not joining a domain), you are asked to specify both a user name and a password for the server's administrator account.

29. Specifying Virtual Memory Settings

The Virtual Memory dialog box enables you to change the default virtual memory settings. Virtual memory is described in Chapter 18, "Managing the Server." You can refer to that chapter for complete information, or select the default value that is presented.

30. Setting Up Applications

If you chose Set Up Applications in step 18, the next dialog box you see is titled Set Up Applications. You can select drives to designate where Setup should look for existing applications. Choose Search Now to start the search.

After application files are identified, you will have the option of adding them to the desktop.

Note Searching for an application will not install the application in Windows NT. It will only add an application icon to the desktop. If the application uses a special installation procedure to configure INI files or the Registry for the application, you must run the setup program for the application.

continues

If you are upgrading from another version of Windows, the settings for most applications will be incorporated into Windows NT.

31. Entering Date and Time Parameters

For many domain functions to operate, servers in the domain must be in reasonable agreement regarding the date and time. A Date/Time dialog box appears next, enabling you to set the Date, local Time, and Time Zone of the server.

Be sure to check the box Automatically Adjust for Daylight Saving Time appropriately for your locale.

Choose OK to accept the settings and continue.

32. Configuring the Display

Setup won't permit you to configure a video display setting that is non-functional with your equipment. The next dialog box, Display Settings, enables you to select settings that are appropriate to your display type. To set the video display mode, use the following steps:

1. Confirm that the adapter Setup has identified is correct. If not, choose Change Display Type and select a different video adapter.
2. Select the video display modes you want, such as the number of colors, pixel size of the desktop, font size, and so forth.
3. Choose Test. Setup displays a grid that tests the display mode you have selected. After a few seconds, the grid is cleared.
4. If the display appeared to be correct, choose OK to confirm that it functioned properly. This mode can then be selected for the display adapter.
5. Some trial and error might be required to identify the best settings for your monitor. Keep going until you find a mode that passes the test. You cannot select a mode that you have not identified as OK.
6. After selecting a video display mode, choose OK.

Setup now saves the configuration for the server.

33. Creating the Emergency Repair Disk

An Emergency Repair Disk contains information about the hardware configuration of your server and can be used to recover the server from corruption in system files that prevents the server from starting up.

When Setup asks you if you want to create an Emergency Repair Disk, you should respond Yes and follow the prompts.

34. Restarting the Computer

Next, you will need to restart the computer. Remove all floppy disks and click Restart Computer to continue.

The first time a new server restarts, the process can be lengthy. For one thing, if you specified that the system domain should use NTFS files, the FAT partition that was created during Setup must be converted to NTFS.

Installation is now complete.

Logging On and Off, Restarting, and Shutting Down the Server

After the server restarts, the Welcome box invites you to Press Ctrl+Alt+Del to log on. Give the computer a three-finger salute to bring up a Welcome dialog box.

To log on, supply the following information in the Welcome dialog box:

- **Username.** If this is the first time a primary domain controller has been started, only the Administrator account will exist.
- **From.** This is the domain to be logged on from. By default, this will be the domain you declared in step 26a.
- **Password.** For new PDCs, this password was declared during Setup in step 28.

To log off, press Ctrl+Alt+Del any time when you are logged on. Unlike DOS, the Ctrl+Alt+Del key sequence does not immediately reboot the system. Instead, it produces a dialog box with the following options:

- **Lock Workstation.** Choose this option to lock the station when logged on. You will stay logged on, but will be required to enter your user password to regain access to your session.
- **Change Password.** Choose this option to change your password.
- **Logoff.** Logs out of the current session and displays the Welcome banner.
- **Task List.** Displays a list of running tasks and enables you to switch to a task or end the task. This option is especially useful to cancel a task that has hung or malfunctioned.
- **Shutdown.** This option gives you two further options:
  - **Shutdown.** After Windows NT performs a controlled shutdown, the server does not restart. Use this option if you need to turn the server off.
  - **Shutdown and Restart.** Use this option if you have made changes that require a server restart to be activated.

Reinstalling Windows NT

You might need to reinstall Windows NT for several reasons, for example:

- To change a computer security role. You can't upgrade a server to a domain controller without reinstalling Windows NT, for example.
- To repair corrupt files.
- To upgrade the operating system
- To move this computer to a new domain

To reinstall and change settings follow the original installation procedures and choose New Version installation.

To upgrade the operating system or reinstall damaged files without changing any configuration settings choose Upgrade installation.

There are some differences from first-time setup when you are upgrading. When Setup detects an existing Windows version after step 5, press Enter to upgrade. Do not press N to begin a new installation or the existing software will be overwritten.

If you upgrade, your existing partitions are used, along with all configuration information from the preceding version.

Stop Reinstalling a primary domain controller is particularly tricky business. See Chapter 9 before you are tempted to try it.

Actually, reinstalling any Windows NT computer can cause problems. You might think that no problems will arise provided you don't change the computer's name. Unfortunately, a computer is known by more than it's name. It also has a security ID (SID) that is created when you install Windows NT. When you reinstall and replace the old installation, a new SID is created. Even though the computer name might be the same, no other computers on the network will recognize the newly installed computer.

Repairing Windows NT

To repair Windows NT, it is best to have an Emergency Repair Disk (see step 32) that is up-to-date for your system. See Chapter 16 for information on updating the Emergency Repair Disk. You may be able to repair your problem without the Emergency Repair Disk, however.

To repair Windows NT:

1. Boot the server with the Setup Boot Disk.
2. Select **R** to Repair the system.
3. Check the areas you want Setup to examine. You have four choices:
   - Inspect registry files
   - Inspect startup environment
   - Verify Windows NT system files
   - Inspect boot sector
4. After checking areas you want, select Continue and press Enter.

5. You are now at step 3 in the Setup sequence. Work with Setup to identify the mass storage system drivers for your server.

6. Proceed with steps 3 through 5 of the standard Setup sequence.

7. When you are asked to supply an Emergency Repair Disk, you have two choices:

   - Press Enter if you have an Emergency Repair Disk
   - Press Esc if you don't have an Emergency Repair Disk. Setup will make its best effort to repair Windows NT by looking for Windows NT on your hard drives.

8. When prompted, insert the Emergency Repair Disk. Follow subsequent prompts.

9. Setup will examine your system in the areas you checked in Repair step 3.

10. You can choose to restore Registry files. When prompted select the files to be recovered from the following:

    - SYSTEM (System Configuration)
    - SOFTWARE (Software Information)
    - DEFAULT (Default User Profile)
    - SECURITY (Security Policy) and SAM (User Accounts Database)

    Choose Continue and press Enter to restore Registry files.

Stop Restoring the Registry from this procedure will discard any changes that were made to the system since the Emergency Repair Disk was last updated.

11. If Setup identifies a version problem with a file, you can choose:

    - Press Esc to not repair the file. Use this option if you have manually installed drivers or other files since the system was set up. Otherwise, your manual changes will be backed out.
    - Press Enter to repair the file. It will be restored to the version that existed when the Emergency Repair Disk was created.
    - To repair all files type **A**.

12. When repairs are completed, you will be prompted to remove the disk from drive A and restart the computer.

Managing Network Adapters

Figure 7.1 shows the box that is used to configure network adapters in Windows NT. This dialog box appears during Setup at step 24, as described during the Setup walk through in this chapter. It can also be accessed using the Network utility in the Control Panel.

To start Network utility:

1. Locate the Control Panel icon in the Main program group, and double-click on the icon.

2. Double-click on the Network icon in the control panel. The Network Settings dialog box is displayed.

This dialog box is the focus for changing a large number of network settings including adding and removing adapters and network protocols. It's worth taking some time to understand how these procedures work.

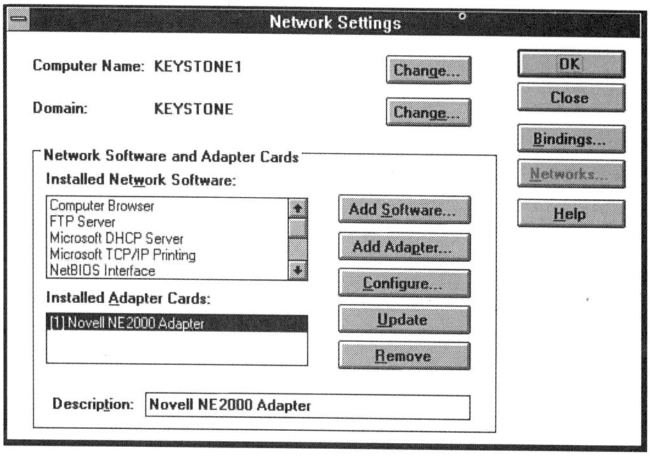

Figure 7.1

The Network Settings dialog box.

Changing the Computer Name and Domain Name

These options look simple, but are loaded with potential traps. Changing a computer name is risky business because on an established network many computers reference this computer by name, when, for example, they are accessing shared files. If you change the name, all those references will be made invalid by a name change.

The Network Settings dialog box makes it look like you can rename a domain here. This option is available only for primary domain controllers. Changing the domain name doesn't rename the domain. It creates a new domain with the name you specify and makes this computer the PDC for the new domain. If this computer is the only domain controller for the original domain, changing the domain orphans all of the computers that were in the domain. They will look for a domain controller with the old name, completely unaware that the controller is now in a new domain. When you change the domain of a controller, you need to change the domain of all of the computers that log on to the domain as well.

Adding Software

Many different options are available under the heading of Adding Software. This is the place you add protocols, network services, application environments such as Streams, network monitor agents, and a wide variety of features. Although this section won't describe all of the items you can add, many features are described in other chapters.

To add software:

1. Choose Add Software to display the Add Network Software dialog box shown in figure 7.2.
2. Pull down the Network Software list by clicking the arrow to the right of the box.
3. Select an item from the list.
4. Choose Continue.
5. You are shown a configuration dialog box for some software. Figure 7.3 shows the configuration box for NWLink (see the note on NWLink for an explanation). Make the appropriate settings and choose OK to continue.
6. You need to restart the computer to activate the new software.

The software you specified is added to the Installed Network Software list.

Note NWLink is the standard network protocol for Windows NT version 3.5. NWLink was developed by Microsoft as a transport that is compatible with Novell's IPX/SPX protocols. The IPX/SPX protocols perform well and require little configuration.

One configuration item that you might need to attend to is the frame type for Ethernet or token ring networks. A frame type is a variation on the basic frame format for a network. Novell NetWare supports four frame types for Ethernet and two for token ring. The primary reason for changing the frame type is to enable the Windows NT network to be compatible with another network.

Current Novell networks run the following default frame types:

- **Ethernet_802.2 for Ethernet networks.** This frame type fully conforms to the IEEE 802 standards and is the default frame type for current NetWare versions.
- **Token_Ring for token ring networks.** This frame type conforms to IBM Token Ring and to IEEE 802.5 standards and is the default token ring frame type on NetWare networks.

The following frame types are also supported:

- **Ethernet_802.3.** An older Ethernet frame type Novell developed before the IEEE 802.2 standard was set. This frame type continues to be supported on Novell networks but is not preferred.
- **Ethernet_II.** The frame type that predated the IEEE 802.3 standard. This frame type is used on TCP/IP networks.
- **Ethernet_SNAP.** A variation used to support Macintosh EtherTalk networks.
- **Token_Ring_SNAP.** A token ring variant that supports Macintosh TokenTalk networks.

Because Novell networks can bind multiple protocols, the best course of action is to have all networks bind to the Ethernet_802.2 or Token_Ring frame types. If your NetWare administrator is unable or unwilling to do that, you can add frame types to NWLink in the Protocol Configuration dialog box.

When you set NWLink to the recommended setting of `Auto` Frame Type Detection, NWLink examines the network and selects an active frame type. If Ethernet_802.2 frames are detected, or no frames are detected, the Ethernet_802.2 frame type is selected. Otherwise, NWLink selects the frame type that is observed on the network.

NetWare servers also support an internal network number that supports inter-process communication among servers. If you change the default number of 00000000, be sure that the number you enter does not conflict with other internal NetWare network numbers on the network.

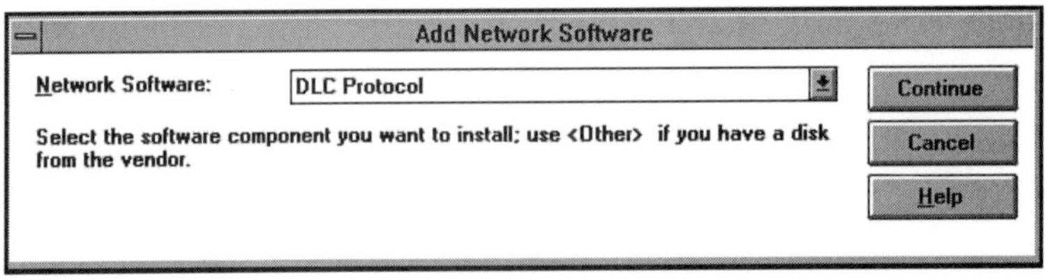

Figure 7.2
Adding network software.

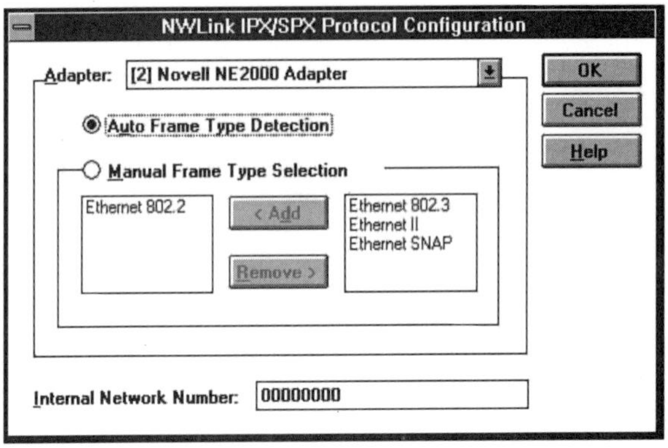

Figure 7.3
Configuring network software.

Configuring Network Software

Many of the network software items accept configuration parameters. To change the settings for a software item:

1. Select the software to be configured in the Installed **A**dapter Cards box.
2. Choose **C**onfigure to display a configuration dialog box. Figure 7.3 shows an example.
3. Enter the required configuration changes.

Adding Network Adapters

Figure 7.1 shows a single installed network adapter. You can have several if required. Before you install additional adapters, be sure that they are configured for non-conflicting settings.

To add an adapter:

1. Choose Add Ada**p**ter to display the Add Network Adapter dialog box shown in Figure 7.4.

2. Pull down the Network Adapter Card list by clicking the arrow to the right of the box.

3. Select an item from the list. If a driver for your card is not listed, choose Other. You are required to supply the drivers on a floppy disk in the next step.

4. You are informed that an adapter already exists of this type. Confirm your request to install the adapter.

5. You are asked to confirm hardware settings for this adapter.

6. You might be asked to confirm adapter settings for installed protocols such as NWLink and TCP/IP. Protocol Configuration dialog boxes will be displayed. Make any desired changes. (See the section "Adding Software" for an example of configuring a protocol. TCP/IP configuration is discussed in Chapter 15.)

7. You need to restart the computer to activate the new adapter.

The adapter you specified will be added to the Installed Adapter Cards list. If you have installed two cards with the same driver, they will be identified as [1], [2], and so forth.

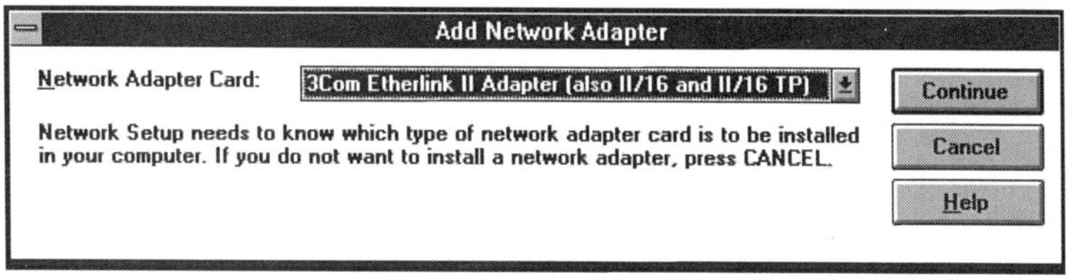

Figure 7.4
Adding a network adapter.

Configuring Network Adapters

After you add a network adapter, and whenever you change an adapter's hardware settings, you must change the network adapter configuration in the Network Settings.

To change the configuration of a network adapter:

1. Select the adapter to be configured in the Installed Adapter Cards box.

2. Choose Configure to display the Adapter Settings dialog box shown in figure 7.5.

3. Enter the hardware settings for your adapter.

Updating a Network Adapter

If you receive an updated version of a network adapter driver file, use the Update option to install the new file.

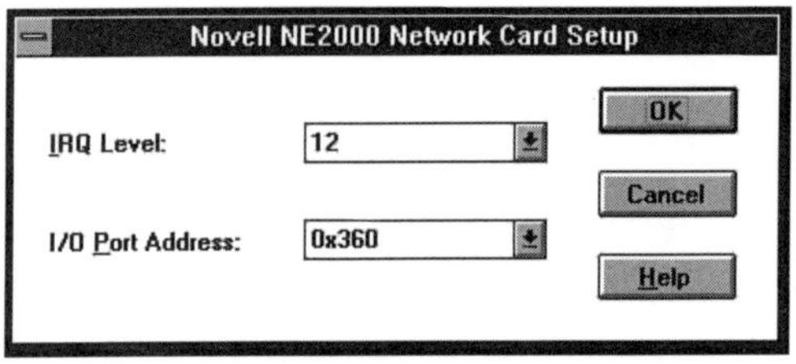

Figure 7.5
Configuring a network adapter.

Removing a Network Adapter

To remove a network adapter:

1. Select the adapter in the Installed Adapter Cards list.
2. Choose Remove.

Stop Removing software or an adapter, or entering improper configuration settings, can disrupt network functionality. Be careful what you modify, and make changes when you have time to pick up the pieces if something gets broken.

Managing Bindings

When network drivers and hardware are associated with one another, they are *bound* to one another. To display the bindings that are active on your computer, select Bindings. The bindings box is shown in figure 7.6.

Each line in the binding list shows a series of software and hardware items that are bound together. Lower bindings are closest to the computer hardware (lower in the protocol stack). Higher bindings are closer to the operating system (higher in the protocol stack).

In the figure, the NWLINK IPX/SPX Compatible Transport is bound to the Novell NE2000 Adapter Driver which, in turn, is bound to each of the installed NE2000 adapters. Through this series of bindings, NWLink protocol support is enable for the NE2000 adapter hardware.

The light bulb at the left is generally lit (yellow), indicating that the bindings are enabled. You can disable any set of bindings by selecting the entry and choosing Disable.

All bindings are established for you by the Network Settings dialog boxes.

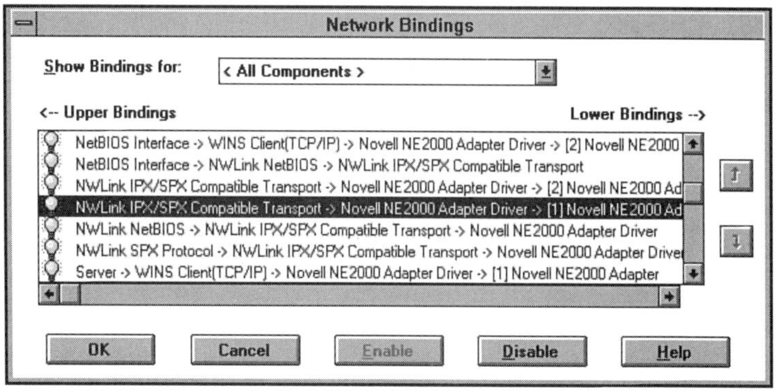

Figure 7.6

Network Bindings.

CHAPTER 8

Understanding User Accounts, Groups, Domains, and Trust Relationships

If networks were always simple, if they never had more than a single server or a few users, they would be easy to administer and to use. All resources would be in one place, and all users would be local. There would be no confusion regarding where a resource was located or how to gain access.

Today, however, increasing numbers of networks are not simple. They incorporate multiple servers (file, print, fax, mail, and so on) and often span multiple locations. More often than not, servers will be storing many gigabytes of files. Clearly, expecting users to simply know where things are under those circumstances is not very realistic.

Network designers, therefore, have sought ways to simplify the location of network resources. This chapter introduces you to the technique chosen by the designers of Windows NT Server, which is based on domains and trust relationships. These building blocks enable you to build enterprise networks that are easy for you to manage and easy for your users to use.

Organizing LAN Resources

In Chapter 1, "Understanding Networks," you learned that LANs provide services in two ways: through peer-to-peer resource sharing or through central servers. Whichever method your network uses, the problem remains of enabling users to locate the resources that are available for use. This section surveys some of the following techniques, which have been used for organizing network resources:

- Stand-alone services
- Directory services
- Workgroups
- Domains

Stand-Alone Services

The vast majority of early LANs incorporated only one server, so users had little difficulty locating files, printers, and other resources to be shared. NetWare 2.*x* and 3.*x* have long been the dominant network operating systems on small LANs, and statistics indicate that the average Novell 2.*x* and 3.*x* networks include a single server and 30 or fewer workstations.

With such an arrangement, there is little need for a sophisticated resource-management service. Files can be found using DOS DIR commands, and printers easily can be selected from a list. In most cases, users' LAN environments are entirely precon-figured for them by the LAN administrator. Users are given access to specific printers, file access is preset, and users do not need a great deal of knowledge about the LAN to use it effectively.

Adding a second server can significantly complicate things, however. The problem arises because each stand-alone server maintains its own lists of users and resources. Figure 8.1 illustrates the problem. Server A is the host for applications such as WordPerfect and Lotus 1-2-3. Server B is the host for the company's e-mail, accounting applications, and sales database. Users who need to access the sales database and use the applications must be given accounts on both servers. Each of these user accounts must be created and maintained separately. Notice that some users have accounts on only one server. It is easy for servers to get out of synchronization when they must be updated manually.

The situation complicates matters from the user's standpoint as well. The user must log on to and maintain a password on each server separately. This process can be automated, but is a bit error prone. Administrators of networks with several stand-alone servers are used to getting calls to resynchronize user passwords among servers.

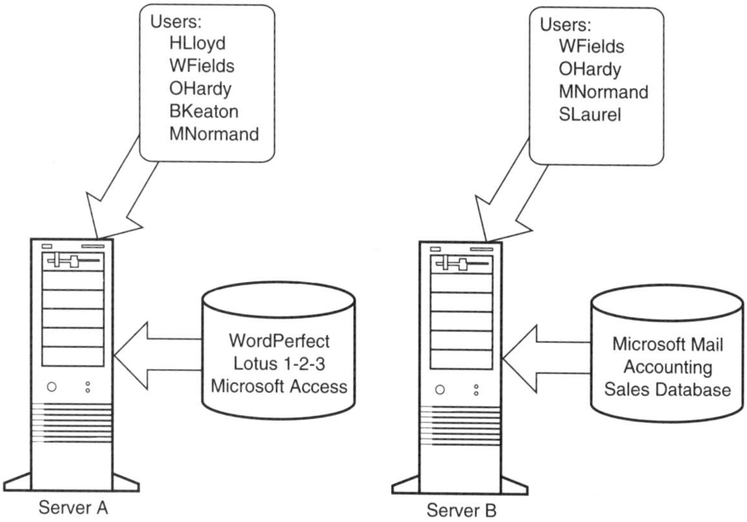

Figure 8.1

Administering two stand-alone servers.

Two servers are about the most you would want to administer in this way, but even two servers can be too much. Assuming all users need to access all server resources, each user must be given an account on each server. It is easy to see how errors could occur in busy office environments where staff changes are frequent.

Users also have a problem with multiple stand-alone servers. To use a printer, the user must know which server hosts the printer. To access a file or program, the user must be aware of the server that maintains the file. Unless the user is given friendly tools for locating services, many of the network's capabilities will be difficult to access. The situation is much like trying to locate a plumber by using only the telephone directory's White Pages. Unless you already know the name of the plumber you want, finding one in your area of the city would be extremely difficult.

Given these limitations, LAN vendors have made considerable investments in making large LANs more manageable and usable. Two techniques have arisen: directories and browseable services.

Directory Services

A network directory works much like a telephone directory's Yellow Pages. Resources can be grouped logically to make them easier to locate. Users can search the directory for the information they want, or they can browse the directory in a sensible fashion.

Directory services can be used to organize the resources on extremely large LANs. Several approaches are available:

- Banyan has long offered the StreetTalk directory service as part of its VINES network operating system. Banyan is now marketing StreetTalk as a directory service that can be used to integrate various network platforms.
- X.500 is an international standard for a directory service. It currently is not implemented in any LAN products.
- NetWare Directory Services (NDS) is incorporated into Novell's NetWare 4.*x* product line. NDS is based on X.500, but is not entirely compliant with the standard. At present, NDS can be used only with NetWare 4.*x* networks.

The concept of a directory service is attractive. Instead of logging on to several servers, a user now logs on to a network and is granted access to network resources by the directory service, regardless of which server is providing the service. The user sees a network directory with no indication of which server supports the user's account.

A directory service is an extremely formal way to organize network resources. Setting up such a service calls for careful planning that involves all departments in the organization. And directory services work best when one organization (such as a central MIS department) is responsible for maintaining the directory. Some directory services enable departments to have responsibility for portions of the directory, but one department must take primary responsibility. In organizations that do not have a central MIS department, it might be difficult to identify a primary directory manager.

In many organizations, LANs happened in departments long before they were discovered by the central MIS department. The departments that pioneered LANs often are reluctant to give up control and prefer to retain responsibility for managing their LAN resources. In Chapter 2, "Introducing Windows NT Server," you were cautioned that managing a LAN has political overtones. Setting up a directory service in a company that has well-established departmental networks can appear to threaten department autonomy and can run smack into those company politics. In most cases, users who are logged on to one directory structure cannot access resources that are controlled by another directory structure, making interdepartmental cooperation essential.

Directory services often add new complications as they solve old problems, and administrators of a directory need to be more skilled than administrators of stand-alone servers.

Almost any technology has up and down sides, and directory services are no exception. Although they can be very effective at organizing the resources of the largest LANs, directory services require skill and planning to administer correctly. They represent a formal approach to managing a network, and some organizations will take to directories more readily than others.

Workgroups

Workgroups are the complete opposites of directory services. Directories are formal and centrally administered; workgroups are informal and are operated by the users who are pooling their computing resources.

With a peer-to-peer approach to networking, users share the resources on their computers with other users. They might enable other users to print through their printers, access their files, or share a modem or CD-ROM. Individual users manage the sharing of resources on their PCs by determining what will be shared and who will be allowed access.

Peer-to-peer networking runs into two problems in large organizations:

- So many resources are available that users might have trouble locating them.
- Users who want to share resources often need an easy method of sharing resources only with a limited group of coworkers.

Microsoft introduced the metaphor of workgroup computing with the Windows for Workgroups (WfW) product. WfW enables users to share their workstation resources in a peer-to-peer mode, and workgroups make it easy to establish groups of related workers who easily can view and share each other's resources.

After someone joins a workgroup, he or she has access to all resources that are shared in that workgroup. You can share your hard drive with your coworkers simply by giving their workgroup rights to your printer. Figure 8.2 shows the Windows for Workgroups form that is used to share a printer.

Notice that the window in figure 8.2 enables the printer owner to assign a password that can be used to restrict access to specific individuals. Without a password, any member of the workgroup can use the printer. This is the only security provided by Windows for Workgroups.

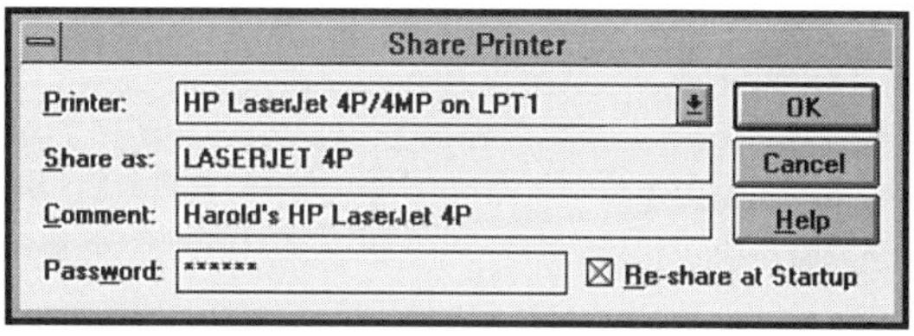

Figure 8.2

Sharing a printer with a workgroup.

To locate resources on a network, Microsoft uses a browsing service. The File Manager and Print Manager can be used to browse the network and identify resources to connect to. In figure 8.3, a user is browsing for sharable directories. Three such directories have been established on the workstation named KEATON.

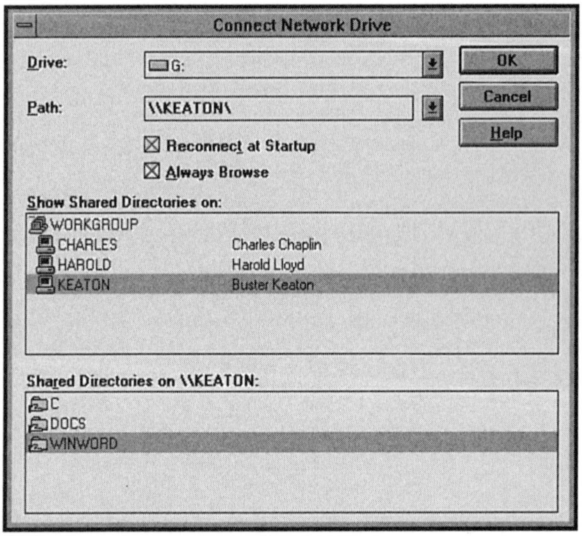

Figure 8.3

Browsing for shared directories.

Workgroups are more a convenience than anything else. They make resource sharing more efficient, but they do not organize services into a directory. Nor do they make it easy to manage the shared resources in an efficient manner. Passwords can be used to restrict access to resources, but with one password for each resource, passwords proliferate rapidly. To change a password, everyone who uses the resource must be notified. If each resource has a different password, things get really complicated. It is difficult to maintain much security under those circumstances.

Figure 8.4 illustrates some of the problems with passwords in workgroups. When separate passwords are assigned by individual users, the number of passwords a user must remember can multiply rapidly. To make things easier, users tend to select passwords that are easy to remember, but such passwords also tend to be ones that are easy to guess.

To make matters worse, imagine that the network has dial-up capability and that an employee has just left to work for your biggest competitor. You want to change all the passwords so that the employee cannot call in and get to your data. Obviously, changing all those passwords and informing everyone of the changes is going to be a big hassle.

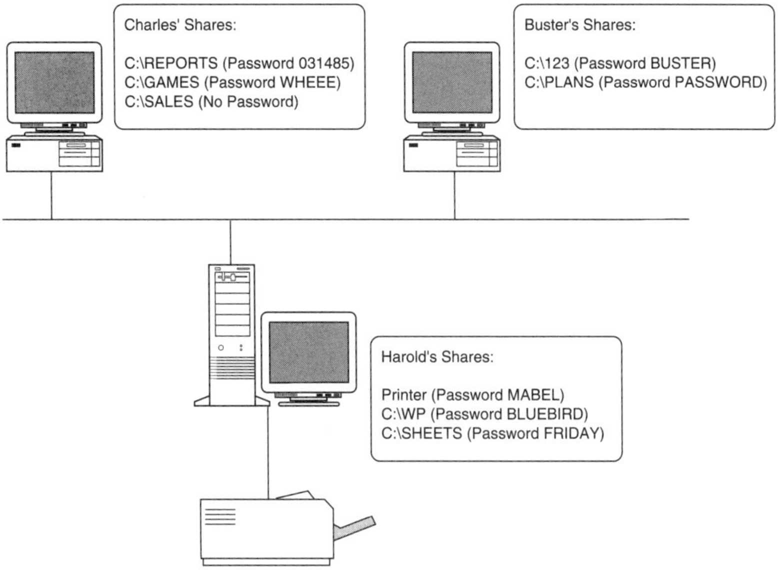

Figure 8.4
Passwords and shared resources in workgroups.

The following Microsoft products can share their resources in workgroups:

- Windows for Workgroups
- Windows NT Workstation
- Windows NT Server 3.5
- MS-DOS with the Workgroup add-on feature

These Microsoft products enable workstations to access workgroup resources:

- Windows 3.*x* with the Workgroup Connection
- MS-DOS with the Workgroup Connection feature
- LAN Manager for MS-DOS Enhanced and Basic Clients (not covered in this book)
- LAN Manager for MS OS/2 Client (Since this client has not been updated for the most recent versions of OS/2, it is not covered in this book.)

Organizations that are large or that want more control over their networks need something more than workgroups. Therefore, Microsoft has incorporated the domain concept into Windows NT Server.

Domains

Domains borrow concepts from workgroups and from directory services. Like workgroups, domains can be fairly informal and can be administered using a mix of central and local controls. Domains can evolve fairly easily and can be set up with less planning than typically is required for a directory.

Like a directory, a domain organizes the resources of several servers into one administrative structure. Users are given logon privileges to a domain rather than to each individual server. Because a domain controls the resources of several servers, it is easier to administer than a network with many stand-alone servers.

Servers within the domain advertise their services to users. Users who log in to a domain gain access to all resources in the domain for which they have been granted access. They can browse the resources in a domain much as they would browse the resources in a workgroup; however, domains are hosted by Windows NT Servers and can be made more secure than workgroups.

When networks become large enough to require several domains, administrators can establish trust relationships among domains. Trust relationships simplify administration, because a user is required to have an account in only one domain. Other domains that trust the user's logon domain can rely on the logon domain to authenticate the user's logon.

Note Windows NT Server domains are not the same as domains found on TCP/IP networks. TCP/IP domains are discussed in Chapter 15, "Using TCP/IP."

Domains and Trust Relationships

Domains are essentially improved workgroups. Access to domain resources is controlled by a domain controller. The user is assigned a single domain account and a password that is used to control access to all domain resources. Windows NT Server domains also support the use of groups that enable administrators to assign and change permissions for large numbers of users more efficiently. You will learn about managing users and groups in Chapter 10, "Managing Users and Groups."

Domains and Domain Servers

A server in a domain has one of three roles:

- **Primary domain controller.** One Windows NT Server stores the master copy of the domain's user and group database.

- **Backup domain controller.** Other Windows NT Servers can store backup copies of the domain's user and group database.
- **Server.** Servers can participate in a domain without being designated as primary or backup domain controllers.

Each of these roles is described more fully in the following sections.

The Primary Domain Controller

The first Windows NT Server in the domain is configured as a primary domain controller. The User Manager for Domains utility is used to maintain user and group information for the domain. This information is stored in a database on the primary domain controller.

Backup Domain Controllers

Other Windows NT Servers in the domain can serve as backup domain controllers. Each backup domain controller stores a replica of the database on the primary domain controller. Replication of the database has several values.

If the primary domain controller experiences a hardware failure, one of the backup domain controllers can be promoted to the primary role. Having one or more backup domain controllers builds a degree of fault tolerance into your network.

Backup domain controllers also can participate in the log-in process. When a user logs in to a domain, the logon request can be handled by any primary or backup domain controller. This spreads the logon processing load across the available servers and improves logon performance. This can be an important benefit in domains with large numbers of users.

Servers

Windows NT Servers also can function as independent servers, which may or may not participate in domains. These servers do not function as primary or backup domain controllers. However, they can take advantage of the user and group databases that are maintained for a domain, and you can assign user and group permissions for the server using the User Manager for Domains.

The server also can maintain its own database of users, and users can log on to the server independently of the domain. When this is done, the server cannot utilize the user and group database of a domain, and the server handles accounts much like computers running Windows NT Workstation.

You might choose to configure an independent Windows NT Server for several reasons:

- So that the server can be administered by different staff members. Many Windows NT Servers are used for application servers such as SQL databases. If you configure a database server as an independent server, you can assign a member of your database staff as the server administrator.

- Attending to logon requests can use a significant part of a server's processing capability. If you configure the server as an independent server, it can concentrate on servicing a single function, such as providing application services.

- When a server is functioning as a primary or backup domain controller, it is difficult to move the server to a new domain. If there is a chance the server will move to a different domain, configure it as an independent server.

Trust Relationships

Many organizations own several LAN servers—that's fine because domains make multiple servers easy to administer. But what happens when an organization needs to have several domains? Reasons why this might be the case follow:

- If too many servers are put in a domain, performance can suffer.

- Some departments prefer to manage their own resources, which is easiest if they have their own domains.

So your organization decides to have several domains. If a user needs to access resources in several domains, is it necessary to create an account for that user in each domain? That could be just as bad as administering several stand-alone servers.

Fortunately, Windows NT Server enables you to establish trust relationships between domains. Figure 8.5 illustrates a simple, two-domain trust relationship. Domain B is configured to trust Domain A. As a result, if a user is successful at logging on to Domain A, Domain B assumes that the user has been authenticated properly. Therefore, Domain B accepts the user without forcing the user to explicitly log on to Domain B.

Trusts can flow both ways. In figure 8.6, Domains C and D are configured to trust each other. You will see several examples of network designs that use two-way trust relationships.

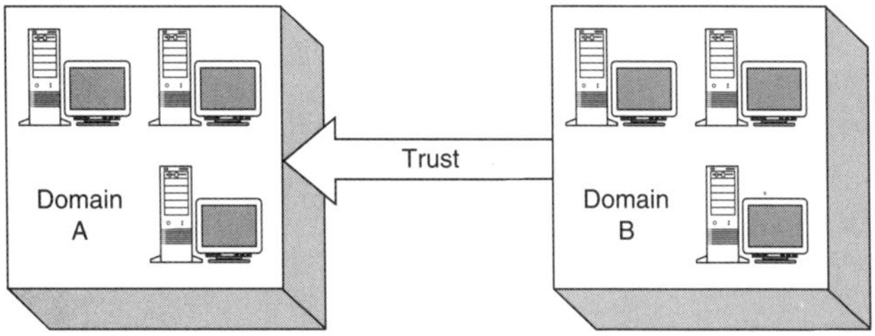

Figure 8.5

A simple trust relationship.

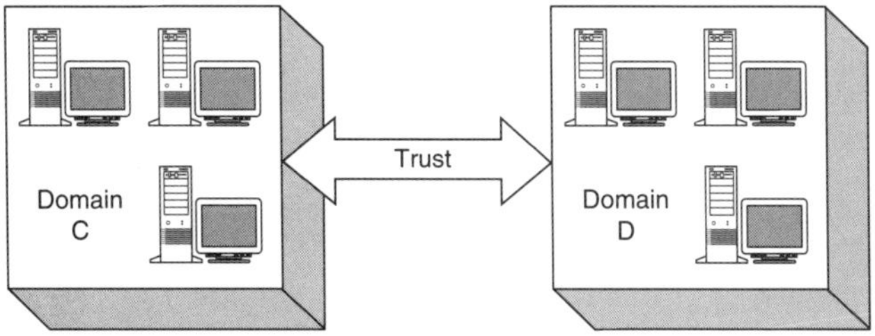

Figure 8.6

Domains configured to trust each other.

One more thing you should know about trust relationships is that trust does not flow through a domain. (Microsoft's term is that trusts are not *transitive.*) Figure 8.7a shows three domains that have established two-way trust relationships. Domains E and F trust one another, as do domains F and G. However, Domains E and G do not trust each other because trusts do not pass through Domain F.

If all domains should trust each other, it is necessary to establish trust relationships between each pair of domains. Figure 8.7b shows how three domains can be made to trust each other.

Note Trust relationships do not automatically grant users access to resources in a trusting domain. A domain that trusts another domain relies on the trusted domain to authenticate users when they log on. The trusting domain still must grant those users access to resources.

Domain Models

Proper use of trust relationships enables organizations to build enterprise networks that still require only a single logon procedure for resource access. Microsoft has defined four models for domain trust relationships. If you are configuring a multidomain network, you will want to consider the merits and disadvantages of each model.

Figure 8.7

Multidomain trust relationships.

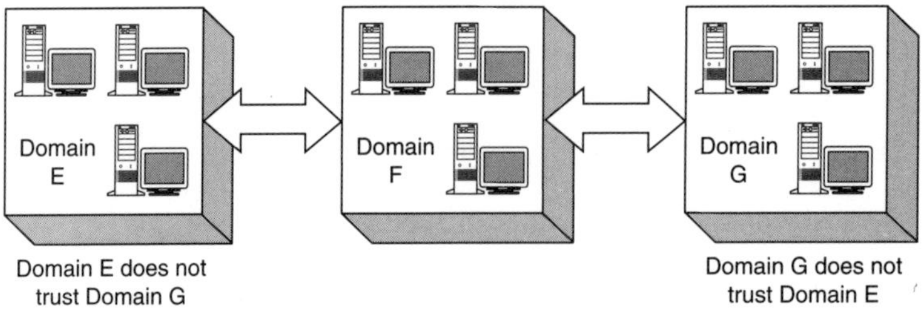

Figure 8.7a

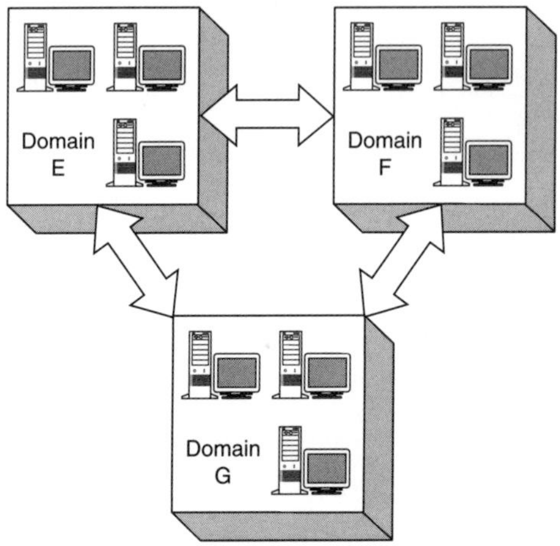

Figure 8.7b

There are two reasons for adding domains, as follows:

- For organizational reasons
- To improve network performance

Regarding network performance, you will find that Microsoft's descriptions are a bit vague. You can use a single domain model, for example, "if your network doesn't have too many users...". That doesn't give you much help during the planning stages. Unfortunately, there are many variables, and it's difficult to come up with a simple prescription for adding domains. Windows NT Server can, after all, run on everything from an Intel 80486 PC to a multiprocessor RISC system. Such a broad range of hardware makes performance generalizations difficult. Fortunately, Windows NT Server domains make it easy to reorganize the LAN as it grows.

The four domain models defined by Microsoft follow:

- Single domain
- Master domain
- Multiple-master domains
- Complete trust

Each domain is discussed in the following sections.

The Single Domain Model

Figure 8.8 illustrates the *single domain model*—the preferred model for small organizations. (Remember, size descriptions are very vague. More powerful servers enable a single domain to grow in size.) When all servers are located in a single domain, administration is simplified greatly. Also, there is no need to administer trust relationships—an activity that can get quite involved.

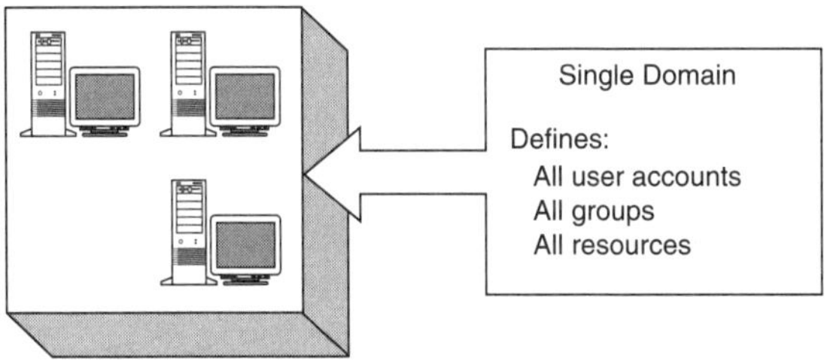

Figure 8.8
A single domain network.

Large amounts of logon or browsing activity might degrade the performance of the domain. When a domain has a large number of servers, browsing can be inefficient, and you might find it advantageous to move some of the servers to another domain. Be alert to performance issues so that you can anticipate when you need to move to a different domain model.

A single domain network has several advantages:

- It is easier to manage because resources are centralized
- No trust relationships are required
- Group definitions are simpler

You need to consider a multidomain model in the following situations:

- ◆ If browsing is slow
- ◆ If too many users are degrading performance
- ◆ If your organization wants to assign domains to departments
- ◆ If you want to have some resources in their own domains

The Master Domain Model

The *master domain model* designates one domain to manage all user accounts. The master domain also supports global groups. *Global groups* can export group information to other domains. By defining global groups in the master domain, other domains easily can import the group information.

Figure 8.9 illustrates a network based on a master domain model. The master domain is named Keystone, and is managed centrally by the MIS staff. All users are defined in Keystone, as well as some groups that will make administration easier. Therefore, only the primary and backup domain controllers in the Keystone domain are used to store user and group account information. Because users cannot log on to the network without a working domain account database, a master domain always should include at least one backup domain controller in addition to the primary domain controller.

When users log on to the network, they always log on to the Keystone master domain. After they have logged on, they can access resources in other domains that trust Keystone.

In this example, the other domains are organized according to departments. After a user logs on through the master domain, most of the user's network activity relates to one of the department domains. Therefore, user network activity is distributed across several domains, removing much of the processing responsibility from the Keystone domain.

Each of the department domains is configured to trust Keystone. The assumption is that Keystone security will be sufficiently tight and that other domains do not need to take special precautions of their own.

The department domains could be administered by MIS or by the individual departments. The master domain model makes it possible to delegate some management tasks while keeping the critical security function under the control of a central network authority. So that department domains are comfortable with the network security, administrators of the master domain should be well-trained and security policies carefully defined.

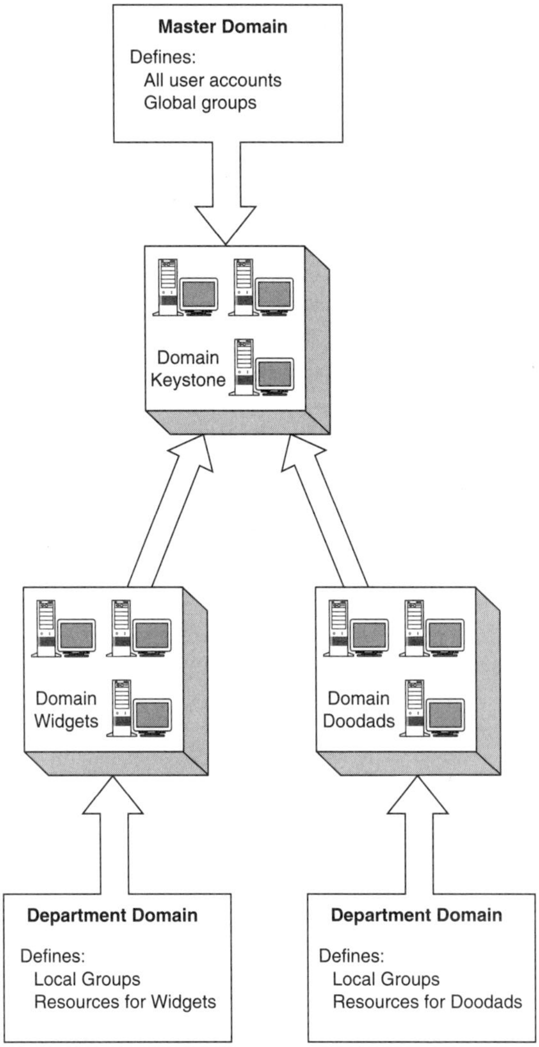

Figure 8.9

A network with a single master domain.

A master domain network has several advantages:

- Security management is centralized.
- Nonmaster domains can be used to organize resources logically.
- Browsing activity is distributed through the department domains.

- Global groups in the master domain enable departments to easily establish local permissions.
- Departments that want to can manage the resources in their own domains.

The chief liability of the master domain model is that all logon activity takes place in a single domain. When performance begins to suffer in the master domain, you need to be prepared to move to a multiple master domain model.

Note *Groups* are essential ingredients of effective Windows NT Server management. Groups enable you to manage the privileges of large numbers of users more efficiently than would be possible if privileges were assigned to users individually.

Windows NT Server uses two types of groups: local and global. It can be difficult to grasp the differences between these group types and the appropriate uses of each. Consequently, this section does not dwell on that topic. Later in this chapter, the sections "Global Groups" and "Local Groups" investigate Windows NT Server groups thoroughly.

The Multiple Master Domain Model

The master domain model can be extended by introducing additional master domains. This is the primary technique used to scale Windows NT Server networks for larger enterprises. Figure 8.10 shows networks with two master domains and three department domains.

Each master domain supports about half the user accounts. This spreads the processing of logons over several domains. Each domain supports some of the groups that are accessed by the department domains.

Under this model, each master domain trusts every other master domain. This is a convenience for administrators, but is necessary for users only if they actually will be using resources on one of the master domains.

Each department domain trusts each master domain. It is not necessary for department domains to trust each other.

Because users are granted most privileges based on their memberships in master domain groups, it is a good idea to group related users into the same master domains. All your users in Accounting should log on to the same master domain, for example. Otherwise, you are forced to establish similar groups in each master domain. With more groups, it becomes far more difficult to establish privileges in the department domains.

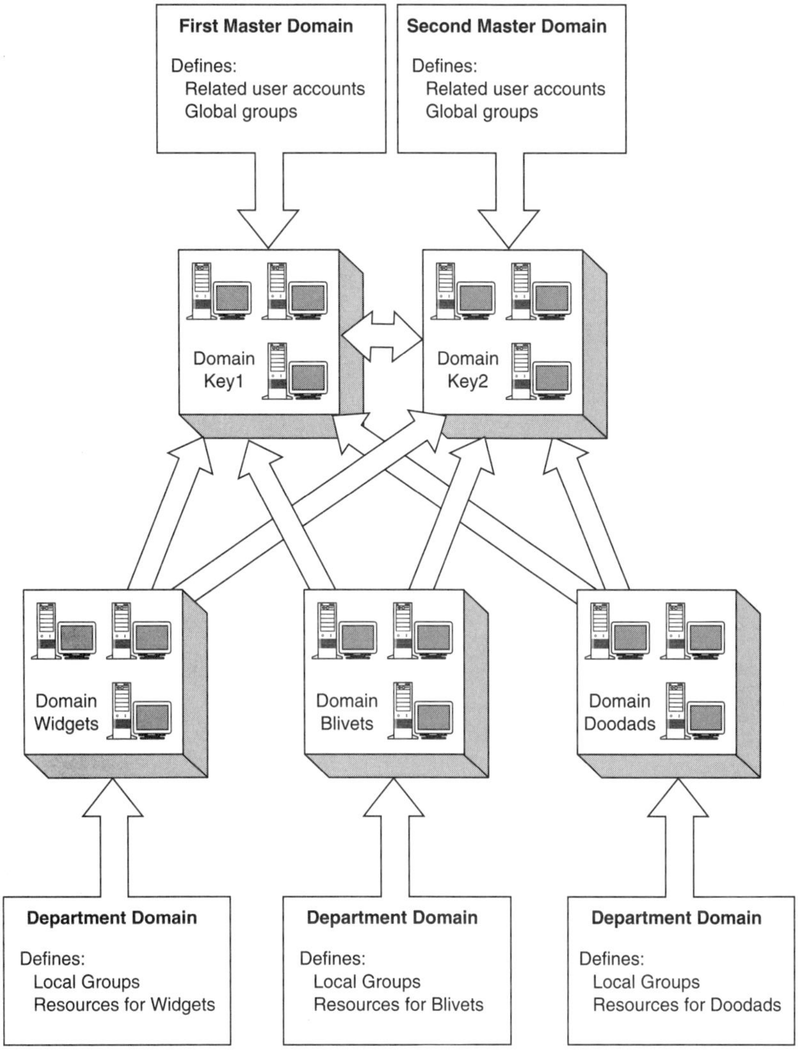

Figure 8.10
Networks with multiple master domains.

The required number of trust relationships increases rapidly as you add domains. Figure 8.11 illustrates a network with three master domains and four department domains. The network in figure 8.10 required eight trust relationships (two trust relationships are required to enable the two master domains to trust one another). The slightly larger network in figure 8.11 requires 18 relationships! Obviously, you don't want to expand the number of domains in your network unnecessarily.

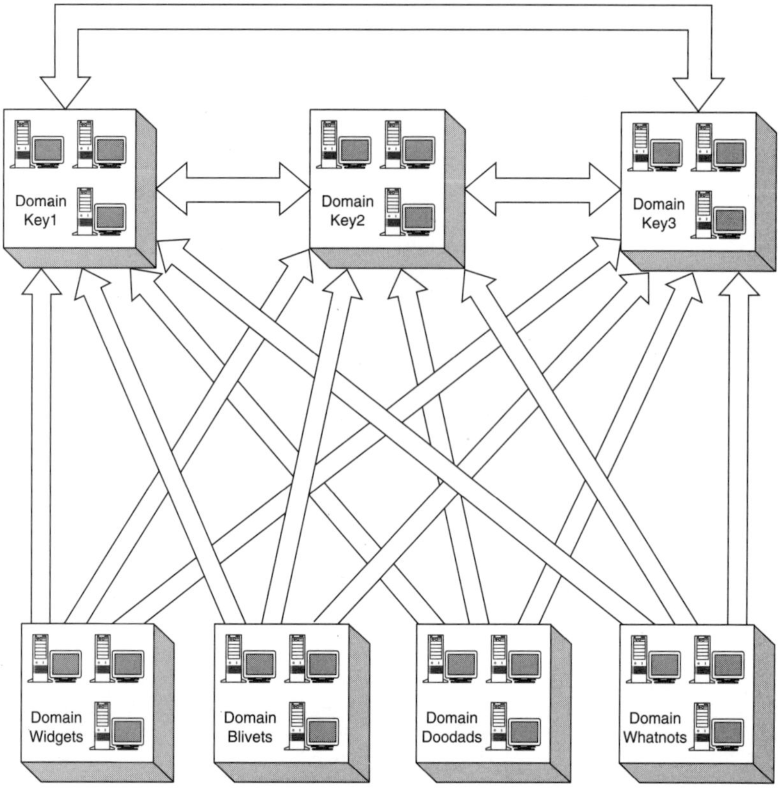

Figure 8.11
A larger network with multiple master domains.

The multiple master domain model has many desirable features:

- It is scalable to any organizational size.
- Security is managed centrally.
- Departments can manage their local domains, if desired.
- Related users, groups, and resources can be grouped logically into domains.

Disadvantages of the multiple master domain model include the following characteristics:

- The number of groups and trust relationships multiply rapidly as the number of domains increases.
- User accounts and groups are not located in a single location, complicating network documentation.

The Complete Trust Model

The master domain models assume that a central department exists that can take responsibility for managing user and group security for the complete organization. If no such department exists, or if departments want to retain full responsibility for managing their own domains, you might choose to implement a *complete trust model.* An example of a complete trust network is shown in figure 8.12.

In the complete trust model, every domain is configured to trust every other domain. Users log in to their department domains and then access resources in other departments by means of trust relationships.

As with the multiple master domain model, the number of trust relationships required increases rapidly as domains increase. Three domains require six trust relationships (two between each pair of domains), whereas five domains require 20 trust relationships. If n is the number of domains, then the network requires $n \times (n-1)$ trust relationships.

Stop As a believer in tight network security, I find the implications of the complete trust model extremely disturbing. The administrators of each domain must have complete faith that the administrators of every other domain will maintain a high level of security. That for me is carrying trust a little too far.

If your organization does not have a central MIS department, networking is a great reason for establishing one. Besides the need to maintain tight security, several other functions are best when centralized. Here are some examples:

- File backup
- Communications services
- E-mail maintenance
- Management of the network infrastructure (media, hubs, and so on)

Few departments have personnel who possess the expertise to do these jobs well. Also, network management in a large organization calls for personnel who are devoted completely to the task.

Therefore, I don't put much credibility into the advantages that Microsoft attributes to the complete trust model, but here they are nevertheless:

- No central MIS department is required.
- The model scales to any organizational size.

- Departments retain control of their users and resources. (But, it can be argued, they surrender that control by trusting everybody.)
- Users and resources are grouped logically by departments.

Figure 8.12
A network using a complete trust model.

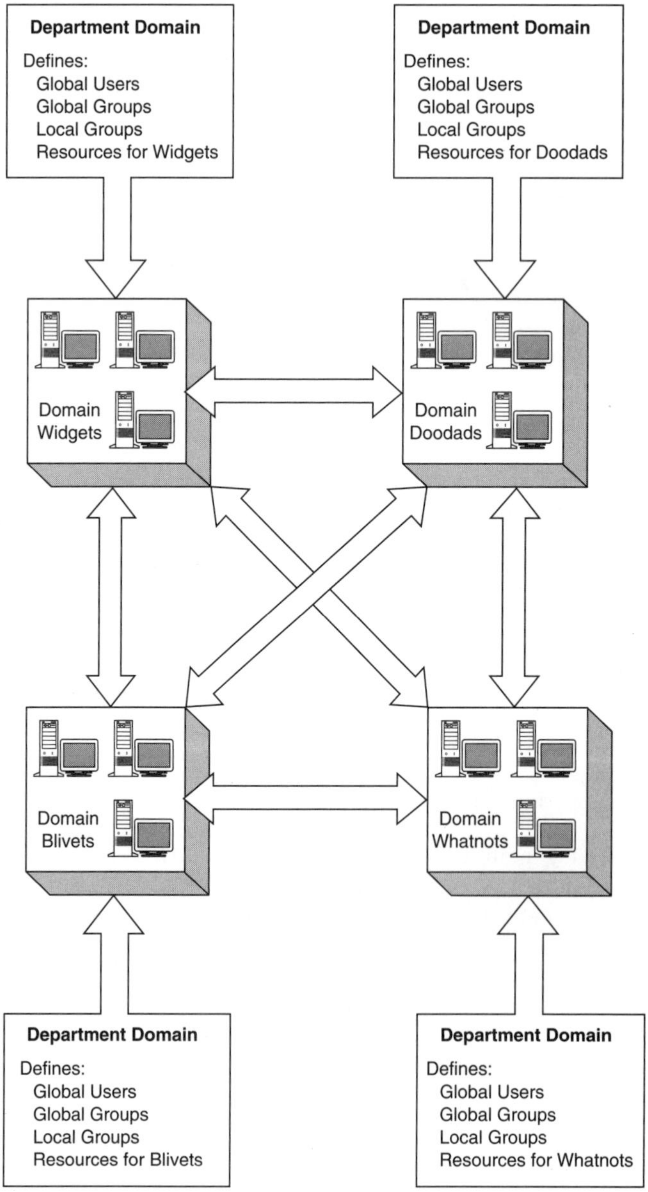

A few of the disadvantages of the complete trust model follow:

- Central security control is lacking.
- Large numbers of trust relationships are required.
- Departments are dependent on the management practices of other departments.

Domains and Workgroups

Microsoft has designed its network products so that users and network administrators can use a mix of peer-to-peer and centralized services. Users can participate in a workgroup at the same time they are logged on to a Windows NT Server domain. This capability enables you to mix formal and informal network services to meet the needs of your users. It also enables you to manage some resources centrally, while other resources are shared under user control.

Mixing workgroup and domain models can complicate your life as a LAN administrator, however. When a user reports a problem, it might be unclear whether the problem is related to the Windows NT Server network or to the user's workgroup. My recommendation is that you use a centralized approach whenever possible.

Files can always be shared simply by placing them on a network server. Although Windows for Workgroups users cannot share their printers with a Windows NT Server network (except through peer-to-peer resource sharing in a workgroup environment), users of Windows NT Workstation can configure their workstations as network print servers, enabling them to share their printers as domain resources. Thus, most of the resource sharing that is made possible by workgroups also is possible under domain management. Windows NT Server domains are, however, much easier to manage and troubleshoot.

Users and Groups

Windows NT Server security is based on the following four types of entities:

- **Global user accounts.** User accounts that originate in the Windows NT environment.
- **Local user accounts.** User accounts that originate in server environments other than Windows NT.

- **Global groups.** Used to manage groups in a domain. Also can be used to export groups of users to other domains.
- **Local groups.** Used to manage users and to import global groups from other domains.

These entities are discussed in detail in the following sections.

Global User Accounts

In Windows NT Server terminology, a *global* entity can be used by domains other than the domain in which the entity was created.

User accounts that are created on Windows NT Servers have a *global scope*—they can be used in any domain that trusts the domain in which the user account was created.

User accounts can be granted network privileges individually. It is more common, however, to include user accounts in groups and to grant privileges to the groups. This method makes it easier to alter the privileges of large numbers of users.

Because multidomain Windows NT Server networks rely heavily on trust relationships, it is easy to see why global user accounts are desirable. A domain that trusts another domain can make use of any global user accounts that have been created in the trusted domain. This fact makes it unnecessary to give a user an account in more than one domain on the network.

Because global user accounts are the most common account types in Windows NT Networks, they simply are called *user accounts* in most situations.

Local User Accounts

When a user account originates on a network not running Windows NT, the account is a *local account.* Local entities cannot be used outside the domains in which they are created. Local user accounts can be placed in both global and local groups, however.

Local user accounts enable users from LAN Manager, IBM LAN Server, or NetWare environments to participate in Windows NT Server domains. Because they can be used only in the domains in which they are created, however, local user accounts are somewhat more difficult to administer than global user accounts.

Global Groups

Global groups are lists of user accounts from within a single domain. A global group can include user accounts only from the domain in which the global group was created. Global groups cannot contain other groups.

A global group created within one domain can be granted permissions in another domain. Figure 8.13 illustrates a two-domain network. The domain Keystone is used by all users to log on to the network. In Keystone, the administrator has created a global group named Domain Users. Users SLaurel, HLloyd, MNormand and CChaplin have been established as members of Domain Users.

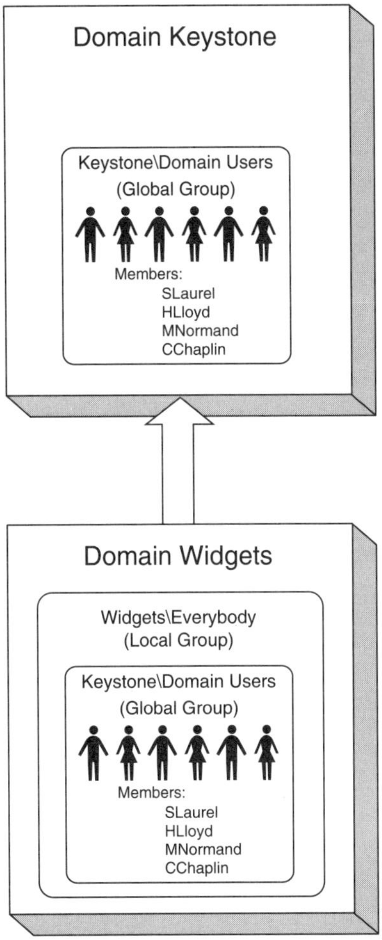

Figure 8.13

Global groups created in one domain can be granted privileges in domains that trust the host domain.

When Windows NT Server utilities reference the names of global groups they frequently include the name of the domain in which the group was created. In the figure, the full name of the Domain Users group would be Keystone\Domain Users because the group is created in the Keystone domain. This notation is commonly used to describe a group in a domain other than the current domain.

The domain named Widgets trusts Main. This enables the Widgets administrator to assign permissions in the Widgets domain to the Keystone\Domain Users group. In Figure 8.13, the administrator of Widgets has added the Keystone\Domain Users group as a member of the Widgets\Everybody local group. Any permissions that are assigned to the Widgets\Everybody group will be inherited by the members of Keystone\Domain Users.

Because it is important to understand this mechanism, let me express the idea a second way. When Widgets trusts Keystone, the Widgets administrator says, "I will accept the logon procedures in Keystone. Users who are authenticated by Keystone are also welcome in Widgets." Then the Widgets administrator proceeds to include global groups in Keystone as members of local groups in Widgets. By giving members of Keystone memberships in the Widgets local groups, those members are given permissions as though their accounts had been created directly in the Widgets domain.

The characteristics of global groups that you should remember follow:

- Global groups can contain users from the domain in which the group was created.
- Global groups cannot contain users from other domains.
- Global groups cannot contain other groups.
- Global groups can be assigned privileges in the domain in which the group was created.
- Global groups also can be assigned privileges in domains that trust the domain in which the group was created.

The word *global* indicates that global groups can be assigned privileges anywhere in the network (globally).

Local Groups

Local groups can be assigned privileges only in the domain in which they were created. Local groups can contain both users and global groups. This capability enables you to use a local group to collect entities from several domains and to manage them as a group in a local domain. When you assign privileges to a local group, all users and global groups in the local group inherit those privileges.

Figure 8.14 illustrates a three-domain network with the following features:

- The domain Blivets includes global users CChaplin, HLloyd, SLaurel, and MNormand.

- The domain Blivets includes a global group named SomeUsers. Users SLaurel, HLloyd, and MNormand are members of SomeUsers.
- Global users in the domain Doodads are BKeaton, FArbuckle, and OHardy.
- The domain Doodads includes a global group named MoreUsers. Only user OHardy is a member of MoreUsers.

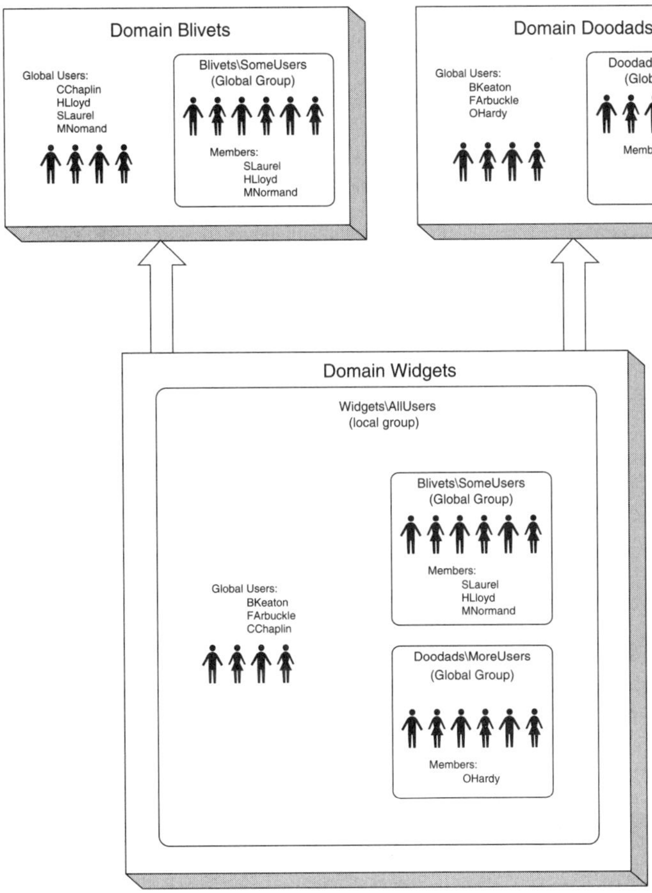

Figure 8.14
Configuring a local group.

The administrator of the domain Widgets would like to assign privileges to all the users in the Blivets and Doodads domains. One way to do that is to create a local group. In the figure, the local group is named Widgets\AllUsers. All the following entities can be added to AllUsers:

- **Blivets\SomeUsers.** A global group.

- **CChaplin.** A global user in the Blivets domain, who must be explicitly included since he is not a member of Blivets\SomeUsers.
- **Doodads\MoreUsers.** Another global group.
- **BKeaton and FArbuckle.** Global users in the domain Doodads, who must be explicitly included because they are not members of Blivets\SomeUsers.

A preferable approach would be to add all the users to the global groups Blivets\SomeUsers and Doodads\MoreUsers. This, however, would require the cooperation of the other domains. Fortunately, local groups enable you to include users when the global groups are not configured as you want.

The characteristics of local groups that you should remember follow:

- Local groups can contain users from the domain in which the local group was created.
- Local groups can contain global users from other domains that are trusted by the group's domain.
- Local groups can contain global groups from domains that are trusted by the local group's domain.
- Local groups can be assigned privileges in the group's local domain.
- Local groups cannot be assigned privileges in other domains.

Built-In Groups and Users

When you install Windows NT Workstation or Windows NT Server, several users and groups are created. These users and groups define various levels of access to workstations and servers and are the building blocks you use to secure your network.

The default users and groups can be modified by users with sufficient privileges. These groups cannot be deleted, however.

Built-In User Accounts

Every Windows NT Server or Windows NT Workstation has two default user accounts.

The *Administrator user account* enables you to manage the server when it first is installed. So that you cannot be locked out of the server, this account cannot be deleted or disabled, although it can be renamed. After you create other administrators, you can choose to give the Administrator account an especially secure password, store the password in a safe place, and put the Administrator account into semi-retirement.

The *Guest user account* cannot be deleted, but it can be disabled and renamed. Guest is disabled by default, but can be enabled if you want to permit guest users to have limited access to your domain or server.

Built-In Groups

You grant a user a set of capabilities on a domain, workstation, or server by adding the user to the correct group. The built-in groups are available in both global and local varieties to make management of the network more versatile.

Users can be assigned to multiple groups if required. To enable a user to manage printers and back up the system, add the user to the Print Operators and Backup Operators groups. These groups make it easy to configure layers of security on your network so that you can distribute responsibilities to various personnel.

Table 8.1 summarizes the built-in groups and whether they are installed on domains, workstations, or servers. Each of the groups is discussed in the following sections.

TABLE 8.1
Windows NT Built-In Groups

Group	Local/ Managed by Global	Windows NT Server Domains	Workstations and Servers	Automatic Contents
Administrators	Local Administrators	Yes	Yes	Domain Admins Administrator (user)
Domain Admins	Global Administrators	Yes	No	Administrator
Backup Operators	Local Administrators	Yes	Yes	None
Server Operators	Local Administrators	Yes	No	None
Account Operators	Local Administrators	Yes	No	None
Print Operators	Local Administrators	Yes	No	None

continues

Table 8.1, Continued
Windows NT Built-In Groups

Group	Local/ Managed by Global	Windows NT Server Domains	Workstations and Servers	Automatic Contents
Power Users	Local Administrators Power Users	No	Yes	Setup user
Users	Local Administrators	Yes	Yes	Domain Users
	Account Operators			Administrator (user)
Domain Users	Global Administrators	Yes	No	Administrators
	Account Operators			New users
Guests	Local Administrators	Yes	Yes	Domain Guests Guest (user)
	Account Operators			
Domain Guests	Global Administrators	Yes	No	Guest
	Account Operators			
Replicator	Local Administrators	Yes	Yes	None

Administrators

- Local
- Domains, workstations, and servers

Members of Administrators local groups have nearly complete authority over the domain, workstation, or server on which the group resides. Adding a user account to the Administrators group is all that is necessary to make the user an administrator.

Administrators are limited in one respect: They cannot automatically access files on NTFS file systems. Each NTFS file has an owner who, by default, is the person who created the file. Unless the owner grants access permissions, even an administrator cannot access the file. Administrators can, however, take ownership of any file, as described in Chapter 11, "Sharing Drives, Directories, and Files."

Domain Admins

- Global
- Domains

Each domain also includes a built-in global group named Domain Admins. This group is added automatically to the Administrators local group, making all members of Domain Admins domain administrators.

You therefore have two ways to make a user a domain administrator: by adding the user directly to the Administrators local group, or by adding the user to the Domain Admins global group. The advantage of adding the user to the Domain Admins group is that this group can be included in the Administrators local group of other domains that trust this domain. This enables you to easily give administrators the capability of managing several domains.

When a Windows NT Workstation or a stand-alone Windows NT Server is brought into a domain, the Domain Admins group is added automatically to the workstation or server's Administrators group. If you want to prevent members of Domain Admins from managing the workstation or server, you manually must remove that entry from the Administrators group.

Backup Operators

- Local
- Domains, workstations, and servers

This group solves an old problem in LAN administration. Frequently, tape backups are performed by operators who really should not have administrator privileges. Members of the Backup Operators group can back up and restore files, log on to the system locally, and shut down the system, but they are not granted the capability to manipulate security or perform other administrative functions.

Server Operators

- Local
- Domains

Each primary or backup domain controller has a Server Operators local group. Users in this group can perform many administrative functions, but cannot manage security. They can share and unshare resources, format server disks, back up and restore files, log in locally to servers, and bring down servers.

Account Operators

- Local
- Domains

Account operators can manage user accounts and groups in the domain. They can create, delete, and modify most users, local, and global groups but cannot assign user rights. Account Operators cannot manage the accounts of administrators, or modify the local groups' Administrators, Server Operators, Account Operators, Backup Operators, or Print Operators.

Print Operators

- Local
- Domains

Members of Print Operators can share, stop sharing, and manage printers running in a Windows NT Server domain. They can also log on to servers locally and shut them down.

Users

- Local
- Domains, workstations, and servers

Most users will be members of the Users local group. Members of Users are not permitted to log on locally to primary or backup domain controllers. They can access resources in the domain only through clients on the network. Users also can maintain a profile on a Windows NT Workstation (see Chapter 14, "Using Windows NT Clients"). However, users can log on to domains, workstations, and servers.

Power Users

- Local
- NT Workstations and stand-alone servers

Members of Power Users can perform user functions on workstations and servers. They can also create user accounts and modify the accounts they have created. Power

Users can add user accounts to the built-in groups Users, Guests, and Power Users. And they can start and stop sharing of printers and files on the workstation or server.

If a Windows NT Workstation is operating in a Windows NT Server domain, a recommended strategy is to put the user's domain account into the Power Users group at the workstation. In that way, a single account enables the user to be a user in the domain and to administer the workstation.

Domain Users

- Global
- Domains

All user accounts in a domain automatically are included in the Domain Users global group. The Domain Users global group is in turn included in the local Users group, establishing all members of the Domain Users group as users of the domain.

In multidomain networks, you can include the Domain Users group in the local Users groups of other domains that trust the logon domain. This is an easy way of granting users privileges on multiple domains.

Guests

- Local
- Domains, workstations, and servers

In domains, members of Guests are similar to members of Users. They can utilize domain resources, but may only do so by logging on through the network. Local server logons are not permitted.

Members of the Guests group on workstations and servers have limited rights. They can maintain a profile on a Windows NT Workstation, but they cannot manage local groups or lock the workstation.

Domain Guests

- Global
- Domains

The Guest user normally is included in the Domain Guests global group, which is included in the local Guests group. Other user accounts also can be added to the Domain Guests group. Members of the Domain Guests or Guest group have guest privileges in the domain.

In multidomain networks, you can include the Domain Guests group in the local Guests groups of other domains that trust the logon domain. This is an easy way of granting users guest privileges on multiple domains.

Replicator

- Local
- Domains, workstations, and servers

Members of the Replicator group can manage the replication of files on the domain, workstation, or server.

CHAPTER 9

Managing Domains and Trust Relationships

As you probably have gathered from reading the preceding chapter, proper management of domains and trust relationships is extremely important and can have critical implications for network security and performance. Chapter 8 focused on giving you background information about domains and trust relationships. In this chapter, you will learn to apply that understanding to real network-management operations.

Several terms are used frequently in this chapter, and it's worth reviewing their definitions:

- **Primary Domain Controller (PDC).** A computer running Windows NT Server, on which the primary domain user database is stored.
- **Backup Domain Controller (BDC).** A computer running Windows NT Server, on which replicas of the domain user database are stored.
- **Server.** A computer running Windows NT Server that is participating in a domain but is not serving as a domain controller.

- **Workstation.** A computer running Windows NT Workstation that is permitted access to a domain. Sometimes Microsoft also calls a Windows NT Workstation or Server a *computer.* For consistency and clarity, the terms *workstation* and *server* are used here.

Microsoft doesn't have a unique term for computers that are clients on a Windows NT Server network but are not running Windows NT software. Procedures for managing nonNT clients are somewhat different from procedures for Windows NT computers.

Creating Domain Controllers

Primary and backup domain controllers can be created only by the Setup process, which you examined in Chapter 7, "Installing Windows NT Server."

Selecting a Server Role

During Windows NT Setup, you are prompted to define the Windows NT Server Security Role. The following two choices are available:

- Domain Controller (Primary or Backup)
- Server

If you specify that the server is to be a Domain Controller, Setup takes you through the steps required to connect the server to the network. These steps were described in Chapter 7. Network communication is required so that Setup can determine which domains already are present. Each domain on the network must be named uniquely. A PDC cannot be added to an existing domain, and a BDC can be added to a domain only when the domain is available.

After a connection to the network has been established, the Domain Settings dialog box prompts you to specify whether the server will be a Primary or a Backup Domain Controller.

Creating a Primary Domain Controller (PDC)

If you select Primary Domain Controller, you also must specify a domain name in the Domain Settings dialog box. Domain names cannot contain spaces.

Setup searches the network to ensure that a domain with the name you specify does not already exist. You are permitted to proceed only if the domain name specifies a new domain.

Setup creates an Administrator user for each new domain. The default Administrator user account has complete administrative authority for the domain. After the domain name you specified is approved, the Administrator Account Setup dialog box prompts you for a password for the Administrator user. Blank passwords are permitted, but Setup warns you that `No password has been entered`. You need to choose OK to confirm your decision to leave the password blank.

You are required to enter the password twice as confirmation. Record this password in a safe place. If the Administrator password is lost before other administrator accounts are created, the only way to change the password is to reinstall Windows NT Server.

After installation is completed and Windows NT Server is restarted, this server is the primary domain controller for the domain.

How Domain Security IDs Work

When you create the Primary Domain Controller for a domain, Windows NT Server assigns the PDC a Security ID (SID) that is used to identify everything in the domain. In fact, each time you add a backup domain controller or a computer to the domain, the domain SID is added as a prefix to the computer's own SID. It is the SID, not the domain name, that you see that actually defines the identity of the domain. This has several potentially troublesome consequences.

Never perform a New installation of Windows NT Server on an existing primary domain controller. Even though you specify the same domain name, Setup will create a new SID for the PDC. Computers that have already been added to the domain were configured with the old SID and will be unable to find the new PDC. As a result, computers that could once attach to the domain will mysteriously be unable to do so.

Never install a domain controller when the PDC is down. Because Setup cannot find a PDC, the new computer is installed as a PDC, creating a second SID for the same domain name. (Should this condition be called SIDling rivalry?) The new PDC will never be able to participate in the same domain as the old PDC. If you want to install a new computer to act as a PDC in a domain, install it as a BDC while the current PDC is running. Then promote the new computer to a PDC when both domain controllers are running.

Creating a Backup Domain Controller (BDC)

A BDC can be added to a domain in two ways:

- By first adding a computer account to the domain using the Server Manager utility, a procedure described later in this chapter. You then can install the BDC to that computer account.
- By creating the computer account during Setup, in which case, you must enter a User Name and a Password that has administrative privileges in the domain. This is the more common approach and the one that will be described in this section.

If, during installation, you select Backup Domain Controller in the Server Security Role dialog box, you also must specify the name of the domain that the backup domain controller will be joining.

If this computer already has been added to the domain (the procedure for doing so follows), you can choose OK. If the computer is being added to the domain during installation, you must specify the following:

- A User Name that has administrator privileges in the domain to be joined
- The Password for the user name you have entered

You can use an administrator account that originates in a domain that is trusted by the current domain. If Max is an administrator in the trusted domain Keystone, for example, you would enter the name as **Keystone\Max**.

Note If you are moving existing Backup domain controllers to new domains, you will be required to reinstall Windows NT. During installation, Setup will determine that Windows NT is already installed on the hard drive and will ask you to choose between the following actions:

- To upgrade Windows NT in the directory shown, press Enter.
- To cancel the upgrade and install a fresh copy of Windows NT, press **N**.

Be sure to request a New Version installation. Upgrading the current software retains the current system configuration and does not permit you to redefine the server's security role.

Selecting New Version reinstalls Windows NT Server over the previous installation, and you lose your previous user account database. (You retain any applications and other files that have been installed on the computer's hard drives, however.)

The only way to retain a user account database while changing a server's security role is to move a primary domain controller to a new domain. However, this isn't really something you should count on, because it is probable that most of the permissions no longer will make sense because they pertain to the old domain name.

If you are reinstalling a backup domain controller to a new domain, it receives a copy of the domain user account database from the PDC after it joins the domain.

Creating New Domains

New domains can be created in two ways:

- By installing a new primary domain controller into a new domain using the procedure described earlier in the section "Creating a Primary Domain Controller."
- By using the Control Panel on a primary domain controller to create a new domain and set the server as the primary domain controller of the new domain. This procedure is described in the following section.

Creating a New Domain by Moving a Primary Domain Controller

On the primary domain controller, follow these steps:

1. Choose the Network utility in the Control Panel. This displays the Network Settings dialog box, which is shown in Figure 9.1.
2. Next to the Domain name, choose the Chang<u>e</u> button to bring up the Rename Domain dialog box, shown in Figure 9.2.
3. In the Rename Domain box, enter a <u>N</u>ew Domain Name that does not already exist on your network. Figure 9.2 shows the establishment of a new domain named Widgets.

   The Network Settings warning message appears to warn you of possible consequences of this action (see fig. 9.3).
4. Choose <u>Y</u>es to complete the change. After a pause, you are greeted with a message welcoming you to the new domain.
5. Restart the server to make the change effective.

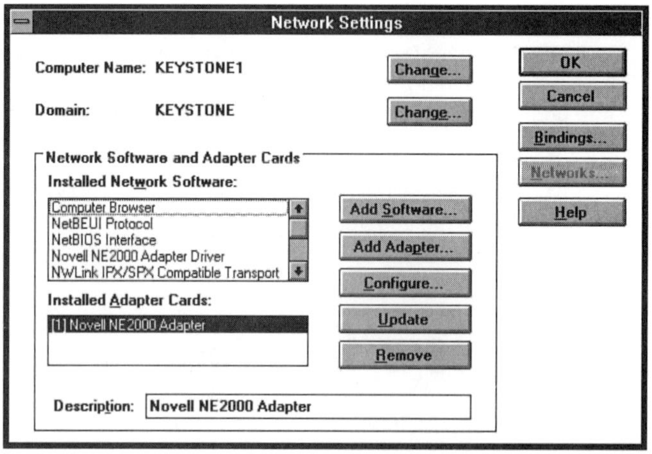

Figure 9.1

The Network Settings dialog box.

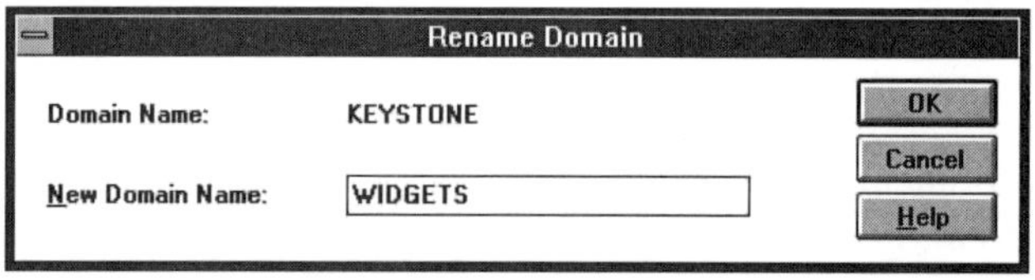

Figure 9.2

Renaming a domain.

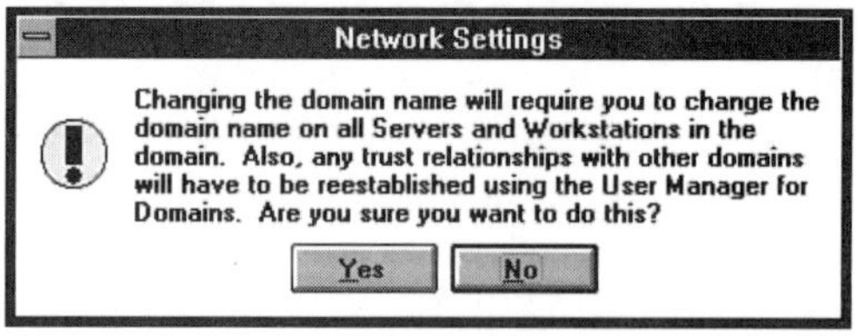

Figure 9.3

The Network Settings warning message.

Stop Moving primary domain controllers is not for the faint of heart. After you move the PDC, you might have a great deal of cleanup to do. You need to reinstall any backup DCs that you want to move to the new domain. You also need to update all the workstation logon configurations so that they will log on to the new domain.

Moving a Domain Controller to a New Domain

A primary domain controller can be moved to a new domain by using the procedures described in the previous section, "Creating New Domains." You can use the Control Panel to move a PDC only (not a BDC), and you can move a PDC only if it is being moved to a domain that does not already exist.

A DC can be moved to another domain by reinstalling Windows NT Server. You can reinstall a primary domain controller to a domain only if the domain does not exist. If the domain exists, a PDC already is established in the domain. You have to install the computer as a BDC and promote it to a primary DC after setup.

To move a backup domain controller to another domain, you must reinstall Windows NT Server. During the Setup procedure, you can use the procedures described in the earlier section, "Selecting a Server Role," to specify the new domain for the server.

Renaming a Domain

You don't directly rename a domain. You create a new domain by moving a PDC to a new domain and then moving computers into the domain that was created. Changing a domain name can be a time-consuming task. You can change a domain name only by changing the domain for each Windows NT machine in the domain. Other tasks to be performed follow:

- Changing parameters for any resource connections that are made by computers that log on to the domain.
- Reinstalling all the backup domain controllers to move them to the new domain. Backup domain controllers cannot be moved using the Control Panel.
- Using User Manager for Domains to reconfigure the trust relationships that affect the renamed domain.
- Reconfiguring a user's logon procedures so that they will begin to use resources in the new domain.

Renaming a large, established domain is not something you want to do even once. Life is too short.

Promoting Domain Controllers

You might need to promote a backup domain controller to the primary role for several reasons:

- If the server functioning as a primary domain controller will be shut down for maintenance, you should promote a backup domain controller so that the domain remains in operation. Users will be unable to access resources on the downed server, but still will be able to log on to the domain. This procedure is particularly significant in a logon domain. You can shut down a server without preventing users from accessing the network.

  If a backup domain controller is promoted while the primary domain controller is available, a copy of the current user account database is replicated to the new primary domain controller. Also, the old primary domain controller is demoted to the role of backup domain controller.

- If the primary domain controller is unavailable, the user account database on the backup domain controller will be established as the account database for the domain. After it comes back online, you need to demote the old primary domain controller to a backup role.

To promote a server to a primary domain controller, follow these steps:

1. Start the Server Manager utility (in the Administrative Tools group).
2. Choose Servers from the View menu. You then see a display similar to figure 9.4 that clearly indicates the domain controller function of each server. Notice the different icons that are used for primary and backup DCs.
3. Select the BDC to be promoted from the list.
4. Choose Promote to Primary Domain Controller from the Computer menu.

   The warning shown in figure 9.5 appears.
5. Clearly, you should not promote a server when users are active in the domain. Choose Yes to proceed or No to cancel.

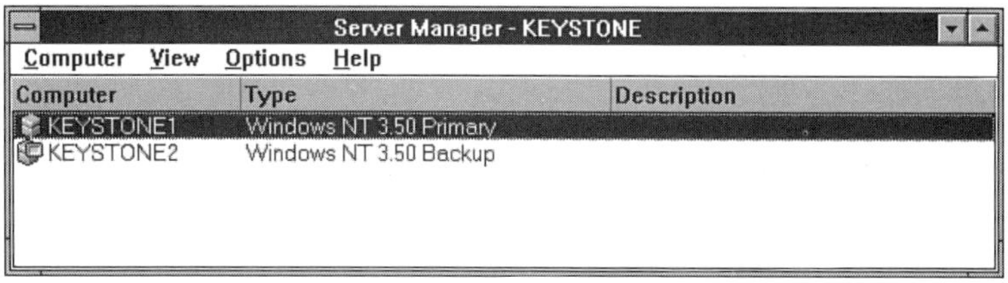

Figure 9.4
The servers list in Server Manager.

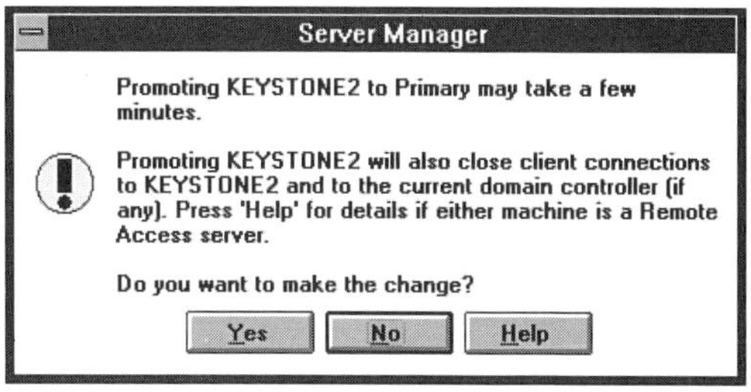

Figure 9.5
The warning you see when promoting a server.

Demoting a Primary Domain Controller

If a backup DC is promoted while the primary DC is off-line, you should be aware of the following differences from the procedure described in the last section:

- You are warned that the primary DC is unavailable and that promoting the backup DC might result in errors when the primary DC returns to service.
- The status of the old PDC when it comes back online is uncertain. While experimenting with this scenario, I encountered two results:

  The old PDC came online as a workstation.

  The old PDC came online as an inactive PDC.

When a primary DC attempts to reenter the domain after another server has been promoted to PDC status, Windows NT Server displays the message `At least one service or driver failed during system startup`. You are prompted to examine the Events log. Using the Events Viewer is covered in Chapter 18, "Managing the Server."

One event in the log has the source of NETLOGON. The Detail Description states that `A Primary domain controller is already running in this domain.`

If you examine the Servers list in System Manager on the new primary DC and discover that two servers are shown as primary, the old PDC is not functioning (its icon appears as an outline) and must be demoted.

If you select a server that needs to be demoted, a new menu choice appears on the Computer menu. This new choice is Demote to Backup Domain Controller. This option is unavailable unless the selected computer is a duplicate PDC.

Choose the Demote to Backup Domain Controller option to demote the old server.

Synchronizing Domain Computers

Under normal circumstances, Windows NT Server keeps all BDCs synchronized with the PDC in a domain. It seldom is necessary for you to force a domain to resynchronize. Because it is possible for BDCs to lose sync with the domain, however, Windows NT Server provides a manual synchronization procedure.

To synchronize a BDC with the PDC, follow these steps:

1. Choose View Servers in the Server Manager utility.
2. Select the backup domain controller to be resynchronized.
3. Choose Synchronize with Primary Domain Controller from the Computer menu.

To synchronize an entire domain with the PDC, follow these steps:

1. Choose View Servers in the Server Manager utility.
2. Select the primary domain controller.
3. Choose Synchronize Entire Domain from the Computer menu.

Adding Workstations and Servers to the Domain

Clients that are not running Windows NT enter a domain simply by running the correct protocols and logging on to a valid user account.

Because they participate more intimately in the domain, Windows NT Workstations and Servers must be explicitly added to a domain before they are permitted to access domain services. They simply cannot connect up and log on.

Servers and workstations can join a domain in three ways:

- By adding the server or workstation computer to the domain first using the Server Manager utility.
- By adding the server or workstation to the domain during installation.
- By adding the server or workstation to the domain from the Control Panel.

Adding Workstations and Servers to a Domain with Server Manager

You can prepare the way for a server or workstation to join a domain by adding it to the domain configuration with the Server Manager. To add a workstation named Harold, for example, follow these steps:

1. Log on to the domain as an administrator.
2. Run the Server Manager utility in the Administrative Tools folder. The Server Manager box displayed by the utility is shown in figure 9.6. At present, this box lists only the primary domain controller computer KEYSTONE1.
3. Choose Add to Domain from the Computer menu. The Add Computer to Domain dialog box appears.
4. Figure 9.7 shows the Add Computer to Domain dialog box being used to add a server or workstation named HAROLD. You also can use this dialog box to add a backup domain controller to the domain prior to installing software on the BDC computer.
5. Choose Add to add the computer you have specified.
6. After you add all required computers, click on Cancel.
7. The computer(s) you add appear in the Server Manager list (see fig. 9.8).

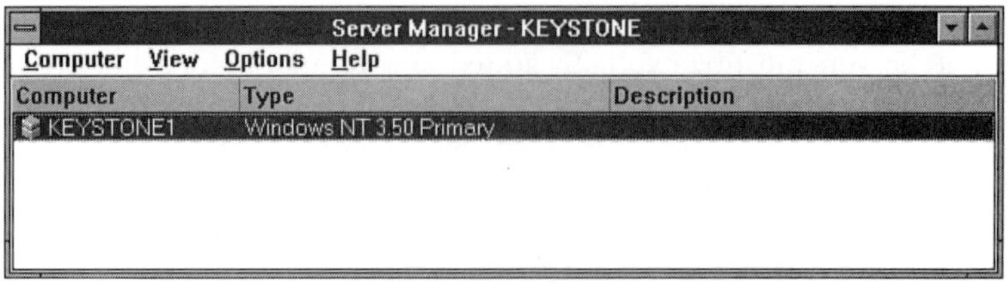

Figure 9.6
Server Manager with a single computer installed.

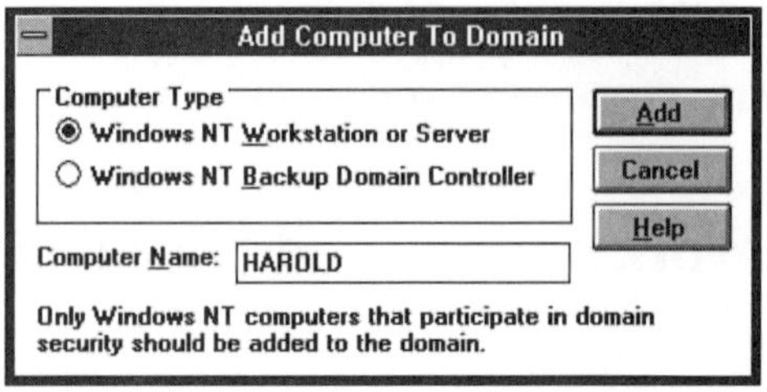

Figure 9.7
Adding a computer to a domain.

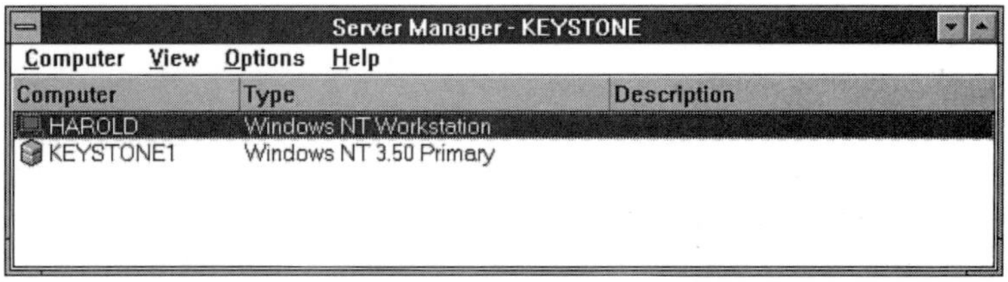

Figure 9.8
Server Manager after a new computer has been added.

Once a computer account has been created, you can then join the domain from the Workstation or Server. To join a domain from a Windows NT Workstation follow these steps:

1. Choose the Network utility from the Control Panel.
2. Check the Computer Name entry to ensure that it matches the name that was specified in the Server Manager. If it does not match, choose the Change button next to the Computer Name field. A Computer Name dialog box enables you to enter a new computer name. You need to restart the computer to put the new computer name into effect before you resume this procedure from step 1.
3. Depending on whether the computer is configured as a workgroup or a domain member, the second item down in the Network dialog box may be labeled

Workgroup or Domain. Click on the Chang**e** button next to the Workgroup or Domain field. The Domain/Workgroup Settings dialog box appears, as shown in figure 9.9.

4. Select the **D**omain button.
5. Enter the domain to which the computer will be added in the **D**omain field. The Domain/Workgroup Settings dialog box shown in figure 9.9 is being used to add the computer to the domain KEYSTONE.

   Because the computer already has been created, you do not need to check the **C**reate Computer Account in Domain check box or use the other fields of the dialog box. If the computer successfully enters the domain, you will see a message "Welcome to the...domain."
6. When you exit the Network utility, you will be prompted to restart the computer to activate the network changes.
7. Press Ctrl+Alt+Del to log on again.
8. In the Welcome dialog box, change the **F**rom entry to the name of the domain you want to log on to. Be sure that the **U**sername and **P**assword entries match a valid user account in the domain.
9. Choose OK to log on.

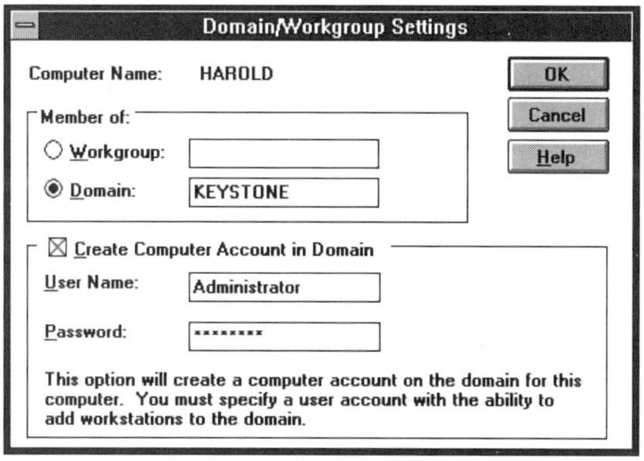

Figure 9.9

The Domain/Workgroup Settings dialog box on a Windows NT Workstation.

Note You might want to look at the computer list in Server Manager before and after a new computer has logged on for the first time. Prior to the logon, the computer's icon is presented as an outline. Following a successful logon, the icon is filled in.

Adding Workstations or Servers to a Domain During Installation

Windows NT Workstations and Servers also can join a domain during installation. In this case, installation must be performed by a domain administrator, because an administrator logon is required to access the domain database and add the new workstation or server.

During Windows NT Server installation, you are prompted to define the Windows NT Server Security Role. Two choices are available:

- Domain Controller (Primary or Backup)
- Server

When you are installing Windows NT Workstation or Windows NT Server in Server mode, after Setup connects to the network, it presents a Domain/Workgroup Settings dialog box, which has features similar to the dialog box shown in figure 9.9.

To add the computer to the domain, follow these steps:

1. Choose Domain and enter the name of the domain of which the computer will be a member.
2. Check the Create Computer Account in Domain box. This activates the User Name and Password fields.
3. In the User Name field, enter a name that is an administrator in the domain that you specified in the Domain field.
4. In the Password field, enter the User Name you specified.
5. Click on OK.

Adding Workstations or Servers to a Domain from the Control Panel

Windows NT Workstations and Servers also can join a domain after setup is completed. This procedure must be performed by a domain administrator, because an administrator logon is required to access the domain database and add the new workstation or server.

Choose the Network utility from the Control Panel. Network displays the Domain/Workgroup Settings dialog box, which is shown in figure 9.9.

To add the computer to the domain, follow these steps:

1. Choose **D**omain and enter the name of the domain of which the computer will be a member.

2. Check the **C**reate Computer Account in Domain box. This activates the **U**ser Name and **P**assword fields.

3. In the **U**ser Name field, enter a name that is an administrator in the domain you specified in the **D**omain field.

4. In the **P**assword field, enter the user name you specified.

5. Click on OK.

Note Just as installing a primary domain controller defines a security ID (SID) for the domain, each computer that is added to the domain is assigned a SID that uniquely identifies it in the domain.

It is the computer SID that permits the computer to participate in the domain. The computer's name is included as a convenience for users. This approach makes it difficult for another computer to masquerade as a computer that already has been added to a domain. Suppose that a computer named Harold has been added to a domain. Another Windows NT computer cannot log on to the domain simply by changing its name to Harold. It also is required to duplicate the SID that was created for the first Harold.

Removing Computers from Domains

Computer accounts are not deleted when a computer stops using a domain. When you move a domain controller to a new domain, for example, the old domain retains a computer account. If a user's workstation begins to access the network from a new domain, its computer account remains in the old domain.

There will be times, therefore, when you need to remove a computer from a domain. This is performed from the Server Manager using the following procedure:

1. Log on to the domain as an administrator.

2. Run the Server Manager utility in the Administrative Tools folder.

3. Select the computer to be removed from the domain.

4. Choose Remove from Domain from the Computer menu. You are asked to confirm your decision.

The computer might not be removed from the Server Manager computer list immediately. It might be several minutes before periodic server housekeeping updates the computer list.

Setting Trust Relationships

The operations required to add and remove trust relationships can be illustrated in a simple two-domain network. The example network has two domains:

- **Keystone**, which will be trusted by Widgets
- **Widgets**, which will trust Keystone

Each trust relationship is the result of two actions:

- The trusted domain must be configured to allow another domain to trust it.
- The trusting domain then must be configured to trust the trusted domain.

The following example demonstrates the steps required to enable the Widgets domain to trust the Keystone domain.

Permitting Widgets to Trust Keystone

First, an administrator of Keystone must add Widgets to the list of domains that are permitted to trust Keystone. The steps to accomplish this follow:

1. Start the Server Manager utility in the Administrative Tools folder. The Trust Relationships dialog box shown in figure 9.10 appears.
2. Click on the Add button beside the Permitted to Trust this Domain list. This brings up the Permit Domain to Trust dialog box. The example shown in figure 9.11 is adding Widgets to the list of domains that are permitted to trust Keystone.
3. An optional password can be specified. The password must be used to enable the trusting domain to complete the establishment of the trust relationship.
4. Click on OK. When you return to the Trust Relationships dialog box, the domain you specified is added to the Permitted to Trust this Domain list.

5. The Cancel button changes to Close after a domain has been added or removed. Click on Close to exit the dialog box.

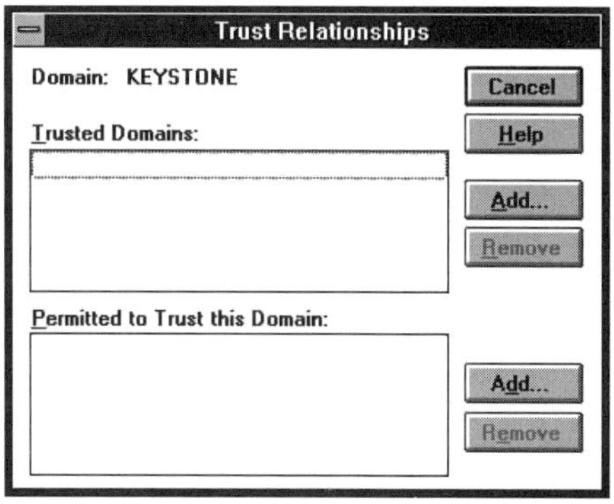

Figure 9.10

The Trust Relationships dialog box.

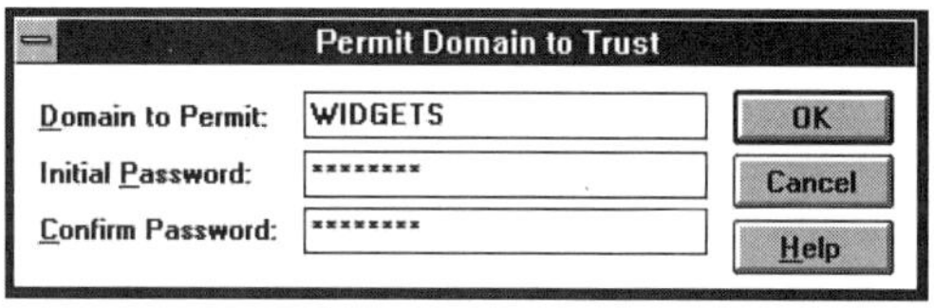

Figure 9.11

Adding a domain to the Permit Domain to Trust dialog box.

Trusting Keystone

Next, an administrator must add Keystone to the list of trusted domains for the Widgets domain. After logging on to Widgets, an administrator should perform the following actions:

1. Start the User Manager for Domains utility in the Administrative Tools folder.
2. Choose Trust Relationships from the Policies menu to display the Trust Relationships dialog box.
3. Click on the Add button next to Trusted Domains. The Add Trusted Domain dialog box shown in figure 9.12 appears.

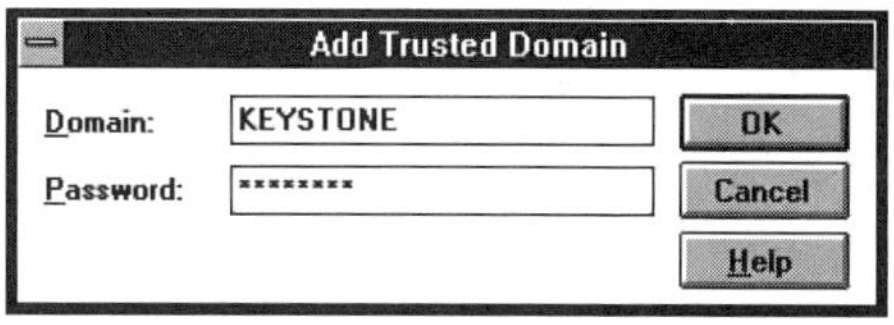

Figure 9.12

The Add Trusted Domain dialog box.

4. Figure 9.12 shows a completed dialog box that adds Keystone to the domains that are trusted by Widgets. After specifying the domain to be trusted, the administrator must enter the password that was established by the administrator of Keystone.

5. Click on OK to return to the Trust Relationships dialog box.

6. If all goes well, a message is displayed stating `Trust Relationship with KEYSTONE successfully established.`

   An error message results if the domains are unable to establish contact to confirm the trust relationship. An error also results if you have specified a domain name that doesn't exist or a password that does not match the password specified by the trusted domain.

7. Confirm that the domain has been added to the list of domains in the **P**ermitted to Trust this Domain list.

8. Click on Close to close the Trust Relationships dialog box.

The domain Widgets now trusts Keystone.

Note Trusting another domain does not immediately give users in the trusted domain access to resources in the trusting domain. You also must grant permissions that enable users who log on through the trusted domain to access resources in the trusting domain. The procedures for assigning permissions are described in Chapter 10, "Managing Users and Groups."

Removing Trust Relationships

Two steps are required to remove a trust relationship. The trusting domain must stop trusting the trusted domain, and the trusted domain must cancel its permission to be trusted.

Removing a Trust Relationship

Removing a domain from the **T**rusted Domains list is accomplished by following these steps:

1. Log on as a domain administrator for the trusting domain and start the User Manager for Domains utility in the Administrative Tools folder.

2. Select the Widgets domain from the **S**elect Domain option in the **U**ser menu.

3. Choose Trust Relationships from the Policies menu to display the Trust Relationships dialog box.

4. In the Trusted Domains list, select the domain to be removed. Then click on the Remove button beside the Trusted Domains list.

   Because canceling a trust relationship can have far-reaching effects, User Manager for Domains displays the warning shown in figure 9.13.

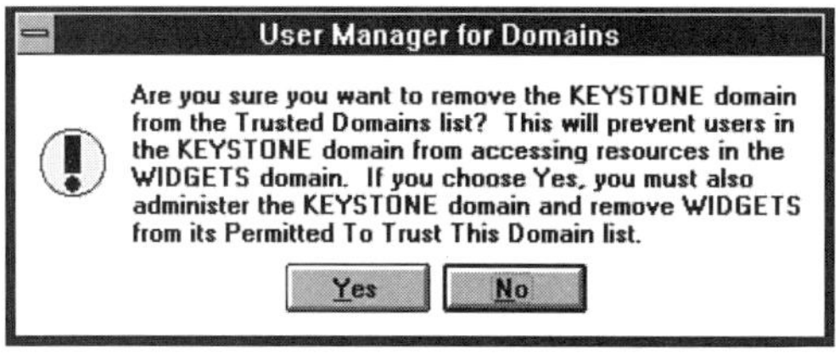

Figure 9.13
The warning displayed when removing a trust relationship.

5. Click on Yes to complete the action. You are returned to the Trust Relationships dialog box, and the domain you removed is no longer listed.

6. Click on Close to exit the Trust Relationships dialog box.

Canceling Permission to Trust a Domain

Next, an administrator on the trusted domain must cancel permission to trust the domain. Canceling a trust permission is accomplished with this procedure:

1. Log on as a domain administrator and start the User Manager for Domains utility in the Administrative Tools folder.

2. Choose Trust Relationships from the Policies menu to display the Trust Relationships dialog box.

3. In the Permitted to Trust this Domain list, select the domain to be removed. Then choose the Remove button beside the Permitted to Trust this Domain list.

   Because this action also can create havoc on the LAN, User Manager for Domains displays a warning message.

4. Choose Yes to complete the action. You are returned to the Trust Relationships dialog box, and the domain you removed no longer is listed.

5. Click on Close to exit the Trust Relationships dialog box.

After the trust relationship has been removed on both the trusting and the trusted server, the complete trust relationship has been removed.

CHAPTER 10

Managing Users and Groups

LAN administration would be considerably more pleasurable if LANs did not have to have users. You can set up your network perfectly, install your software, and test everything for days until every last problem is ironed out, but it will do you no good. The moment you add the first user is the moment your problems really begin. Applications that once worked perfectly will begin to have bugs. Files that are critical to your organization will disappear mysteriously. Your phone will ring off the hook. Users! You might begin to wish that you had chosen a more secluded way to make a living.

Without users, however, your LAN can't pay its keep, so you have no choice but to let them in. The key is to let users into the LAN the right way. There are several key ingredients to configuring the user environment:

- Establishing solid user security
- Creating productive environments for users
- Training users on anything you can't make self-evident

Part Three of this book delves into the details of setting up user environments for Windows and DOS clients. The groundwork for your users' working environments begins in this chapter, however.

User accounts enable users to log on to the network and access network resources. Setting up user accounts involves two almost contradictory goals:

- Helping users access the resources they need
- Keeping users away from everything else

To meet these goals, you will grant users permissions to use network resources. Doing so involves assigning privileges to users themselves and to groups to which the users belong.

The tool you will use for managing users and groups is User Manager for Domains; most of its features are covered in this chapter.

Note Windows NT Workstation includes a similar tool called User Manager to manage user accounts and groups on the workstation. Because User Manager is designed to manage the resources of a single workstation, there are many differences, but experienced users of Windows NT Workstation should have no difficulty making the transition to User Manager for Domains.

Who Can Manage Users and Groups

Rights to administer user accounts and groups are conferred on members of three Windows NT groups:

- **Administrators.** Members of this local group can perform all user and group management functions.
- **Domain Admins.** In most domains, the Domain Admins global group is a member of the Administrators local group. All users who are members of Domain Admins therefore are granted Administrator privileges for the domain.

  To enable Administrators to manage users and groups in other domains, first trust the Administrators' logon domains. Then add the Domain Admins global group from the logon domain to the Administrators local group of the domain you want the Administrators to manage.
- **Account Operators.** Users in the Account Operators group can create user accounts and groups, delete most users and groups, and manage many characteristics of user accounts and groups.

  Members of the Account Operators group cannot manage the administration groups set up by Windows NT Server: Administrators, Domain Admins, Account

Operators, Server Operators, Print Operators, or Backup Operators. Also, members of the Account Operators group cannot manage the accounts of domain Administrators or establish domain security policies.

Getting Started with User Manager for Domains

User Manager for Domains can be used to manage any domains for which you have been given administrative access.

In most cases, you will run User Manager for Domains by choosing the User Manager for Domains icon in the Administrator Tools group. The User Manager for Domains window, shown in figure 10.1, is displayed when you start the utility. When started from the icon, User Manager for Domains displays the domain where your user account is defined.

You also can run User Manager for Domains from the command line by following these steps:

1. Choose Run from the File menu.
2. To start User Manager for Domains in the domain that supports your user account, type **usrmgr** in the Command Line box.

   To start User Manager for Domains in a specific domain, include the domain name after the command. To start in the Keystone domain, for example, use the command **usrmgr keystone**.

   To start User Manager for Domains for a specific computer, include the computer name after the command. To start with the computer named Charles, for example, use the command **usrmgr \\Charles**, as shown in figure 10.2. Be sure to precede the computer name with two backslashes. (Specifying the computer domain of a primary or backup domain controller displays the users and groups for the domain that the domain controller supports.)
3. Click on OK.

Note Microsoft uses a system called the universal naming convention (UNC) to name computers and their resources. UNC rules require the computer name to be preceded with two backslashes, for example, \\Keystone1.

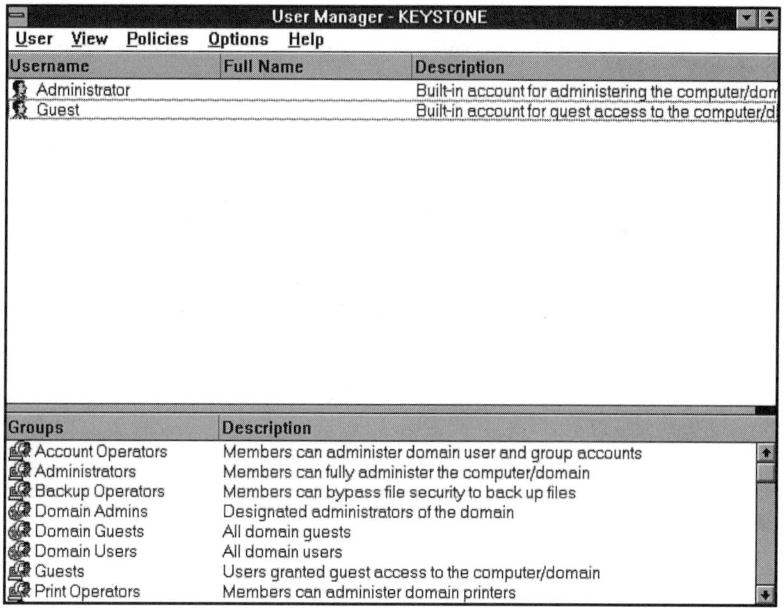

Figure 10.1

The opening window for User Manager for Domains.

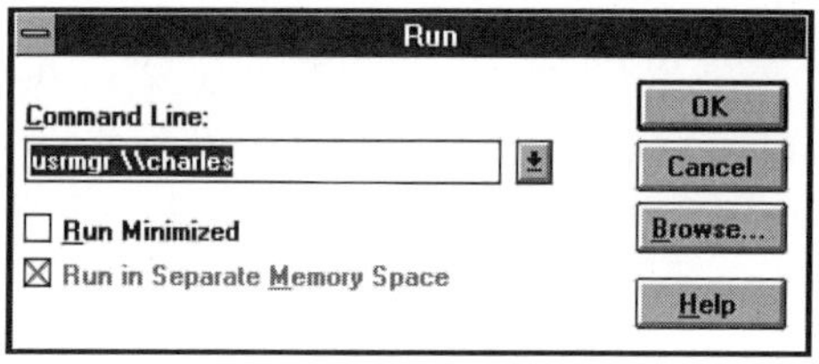

Figure 10.2

Using the Run command to start User Manager for Domains.

Note

Remember that Windows NT is a multitasking operating system and that you can run multiple copies of an application. You might find it convenient to start several copies of User Manager for Domains, with each copy managing a separate domain.

You can create multiple application icons and configure each copy to start up in a separate domain. To create an icon to start User Manager for Domains in the domain Widgets, for example, follow these steps:

1. Create a copy of an icon by holding down the Ctrl key while you use the mouse to drag a copy of the icon to a new location.
2. Highlight the copy of the icon and press Alt+Enter to display the icon's property list.

3. Edit the Command Line entry in the property list to add the name of the domain that User Manager for Domains should access when this copy of the icon is chosen.
4. Edit the Description entry to describe this copy of the User Manager for Domains icon.

Selecting a Domain

You can change the domain or computer that is being managed by User Manager for Domains. Follow these steps:

1. Choose Select Domain from the User menu.
2. Choose a domain from the Select Domain box;

   Or you can enter a domain name in the Domain box;

   Or you can enter a computer name in the Domain box. Remember to precede a computer name with two backslashes. For example, **Keystone1**. Specifying the computer name of a backup or primary domain controller displays the domain.
3. Select the Low Speed Connection option if you will be accessing a domain or a computer using a low-speed communication channel. Low-speed operation is described later in this chapter.
4. Click on OK.

Using Low Speed Connections

When User Manager for Domains is managing a domain or computer, a fairly large amount of data is required to pass between the computer running User Manager and other computers on the network. When the connection is made through a LAN, the volume of data is not a problem. When communicating through a low-speed connection such as a modem or most wide area networks, however, the large amount of traffic might result in slow operation.

You can improve performance over a slow channel by selecting Low Speed Connections when you specify a domain or computer to be managed. Choosing Low Speed Connections restricts the operation of User Manager for Domains in the following ways:

- User accounts no longer will be listed in the main window, and the Select Users option on the User menu is inactive. You will need to specify user account names to manage them.

- Groups no longer will be listed in the main window. Local groups can be created and managed using options from the User menu. Global groups cannot be created or managed. Global group memberships must be managed by setting group memberships in users' accounts.

- The View menu commands are inactive.

User Manager for Domains remembers the connection speed setting for the last 20 domains or computers that you have administered. The Low Speed Connections option already will be checked for you when you specify a domain or computer that recently was accessed with that option.

You also can turn low-speed connection service on or off by choosing the Low Speed Connections command from the Options menu. You also can include the /l and /h parameters on the command line to force User Manager for Domains to start up with Low Speed Connection selected.

Refreshing the User Account List

User Manager for Domains immediately posts changes to the User and Group lists. However, this utility only searches the network for changes made by other Administrators at intervals. Changes made to the domain by another Administrator are not displayed until the next time User Manager for Domain examines the network.

If you want to ensure that the information being displayed to you is current, choose the Refresh command from the View menu. (This command is unavailable when the Low Speed Connection option is selected.)

Sorting User Accounts

By default, user accounts are listed in alphabetical order. You can control the order in which user accounts are listed by choosing a sort order from the View menu. Two commands are available:

- Sort by Full Name

- Sort by Username

These options are unavailable when Low Speed Connection is specified.

Managing User Accounts

A user account enables users to access resources on domains and Windows NT computers. When you manage a user account, you configure a wide variety of security features that restrict how, where, and when the user can access the network. You also grant privileges that permit the user to access resources.

This user information is stored in a user account database, and it is that database on a primary domain controller that you are actually managing as you use User Manager for Domains. The database is replicated to any backup domain controllers that are included in the domain.

Managing Built-In User Accounts

Two user accounts, Administrator and Guest, are created when Windows NT is installed. These accounts cannot be removed, but can be managed in specified ways.

The Administrator User Account

The Administrator user account is created to enable you to manage Windows NT after the software is installed. You can rename the Administrator user account, but you cannot remove it from the domain.

Administrator is a member of the following built-in groups, from which it cannot be removed:

- Administrators (local group)
- Domain Admins (global group)
- Domain Users (global group)

To create other user accounts that are equivalent to Administrator, you must include them as members of these three groups.

By default, the Domain Admins global group is added to the Administrators group for every Windows NT computer in the domain. A user logged on as Administrator can manage the domain and all Windows NT computers in the domain.

Note Administrator users (members of the Administrators group) are extremely powerful and operate with very few restrictions. When logged on as an Administrator, take care not to perform actions that could damage network operations. It can be very easy, for example, to accidentally delete files that are crucial to network operation by selecting the wrong file or directory in File Manager.

An Administrator has unrestricted access to most files in the domain and easily can disseminate viruses throughout the network. Make frequent use of virus-detection software to ensure that viruses are not present on an Administrator's computer.

You also should assign Administrators two user accounts: one with Administrator privileges to be used when administering the network, and another with user privileges to be used at other times. When logged on under the user account, the risk of infecting the network with a virus is reduced considerably. Administrators will find it extremely useful to use Windows NT Workstation on their personal computers because the process of logging on and off is simplified greatly.

The Guest User Account

The Guest user account is a member of the Domain Guests built-in group, and initially is disabled. You can enable the account by using the Disable Account option described in the section "Modifying User Account Properties," later in this chapter. The Guest user account can be renamed, but it cannot be removed.

The initial account password for Guest is blank. Unless a password is added to the account, users can use Guest to access the domain even from untrusted domains.

Activate the Guest user account if your network supports resources that should be accessible to individuals who do not have formal user accounts.

I am not greatly in favor of Guest accounts. Adding a user account requires little effort but is repaid in substantially improved security. Few of the programs or data that you will put on the LAN are so unimportant that security ceases to be a concern.

Adding a User Account

You need to create a user account for each user who requires access to the network. User accounts are created and managed from the New Users window, which is accessed by choosing the New User command from the User menu of User Manager for Domains. The New User window is shown in figure 10.3. The figure illustrates an example of a completed New User form.

After the fields in the New User window have been completed, click on Add to create the user account. Each of the fields in the window is discussed in the following sections.

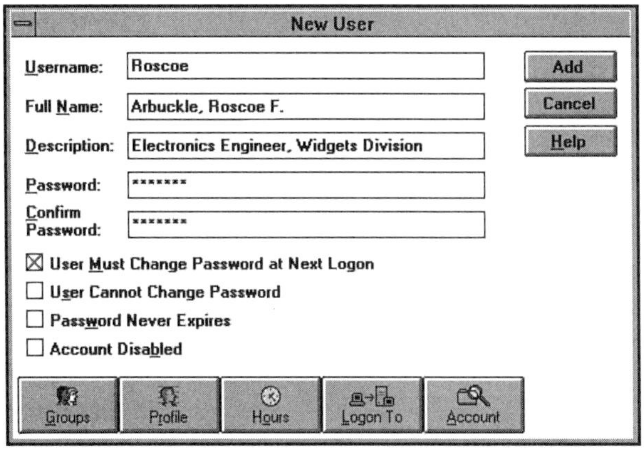

Figure 10.3

The New User window.

Username

Each user in a domain or computer must have a unique user name. A user name can include up to 20 characters, including upper- and lowercase letters, numbers, and punctuation. The following characters cannot appear in a user name:

```
= + [ ] / \ < > ; : ' " * ?
```

You should establish a network policy for user names. Consistent naming conventions make it easier to remember user names and to find them in lists. First names are used for user names in the examples in this book, but that approach works only for very small LANs. You might work in a 15-person department that includes three Roberts, for example.

If your network includes users of DOS and Windows 3.1, it makes some sense to restrict user names to eight characters. Then, user names also can be used as the names of users' home directories.

Some alternative naming standards follow:

- First name plus a number, such as Jim338. User names of this type can be difficult to remember and recognize.
- First name plus last initial, such as JimA. Numbers can be added in case of duplicates. You might create accounts for JimA1 and JimA2, for example.
- First initial plus last name. An example is JAnderson (or JAnderso if you want to restrict the user name to eight characters). In case of duplication, include a digit, as in JAnders1 and JAnders2.

The third option is probably the best because it results in fewer name duplications. The number of first names in common use is surprisingly limited, and user names based on first names quickly produce duplications in organizations of any size.

Full Name

This optional field enables you to specify a more complete name for the user. The full name appears in several lists of user names that are presented by network utilities. Use of the Full Name field is especially important when the convention you select for the user name does not produce names that are easily recognizable.

As with user names, you should establish a convention for full names. These names can be used by programs on the network, and might provide the user name directory for your network's e-mail program, for example. In such cases, it probably is preferable to enter the last name first (Lloyd, Harold H.), rather than the first name first (Harold H. Lloyd).

Description

The Description field is optional. You might, for example, want to use it to identify the user's job title and department.

Password and Confirm Password

If you choose to specify an initial password, enter it in both fields. Passwords are never displayed in open text when they are entered, and the Confirm Password field verifies that you have correctly typed the password.

Passwords are case-sensitive and can consist of up to 14 characters. Administrators can set policies that establish the types of passwords that are permitted. See the section "Managing the Account Policy," later in this chapter, for more information.

User Must Change Password at Next Logon

If User Must Change Password at Next Logon box is checked (the default value), the user is forced to change the password the first time he or she logs on.

Windows NT Server security is so versatile that even Administrators can be restricted from openly accessing some user resources. By forcing users to select a password that is unknown to the Administrator, you can enforce this capability.

You always should check this field if you are entering blank passwords for newly created user accounts.

User Cannot Change Password

There are at least two reasons for using the User Cannot Change Password option:

- Several users share an account
- Passwords are entered manually by the network Administrator, and users are not permitted to enter passwords.

Users have a tendency to enter passwords that are easy for them to type and remember. Unfortunately, these passwords tend to be easy to guess—such as children's names, birthdates, and so on.

Some organizations that require especially high levels of security assign passwords centrally so that they cannot be guessed easily. Because Administrators cannot examine user-entered passwords to determine whether they meet security guidelines, it is necessary for such passwords to be administered by a central security staff.

Password Never Expires

Your account policy probably will specify the number of days that a password is valid before a user is forced to specify a new password. In rare instances, you might want to override automatic password expiration for some accounts.

If you choose the Password Never Expires option, the value of the User Must Change Password at Next Logon field is overridden.

Account Disabled

Check this box to prevent users from accessing a user account. Here are several reasons for using the Account Disabled option:

- To disable an account while a user is on extended leave
- To disable an account that is used by a person filling a particular role when the position is vacant
- To create a template account that is used only to create other accounts

Additional Account Properties

At the bottom of the New User window are five buttons: Groups, Profile, Hours, Logon To, and Account. Each button produces a window that enables you to specify additional properties for user accounts. Each of these sets of properties is discussed later in this chapter.

Copying a User Account

If an existing user account is substantially similar to a new user account you want to create, you can copy the existing account and modify it as required for the new user. To copy a user account, follow these steps:

1. Select the account to be copied in the User Manager for Domains window.
2. Choose Copy from the User menu. This produces a window labeled `Copy of` *`username`*, where *`username`* is the name of the account you are copying.
3. In the Username field, enter the user name and other user-specific information.
4. Make any modifications you want to other user properties.
5. Click on Add to create the user account.

Note You will find it useful to configure a template account that is used to create other accounts. After you have configured the properties of the template, check the Account Disabled box in the New User window so that the account cannot be used. Create new users by copying the template account.

Modifying User Account Properties

You can modify user accounts one at a time or in groups. The following sections explain the ways in which to do this.

Modifying Individual User Accounts

You can select a single user account for modification in three ways:

- Locate the user account entry in the User Manager for Domains window and double-click on the entry.
- Select the user account entry in the User Manager for Domains window and press Enter.
- Select an entry in the User Manager for Domains window and choose the Properties command from the User menu.

Either way, the user account properties are presented in the User Properties window, which is nearly identical to the New User window that was used to create the account. The User Properties dialog box is shown in figure 10.4.

Make any required changes in the properties in this window. Notice that you cannot change the Username field. You can access any of the additional property windows by clicking on the appropriate button at the bottom of the window.

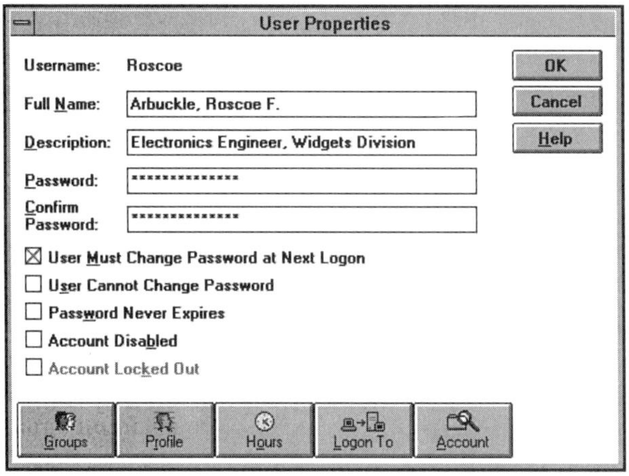

Figure 10.4
The User Properties dialog box.

Disabling User Accounts

You might want to disable a user account without removing it from the domain. To disable a user account, check the Account Disa**b**led check box.

Unlocking User Accounts

The Account Loc**k**ed Out field usually is inactive (shown in gray). Under certain circumstances, a user account can be locked out by Windows NT Server. If that is the case, the Account Loc**k**ed Out field will be active. You can unlock the account by checking this field.

Modifying Two or More User Accounts

If you need to perform the same action on several user accounts, you can do so by selecting the accounts in the User Manager for Domains accounts list. You can select accounts in several ways:

- Select individual accounts by holding down the Ctrl key as you click on each account. If you select accounts by pressing Ctrl and clicking, previously selected accounts remain selected.

- Select a range of accounts by selecting an account at one end of the range. Then locate the account at the other end of the range and hold down the Shift key as you click on the account. A range of accounts is selected, starting with the account you first selected and extended to the account you Shift+clicked.

- Use the S**e**lect Users command in the Users menu to display a Select Users list of groups, as shown in figure 10.5.

If you highlight a group and click on Select, users in that group are added to the selected users in the main window.

If you highlight a group and click on Deselect, users in that group are deselected in the main window.

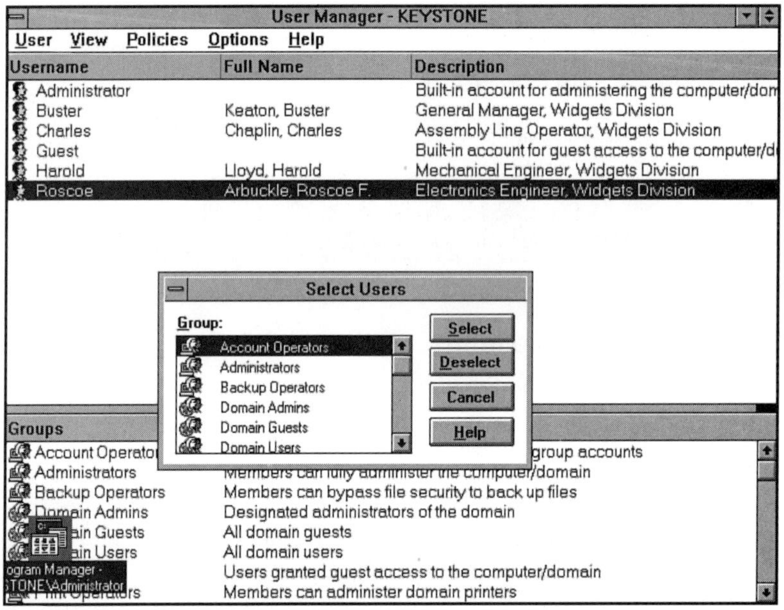

Figure 10.5
The Select Users list.

After you select the user accounts to be modified, choose the Properties command from the Users menu to reveal the User Properties window. The User Properties window in figure 10.6 is being used to modify properties for four users.

When you are modifying two or more users, some options in User Manager will be unavailable:

- The User Properties window does not permit you to modify these fields:

  Full Name

  Description

  Password and Confirm Password

  Password Never Expires

- The Group Memberships window permits you to manage only group memberships that are common to all the users you have selected.

- The User Environment Profile window can be used to assign common or custom profile assignments.
- The Logon Hours window can be used only to set the same logon hours for all selected users.
- The Logon Workstations window can be used only to set the same logon workstations for all selected users.
- The Account Information window can set uniform properties for all selected users.

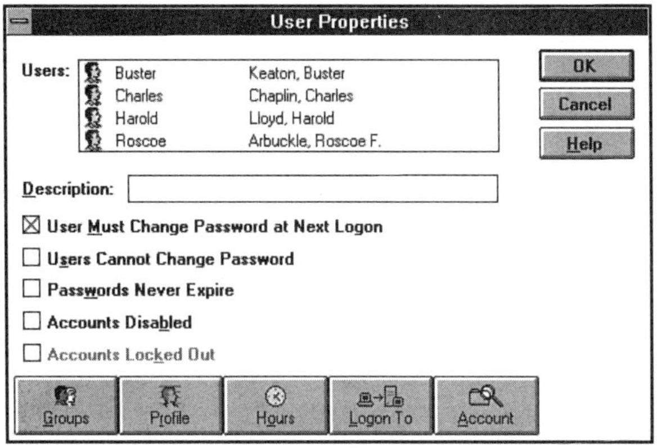

Figure 10.6

Managing properties for multiple users.

Assigning Group Memberships

The <u>G</u>roups button in the New User, Copy of, and User Properties windows enable you to assign group memberships. Clicking on <u>G</u>roups reveals the Group Memberships window shown in figure 10.7. The options in this window are described in the following sections.

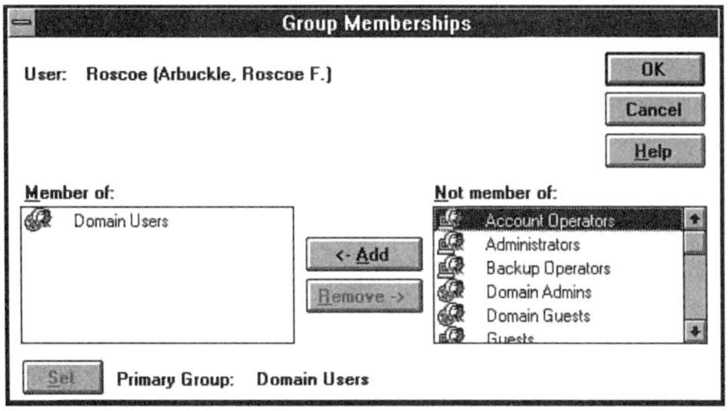

Figure 10.7

The Group Memberships window.

Adding a Group Membership to a User Account

The Not Member Of list box lists groups to which this user account does not belong. To add a group membership to the user's account, select the group name and click on the Add button. The group name is removed from the Not Member Of box and added to the Member Of box.

You are permitted to select multiple groups in the Member Of box prior to removing them from the user account.

You are not permitted to remove the group that is designated as the user's primary group. If you want to remove that group, you first must designate a different group as the user's primary group, as described in the following section.

Removing a Group Membership from a User Account

The Member Of list box lists the groups to which this user account does not belong. To remove a group membership from the user account, select the group name in the Member Of box and click on Remove. The group name is removed from the Member Of box and added to the Not Member Of box.

You are permitted to select multiple groups in the Not Member Of box prior to adding them to the user account.

Setting the Primary Group for a User Account

The primary group is used only by users who are accessing Windows NT Server through Services for Macintosh. When a Macintosh user creates a folder, the user's primary group is associated with the folder.

Whether or not they are using a Macintosh, each user account must designate one group as its primary group. To set the primary group, select a group in the Member Of list box and click on Set.

Managing Group Memberships of Two or More Users

When you select two or more users in the User Manager for Domains window, the Group Memberships window resembles figure 10.8.

This window has the following features:

- The Users box lists the names of the users you have selected.

- The All Are Members Of box lists only the groups that are assigned to all the users in the Users box. In figure 10.8, no groups are listed because Administrator is not a member of any groups to which Buster and Charles belong.
- The Not All Are Members Of box lists all groups that are not already assigned to all users in the Users box.
- The Set button for the Primary Group selection is inactive.

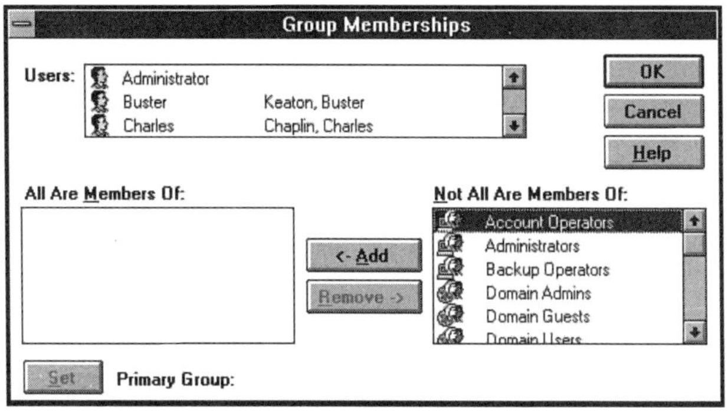

Figure 10.8
Managing group assignments for multiple users.

When you add or remove a group, it is added or removed from all groups in the Users list box.

To ensure that none of the selected users is a member of a group, follow these steps:

1. Select the group in the Not All Are Members Of box and click Add to add the group membership to all listed users.
2. Click on OK to save the change and return to the User Properties window.
3. Click on Groups in the User Properties window.
4. Select the group in the All Are Members Of box that is to be removed from all user accounts and click on Remove.
5. Click on OK to save the changes.

Managing User Profiles

The Profile button in the New User, Copy of, and User Properties windows enables you to assign user profile information. Clicking on Profile reveals the User Environment Profile dialog box shown in figure 10.9. This dialog box has fields for several items which are explained in the following sections.

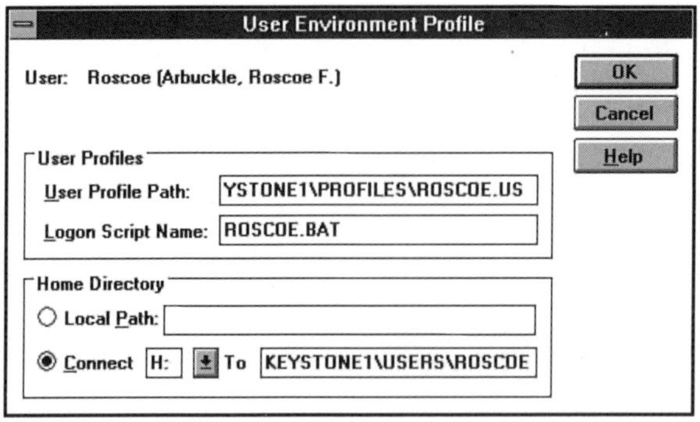

Figure 10.9

The User Environment Profile dialog box.

User Profile Path

Users of Windows NT can take advantage of *user profiles*—the most powerful means provided by Windows NT Server to configure users' network environments. A user profile can specify most of the startup features of a Windows NT session, including program groups and available applications. Profiles can be managed by users, or Administrators can take over profiles for users when it is necessary to exercise greater control over actions users can perform on the network.

When working on a Windows NT computer, each user maintains a user profile that is associated with the user's user name on the computer. This profile is stored on the workstation computer, and users who access several computers must maintain a profile on each computer.

Users who log on to a Windows NT Server network have the option of maintaining their profiles on the network server. This capability enables them to access the same profile regardless of the Windows NT Workstation from which they are logging on.

Windows NT Server supports two types of user profiles:

- **Personal user profiles.** An individual profile is assigned to each user. Personal user profiles are stored in files with the file name extension USR.
- **Mandatory user profiles.** Administrators also can assign mandatory profiles that users are not permitted to modify. Mandatory user profiles ensure that users work in a common environment and prevent problems that can result from users modifications to profiles. Mandatory user profiles are stored in files with the file name extension MAN.

The location of a user's profile file is specified in the User Profile Path field of the User Environment Profile window.To specify a personal user profile, follow these steps

1. Enter the path to the file in the User Profile Path field. Be sure to specify a USR extension in the file name. For user Roscoe on server Keystone1, for example, you might specify this path:

   \\KEYSTONE1\PROFILES\ROSCOE.USR

2. Optionally, use User Profile Manager to create the ROSCOE.USR profile file. If you do not create a user profile file, the user will access the default profile on the workstation when next logging into the network. This default profile, along with changes the user makes, is saved to the user profile path you specified in step 1.

Because Administrators are not required to create personal user profiles, it is easy to create large numbers of user accounts.

To specify a mandatory user profile, follow these steps:

1. Enter the path to the file in the User Profile Path field. Be sure to specify a MAN extension in the file name. You can assign a mandatory profile to be shared by all users in the Widgets division, for example, by specifying the same profile path for all users:

   \\WIDGETS1\WIDGETS\WIDGETS.MAN

2. Create the mandatory profile. Users cannot create mandatory profiles. You must use User Profile Manager to create the WIDGETS.MAN profile file. If you fail to create the mandatory profile file, users will not be permitted to log into the domain.

The user profile files are maintained with the User Profile Editor, which is described in Chapter 14, "Using Windows NT Clients."

Note

In the next section, you will learn that logon script files generally are replicated to each domain controller in the domain. This is possible because all logon script files can be maintained in a single place and replicated to other specific places. It does not matter which copy of the logon script actually is used during the logon process.

Replication is a one-way street. Administrators specify export and import directories on Windows NT computers, and files are copied from the export directories to the import directories by the Replicator service. Replication is not sophisticated enough to identify which of several copies of a file is most current and replicate that copy to all other servers.

continues

For this reason, personal user profiles cannot be replicated in the same manner as logon scripts. Suppose that the Replication service was configured to replicate a profile file from Keystone1 to Keystone2. If users attached to replicas of their user profiles on Keystone2 and made modifications, those changes would not be replicated back to the master copies of the profiles on Keystone1.

Logon Script Name

Logon scripts are batch files that are executed when users log on from Windows NT, DOS, Windows for Workgroups, and OS/2. Logon scripts are less versatile than profiles, and you probably will want to use profiles for users of Windows NT computers.

Logon scripts have the extension BAT for DOS, Windows for Workgroups, and Windows NT workstations. The CMD extension is used when users log in from OS/2 workstations. Because logon script files are tailored for specific client operating systems, users who log in from both Windows and OS/2 operating systems might require more than one user account.

By default, logon scripts are stored in the directory C:\WINNT35\SYSTEM32\REPL-\IMPORT\SCRIPTS. The directory can be modified by changing a logon script path specification using the Server Manager. This feature is part of the Windows NT Server directory Replicator service and is discussed in Chapter 21, "Managing Directory Replication."

In most cases, a master copy of each logon script is kept on one domain controller—usually the PDC. The directory Replicator service then is configured to replicate the logon script files to other domain controllers. In this way, the logon scripts are available to users regardless of the DC that is used to authenticate their connection to the domain.

The Logon Script Name may be expressed as a relative path specification in the following situations:

- If you specify only a file name such as HAROLD.BAT, Windows NT Server will look for the file in the default logon script directory.

- If you specify a relative path name (one that does not begin with a drive letter or a backslash), Windows NT Server looks for the logon script file in a subdirectory of the logon script default directory. If you enter **WIDGETS\ALLUSERS.BAT**, Windows NT Server looks for a file named ALLUSERS.BAT in the WIDGETS subdirectory of the logon script directory. For the default logon script directory, the complete directory path would be as follows:

  C:\WINNT35\SYSTEM32\REPL\IMPORT\SCRIPTS\WIDGETS\ALLUSERS.BAT.

You can assign individual logon script file names for each user or the same file for a group of users. By sharing the same logon script with groups of users, you can ensure that they are working in a consistent network environment.

Specific information about logon scripts is presented in the following chapters:

- Chapter 13, "Using Windows and DOS Clients"
- Chapter 14, "Using Windows NT Clients"

Home Directory

In most cases, each user should be assigned a home directory on the network. This directory can be used by the user to store personal files. It also can be designated by the system Administrator as a location for certain user-specific files.

The home directory can be located on the user's local hard drive. In this case, the user will be able to access only the home directory from a single workstation. To specify a local logon script path, follow these steps:

1. Select the Local Path option in the User Environment Profile dialog box.
2. Enter a local path in the Local Path field, such as **C:\HOME**.

Generally speaking, you will want to locate home directories on the network. Users can access a network home directory when they log on to any client on the network. To specify a network home directory, follow these steps:

1. Select the Connect option in the User Environment Profile window.
2. Specify a drive letter that will identify the home directory. Click on the arrow button to choose an available drive letter from a list.
3. Enter a complete path to the home directory. You should use UNC notation and specify the server so that the user can log on from any domain controller. To place Roscoe's home directory on the KEYSTONE1 computer in the USERS directory, for example, you enter **KEYSTONE1\USERS\ROSCOE** as the home directory path.

Windows NT Server will create a user home directory following the home directory path name you have entered. Privileges for user home directories are configured so that only the specified user has access to the directory contents.

Managing User Profiles for Two or More Users

You probably will configure your users with nearly identical user profiles, and you often will want to configure all their profiles in a single operation.

When you select two or more users in the User Manager for Domains window, the User Environment Profile window resembles figure 10.10. The window in the figure has been preconfigured to illustrate techniques for defining group user profiles.

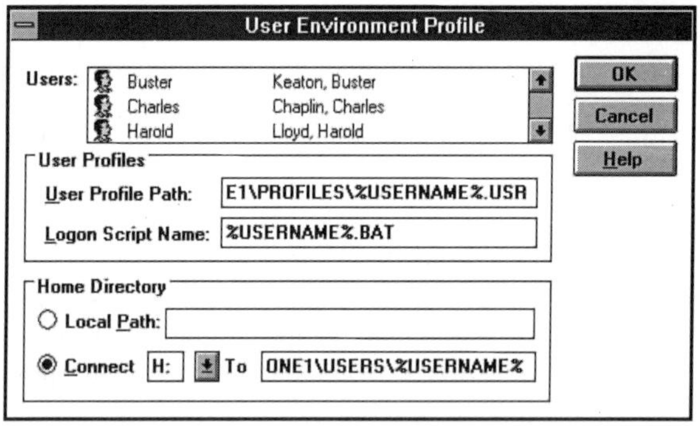

Figure 10.10
Specifying user profiles for two or more users.

The trick is to use one of the variables available on Windows NT Server computers. The variable %username% stores the user name of the current user. This variable is used in two fields in the figure.

Specifying User Profiles for Two or More Users

The User Profile Path field in figure 10.10 establishes a personal user profile for each user. For the user named Buster, the user profile path will be \\KEYSTONE1\PROFILES\BUSTER.USR.

If you will be using a mandatory profile, it is probable that you will be assigning the same profile to several, or even all, of your users. In that case, you might specify a user profile path such as \\KEYSTONE\PROFILES\ALLUSERS.MAN. (Be sure to create the ALLUSERS.MAN profile, or users will be unable to log on.)

Specifying Logon Scripts for Two or More Users

If you want to create personal logon scripts for users, you can specify the file names in the Logon Script Name path by entering **%USERNAME%.BAT** (or **%USERNAME%.CMD**, as appropriate). Remember that DOS and Windows users can access only files that conform to the 8.3 format. If you use this technique, be sure that the user names you have selected do not exceed eight characters.

Creating Home Directories for Two or More Users

Figure 10.10 also shows the use of the %username% variable to create personal home directories. A user named Roscoe will be assigned a home directory on the KEYSTONE2 server in the directory \HOME\ROSCOE. When users log on, Windows NT Server assigns drive letter H to each user's home directory.

Note If your network includes DOS and Windows workstations, remember that those users can access only directories that conform to the 8.3 character-naming convention. User names can consist of up to 20 characters, but a file name in DOS and Windows can consist of eight characters at most.

If your server is configured with NTFS volumes, long directory names are supported, and you can use the %username% variable even though user names might exceed eight characters. Your DOS and Windows users might have trouble recognizing their directory names from their workstations because the long NTFS names are converted to an 8.3 format when viewed from DOS or Windows.

If your server is configured with FAT volumes, you cannot create directory names that do not conform to the 8.3 format. If any of the user names you have selected are longer than eight characters, do not use the %username% variable to create user profiles or home directories.

Stop Officially, this technique for creating home directories should work, but in my experience, it is not always reliable. Check things out with File Manager to determine that directories were created and properly secured. You might need to do part or all of the job manually.

Managing Logon Hours

The Hours button in the New User, Copy of, and User Properties windows enables you to restrict the hours during which a user can log on to the network. Clicking on Hours reveals the Logon Hours window shown in figure 10.11.

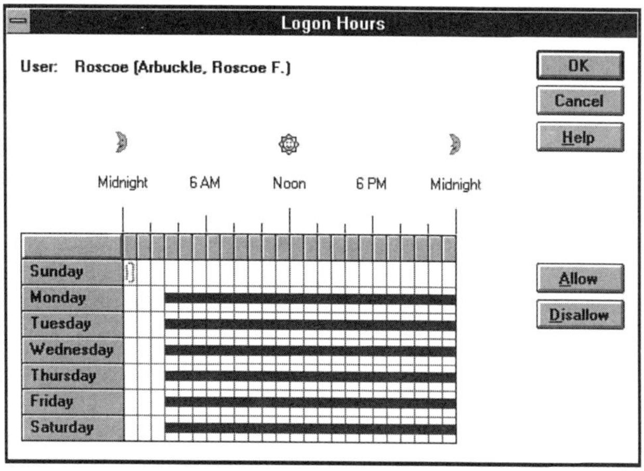

Figure 10.11

The Logon Hours window.

The Logon Hours window shows a weekly schedule of hours during which the user is permitted to log on to the network. Hours that are marked with a dark bar are hours when the user is permitted to log on. Hours that are cleared are hours when the user is not permitted to log on.

The example in figure 10.11 gives the user the following log restrictions:

- The user is permitted to log on daily from 3 a.m. through Midnight.
- The user is not permitted to log on between Midnight and 3 a.m. because this is the time during which daily backups are performed.
- The user is not permitted to log on on Sunday because that day is reserved for comprehensive network backups and system maintenance.

To permit logon during a time period, select the hours and click on **A**llow. The hours you selected are marked in black with a horizontal bar, indicating that these hours will be allowed after you click on OK.

To prevent logon during a time period, select the hours and click on **D**isallow. The hours you selected are marked in black, indicating that these hours will be disallowed after you click on OK.

You can select hours in several ways:

- Click on a specific hour.
- Click on a day label to select that entire day.
- Click at the top of an hour column to select that hour for all days.
- Click on the square above Sunday to select the entire week.

After you make your changes, click on OK to save the changes.

Managing Logon Hours for Two or More Users

When you select two or more users in the User Manager for Domains window, and those users are configured with different logon hours, clicking on H**o**urs in the User Properties window produces an information box warning you that `The selected users have different Logon Hours settings`. If you choose to continue, the logon hours for all selected users are reset. You then can configure new logon hours for all users with the procedure described in the preceding section.

Note Users of Windows NT computers are fully affected by the log-in hours you specify for their accounts. Users are permitted to log on only during hours allowed in their account properties. If they are logged on when their hours expire, the effect is determined by settings made by the Domain Administrator in the Account Policy window (described later in the section "Managing the Account Policy").

- Normally, users are allowed to remain logged on but they cannot make new connections.
- If the Administrator has selected "Forcibly disconnect remote users from server when logon hours expire" in the Account Policy window, users will receive a warning to log out. Users who have failed to log out when the time expires are disconnected.

Users of non-NT computers are not disconnected when the logon time interval expires, and they can continue to use the network without restriction. However, they are not permitted to log on to the domain during a restricted time interval.

Managing Permitted Logon Workstations

The Logon To button in the New User, Copy of, and User Properties windows enables you to restrict the computers from which users can log on to the domain. Clicking on Logon To reveals the Logon Workstations window shown in figure 10.12.

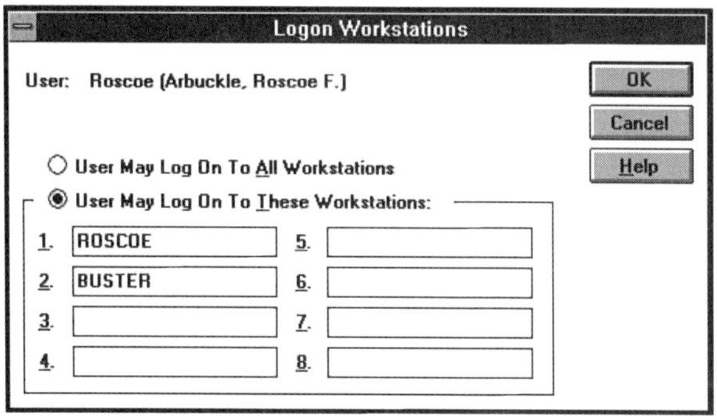

Figure 10.12
The Logon Workstations window.

By default, the User May Log On To All Workstations option is selected, and no workstation restrictions are in effect.

If you select the User May Log On To These Workstations button, you may enter up to eight workstation names from which the user is permitted to log on.

Managing Permitted Logon Workstations for Two or More Users

When you select two or more users in the User Manager for Domains window, clicking on Logon To in the User Properties window produces a Logon Workstations window that displays only information that is true of all workstations.

If you select one of the buttons, that option will be selected for all the users you have selected.

The workstations you enter replace the workstation lists that were established previously for the selected users.

Note Users of non-NT workstations are not restricted by any logon workstation properties you assign to their accounts.

Managing Account Information

The **A**ccount button in the New User, Copy of, and User Properties windows enables you to assign user account information. Clicking on **A**ccount reveals the Account Information window shown in figure 10.13. You use this window to configure two properties of user accounts.

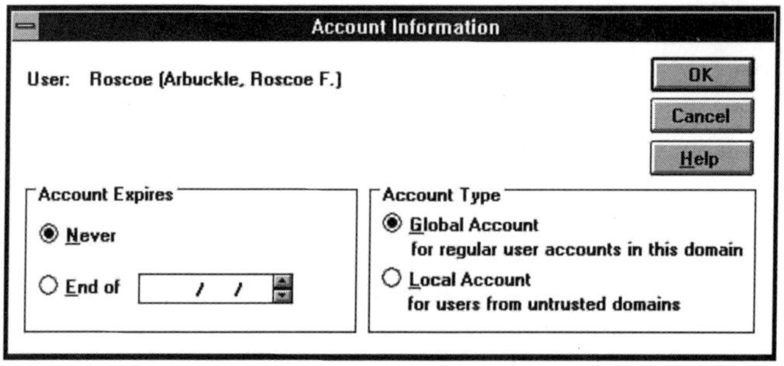

Figure 10.13
The Account Information window.

By default, user accounts never expire. You can configure an account to expire by choosing **E**nd Of and specifying a date. Automatic account expiration is useful in several situations. Two follow:

- ◆ You receive notice that an employee will terminate on a certain day, and you want to ensure that the account will become inactive at that time.
- ◆ A temporary employee requires access for a specific period of time. This might be a good use of the Guest account. Or, you could set up a user account named Temp to reuse in similar situations.

The Account Information window also enables you to specify whether the user account will be a local or global account:

- ◆ Select **G**lobal Account if you want the account to be recognized by other domains that trust the user's logon domain.

- Select Local Account if this user will be logging on to the domain from an untrusted domain such as LAN Manager 2.*x*.

Managing Account Information for Two or More Users

When you select two or more users in the User Manager for Domains window, clicking on Account in the User Properties window produces an Account window that displays only information that is true of all workstations. When workstations do not share a common configuration for a given set of buttons, neither button is selected.

Any changes you make in the window replace the previous settings for all the accounts you have specified.

Managing the Account Policy

The account policy determines password and lockout policies that affect all users in the domain. You can access the Account Policy window, shown in figure 10.14, by choosing the Account command from the User Manager for Domains Policies menu. Figure 10.14 does not show default settings. Instead, it presents minimum settings that I recommend you establish on your network.

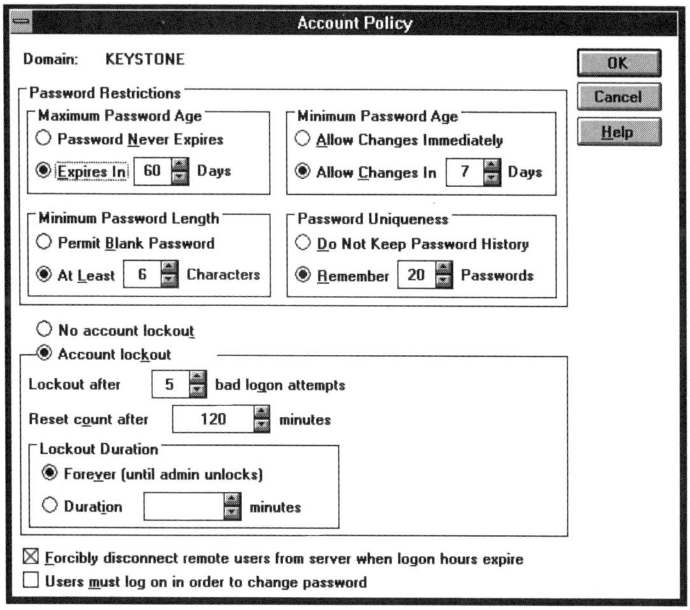

Figure 10.14

The Account Policy window.

Setting Password Restrictions

The account policy can define four password restrictions:

- **Maximum Password Age.** This setting determines how long passwords can be in effect before they expire. If you select the Expires In button, users are forced to change their passwords after the specified number of days. The default for this setting is Password Never Expires. I recommend that you allow a maximum of 60 days before users are forced to change their passwords.
- **Minimum Password Age.** In most cases, you want Windows NT Server to remember users' recent passwords so that they don't simply enter the same old password when their passwords expire. Unless you establish a minimum password age, some users simply will enter some dummy passwords until they can reuse their favorite old password. The default for this setting is Allow Changes Immediately. A minimum setting of seven days is recommended.
- **Minimum Password Length.** Short passwords are easier to guess or determine by trial and error. The default setting is Permit Blank Password. To ensure security, you should require a minimum password length of at least six characters.
- **Password Uniqueness.** If you choose the Remember option, Windows NT Server remembers the users most recent passwords. I recommend that you select Remember and set the number of remembered passwords to 10 or more. Otherwise, users tend to reuse the same, easily guessed passwords.

Setting Policy for Changing Expired Passwords

At the bottom of the Account Policy window, you see a box labeled "Users must log on in order to change password." If you check this box, a user whose password has expired will not be permitted to log on and must obtain assistance from an Administrator.

Setting Account Lockout Actions

Many passwords can be guessed if you give an intruder enough opportunities. To prevent someone from attempting to determine passwords by trial and error, establish account lockout properties. If you select Account Lockout, the following options are active:

- **Lockout after n bad logon attempts.** Generally speaking, if a user cannot log on after five attempts, it is due to a forgotten password.
- **Reset count after n minutes.** This field determines the interval (from 1 to 99999 minutes) in which the minimum number of bad logon attempts will lock

out the account. I'm in favor of setting the reset count to a fairly high value, even to the maximum value of 99999. A high value ensures that a user will contact an administrator when the account is locked out. In that way, you learn if a user is having problems, and may be tipped off to attempts to breach security.

- **Lockout duration.** If a user cannot successfully log on after five attempts, it is a good bet that the user has forgotten the password or is an intruder. If an intruder locks up a user's workstation, and you have set the reset count to a low value, the lockout condition will have cleared when the legitimate user attempts to access the network and both of you will be unaware of the intrusion attempt. Therefore, it is recommended that you set the value to Forever (until admin unlocks), forcing users to contact an Administrator when they have been locked out.

Restrictive account lockout policies are particularly important if your network can be accessed from outside your organization through a wide-area network or a dial-up connection. There is a myth that all computer intruders are exceptionally clever computer geeks who know how to crack their way into the most secure systems. In fact, most intruders are successful because system administrators have been careless in setting security policies.

Setting Disconnection Policy

At the bottom of the Account Policy window is the "Forcibly disconnect remote users from server when logon hours expire" option. If time restrictions have been established for a user account, checking this option instructs Windows NT Server to disconnect users whose time has expired.

Users of non-NT computers are unaffected by this option.

Managing Groups

The bottom portion of the User Manager for Domains window lists groups that have been defined in the domain. A number of groups are created for you when Windows NT is installed. These groups were described in Chapter 8, "Understanding User Accounts, Groups, Domains, and Trust Relationships."

Take a moment to examine the group listing shown in figure 10.15. You will notice that global groups are identified by an icon that includes a world globe in the background. Local groups are identified by an icon that includes a workstation in the background.

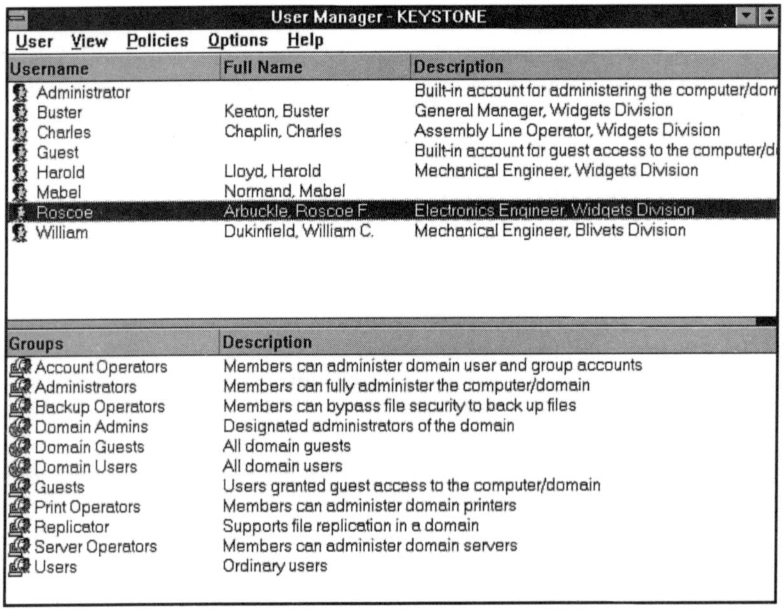
User Manager - KEYSTONE
User View Policies Options Help
Username
Full Name
Description
Administrator
Built-in account for administering the computer/dom
Buster
Keaton, Buster
General Manager, Widgets Division
Charles
Chaplin, Charles
Assembly Line Operator, Widgets Division
Guest
Built-in account for guest access to the computer/d
Harold
Lloyd, Harold
Mechanical Engineer, Widgets Division
Mabel
Normand, Mabel
Roscoe
Arbuckle, Roscoe F.
Electronics Engineer, Widgets Division
William
Dukinfield, William C.
Mechanical Engineer, Blivets Division
Groups
Description
Account Operators
Members can administer domain user and group accounts
Administrators
Members can fully administer the computer/domain
Backup Operators
Members can bypass file security to back up files
Domain Admins
Designated administrators of the domain
Domain Guests
All domain guests
Domain Users
All domain users
Guests
Users granted guest access to the computer/domain
Print Operators
Members can administer domain printers
Replicator
Supports file replication in a domain
Server Operators
Members can administer domain servers
Users
Ordinary users

Figure 10.15
Groups listed in User Manager for Domains.

User Manager for Domains can be used to create and delete groups and to add and remove user accounts from groups. Later, you will examine how to determine the rights that a group can exercise.

Adding a Global Group

To create a new global group, follow these steps:

1. Choose the New **G**lobal Group command from the **U**ser menu. The New Global Group dialog box appears, as shown in figure 10.16. Figure 10.16 illustrates an example global group.

2. The group name is required. Enter a group name of up to 20 characters in the **G**roup Name field.

3. The description is optional. In long listings of groups, descriptions can be extremely useful, and it is recommended that you make an entry.

4. Only user accounts can be members of global groups. To add users to the group, select the user or users in the **N**ot Members list. Then click on **A**dd.

5. To remove users from the group, select the user or users in the **M**embers list. Then click on **R**emove.

6. Click on OK to add the group.

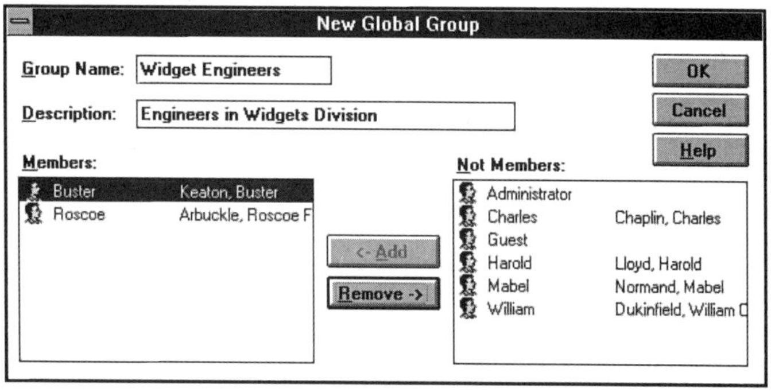

Figure 10.16
Adding a new global group.

Adding a Local Group

To add a local group, follow these steps:

1. Choose the New Local Group command from the User menu. The New Local Group window is shown in figure 10.17. This figure illustrates a local group. Group members include two global groups and two user accounts.

2. The group name is required. In the Group Name field, enter a group name of up to 20 characters.

3. The description is optional. In long listings of groups, descriptions can be extremely useful, and making an entry is recommended.

4. To add names to the group, click on Add. The Add Users and Groups window shown in figure 10.18 appears. Members of local groups can include users and global groups from the local group's own domain as well as global users and global groups from other domains that this domain trusts. You have several options in this window:

   - **List Names From.** Local groups can include users and groups from other domains that this domain trusts. To select names from a trusted domain, click on the arrow for this option and choose a domain from the list that is provided.

   - **Add.** To add a user account or a group to the members of the group, select the entry in the Names list and click on Add. The name is added to the Add Names box.

   - **Members.** To view the members of a global group, select the group in the Names list and click on Members. You can choose members of the global group to add to the group you are creating.

- **Search.** Because the list of domain names may be quite long, you might want to click on Search to find a particular entry. After you find a user or group, you can add it to the members of the group you are creating.

After you choose the names you want to add, click on OK.

5. To remove names from the group, select the name or names and click on Remove.

6. Click on OK when you have defined the group's members as you want.

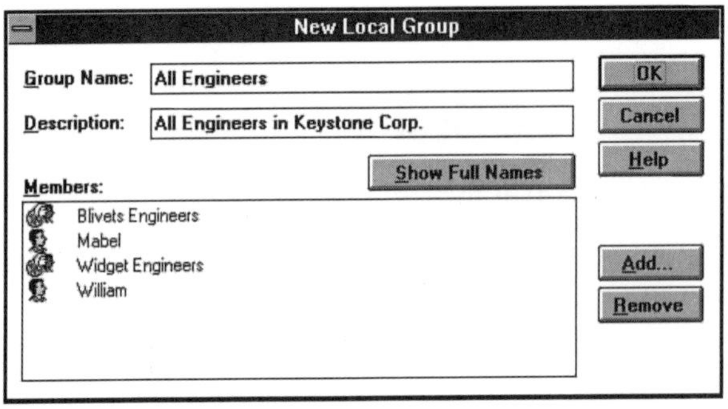

Figure 10.17
Adding a new local group.

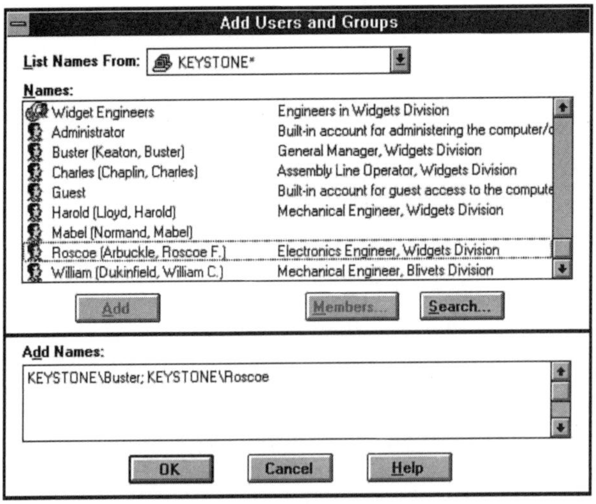

Figure 10.18
Adding users and groups to a local group.

Managing Group Properties

To manage the properties of a global or local group, double-click on the group entry in the Groups list. Or, select a group name from the list and choose Properties from the Users menu. The Global Group Properties window and the Local Group Properties window enable you to manage group properties.

Copying a Group

To create a copy of a group, select a group in the User Manager for Domains window. Then choose Copy from the User menu. A New Group window enables you to configure a new group with the same list of members. You will, of course, need to specify a unique name for the new group.

Deleting a Group

Groups that have been created by domain administrators can be deleted, but built-in groups cannot.

Deleted groups cannot be recovered. Like other entities in Windows NT Server networks, groups are identified by a security ID (SID). If you delete a group and then re-create it, the SID for the new group is different from the original SID. The newly created group does not have the rights and privileges of the old group, and it is not recognized by other groups that once recognized the SID of the old group.

To delete a group, follow these steps:

1. Select the group in the User Manager for Domains Window.
2. Choose Delete from the User menu (or press the Delete key). The warning in figure 10.19 appears.
3. Click on OK to delete the group or click Cancel to cancel the action.
4. A second box asks you to confirm your decision. Click on Yes to delete the group.

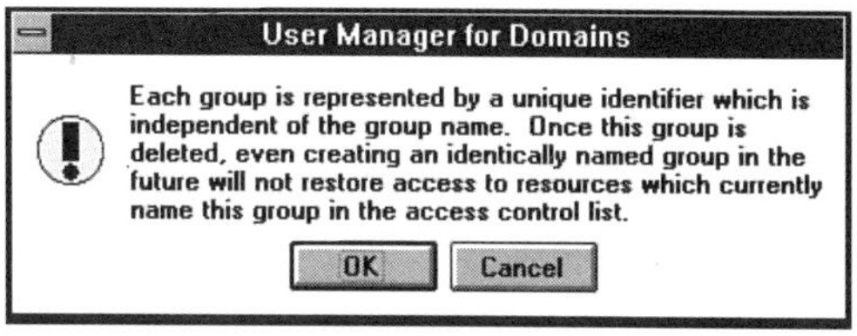

Figure 10.19

The warning you see when deleting a group.

Enabling Users in Trusted Domains to Access Resources in Trusting Domains

In Chapter 9, you were shown how to enable a domain to trust another domain. If the domain Widgets trusts the domain Keystone, users who log on to the network through Keystone can be given permissions to access resources in Widgets. Without trust, users would be required to log on to Widgets directly.

Setting up a trust relationship does not grant users in Keystone to access resources in Widgets, however, until an Administrator in Widgets has given Keystone users permissions in Widgets.

This is most commonly done by adding global groups from the trusted domain to local groups in the trusting domain. Here are some memberships you might set up:

- Add Keystone\Domain Users to Widgets\Users
- Add Keystone\Domain Adminis to Widgets\Administrators
- Add Keystone\Domain Guests to Widgets\Guests

You can create other global groups in trusted domains. This is the easiest way to give users in trusted domains access to trusting domains.

Suppose that you want to have one set of backup operators back up multiple domains. Windows NT Server does not have preconfigured groups for doing this, but you easily could make the arrangements by doing the following:

- Make sure that each domain to be backed up trusts the backup operator's logon domain.
- In every domain to be backed up, create a local group named Backup.
- Add the Backup Operators global group from the logon domain to the Backup local group in each domain to be backed up.

This approach can be used for any user group that you want to have access to a trusting domain. It seldom should be necessary to assign individual user accounts permissions in trusting domains.

The User Rights Policy

The actions that users and groups can perform depend on the rights and privileges they have been assigned. Rights and privileges are distinct sets of capabilities:

- *Rights* apply to the system as a whole. Because rights are assigned with User Manager for Domains, they are covered in this chapter.
- *Permissions* apply to specific objects such as files, directories, and printers. You will learn about permissions in other chapters, including Chapter 11, "Sharing Drives, Directories, and Files."

Rights have fundamental effects on the tasks that a user can perform on the network. In fact, rights can exceed the privileges that the user has been assigned.

Consider the Backup Operators group. Users in this group must be able to back up all files on the network—even files that they are not explicitly permitted to read. This capability is given to the Backup Operators group by assigning the Backup files and directories right.

The various built-in groups you have learned about are distinguished by the default rights that have been assigned to them by Windows NT Server.

What Are the Windows NT Server Rights?

Two categories of rights are defined: basic and advanced. The basic rights are listed here. After basic rights are discussed, the advanced rights will be examined.

Because the capabilities of the built-in groups are in part the result of the rights that initially are assigned to the groups when they are created, each right is identified with the groups to which it is assigned by Setup.

- **Access this computer from network.** Permits users to log on to the computer through the network.

  Administrators

  Power Users (Windows NT Workstation)

  Everyone

- **Add workstations to domain.** Enables users to create computer accounts in a domain.

- **Back up files and directories.** Allows users to back up all files on the computer.

  Administrators

  Backup Operators

  Server Operators

- **Change the system time.** Permits users to set the time on the computer's clock.

  Administrators

  Power Users (Windows NT Workstation)

  Server Operators

- **Force shutdown from a remote system.** This right is not implemented in current versions of Windows NT.

  Administrators

  Power Users (Windows NT Workstation)

  Server Operators

- **Load and unload device drivers.** This right may show as an advanced right if the server was upgraded to Windows NT Server 3.5 from a previous version.

  Administrators

- **Log on locally.** Enables users to log on to a Windows NT computer. Without this right, a user cannot log on to a computer that is running Windows NT Server.

  Account Operators

  Administrators

  Backup Operators

  Power Users (Windows NT Workstation)

  Print Operators

  Server Operators

- **Manage auditing and security log.** Permits users to specify resources to be audited and to manage the security logs. This right does not enable users to set up system auditing—an ability that is held by Administrators.

  Administrators

- **Restore files and directories.** Allows backup operators to restore all files and directories, regardless of any permission restrictions.

Administrators

Backup Operators

Server Operators

- **Shut down the system.**

  Account Operators

  Administrators

  Backup Operators

  Power Users (Windows NT Workstation)

  Print Operators

  Server Operators

- **Take ownership of files or other objects.**

  Administrators

Additionally, there are several advanced rights. Most of these rights are of interest only to programmers and will not be discussed. If you cannot control your curiosity, you can read about these rights in the *Windows NT Server System Guide.*

The following advanced user rights may be useful when operating a Windows NT network:

- **Bypass traverse checking.** Permits a user to traverse a directory tree even if permissions to access the directory have not been assigned.

  Everyone

- **Load and unload device drivers.** This right appears as an advanced right if the server was upgraded to Windows NT Server 3.5 from an earlier version.

  Administrators

- **Log on as a service.** Enables users to log on as a service. The Replicator service uses this right.

  (None)

Managing the User Rights Policy

You seldom will need to redefine the default rights assignment. Microsoft has done a thoughtful job of setting up the built-in groups. At the very least, don't try to outguess Microsoft until you have gained some experience with Windows NT Server.

Note One change you might need to make is to permit users to log on to the server computer directly rather than through the network. To enable a user to log on at the server, assign the Log on locally right. In the next chapter, you will learn there's a risk to granting users this capability because share restrictions do not apply to local logons.

To manage the user rights policy, follow these steps:

1. Choose the User Rights command from the Policy menu of User Manager for Domains. This action displays the User Rights Policy menu, which is shown in figure 10.20.
2. To include advanced rights in the Rights list, check the Show Advanced User Rights box. This seldom will be necessary.
3. Click on the arrow beside the Right box to display a list of rights.
4. Select the right you want to examine. As you select rights, the Grant To box shows you the groups and users who have been assigned that right.
5. To add a group or user to the Grant To list, click on Add and choose users and groups from the Add Users and Groups list. This list permits you to specify users and groups in the current domain or in trusted domains.
6. To remove a group or user, select it in the Grant To list. Then click on Remove.
7. To confirm your changes, click on OK. To cancel changes, click on Cancel.

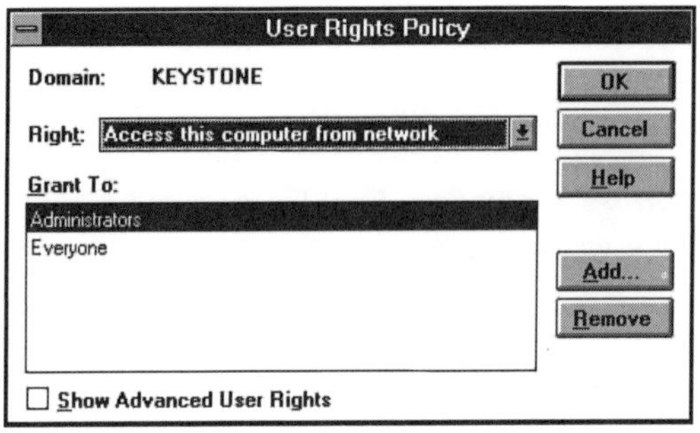

Figure 10.20
Managing the user rights policy.

The Abilities of Built-In Accounts

The special characteristics of built-in accounts are determined by two sets of capabilities:

- *Rights*, which can be administered as you learned in the previous section
- *Capabilities*, which are assigned by Windows NT Server to each built-in account and cannot be altered or assigned to new accounts

You have examined rights, and you should take a moment to examine the following list of capabilities, along with the local groups that possess those capabilities:

- Assign user rights

  Administrators

- Create and manage local groups

  Administrators

  Power Users (Windows NT Workstation)

  Users (can modify only local groups they create)

- Create and manage user accounts

  Administrators

  Power Users (Windows NT Workstation)

- Create common groups

  Administrators

  Power Users (Windows NT Workstation)

- Format computer's hard disk

  Administrators

- Keep local profile

  Administrators

  Power Users (Windows NT Workstation)

  Everyone

- Lock the computer

  Administrators

  Power Users (Windows NT Workstation)

  Everyone

- Manage auditing of system events

  Administrators

- Override the lock of the computer

  Administrators

- Share and stop sharing directories

  Administrators

  Power Users (Windows NT Workstation)

- Share and stop sharing printers

  Administrators

  Power Users (Windows NT Workstation)

CHAPTER 11

Sharing Drives, Directories, and Files

Unless users can access network resources, they have no reason to access the network at all. In previous chapters, you learned how to set up computers so they could communicate, and you learned how to set up user accounts so users could log on. Before users can benefit from the network, however, you need to share the network's resources with its users.

Sharing is the basic technique used by all Microsoft networking products to make directories and files on servers available to clients. The capability to share files in a workgroup setting is available in Windows for Workgroups and Windows NT Workstation. Workgroup file sharing is informal and is not always suitable for large numbers of users or for sharing critical files. It is difficult to maintain a high level of security and to back up files in a workgroup environment, for example.

Windows NT Server contributes the capability to share files in a robust, centrally controlled environment. An extremely high level of security is possible, and files are located on central servers where they can be accessed by many users.

Merely sharing files with Microsoft networking products is easy. Any user can learn to share files on Windows for Workgroups in a few minutes. Taking advantage of the advanced security offered by Windows NT Server is a more involved topic, and it is the focus of this chapter.

Windows NT Server security is based on four sets of capabilities that can be given to users:

- **Abilities.** Users gain these by being assigned to built-in groups.
- **Rights.** Initially are assigned to built-in groups but can be assigned to groups or users by an Administrator.
- **Shares.** Pools of files that are shared on the network and can be assigned share-level security.
- **Permissions.** File system capabilities that can be assigned to groups or directly to users.

Administrators seldom get deeply involved in rights and have no direct control over abilities. Your involvement with rights and abilities probably will be limited to granting users membership in built-in groups.

You will be heavily involved in sharing files and setting permissions, however, and the activities related to sharing and permissions are the focus of this chapter.

Understanding File Sharing

Until at least one directory has been shared, users are unable to access files on the server by logging on through the network. This section shows you a very basic example of setting up and using a directory share.

Figure 11.1 illustrates a directory tree on a Windows NT Server, as shown in the File Manager utility. Before users can access any of the directories through the network, the directories must be shared. One directory is shared. The icon for the \WINNT35 directory shows a hand, indicating that it is shared. This directory is shared only for Administrators, and the share was established when Windows NT Server was installed.

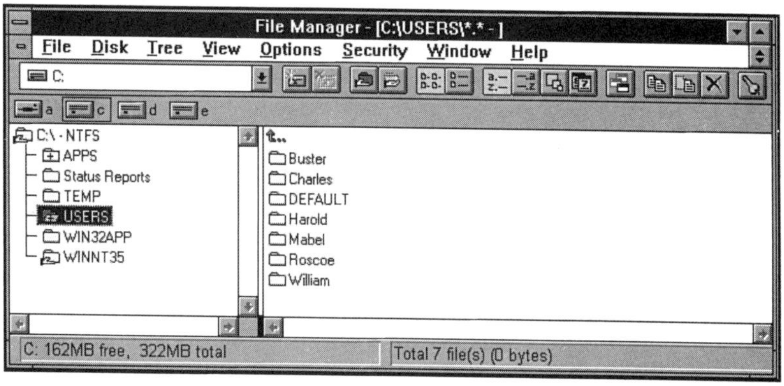

Figure 11.1

A directory tree in File Manager.

Note One other directory is shared by default. A share named NETLOGON enables users to access their logon scripts. Do not remove this share.

To share a directory in File Manager, follow these steps:

1. Select the directory to be shared by clicking on it with the mouse.

2. Choose the Share **A**s command from the **D**isk menu to display the Shared Directory window shown in figure 11.2.

3. In the **S**hare Name field, enter a name that will be used to advertise the share. Other information that can be added to the share definition is discussed later in the chapter.

4. If you want to limit the number of users who can access a share, select **A**llow and specify a number in the Users field. You might want to limit users to conform to software licensing requirements or to reduce activity on busy servers. Remember, though, that users must explicitly stop sharing a directory to free a share count for other users. Users tend to forget such housekeeping details.

5. Choose OK to save the share information. Check the File Manager display to see the new icon assignment for the shared directory.

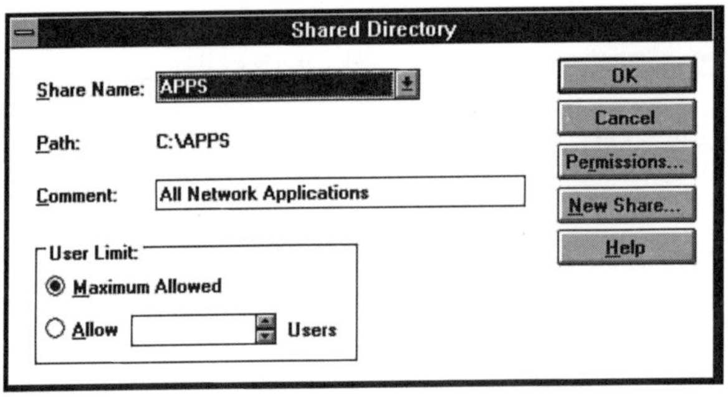

Figure 11.2
Sharing a directory.

Now that a directory has been shared on the server, users can log on to the server and access the shared directory. On a Windows client, this task is also performed with File Manager. (DOS and OS/2 users must access shared files by using the command line.)

To use a shared directory, a user must connect the share to a free drive letter. On most PCs, drive letters E through Z are available for use as network drives. After a shared directory is connected to a drive letter, the user can access the shared directory as if it were an extra hard drive on the local computer.

To connect a network drive, the user must run File Manager and perform the following steps:

1. Choose the Connect Network Drive command from the File Manager Disk menu. This produces a Connect Network Drive window similar to the one shown in figure 11.3.

2. First, the user specifies a drive letter that will be used. File Manager suggests the first available drive letter in the Drive field.

3. Then, the user can browse the network for available shares. Charles, the user in this example, can see two Windows NT Server domains (KEYSTONE and WIDGETS) as well as a Windows for Workgroups computer (BUSTER). Charles can open any of these items to look for available shares.

4. In figure 11.4, Charles has performed the following actions:

He selected G in the **D**rive field.

He opened the KEYSTONE domain by double-clicking on the domain icon. When KEYSTONE opened, the computers in the domain were displayed. In this case, one computer named KEYSTONE1 is in the domain.

He opened KEYSTONE1 to display the shares that were available. These shares are shown in the Sha<u>r</u>ed Directories on \\KEYSTONE1 box.

He selected the share named APPS to connect drive G to the shared directory associated with that name. The path is displayed in the **P**ath field.

He checked Reconnec<u>t</u> at Startup so that the connection would be reestablished each time he logs on.

5. After Charles chooses OK, he can access the APPS directory in File Manager by selecting drive G, as shown in figure 11.5. Notice that the subdirectory APPS displays as though it were the root of drive G.

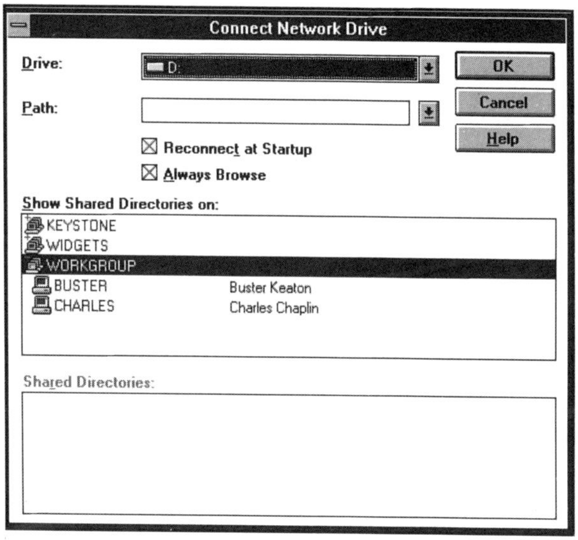

Figure 11.3

Connecting a network drive.

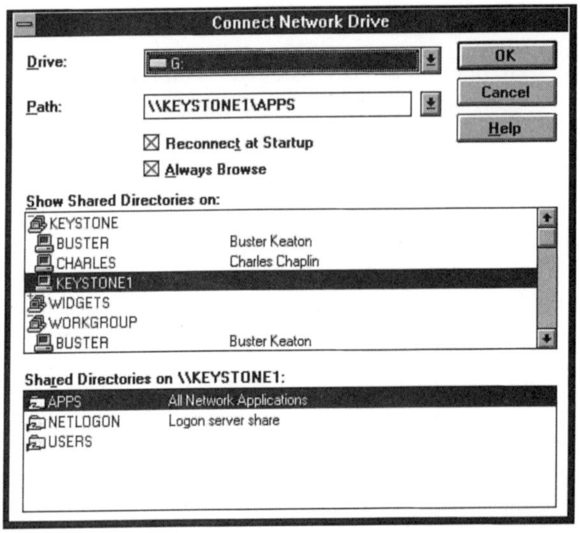

Figure 11.4

Browsing a directory tree to select a share.

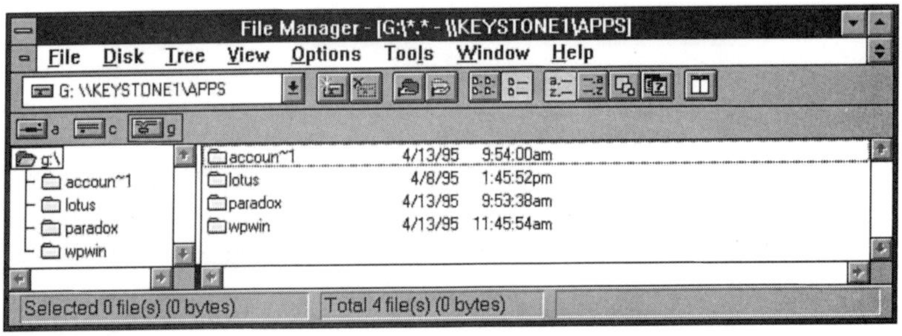

Figure 11.5

Accessing a connected network directory.

As you can see, sharing directories is extremely easy from the user's viewpoint. Additionally, users access shared directories using the same technique, whether the files are on a Windows NT Server or a workgroup computer running Windows NT Workstation or Windows for Workgroups. The network appears to the user as a large pool of shared resources, and the user doesn't need to know much about how the resources actually are being provided.

Using File Manager

If you have been using any version of Windows, you certainly are familiar with File Manager. File Manager is such an important tool, however, that I want to make sure you are familiar with its features before getting into the details of sharing files and setting file-system permissions.

If you have been using File Manager for a while, you can skip to the next major heading, "Managing Directory Shares." If you think you need a basic lesson about File Manager, read on.

Many of the actions in File Manager can be performed from menu commands or from mouse actions. In those cases, you are shown both techniques.

Displaying Drives

Figure 11.6 shows File Manager running on Windows NT Server. Several of the features of the window are identified. Below the toolbar, an icon appears for each drive to which File Manager is connected. At present, all the drives are local.

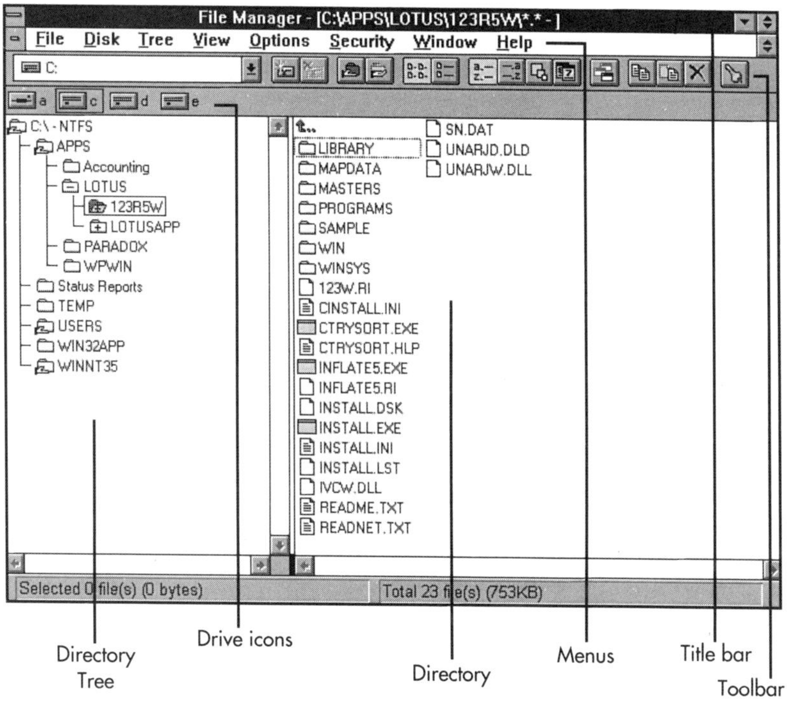

Figure 11.6

Displaying a drive in File Manager.

Beside the drive letter in the directory tree window, File Manager displays the file system used on the volume being displayed: FAT, HPFS, or NTFS. The volume shown uses the NTFS file system. Figure 11.6 illustrates the use of upper- and lowercase letters. If this volume used the FAT file system, you would see all file names in uppercase and all file names restricted to the 8.3 format.

You can use four techniques to change the drive that is displayed:

- Choose the Select Drive command from the Disk menu. Then select the desired drive from the Select Drive list.
- Press the Ctrl key and type the letter of the drive you want to display.
- Pull down the drive list in the toolbar by clicking on the arrow next to the box displaying the current drive letter. Then select the desired drive from the drive list that is provided.
- Click once on a drive icon in the drive bar.

Notice that the title bar for the File Manager window identifies the drive window that is displayed.

Moving and Sizing Windows

Figure 11.7 shows several points that you can drag with a mouse to control the size and position of a window. To drag, point the mouse to the control point, hold down the left mouse button, move the mouse to the new location for the dragged object, and release the mouse button.

Figure 11.7 also identifies five buttons that can be used to manage windows.

Figure 11.7

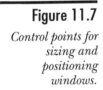

Control points for sizing and positioning windows.

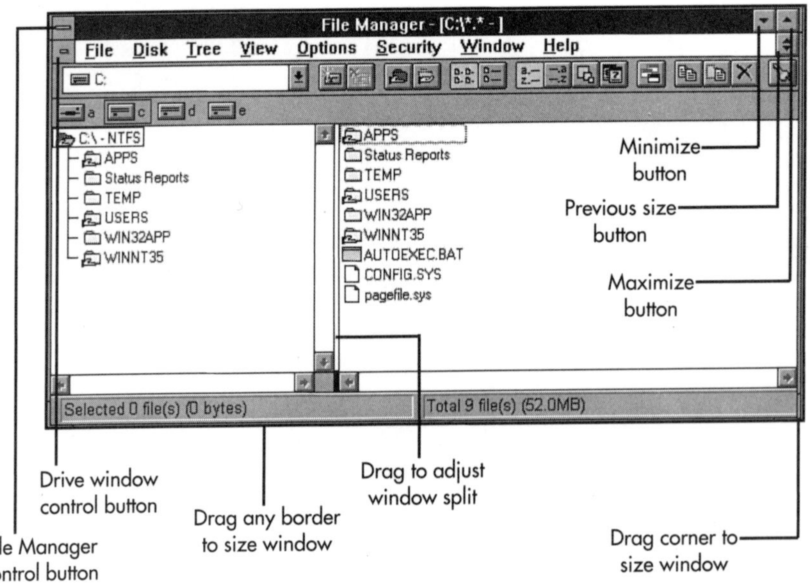

Opening Additional Drive Windows

You can have several active drive windows at one time, and it is often very handy to do so. Two techniques are available for creating a new window:

- Choose New Window from the Window menu. A window is added to the display. If the title bar identified the previous window as [C:*.*-], the new window will be identified as [C:*.*:2-]. You now have two windows displaying drive C.

  You can change the drive displayed by the new window by clicking on a drive icon or by using one of the other techniques described in the previous section, "Displaying Drives."

- Using the mouse, double-click on a drive icon. (If you double-click too slowly, File Manager reads it as a single click and simply switches the display to the new drive.)

If your current File Manager window is maximized, the window for the new drive will fill the available space so that you still see only one drive.

Cascading and Tiling Windows

If you have opened more than one drive window, you can display them together in one of three formats by using commands on the Window menu:

- Cascade displays all the windows overlapping one another.
- Tile Horizontally displays all open windows, arrayed one above the other. The windows do not overlap.
- Tile Vertically displays all open windows, arrayed side by side. The windows do not overlap. This view is shown in figure 11.8.

Selecting the Active Window

One window at a time is the *active window.* The title bar of the active window is highlighted. You can perform actions only on the active window, and if you want to work with another window, you must make it active. There are several ways to change the active window:

- Click anywhere on the desired window. This works only if the window is at least partially revealed on-screen.

- ◆ Choose the desired window from those listed at the bottom of the **W**indow menu.
- ◆ Press Ctrl+Tab or Ctrl+F6 until the desired window is made active.

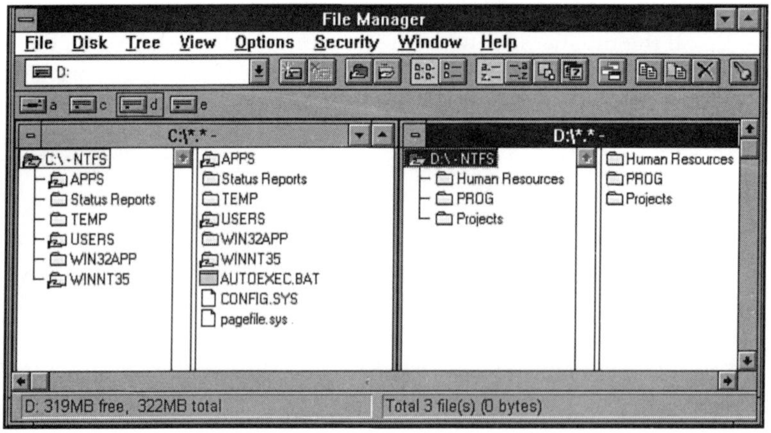

Figure 11.8

Drive windows tiled vertically.

Minimizing Windows

If you have opened several windows, it can be useful to minimize some of them to icons. Windows that have been minimized to icons are out of the way and will not appear in tiled or cascaded displays, but they remain quickly available when needed. Two techniques are available:

- ◆ Click once on the window's Control button and choose the Mi**n**imize command from the menu that is displayed.
- ◆ Click on the Minimize button. If the window has been maximized, you might need to click the Previous Size button before the Minimize button is displayed.

Maximizing Windows

You can enlarge a window to fill available space by doing one of the following:

- ◆ Click on the window's Control button and choose the Ma**x**imize command.
- ◆ Click on the window's Maximize button.
- ◆ Click on a minimized icon and choose Ma**x**imize from the menu that appears.

Closing Windows

You can close all the drive windows but one. To close a drive window, do one of the following:

- Select the window and press Alt+F4.
- Click on a minimized window icon and choose Close from its menu.
- Click on the Control button and choose Close.
- Double-click on the Control button.

Customizing the Toolbar

You can customize the toolbar in File Manager. You might want to add buttons for tiling windows, for example. To add a button to the toolbar, do the following:

1. Choose the Customize Toolbar command from the Options menu. The Customize Toolbar window shown in figure 11.9 appears.
2. Select the location for the new icon in the Toolbar Buttons box.
3. Select the button you want to add in the Available Buttons box.
4. Click on Add.
5. Click on Close.

In figure 11.9, the Tile Vertically icon was added to the toolbar. Icons are placed above the item you select in the Toolbar Buttons box.

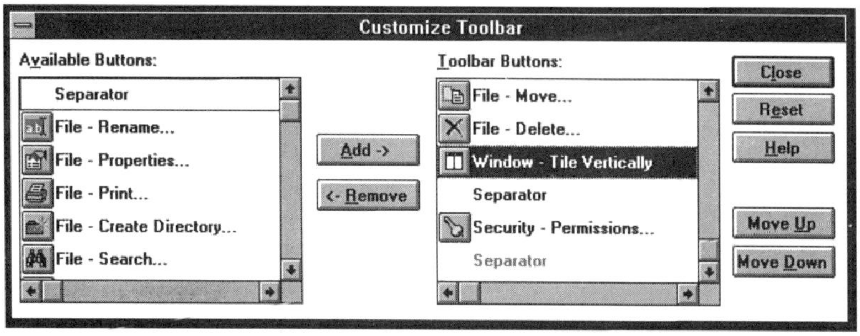

Figure 11.9

Customizing the toolbar.

Customizing the View

You might want to customize the manner in which File Manager displays directories and files. The View menu supplies a number of options that enable you to tailor your display.

Three commands specify whether File Manager should display files, directories, or both:

- **Tree and Directory.** Displays all files, directories, and subdirectories. This is the default view.
- **Tree.** Displays the directory tree but no directory contents.
- **Directory Only.** Displays only the contents of the current directory. The directory tree is not displayed.

You can move the split bar that divides the Tree window from the Directory window enabling you to display more Tree or more directory information. Two techniques for adjusting the way the window is split follow:

- Choose the Split command from the View menu and use the handle it produces to position the split bar.
- Point to the split bar directly and drag it with the mouse.

You can determine what file information will be listed with the following three options:

- **Name.** Lists the file names only. This is the default view.
- **All File Details.** Lists file names along with the files' sizes, creation date and time, and attributes. You need to adjust the split to display all this information.
- **Partial Details.** Enables you to specify which file details are displayed by selecting them from check boxes.

Five commands are available for controlling the order in which listed files are sorted:

- Sort by Name
- Sort by Type
- Sort by Size
- Sort by Date
- Sort by Type

The Sort by Type command reveals the By File Type box shown in figure 11.10.

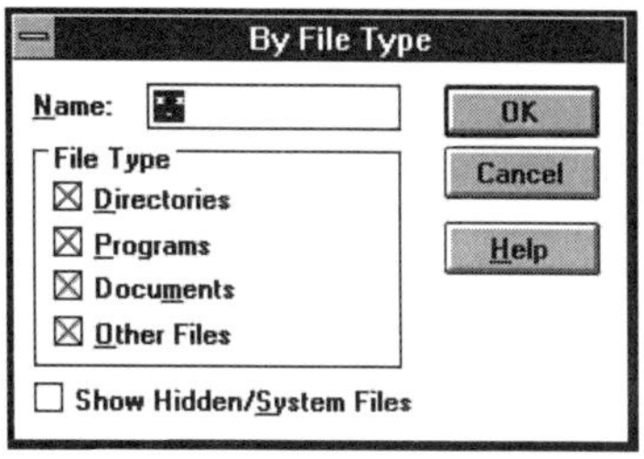

Figure 11.10
Specifying the file type for sorting.

This box can be a very handy administration tool. The options in this box follow:

- **Name.** Accepts a file name pattern that can include wild cards. Only files that match the file name pattern are displayed. Directories on network servers can fill up with large numbers of files, and you can use the Name box to focus your attention on a subset of all the files on the server.
- **Directories.** Determines which directories are displayed along with files in the directory contents box.
- **Programs.** Determines whether program files are displayed. Program files are files with EXE, COM, PIF, and BAT extensions.
- **Documents.** Controls the display of files that are associated with applications. See the section "Associating Files with Applications," later in this chapter.
- **Other Files.** Restricts display of files that don't meet the requirements to be programs or documents.
- **Show Hidden/System Files.** Determines whether files marked with the H or S attributes are displayed. As a system administrator, you often will need to examine hidden and system files.

Note If you check the Save Settings on Exit command in the Options menu, File Manager remembers your settings from session to session. Otherwise, File Manager starts up displaying the current directory of your current drive.

Viewing Directories

Before you work further with directories, choose the Indicate Expandable Branches command from the Tree menu. When active, this command instructs File Manager to mark with a plus sign (+) the icons of any directories that contain subdirectories.

Take a moment to examine the File Manager display in figure 11.11.

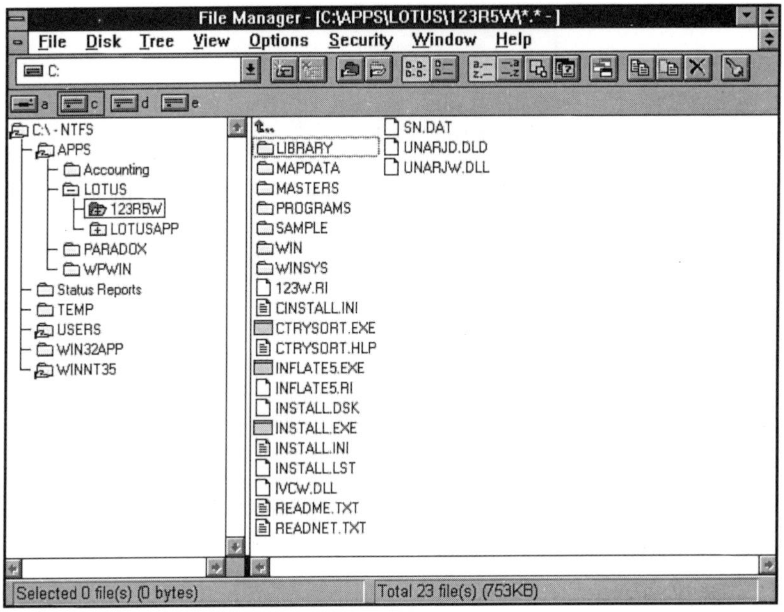

Figure 11.11

Features in the File Manager window.

Following are some items of interest:

- ◆ The icon for the 123R5W directory is marked with a + indicating that it contains unexpanded subdirectories. The icon shows an opened folder, indicating that the directory is open in the Directories area.
- ◆ The \APPS\Accounting directory has no subdirectories. Notice that the icon does not display with a +.
- ◆ Three directories are being shared: APPS, USERS, and WINNT35. The icons for these directories include a hand.

Expanding and Collapsing Directories

You can explore directories and determine which branches are displayed in four ways. In most cases, you are introduced to menu, keyboard, and mouse options:

- Expanding the branch one level:

  Select the folder icon of the directory to be expanded and choose Expand One Level from the Tree menu.

  Select the folder icon of the directory to be expanded and press the + key.

  Double-click on the folder icon.

- Expanding the entire directory tree beneath a directory (this can produce some large directory trees—try it on SYSTEM32):

  Select the folder icon of the directory to be expanded and choose Expand Branch from the Tree menu.

  Select the folder icon of the directory to be expanded and press the asterisk (*) key.

- Expanding the entire directory tree from the root:

  Choose Expand All from the Tree menu.

  Select the folder icon of the directory to be expanded and press the asterisk (*) key.

- Collapsing a branch:

  Select the folder icon of the directory to be collapsed and choose Collapse Branch from the Tree menu.

  Select the folder icon of the directory to be expanded and press the minus sign (–) key.

  Click on the parent directory icon in the file/directory listing. This icon is marked with two periods (..), which is Microsoft shorthand for the parent directory.

Tips on Selecting Files

- For selecting individual files and directories.

  With the mouse, click on the item.

  With the keyboard, press the Tab key to select the desired box, then highlight the desired item with the arrow keys.

  Several File Manager operations can be performed on groups of files. (You can select only one directory at a time.) Following are some techniques for selecting two or more files at one time:

- For selecting a range. If the files are listed together in a window, you can select a range of files. You may be able to use one of the sort or view options from the View menu to bring the files you want together. To select a range of files, first select a file at one end of the range, and then do one of the following:

  With the mouse, hold down Shift and click on the other end of the range. The entire range is selected.

  With the keyboard, hold down Shift and use the arrow keys to extend the selection range.

- *Extending a selection.* If files already are selected, you can add files one at a time with one of these methods:

  With the mouse, hold down Ctrl and click on the other selections.

  With the keyboard, highlight an item using the arrow keys and press Shift+F8. Highlight additional items and select them by pressing Shift+F8.

- For selecting files that fit a file name pattern. Choose the **S**elect Files command from the **F**ile menu. In the **F**iles box, specify a file name or a wild-card pattern. The files that match the file name pattern you specify are selected.

Creating Directories

To create a directory, follow these steps:

1. Select the parent directory that will contain the new directory.

2. Choose Cr**e**ate Directory from the **F**ile menu. The Create Directory dialog box appears.

3. Enter a name for the directory, as shown in figure 11.12.

4. Click on OK to create the directory.

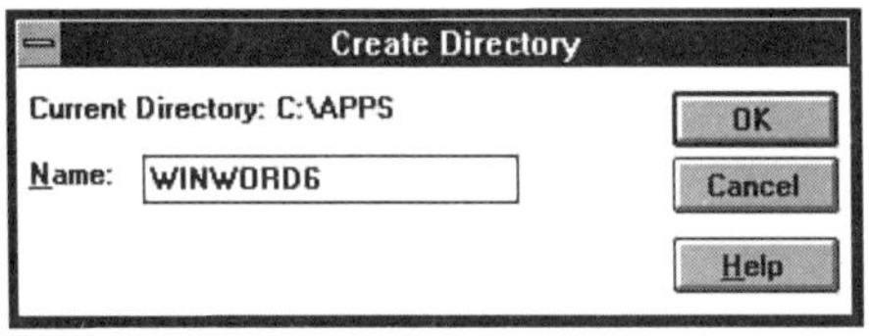

Figure 11.12
Creating a directory.

Naming NTFS Directories Files

The NTFS file system supports long file names, which can consist of up to 255 characters. The following characters may not be used:

? * / \ < > | :

Although NTFS supports upper- and lowercase letters, case is not significant. These file names are functionally identical: barney, Barney, BaRNey, and BARNEY.

Remember that your DOS and Windows 3.1*x* users cannot display long file names. When a DOS or Windows user displays a long NTFS file name, it is shortened and converted according to the following rules:

- ◆ All spaces are removed.
- ◆ Characters not allowed in DOS are converted to underscore characters (_).
- ◆ The name is shortened to the first six characters, unless a period appears in the first six characters, in which case only the characters that precede the period are retained.
- ◆ A tilde (~) and a digit are added to the characters that are retained. The digit is incremented if files are encountered that duplicate the first six characters.
- ◆ If a period is found in the long name, the first three characters following the period are used as a file-name extension.

continues

For example, the file name

Sales report for 10/94 by Sam R. Green

is converted to

SALESR~1.GRE

Because the resulting file names can be illogical or confusing, you might want to conform to DOS file-naming conventions on a network that includes DOS or Windows clients.

Deleting Directories and Files

To delete directories or files, select the items then:

- Press the Delete key

  or

- Choose Delete in the File directory

Copying Directories and Files

After you select a directory, file, or files, you can copy them to a new location by using menu commands or mouse actions.

To copy a directory or files from the menu, follow these steps:

1. Choose the Copy command from the File menu. This action displays the Copy dialog box shown in figure 11.13.

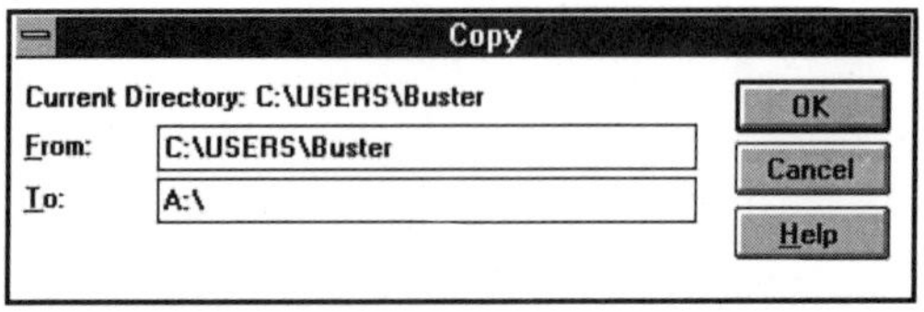

Figure 11.13
Copying files with the Copy command.

2. Edit the entry in the From field if desired.

3. Enter a suitable destination in the To field. This can be any destination that would be legal as the destination of a COPY command, including the following:

- A drive letter
- A directory
- A file name wild card if you want to rename files

You can drag selected directories or files to their destinations with the mouse. Be aware of the following:

- Dragging a directory or files to a different disk drive makes a copy of the items on the new drive. If you want to move an item(s) to a new drive, removing the item(s) from the original drive, hold the Shift key while dragging and dropping.
- Dragging a directory or files to a location on the same drive moves them. The directories and files are removed from the old location and stored in the new location.
- To copy files to a new location the same drive, you must hold down the Ctrl key as you drag the files.

To drag directories or files, you must be able to see both the source and destination screen. At times, you might need to open two directory windows in order to accomplish this. You can have two windows displaying the same hard drive if needed.

To copy or move a selected directory, file, or files with the mouse, simply drag the selected files and drop them in the appropriate destination directory. Use the Ctrl+drag technique if you want to copy on the same drive.

To copy directories or files to the current directory of a disk, you also can drag the selected items to the appropriate disk icon. This relieves you of the need to open a directory window for the drive. Be sure to confirm the current directory for the destination disk before you use this technique.

File Manager Confirmations

You eventually will get irritated with the number of times File Manager asks you to confirm your actions. You can turn off some or all of the File Manager confirmation messages by choosing the Confirmation command from the Options menu. The Confirmation window contains check boxes that determine whether you receive confirmation messages on various actions. Clear the check marks to cancel messages.

Deleting a directory erases the entire directory tree, starting with the directory you specify. You should leave Directory Delete checked in the Confirmation box to ensure that you don't accidentally delete a vital directory tree.

continues

> Administrators should never turn off confirmations for modifying System, Hidden, Read Only files! Doing so enables Administrators to remove without notice files that are critical to the operation of the network.

Managing Directory and File Properties and Attributes

Directories and files have several properties that are managed by Windows NT.

Files and directories also can be assigned several attributes that determine actions that can be performed with them. The attributes follow:

- **Read Only.** Files and directories cannot be erased or modified.
- **Hidden.** Files and directories do not usually appear in directory lists. You can direct File Manager to display hidden files by choosing the View/By File Type command and checking the Show Hidden/System Files box.
- **System.** Files usually are given this attribute by the operating system or by the OS Setup program. This attribute rarely is modified by Administrators or users. System files and directories behave as if they have both the Read Only and Hidden attributes. You can display the attributes in File Manager listings using the technique described for hidden files.
- **Archive.** Assigned by the operating system to indicate that a file has been modified since it was backed up. Backup software usually clears the archive attribute. The archive attribute makes it possible to identify modified files when performing incremental backups.

Managing Properties and Attributes for Directories

To display the properties for a directory, select the directory then:

- Press Alt+Enter

  or

- Choose the Properties command in the Files menu

The Properties window for directories is shown in figure 11.14. This window lists the directory name, the directory path, and when the file was last changed. You can use the check boxes to change the attributes for the directory.

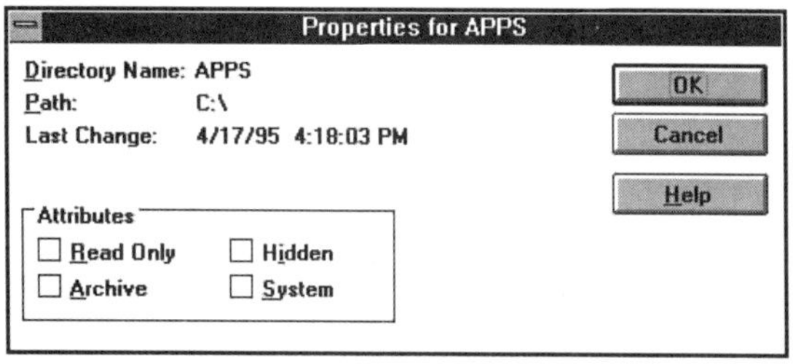

Figure 11.14

The Properties window for a directory.

Note If you mark directories or files with the Hidden or System attribute, or if you make some other changes, they remain in the directory listing when you return to the File Manager window. File Manager does not refresh the window until you change the directory. You can force a refresh of the window by pressing F5 or by choosing the **R**efresh command from the **W**indow menu.

Hidden and system files remain displayed if you have checked the Show Hidden/**S**ystem Files check box in the View/By File Type window.

Managing Properties and Attributes for Files

To display the properties for a file, select the file then:

- Press Alt+Enter

  or

- Choose the Properties command in the Files menu

The Properties window for a file is shown in figure 11.15. Not all files will show all the information displayed for the file in the example. You can modify the attributes for the file, but other information in the window is for your information only.

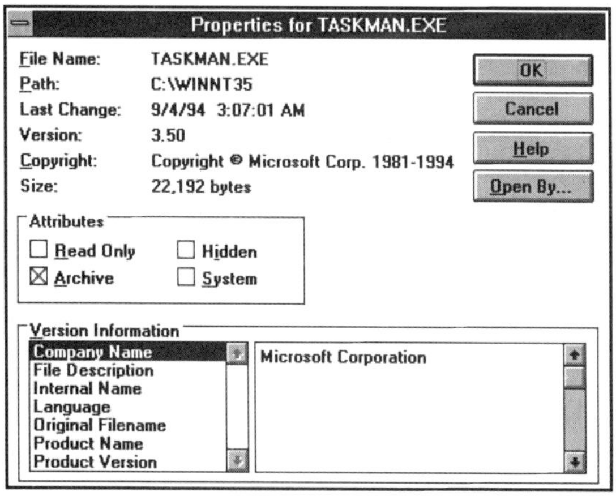

Figure 11.15

The Properties window for a file.

If a file is open and you click on the Open By button in the Properties window, File Manager displays additional properties for the file, including who currently has the file open.

If you select two or more files before displaying the Properties window, you are shown only the file attribute check boxes, which indicate the attributes the files have in common. You can change the attributes for all the files you selected by checking the appropriate boxes.

Managing Disks

You can format and copy floppy disks from File Manager. Hard drives can be formatted only by an Administrator using the Disk Administrator utility described in Chapter 16, "Managing Disk Storage."

To format a floppy disk, first insert the disk to be formatted. Then choose Format Disk from the Disk menu. Fill in the information in the Format Disk window and click on OK.

To copy a floppy disk, choose Copy Disk from the Disk menu, and then follow the prompts. When performing a copy to the same disk drive, you are required to swap disks only once.

One of the great things about Windows NT is that it is really multitasking so it doesn't lock up your system when formatting or copying a disk. Each operation offers you a Hide button that conceals its operation until it requires attention.

Searching for Files

Servers typically have many files in large directories on very large drives. If you had to remember where every file was located, you would be in trouble. Fortunately, File Manager provides a search option. To search for a file, follow these steps:

1. Choose Search from the File menu to display the Search dialog box shown in figure 11.16.

2. Enter a search file name in the Search For box. This can be a specific file name or a wild-card pattern.

3. In the Start From field, specify the directory from which the search should start, if it is not the current directory.

4. Check the Search All Subdirectories check box if you want subdirectories to be examined.

5. Click on OK to start the search.

When the search is complete, File Manager displays a Search Results window that lists all files that met your specifications, along with the directories in which they were located.

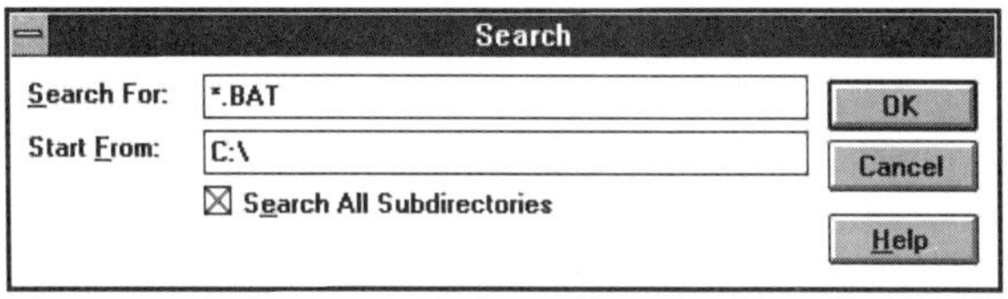

Figure 11.16
Specifying parameters for a file search.

Running Applications from File Manager

You can start applications directly from File Manager. An application file is any file with an extension of EXE, COM, BAT, or PIF. (PIF files are Program Information Files that can be used to configure the operating environment for an EXE or COM file. Running a PIF file automatically executes the program file specified in the PIF file.) Several techniques can be used to run an application from File Manager:

- Double-click on the icon for the application file.
- Select an application file icon and choose **Open** from the **File** menu.
- Drag a data file icon to the icon for the appropriate application file. This approach works only if both icons are visible.
- Double-click on a data file that has been associated with an application, as described in the next section.

Associating Files with Applications

You can associate file-name extensions with particular applications. Doing so informs Windows NT to run the associated application whenever you open the data file.

If files with the extension DOC are associated with Microsoft Word, for example, the Word word processing software is launched whenever you open a file with a DOC extension by double-clicking on its icon.

File-name associations are managed by choosing the **Associate** command from the **File** menu. The Associate dialog box shown in figure 11.17 can be used to display and modify associations that already have been created. The **Files** with Extension list shows you file extensions that already have been entered into Associate. In figure

11.17, the WRI extension was selected, showing that it is associated with the Windows Write program. You can associate the WRI extension with another application by choosing the application from the **A**ssociate With list.

You can associate one application with several extensions. However, a given extension can be associated with only one application. You can, for example, associate both the DOC and the TXT extensions with Word. You cannot, however, associate the TXT extension with both Word and the Windows Notepad.

Figure 11.17

Associating extensions with programs.

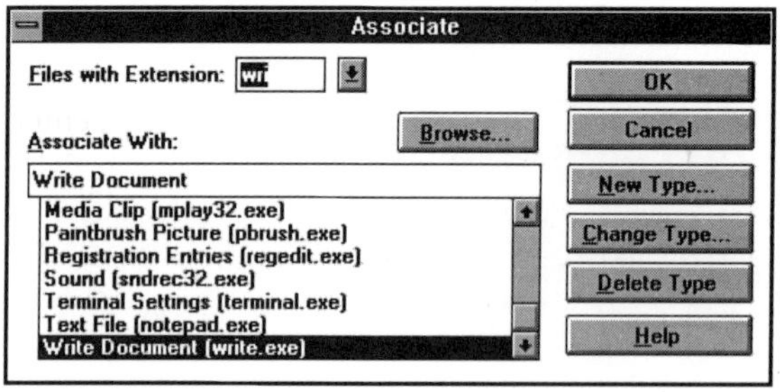

To create a new association, click on the **N**ew Type button. A Change File Type dialog box similar to the one shown in figure 11.18 appears. This figure shows how the Windows Write application was associated with the WRI extension.

Figure 11.18

Creating a new association.

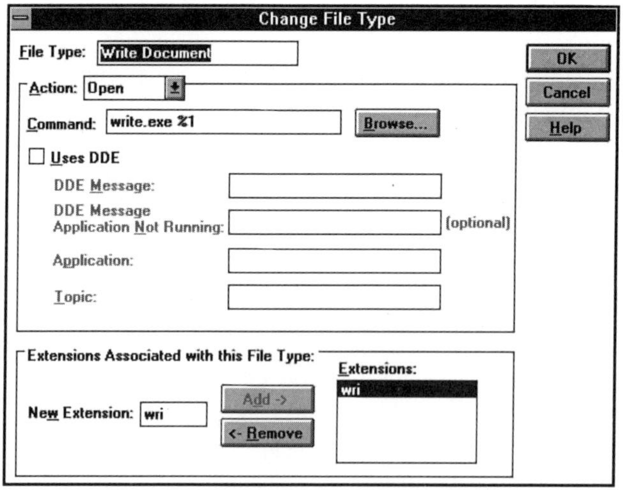

To define a new association, follow these steps:

1. Enter a description in the **F**ile Type field. Notice that this description appeared in the **A**ssociate With list of the Associate dialog box.

2. Specify an action in the Action field. An association can open a data file in an application or cause the application to print the data file. Choose Open or Print for this field. Not all applications can accept a Print request, but most should accept an Open request.

3. Enter the command line in the Command field. The %1 parameter following `write.exe` passes the file name to the application so that the file will be opened automatically. You can use the Browse function to locate the application program file and enter the path in the Command field.

4. Enter the DDE information if it is known.

5. To associate an extension with the application, enter the extension in the New Extension box and click on Add.

6. To disassociate an extension from an application, select the entry in the Extensions box and click on Remove.

Managing Directory Shares

Unless a directory is shared, it is unavailable to users who access the server through the network. Even Administrators, who have free access to all directories and files when logged on to the server, cannot access unshared resources through the network. Early in this chapter, you saw a brief demonstration of the way in which shares are created and used. This section covers the details.

Sharing works with FAT, HPFS, and NTFS file systems. However, you will find that the security you can implement with sharing is pretty limited. To enhance share security, you need to be able to assign directory and file permissions, which are available only with the NTFS file system. Directory and file permissions are discussed in the section "Directory and File Permissions."

Keep in mind some of the significant limitations of shares:

- Shares control user access only with remote logins. Shares have no effect on users who are permitted to log on locally to the server.

- Because shares have no effect on security for users who log on locally to the server, security on FAT and HPFS volumes is practically nonexistent for users who have physical access to the server.

- When you share a directory, you share all its files and subdirectories. If you need to restrict access to part of a directory tree, you must use file and directory permissions and the NTFS file system.

Sharing a Directory

To share directories, you must be logged on as a member of the Administrators or Server Operators group.

All file sharing procedures are performed in File Manager. To share a directory, use these steps:

1. Select a directory that is not already shared in the directory tree window.
2. Choose the Share **A**s command from the **D**isk menu to access the Shared Directory window shown in figure 11.19.

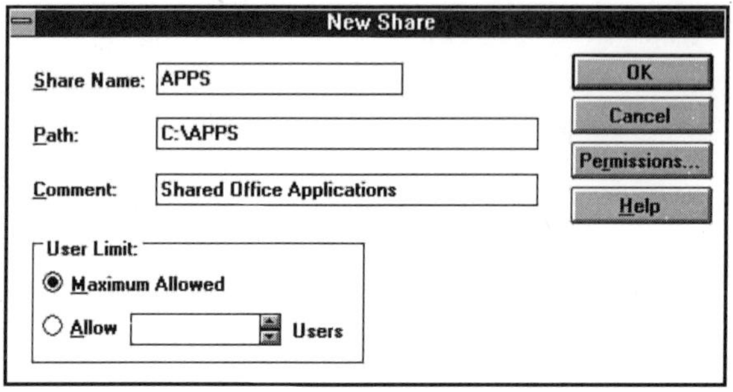

Figure 11.19
Sharing a directory.

3. Enter a share name in the **S**hare Name field. The name of the directory you selected is displayed as a default, but you can change the share name if desired. The share name can consist of up to 12 characters.

Stop

Share names that exceed the limitations of a DOS file name are not available to DOS or Windows users. Windows NT Server converts long file and directory names to a format that can be displayed on DOS and Windows clients, but it does not do so for share names.

4. Edit the path, if required.
5. Enter a comment. This comment can describe the share to your users in greater detail than the short share name.
6. Set a user limit. By default, an unlimited number of users can access a share, but you can set a fixed limit by selecting **A**llow and entering a number.

7. By default, everyone in the network has full control of the directory you share. If you want to restrict access, click on the Permissions button. Setting share permissions is described in the next section.

8. Click on OK.

The icon for the directory you shared now includes a hand to indicate that it is shared.

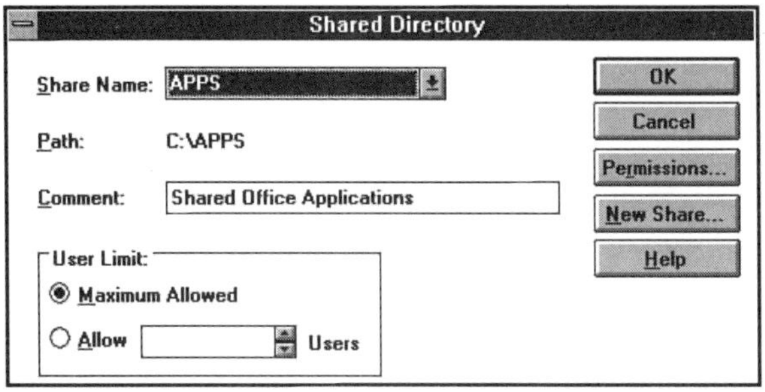

Figure 11.20
Changing a shared directory definition.

Managing Existing Shares

If you select a shared directory and choose Share As from the Disk menu, a slightly different window appears. The Shared Directory window enables you to modify all aspects of a share except the directory (see fig. 11.20). To change the directory, you must stop the share and create it again.

Creating a New Share for a Shared Directory

You might want to share the same directory more than once. You might have one share with full control for Administrators and a more restricted directory for users, for example. To add a new share to a shared directory, follow these steps:

1. Select the shared directory in the directory tree.

2. Choose the **S**hare As command from the **D**isk menu to display the Shared Directory window shown in figure 11.20.

3. Click on New Share to create a new share.

Each share must have a unique name. If you are creating two or more shares for the same directory, be sure your share names and comments explain what each share is for and who can use it.

Understanding Special Identities

You have been introduced to most of the entities that can be assigned permissions on Windows NT Server: local and global users, as well as local and global groups.

Permissions also can be assigned to five entities that Microsoft calls *special identities* or *special groups*:

- **Everyone.** Includes all users and can be used to assign permissions that all users in a domain hold in common, including guests and users from other domains.
- **SYSTEM.** Represents the operating system. Setup assigns initial permissions to SYSTEM that you should not modify. In fact, you should seldom, if ever, need to directly manipulate the permissions for SYSTEM.
- **NETWORK.** Includes all users who access a file or directory through the network. Rights assigned to NETWORK are active only when a user logs on remotely.
- **INTERACTIVE.** Includes users who log on locally to the server. Rights assigned to INTERACTIVE are in force only when a user logs on to the server computer itself.
- **CREATOR OWNER.** Represents the user who creates a directory or file. Permissions given to CREATOR OWNER for a directory are assigned to any files or subdirectories that are created in the directory. As a result, users are given the rights assigned to CREATOR OWNER for any subdirectories or files they create.

Of these five special identities, only Everyone and CREATOR OWNER apply to shares. Because share permissions affect only users who log on through the network; SYSTEM, NETWORK, and INTERACTIVE have no genuine role with regard to share security even though you can choose to assign share rights to those groups.

All special identities can be used with directory and file permissions, which are discussed later in this chapter.

Setting Share Permissions

Share permissions establish the maximum set of permissions that are available within a shared directory tree. Other permission assignments can further restrict access, but cannot add to the permissions established by the share permissions.

Four types of permissions can be assigned to shared directories. From most restrictive to least restrictive, the permissions follow:

- **No Access.** No permissions are granted for the share.
- **Read.** Users have the following capabilities:

  Displaying subdirectory names and file names

  Opening subdirectories

  Displaying file data and file attributes

  Running program files
- **Change.** Users have Read permissions plus the following capabilities:

  Creating subdirectories and files

  Modifying files

  Changing subdirectory and file attributes

  Deleting subdirectories and files
- **Full control.** Users have Change permissions plus the following capabilities (which are effective only on NTFS files):

  Changing permissions

  Taking ownership

These share permissions can be assigned to users; groups; and to the special identities Everyone, SYSTEM, NETWORK, INTERACTIVE, and CREATOR OWNER. See the sidebar "Understanding Special Identities," in the last section, for information about those groups.

To set share permissions, click on the Permissions button in the New Share or the Shared Directory window. The Access Through Share Permissions window shown in figure 11.21 appears.

When you create a new share, the default permissions give Everyone Full Control over the share. This default assumes that you will be assigning directory and file permissions when it is necessary to restrict users' access to other directories. If your server uses NTFS and you will be setting file and directory permissions, you do not need to restrict share permissions.

If you are using FAT or HPFS volumes, share permissions are all you have to work with. Here are some suggestions:

- Users often need only Read permissions in application directories because they don't need to modify files.
- In some cases, applications require users to share a directory for temporary files. If that directory is the same as the application directory, you can enable users to create and delete files in the directory by assigning Change access to CREATOR USER.
- Users generally need Change permissions in any directory that contains shared data files.
- Often, the only place you will permit users to have Full Control privileges is in their personal directories.

The permissions a user can exercise are cumulative. Take the case of a user who belongs to a group named Widgets. If Everyone is given Read permission to a directory and Widgets is given Change permission, the user can exercise Change authority in the directory.

As a general rule, create shares and grant permissions on a group basis. You will quickly become overwhelmed if you attempt to manage permissions for individuals.

Modifying Permissions

You can modify permissions easily from the Access Through Share Permissions window. To change share permissions for a group or user, follow these steps:

1. Select the shared directory in the directory tree.
2. Choose the Share **As** command from the **D**isk menu to reveal the Shared Directory window.
3. Click on the Pe**r**missions button to display the Access Through Share Permissions window shown in figure 11.21.
4. Select the entry in the **N**ame box.
5. Pull down the **T**ype of Access list.
6. Select the access privilege you want to assign.

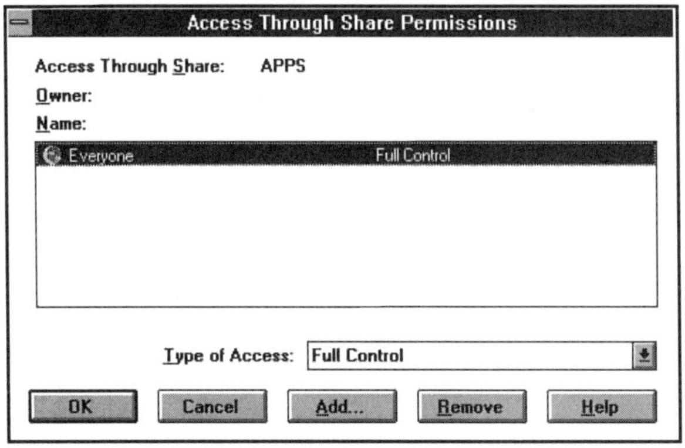

Figure 11.21
Setting share permissions.

Removing a User or Group from Share Permissions

To cancel permissions for a user or group, you can change the permissions to No Access or you can remove the group. Use the following steps:

1. Select the shared directory in the directory tree.
2. Choose the Share **A**s command from the **D**isk menu to display the Shared Directory window.
3. Click on the Pe**r**missions button to display the Access Through Share Permissions window.
4. Select the entry in the **N**ame box.
5. Click on **R**emove.

Adding User or Group Permissions to a Share

You can add a user to the **N**ame list. Of course, it only makes sense to do this if you have changed the privileges of Everyone from Full Access.

To add privileges for a group or user, follow these steps:

1. Select the shared directory in the directory tree.
2. Choose the Share **A**s command from the **D**isk menu to display the Shared Directory window.
3. Click on the Pe**r**missions button to display the Access Through Share Permissions window.

4. Click on Add in the Access Through Share Permissions window. This displays the Add Users and Groups window shown in figure 11.22.

Figure 11.22

Adding a group to a share permissions list.

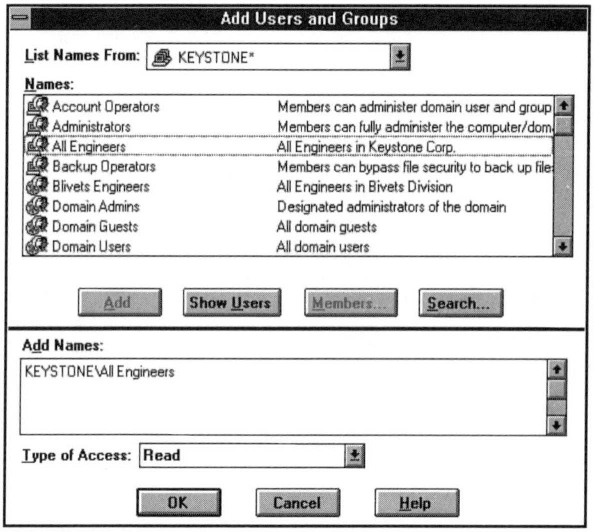

5. Pull down the List Names From list if you need to select a domain. You can specify share privileges for the following:

   - Local users in this server's domain
   - Global users in domains this server's domain trusts
   - Local groups in this server's domain
   - Global groups in domains this server's domain trusts
   - Special identities in this server's domain or in trusted domains

6. Click on Show Users to display user accounts in the selected domain. (Remember that it is not a good idea to assign permissions to individual users.)

7. Select a name to which permissions are to be assigned and click on Add. The name is added to the Add Names list.

8. Pull down the Type of Access list and select the access to be granted to the names you have selected.

9. Click on OK. The names are added to the Names list for the share.

Stopping Directory Sharing

To stop sharing a directory, follow these steps:

1. Choose Stop Sharing from the Disk menu. The Stop Sharing Directory window shown in figure 11.23 appears.

2. Select the share you want to remove and click on OK. That's it! The share is gone.

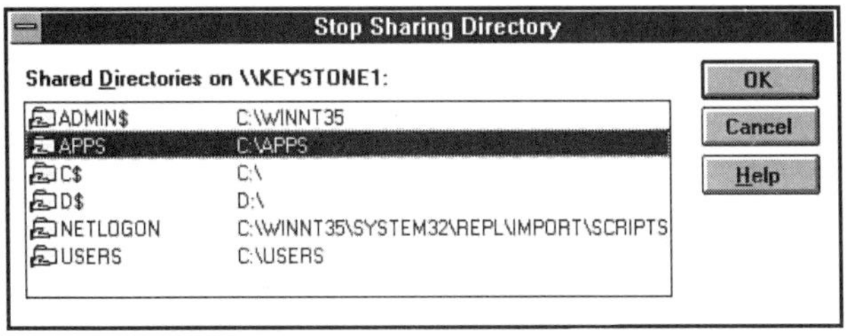

Figure 11.23
Stopping a shared directory.

Stop Obviously, you need to be careful. File Manager doesn't ask you to confirm your action when stopping a share, and stopping a share can seriously disrupt a network.

Using Administrative Shares

Look again at figure 11.23. In the Shared Directories on \\KEYSTONE1 list, you will see several shares that include a dollar sign ($) at the ends of their names. These shares don't show up when you list available shares with the Connect Network Drive command.

Windows NT Server creates several administrative shares to assist Administrators who need to access server drives through the network:

- An ADMIN$ share on each server is associated with the directory that stores the Windows NT Server operating system files—usually C:\WINNT35.

- An administrative share is created for each hard drive on the server. C$, for example, is an administrative share that is associated with the root of drive C.

To connect to an administrative share, you must type the path in the Connect Network Drive window, as shown in figure 11.24.

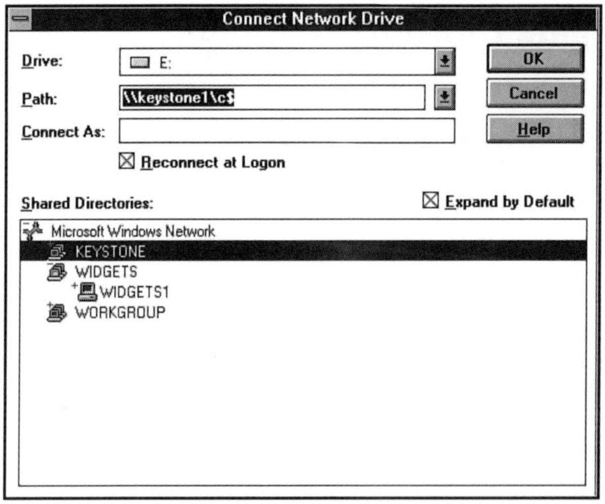

Figure 11.24

Connecting to an administrative share.

Administrators can use administrative shares to manage remote servers. After connecting to an administrative share, you can even add and manage shares on the drive.

You might need to create shares that are not publicly known. Any share whose name ends with a $ will not appear in the Connect Network Drive window. To use the shares, users must be aware that the share exists and enter the share path manually.

Note Don't be worried that users will discover administrative shares and get into the roots of your server drives. To access the root of a server's drive from a remote location, you must be logged on as a member of the Administrators, Server Operators, or Backup Operators group.

Connecting Network Drives

Users can connect a network drive to any share for which they have access permissions. A connection to a shared directory appears to a user to be a local hard drive.

Figure 11.25 shows how a shared directory appears on a user's local computer. The share shown is for the APPS subdirectory, which is not the root directory of the server. When the user connects to the share as drive F, however, APPS is treated as the root directory of F. No matter how deeply nested the shared directory is in the server directory structure, the same effect applies. As a result, users are shown a simplified view of what might be a very complex directory structure.

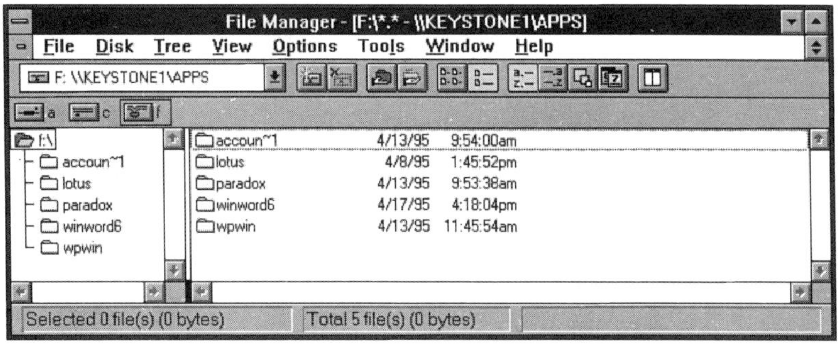

Figure 11.25

How connections to shared directories work.

Connecting a Network Drive

The technique for connecting to a share differs depending on the client operating system. DOS and Window are considered in separate chapters. Here, Windows for Workgroups is used as an example.

To connect a network drive, a user performs the following actions:

1. Choose the Connect Network Drive from the Disk menu to display the Connect Network Drive window shown in figure 11.26.

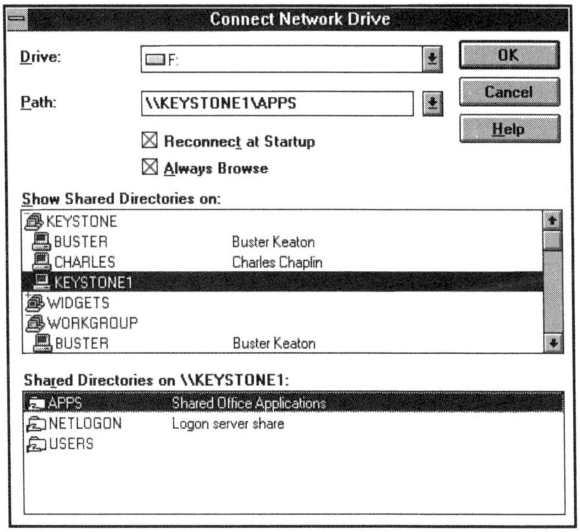

Figure 11.26

Connecting a network drive with Windows for Workgroups.

2. If desired, pull down the **D**rive list and select an available drive letter.

3. To select the **P**ath entry, use one of these techniques:

   ◆ Browse the network tree in the Sha**r**ed Directories box to locate available shares. When you identify the share you want, double-click on it to copy it to the **P**ath field.

   ◆ Type the computer and share name in the field. For example, type **\\keystone1\apps**.

4. If you want this connection to be established each time you log on to the network, check the **R**econnect at Startup check box. If this box is cleared, the connection will be for this logon session only.

5. Click on OK.

The drive letter specified in step 2 is added as an icon to the drive bar. This drive can be used as a local resource, subject to any permissions that might apply.

Disconnecting a Network Drive

To disconnect a network drive, follow these steps:

1. Choose **D**isconnect Network Drive in the **D**isk menu.

2. Choose a network drive from the Disconnect Network Drive window and click on OK.

Ownership

All directories and files in Windows NT have an owner who has a special status. Although a user usually must be an Administrator to manage permissions, a user can grant permissions for directories and files the user owns.

When you read about directory and file permissions in the next section, you will learn that a user can restrict directories and files he or she owns to prevent even Administrators from accessing them. This enables users to configure their personal directories for complete privacy.

Users cannot give away ownership of directories and files that they own. They can give another user permission to take ownership, however. This approach prevents users from creating files and then making them appear to belong to another user.

Administrators can take ownership of any file or directory on the network. This is necessary because Administrators must be able to access files of users who leave the company or change departments. However, because Administrators cannot return ownership to the original owner, they cannot casually access private files without leaving some evidence behind.

Directory and File Permissions

Directory and file permissions enable Administrators and owners to fine tune security on directories and files down to the individual file level. Directory and file permissions are available only on volumes that use the NTFS file system.

How File and Directory Permissions Work

Six individual permissions can be assigned to directories and files. Each permission has an abbreviation, which is included in parentheses in the following list. Permissions can be assigned to directories and files. The list describes the effect of each permission on a user's capabilities with directories and files.

- **Read (R)**
  Directory: Permits viewing the names of files and subdirectories
  File: Permits reading the file's data

- **Write (W)**
  Directory: Permits adding files and subdirectories
  File: Permits changing the file's data

- **Execute (X)**
  Directory: Permits changing to subdirectories in the directory
  File: Permits running of the file if it is a program file

- **Delete (D)**
  Directory: Permits deleting the directory
  File: Permits deleting the file

- **Change Permissions (P)**
  Directory: Permits changing the directory's permissions
  File: Permits changing the file's permissions

- **Take Ownership (O)**
  Directory: Permits taking ownership of the directory
  File: Permits taking ownership of the file

Assigning Standard Permissions

To simplify the task of assigning permissions, Microsoft has defined a series of standard permissions that can be used to assign useful sets of permissions in a single operation. Table 11.1 summarizes the standard permissions for directories.

Table 11.1
Standard Permissions for NTFS Directories

Standard Permission Name	Individual Permissions for Directory	Individual Permissions for Files	Explanation
No Access	None	None	No access to directory or to files
List	RX	Not Specified	List directory contents Change to subdirectories No access to files unless otherwise given
Read	RX	RX	List directory contents Change to subdirectories Read data from files Execute programs
Add	WX	Not Specified	Create subdirectories Create files No access to existing files unless otherwise given
Add & Read	RWX	RX	List directory contents Create subdirectories Change to subdirectories Read file data Execute programs
Change	RWXD	RWXD	List directory contents Create subdirectories Change to subdirectories Delete subdirectories Read file data Create and modify files Execute programs Delete files

Standard Permission Name	Individual Permissions for Directory	Individual Permissions for Files	Explanation
Full Control	All	All	All directory permissions All file permissions Change directory and file permissions Take ownership

Each of the standard permissions defines two sets of privileges:

- Permissions that will be assigned to the directory, which are shown in the second column of the table.
- Permissions that will be assigned to files that are created in the directory. These are the permissions shown in the third column of the table. When you assign permissions, you have the option of assigning these file permissions to the existing files as well.

When the third column states that permissions are `Not Specified`, it means that users are not granted any file-access permissions by the standard permissions. If you want users to have access to files in the directory, you can specify file permissions separately. However, under that scenario, users will not have access to files that are subsequently created in the directory, because permissions for those files will be Not Specified.

Windows NT Server also offers standard permissions for files:

- No Access
- Read (RX)
- Change (RWXD)
- Full Control (All)

How Working Permissions Are Determined

The operations a user can apply to a directory or file are the sum of the permissions the user acquires through the following sources:

- Membership in a special identity (special group)

- All group memberships
- Permissions directly assigned to the user

Here is an example. The Widgets division maintains a directory of engineering specification documents named \SPECS. Several groups have privileges in \SPECS:

- **Engineers.** Members have read privileges (R)(R)
- **Sr_Eng.** Members can add and update documents (W)(W)
- **Eng_Mgt.** Members can delete documents (D)(Not Specified)

Mabel is a member of all three groups. In addition, her user account has been given the privilege (X)(D) so that she can administer the directory. Consequently, her privileges in the \SPECS directory are the sum of all the following:

```
(R     )(R     ) from the group Engineers
( W    )( W    ) from the group Sr_Eng
(     D)(      ) from the group Eng_Mgt
(   X  )(     D) from assignment to Mabel's user account
```

Mabel's working privileges to files in the directory are (RWXD)(RWD).

Any permissions a user has for a file augment permissions the user has from directories.

There is one big exception to all of this: the No Access standard permission. If a user is assigned No Access permissions in any group, all permissions for the directory are revoked, even if the user is an Administrator. Try it. Log on as an Administrator and assign the No Access permission to Everyone for the USERS directory. Even as an Administrator, you will be unable to access the directory.

If the No Access permission has been used to lock users out of a directory, only the owner can remove the No Access permission. An Administrator can take ownership of the directory and remove the No Access permission if necessary.

Assigning Standard Directory Permissions

To assign standard permissions for a directory, use the following steps:

1. Select the directory in the File Manager directory tree.
2. Choose Permissions from the Security menu (or select the Security icon in the icon bar—the one that looks like a key). The Directory Permissions window shown in figure 11.27 appears.

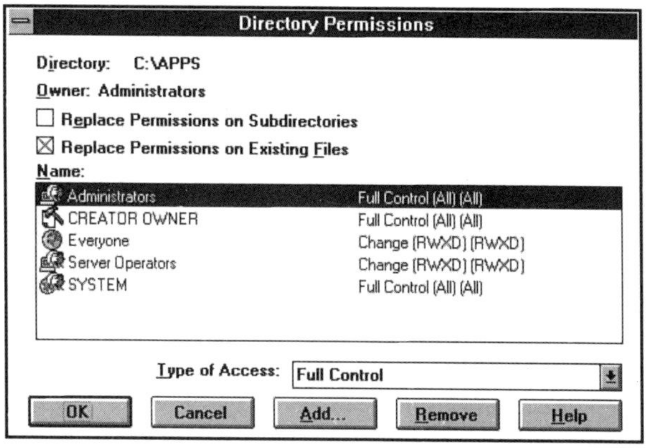

Figure 11.27

Managing directory permissions.

The example in figure 11.27 shows a newly created directory named APPS. New directories inherit the permissions of the directory in which they were created. APPS was created in the root directory, which is configured with default permissions.

3. To change permissions for a group or user that is already in the Name box,

   - Select the group or user.

   - Pull down the Type of Access list and select one of the standard permissions. This list is shown in figure 11.28.

4. To add a group or user:

   a. Choose Add to display the Add Users and Groups window shown in figure 11.29.

   b. To display names from another domain, pull down the List Names From list and choose a domain.

   c. To show users in the Names list, click on the Show Users button.

   d. Double-click on the groups or users to be added from the Names list. Each group or user you select is added to the Add Names list.

   e. Select standard permissions from the Type of Access list. All names in the Add Names list will receive the same standard privileges.

   f. Click on OK to add the names and return to the Directory Permissions window.

Figure 11.28

Selecting a type of access.

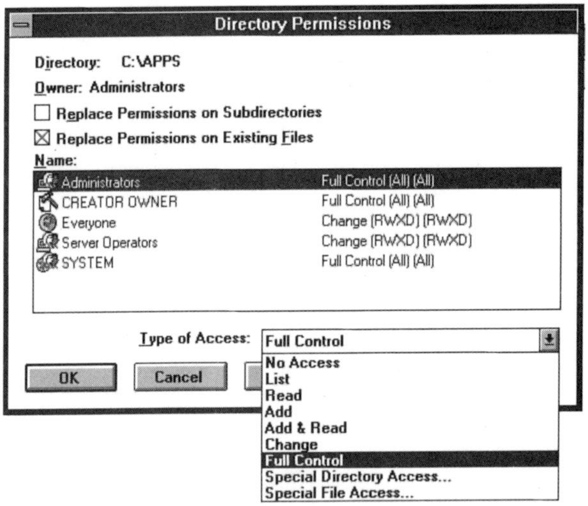

Figure 11.29

Adding a group to directory permissions.

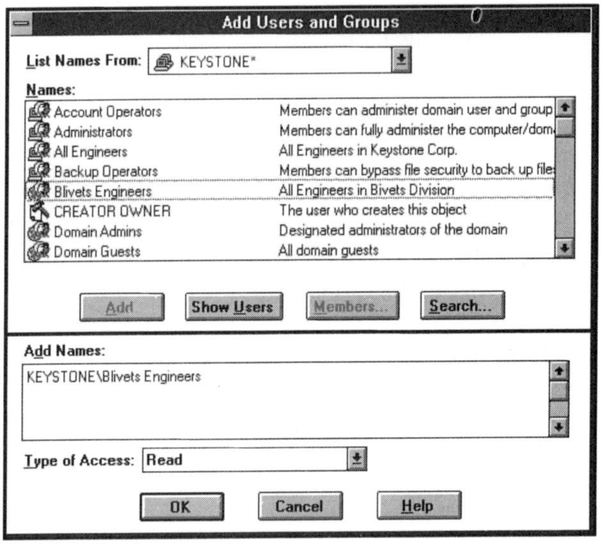

5. If you want existing files in the current subdirectory to be assigned the file permissions you have specified, check the Replace Permissions on Existing **F**iles box in the Directory Permissions window. (If you do not choose this option, files retain the permission assignments they already have.)

6. If you want to assign the rights you have selected to all subdirectories of this directory, check the R**e**place Permissions on Subdirectories box. (If you do not choose this option, subdirectories retain the permission assignments they already have.)

7. Click on OK to save the directory permissions.

Assigning Special Access Permissions

When the Directory Permissions window is displayed, you can assign special directory and file access permissions to any name in the **N**ame list.

To assign directory access permissions, use these steps:

1. Pull down the **T**ype of Access list and choose Special Directory Access to display the Special Directory Access window shown in figure 11.30. The currently assigned privileges are checked.

2. Check the boxes of the privileges you want to assign.

3. Click on OK to assign the checked privileges.

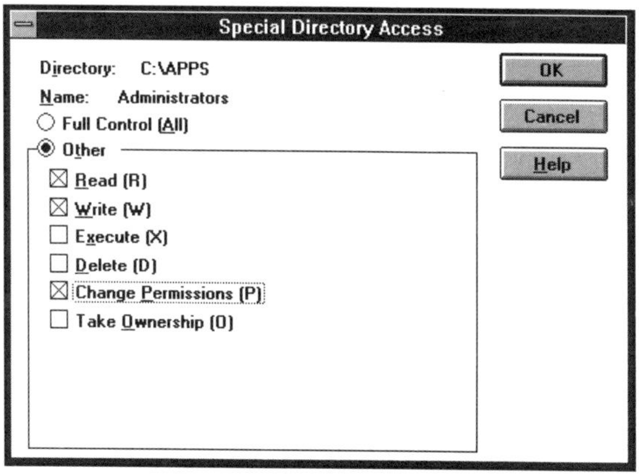

Figure 11.30

Assigning special directory access permissions.

To assign file access permissions, follow these steps:

1. Pull down the Type of Access list and choose Special File Access to display the Special File Access window shown in figure 11.31. The currently assigned privileges are checked.

2. Check the boxes of the privileges you want to assign.

3. Click on OK to assign the checked privileges.

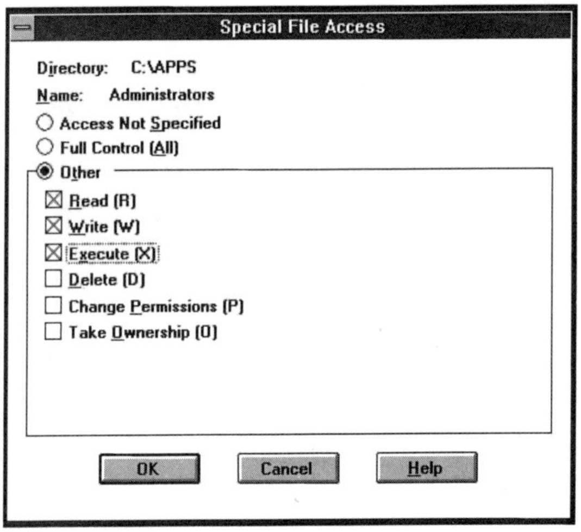

Figure 11.31
Assigning special file-access permissions.

Managing File Permissions

File permissions are managed in much the same way as directories. Follow these steps:

1. Select the file or files you want to manage. Unlike directories, you can assign privileges to multiple files at one time.

2. Choose the **P**ermissions command from the **S**ecurity menu or select the Permissions icon in the icon bar.

3. Manage **n**ames and permission assignments as described for directories. The Special File Access choice in the Type of Access list enables you to specify custom file privileges. If you have selected two or more files, permissions that are not held in common by all selected files are shown with gray Xs.

Changing Ownership of Directories and Files

Directory and file owners cannot give away ownership, but can grant permission to other users to take ownership. In emergencies, Administrators can take ownership of directories and files owned by users.

If you see that a user or group has All privileges for a file or a directory, remember that All includes the Take Ownership privilege.

Giving Users the Right to Take Ownership

Use the procedures described for assigning special directory or file access permissions. Assign the Take Ownership right to the group or user you want to have that privilege.

Taking Ownership

To take ownership, follow these steps:

1. Select the directory or file that you want to own.

2. Choose Owner from the Security menu.

3. If you do not have Take Ownership privileges for the directory or file, you see the message shown in figure 11.32. If you want to take ownership, click on Yes. To cancel, click No.

   The Owner dialog box shown in figure 11.33 appears, showing who currently owns the item you selected.

4. To take ownership, click on Take Ownership.

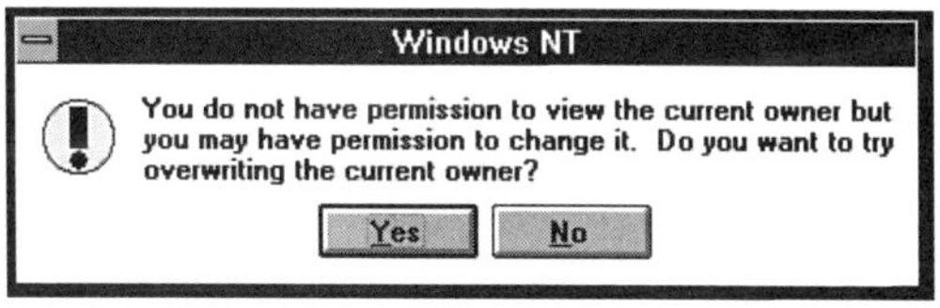

Figure 11.32
Overriding permissions to take ownership.

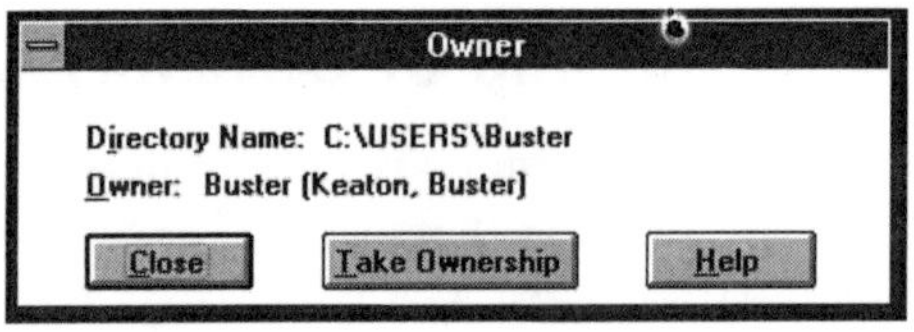

Figure 11.33
Taking ownership of a directory.

Using No Access Permissions

Remember, if you assign No Access privileges to a directory or file for any group a user belongs to, the user loses all privileges for the directory. No Access overrides permissions from other groups and permissions made directly to the user's own user account. Even Administrators lose access to directories if a No Access permission has been assigned. Obviously, No Access should be used with caution. It often is preferable to revoke permissions instead of using No Access because revoking permissions from one group does not affect permissions for another group.

Use No Access when you want to be absolutely certain that users do not have access, but be aware of potential side-effects.

Default Directory Permissions

When Windows NT Server is installed, default permissions are assigned to all directories on the server. You seldom will need to change these permissions. Because newly created directories inherit privileges from the directory in which they were created, it is useful for you to be aware of the default permissions created during system setup. Here is a summary:

- \(Root directory of an NTFS volume)

Administrators	Full Control
Server Operators	Change
Everyone	Change
CREATOR OWNER	Full Control
SYSTEM	Full Control

- \SYSTEM32

Administrators	Full Control
Server Operators	Change
Everyone	Change
CREATOR OWNER	Full Control
SYSTEM	Full Control

- \SYSTEM32\C0NFIG

Administrators	Full Control
Everyone	List
CREATOR OWNER	Full Control
SYSTEM	Full Control

- \SYSTEM32\DRIVERS

Administrators	Full Control
Server Operators	Full Control
Everyone	Read
CREATOR OWNER	Full Control
SYSTEM	Full Control

- \SYSTEM32\SPOOL

Administrators	Full Control
Server Operators	Full Control
Print Operators	Full Control
Everyone	Read
CREATOR OWNER	Full Control
SYSTEM	Full Control

- \SYSTEM32\REPL

Administrators	Full Control
Server Operators	Full Control
Everyone	Read
CREATOR OWNER	Full Control
SYSTEM	Full Control

- \SYSTEM32\REPL\IMPORT

Administrators	Full Control
Server Operators	Change
Everyone	Read
CREATOR OWNER	Change
Replicator	Change
NETWORK	No Access
SYSTEM	Full Control

◆ \SYSTEM32\REPL\EXPORT

Administrators	Full Control
Server Operators	Change
CREATOR OWNER	Full Control
Replicator	Read
SYSTEM	Full Control

◆ \USERS

Administrators	RWXD
Account Operators	RWXD
Everyone	List
SYSTEM	Full Control

◆ \USERS\DEFAULT

Everyone	RWX
CREATOR OWNER	Full Control
SYSTEM	Full Control

◆ \WIN32APP

Administrators	Full Control
Server Operators	Full Control
CREATOR OWNER	Full Control
Everyone	Read

◆ \TEMP

Administrators	Full Control
Server Operators	Change
CREATOR OWNER	Full Control
Everyone	Change
SYSTEM	Full Control

You probably are surprised that groups like CREATOR OWNER and Everyone have privileges dispersed throughout these directories. Remember that these privileges can be exercised by network users only if they access a directory through a share. If you don't share a directory where Everyone has permissions, they cannot exercise their permissions in the directory.

This restriction does not apply to users who can log on to the server directly, however. If you will be permitting non-Administrators to log on to the server computer, you should consider adjusting permissions, especially to Everyone.

Examples of Directory and File Permissions

Figure 11.34 shows a simplified directory tree that illustrates how shares and permissions can be set up. Because permissions can be assigned only to NTFS volumes, these examples apply only to servers that are using the NTFS file system.

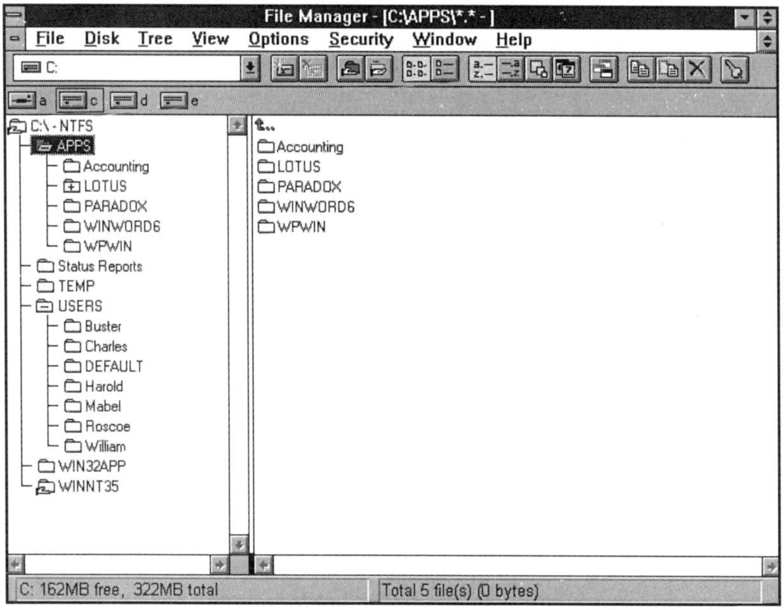

Figure 11.34
Example of a directory tree.

This directory tree has several directories that will be shared on the network:

- **\APPS.** The location for all shared application files. All these applications are capable of being shared on a network. Users will need to be permitted to read files from these directories, but personalized files will be kept in their home directories or on their C drives. Therefore, only Read and Execute permissions are required and the standard List permission can be assigned.

- **\APPS\Accounting.** Contains the company's accounting application. Of course, only members of the accounting department should have access, so an Accounting group will be created and given appropriate permissions. Permissions are revoked for all other users.

- **\USERS.** Contains a personal directory for each user. Personal directories are secured so that only the directory owner has access to the files.

- **\Status Reports.** A directory in which all employees maintain their weekly status reports. Each user must have the capability to modify his or her own files. Only engineering managers should be permitted to read the reports.

The first step in securing the directory tree is to create the following groups:

- **Accounting.** Membership is restricted to the accounting staff.
- **Eng Managers.** Includes all managers who should have access to status reports.

Users of the \APPS directory require only List permissions. They will read and execute files, but they will not create or modify files. Figure 11.35 shows the permissions assigned for \APPS. Notice that the check boxes are selected so that files and subdirectories inherit the appropriate permissions.

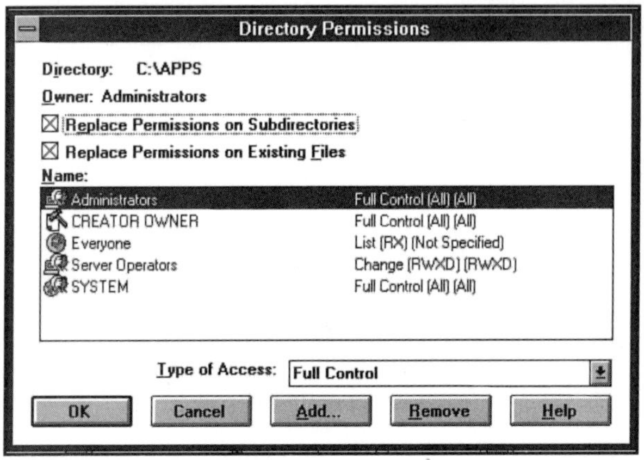

Figure 11.35

Setting permissions for the \APPS directory.

The \APPS\Accounting directory must have different permissions. In figure 11.36, notice that the \Accounting group has been added with Change permissions given to \Accounting, but no other users, including Administrators, have access.

To configure the \Status Reports directory, use the special identity CREATOR OWNER. By assigning Change permissions to CREATOR OWNER, users are given the capability of modifying the status reports they create. The group Everyone is given Add privileges in the directory to enable users to create the files in the first place. The group Eng Managers is given Change permissions. Permissions for \Status Reports are shown in figure 11.37.

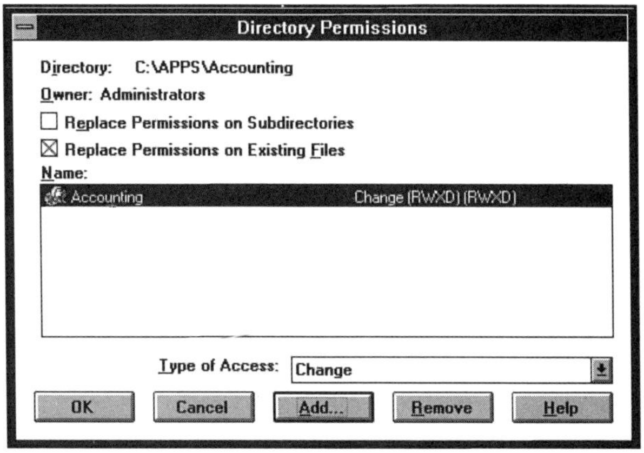

Figure 11.36

Setting permissions for the \APPS\Accounting directory.

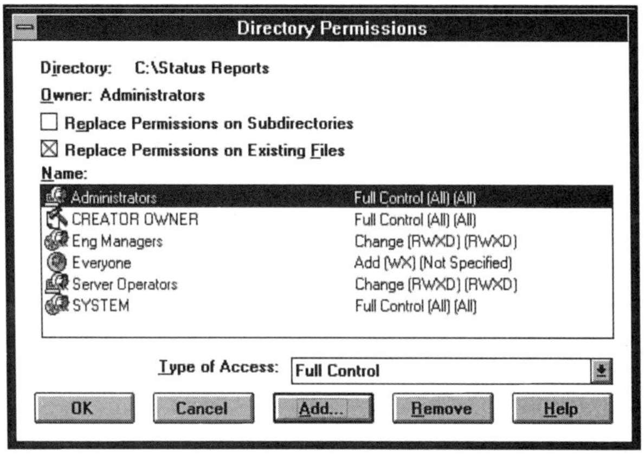

Figure 11.37

Setting permissions for the \Status Reports directory.

No action should be needed to secure the home directories. The user directories were created using the technique described in Chapter 10 in the section "Creating Home Directories for Two or More Users." When home directories are specified in the User Profile window of User Manager for Domains, the directories are created, the user is established as the owner, and default permissions are assigned. The default permissions for a home directory permit Full Control for the directory's owner. No other users, including Administrators, have access.

Now that the required permissions have been assigned, the only remaining step is to assign shares so that networked users can access the directories. One approach is to create the following shares:

- USERS for the \USERS directory
- APPS for the \APPS directory
- STATUS for the \Status Reports directory

Note Even though Status Reports has a long directory name, it will have no effect on DOS and Windows users because they will not see the directory name when they connect to the share. Remember, however, that shares must have 8.3 format names to be used by DOS and Windows users.

CHAPTER 12

Managing Printing Services

Even though printer prices have fallen dramatically in recent years, it continues to make good sense to share printers on a network. If there are any personal printers in your office, keep an eye on them. What percentage of the time are they actually busy printing? At most times, most printers are idle. An idle personal printer might be a nice status symbol, but many organizations feel that idle printers make little economic sense.

Today, a high-capacity printer, capable of printing 16 pages per minute, can be purchased for less than $2,000. Such a printer easily can fill the needs of 20 or more typical users if it is configured properly for sharing. Windows NT is quite capable of sharing such printers effectively.

Selecting Network Printers

Practically any printer can work in a network environment, but some printers are a better fit than others.

An important consideration for shared printers is the duty cycle. Just because a printer can print 10 pages per minute doesn't mean that it can work at that rate constantly, eight or more hours a day. The *duty cycle* of a printer is a statement of the maximum number of pages a printer should be expected to produce in a given period of time, often a month. Forcing a printer to exceed its recommended duty cycle significantly shortens its life and probably makes it less reliable.

A wide variety of printers are designed with networks in mind. One of the special characteristics of network-ready printers is that they are designed for high duty cycles. Often, the difference in cost between printers doesn't show up in speed or print quality, but appears in different duty cycles. Unfortunately, the duty cycle is a specification that tends to be left off most product data sheets. You might have to call the manufacturer to get this information.

Virtually all network-ready printers provide the option of directly connecting to an Ethernet network. Most also have the option to be connected to a Token Ring. Of these printers, the vast majority are capable of participating in a Windows NT network. Depending on the exact hardware and the level of network activity, DIRECT network attachment might not make a big difference in performance, because documents still must be managed by a print server and data must be transmitted over the network. The chief advantage of network attachment is that printers can be placed anywhere on the network. They do not need to be within 100 feet of a print server, as do printers that must connect through a serial port.

Hewlett-Packard produces a wide variety of printers that can attach to networks using HP's JetDirect network interfaces. Windows NT directly supports network-attached HP printers.

Other printer brands might provide support for Windows NT, but you will be dependent on the manufacturers to provide the necessary software to make the connections.

A feature that might be more important than speed is paper capacity. When many users are printing, paper supplies are exhausted rapidly. If you are selecting a printer for a busy office, be sure that it has the paper capacity required to handle the printing volume.

If your office needs a special-purpose printer such as a high-quality color printer or a 1,200 dpi black-and-white laser, a network is an excellent way to connect users to the printer. Such printers are far too expensive to be dedicated to the use of one individual, and because color printers are expensive to use, you don't want them used to print the office football pools. Network security enables you to restrict the users who can access the printer and to audit the activity.

Expensive printers aren't the only ones you should consider sharing. If your office has a Windows NT Server network, you have everything in place to share any printer you want. By all means, share the personal laser printers in your office. Just be sure they are suited to the job you are asking them to perform.

Windows NT enables you to place printers anywhere on your network. Any Windows NT computer can function as a print server. You can dedicate the Windows NT computer for use as a print server or permit it to be used as a workstation as well. Of course, if a workstation is supporting a great deal of printing its performance as a workstation could suffer.

Planning Network Printing

Network printing must cope with a couple of problems:

- Many users send jobs to a few printers. Orderly procedures must be established so that all users' printing needs are served.
- Access to some printers should be restricted, or should be restricted to certain times of day.
- Some users' jobs require special treatment. Some jobs must be printed immediately, while others can wait for overnight printing.

These problems are solved through a mechanism called *spooling*. Figure 12.1 illustrates the process:

1. When a user prints a job, it is not sent directly to a printer. Instead, it is stored in a file on a print server. The print server software is capable of accepting print jobs from many users at one time. All jobs are stored in the spooler files.
2. When a printer becomes available, the print server retrieves jobs one by one from the spooler files and directs them to the printer. Print servers can despool jobs to several printers at once.

Figure 12.1

Spooled printing.

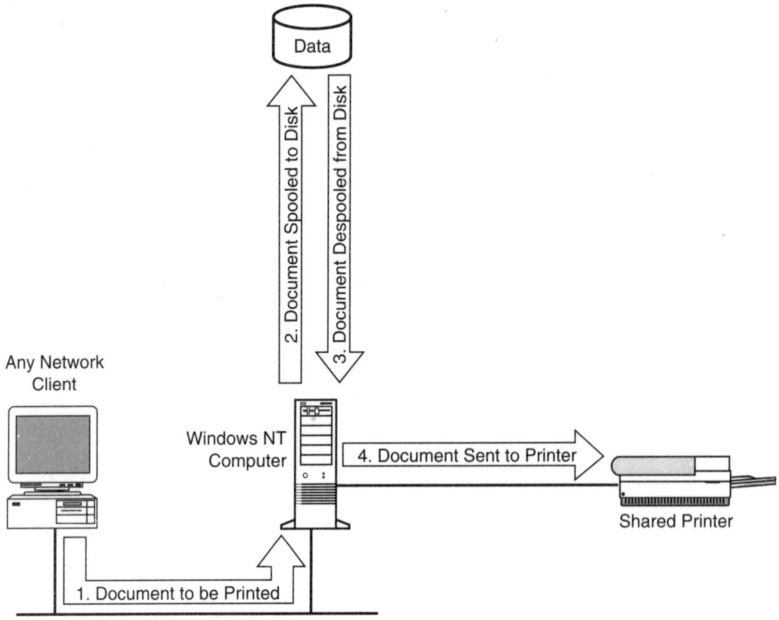

The print spooler serves as a gigantic buffer that can store many megabytes of printer data until printers become available. Print servers can be configured in a wide variety of ways to meet different printing requirements.

Because the entire shared printing process is controlled centrally, a wide variety of special printing needs can arise, such as the following:

- Delayed printing of low-priority jobs—even delaying for overnight printing
- Restriction of users' access to printers
- Printing of identification pages (banners) to identify jobs
- Printing of spooled jobs on the first available printer in a printer pool

The need for some of these functions becomes clearer when more than one printer is on the network. In that case, there is a wide variety of ways that the printers can be shared.

Users print to the print spooler by printing to logical printers. A *logical printer* consists of software that is running on a Windows NT computer. Users use a logical printer just as they would a printer that was attached to their computer, but the data that is printed to a logical printer is directed through the network to a shared network printer.

A Windows NT computer that supports logical printers is called a *print server.* Both Windows NT Workstation and Windows NT Server can function as print servers.

The print server associates logical printers with physical printers (actual printer hardware), and it is the job of the print server to ensure that jobs a user sends to a logical printer are directed to the correct physical printer.

Note Microsoft's terminology is a bit muddy. They generally use the term *printer* to refer to a logical printer—a printer is sometimes a hardware device. When Microsoft talks about "creating a printer," they are discussing the creation of a logical printer. Typically, they refer to a physical printer as a *printing device.* However, there are times when you need to look at the context for the word *printer* to determine whether the manuals are describing a logical or a physical printer.

To avoid confusion, the term *logical printer* is used in this book to refer to a Windows NT printer that is created in the Print Manager and functions as a print spooler. The term *physical printer* is used to describe the hardware printing device.

Figure 12.2 illustrates the three ways in which logical printers and physical printers can be related:

- One logical printer can be associated with a single physical printer. All jobs that are directed to the logical printer eventually wind up being printed by the same physical printer.
- One logical printer can be associated with two or more physical printers. The print spooler sends each job to the first physical printer that becomes available. There is no way to predict which printer actually will service a given job. This approach is called a *printer pool.*
- Two or more logical printers can be associated with a single printer. The advantage to this approach is that the logical printers can be configured differently. One might be configured for normal printing, while another might accept jobs that will be printed overnight, for example. Or, logical printers could be serviced at different priority levels.

The three printer relationships can be mixed up a bit. Figure 12.3 shows one possibility for combining two approaches. The high-priority logical printer is serviced by only one of the printers in the pool.

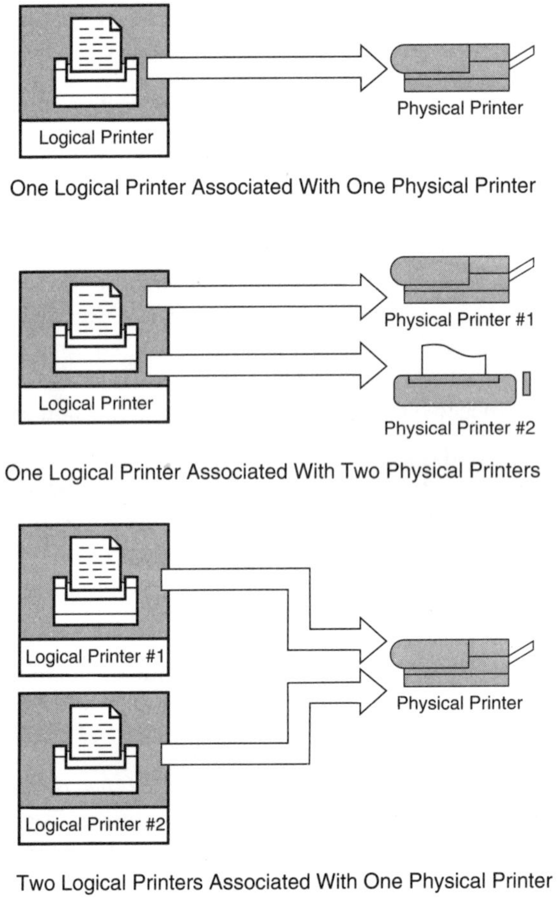

Figure 12.2
Possible relationships between logical and physical printers.

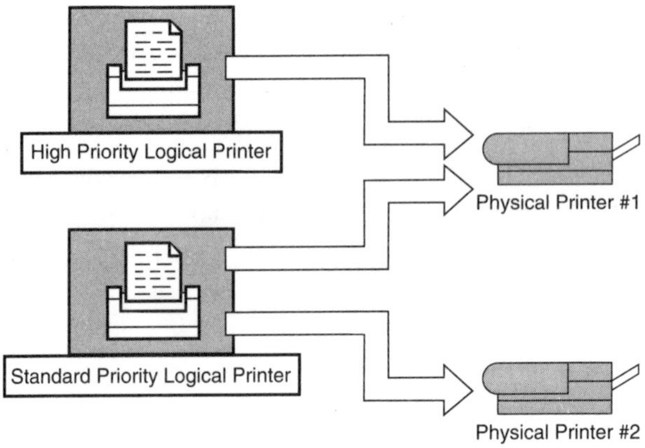

Figure 12.3
A more complex logical and physical printer arrangement.

Installing Printer Hardware

Printers can be attached to print servers through parallel or serial interfaces. Windows NT supports up to 256 COM ports, named COM1 through COM256. Computers based on the Intel/IBM architecture are limited in the numbers of ports they can support. RISC computers are far less limited.

Parallel interfaces are considerably easier to set up than serial interfaces. Most Intel PCs are equipped to support two parallel ports:

- LPT1, which uses IRQ7
- LPT2, which uses IRQ5

A third parallel port can be added. You will need to obtain a parallel port adapter that supports LPT3. Be sure that the adapter can be set for an interrupt that is not in use on the print server. For reliable operation, parallel printer cables should not exceed 20 feet in length.

Serial ports are considerably more difficult to configure. The most common serial interface standard, RS-232, was not designed with printers in mind. Consequently, manufacturers differ in the way they design printers to work with serial interfaces. You will need to obtain a cable that is wired according to the specifications for your printer. Cables for serial ports can be up to 100 feet.

Serial ports typically use the following interrupts:

- COM1 uses IRQ4
- COM2 uses IRQ3

With most serial port hardware, COM3 and COM4 reuse interrupts IRQ4 and IRQ3, respectively. Because COM ports share interrupt real estate, some device combinations work well and others don't. If you want to use both COM1 and COM3 (or COM2 and COM4) simultaneously, your serial port hardware must enable you to configure the interrupts for COM3 and COM4 so that they do not conflict with COM1 and COM2.

With standard hardware, serial ports can be in short supply on Intel/IBM AT computers. You certainly don't want to manage Windows NT without a mouse, and most mice use a serial port. If the computer also has a modem, it has used up standard IRQs for COM ports. Consider getting a mouse that uses an InPort interface card, which doesn't use up a COM port IRQ. InPort mice take a little effort to locate, but it's worth the trouble.

Several vendors provide expansion cards that support 4, 8, or 16 serial ports on a PC. Special drivers are required to enable the operating system to support the expansion card. Because Windows NT is relatively new on the market, not all multiport serial cards provide drivers for Windows NT. Be sure to check with the card's manufacturer to be sure Windows NT is supported by its hardware.

RISC computers don't have these interrupt problems or arbitrary limitations on the number of ports you can add. You can add parallel and serial ports up to the expansion limits of your computer hardware.

Configuring Serial Ports

Serial ports are configured using the Ports utility of the Control Panel. If you run the Ports utility, you see the Ports window shown in figure 12.4. This window shows the ports that Windows NT knows about. In this example, COM1 is dedicated to the computer's mouse and is not available for configuration. COM2 was present when Windows NT was installed.

The Ports window only displays information for COM1 and COM2. If you have added COM port hardware, you need to choose Add and specify the advanced port settings as described in the following sections.

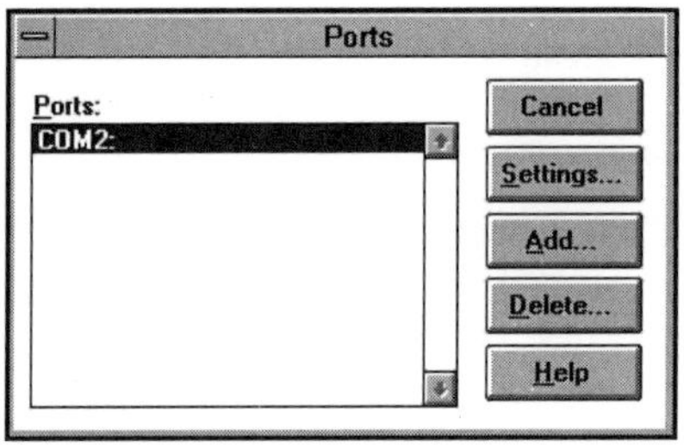

Figure 12.4
The Ports window in the Control Panel.

Configuring Serial Port Settings

If you select a port and choose Settings in the Ports window, you access the Settings dialog box shown in figure 12.5. This box enables you to configure serial communication parameters for the port you selected.

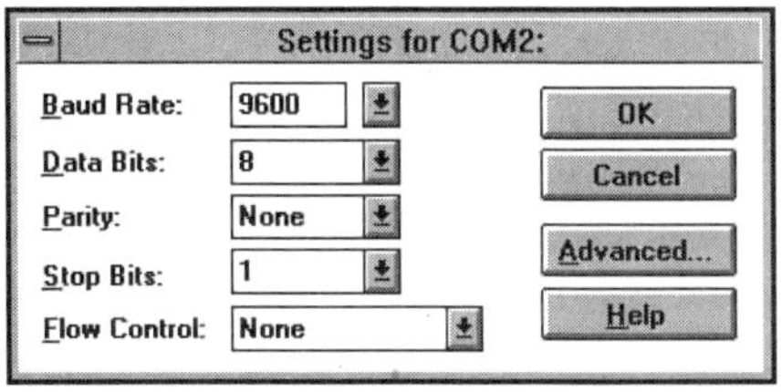

Figure 12.5
Serial port settings.

Serial ports must be configured with a variety of parameters. Both the computer port and the printer port must be configured with the same settings. These settings follow:

- **Baud Rate.** A measure of the bits-per-second rate at which the port will operate. 9600 is the most common setting for printers.
- **Data Bits.** Serial communication takes place one character at a time. Each character contains 4 to 8 bits of data. In almost all cases, you will want to work with 8 data bits, which support advanced character sets and graphics.
- **Parity.** A rudimentary form of error detection that seldom is employed for computer-printer communication. In general, you can configure both devices for None. Other options are Even, Odd, Mark, and Space.
- **Stop Bits.** One or more stop bits signal the end of a serial character. It isn't important how many are used, as long as the computer and printer agree. (However, extra stop bits do waste a bit of the communication bandwidth, and one stop bit will do fine.)
- **Flow Control.** This parameter determines how the computer and printer inform each other when data is ready to transmit and when the printer's input buffer is full. Options for this setting follow:

  Hardware. The computer and printer communicate through extra wires in the serial cable. This is the most commonly implemented handshaking method.

  XON/XOFF. Software handshaking transmits control characters called XON and XOFF to start and stop transmission.

  None. Risky if the volume of data potentially could overflow the printer's input buffer, which is often the case.

Choose OK to save settings. Click Advanced to configure hardware settings for the port.

Configuring Advanced Serial Port Settings

Click on the Advanced button in the Settings for COM*x* window to configure additional settings for a serial port. The Advanced Settings for COM*x* dialog box, shown in figure 12.6, can be used to configure Windows NT if your serial ports use nonstandard hardware settings or exceed the COM1 and COM2 port configurations that Windows NT knows by default.

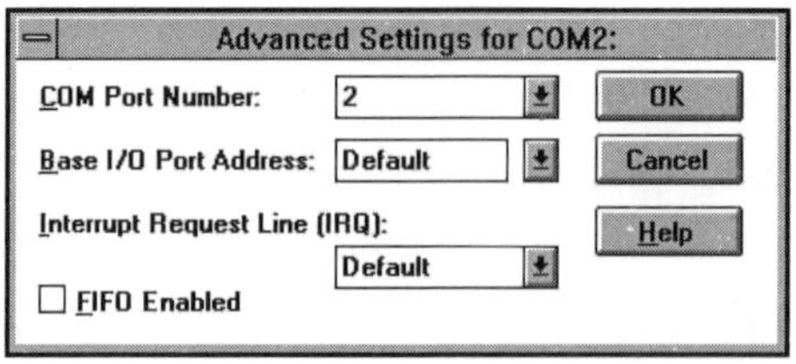

Figure 12.6
Advanced settings for a COM port.

The settings in the Advanced Settings window follow:

- **COM Port Number.** This field enables you to specify the COM port that you want to configure. If you add a new port, it should be numbered COM3 or above.
- **Base I/O Port Address.** COM ports must be configured with an address in the memory range 2E0h through 3ffh. This address supports communication between the OS and the port. Avoid changing the default settings for COM1 through COM4, which have standard and nonconflicting port addresses.
- **Interrupt Request Line (IRQ).** If your serial port hardware permits you to configure custom interrupts, you can configure NT for those interrupts here. To use COM1 and COM3 at the same time (or COM2 and COM4), you need to configure custom, nonconflicting interrupts. Interrupts must be in the range of 2 through 15, although most of the interrupts in this range are unavailable.
- **FIFO Enabled.** Enables Windows NT to take advantage of the capability of some advanced serial chips (called UARTs) to buffer incoming signals. Check your serial port documentation before you enable this feature.

Click on OK to save the settings.

Configuring Network-Attached Printers

To support network-attached printers, you must be sure that the proper protocol support has been installed in Windows NT. To support network-attached Hewlett-Packard printers, the Data Link Control (DLC) protocol is required.

To install DLC, follow these steps:

1. Start the Network utility from the Control Panel.
2. In the Network Settings window, choose Add Software.
3. In the Add Network Software window, pull down the Network Software list and choose DLC Protocol from the list.
4. Select Continue.
5. Provide any disks and path information that are requested.

Installation of TCP/IP is covered in Chapter 15, "Using TCP/IP."

Creating Printers

Microsoft calls the process of setting up a logical printer *creating* a printer. Remember, when you create a printer, your actions do not set up the printer hardware itself. Creating a printer is the process of setting up a logical printer that enables users to print on the network.

Logical printers are created and managed using Print Manager. The icon for Print Manager is installed in the Main program group. This section covers the basics of creating a printer. Later, in the section "Configuring Printer Properties," you will be shown some more advanced features of printers.

Any Windows NT computer can be configured as a print server. You must be a member of one of the following groups to create printers:

- Administrators (NT Workstation and Server)
- Server Operators (NT Server)

- Print Operators (NT Server)
- Power Users (NT Workstation)

To create a new logical printer, follow these steps:

1. Start the Print Manager utility in the Main Program group. The Print Manager window appears.
2. Choose the Crea**t**e Printer command from the **P**rinter menu. Figure 12.7 shows the Create Printer window that appears, as well as example entries for a printer. The Create Printer window enables you to enter the basic configuration of a logical printer.

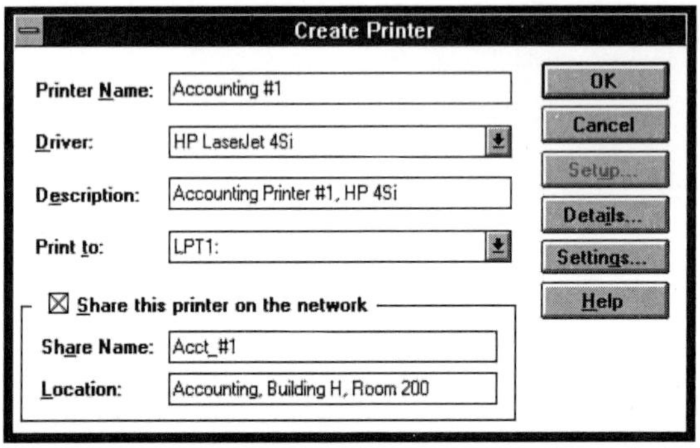

Figure 12.7
Creating a printer.

3. In the Printer **N**ame field, enter a name to identify the printer in Print Manager.
4. In the **D**river field, click the arrow to the right to select a printer driver from the list. Windows NT ships with drivers for a large number of printers. If your printer model isn't found, you might be able to use a driver that is in the list. Check your printer documentation; it might suggest a compatible driver.

   If no compatible driver is in the **D**river list, choose Other at the end of the list. You are asked to supply a disk that contains vendor-provided drivers for your printer.

Note Few printer manufacturers actually design proprietary printer control languages. Virtually all laser printers can emulate a Hewlett-Packard LaserJet by supporting some level of HP's Printer Control Language (PCL). Three versions of PCL have been used in laser printers. Here they are, along with basic drivers that should work with compatible printers:

- PCL3—HP LaserJet Plus
- PCL4—HP LaserJet II
- PCL5—HP LaserJet III

The problem with using HP drivers is that they might not support special features in your printer such as multiple paper sources.

If your printer uses PostScript, try using the Apple LaserWriter Plus driver.

The majority of dot-matrix printers will emulate at least one model in the Epson or IBM Proprinter lines. Here are some possibilities to try:

- IBM compatible—IBM Proprinter (9-pin) IBM Proprinter X24 (24-pin)
- Epson compatible—Epson FX-80 (9-pin standard carriage, Epson FX-100 (9-pin wide carriage), or Epson LQ-1500 (24-pin)

Note Windows NT computers do not require their own copies of driver files to print with a Windows NT print server. The required driver files are read from the print server when a connection is made to a printer.

Different drivers are required for Intel and RISC-based Windows NT computers. If your network includes both hardware platforms, you must install drivers for both Intel and RISC computers on the print server.

5. In the Description field, enter any further information required to identify this printer.

6. In the Print to field, select the destination for printer data. Your choices follow:

   - **LPT or COM ports.**
   - **FILE.** Directs printer data to a file. Users are asked for a file name when they print with this option.

- **Other.** Enables you to direct printing to the following:

  Digital Network Port. To support Digital network-attached printers.

  Hewlett-Packard Network Port. To support a printer that is attached with an HP JetDirect interface. The DLC protocol must be installed for this option to be available.

  LPR Port. To support a TCP/IP printer that is attached to the network or to a Unix computer. TCP/IP protocols must be installed for this option to be available.

  Local Port. To add a port to the print server's configuration. You are prompted for the port name.

  Other. To install third-party drivers.

7. Check the "Share this printer on the network" box if the printer will be shared. The Share Name and Location fields become active.

8. In the Share Name field, enter a name of up to 12 characters to identify the shared printer to users. You must limit the share name to 8.3 format if the share is to be available to DOS and Windows users on your network.

9. In the Location field, enter information to further describe the share to users when they are browsing the network for resources.

10. Choose OK to create the printer. If this is the first printer you are creating for a given print driver, you are asked to supply a path to locate the driver file. Windows NT requires only one copy of a printer driver file, which can be reused for other logical printers.

Note Just as you can create file shares that do not appear when users browse the network, you can conceal printer shares by adding a dollar sign ($) to the end of the share name. Users who want to access the printer share must enter the share name manually when connecting to the printer.

11. If this printer has any configuration options, the Printer Setup window shown in figure 12.8 is displayed. Settings in this window are described in the section "Configuring Printer Properties."

12. Click on OK in the Printer Setup window. The printer you have created is represented in a window in the Print Manager window, as shown in figure 12.9.

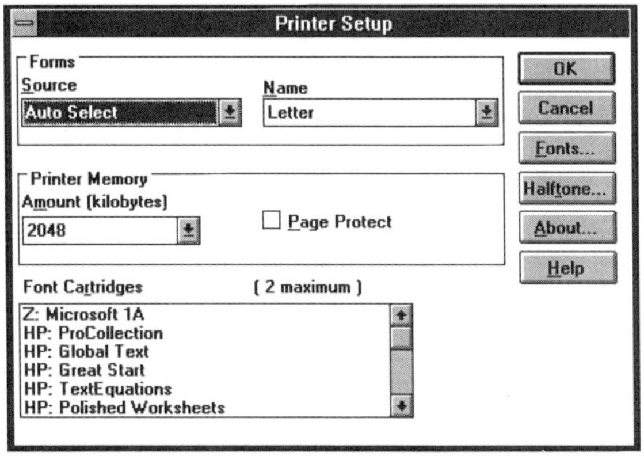

Figure 12.8

The Printer Setup window.

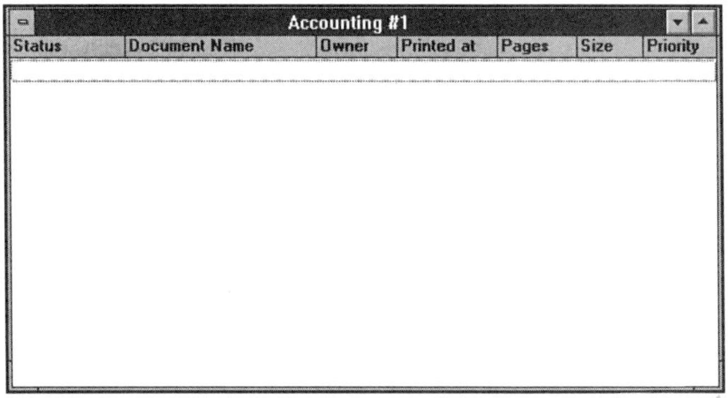

Figure 12.9

A printer window in the Print Manager window.

As with File Manager, you can perform a variety of operations on printer windows. For example, you can do the following:

- Minimize printer windows to icons
- Maximize printer windows to fill available space
- Open multiple windows and tile or cascade the printer windows

These printer windows are used to monitor and manage print jobs that are handled by logical printers.

Connecting to a Network Printer

After a printer has been created, users can connect to the printer. This section shows how to connect a printer in Windows NT. Specific procedures for other operating systems are covered in the chapters devoted to those environments.

Windows NT computers can print to the network immediately. They can access the printer driver that was installed on the print server computer and do not need to have a driver installed locally.

To connect to a logical printer on a Windows NT computer, follow these steps:

1. Open the Print Manager utility in the Main program group.
2. Choose Connect to Printer from the Printer menu to display the Connect to Printer window shown in figure 12.10.
3. Browse the Shared Printers list for printers. One is shown in figure 12.10.
4. Select the desired printer and click on OK. A Printer box is created for the printer in the Print Manager window.
5. If you do not want to monitor printer activity, you can close Print Manager.

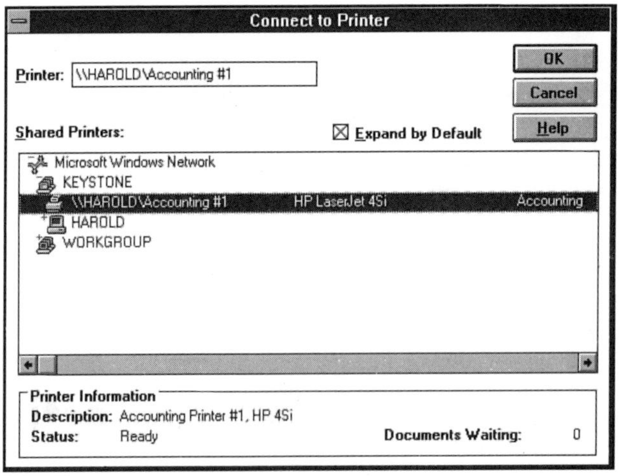

Figure 12.10
Connecting to a network printer in Windows NT.

If you are familiar with printing in Windows for Workgroups, you probably are surprised that the network printer was not connected to a port. In Windows NT, a port assignment is not necessary.

Note Many DOS applications require you to specify a port assignment, which is done with the NET USE command. To assign the printer LASER1 on the server Widgets to your parallel port LPT3, enter the command:

```
NET USE LPT3: \\WIDGETS\LASER1
```

The NET USE command is described in the Appendix.

The logical printer now can be selected for printing in applications. Figure 12.11 shows the Print Setup window in Windows NT Write.

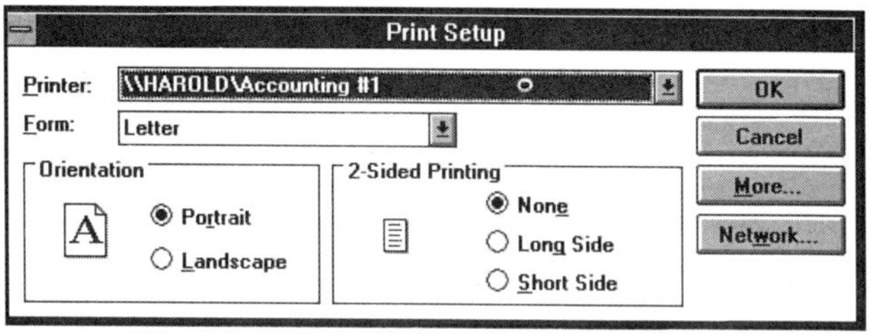

Figure 12.11

Selecting a network printer in Windows NT Write.

Selecting the Default Printer

At any given time, a user can have several printer connections in effect. One of these connections is the default printer, which is used for printing unless the user specifies otherwise.

To select the default printer in Windows NT, pull down the list of connected printers in the Default box in the Print Manager toolbar. Select the printer that you will be using most often to be your default printer.

Configuring Printer Properties

In this section, you will be shown how to configure properties of logical printers. To manage the properties for a printer, select the printer's box or icon in the Print Manager window. Then choose Properties from the Printer menu. The Printer Properties box is displayed.

You already are familiar with most of the printer properties, which are shown in figure 12.7. The Printer Properties box has three buttons that enable you to configure other properties of the printer:

- **Setup.** This button displays the Printer Setup window, which is used to enter information about the physical printer's configuration.
- **Details.** This button displays the Printer Details window, which is used to enter additional properties for the logical printer.
- **Settings.** This button is used to configure settings from the port you specify in the Print to field.

Configuring the Printer Setup

Figure 12.12 shows the Printer Setup box. The properties in this box describe the printer hardware with which this logical printer is associated. The options you see will depend on the printer driver that is being used for this printer.

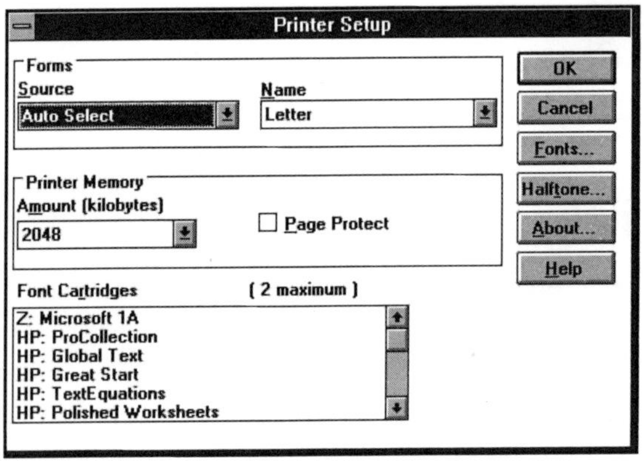

Figure 12.12
The Printer Setup dialog box.

Identifying Available Forms for a Printer

Two options in the Printer Setup dialog box enable you to specify which forms are available on the printer.

- **Source.** If a printer accepts forms from more than one source, this field enables you to associate each source with a form type. Select a source, then select an option in the Name field to specify the form type that is associated with a source.

- **Name.** Use this field with the Source field to specify the form name that will be associated with each form source.

See the section "Managing Forms," later in this chapter, for more information about using these fields.

Specifying Printer Memory

It is particularly important for Windows NT to know how much memory is installed in a laser printer. When graphics are printed to a laser printer, the entire page must be imaged in memory before the page is printed. This cannot be achieved if the memory installed in the printer is insufficient for the graphics being printed.

If the printer has insufficient memory to image the entire page, Windows NT might resort to *banding*—sending the page in sections.

Two options relate to printer memory:

- **Amount (kilobytes).** This field should be set to match the memory that is installed in the printer. The value of the field will be set to the factory default value for the printer model.

- **Page Protect.** Check this option to instruct the printer to image the entire page in memory before printing. Page protection ensures that complex pages can be printed correctly. If the printer supports this feature, the Page Protect box is active.

Specifying Fonts and Color/Halftone Properties

Some printers can accept additional fonts in the forms of font cartridges or soft fonts. Two options in the Printer Setup box relate to fonts. Another option enables you to fine tune the printer for reproducing color and halftone printouts. These options follow:

- **Font Cartridges.** If font cartridges are installed in the printer, specify the installed cartridges by choosing them from this list. The number of cartridges you can select depends on the printer model.

- **Fonts.** This button displays the Font Installer window. Use this window to install drivers for soft fonts.

- **Halftone.** This button displays the Device Color/Halftone Properties window, which enables you to fine tune the printing characteristics of printers that support these features. Halftone and color properties can be set only by users who have Full Control access for the printer (Administrators, Server Operators, Print Operators, and Power Users). Discussion of these features is beyond the scope of this book.

Note Printing devices can use three types of fonts:

- **Hardware fonts.** The font data resides in the hardware of the printing device, either built into the printer or in plug-in cartridges.
- **Screen fonts.** These are fonts that Windows NT can translate into printer-specific output. The standard screen font technology for Windows is called TrueType. Screen fonts are installed using the Font utility in the Control Panel. This is the printing font technology most commonly used with Windows applications.
- **Soft fonts.** These fonts can be downloaded to the printer. The soft font files are stored on the print server, and Windows NT will download the fonts to printers as required. DOS and Windows computers must have their own copies of soft-font files and are responsible for downloading the fonts to printers. The time required to download soft fonts can slow printing performance.

Identifying the Printer Driver

Printer vendors periodically issue new printer drivers to fix bugs or to offer new features. Click on the About button to view the version specifications of the driver that is installed for this printer.

Configuring the Printer Details

Click on the Details button in the Printer Properties box to configure the logical printer. The Printer Details dialog box appears, as shown in figure 12.13.

Restricting Printing Hours

It can be extremely useful to delay print jobs for later printing. This is most commonly done so that large or low-priority jobs can print overnight when printers ordinarily are idle.

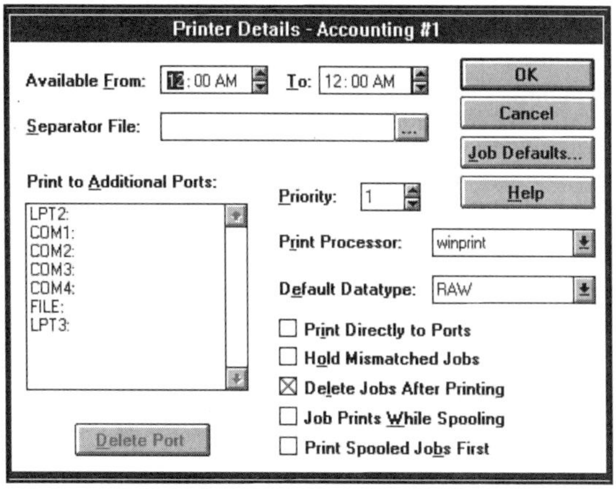

Figure 12.13

The Printer Details dialog box.

Jobs will be sent to the printer only between the hours specified in the Available From and Available To fields. Printing normally is permitted between 12:00 midnight and 12:00 midnight—all day, in other words. Use the arrow buttons to set times in these fields.

You can establish several logical printers with different printing-hour restrictions if you want to have different time restrictions for different users or for different types of jobs.

Specifying a Separator File

The Separator File field enables you to specify a file that will be used to print a separator page between each print job. Separator pages identify the user who requested the job and are useful for routing jobs to their requesters in large organizations. By default, no separator file is identified, and separator pages are not printed.

To print separator pages, click on the ... button in the Separator File field and select a separator file from the list. The file must match the printer type. Three standard files are included with Windows NT:

- **PCL.SEP.** For use with Hewlett-Packard printers and other printers that use the HP Printer Control Language (PCL). In dual-protocol printers, PCL.SEP switches the printer into PCL mode.
- **PSCRIPT.SEP.** For use with HP printers equipped with PostScript. In dual-protocol printers, PSCRIPT.SEP switches the printer into PostScript mode.
- **SYSPRINT.SEP.** Prints a separator page on PostScript printers.

Each of these files can be edited, and you easily can create custom separator pages. The section "Creating Separator Files," later in this chapter, describes the procedure.

To cancel use of a separator file, select the text in the **S**eparator File box and delete it.

Setting Printer Priority

When several logical printers are serviced by the same physical printer, you might want to adjust the priorities of the logical printers. Figure 12.14 shows how priorities work. LoP is a printer with a priority of 1, and HiP is a printer with a priority of 2. Any jobs in HiP will be printed before jobs waiting in LoP, regardless of the time LoP jobs have been waiting.

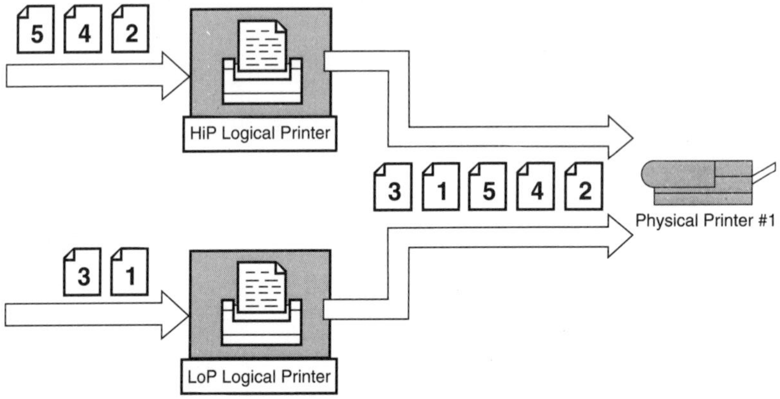

Figure 12.14
How printer priorities work.

Set the priority for a logical printer by adjusting the value of the **P**riority field, which has a range of 1 (lowest priority) to 99 (highest priority). If only one logical printer is assigned to a physical printer, priority has no effect.

Creating a Printer Pool

A logical printer can send jobs to several printers. This arrangement is called a *printer pool,* and was described earlier in the chapter. Two conditions apply:

- The printer devices must be connected directly to the same print server, although you can mix different types of ports.
- The printer devices must be identical. Otherwise, the configuration information entered in Print Manager will not apply to all printers. If printers differ,

configure the logical printer so that it matches the specifications of the most limited printer hardware.

To create a printer pool or to add a physical printer to an existing pool, select the ports by clicking the entry in the Print to Additional Ports box.

To deselect a port, click the selected entry in the Print to Additional Ports list box.

To delete a port from the list, select the port and click the Delete Port button. You might want to remove a port if it is not available in the print server's hardware configuration.

To add a port to the list, follow these steps:

1. Go to the Printer Properties dialog box.
2. Pull down the Print to drop-down list and select Other.
3. In the Print Destinations dialog box, select Local Port and click on OK.
4. In the Port Name dialog box, enter a port name such as LPT3 in the Enter a port name field. Then choose OK.

Selecting the Print Processor and Data Type

Windows NT includes only one print processor named WINPRINT. You need to change the entry in the Print Processor box only if you install software that provides its own print processor. Consult the software documentation for details.

In rare instances, you might need to change the Default Datatype entry. Choices for this field include the following:

- **RAW.** Data is passed to the printer as raw bit streams. Required for printing graphics jobs, for PostScript, and for printing with Windows TrueType fonts. In fact, this setting is required for most printing and works for most other printing as well. You seldom will need to use other options.
- **RAW [FF appended].** Use in the rare instances when an application does not force a form feed at the end of a print job.
- **TEXT.** Use this choice for printing with applications that print only ASCII text. A form feed is forced at the end of the print job. Some text-mode DOS applications print more effectively with this setting.

Configuring Spooler Operation

Several check boxes in the Printer Details dialog box enable you to specify how the spooler will handle print jobs:

- **Print Directly to Ports.** Select this box to bypass the spooler. Print jobs will be sent directly to the printer instead of being spooled to a file. When direct-mode printing is selected, users do not regain use of their applications until printing is completed. Generally speaking, spooled printing is a more efficient use of computing resources.

- **Hold Mismatched Jobs.** For printers that accept multiple form types, you can specify two methods of printing jobs:

  - Check this option to have the spooler hold jobs that do not match a currently mounted form. Jobs that match a current form continue to be printed, even though they might have entered the spooler at a later time.

  - Leave this option unchecked if you want documents to print regardless of the forms that are mounted.

  Changing forms might require you to change the form mounted in the printer, to change the form in the Printer Setup dialog box, or both. See the section, "Managing Forms," later in this chapter.

- **Delete Jobs After Printing.** By default, this option is checked and jobs are deleted automatically. If this box is not checked, jobs must be deleted manually after printing.

  One time you might want to use this option is when it takes considerable time to generate a document for printing. Some reports from large database programs can take hours to generate. This option enables you to be absolutely sure that you have a good printout before the document is deleted. It also lets you preview the printout and request additional printouts if needed.

- **Jobs Print While Spooling.** Ordinarily, a job must be spooled to disk completely before it is printed. If this box is checked, printing begins even while the job is spooling. Checking this option can improve printer throughput by enabling a spooler to receive and print jobs simultaneously, but it might place a performance burden on heavily used print servers.

- **Print Spooled Jobs First.** When this box is disabled, print jobs are selected on the basis of priority. When the box is enabled, jobs that have been spooled completely are printed before partially spooled jobs, even though the partially spooled jobs might have a lower priority.

Specifying Print Job Defaults

If you click on the Job Defaults button, you can use the Document Properties dialog box shown in figure 12.15 to specify default job settings for the printer. Options will be active only if they are supported by the printer device you have specified.

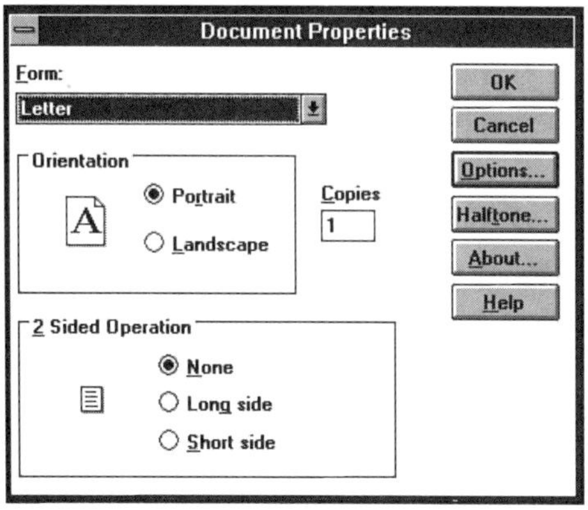

Figure 12.15

Specifying job defaults in the Document Properties dialog box.

You can specify the following job defaults:

- **Form.** Specifies the initial form that the logical printer will select.
- **Orientation.** Specifies whether the printer defaults to Portrait or Landscape printing.
- **Copies.** Specifies the number of copies the printer produces.
- **2 Sided Operation.** Specifies whether the printer produces one-sided or two-sided prints. Two two-sided options are available:

  Long side. Arranges prints so that the pages can be arranged in standard, side-bound book format.

  Short side. Arranges prints so that they can be bound at the top.

Configuring Port Settings

The Settings button in the Printer Properties dialog box enables you to configure the printer port to which the printer is connected.

If a COM port is specified in the Print to box, the Settings button branches to the COM ports configuration dialog box described earlier in the section "Configuring Serial Ports."

If an LPT port is specified in the Print to box, the Configure LPT Port dialog box is displayed, as shown in figure 12.16. Only one setting is required for LPT ports. The Transmission Retry setting determines how many seconds the Print Manager waits for a printer to become available before announcing that a printer error has occurred.

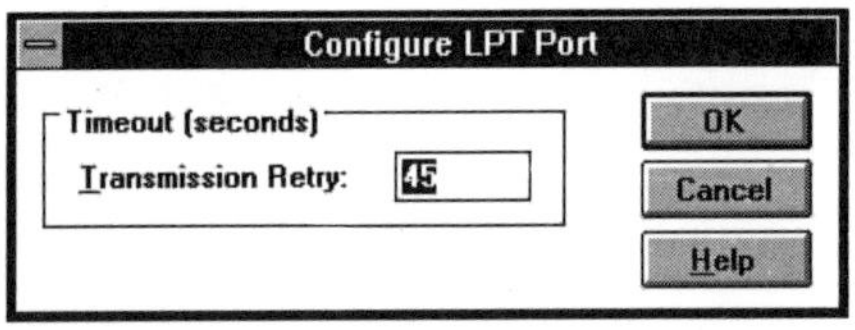

Figure 12.16
Configuring an LPT port.

Adding Logical Printers to a Physical Printer

Here are three good reasons for creating several logical printers that are serviced by the same physical printer:

- To set up a spooler that holds jobs to be printed overnight
- To enable some users to print with a higher priority than others
- To package several logical printer configurations in an easy-to-use manner

To create a second logical printer for a physical printer, follow these steps:

1. Choose the Create Printer command from the Printer menu.
2. Enter a name in the Printer Name field that is different from other logical printers on this print server.
3. In the Driver box, select the same driver that was specified for other logical printers that will service the physical printer you want to service.
4. In the Print to box, select the port that connects to the physical printer you want to service this logical printer.
5. Share the printer and enter a name in the Share Name box that is different from other shared printers on this print server.
6. Set other properties as required.
7. Click on OK to save the printer.

Printer Security

Printer security can be managed by the owner of the printer or by users who have Full Control permissions. Four permissions can be assigned to printers:

- No Access
- Print
- Manage Documents
- Full Control

Users with the Manage Documents permissions can perform the following actions:

- Controlling document settings
- Pausing, resuming, restarting, and deleting documents

Users with Full Control permissions can perform the actions permitted by Manage Document permissions. In addition, they can perform these actions:

- Changing document printing order
- Pausing, resuming, and purging logical printers
- Changing logical printer properties
- Deleting logical printers
- Changing logical printer permissions

Note The user who creates a document is established as the document's owner. All users can perform Manage Document operations on documents they own.

Taking Printer Ownership

The user who creates a printer is the printer's owner and can administer all characteristics of the logical printer. The owner can enable other users to administer the printer by giving the users Manage Documents or Full Control permissions.

Any user who has Full Control permissions can take ownership of the printer by selecting the Owner command from the Security menu.

Managing Printer Permissions

The procedure for setting printer permissions is nearly identical to the procedure for setting file permissions. Use the following steps:

1. Select the printer window or icon in the Print Manager window.
2. Choose the Permissions command from the Security menu to display the Printer Permissions box shown in figure 12.17.
3. To change permissions for a user or group,
   - Select a name in the Name box.
   - Pull down the Type of Access list and select the desired access.
4. To add a user or group to the permissions list,
   - Click Add in the Printer Permissions box. The Add Users and Groups dialog box appears, as shown in figure 12.18.
   - If required, select a different domain from the List Names From drop-down list.
   - To display user names in the Names box, click on Show Users.
   - Add names to the Add Names box by double-clicking entries in the Names box or by selecting entries in the Names box and clicking on Add.
   - In the Type of Access box, select the permissions to be assigned to the names you have selected. All selected users and groups receive the same permissions.
   - Click on OK to add the users or groups to the permissions list for the printer and return to the Printer Permissions box.
5. To remove a name, select the entry in the Names box of the Printer Permissions dialog box, and click on Remove.
6. Choose OK to save the permissions.

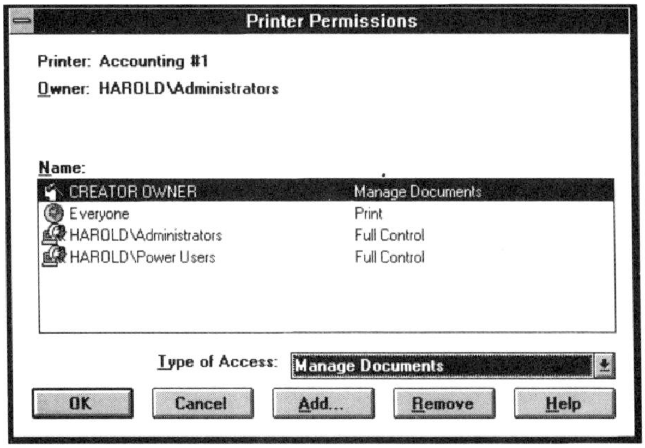

Figure 12.17

Setting printer permissions.

Figure 12.18

Adding users and groups to printer permissions.

Managing Printer Operation

Print Manager can be used to view the documents in a logical printer and to manage them in a variety of ways. Users always can manage documents that they create. To manage other users' documents, you must be the owner of the logical printer, or you must be logged in as a member of one of these groups: Administrators, Server Operators, or Print Operators. You also can manage documents on a logical printer if you have been given Full Control or Manage Documents (limited capabilities) permissions for the printer.

To view documents in a printer, display the window for the printer. An example of a printer window is shown in figure 12.19.

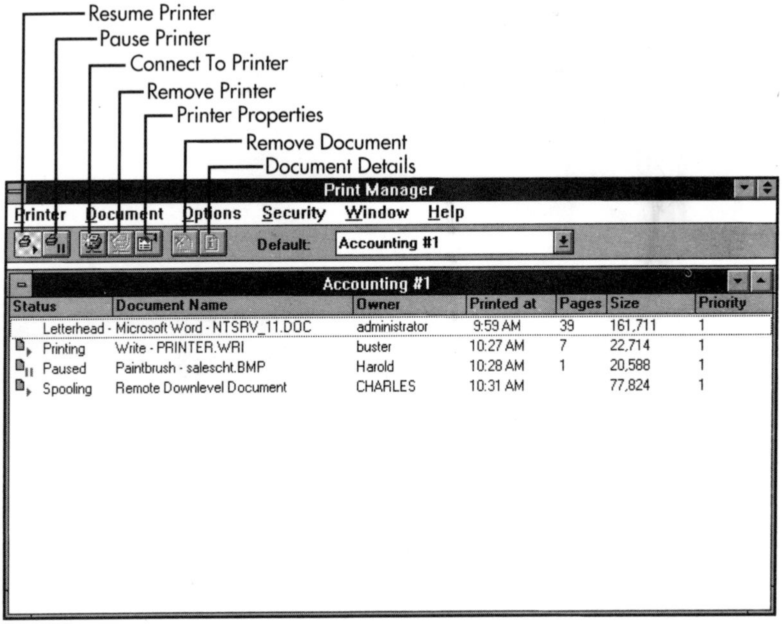

Figure 12.19
Viewing documents in a printer.

For each document in the printer, you see the following information:

◆ **Status.** `Printing`, `Spooling`, `Paused`, and `Deleting` are the most common messages. If no status is displayed, the document is waiting to be printed.

If a document is waiting to have a form mounted, the name of the form is shown in the Status field.

◆ **Document Name.** The detail you see depends on the environment that originated the document. In some cases, you see the file name, along with the application that created it. Other messages are less informative. The entry `Remote Downlevel Document` was printed from Microsoft Word on a Windows for Workgroup computer.

- **Owner.** The owner of the document.
- **Printed at.** The time spooling was completed.
- **Pages.** The number of pages in the document.
- **Size.** The document size in bytes.
- **Priority.** The priority of the document.

Authorized users can perform a number of operations to manage documents in a printer.

Tip

You can change the column widths of the items that are displayed in the printer status box. Between each column name you will find a separator bar. This bar can be dragged to the left or right to expand and contract the width of columns.

Pausing the Printer

In some cases, you might want to pause the logical printer. This often is necessary when a printing device requires attention, for example. Users can continue to spool documents, but none will be printed.

To pause the logical printer, follow these steps:

1. Select the box or icon for the printer.
2. Choose Pause from the Printer menu or choose the printer Pause button in the toolbar.

While a printer is paused, the title bar for the printer includes the word `Paused` after the name of the printer.

Resuming Printing

To resume printing with the logical printer, follow these steps:

1. Select the box or icon for the printer.
2. Choose Resume from the Printer menu, or choose the printer Resume button in the toolbar.

Pausing Document Printing

You can pause and resume individual documents. You might want to do this to hold an especially large document or to hold a document until a special form becomes available.

To pause a document, follow these steps:

1. Select the document in the logical printer. (Deselect a selected document by pressing the right mouse button or by pressing the space bar.)

   When you select a document, the Pause and Resume buttons in the toolbar change from printer icons to document icons. They now can be used to pause and resume documents.

2. Choose Pause from the **D**ocument menu, or choose the document P**a**use button in the toolbar.

Resuming Document Printing

To resume a document's printing, follow these steps:

1. Select a paused document.
2. Choose R**e**sume from the **D**ocument menu or choose the document Resume button in the toolbar.

Changing Document Printing Order

To change the position of a document in the printing order, follow these steps:

1. Select the document.
2. Drag the document to the new position, or move the document by pressing Ctrl+↑ or Ctrl+↓.

Restarting Documents

Occasionally, you will find it handy to restart a document from the beginning. This need arises most often when printers malfunction and damage pages in the printout. Until the document is deleted from the spooler, you can restart it from the beginning.

To restart a document, follow these steps:

1. Select the document being printed.
2. Choose Restart from the Document menu.

Removing Documents

If a document is waiting to print, it can be removed from the spooler. To remove a document, follow these steps:

1. Select the waiting document.
2. Choose Remove Document from the Document menu, press Del, or choose the Remove Document button in the toolbar.

To remove all documents from a logical printer, follow these steps:

1. Select the window or icon of the printer.
2. Choose Purge Printer from the Printer menu.

Note Removing a document that is printing is a bit problematic, because most printers have input buffers that hold several pages of data. Therefore, the printer might continue to print for several pages after the document has been removed from the spooler. Additionally, if a document was removed from the spooler in mid-page, no form feed will be sent and a page might remain in the printer. You might be required to force a form feed manually to clear the partially printed page from the printer.

Displaying and Managing Document Details

You can display a detailed information box for each document in the printer. An example is shown in figure 12.20. Qualified users can change some of these details.

To display and manage document details, follow these steps:

1. Select a document in the printer window.
2. Choose Details from the Document menu, press Enter, or choose the Details button in the toolbar.

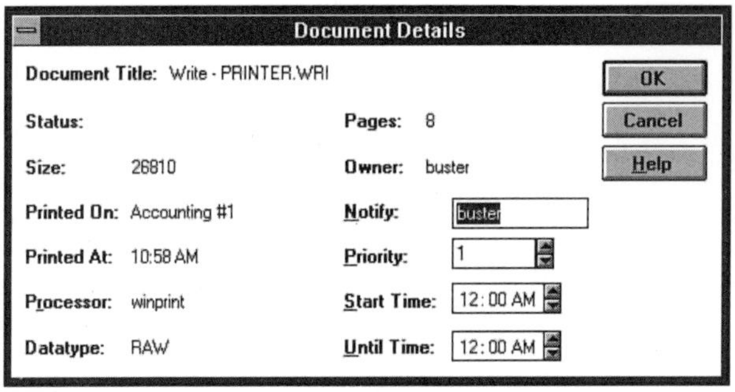

Figure 12.20
The Document Details dialog box.

From the Document Details box, you can manage several characteristics of the document.

Changing Print Notification

By default, the user who originated a document will be the user who is notified when the document has printed.

If a different user should be notified that a document has been printed, enter the user's name in the Notify field.

Changing Printing Priority

By default, documents are given the same priority as the logical printer to which they were printed. You can adjust priorities for individual documents by adjusting the number in the Priority field from 1 (lowest) to 99 (highest).

Changing Printing Times

You can schedule individual documents to print in a specified time period by adjusting the Start Time and Until Time fields.

Administering Print Servers Remotely

If you are logged on with proper authority, you can manage a printing operation remotely. You must be a member of the Administrators, Server Operators, or Print Operators group, or you must have been granted Full Control for the printer to be managed.

To select and manage a different print server, follow these steps:

1. Start Print Manager on the remote computer.
2. Choose Server Viewer from the **Printer** menu. The Select Computer dialog box shown in figure 12.21a appears.

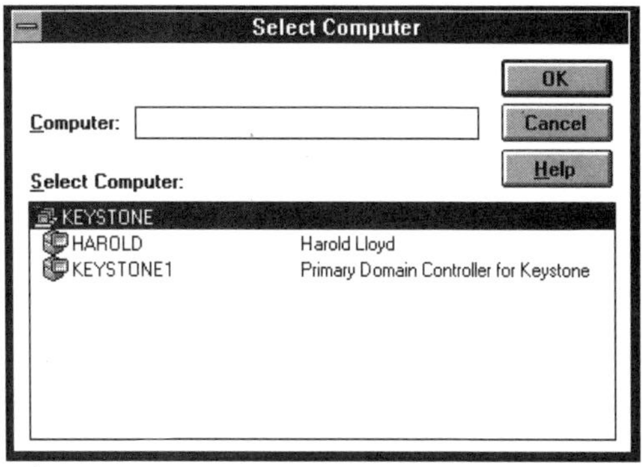

Figure 12.21a

Selecting a computer to be managed.

3. Double-click a domain to display print servers in the domain.
4. Select a print server and click on OK.
5. Print Manager displays a new box showing the printers on the remote print server (see fig. 12.21b). You can manage printers from this box. Printers can be created and removed, and printer properties can be changed.

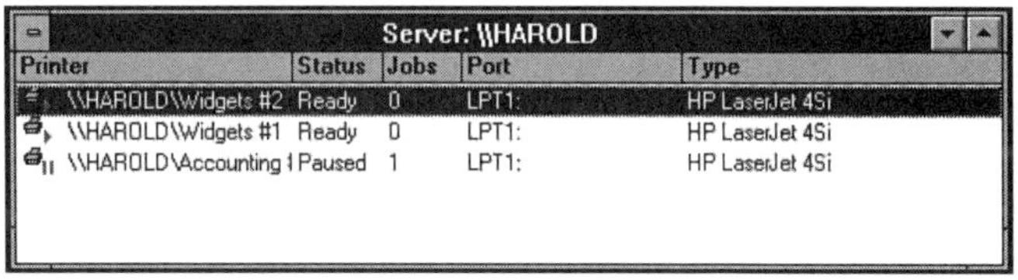

Figure 12.21b

Selecting a server to manage.

Managing Forms

Most organizations use more types of printer forms than they have paper drawers in their printers. In many offices, you see users sprinting for the nearest printer so that they can shove a sheet of letterhead in before their job starts to print. You also see users losing patience because their document has printed on the wrong form.

Windows NT printing has a useful forms-management system that can eliminate forms-management problems. To prepare your print servers to support forms, you need to configure two sets of printing characteristics:

- Windows NT includes definitions for a wide variety of forms. You might need to create custom form definitions to match the forms used in your office.
- You also need to update the properties of your printers to reflect the forms that are mounted on them.

If your office uses more than one form type, you should seriously consider a printer that has at least two paper bins. Keep one bin loaded with the paper that is used most often—often plain white bond. Purchase extra paper holders for the other bin so that it is easy to change forms. A manual-feed slot is an advantage for forms that are used infrequently or in single-sheet quantities.

Note Unfortunately, the Windows NT forms capability works only with Windows NT clients, because they obtain their print drivers from the print server.

DOS and Windows clients maintain their own print drivers, which may or may not include definitions of forms. The forms DOS and Windows drivers can control print formatting, but cannot request form changes from Windows NT printers.

Defining Custom Forms

Each print server maintains a database of forms. A large number of standard form types are predefined and cannot be edited. You can create custom forms that fit your needs, however.

To define a form, follow these steps:

1. Choose Forms from the Printer menu to reveal the Forms window shown in figure 12.22. When you select a form in the Forms on this Computer box, the characteristics for that form are displayed in the Form Description area.
2. The easiest way to define a new form is to select a standard form that is similar to the form you are defining. If you want to start this way, select a form.
3. Enter a name for the form you are designing in the Name field.
4. Choose the units in which you want measurements to be expressed: Metric (centimeters) or English (inches). When entering measurements in other areas of the page, you do not need to specify the unit of measure (centimeters or inches). The unit of measure is supplied based on your selection in the Units box.

5. Enter the dimensions for the form in the Paper Size box.

6. If printing should not extend to the borders of the form, enter margin measurements in the Print Area Margins box.

7. Click Add to save the form definition.

In figure 12.22, a Letterhead form is being created. The margins are set to enlarge the top margin so that printing will not overlap printing at the top of the page.

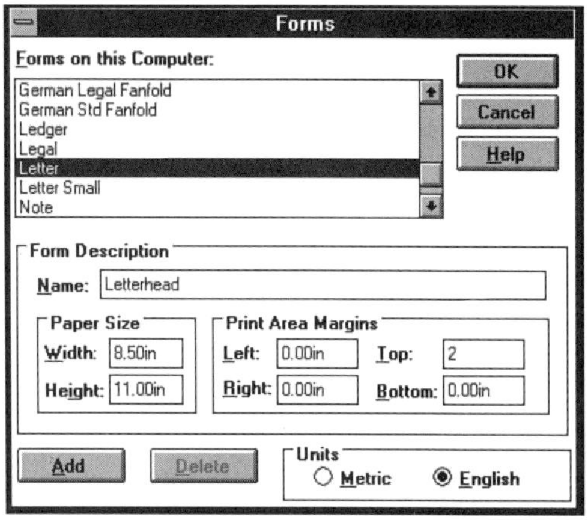

Figure 12.22

Creating a custom form definition.

Preparing the Logical Printer for Forms

After required forms have been defined, some minor setup is required for printers on which you will be changing forms.

For each printer that will support multiple forms, follow these steps:

1. Select the printer box or icon.

2. Choose Printer, Properties, Details to display the Printer Details form.

3. Check the Hold Mismatched Jobs box.

4. Choose OK.

5. In the Printer Properties box, choose Setup to display the Printer Setup form.

6. Pull down the Source drop-down list. This shows all the paper sources that are available for the printer you are configuring.

7. For each entry in the **S**ource box,
   - Select the entry
   - Select a form type in the **N**ame list
8. After you have associated a form name with each form source, click on OK.
9. Choose OK in the Printer Properties window to save the property changes for the printer.

Printing with Forms

When Windows NT users select a printer on a Windows NT print server, they have the option of specifying a form that will be used on the printer. In most cases, this is done using the Print Setup command in the File menu of an application.

Figure 12.23 shows the Print Setup window for Windows Write. After a printer has been selected, you can select a form that should be used to print the document.

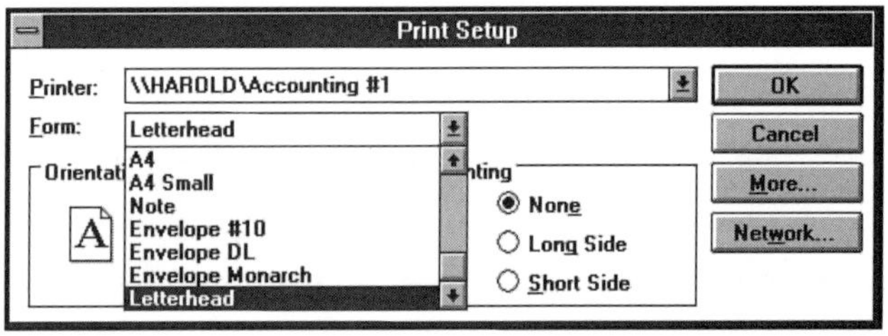

Figure 12.23

Selecting a form in Windows Write.

If the form you selected already is available on the printer, your document is printed immediately.

If the form you selected is not available, the document is held in the spooler until a printer operator changes the form. Figure 12.24 shows a printer window with a document being held while awaiting a form change.

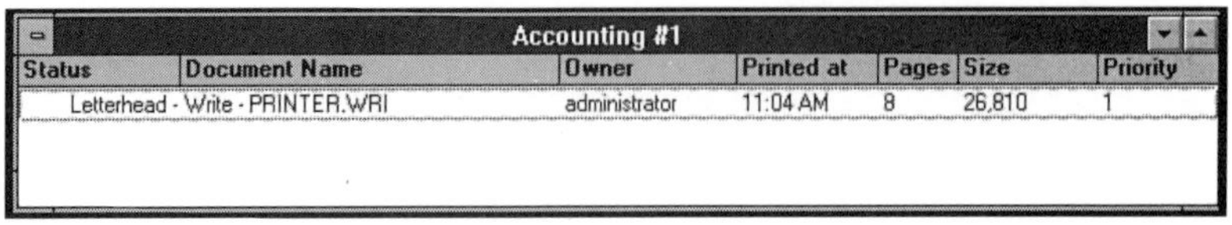

Figure 12.24

A document held pending a form change.

Note Some applications use Windows NT forms more effectively than others. Not all applications will use the form size and margin information you enter in the form properties to set form size and margins in documents.

However, all applications that can select Windows NT forms can take advantage of the forms-management feature. Documents that require a form change are held until the proper form has been mounted.

As a printer operator, you must take the following steps to change the form and print the document:

1. Install the form on the printer by changing paper, changing paper trays, or inserting a sheet in the manual-feed slot.
2. Select the printer window or icon for the printer.
3. Choose **P**rinter, **P**roperties, Set**u**p to display the Printer Setup window.
4. Select the paper source that now holds the form in the **S**ource box.
5. Select the form name that matches the document's requirements from the **N**ame box.
6. Click on OK twice to save the printer properties. The document begins to print.

You might want to restore the default form settings for the printer after the document has printed.

Creating Separator Files

You can create custom separator pages, or you can edit the standard separator pages that are included with Windows NT. A separator page file is a standard text file with a SEP file-name extension. SEP files are created with a text editor, or you can use Windows Write, which is included with Windows NT.

Note Separator page files must be stored on the print server. By default, files are stored in \WINNT35\SYSTEM32.

Table 12.1 lists the codes that are used in separator files. These codes are called *escape codes,* because they begin with an escape character that signals the start of a script command. Any character that will not appear in the text of a file can be used as the escape character. Microsoft has used the \ character as the escape character in the standard SEP files, so \ is used in table 12.1.

Table 12.1
Escape Codes Used in Windows NT Separator Files

Escape Code	Function
\B\M	Starts printing in double-width block characters. Block printing continues until \U occurs.
\B\S	Starts printing in single-width block characters. Block printing continues until \U occurs.
\D	Prints date. The date format is determined by the date format in the International section of the Control Panel.
\E	Forces a page eject. Remove this code if you are getting extra blank separator pages.
\F*pathname*	Starts a new line and prints contents of a file specified by *pathname.*
\H*nn*	Sends a printer control code where *nn* is a hexadecimal number. Codes are defined by the printer's control language. Consult printer documentation for information.
\I	Prints job number.
\Lcccc	Prints the string of characters represented by cccc. The string is terminated by the next occurrence of an escape character.
\N	Prints user name of user who submitted the job.
\T	Prints time job is being printed. The time format is set by the International section of the Control Panel.
\U	Terminates block-mode printing.
\W*nn*	Sets the page width, where *nn* is a width from 1 through 256. Default width is 80.
n	Creates *n* line feeds where n is in the range of 0 through 9. Use \0 to end the current line of text and start a new line. Otherwise, printing continues on the same line.

Following is a custom separator file that I created by modifying PCL.SEP. This file ensures that a PCL printer is switched into PCL mode and then prints identification information on the separator page. Line numbers have been added to assist discussion.

```
1.  \
2.  \H1B\L%-12345X@PJL ENTER LANGUAGE=PCL
3.  \L*********************************************************
4.  \1\B\S\N\U\1
5.  \L*********************************************************
6.  \4\D\L    \T\1
7.  \LJob #  \I
8.  \E
```

Here is a line-by-line explanation of the file:

1. This line establishes the character that will serve as the escape character for the rest of the file. The character on this line can function only as an escape character and may not appear in any other text in the file.

2. \H1B sends a hexadecimal 1B code to the printer. This is the ASCII escape character that is used as the escape character in PCL. This code readies the printer to accept a command sequence.

   The text following \L is the PCL command. This text contains the command that sets the printer into PCL mode.

3. This line uses the \L ("literal") command to print a line of asterisks above the user name.

4. After skipping one line (\1), this line switches into block mode (\B\S) and prints the user's name.

5. Same as 3.

6. First skipping four lines, this line then prints the date (\D) and time (\T). An \L command inserts some spaces between the two items.

7. \L is used to print the text "Job #" and is followed by a \I to print the actual job number.

8. \E forces a page eject so that the print job starts on a new page.

Here is an example of the separator page that would be printed by this file:

```
********************************************************


HH   HH                          lll        ddd
HH   HH                           ll         dd
HH   HH   aaaa   rr rrr   oooo    ll         dd
HHHHHH      aa    rrr rr oo   oo   ll      ddddd
HH   HH   aaaaa   rr   rr oo   oo   ll    dd   dd
HH   HH  aa   aa   rr      oo   oo   ll    dd   dd
HH   HH   aaa aa rrrr      oooo    llll    ddd dd


********************************************************



 4/20/1995     8:29:21 AM

Job #  9
```

Part III

Installing and Using Clients

CHAPTER 13

Using Windows and DOS Clients

The overwhelming popularity of Microsoft MS-DOS and Windows practically ensures that your network will include DOS and Windows clients. Microsoft produces two distinct families of Windows products:

- Windows versions that run over MS-DOS:

  Windows 3.1. A Windows product that is intended primarily for stand-alone computing but is capable of being networked.

  Windows for Workgroups 3.11 (WfW). An extended version of Windows 3.1 that has many built-in networking features.

  Windows 95. Microsoft's next-generation Windows product that replaces the 16-bit Windows 3.*x* architecture with a 32-bit architecture. Much of the underlying technology of Windows 95 can be traced back to MS-DOS.

- Windows NT (new technology):

  Windows NT Workstation. Version 3.5 has a user interface that looks much like Windows 3.1, but Windows NT was designed from the ground up as an advanced 32-bit operating system, completely free from any dependence on DOS technology.

  Windows NT Server. Version 3.5 is an extended version of Windows NT Workstation that provides a full range of network server features.

Because Windows NT is so dramatically different from DOS-based Windows products, the two product groups will be considered in separate chapters. Look for coverage of Windows NT clients in the next chapter.

Windows for Workgroups (WfW) is ready to network out of the box and is considered first.

To network MS-DOS with Windows 3.1, you must install and configure a network add-on called the Workgroup Connection. Procedures are similar for both environments, and they will be considered together.

Finally, the chapter looks at networking with Microsoft's new Windows 95.

Windows for Workgroups 3.11

Windows for Workgroups can be used by itself to build peer-to-peer networks that support file and printer sharing. The utilities included with WfW are network-ready. Print manager can share local printers and connect to shared printers elsewhere on the network. File Manager can share files and connect to shared files. Although you can network Windows 3.1, the utilities in Windows 3.1 cannot participate in the network with the same facility as the utilities in WfW.

Everything you need to configure a WfW 3.11 client is included with the product. In this section, you will learn how to install networking software, connect to a domain, and access domain resources.

Installing WfW Network Software

When WfW is installed on a networked computer, SETUP will normally install the network software and configure WfW to participate in a workgroup. If the WfW computer is already participating in a workgroup, the network software is already installed, and you can skip this section and go to the section "Connecting to a Domain."

Here are step-by-step procedures for adding network software to an installed copy of Windows for Workgroups:

1. Run the Windows Setup utility. The icon for Windows Setup is normally stored in the Main program group. In the Windows Setup dialog box, the Network field will indicate "No Network Installed."

2. Choose the Change Network Settings command in the Options menu. The Network Setup dialog box will be displayed as shown in figure 13.1. This box is the focus for most WfW network configuration procedures. In figure 13.1, no networking features are enabled.

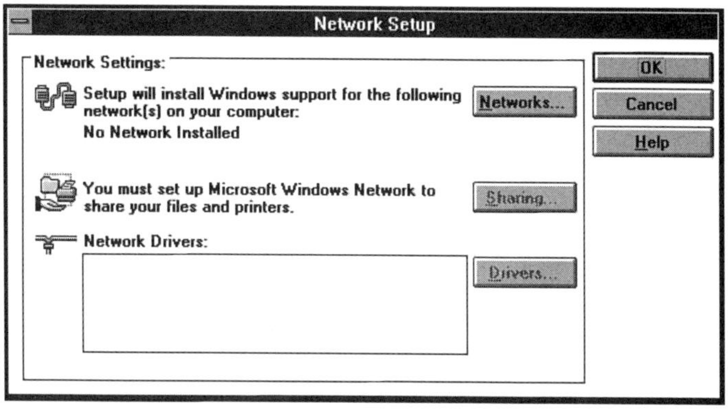

Figure 13.1
The Network Setup dialog box.

3. To install network support, choose Networks to display the Networks dialog box shown in figure 13.2.

   Although WfW can be configured with protocol stacks provided by other vendors, such as the Open Datalink Interface (ODI) stack from Novell, you will probably want to use the NDIS stack that is provided by Microsoft. NDIS supports multiple, simultaneous protocols including NetBEUI, NWLink (a transport that is compatible with Novell's IPX/SPX), and TCP/IP.

4. To install the protocols, select the button Install Microsoft Windows Network and choose OK. (If your network includes NetWare or other supported networks, you will also need to select Other and follow the required procedures for the other network type.)

   You will be returned to the Network Setup dialog box, which now indicates that Setup will install the Microsoft Windows Network (version 3.11). Choose OK to continue.

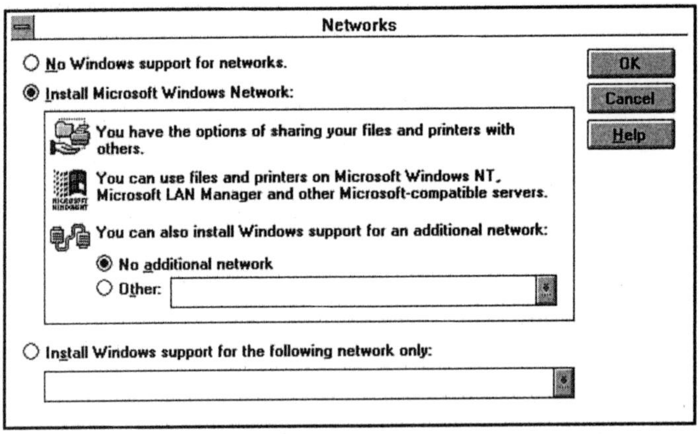

Figure 13.2

Selecting Network support options.

5. Setup attempts to discover any network cards in the PC and will probably be successful.

   Some cards will fool the detection programs. If the card Setup detects is incorrect, you must choose No to enter the Add Network Adapter dialog box.

Note In my case, the computer had a card that was compatible with the Novell/Eagle NE2000. Setup thought it was an NE1000, and displayed the message shown in figure 13.3. I had to choose **N**o and select the card manually.

Incidentally, I was not using a standard NE2000, which supports interrupts 2, 3, 4, and 5 only. I was using a card which provides NE2000 compatibility but supports high interrupts. My card was configured for IRQ 10. Setup was aware only of the standard NE2000 interrupts, however, so I had to select an invalid interrupt and fix it later manually by editing the PROTOCOL.INI file.

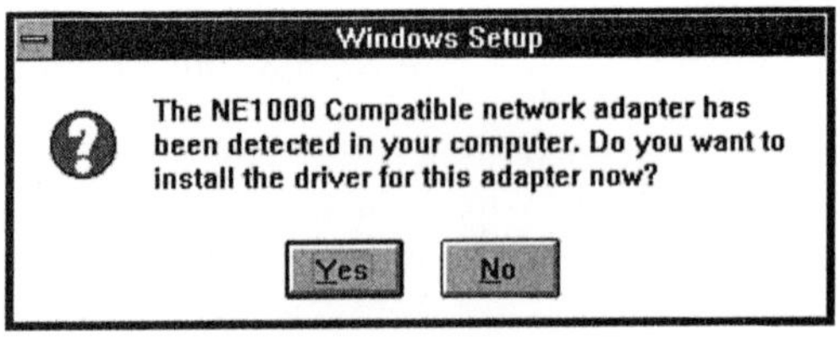

Figure 13.3

Setup requesting confirmation of a discovered network card.

6. If you must manually select a network card driver, you will do so from the list in the Add Network Adapter dialog box, shown in figure 13.4. In the figure, an NE2000 has been chosen.

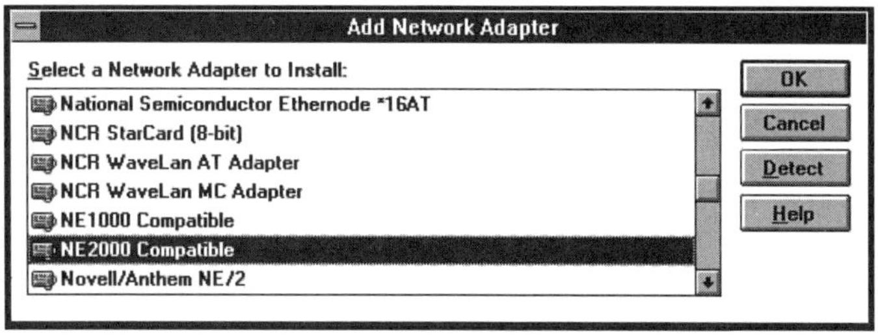

Figure 13.4
Choosing a network adapter.

7. Next, a series of boxes enables you to specify settings for your network card. In the case of the NE2000, the interrupt and the I/O port had to be confirmed.

   If you select an interrupt that is normally dedicated to another resource, Setup warns you. Figure 13.5 shows the warning shown when Interrupt 3 was selected.

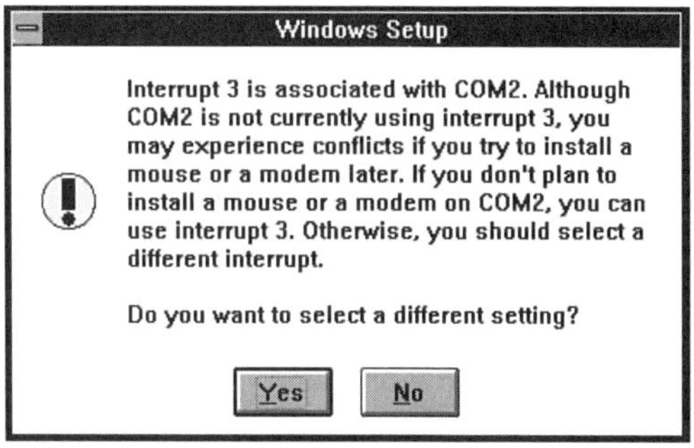

Figure 13.5
Setup warning of a potential resource conflict.

8. After specifying card settings, Setup presents the Microsoft Windows Network Names dialog box shown in figure 13.6. Here you must specify the following:

   ◆ **User Name.** Should match a user name that is recognized by the domain this user will access.

   ◆ **Workgroup.** Can be a WfW workgroup (the default is WORKGROUP) or a domain. It is suggested that you leave this setting at WORKGROUP and connect to the NT domain as described in the next section.

   ◆ **Computer Name.** Should uniquely identify this computer on the network.

   Workgroup and computer names can consist of up to 15 characters and may include the following characters:

   ! # $ % ( ) - _ . @ ^ ' ~

   Spaces are not permitted.

Note

The entry specified in Workgroup determines which computers a WfW computer can share resources with. If the entry is the name of a workgroup, the WfW computer can share resources with other computers in the Workgroup but not with Windows NT computers or with computers that are connected only to a domain.

If the entry in Workgroup is the name of a domain, the WfW computer can share resources with Windows NT computers, WfW computers, and with DOS computers that are running Microsoft Network software. The computer will not, however, enable the WfW computer to share resources with computers that are not logged on to the domain.

A WfW computer can share resources with a workgroup and log onto a domain by specifying a workgroup in the Workgroup entry and entering a domain, as described in the later procedure, "Connecting to a Domain."

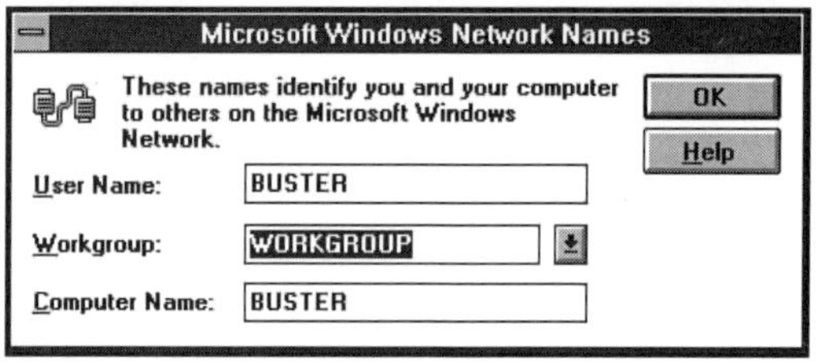

Figure 13.6
Specifying network names.

9. Choose OK when network names have been specified. Setup will begin to install files. Insert disks and specify file locations when prompted.

   You are notified that Setup will modify the files AUTOEXEC.BAT, SYSTEM.INI, and PROTOCOL.INI. The changes made to these files will be discussed later in the chapter.

10. After files are installed, the computer must be rebooted to activate the network software. You are given the option `Restart your computer now?`. Choose **R**estart Computer to activate the network.

11. When you restart Windows, you will see a Welcome to Windows for Workgroups dialog box. This dialog box has the following two fields:

   - **Logon Name**. Matches the name you specified in Step 8.
   - **Password**. You should enter the password this user will enter to access the workgroup network.

Note WfW is capable of logging users on to a variety of resources while it is starting up. For this to work smoothly, a user should have the same User Name on each network. It is also useful to enter the same password on each network. There is no way to discover a password once it has been created, and one password is easier to remember than three or four.

12. Next you will see the message `There is no password list file for the user name. Do you want to create one now?`. Respond by choosing Yes.

13. A Confirm User Password dialog box requests that you enter the password a second time. Type the password again in the Confirm New Password dialog box and click on OK.

    WfW will encrypt the password you entered and store it in a file named *username*.PWL in the Windows directory (where *username* matches the user's logon name). The next time this user logs into WfW, a password will be requested and checked against the password in the PWL file. If a blank password was entered, no password is requested when WfW starts.

The computer is now set up to participate on a network, but cannot yet log onto a domain. The next section covers the steps to connect the computer to a Windows NT domain.

Connecting to a Domain

After a WfW computer has been configured to connect to a network you can enable it to log in to a domain. Start the Network utility in the Control Panel. The Microsoft Windows Network dialog box that is shown can be used to reconfigure many WfW network settings (see fig. 13.7).

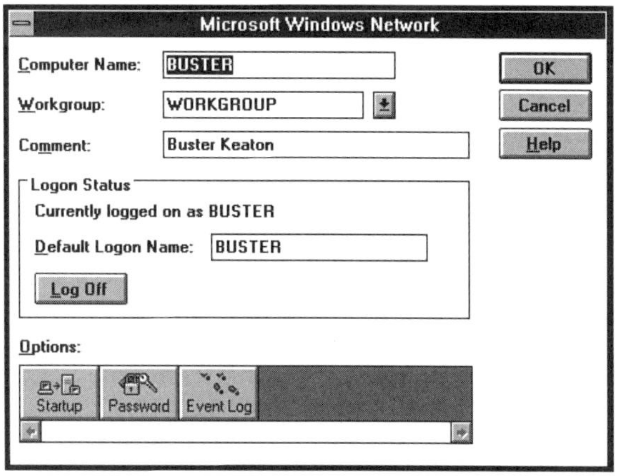

Figure 13.7
Windows for Workgroups network settings.

To configure WfW to log on to a domain when starting do the following:

1. Choose the Startup button to display the Startup Settings dialog box shown in figure 13.8. Several check boxes are included:

   - **Log On at Startup.** Check this box to have WfW log you on automatically when it starts.

   - **Enable Network DDE.** If you will be using network DDE with your applications, check this box. Check the box only if network DDE is required because enabling this option uses about 50 KB of memory.

   - **Ghosted Connections.** Selecting this option saves time at startup by not establishing connections to resources until they are actually placed in use. Drive letters are reserved for persistent connections, but connections are not established.

   - **Enable WinPopup.** WinPopup is a message display utility that displays network messages in Windows. If you will be broadcasting messages to users, enable this option. WinPopup also receives confirmation messages from domain print servers.

2. Check the box labeled Log On to Windows NT or LAN Manager Domain to enable Windows NT Server logon when WfW starts up.

3. Enter the log on domain name in the Domain Name box.

4. Choose Set Password to enter the logon password at this time.

5. If you do not want to receive a message confirming a successful logon, check the box Don't Display Message on Successful Logon.

6. Click on OK. You will be prompted to restart the computer.

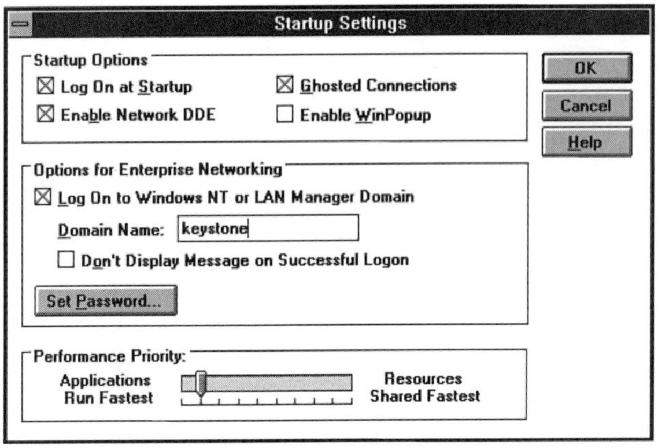

Figure 13.8

Specifying WfW network startup settings.

7. When WfW restarts, you will be presented with the Domain Logon dialog box shown in figure 13.9. Enter the password for the domain that was selected. If desired, you can change the domain, or Browse for one.

8. If you check the box Save this Password in Your Password List, WfW will encrypt the domain password and store it in this user's PWL file.

9. Following a successful domain logon, WfW displays a confirmation message similar to the one shown in figure 13.10. (This box will not display if Don't Display Message on Successful Logon was checked in Step 2.)

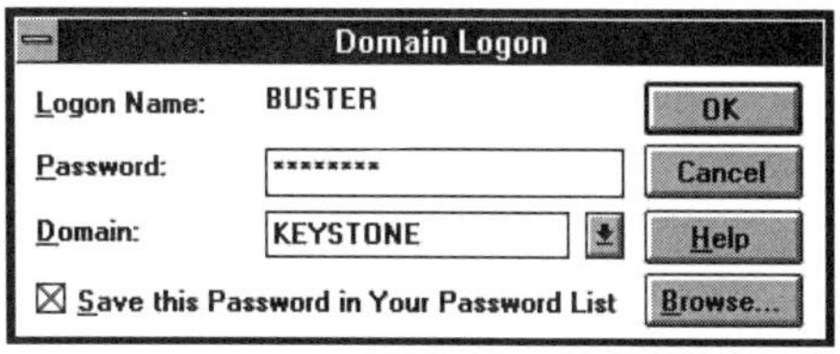

Figure 13.9
Logging on to a domain.

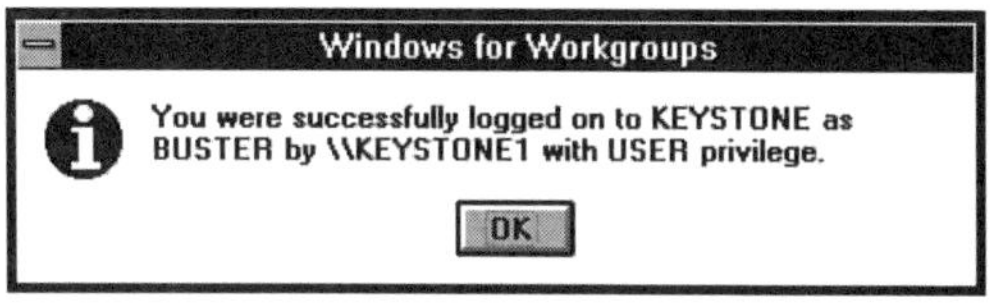

Figure 13.10
Confirmation of a successful domain logon.

After workgroup and domain passwords have been stored in a password file, WfW will not request them when starting unless they are refused by the workgroup or the domain.

If a password has changed, or if you want to change your password do the following:

- Change your domain password by selecting the Set Password button in the Startup Settings window (see figure 13.8).

- Change your workgroup password by selecting the Password button in the Microsoft Windows Network window, shown in figure 13.7.

If you have not logged on to a domain and attempt to browse domain resources, you will be shown the logon message displayed in figure 13.11, giving you the option of logging on to the domain.

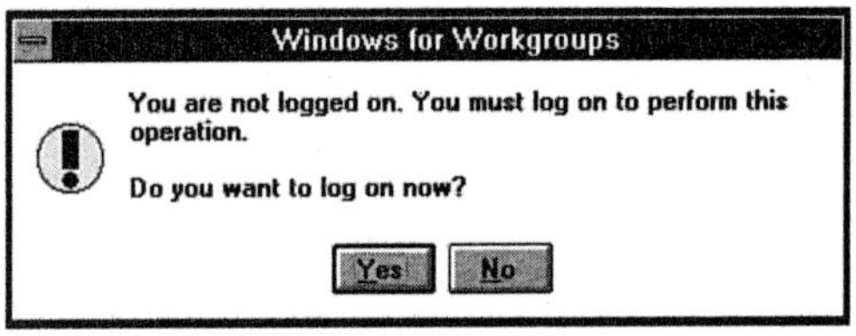

Figure 13.11
Logging on to the domain in mid-session.

Connecting to Shared Directories

WfW computers can connect to shared directories on Windows NT computers, using File Manager:

1. Run File Manager.
2. Choose the Connect Network Drive command in the Disk menu.
3. Specify a drive letter and browse the network for a shared directory.
4. Specify whether the disk should be reconnected at startup.
5. Click on OK.

The disk connection can be used as a virtual hard drive.

Connecting to Shared Printers

Unlike Windows NT, WfW computers cannot read print drivers from a print server. Before a WfW computer can use a printer that is shared by a Windows NT print server, the proper print drivers must be installed on the WfW computer.

To install a printer driver in Windows for Workgroups:

1. Start the Print Manager.
2. Choose the Printer Setup command from the Options menu.
3. In the Printers box, choose Add to display the List of Printers dialog box, shown in figure 13.12. Browse the list to determine if a driver is available to support your printer. If so, select the driver and choose Install. You will be prompted to insert disks from the WfW installation set.

   Unfortunately, the drivers that are included with Windows for Workgroups haven't been updated since the product was introduced two years ago, and many newer printer models are not directly supported. You might need to supply drivers on a floppy disk. To do so choose Install Unlisted or Updated Printer from the List of Printers and then choose Install. You will be prompted to enter a path where WfW can locate the print drivers, usually on drive A.

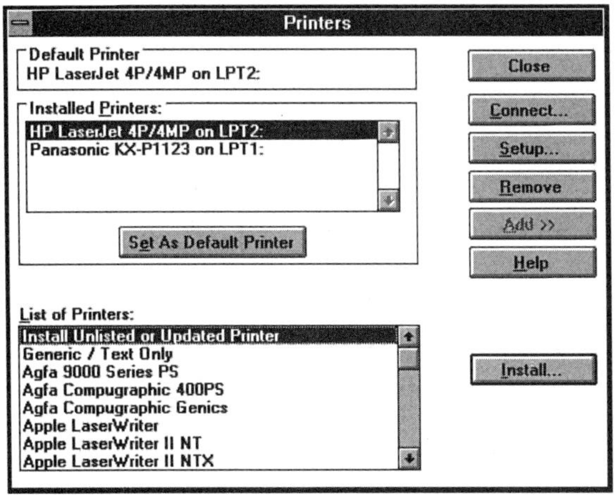

Figure 13.12

Installing a printer in Windows for Workgroups.

4. The new printer will be automatically installed on LPT1: even if another printer already occupies that port. If you are sharing a workgroup printer on LPT1:, you must assign the network printer to a new port. To do so do the following:

   - Choose Connect in the Printers window. This will reveal the Connect dialog box shown in figure 13.13.

   - Select an unoccupied port in the Ports box.

   - Click on OK. You will be returned to the Printers dialog box. The printer will now be installed on the port you have selected.

Note Windows uses background printing through the print manager to enable applications to print without waiting for a printer to become available. The approach works much like spooled printing on a network. Since printing on a network is already being spooled, you can improve network printing performance by enabling WfW to print directly to a port. To make the change, check the box Fast Printing Direct to Port in the Connect dialog box.

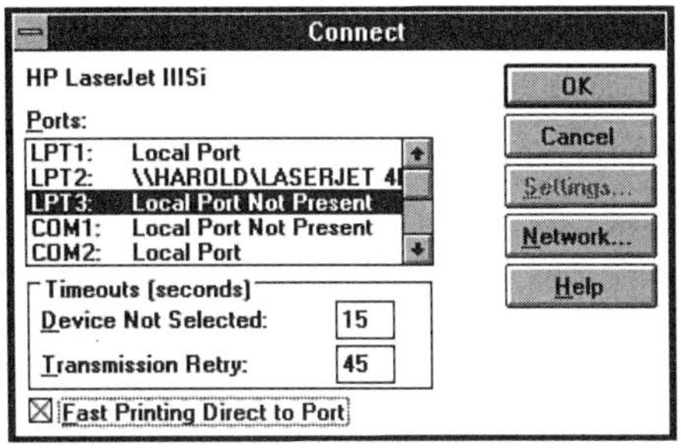

Figure 13.13

Connecting a printer to a port in Windows for Workgroups.

To enable an installed printer to print to the network, you must connect it to a shared printer. This is also done in Print Manager:

1. Start the Print Manager.
2. Select a printer that is labeled (not shared).
3. Choose **C**onnect Network Printer... from the **P**rinter menu. This will display the Connect Network Printer dialog box in which you can browse for a network printer. (See figure 13.14.)
4. Browse for a shareable printer and select it to store the path in the **P**ath box, or enter the path manually.
5. Indicate whether the printer should Reconnec**t** at Startup by checking the box.
6. Choose OK to return to the Connect dialog box. The **P**orts box will now show that the port you specified is connected to the shared network printer.
7. Click on OK to return to the Printer Manager. The printer list will now indicate the resource path to which the printer is connected.

Print Manager need not be running to print to the network unless you are sharing a local printer with a workgroup. WfW will open Print Manager if it is required.

Figure 13.14

Browsing for printers in Windows for Workgroups.

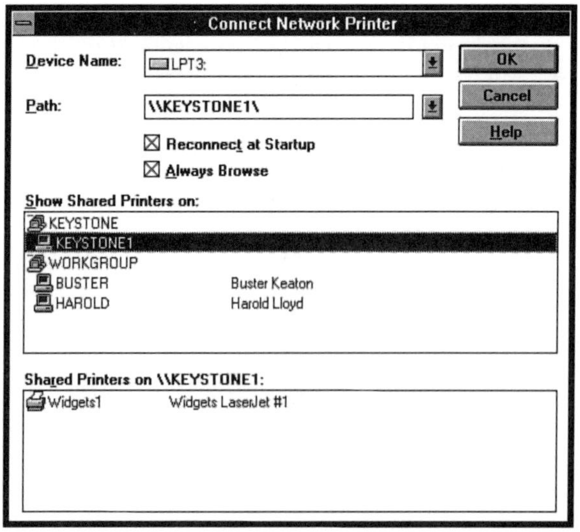

MS-DOS

Windows NT Server includes software that enables MS-DOS and Windows 3.1 computers to function as clients on an Windows NT Server network. The client software is called Microsoft Network Client 3.0 for MS-DOS.

Note Do not use software called the Workgroup Connection, which is available from several sources including CompuServe and the Microsoft TechNet CD-ROMs. The Workgroup Connection uses very old technology from the first version of Windows for Workgroups, version 3.1. Workgroup Connection will enable workstations to log onto the network, but does not enable them to take advantage of many Windows NT Server features such as logon scripts.

Creating an Installation Disk

You will need to create installation disks before the client software can be installed on the workstation. Disks are created using the Network Client Administrator utility, which is installed in the Network Administration program group.

When you start the Network Client Administrator, you will see the Network Client Administrator dialog box with several options, shown in figure 13.15.

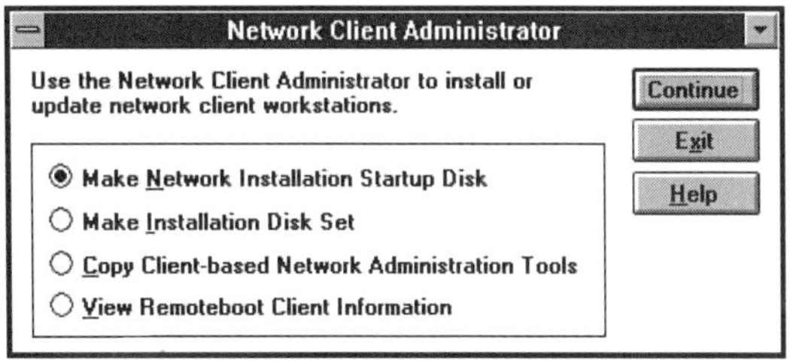

Figure 13.15
The Network Client Administrator options.

The DOS client can be installed in the following two ways:

- Using a network installation startup disk that you boot on the workstation. This disk has enough information to connect to the network and download client software from a directory on the server.
- Using client installation disks that enable you to manually install the software on the workstation.

Using a network installation startup disk has a number of catches:

- ◆ The disk must be formatted as a system disk using the same DOS version as the computer on which it will be installed. This can be problematic unless all your PCs have exactly the same DOS version.
- ◆ The disk must include a driver for the network card that will be on the workstation. Unless all your computers use the same network card, you will need several disks.
- ◆ It doesn't always work, and you might have to resort to manual installation in any case.

Therefore, the procedure I will describe involves use of a conventional client installation disk set.

To create the disk set, select the option Make Installation Disk Set and choose Continue. This will take you to the Share Network Client Installation Files dialog box, shown in figure 13.16.

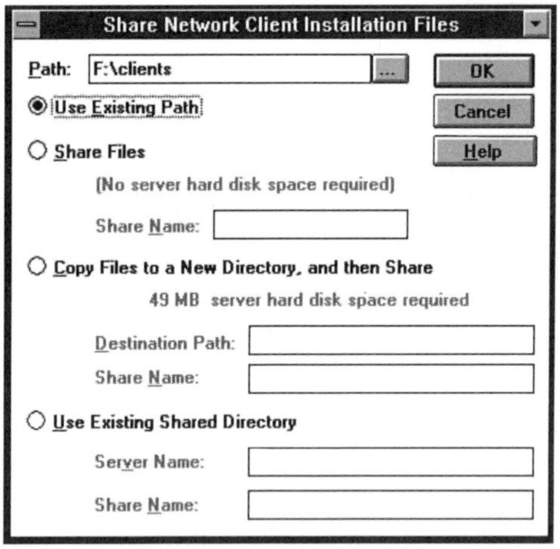

Figure 13.16
Network client installation options.

Network Client Administrator can copy the drivers for various network clients to the server, where they can be available to support client installation using network installation startup disks. Since the method described here uses the client installation disk set, it is not necessary to copy files to the server. They can be copied directly from the Windows NT Server installation media (in my case a CD-ROM) to the floppies.

To create the installation disk set:

1. Locate two high density disks. All files on these disks will be erased. Label these disks Network Client v3.0 Disks 1 and 2.

2. Start Network Client Administrator, select the Make **I**nstallation Disk Set option, and choose Continue.

3. In the Share Network Client Installation Files dialog box, select Use **E**xisting Path. Be sure that the drive letter in the **P**ath box is correct for your CD-ROM.

4. Click on OK to display the Make Installation Disk Set dialog box shown in figure 13.17.

5. In the **N**etwork Client or Service select Network Client 3.0 for MS-DOS and Windows.

6. Select the **D**estination Drive you will be using.

7. Check the **F**ormat Disks box. It is always a good idea to format. A quick format will be performed if possible to save time.

8. Click on OK and follow the prompts to create the disks.

Figure 13.17
Preparing to create client installation disks.

Installing Network Client for MS-DOS

Network Client requires MS-DOS version 3.3 or later. To install the Network Client on a DOS PC:

1. Insert Disk 1 and, depending on the drive that holds the disks, type **A:SETUP** or **B:SETUP** from the C: prompt.

2. Press Enter once to reach a screen where you can enter a directory in which files will be installed. The default is C:\NET. Change this path if desired and press Enter.

3. SETUP will examine your PC hardware. You might see the message shown in figure 13.18. Network Client requires a substantial amount of DOS memory. Unless you will be using a memory manager to move programs to upper memory you will need to do everything you can to conserve memory.

   Press Enter if SETUP should maximize performance at the expense of higher memory overhead.

   Press **C** to conserve memory at the cost of reducing performance.

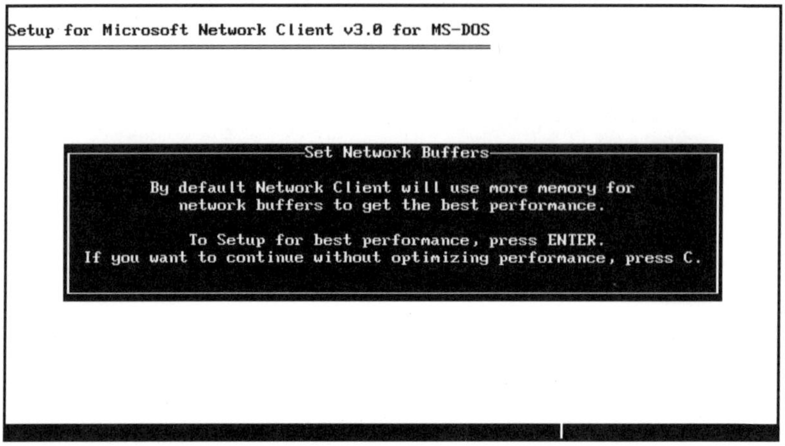

Figure 13.18
The Set Network Buffers message.

4. Enter a computer name of up to 15 characters. The name can include letters, numbers, and these characters: ! # $ % ^ & ( ) _ ' { } ~, but not spaces.

   After you enter a computer name, you will see the screen shown in figure 13.19. This screen accesses three other screens that configure the Network Client. Use the arrow keys to highlight an option, and press Enter to select the option.

5. Select the Change Names option to display the screen shown in figure 13.20. The computer name you entered in Step 4 will appear in the Change User Name and Change Computer Name fields.

   The other fields will show the default entry of WORKGROUP. In the figure, the domain name has been edited.

   To change a field, highlight it with the arrow keys and press Enter. Modify the entry in the Change Domain Name field to match the domain this computer will log on to.

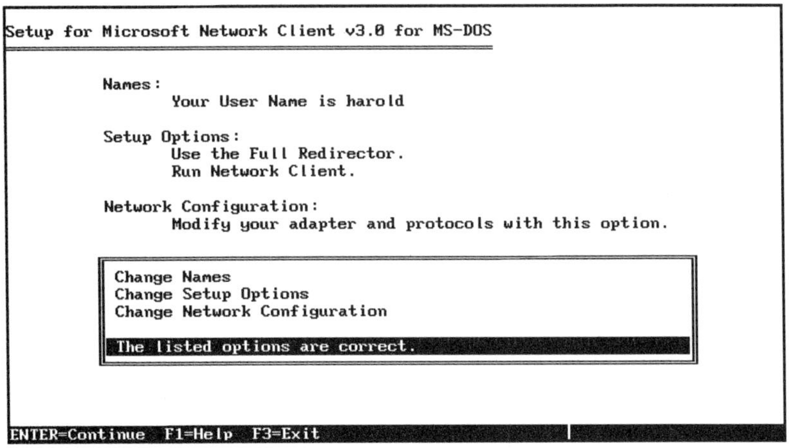

Figure 13.19

The main menu in Setup for Network Client v3.0.

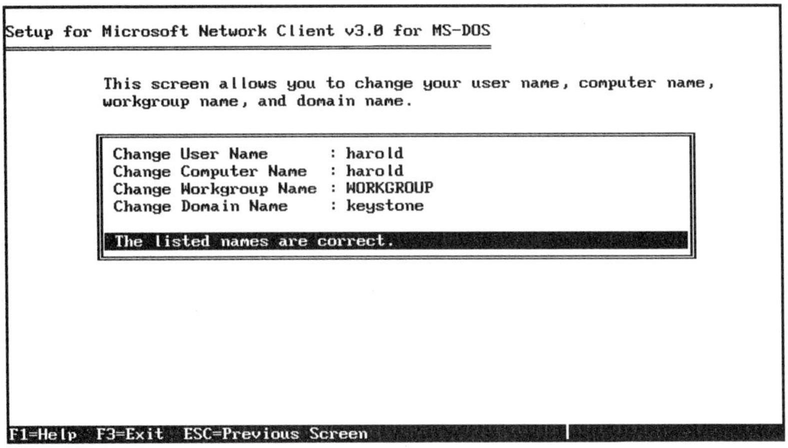

Figure 13.20

Changing Network Client names.

6. Select The listed names are correct, and press Enter to save the changes and return to the Setup menu.

7. Select Change Setup Options. This will bring up the screen shown in figure 13.21. This screen has four options that you may choose to modify:

   - **Change Redir Options.** You can choose to use the Full Redirector or the Basic Redirector. The Basic Redirectory works for many users and saves memory. The Full Director is required to support Microsoft Windows, Remote Access Service, and other advanced functions.

- **Change Startup Options.** You can choose to:

  Run Network Client. The client runs when the computer is booted.

  Run Network Client and Load Pop-Up. The pop-up is a utility that enables you to connect to network resources from a menu interface. It can be easily loaded later if needed.

  Do Not Run Network Client. The client software must be started manually.

- **Change Logon Validation.** You can choose the following:

  Do Not Logon to Domain.

  Logon to Domain.

- **Change Net Pop Hot Key.** When the NET pop-up utility is loaded, it can be displayed with a hot key, normally Alt+N. You can change the letter for the hot key if it is used by another utility.

When you have configured these options choose `The listed options are correct.`

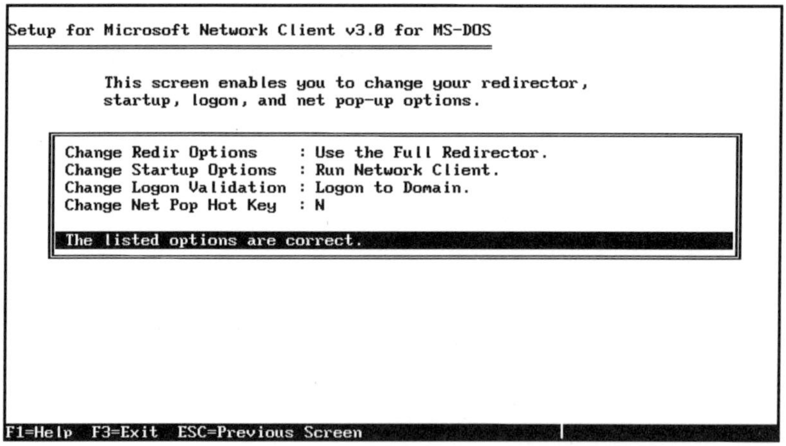

Figure 13.21
Entering setup options.

8. Select Change Network Configuration to display the screen shown in figure 13.22, which is used to configure network adapters and protocols.

9. Examine the network adapter in the Installed Network Adapter(s) box.

   This screen has two boxes: Installed Network Adapters and Protocols and Options. To change the active box, press Tab.

10. If the listed adapter is incorrect, select Remove in the Options box. You will be asked immediately to add a network adapter. Select an adapter from the list provided.

11. To add an adapter choose Add Adapter and select an adapter from the list provided. To supply a driver for a card that is not listed, choose `Network adapter not shown on the list below....`

12. Choose Change Settings and review the settings for your adapter. Figure 13.22 shows the settings screen. Change any setting by selecting it and choosing new values from a list.

    The default protocol NWLink is probably the only protocol you will require. If you want to install other protocols, choose Add Protocol.

    - Microsoft NetBEUI. Add this protocol if you want to access shared resources on workgroup computers that are not running NWLink.
    - Microsoft TCP/IP. Add to support the TCP/IP protocol suite. *See Chapter 15, " Using TCP/IP, " for more information.*

13. Choose Network configuration is correct to return to the SETUP menu.

14. After all settings are correct, continue installation by choosing The listed options are correct in the setup menu.

15. You will be prompted to reboot the computer to activate the network software.

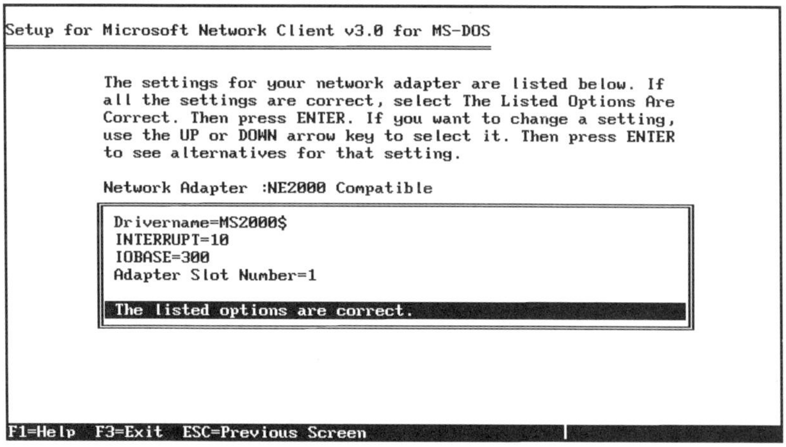
Setup for Microsoft Network Client v3.0 for MS-DOS
The settings for your network adapter are listed below. If all the settings are correct, select The Listed Options Are Correct. Then press ENTER. If you want to change a setting, use the UP or DOWN arrow key to select it. Then press ENTER to see alternatives for that setting.
Network Adapter :NE2000 Compatible
Drivername=MS2000$
INTERRUPT=10
IOBASE=300
Adapter Slot Number=1
The listed options are correct.
F1=Help F3=Exit ESC=Previous Screen

Figure 13.22

Configuring network adapter settings.

Tip You may rerun the SETUP utility in the network directory to reconfigure options. This is much more efficient than attempting to edit configuration files manually. Do not reconfigure by running SETUP from the client installation disks.

Note Network Client v3.0 uses a significant amount of DOS memory. Unless you optimize memory, you might find that some applications will not run. You might also find that NET commands in logon scripts cannot be run due to memory limitations.

It is strongly recommended that you run a memory manager on all DOS clients. If possible, configure your system without expanded memory since EMS page frames occupy high DOS memory that could be used to relocate DOS TSRs and drivers.

Logging On with Network Client

After the system boots, you can log on to the network.

1. The logon procedure depends on the option you chose for the Startup Option field in Setup.

   - If you chose `Run Network Client` and `Logon to Domain`, you will receive the prompt `Type your user name`. The user name you entered during setup will be presented as a default. Enter a user name or press Enter to accept the default.

   - If you chose `Do Not Logon to Domain`, you must type the command **NET LOGON** at the DOS prompt when you want to connect to the network.

2. After you log on, you will be prompted for a workgroup password. Workgroup passwords might be stored in a file, you will be asked if you want to create a password file for this user.

3. If the DOS client is logging on to a Windows NT Server domain, you will be prompted to enter a domain password.

4. If the full redirectory has been loaded, after logging on, any commands in the user's login script will be executed.

Connecting Drives and Printers with the Workstation Connection NET Pop-Up

Network functions are accessed with the NET utility, which has both a command-line and a pop-up interface. The default hot key for the pop-up utility is Ctrl+Alt+N.

To connect a drive:

1. Activate the NET pop-up by typing **NET**. If it is already loaded, press the hot key to display the Disk Connections dialog box, shown in figure 13.23. Select fields in Disk Connections by pressing the Tab key.

2. If desired, change the drive letter in the Drive field.

3. Connect to a shared directory by entering a path in the **P**ath field and choosing **C**onnect.

4. Choose **R**econnect at startup if you want this connection to be reestablished when the Network Client starts up.

5. Press Esc when done.

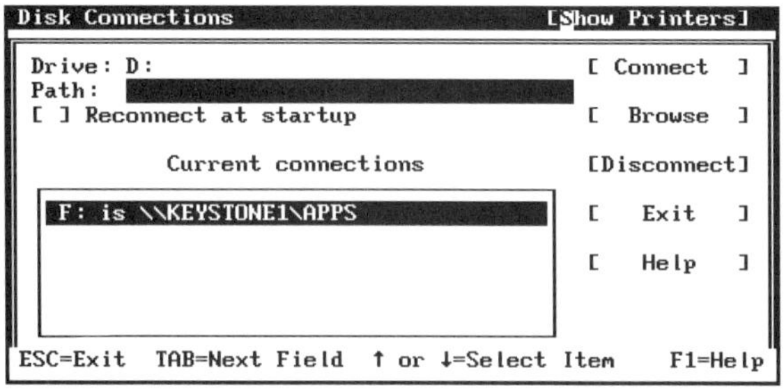

Figure 13.23

Connecting drives with the NET pop-up utility.

To connect a printer:

1. Start the NET utility by typing **NET** or by pressing the hot key if NET is already loaded.

2. Select **S**how Printers to display the Printer Connections box shown in figure 13.24.

3. Select a Port. No default value is provided.

4. Enter a printer path in the Path field and choose **C**onnect to make a connection.

5. Check **R**econnect at Startup to have this printer connect when the Network Client is started.

6. Press Esc to leave the pop-up utility.

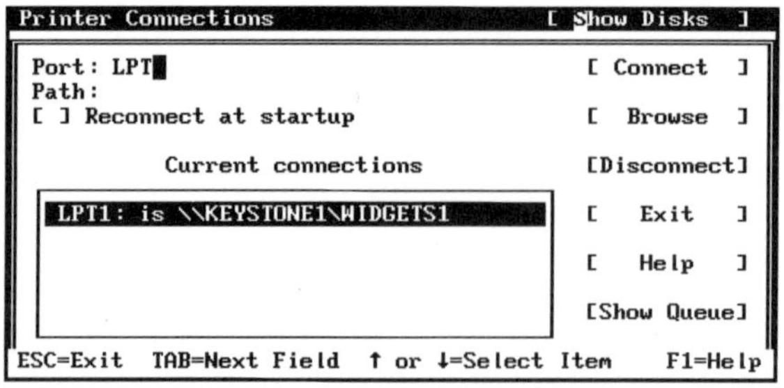

Figure 13.24
Printer Connections in the Network Client pop-up.

Using Network Client Commands

The NET command accepts several command arguments that control functions such as logon, logoff, and resource connections. These commands can be used interactively, but are probably most valuable when included in logon scripts. Examples of logon scripts will be provided in the `Logon Scripts` section later in this chapter.

Because the NET commands can be used with a variety of network clients, they are summarized in the Appendix. Some of the most useful are briefly discussed here.

NET HELP

NET HELP displays a summary of the NET command options. You can display details about any command by including a command as a option. For example, to see a help listing on the LOGON command type:

```
NET HELP LOGON
```

NET LOGON

NET LOGON initiates a logon dialog. Entered alone, NET LOGON prompts you for a user name and a password. You can also enter the name and password as parameters, for example, buster would log on the default domain or workgroup with the password general like this:

```
NET LOGON BUSTER GENERAL
```

A different domain can be specified with the /domain:*domainname* option. For example:

```
NET LOGON HAROLD CLOCK /DOMAIN:WIDGETS
```

NET LOGOFF

NET LOGOFF breaks your logon connection with the network. If you include the /YES option, you will not be asked to confirm your logoff request.

NET USE

Disks and printers are both connected and disconnected with the NET USE command. To connect drive C to the APPS share on KEYSTONE1, use this command:

```
NET USE C: \\KEYSTONE1\APPS
```

The following command connects LPT1: to printer WIDGETS1 on server KEYSTONE1:

```
NET USE LPT1: \\KEYSTONE1\WIDGETS1
```

Add the option /PERSISTENT:YES to specify connections that should be made when the Workstation Connection starts up.

To see a list of your connected resources, enter the NET USE command without options.

NET VIEW

Use the NET VIEW command to list computers and shared resources. Enter NET VIEW without options to list computers that are sharing resources in your domain.

Include a computer name to list shared resources on the computer. NET VIEW \\KEYSTONE1 lists shared resources on KEYSTONE1.

NET TIME

NET TIME provides a convenient means of synchronizing a computer's clock with the clock on another computer. It is generally preferable to synchronize clocks in a share environment so that users can be assured that time and data stamps are meaningful.

To synchronize a client clock with the computer \\KEYSTONE1, you would use this command:

```
NET TIME \\KEYSTONE1 /SET /YES
```

The `/YES` parameter carries out the NET TIME command without prompting you for confirmation.

NET STOP

The NET STOP command unloads services. To unload the pop-up, enter the command:

```
NET STOP POPUP
```

You can stop the default redirector, which disconnects you from the network, by entering the command:

```
NET STOP WORKSTATION
```

NET PASSWORD

Change your password with the NET PASSWORD command. Remember that users can have passwords in several places, including the password list file on the client and the user name database on a domain or workstation.

Entered without parameter, the command prompts you for old and new passwords. You can also include old and new passwords as parameters. To change the password in the client password list file, the command syntax would be:

```
NET PASSWORD oldpassword newpassword
```

To change a password on a specific computer, include the computer name as a parameter. A user name is also required:

```
NET PASSWORD \\WIDGETS1 MABEL oldpassword newpassword
```

To specify a domain, use the /DOMAIN option:

```
NET PASSWORD /DOMAIN:KEYSTONE oldpassword newpassword
```

Windows 3.1

The Network Client can be used to enable Windows 3.1 computers to access Windows networks. Although Windows 3.1 workstations lack the workgroup features of Windows for Workgroups, they can become clients of Windows NT Server domains and of Windows workgroups.

Installing Networking for Windows 3.1

Network Client should be installed as described in the section "Installing Network Client." This is a standard DOS installation, and no differences are required when Windows will be supported.

You might be tempted to install the Network Client files in the same directory as Windows, but this will not be permitted. The primary reason is probably that both Windows and Network Client rely on files named SYSTEM.INI, and Setup is not permitted to overwrite the Windows SYSTEM.INI file. (Windows for Workgroups is more fully integrated for networking and one SYSTEM.INI file serves both WfW and the network drivers.)

After Network Client is installed, reboot the computer. Then start Windows and configure networking as follows:

1. Start the Windows Setup utility in the Main program group.
2. Choose **C**hange System Settings in the Windows Setup **O**ptions menu. This will display the Change System Settings dialog box.
3. Pull down the **N**etwork box in Change System Settings to display a list of network options. From this list, choose the entry `Microsoft Network (or 100% compatible)`.
4. Click on OK to save the settings. Then close Windows Setup.
5. When you exit Windows setup, You will be told that `You need to exit Windows so that the changes you made will take effect`. Choose **R**estart Windows to activate networking.
6. You should check two settings in the Control Panel. Start the Network utility in the Control panel.
   - If you want to have connections established in Windows reestablished when Windows starts, check the box **R**estore all connections at startup.
   - Normally, you will receive warning messages if network services are not running. To eliminate these messages, check the box **D**isable warning when network not running.

   Click on OK when network settings have been made.

You are now ready to connect to network resources.

Connecting to Network Resources

You can connect to network resources in the following ways:

- By entering NET USE commands before starting Windows or from an MS-DOS prompt in Windows. These connections will be reestablished if you include the /PERSISTENT:YES option.

- By connecting to files with File Manager and printers with Print Manager. These connections will be reestablished when Windows restarts if you checked the box in the Network utility of the Control Panel Restore all connections at startup.

Connecting Drives with File Manager

To connect a drive with File Manager do the following:

1. Choose Network Clients in the Disk menu. The Network Clients dialog box (figure 13.25) is somewhat different from the same box in Windows for Workgroups.
2. Select an available drive letter in the Drive box.
3. Enter the path in the Network Path box. The Windows Networking driver does not enable you to browse for network resources.
4. If a password is required for this share, enter it in the Password box.
5. Choose Connect.
6. Click on Close when all required connections are established.

The drives you have connected can now be used by any Windows program.

Figure 13.25

Connecting a drive in Windows 3.1.

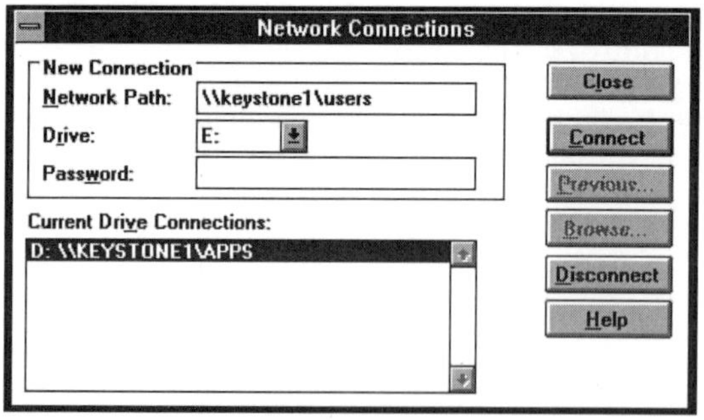

Connecting Printers with Print Manager

To connect a printer:

1. Choose Network Clients in the Options menu. The Printers-Network Clients dialog box, shown in figure 13.26, will be displayed.
2. Enter a path in the Network Path box. As with File Manager, you will be unable to browse for resources.

3. If a password is required for this share, enter it in the Password box.

4. Choose Connect. The printer connection will appear in the Current Printer Connections box.

5. Add other printer connections if desired by selecting other ports and entering the desired paths. Choose Connect to complete each connection.

6. Click on Close to return to the Print Manager.

The printers you have connected can now be used for printing with any Windows program.

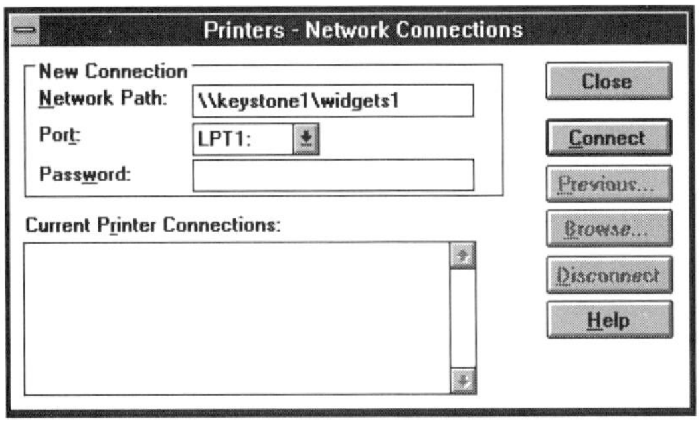

Figure 13.26

Connecting printers with Print Manager.

Files Used with DOS and Windows Clients

When Microsoft network software is installed on a computer, several files are modified or added. Some of these modifications define parameters that you might need to modify, so it is a good idea to take the time to familiarize yourself with the files discussed in the following sections.

CONFIG.SYS

Windows for Workgroups 3.11 and Network Connection 3.0 require two new lines in the CONFIG.SYS file:

```
LASTDRIVE=Z
DEVICE=C:\NET\IFSHLP.SYS
```

`LASTDRIVE=Z` configures DOS to support drive letters up to Z. (By default, DOS supports drives A through E.)

AUTOEXEC.BAT

If you have configured the computer to start the network automatically when booting, the NET START command will be added to the AUTOEXEC.BAT file, along with an appropriate path to locate the NET.EXE file. For example:

```
C:\WINDOWS\NET START
```

Windows for Workgroups performs most network functions within Windows. The Workgroup Connection must perform all network configuration functions from DOS. Therefore, Workgroup Connection 3.0 adds some other lines to AUTOEXEC.BAT.

With Network Connection, when protocols other than NetBEUI are loaded, the following command is added to the beginning of AUTOEXEC.BAT to load protocols and drivers without binding them to the Protocol Manager:

```
C:\NET\NET INITIALIZE
```

If you are using NWLink with Network Connection 3.0, you will see this line in the AUTOEXEC.BAT file, which loads the NWLink protocol:

```
C:\NET\NWLINK
```

Finally, Network Connection adds a NET START command. With Network Connection, NET START can be configured to log the user onto the network. Windows for Workgroups logs the user on after WfW starts.

PROTOCOL.INI

The PROTOCOL.INI file defines the configuration for the NDIS drivers. If several network card drivers or protocols are being loaded, PROTOCOL.INI can get quite elaborate, so we will examine only a simple example that loads an NE2000 adapter and the NETBEUI protocol. In general, you will find it much easier to let Microsoft setup programs build the PROTOCOL.INI file for the hardware you want to support. You will be required to make only small manual modifications to PROTOCOL.INI if any are needed at all. The file can be modified by any text editor, including the Windows Notepad.

Windows for Workgroups places the PROTOCOL.INI file in the Windows installation directory (usually C:\WINDOWS). Network Client setup places PROTOCOL.INI in the Network Client installation directory.

Here is a listing of a PROTOCOL.INI that was created by Network Client. I have added numbers to the lines to simplify discussion. This section won't go through the file line-by-line, but it will point out some significant features.

```
[network.setup]
version=0x3110
netcard=ms$ne2clone,1,MS$NE2CLONE,1
transport=ms$nwlink,MS$NWLINK
transport=ms$ndishlp,MS$NDISHLP
lana0=ms$ne2clone,1,ms$nwlink
lana1=ms$ne2clone,1,ms$ndishlp

[MS$NWLINK]
FRAME=ETHERNET_802.2
DriverName=nwlink$
BINDINGS=MS$NE2CLONE
[MS$NE2CLONE]
IOBASE=0x300
INTERRUPT=10
DriverName=MS2000$
[MS$AE2]
IOBASE=0x300
INTERRUPT=3
[MS$NE1CLONE]
IOBASE=0x300
INTERRUPT=3

[protman]
DriverName=PROTMAN$
PRIORITY=MS$NDISHLP

[MS$NDISHLP]
DriverName=ndishlp$
BINDINGS=MS$NE2CLONE
```

This file is divided into several sections, each beginning with a label in square brackets, for example `[MS$NDISHLP]`. These labels enable network components to locate the lines that are relevant to them.

The `[network.setup]` section defines the basic characteristics of the network by cross-referencing other sections. The line beginning with netcard, for example, states that the driver to be used is MS$NECLONE and that parameters for the card can be found in the section `[MS$NE2CLONE]`.

The `[protman]` section defines parameters for the protocol manager. If additional protocols are added to the NDIS protocol stack, this section tells the protocol manager which protocols have priority.

The [MS$NDISHLP] section supports configuration of the NDIS protocol stack and binds the NE2CLONE driver to the stack. You should not need to edit this section.

Each network board will have a section dedicated to it, in this example [MS$NECLONE]. This is the only section that is likely to require manual attention if a card is reconfigured or if the setup program will not permit you to enter a setting that your hardware supports.

SYSTEM.INI

A file named SYSTEM.INI is used by Windows and by Network Client. For Windows, this file is located in the Windows installation directory, which is C:\WINDOWS by default.

Network Client Setup will not permit you to install Network Client in the same directory as Windows, so you will have SYSTEM.INI files for both Windows and for Network Client.

SYSTEM.INI in Network Client

For Network Client, SYSTEM.INI has the following structure:

```
[network]
sizworkbuf=1498
filesharing=no
printsharing=no
autologon=yes
computername=HAROLD
lanroot=C:\NET
username=HAROLD
workgroup=WORKGROUP
reconnect=yes
dospophotkey=N
lmlogon=1
logondomain=KEYSTONE
preferredredir=full
autostart=full
maxconnections=8

[network drivers]
netcard=ne2000.dos
transport=ndishlp.sys,*netbeui
devdir=C:\NET
LoadRMDrivers=yes
```

```
[Password Lists]
*Shares=C:\NET\Shares.PWL
HAROLD=C:\NET\HAROLD.PWL
```

You will recognize in this file many of the parameters that you entered when you set up the software. In fact, you can reconfigure most of the startup features of Network Client by editing this file. It is generally more prudent, however, to make changes with the SETUP utility.

Each user who establishes a password list file (PWL extension) on the client will be given an entry in the `[Password Lists]` section.

SYSTEM.INI in Windows for Workgroups

Windows has a SYSTEM.INI file that contains settings both for Windows and for the network. The changes made to SYSTEM.INI are different for Windows for Workgroups 3.11 and network-enabled Windows 3.1. You will find it useful to scan SYSTEM.INI using either the Windows NOTEPAD or SYSEDIT utilities to identify features that are modified or added when networking is configured.

In WfW, you will find `[network]` and `[Password Lists]` sections that serve similar purposes to the sections defined for Network Client but might be more elaborate. WfW can share resources in addition to connecting to shares, and extra settings are required in the WfW SETUP.INI file.

Most of the network-related features of SYSTEM.INI can be reconfigured in Windows using the Control Panel or Windows Setup utilities. If you will be editing this file (or any configuration file for that matter), save a backup copy in case you introduce an error.

Windows 95

Microsoft's newest Windows product, Windows 95, should be available at about the time this book is published. Windows 95 integrates effortlessly into most networks. The details of installation won't be discussed here, but some of the most important features of using Windows 95 in a Windows NT Server network will be covered.

Despite being a 32-bit operating system and a significant enhancement over Windows 3.*x*, Windows 95 retains many of the underlying technologies that are found in Windows for Workgroups and DOS. If you browse the WINDOWS directory, you will find a PROTOCOL.INI file, for example. All features of Windows 95 networking, however, can be set up from the Control Panel, and manual editing should seldom, if ever, be required.

Installing Windows 95 Networking

The installation program for Windows 95 uses Microsoft's Wizard technology to take you through the procedure step-by-step. Network installation and configuration is highly automated, and you will need to do little more than answer a few questions.

During installation, you are asked if you want to identify network adapters in your computer. If you check the Network Adapter box, the Setup Wizard will scan your system for an adapter and will probably succeed in identifying not only the adapter but its settings as well.

Note If you are using a compatible card, automatic card identification may fail. My card can be configured in two modes including NE2000 compatible. Windows 95 identified the card by its default mode, and manual configuration was required. It is difficult for automatic configuration to cope with hardware that has multiple personalities. By and large, however, Windows 95 should set up without a hitch with most hardware.

After Windows 95 is set up, you can add or reconfigure network adapters using the Network utility, which you start by opening the My Computer icon on the desktop and then choosing Control Panel. Figure 13.27 shows the Network utility after a network adapter has been added and configured. (If you haven't seen Windows 95, take note of the new tabs, which make it easy to flip through various configuration boxes. Just click the tab to select a different set of configuration options.) The following procedures demonstrate how to get to this point.

To add a network adapter, do the following:

1. Choose Add in the Configuration tab to display the Select Network Component Type dialog box shown in figure 13.28.

2. In most cases you will select an adapter and permit Windows 95 to select protocols. To select an adapter, click Adapter and choose Add to display the Select Network Adapters window shown in figure 13.29.

3. Select Network Adapters has two lists of options. First select an entry in the Manufacturers list. Then select a specific card in the Network Adapters list. If your card is not supported by drivers shipped by Windows 95, you can supply drivers on a disk by choosing the Have Disk... button. After specifying an adapter, you will be returned to the Network window, which will be completed as shown in figure 13.27.

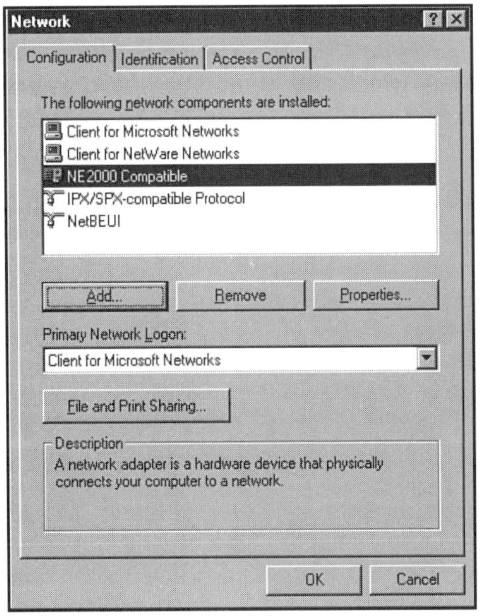

Figure 13.27

The Network window with an installed and configured network adapter.

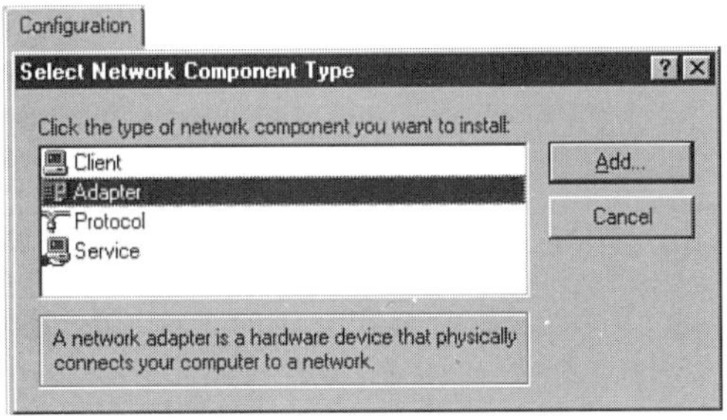

Figure 13.28

Selecting a network component to install.

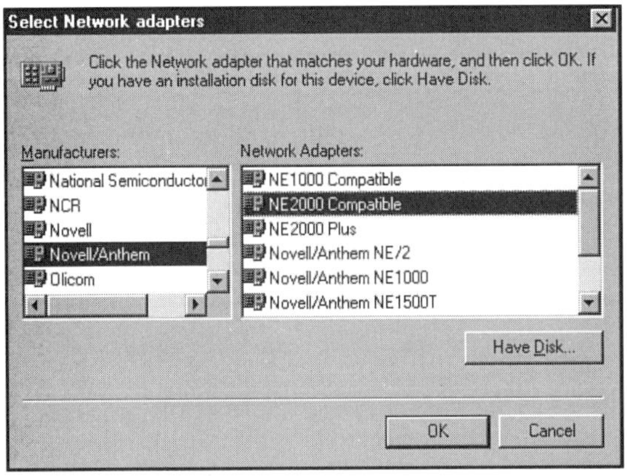

Figure 13.29

Selecting a network adapter.

Notice that support is automatically installed for both Microsoft and NetWare networks. Also, both the NWLink (IPX/SPX compatible) and the NetBEUI protocols are installed. In its default configuration, Windows 95 will integrate smoothly into Windows NT Server, Microsoft workgroup, and NetWare networks.

4. By default, the Primary Network Logon field will be set to Client for Microsoft Networks. You can pull down this list to change the default logon to Client for NetWare Networks or to Windows Logon. Choose Windows Logon if you do not want Windows 95 to access the network each time it is started.

5. To enable sharing click the File and Print Sharing button. You can check the following options:

   - I want to be able to give others access to my files.
   - I want to be able to allow others to print to my printer(s).

   After you enable these options, the network components list will include File and printer sharing for Microsoft Networks.

6. Click the Identification tab to enter the following information:

   - **Computer Name.** If you will be logging in to a Windows NT Server network, enter your user name.
   - **Workgroup.** Enter a workgroup name or the name of an Windows NT Server domain.
   - **Computer Description.** Enter a more extensive identification of the computer, such as your full name.

7. To configure adapter settings, select the adapter in the network components window and choose Properties. Figure 13.31 shows an example of a Properties dialog box. The options you will have in Properties will depend on your network adapter. The NE2000 Compatible Properties dialog box has three tabs:

   - Driver type (16- or 32-bit)
   - Bindings (protocols)
   - Resources (network adapter settings)

8. After you have configured network settings, click on OK in the Network window. Respond to the prompts if disk changes are required. Then restart the computer when prompted to activate network support.

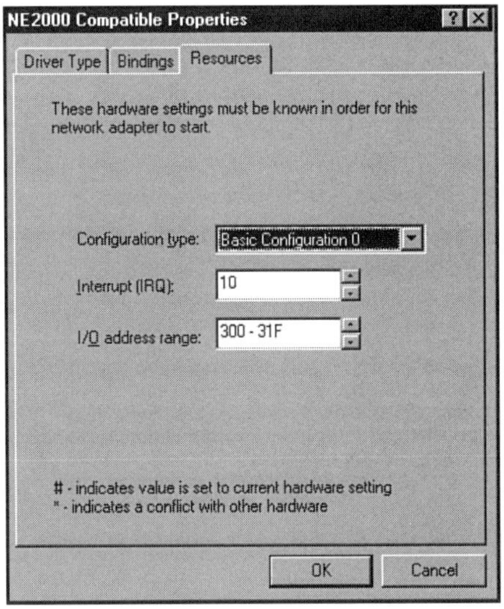

Figure 13.30
Configuring resources for an NE2000 compatible.

Logging On to the Network

When Windows 95 restarts, it should connect to the network. Assuming that you entered a domain name in the workstation identification dialog box, you will be asked to "Type your password to enter the Microsoft Network."

Windows 95 does not remember your Microsoft Network password, and it must be reentered each time you log onto the network.

Accessing Shared Directories with Windows 95

Windows 95 has a terrific browsing tool called the Network Neighborhood, which is installed as a desktop icon. Figure 13.31 shows a series of windows that were opened starting with the Network Neighborhood icon. Eventually, a window for the Keystone1 server was encountered which shows all resources that the server is sharing. Connections to shared directories and printers can be established starting from this window. (Notice that I could have gotten directly to Keystone1 in the Network Neighborhood window, but I wanted to give you a more extensive tour.)

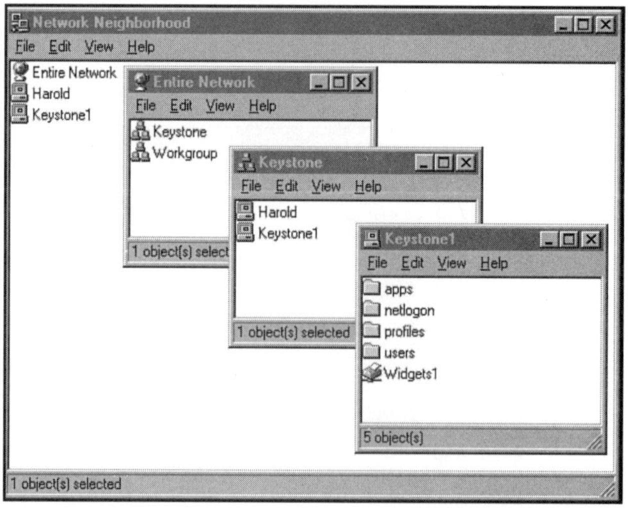

Figure 13.31

Browsing for resources in Windows 95.

Connecting to a Shared Directory

To connect to a shared directory:

1. Browse the network neighborhood to find the icon for the directory.
2. Point to a shared directory and click the right mouse button (That's right. Finally a version of Windows has put that right mouse button to good use.) to open a command menu that includes the option **Map** Network Drive.
3. Choose **Map** Network Drive to display the Map Network Drive dialog box shown in figure 13.32.
4. Choose a different drive letter in the **Drive** box if desired.
5. Check Reconnect at logon to have this connection reestablished when Windows 95 logs you onto the network.
6. Click on OK when settings are complete. A new drive window will be created on your desktop. It will also be added to the My Computer window.

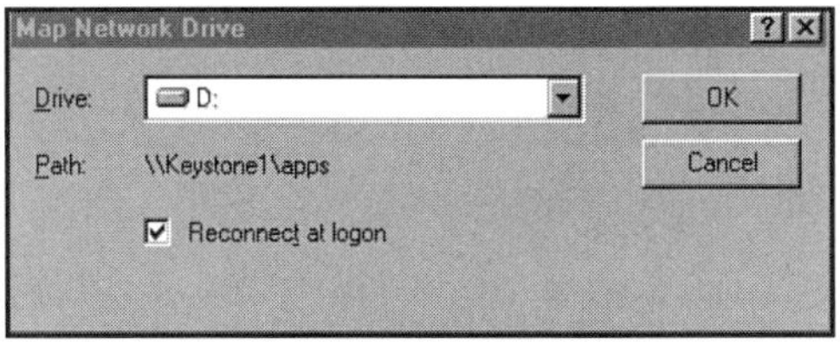

Figure 13.32

Connecting to a shared directory with Windows 95.

Connecting to a Shared Printer

Before you can connect to a shared printer, you must first install printer drivers on Windows 95. Adding printers is controlled by a Wizard that you start by choosing the Add Printer Icon in the Printers folder of the My Desktop window.

The Add Printer Wizard asks you if you are creating a local or network printer. If you create a network printer, The Wizard will give you the option of selecting a shared printer. Windows 95 can identify the printer driver that is required for the shared printer, but cannot load the driver from the server as Windows NT can do. After identifying printer type, the Wizard will copy appropriate drivers from your installation disks.

After a printer has been installed, to connect to a shared printer:

1. Browse the network neighborhood to find the icon for the printer.
2. Point to a shared printer and click the right mouse button to open a command menu that includes the option Capture Printer Port.
3. Choose Capture Printer Port to open the Capture Printer Port dialog box shown in figure 13.33.
4. Change the port in the Device box if desired.
5. Check Reconnect at logon to have this connection reestablished when Windows 95 logs you onto the network.
6. Click on OK when settings are complete.

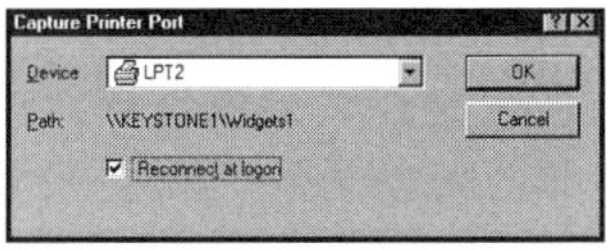

Figure 13.33

Capturing a printer port in Windows 95.

Logon Scripts

Logon scripts are an effective way to configure Windows NT Server clients when they are logging onto the network. Logon scripts are particularly effective for configuring a group of users so that they log on with the same set of drive and printer connections.

A logon script is usually a batch file, and has a BAT file name extension for DOS and for Windows clients. Program files with the EXE extension can also be executed as logon scripts.

The name of a user's logon script is specified in the user's account profile. The procedure for specifying logon script names was described in Chapter 10, "Managing Users and Groups."

By default, logon scripts are stored in the directory C:\WINNT35\SYSTEM32\REPL-\IMPORT\SCRIPTS. In most cases, you won't want to change this location, particularly if you are operating a domain with more than one domain controller because you will want to use directory replication to copy logon scripts to all domain controllers in the domain.

When users log in to a domain, their logon can be authenticated by any active domain controller. If a logon script is specified for the user, the domain controller will look for the script on the local directory that matches the logon script directory location defined for the domain. In other words, each domain controller looks for logon scripts on its local C drive.

You can use the Windows NT Server Replicator service to replicate copies of logon scripts from one domain controller to all other DCs in the domain. The procedure for replicating files is described in Chapter 21, "Managing Directory Replication."

Logon Script Example

Logon scripts don't need to be elaborate. The following is an example of a logon script that defines resources by department. It might be set up for Widgets Engineering:

```
@echo off
net time \\keystone1 /yes
net use g: \\keystone1\apps /yes
net use s: \\widgets1\status /yes
net use lpt1: \\widgets1\laser1 /yes
```

This script uses NET TIME to synchronize each client workstation to the clock of KEYSTONE1. By synchronizing all clients to the same clock, you know that you can rely on the time and date stamps on files.

The /YES option is included with each command and has two effects. First, /YES eliminates the need for users to respond to any prompts. Second, /YES ensures that these settings will replace any persistent settings that users have established.

Note

Because Windows for Workgroups users generally log on to the network after WfW has started, logon scripts execute in a virtual DOS session.

There has been trouble getting logon scripts to work with the Windows 95 beta. Don't be surprised if this feature is not supported by Windows 95.

Tip

Logon scripts are simply batch files, and they can contain any batch file commands that are valid in the user's operating system environment. If you want to know more about DOS batch files, I recommend NRP's outstanding and extensive *Inside MS-DOS 6.22*.

CHAPTER 14

Using Windows NT Clients

Because Windows NT computers are the most capable clients of a Windows NT Server network, I have used Windows NT to demonstrate most of the functions discussed in this book.

In Chapter 11, "Sharing Drives, Directories, and Files," you saw how Windows NT computers could connect to shared directories. And in Chapter 12, "Managing Printing Services," you saw how easy it is to access a shared printer from a Windows NT computer.

Because most topics regarding Windows NT clients are discussed in other chapters, this chapter focuses on features that distinguish Windows NT from other network clients.

Personal and Common Program Groups

Windows NT is designed to accommodate multiple-user accounts, enabling each user to maintain a custom desktop environment. Whereas Windows 3.*x* supports only program groups that are available to all users on the workstation, Windows NT enables users to create the following two types of program groups:

- *Personal program groups* that are stored as part of each user's logon information and presented only to the user who created the group
- *Common program groups*, which appear for all users

Personal and common program groups have different icons. Both are illustrated in figure 14.1.

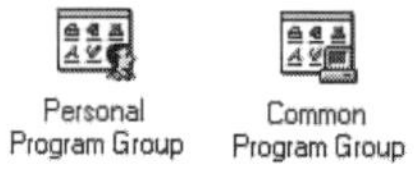

Figure 14.1
Icons for personal and common program groups.

Windows 3.*x* users are comfortable with using the New command in the Program Manager File menu to create program items and program groups. When you choose File, New in Windows NT, a third option is presented, as shown in figure 14.2.

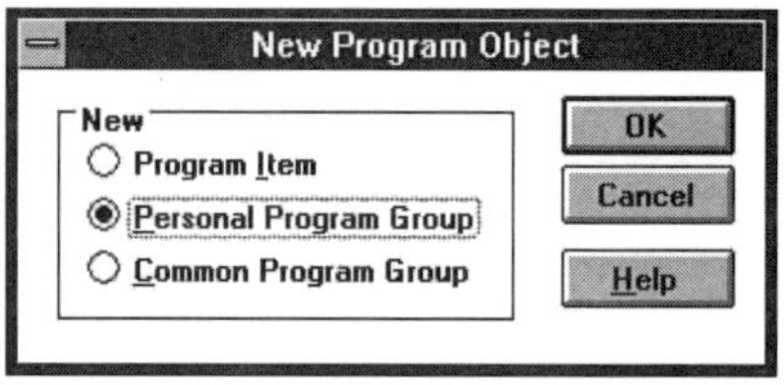

Figure 14.2
Choices presented by the New command in Windows NT.

Note

To create, change, or delete a common program group on Windows NT Server, a user must be logged on as a member of the Administrators or Server Operators group.

To create, change, or delete a common program group on Windows NT Workstation, a user must be logged on as a member of the Administrators or Power Users group.

Any user can copy a program icon from a common program group to a personal program group. Only Administrators, Server Operators, and Power users, however, can copy icons to common program groups.

User Profiles

User profiles are exceptionally rich tools for configuring users' network environments. Unfortunately, profiles can only be used with Windows NT clients, but that's simply because profiles take advantage of capabilities that aren't supported by other operating systems.

In Chapter 10, "Managing Users and Groups," you learned the following about profiles:

- User-defined profiles are identified by a USR extension on the profile file.
- Mandatory profiles are identified by a MAN extension.
- Profiles can be assigned to individuals or to groups.
- Profile files generally are stored in the C:\PROFILES directory but can be stored in any directory. You might, for example, place USR profiles in the users' home directories since all users have access to their home directories.

What you haven't seen is how versatile and powerful profiles are. Profiles can do everything that logon scripts can do, but they also are capable of almost fully describing the user's Windows NT computing environment. Table 14.1 summarizes the configuration features that are stored in profiles.

Table 14.1
Windows NT Settings Stored in User Profiles

Source	Settings
Accessories	User-specific settings in accessories including Calculator, Calendar, Cardfile, Notepad, Paintbrush, and Terminal.
Applications	Applications written for Windows NT can save settings in user profiles.
Command prompt	All user-defined command prompt features including font, color, screen size buffer settings, and window positions.
Control Panel	Settings for the Color, Cursor, Desktop, International, Keyboard, and Sound utility. Entries in the User Environment Variables box of the System utility.

continues

Table 14.1, Continued
Windows NT Settings Stored in User Profiles

Source	Settings
File Manager	User-definable settings including network connections.
Print Manager	Network connections and all user-definable settings.
Program Manager	All user-definable settings. Personal program groups and their properties.
Online Help	User-defined bookmarks.

Planning User Profiles

When users work on a stand-alone Windows NT Workstation, each user account maintains a personal profile that is stored on the workstation. Local user profiles maintain users' personal settings from session to session. These local profiles are created automatically when the user account is created. Guests are the only users who do not maintain local user profiles.

Things change when a user of a Windows NT Workstation logs on to a Windows NT Server network. If a user account is assigned a network profile, the network profile will replace the local profile when the user logs on. This approach has the following two benefits:

- Profiles can be centrally administered
- Users can obtain the same profile when logging on to different Windows NT computers

User profiles can be deployed in several ways:

- Individual users can be given personal profiles that maintain their settings on an individual basis.
- Individual profiles can be configured to restrict the modifications users can make. This ensures that the user always logs on to a standard environment.
- Groups of users can be given the same profile, which they can modify for a specific session only.
- Users and groups of users can be given a common profile that they are restricted from modifying.

Two types of profiles can be defined: personal and mandatory. In addition, there is a default profile which users access if they have not been assigned a profile. Each profile type has useful features.

Note Users on a Windows NT computer also have a *locally cached profile* that is used when the network profile is unavailable, for example, when the user logs on to a workstation local account rather than a domain account. The locally cached profile also is used when the user account has not been assigned a network profile.

Locally cached profiles exist on individual computers only. If a user logs on to another Windows NT computer, a different locally cached profile will be used.

The Default Profile

Every Windows NT computer has a default user profile that is used in the following circumstances:

- A profile has not been assigned to a user account
- A user's assigned profile cannot be accessed during logon
- A user logs on using the Guest account

You can edit the default profile if you want to tighten restrictions that will be inherited by all user profiles.

Personal Profiles

Personal profiles are stored in files with a USR extension. Users can permanently change their personal profiles. A user will access his or her personal profile by logging on to the domain from any Windows NT computer on the network.

When a user has been assigned a personal user profile but the profile file has been created, the user logs on with the default user profile. The default user profile, along with changes the user makes, is used to create the user's personal profile (unless the user has not been given the permissions required to create and modify files in the profile directory).

Note Personal profiles should never be shared by multiple users because user's changes will affect the environment of other users who share the profile.

Mandatory Profiles

Mandatory profiles are stored in files with a MAN extension. Although users with mandatory profiles may be permitted to modify their desktops, changes are not saved to the profile. As a result, the user always logs on with the same environment settings.

Mandatory profiles are especially useful when they are assigned to groups of users. In many cases, users perform a well-defined and restricted set of tasks, such as order entry or entering bank transactions. For users in restricted work environments, it is essential to prevent users from introducing changes that could impair performance of a critical function. Mandatory profiles can be locked up tight, which is done automatically.

Mandatory profiles also provide a great way to manage applications locally. If you need to deploy a new application to the users of a mandatory profile, you need only to install the application in one place. All users of the mandatory profile will automatically receive the application on their desktops.

Note Users can share mandatory profiles. When users make changes to a mandatory profile, the changes are not saved to the network profile. Instead, they are saved to the locally cached profile on the user's Windows NT computer.

Tip If you want to give users the benefits of personal profiles while retaining some ability to set up environments locally, consider using a combination of profiles and logon scripts. You can, for example, include NET USE commands in logon scripts to create a consistent environment of network connections. Printer connections can be established in the logon script, and users can be prevented from creating new printer connections from the desktop.

Restricting Users' Actions with Profiles

In some cases, it might be desirable to restrict users' abilities to modify their personal profiles. Many LAN users don't need to tinker with their desktops, but do so anyway. If you are getting calls from users who can't run programs because they have deleted the program icon, or because someone has renamed the program item, you can greatly simplify your life by assigning restricted profiles to most users. It is much easier to support a LAN when the majority of your users are working in a uniform environment.

Users' profiles can be configured to prevent them from performing the following actions:

- Creating program items and program groups
- Modifying the contents of program groups
- Changing properties of program items
- Making new connections to network printers
- Running programs from the Program Manager File menu

Planning Profiles for Different Workstation Hardware

Some of the settings that are stored in user profiles are hardware dependent, particularly video display cards and monitors. Ideally, therefore, all users of a shared profile should have the same video hardware.

Virtually all graphics adapters and monitors are capable of functioning in standard 640×480 VGA mode, and you can use this mode as a common configuration for shared profiles regardless of computer hardware variations. When users must use more advanced graphics modes, you might need to create several mandatory profiles for each hardware configuration.

When you create a profile, you should create the profile on a computer that has a hardware configuration that matches the machine on which the profile will be used.

Planning Profiles for Applications

All users who share a profile share a common application setup. The properties for each application icon determine where the application files can be found. The information in the shared icons must be valid for all users of the profile. You can ensure that program items are valid for all users in two ways:

- By installing applications on local workstations in exactly the same directories and enter directory paths to local hard drives
- By installing applications on the network file server

The network approach makes a great deal of sense because you can more easily maintain and upgrade one copy of an application on the server than many copies on individual workstations. Further, users can move applications on their personal computers, but can be restricted from moving application files on the file server.

If users have home directories on the server, you can specify individual home directories by using variables in program property paths. The variable string

%HOMEDRIVE%%HOMEPATH%, for example, will always point to each individual user's home directory. You can use each user's home directory as a working directory by specifying %HOMEDRIVE%%HOMEPATH% in the Working Directory box for the properties of an application icon.

Planning Profile Directories

Directories that contain profiles must be shared and secured so that they are accessible to users.

Personal profiles can be stored in user's home directories, if desired. User directories are normally shared, so it's unnecessary to establish a new share, and users have full permissions to manage files in their personal directories. The downside to this approach is that administrators normally cannot access files in home directories, and you will be unable to manage user's personal profiles unless they give you access.

Mandatory profiles should be stored in a common directory where they are easy to maintain. In general, I prefer to place user profiles in a common profiles directory. I create a directory named C:\PROFILES and set it up the following way:

- ◆ Share it with the share name PROFILES and give Everyone Full Control permissions
- ◆ Give Everyone Add & Read permissions for \PROFILES
- ◆ Give CREATOR OWNER Full Control permissions so that users can save changes to their personal profiles

Creating User Profiles

To create a user profile, follow these steps:

1. Configure the desktop environment as desired.
2. Use the User Profile Editor to create and save a profile file.
3. Assign the user profile to users with User Manager for Domains.

Configuring the Desktop Environment

You probably don't want to create user profiles using your personal user account because you might be making extensive changes to the environment. You should create a special user account, which must be a member of the Administrators or Domain Admins group, for administering profiles. I call my user Profile Admin.

The first step in creating a profile is to log in with the profile administrator user account and to configure the desktop as desired. Table 14.1 can serve to remind you of all the features you can customize in a profile.

Don't forget to remove program items and groups that are assigned to administrative applications.

If you want applications to start automatically when the user logs on, copy the program item icon into the Startup program group. You also can designate another program group as the startup group if desired.

Creating User Profiles

User profiles are created and modified with the User Profile Editor. You must be logged in as a member of Administrators or Domain Adminis to use the User Profile Editor.

After you have configured the desktop as desired, open the User Profile Editor. The icon is installed in the Administrative Tools program group. The dialog box for the User Profile Editor is shown in Figure 14.3. From this window, you can define the properties of user profiles.

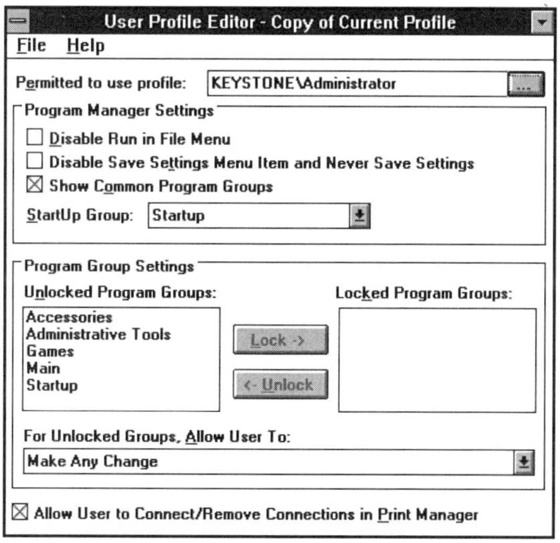

Figure 14.3

The User Profile Editor.

Permitting Users to Use a Profile

Only one user or group at a time can use a profile. You can change the user or group by clicking the ... button for the Permitted to use profile box. This will display a domain browser from which you can add a user or group. The user or group you add will replace the one shown in the Permitted to use profile box.

Managing Program Manager Settings in a Profile

Four settings are found in the Program Manager Settings box:

- **Disable Run in File Menu.** If you check this option, users will be unable to run programs for which program item icons have not been defined.
- **Disable Save Settings Menu Item and Never Save Settings.** If this option is checked, a user will be unable to save permanent changes to the profile. Any changes made will persist for the current session only.
- **Show Common Program Groups.** If you remove the check for this option, users will not see common program groups.
- **Startup Group.** If you want to start up applications in a program group other than Startup, change the program group in this box.

Managing Program Group Settings in a Profile

You can specify which program groups users of the profile can modify and which modifications they can make.

- To lock a program group, select it in the Unlocked Program Groups list and choose Lock.
- To unlock a program group, select it in the Locked Program Groups list and choose Unlock.
- To specify actions users can perform on unlocked groups, choose one of these options from the For Unlocked Groups, Allow Users To box.

  Make Any Change

  Create/Delete/Change Program Items

  Change All Program Item Properties

  Change Program Item Properties Except Command Line

Managing Printer Settings in a Profile

If you remove the check from the box Allow User to Connect/Remove Connections in Print Manager, users are restricted to using the printer connections you establish in their profiles and logon scripts.

Saving Profiles

The User Profile Manager File menu includes four options that can be used to save profiles after they have been configured:

- **Save to Current Profile.** Saves the profile to the profile that is assigned to the current user's account.
- **Save As User Default.** Saves the profile as the default user profile, the profile used by users who cannot access a profile when logging on.
- **Save As System Default.** Saves the profile as the profile used by the system when no users are logged on.
- **Save As File.** Saves the profile as a file with a specified name. Use this option to save personal and mandatory profiles for other users and for groups.

Assigning Profiles to User Accounts

Chapter 10, "Managing Users and Groups," explains how to specify the profile path for a user account.

Creating Profiles as a User

If you assign a personal profile to a user but do not create the USR file, Windows NT attempts to create the USR file automatically the first time the user logs on.

Users cannot create profile files with the User Profile Editor. If, however, the user's account specifies a USR profile in its profile path property, users will automatically create a new profile when they log on to the network for the first time.

When a user has been assigned a profile and the profile is unavailable when the user logs on, the message `Unable to load your central profile` is displayed. This message is produced whenever the user cannot access the profile, which might be the case if the file is missing or the user does not have sufficient permissions to access the file.

If a user has been assigned a profile path and the profile file cannot be accessed when the user logs on, Windows NT retrieves the user's locally cached profile if one exists. The locally cached profile (the user's local profile on the Windows NT computer) will be used to create the user's personal profile on the network.

If the user has been assigned a profile path but the profile file has not been created and the user has never logged on from the existing Windows NT computer, the default user profile on the server is used to create the user's personal profile on the network.

Note Users can only create their personal profiles if they have share access and proper permissions for the directory specified in their user profile path.

Modifying User Profiles

The best procedure for modifying a user profile depends on whether you need to change profile properties or modify the desktop configuration.

If you need to change only properties managed by User Profile Editor, follow these steps:

1. Choose Open in the File menu.
2. Browse for an existing profile file in the Open dialog box. Click on OK when it is selected.
3. Edit the profile as required.
4. Use the Save As File command in the File menu to save the profile. You will need to specify a file name even if you are saving the profile to its original file.

If you need to edit desktop features of a user profile, you must log on with the profile and follow these steps:

1. Open User Manager for Domains.
2. Open the user account for your profile administrator.
3. In the User Properties dialog box, choose Profile.
4. In the User Environment Profile dialog box, edit the User Profile Path to match the profile of the path you want to edit.
5. Log on as profile administrator with the new profile.
6. Make any required changes to the desktop.
7. Open User Profile Editor and edit profile properties as required.
8. Use the Save to Current Profile command in the File menu to save the profile.
9. Restore the User Profile Path box of the profile administrator user account to its original value.

Logon Scripts

The NET commands for Windows NT are more extensive than they are for DOS. The commands are summarized in the Appendix.

Logon scripts for Windows NT clients can make use of several logon variables, listed in table 14.2.

Table 14.2
Windows NT Logon Script Variables

Variable	Description
%HOMEDRIVE%	The drive letter that connects to the user's home directory
%HOMEPATH%	The complete path name of the user's home directory
%HOMESHARE%	The name of the share that contains the user's home directory
%OS%	The operating system running on the user's workstation
%PROCESSOR%	The processor type installed in the user's workstation
%USERDOMAIN%	The domain name in which the user's account is defined
%USERNAME%	The user name of the user

The %USERNAME% variable was encountered in Chapter 10, "Managing Users and Groups," when it was used to specify logon script and profile names. Other variables can be used to enable logon scripts to adjust to changes in the user's environment when moving from computer to computer.

Variables also can be used to enable a single logon script file to service users in different departments. You could use the %USERDOMAIN% printer to enable the logon script to connect different printers depending on the user's home domain, as in the following examples:

```
IF %USERDOMAIN% == WIDGETS NET USE LPT1: \\WIDGETS1\LASER1 /YES

IF %USERDOMAIN% == ACCT NET USE LPT1: \\ACCT\ACCTLASR /YES
```

CHAPTER 15

Using TCP/IP

TCP/IP is without question the most widely used family of network protocols. Several factors contribute to the popularity of TCP/IP:

- **Maturity.** Definition of the TCP/IP protocols began in the 1970s to satisfy a requirement of the Department of Defense for a robust wide-area-networking protocol. TCP/IP gained wide distribution when it was written into Berkeley Standard Distribution (BSD) Unix, and has been a standard feature of Unix implementations for a long time. As a result, TCP/IP received thorough field trials when other protocols were in their early developmental stages.

- **Openness.** TCP/IP is the only protocol suite with an open standards definition process. Discussion takes place in the form of Requests for Comments (RFCs) that are posted and debated publicly on the Internet. Proposals and debates are open, not restricted to members of a standards committee.

- **Non-proprietary ownership.** In a real sense, TCP/IP is owned by the user community. Other protocols, almost without exception, are proprietary protocols, owned by vendors. Users have little or no input into these proprietary protocols, and manufacturers must often pay licensing fees to build proprietary protocols into their products.

- **Richness.** TCP/IP is actually a suite of protocols that provides a vast set of capabilities. Little, if anything, a network should do cannot be done with TCP/IP.
- **Compatibility.** TCP/IP is the only protocol suite that runs on almost anything. Computer system manufacturers now regard TCP/IP as a requirement. Name the hardware, and you will probably find at least one TCP/IP implementation for it.

Unfortunately, a single chapter can only skim the subject of TCP/IP, a subject that would require many volumes to cover thoroughly. The goal in this chapter is to cover the topics that are required to get TCP/IP running in a Windows NT network, along with a few of the configuration techniques you must be aware of.

Before you can appreciate TCP/IP and understand how to set it up, you need to know something more about how small and large networks work.

Networks and Internetworks

On simple networks such as the one in figure 15.1, delivery of messages between devices is quite simple. Each device is assigned a device address (a numeric name). When device A wants to send a message to device C, device A simply adds C's device address to the message and puts the message on the network. C, like every device on the network, is looking at all of the messages that zip by. If C sees a message that bears its device address, it can retrieve the message. Other devices, such as B in the figure, will ordinarily ignore messages not addressed to them.

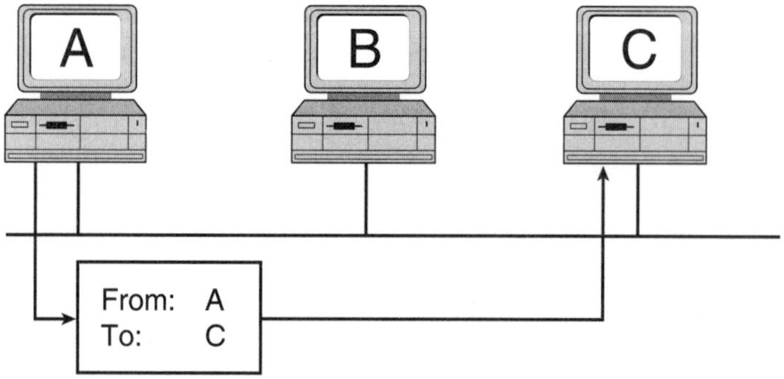

Figure 15.1
Message delivery on a simple network.

Message delivery on a simple network is just like finding your luggage on the conveyor belt at the airport. The baggage handlers aren't aware of where you're standing or even if you're present at all. They just throw your bags on the conveyor, and it's up to you to spot the pieces that have your name on them.

But large networks, and real luggage delivery, are a lot more complicated than simply getting suitcases from the airplane to the owner. Consider what really happens on a long flight with several stops and some plane changes. When you arrive at your departure airport, your bags are marked by a tag that identifies the destination airport. When you change planes, your bags are supposed to change planes with you, and baggage handlers at the intermediate airport must sort through the incoming bags and route them. Each bag is tagged with a destination. Some bags stay at this airport, some go to another airport, and some, whose destination can't be reached directly from this location, need to be routed through another intermediate airport as the next hop toward their destination. If the current airport matches the destination on a luggage tag, the bag needs to go onto the conveyor belt for local delivery. If an item is sent to the wrong airport, a mechanism must be in place to identify the error, discover how to get the item to its correct destination, and start it on its way.

Airport baggage handling is a concrete example of the problems large networks face thousands of times in every second that they operate. Here is a summary of the problems that must be solved to deliver messages through a complex network:

- Each device must have a unique identification on its local network. Imagine if there were two Bill Roberts with the same street address trying to pick up the same luggage with an LAX (Los Angeles International) airport tag.
- Each intermediate and final destination must have an identification. No two networks or airports can use the same identification symbol.
- Procedures must be in place for routing messages between the source and the final destination. Airports use baggage handlers. Networks use routers and routing protocols.
- If an intermediate destination is of a different type from the source and/or destination, all must agree on procedures so that confusion does not arise. Imagine what it would be like flying from New York to Saudi Arabia if every country along the way required you to route your baggage with a completely different procedure.
- When problems occur, as they surely will, mechanisms must be in place to attempt to correct the error.

Figure 15.2 shows a fairly involved wide area network. With this network, a message from A that was addressed to B could hypothetically take several routes to reach its destination. Every place that networks interconnect, devices called *routers* are placed. Routers serve the same function as baggage handlers in an airport; they route packages toward their destinations, hopefully along the fastest route.

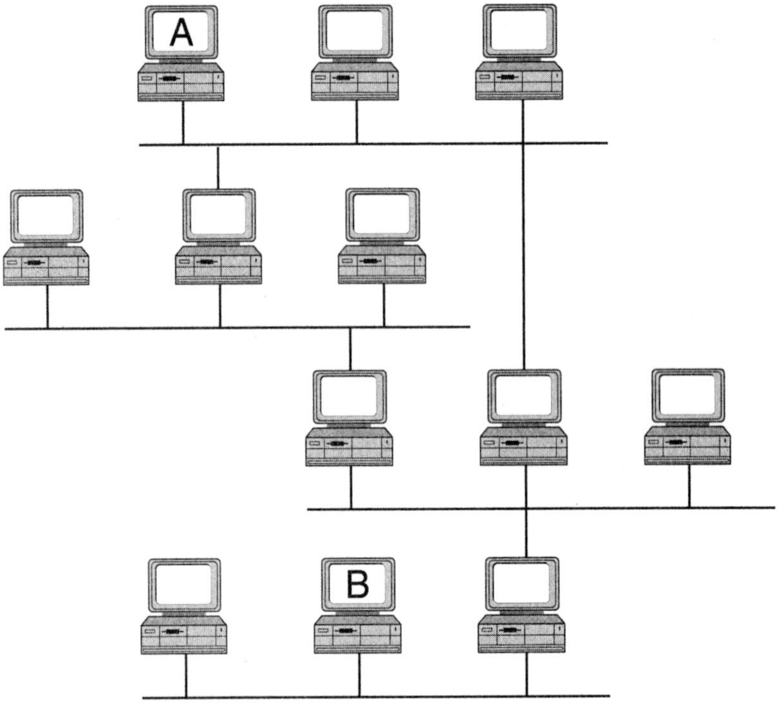

Figure 15.2
A complex network.

The network in figure 15.2 consists of several networks that are interconnected. A "network of networks" is commonly called an *internetwork* or simply an *internet. The* network of networks, a vast, international network that originated from the original Defense Department networks of the late 1970s, is called the *Internet.*

Following are the elements of an internetwork, expressed in somewhat more technical terms:

- **Each device on a network is identified by a unique address, often called a device or node address.** These addresses are frequently permanently coded into the network hardware. Each Ethernet and token-ring card possesses a 48-bit address number that is guaranteed to be unique throughout the world.

- **A local delivery mechanism enables devices to place messages on the medium and retrieve messages that are addressed to them.** Using the OSI reference model discussed in Chapter 1, local delivery is performed by the physical and data link layers.

- **A mechanism for delivering messages that must travel through the internetwork.** In the TCP/IP protocol suite, internetwork delivery is the responsibility of the Internet Protocol (IP).
- **A way to determine good ways of routing messages.** With TCP/IP, routing in complex networks is performed by IP, usually with support of a routing protocol such as Routing Information Protocol (RIP) or Open Shortest Path First (OSPF).
- **A way to detect and recover from errors.** The Transmission Control Protocol (TCP) is responsible for error detection and recovery on TCP/IP networks.

TCP/IP isn't the only way of solving these problems, but it is an excellent approach and the approach with the widest acceptance. If your Windows NT network is participating in an internetwork, there is a good chance that it will need to run TCP/IP.

Protocols and Windows NT

Windows NT ships with support for three transport protocols:

- NetBEUI is the traditional protocol on Microsoft networking products. Its primary limitation is that it can be used only on simple networks because it cannot be routed.
- NWLink is a Microsoft-developed transport that is compatible with Novell's IPX/SPX protocols. A significant advantage of these protocols is that they require virtually no configuration. NWLink is routable and can be used to build large internetworks.
- TCP/IP, as mentioned, is the most commonly implemented network protocol, particularly on internetworks, and has excellent networking capabilities. Unlike NWLink, TCP/IP requires considerable configuration.

All of these protocols can coexist on Windows NT thanks to two technologies:

- NDIS, the Network Driver Interface Specification, which enables multiple protocol stacks to share network adapters.
- TDI, the Transport Driver Interface, which enables various upper-layer Windows NT services to interface freely with the installed protocols.

Figure 15.3 shows how the protocols fit together.

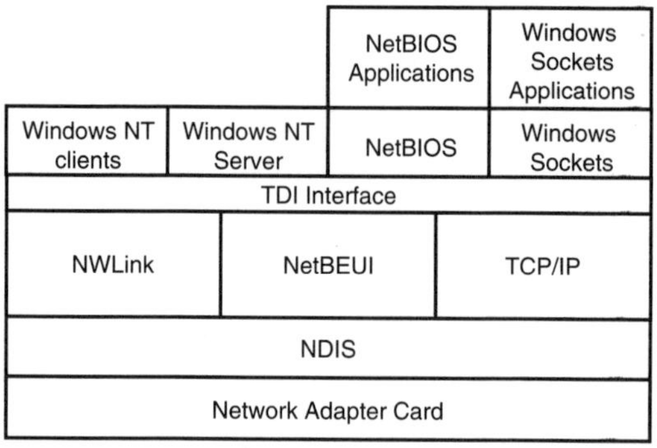

Figure 15.3
NDIS supporting multiple protocols.

Although the TCP/IP protocol stack was developed before the OSI network model was implemented, a fairly close relationship can be drawn between IP and the network layer. Also, TCP is closely related to the OSI transport layer. Purists will argue with trying to forcefit TCP/IP into the OSI model, but for the sake of simplicity, we will regard these protocols and layers as a match.

Note The TCP/IP layer that corresponds to the OSI transport layer is called the *host-to-host* layer. The TCP/IP layer most similar to the OSI Network layer is called the *internet* layer.

TCP/IP and Internetworks

Now that you can see the layered structure of TCP/IP, you can look at how the layers solve the internetwork problems that were introduced earlier.

Local Network Addresses

TCP/IP can use a wide variety of lower layer protocols, including X.25 packet switching, Ethernet, and token ring. In fact, TCP/IP was explicitly designed without data link and physical layer specifications because the goal was to make the protocol suite adaptable to most types of media.

TCP/IP relies on physical addresses to deliver messages on the local network. On LANs, physical addresses are functions of the medium access control (MAC) sublayer of the OSI data link layer. Most LAN standards make provisions for assigning physical (hardware) addresses to cards. Each Ethernet and token ring card has a 48-bit address that is burned into the card's hardware when it is manufactured. A central address registry assigns address ranges to each manufacturer so each card will have a unique address.

Note Computers on TCP/IP networks are called *hosts*. When TCP/IP was being developed, there were no personal computers or workstations. All computers were multi-user computers that were and still are called *hosts*. Today, even a single user computer on a TCP/IP network is called a host.

Local Message Delivery

TCP/IP refers to each local network as a *subnet*. You will see how each subnet is defined later in the chapter. Whenever IP sends a message that is directed to a device on the local subnet, it tags the message with the physical address of the message recipient and sends the message down the protocol stack. The physical layer places the message on the network, where it circulates past all devices on the subnet. The device that matches the physical address retrieves the message.

Routing Messages through Internetworks

When a message is not destined for a device on the local subnet, it must be routed. Each subnet is assigned a subnet address. Each computer is configured with a default router to which it sends messages that must be sent to a remote subnet.

The responsibility of determining how messages should be addressed is one of the tasks of IP, the Internetwork Protocol. IP identifies whether each message is destined for a computer on the local network or whether it should be sent to the default router. The physical address for either the local host or the default router is added to each message that is sent.

IP makes use of addresses called *IP addresses* to logically identify subnets and devices, which are called *hosts* in TCP/IP terminology. IP addresses will be explained later in this chapter, in the section "IP Addresses."

IP receives frames from higher-level protocols. One of IP's responsibilities is to attach to each frame a header containing address information. Once the IP header has been attached to the frame, the combination is generally referred to as a *packet*.

Determining routing paths between routers is usually the responsibility of one of two protocols: Routing Information Protocol (RIP), an older and less-efficient protocol that remains in widespread use, and Open Shortest Path First (OSPF), a newer and more efficient protocol. Thorough discussion of RIP and OSPF is beyond the scope of this book. IP makes use of routing tables built by RIP or OSPF to determine the next router to which a packet should be sent.

Detecting and Recovering from Errors

IP provides what is known as *unreliable network service,* meaning that IP assumes that packets will be delivered correctly and does nothing to verify delivery. Generally speaking, this is insufficient, and a mechanism is required to detect and recover from errors.

Error recovery is the responsibility of the Transmission Control Protocol (TCP), the second protocol that identifies the TCP/IP protocol suite. Among the responsibilities of TCP are the following:

- Fragmentation of large messages from upper layer protocols into *frames* that fit within the limitations of the network. (No network can transmit a 100 megabyte file in a single chunk because that would monopolize the network for too long a time. The file must be broken into smaller units.)
- Reassembly of received frames into messages that are passed to upper layer protocols.
- Error detection and recovery.

When TCP sends a frame, it expects an acknowledgment when the frame is received. When no acknowledgment is forthcoming, TCP assumes that the frame was lost and retransmits. TCP is an extremely robust protocol, enabling TCP/IP to function reliably on surprisingly flaky networks. After all, the protocol was developed with the goal of running critical defense networks when networks weren't all that reliable under normal use, let alone during wartime conditions.

The reliable features of TCP come at the cost of reduced performance. When "best effort" delivery is sufficient, an alternative protocol can be utilized. User Datagram Protocol (UDP) provides unreliable transport service for less critical functions. One use of UDP is to transmit network management information for the Simple Network Management Protocol (SNMP).

IP Addresses

Network addresses, unlike physical addresses, are not burned into any hardware anywhere. Network addresses are assigned by network administrators and are logically configured into network devices.

In addition to logical addresses for subnets, TCP/IP assigns a logical address to each host on the network, as well. Although they complicate network setup, logical IP addresses have some advantages:

- They are independent of the specific physical layer implementation. Upper layer processes can use logical addresses without concerning themselves with the address format of the underlying physical layer.

- A device can retain the same logical IP address even though its physical layer may change. Converting a network from token ring to Ethernet doesn't affect the IP addresses.

IP Address Format

IP addresses are 32-bit numbers that contain both a subnet address and a host address. The method used for encoding addresses in an IP address is a bit confusing for newcomers and is the primary stumbling block for TCP/IP newbies.

Following is an example of an IP address. Please commit it to memory.

```
11000001000010100001111000000010
```

It's not that easy to scan, is it? And it's really hard to quickly identify differences between two numbers. Assuming that the two numbers were not nearby on the same page, how quickly could you spot the difference between the previous number and this one:

```
11000010000010100001111000000010
```

That little change makes a big difference in the way the address functions. To make IP addresses easier to work with, the 32-bit addresses are typically divided into four *octets* (8-bit sections):

```
11000001 00001010 00011110 00000010
```

Still not easy, but the next step considerably simplifies things. Each of the octets can be translated into a decimal number in the range of 0 through 255. This leads us to the more conventional method of representing the example IP address:

```
193.10.30.2
```

This format is commonly called *dotted-decimal notation.*

Note Although IP addresses are most commonly represented in dotted-decimal notation, it is important to keep in touch with the underlying binary numbers. IP functionality is defined by the bit patterns, not by the decimal numbers we commonly use. The vast majority of IP addressing problems result because the network administrator failed to closely examine the bit patterns for the IP addresses that were selected.

Tip

If you are among the 99.44 percent of the population that doesn't think it's fun to convert binary to decimal in your head, make use of the Windows Calculator application. Switch it into Scientific mode by checking the Scientific option in the View menu. Then you can use the Binary and Decimal mode buttons to convert numbers from one representation to another.

IP Address Classes

Each IP address consists of two fields:

- A *netid* field that is the logical network address of the subnet to which the computer is attached.
- A *hostid* field, which is the logical device address that uniquely identifies each host on a subnet.

Together, the netid and the hostid provide each host on an internetwork with a unique IP address.

When the TCP/IP protocols were originally developed, it was thought that computer networks would fall into one of three categories:

- A small number of networks that had large numbers of hosts.
- Some networks with an intermediate number of hosts.
- A large number of networks that would have a small number of hosts.

For that reason, IP addresses were organized into *classes*. You can identify the class of an IP address by examining the first octet:

- If the first octet has a value of 0 through 127, it is a *class A* address. Because 0 and 127 in this octet have special uses, 126 class A addresses are available, each of which can support 16,777,216 hosts.
- If the first octet has a value of 128 through 191, it is a *class B* address. 16,384 class B addresses are possible, each of which can support up to 65,536 hosts.
- If the first octet has a value of 192 through 223, it is a *class C* address. 2,097,152 class C addresses are available, each of which can support up to 254 hosts.

The number of hosts that a class address can support depends on the way the class allocates octets to netids and hostids. Figure 15.4 shows how octets are organized for each class.

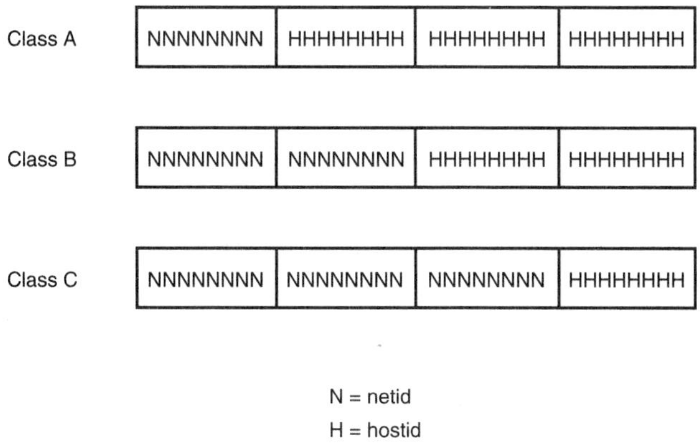

Figure 15.4
Organization of octets in classes of IP addresses.

As you can see, a class A address uses only the first octet for network IDs. The remaining three octets are available for use as host IDs.

Class B addresses use the first two octets to designate the netid. The third and fourth octets are used for host IDs.

Class C addresses use the first three octets for network IDs. Only the fourth octet is used for host IDs.

Note Technically, the class of an address is defined by the leftmost bits in the first octet:

- If the first bit is a 0, the address is class A.
- If the first two bits are 10, the address is class B.
- If the first three bits are 110, the address is class C.
- If the first four bits are 1110, the address is class D.
- If the first four bits are 1111, the address is class E.

Class D and E are not available for standard network addressing and aren't discussed in this book.

Special IP Addresses

You might have noticed that the numbers don't add up to the subnets and hosts that I indicated a particular address class could support. That is because several addresses are reserved for special purposes. If you set up a TCP/IP network, you will be assigning IP addresses and should keep the following restrictions in mind:

- Any address with a first octet value of 127 is a loopback address, which is used in diagnostics and testing. A message sent to an IP address with a first octet of 127 is returned to the sender. Therefore, 127 cannot be used as a netid, even though it is technically a class A address.
- 255 in an octet designates a broadcast or a multicast. A message sent to 255.255.255.255 is broadcast to every host on the internetwork. A message sent to 165.10.255.255 is multicast to every host on network 165.10.
- The first octet cannot have a value above 223. Those addresses are reserved for multicast and experimental purposes.
- The last octet of a hostid cannot be 0 or 255.

Network IDs and Subnets

The rule for configuring TCP/IP subnets is quite simple: Every host on the network must be configured with the same subnet ID. Figure 15.5 shows an internetwork with three subnets:

- A class A subnet with the subnet address 65.
- A class B subnet with the subnet address 140.200
- A class C subnet with the subnet address 201.150.65

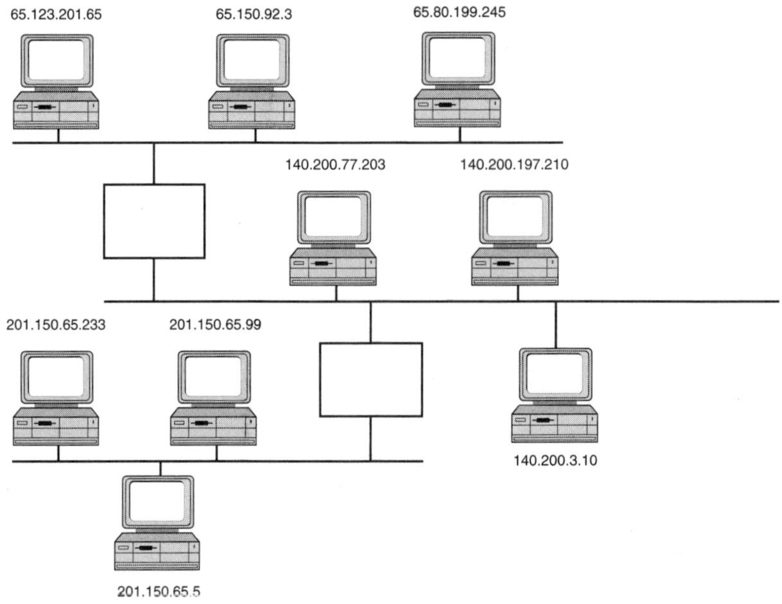

Figure 15.5

An internetwork based on three IP network IDs.

Each host on each subnet is shown with its internet ID. These subnets function in the same fashion. The only difference is that the class A subnet can support many more hosts. The subnets are internetworked with routers. Routing will be described later in this chapter.

Note Actually, you can configure devices on the same cable segment with different netids, and nothing will blow up. However, the devices behave as though they are on different subnets and cannot communicate without a router. As you can see, the netid is the crucial identifier of a subnet, not the cable segment to which the hosts are attached.

Subnet Masks

A *subnet mask* is a bit pattern that defines which portion of the IP address represents a subnet address. Because the octet organization of each IP address class is clearly defined, the purpose of subnet masks is not obvious at first, but subnet masks have good reasons for existing.

Here is a basic example. Consider the Class B address 170.203.93.5. The binary equivalent for this address is

```
10101010 11001011 1011101 00000101
```

The default subnet mask for a class B address is

```
11111111 11111111 00000000 00000000
```

As you can see, the subnet mask has a 1 in each bit position that corresponds to a bit in the netid component of the address. When a 1 appears in the subnet mask, the corresponding bit in the IP address is part of the netid of the subnet. Therefore, the netid of this subnet is

```
10101010 11001011
```

A 0 (zero) in a subnet mask indicates that the corresponding bit in the IP address is part of the host ID.

Like IP addresses, subnet masks are usually represented in dotted decimal notation. The preceding subnet address is 255.255.0.0.

Note The RFCs do not allow a hostid that is all 1s or all 0s. Similarly, the RFCs do not permit the subnet portion of the netid in an IP address to be all 1s or all 0s.

Subnet masks make it easier and faster for IP to identify the netid portion of the IP address. But subnet masks have another benefit, as well; they permit you to suballocate network addresses.

This capability is particularly important when your network is attached to the Internet. This is because you will be assigned your IP addresses, and you probably won't get all the addresses you would like to have. Internet addresses are getting scarce, and you might not be able to secure enough addresses to assign an address to each subnet. Suppose that you have been assigned one class C address but you need to organize your network with three subnets? That's where subnet masks really come in handy.

Consider the class C network address 205.101.55. The default subnet mask would be 255.255.255.0. It is possible, however, to extend the subnet mask into the fourth octet. Consider this binary subnet mask, which would be expressed as 255.255.255.224 in dotted-decimal notation:

```
11111111 11111111 11111111 11100000
```

This mask designates the first three bits of the fourth octet of the IP address as belonging to the subnet ID. To see how this works, apply the subnet mask to an IP address on this network. The IP address 205.101.55.91 would have this binary address:

```
11001101 01100101 00110111 01011011
```

After applying the subnet mask, the network ID for the subnet is

```
11001101 01100101 00110111 01000000
```

The host ID consists of the five bits that correspond to zeros in the subnet mask. Therefore, the host ID is binary 11011, which is decimal 27.

The first three bits of the fourth octet of the IP address can have values ranging from 001 through 110. Because 000 and 111 are not valid subnet IDs, a total of six subnets are made available by a subnet mask of 11100000.

The subnet mask designates that hostids in the fourth octet will fall in the range 00001 through 11110, with decimal values ranging from 1 through 30. (Again, 00000 and 11111 are invalid and decimal addresses 0 and 31 may not be used.) This range of host IDs can be reused with each of the available subnet IDs.

The six subnets designated by a subnet mask of 255.255.255.224 would be associated with the following ranges of values in the fourth octet of the IP addresses:

00100001 through 00111110 (33 through 62)

01000001 through 01011110 (65 through 94)

01100001 through 01111110 (97 through 126)

10000001 through 10011110 (129 through 158)

10100001 through 10111110 (161 through 190

11000001 through 11011110 (193 through 222)

As you can see, the use of the subnet mask has made a considerable number of possible values unavailable. The benefit of creating multiple subnets with a single Class C address must be weighed against the cost in terms of unavailable addresses.

Figure 15.6 shows an internetwork that requires a single class C network ID to implement three network segments. This would not be possible without using subnet masks.

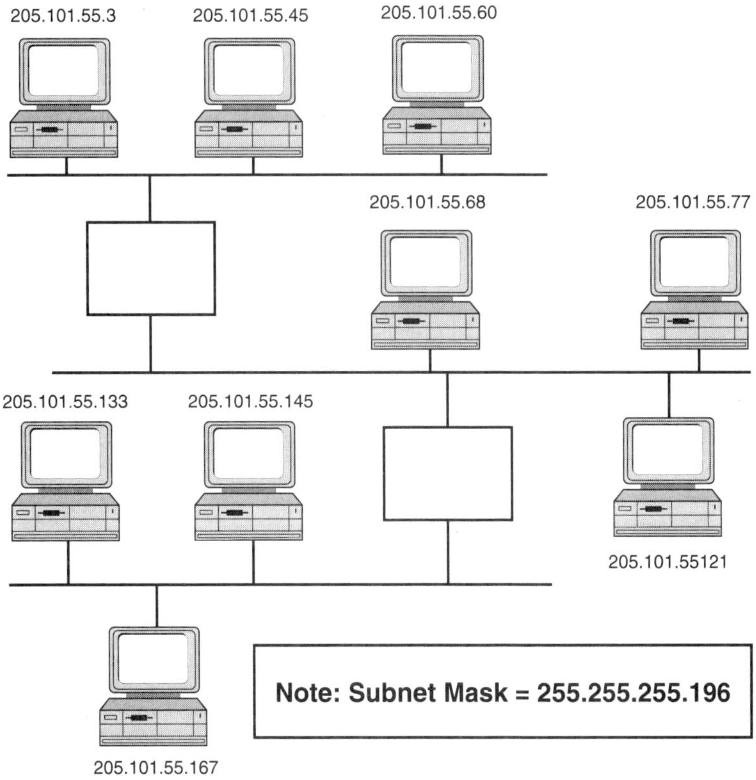

Figure 15.6

An internetwork based on one class C address.

Note When expressed in decimal form, subnet masks can appear to be somewhat of a mystery. For subnet masks to make sense, you must see them in terms of their binary patterns. Fortunately, subnet masks almost always use adjacent, high-order bits, so there are only eight common subnet mask octets:

Binary	Decimal
00000000	0
10000000	128
11000000	192
11100000	224
11110000	240
11111000	248
11111100	252
11111110	254
11111111	255

Delivering Packets on the Local Subnet

One of IP's responsibilities is to determine whether a packet can be delivered on the local subnet or must be routed to another subnet for final delivery. Subnet IDs make it much easier for IP to make this determination.

Before examining how routing takes place, take a look at the steps IP uses to deliver a packet to another host on the local subnet:

1. IP receives a frame from TCP, the next higher layer in the protocol stack. This frame is addressed to a particular IP address.

2. IP compares the subnet ID of the frame's IP address to the subnet ID of the local subnet. If the two subnet IDs match, the frame can be delivered locally.

3. Before sending the frame on the subnet, IP must determine the hardware address of the device that corresponds to the destination IP address. To get this information, IP utilizes the Address Resolution Protocol (ARP). Given an IP address of a host, ARP can determine the associated physical address for the host.

4. IP adds the following information to the frame, which is now referred to as a packet:
   - The source IP address
   - The source hardware address
   - The destination IP address
   - The destination hardware address
5. IP passes the packet with the address information down the protocol stack to the protocols that actually place the packet on the network.

Since the packet is tagged with the hardware address of a host on the local subnet, the destination host will be able to spot the packet and retrieve it.

Routing Packets to Remote Subnets

But what happens if IP determines that the source and destination subnet addresses don't match? That's a clear indication that the packet must be routed through the internetwork. IP in the local host doesn't perform the routing, but IP sends the packet to a device where it can be routed.

When hosts are connected to an internetwork, each host is configured with the IP address of a *default gateway* or *router.* (*Gateway* is an older term for *router.*) When IP determines that the destination of a packet is not on the local subnet, IP addresses the packet to the default router (or an alternative router if the default router is unavailable).

Figure 15.7 illustrates the routing process. For the first time, the devices that connect the subnets have been labeled as routers. A router is essentially a computer running a TCP/IP protocol stack that is equipped with network adapters on all of the attached subnets. The adapter on each subnet is assigned an IP address that is appropriate for that subnet. Thus, a router is assigned two or more IP addresses and has a presence on two or more subnets.

Routing algorithms can be very simple or very complex. To illustrate the simple approach, assume that the default class C subnet mask (255.255.255.0) is configured on all hosts. Suppose that host 200.1.1.5 is sending a packet addressed to host 197.2.2.10. Using figure 15.7 to illustrate, the simple approach works like this:

1. IP on host 200.1.1.5 determines that the destination host is not on the local subnet because the subnet addresses of source and destination don't match.

2. Because the packet must be routed, IP addresses the packet with the following information:

    - Source Hardware Address: 222
    - Source IP Address: 200.1.1.5
    - Destination Hardware Address: 110
    - Destination IP Address: 197.2.2.10

    Notice that the destination hardware address identifies the default router. The destination IP address matches the ultimate destination of the packet.

3. IP on the router receives the packet from subnet 200.1.1 and determines from the IP address that the packet is addressed to a host on subnet 197.2.2.

4. A local network adapter on the router has been configured with an IP address on subnet 197.2.2. Therefore, IP will use that adapter to forward the packet.

5. If it is not already known, IP on the router uses ARP to determine the hardware address of the destination host.

6. IP addresses the packet with this information and sends it on subnet 197.2.2:

    - Source Hardware Address: 600
    - Source IP Address: 200.1.1.5
    - Destination Hardware Address: 500
    - Destination IP Address: 197.2.2.10

7. When host 197.2.2.10 examines the packet, it determines that the addressee of the packet is itself and retrieves the packet from the network.

Notice two things in the routing process:

- The source and destination IP addresses don't change as the frame is routed. They always represent the original source and the ultimate destination of the packet.

- The hardware addresses change to indicate the host that last sent the packet and the host that should receive it.

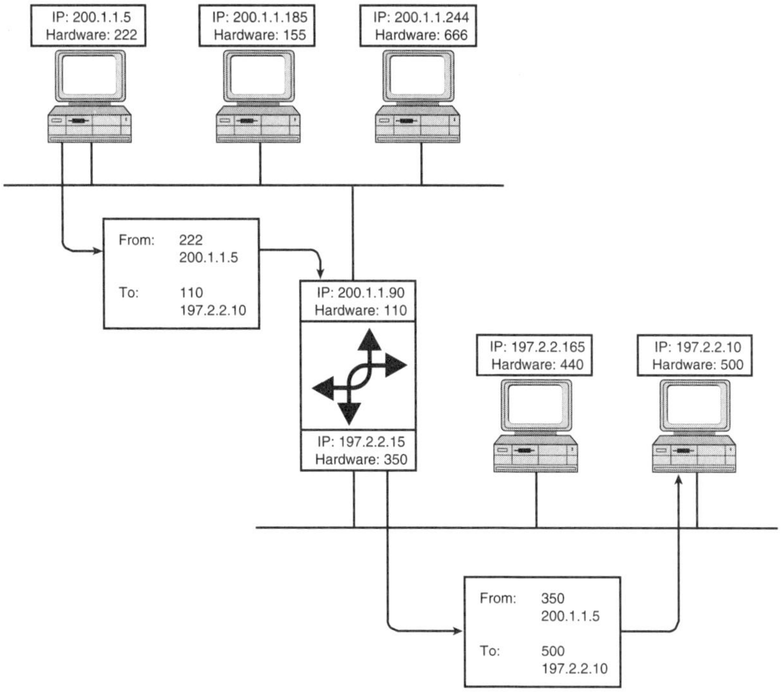

Figure 15.7

Simple IP routing.

Complex IP Routing

IP determines where to route packets by consulting routing tables. The simple routing in the previous discussion is an example of the routing capabilities of Windows NT. Any Windows NT computer can be configured as a basic router by adding a second network adapter card and configuring TCP/IP to enable routing.

By default, Windows NT routing tables only contain information about subnets to which the computer is directly attached. Therefore, a default configuration would be unable to route a packet from subnet 65 to subnet 90 in figure 15.8. Router A is simply unaware that subnet 90 exists and cannot forward the frame.

To route packets through more complex internetworks, it is necessary to enhance the richness of the routing table information that is available to IP. There are two approaches to building routing tables: *static* and *dynamic* routing.

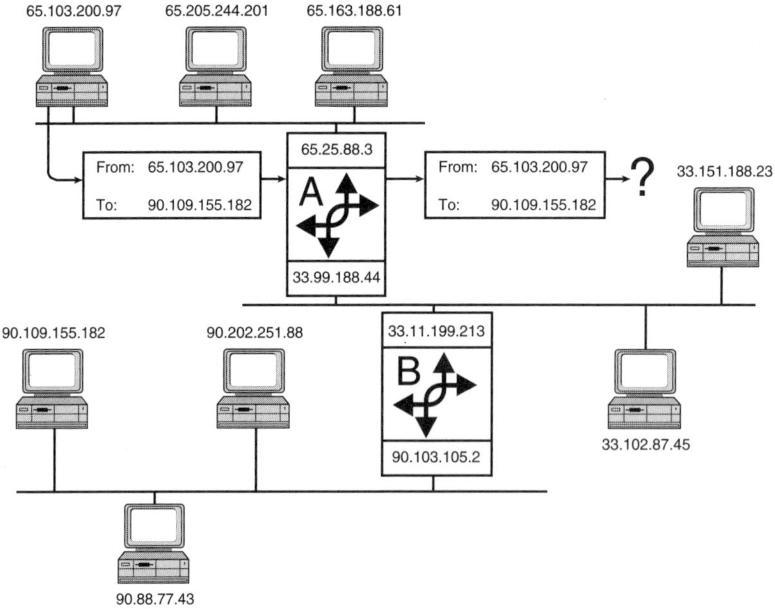

Figure 15.8 *More complex routing.*

Static Routing

A router can be configured with a *static routing table* that contains routing information that is manually defined by a network administrator. The term *static* is used because the table is not automatically updated when the network changes. When you reconfigure TCP/IP, a routing table is maintained on the computer.

Windows NT provides the `route` command-line utility, which can be used to print and directly modify the routing table on a host. The command to display a routing table is `route print`. Figure 15.9 shows the Windows NT routing table that is associated with the router that is set up later in this chapter. A full description of this table and of configuring static routing is beyond the scope of this book. Some essential features are the following:

- The Gateway Address column defines the gateway (router) that should be used next when sending a frame to the address shown in the Network Address column. Network addresses can consist of subnet IDs or complete host IP addresses.
- The Netmask is used to determine whether part or all of the Network Address should be considered when routing packets with this entry.
- The Metric column indicates the cost of reaching the destination address. Cost is measured in hops: a hop count of 1 indicates that the destination is on the local subnet. An additional *hop* is incurred whenever a frame crosses a router.

Each time the network configuration changes, static routing requires a network administrator to use the route command to update the routing table. You can readily see that this could become a time-consuming and error-prone task.

Note With Windows NT version 3.5, static routing information is lost each time the server is restarted. Windows NT 3.51 will correct this problem.

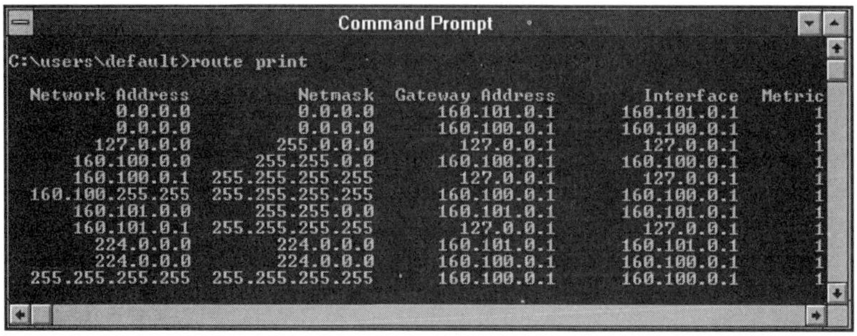

Figure 15.9
Example of a Windows NT routing table.

Dynamic Routing

Because maintaining static routing tables is a pain, most networks rely on routers that can use routing algorithms to dynamically maintain routing tables. Windows NT does not have this capability, and you must turn to commercial routers to get it.

Routing algorithms are quite complex, and the details far exceed the scope of this chapter. Therefore, I will limit discussion to brief descriptions of two algorithms that are commonly employed on TCP/IP internetworks.

Routing Information Protocol

The Routing Information Protocol (RIP) is known as a *distance vector* routing algorithm. If a router knows several routes to a destination, it assigns a cost to the route in terms of the *hops* the route involves. The hop count is incremented each time a packet crosses a router. Each router broadcasts its routing table every 30 seconds. In this way, routers in the internetwork share their routing tables, and routing information gradually propagates through the internetwork.

Distance vector algorithms have a number of practical problems. One, called the *count-to-infinity* problem, has to do with routes that loop back on themselves, causing packets to circulate the network indefinitely. Count-to-infinity is controlled by setting a maximum hop count of 16. Any packet that registers 16 hops is discarded. This limits the maximum number of hops a packet can take to 15 and limits the scope of networks that RIP can manage.

Another problem is that it can take considerable time for a change to propagate through the network. This is called the *convergence* problem.

Finally, because all routers broadcast routing information every 30 seconds, considerable traffic is generated. RIP traffic can really bog down a network, particularly when slower WAN links are involved.

RIP is available in two versions: RIP I and RIP II. RIP II supports the use of subnet masks. Some routers can support both RIP versions simultaneously.

Open Shortest Path First

The Open Shortest Path First (OSPF) algorithm is based on a different approach called *link state*. Each router broadcasts periodic *link state packets* that describe its connections to its neighbors. Using this information, routers build a link state database that is used to identify routes. OSPF enables networks to use costs as high as 65535, enabling designers to build internetworks without the 16 hop limitation.

Link state algorithms do not suffer from the count-to-infinity problem. They also generate much less broadcast traffic than RIP. Link state packets are retransmitted only when the network changes or at infrequent intervals.

As such, OSPF is a significant improvement over RIP and can be expected to become the TCP/IP routing protocol of choice.

Host Names and Naming Services

It would be a real nuisance to have to refer to each host by its IP address. Let's face it, humans don't remember numbers very well. Therefore, a system was developed that enabled users to refer to hosts by name.

Originally, the system involved a file named "hosts," a text file that was stored on each host that mapped IP addresses to host names. A hosts file might contain entries like this:

```
201.150.63.98....widgets.keystone.com
```

Conventionally, the hosts file is stored with other TCP/IP configuration files on Unix computers in a directory named "etc." By default, Windows NT stores the hosts file in C:\WINNT35\SYSTEM32\DRIVERS\ETC.

The hosts file must be manually maintained by the network administrator. One of the big hassles of maintaining a TCP/IP network is updating this file and ensuring that the updates make it onto each computer on the network.

Maintenance of host files should qualify for mental hazard pay, and would be even worse on really large networks. To get around the problem, you need a naming service.

Windows NT offers the Windows Internet Naming Service (WINS), which is discussed later in this chapter in the section "Installing and Managing WINS."

Domain Name Services (DNS) protocol was developed to serve as a central repository of names on the Internet. DNS will be discussed later when we examine issues involved in connecting Windows NT to the Internet. DNS names are discussed in the section "Internet Domain Names."

Note Two categories of names are involved in a Windows NT TCP/IP environment:

- NetBIOS names are the native names used for Windows networking. These are the computer names you enter when you install Windows NT or when you configure Microsoft networking on Windows for Workgroups. NetBIOS names are used when Microsoft network clients are browsing the network.
- DNS names are supported by a TCP/IP Directory Name Service. DNS names identify TCP/IP hosts by name and are recognized by TCP/IP applications.

The Windows Internet Naming System (WINS) permits NetBIOS names to be used in a TCP/IP environment by maintaining a NetBIOS name database.

WINS is a Microsoft-only standard, and names that are maintained by WINS are not usable by non-Windows hosts on an internetwork. If you want your network to have a naming service that is usable by Windows and non-Windows hosts, you need to implement DNS.

Connecting to the Internet

More and more private networks are being connected to the Internet, a giant TCP/IP internetwork descended from the ARPAnet, a network built by the Defense Advanced Research Projects Agency (DARPA) to connect the Department of Defense (DoD) with educational institutions and defense contractors. The Internet has recently been made public and now interconnects millions of hosts throughout the world.

When you connect your TCP/IP network to the Internet, you enter a larger world with restrictions, risks, and responsibilities. One of your responsibilities is to obtain an IP address for your organization that does not conflict with addresses of other organizations on the Internet.

After you obtain an IP address, you will need to obtain a connection to the Internet, usually through a commercial Internet provider.

Obtaining an Internet Address

If you are running a TCP/IP network in isolation, you can use any addresses you choose. On the Internet, however, you need to use an address that is assigned by the Internet Network Information Center (InterNIC).

You can obtain documents from InterNIC by using FTP to connect to is.internic.net. Log in as anonymous and transfer the documents you require.

If you don't have Internet access, contact InterNIC at:

> Network Solutions
> InterNIC Registration Service
> 505 Huntmar Park Drive
> Herndon, VA 22070

Applications and questions can be e-mailed to hostmaster@internic.net.

Incidentally, don't expect to obtain a class A or B address at this late date. Class A addresses were used up long ago by the likes of IBM. Class B addresses are rare enough that they have been listed as business assets by companies offering themselves for sale. Very few class B addresses remain unallocated, but few organizations have the clout to obtain one.

All that's really left are class C addresses, and even those are in short supply. In fact, the Internet will run out of class C addresses in a year or two. To fix the problem, a new generation of TCP/IP protocols is being developed. Next-generation TCP/IP should be seeing the commercial light of day in 1996.

Note It's a good idea to obtain addresses from InterNIC even if your network is not currently attached to the Internet. If you do connect to the Internet in the future, you won't have the headache of reassigning all the IP addresses on your network.

Internet Domain Names

Domain Name Services was mentioned earlier as the solution used on the Internet to assign names to IP addresses. DNS was developed as a means of organizing the nearly 20 million host names that are using the Internet.

An example of a domain name is newriders.macmillan.com.

DNS names are organized in a hierarchical fashion, as shown in figure 15.10.

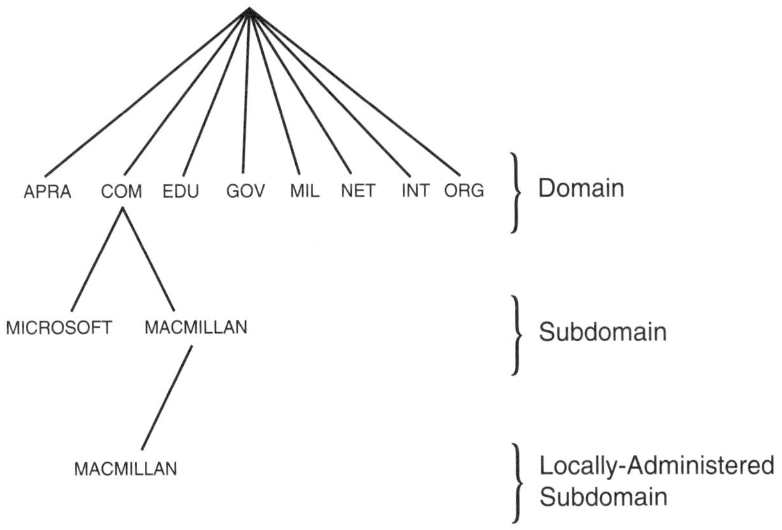

Figure 15.10

The DNS name hierarchy.

The first layer of the hierarchy consists of *domain names* that are assigned by the Network Information Center (NIC). Table 15.1 summarizes the top-level domain names. Each domain is given its own administration authority.

Table 15.1
Top-Level Domain Names

Domain Name	Description
ARPA	Advanced Research Projects Agency network (ARPAnet)
COM	Commercial organizations
EDU	Educational institutions
GOV	Government agencies
MIL	Military agencies
NET	Network support centers, such as Internet service providers
INT	International organizations
ORG	Non-profit organizations
country code	Two-letter X.500 country codes

Second-level domain names, called *subdomain names*, must be registered with the NIC. The application can be found in the file DOMAIN-TEMPLATE.TXT, which can be retrieved by anonymous ftp from hostmaster@internic.net. If you are running a DNS service on your local LAN, register the name even if you are not currently connected to the Internet. When you do connect, you can be sure that the name you want is available.

Third-level domain names usually name a particular host in the subdomain. (You can have as many levels you want, provided that the entire name does not exceed 255 characters.) The NIC only registers domain and subdomain names. Additional levels of the name hierarchy are maintained locally. If you wish to maintain a naming service for hosts, you will need to run a local name service. Windows NT does not ship with one, but a DNS package is included in the Windows NT Resource Kit. Look in the DNS subdirectory of the directory in which you install the Resource Kit.

Getting Access

Unless you are well-connected with an organization that is already connected to the Internet, you will probably gain access through a commercial provider.

Access can be through a dial-up connection if you don't need your site to be consistently accessible from the outside. You can set up a dial-up connection using the Remote Access Server (RAS), which is the subject of Chapter 20, "Using the Remote Access Server." RAS supports dial-up connections through conventional modems using the SLIP and PPP protocols. RAS also enables you to use the high-speed dial-up capabilities of ISDN.

A permanent connection usually means that you will be leasing a dedicated phone line from a local communication provider. This line will connect you with your local Internet access provider. In most cases, you will install a router between your network and the dedicated line to route traffic to the Internet.

When you connect to the Internet, you open your network to the world. There is considerable risk in that because a TCP/IP connection gives outside users significant access capabilities on your network. The Internet is filled with people who know how to infiltrate your system through an Internet connection.

To protect yourself, you should consider installing a *firewall* at your Internet access point. Just as firewalls in buildings slow the spread of fires, a network firewall impedes the ability of outsiders to gain access to your network. NRP offers an excellent book on firewalls named *Internet Firewalls and Network Security*.

Installing and Managing TCP/IP Services

This section covers installation of TCP/IP along with two services that greatly simplify administration of Windows NT TCP/IP networks.

Installing TCP/IP is easy, but proper configuration takes time, planning, and probably some troubleshooting. Much of the time involves planning IP addresses and configuring each host with the correct address information. Because you need to know how to plan and configure hosts with fixed IP addresses, the manual procedures are covered first. You first learn how to set up a network with a single subnet. Then you learn how to configure a Windows NT computer to serve as an IP router between two subnets.

After you know how to assign addresses manually, I'll show you an easier way to assign host addresses. Windows NT provides a protocol that considerably simplifies host addressing. The Dynamic Host Configuration Protocol can assign host names dynamically.

Finally, this section examines the Windows Internet Naming Service (WINS), which provides a naming service for users of Windows network products that are connected to a TCP/IP network.

Setting Up a TCP/IP Subnet with Fixed IP Addresses

Before you start addressing any network, it is essential that you plan your address scheme. If you are using an Internet IP address that was assigned by InterNIC, you need to make the most of the address you have. That means planning any subnetting that will be required.

Let's start with a basic network with a single subnet. With the basics out of the way, it will be easier for you to understand how to set up multiple subnets and routers.

Figure 15.11 illustrates the subnet that will be configured first. It is based on the class B address 160.100. The figure shows only two hosts, but once the basic subnet is configured, adding more hosts is not complicated.

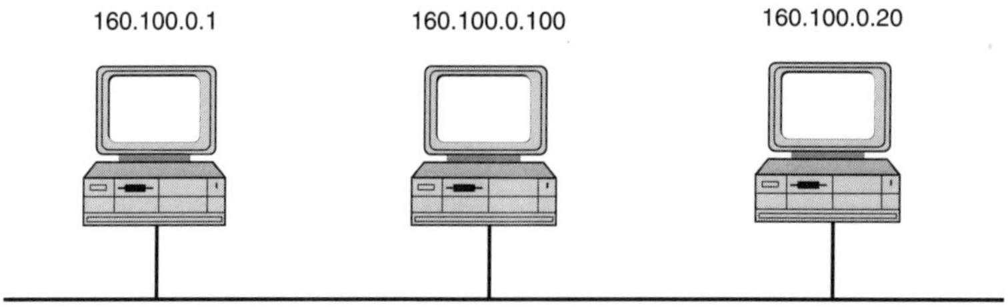

Figure 15.11
A network with one subnet.

The first computer you install is given the IP address 160.100.0.1. To install TCP/IP on the computer, follow these steps:

1. Start the Network utility in the Windows NT Control Panel. This action displays the Network Settings dialog box. (That screen was examined in detail in Chapter 7, "Installing Windows NT Server," so it won't be repeated here.)

2. Click on Add Software to display the Add Network Software dialog box.

3. Pull down the Network Software box and select the entry TCP/IP Protocol and related components. Then choose Continue. The Windows NT TCP/IP Installation Options box is displayed next (see fig. 15.12).

4. Select the required options in the Installations Options. (None of these options is required at this time. However, all of these options will be demonstrated or discussed in this chapter.)

   Choose Continue.

5. The required files will be loaded. You need to specify the path in which the files can be located.

6. After files are installed, you will be returned to the Network Settings dialog box. Click on OK. Network Settings will begin to configure the network software.

7. Network Settings will not permit you to leave without configuring all installed software. Because TCP/IP has not been configured, after you click on OK, the TCP/IP Configuration dialog box will be revealed. This dialog box appears in figure 15.13 with the settings required for the example.

   This example assumes only one adapter card is present. Later, when you learn to configure Windows NT as an IP router, you will see how multiple adapters are listed in the Adapter dialog box.

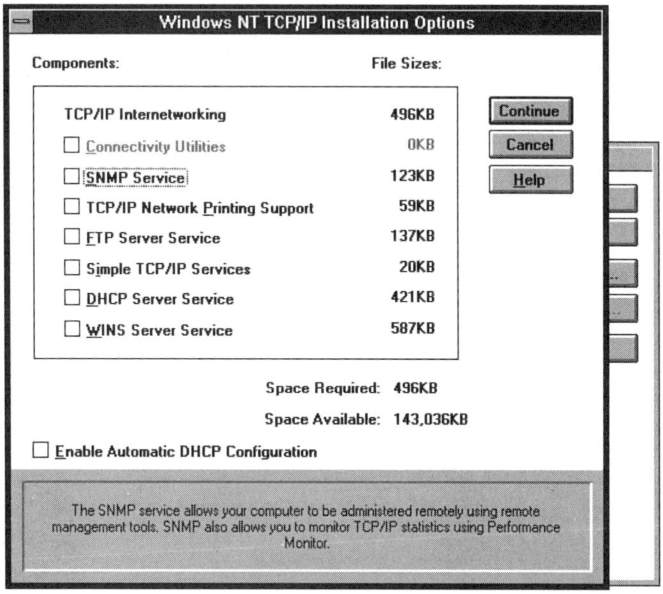

Figure 15.12

Selecting TCP/IP installation options.

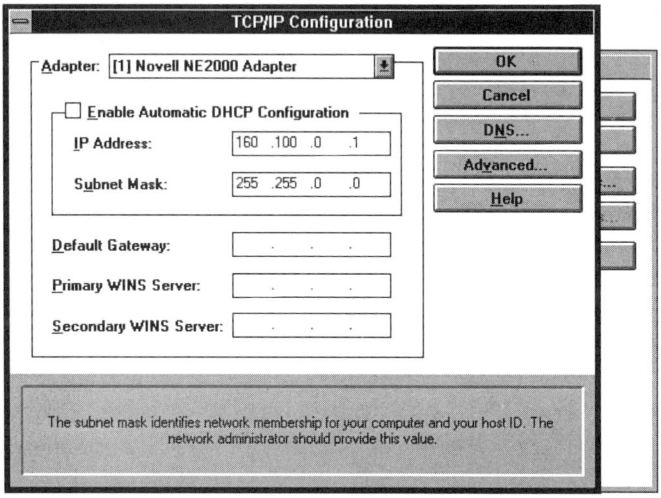

Figure 15.13

Configuration of a TCP/IP host on a single subnet.

8. The only settings required in this example are

   ◆ **IP** Address

   ◆ **Subnet mask.** The dialog box will propose in this field the default mask for the address class you entered in the IP Address box.

No default gateway is specified because a single subnet does not require any routing.

9. Choose OK to save the settings. The warning in figure 15.14 appears. Microsoft expects you to run the Windows Internet Naming Service and wonders why you haven't installed it. For now, choose Yes to complete installation without WINS.

10. When prompted, restart the computer to activate the protocol.

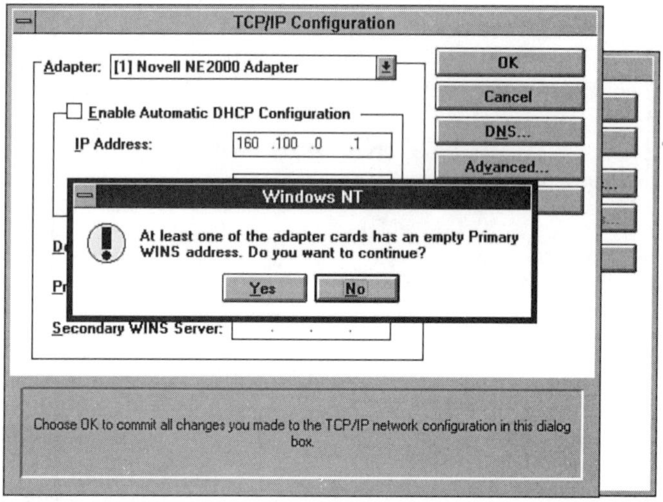

Figure 15.14
Warning that appears when installing TCP/IP without WINS.

The second computer on the subnet will have the IP address 160.100.0.100. This computer is configured using the same procedures; only the IP Address entry differs. After TCP/IP is installed on the second computer and both computers have been restarted, they should be able to communicate through TCP/IP.

Testing the TCP/IP Installation

The basic tool for testing TCP/IP networks is the `ping` command. `ping` accepts an IP address or a name that is recognized by the active naming service. `ping` sends a message to another host that requests a reply. Figure 15.15 shows the result of a successful ping request. When the other host does not respond, the result resembles figure 15.16.

Use the Unix "ping" command to test your network as it is built. Work through the network gradually to ensure that hosts are reachable, particularly when routing is involved.

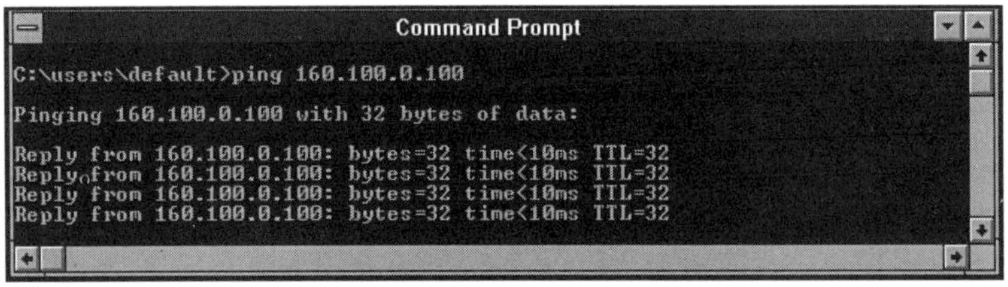

Figure 15.15

Result of a successful ping.

Figure 15.16

Result of an unsuccessful ping.

You can also use ping to test the basic configuration of an individual host. Earlier it was mentioned that IP addresses with a first octet value of 127 were used as loopback addresses. If you ping a loopback address, the attempt loops back without being sent to another host. If ping works with a loopback address, TCP/IP has been properly installed.

Here's a suggested sequence for testing a newly installed host:

1. Ping the loopback address with the command: **ping 127.0.0.1**.

2. Ping the host's own IP address.

3. Ping another host on the segment. If the host's default gateway has been installed, it is a good ping target. Successfully pinging the default gateway is the first step in determining whether the host can reach other segments on an internetwork.

4. Ping a host on another segment that should be attached through a router.

5. If a name service such as WINS or DNS is configured on the network, try pinging host names as well as addresses.

Failure in steps 1 or 2 indicates improper TCP/IP installation.

Failure in step 3 could mean several things:

- You are pinging the wrong address.

- The host you are pinging is improperly configured.

- One of the hosts has a bad network adapter.
- The network media has failed.

Failure in step 4 could indicate the same sorts of failures. First perform tests on the individual segments to ensure that hosts on each segment can ping one another. If the individual segments are functioning, the problem probably lies with the configuration of the router. Setting up Windows NT as an IP router is the subject of the next section.

Setting Up a Two-Segment Network with Routing

Figure 15.17 shows a network with two segments connected by a Windows NT computer that is configured as a router. The router must meet the following requirements:

- A separate network adapter must be installed to connect the computer to both segments
- Each adapter must be configured with an IP address that matches the network segment to which it is connected
- Routing must be enabled on the routing computer.

A router essentially has two network personalities. It functions as a host on each of the networks to which it is attached and is assigned an IP address for each network. Internally, a routing function routes packets as required between the two networks.

The first step in configuring a Windows NT router is to install a second network adapter in the computer. Then some reconfiguration of TCP/IP is required:

1. Install a network adapter card. Be sure it does not conflict with any hardware settings for existing components.
2. Run the Networks utility in the Control Panel.
3. In the Network Settings dialog box, choose Add Adapter.
4. Select an adapter from the list or choose <Other> to install software for an adapter that is not listed.
5. Choose Continue.

   If you are installing a second adapter that is the same model as an existing adapter, you will be asked, "A network card of this type is already installed in the system. Do you want to continue?" Choose OK.

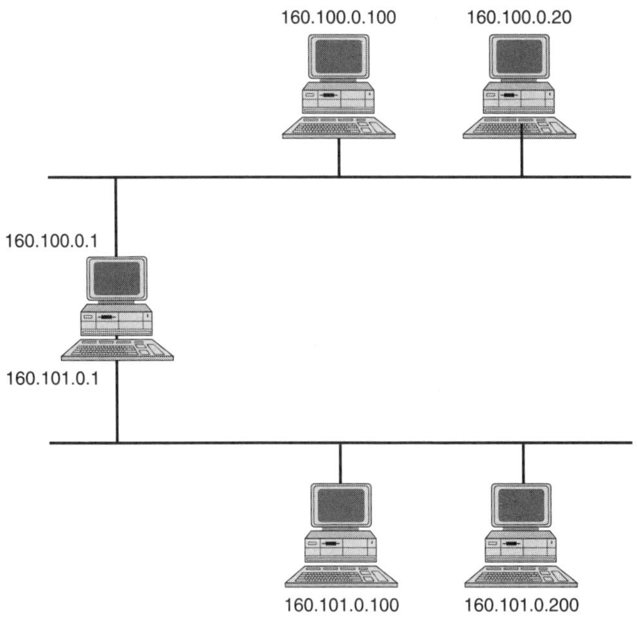

Figure 15.17
A two-segment network with a router.

6. A Network Card Setup dialog box asks you to confirm the hardware settings for the card. Make any required changes and continue by clicking on OK.

   Any required network adapter software will be installed. Supply a file path if one is required. You will be returned to the Network Settings dialog box.

7. Next you must reconfigure TCP/IP. Scroll through the Installed Net**w**ork Software list and select TCP/IP Protocol. Then click on **C**onfigure to display the TCP/IP Configuration box (refer to fig. 15.13).

8. Because you are installing a router, each computer, including the gateway computer, should have a default gateway. Figure 15.18 shows the original adapter reconfigured with its own address as the **D**efault Gateway.

Note If a default gateway is not specified, the computer will not be able to route data to computers on other subnets unless the route command is used to add appropriate routing information to the computer's routing table.

9. You must also configure the new adapter. Pull down the **A**dapter list and locate the newly installed adapter. The new adapter will be identified as number [2]. When you select the adapter, a blank TCP/IP Configuration dialog box is displayed. For the example network, this adapter would be configured as shown in figure 15.19.

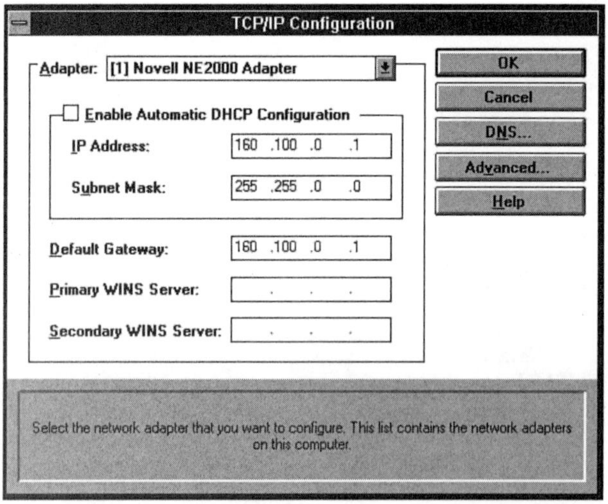

Figure 15.18

Configuring an adapter with a default gateway.

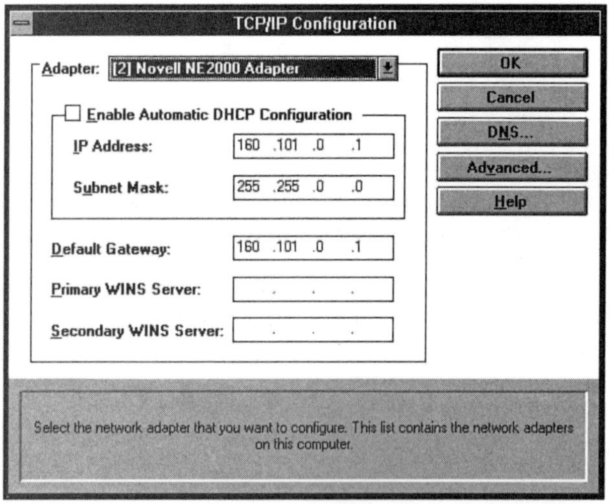

Figure 15.19

The second adapter in a gateway computer.

10. Next, Routing must be enabled. Click on the Advanced button to reveal the Advanced Microsoft TCP/IP Configuration window shown in figure 15.20. The settings in this window will be examined in detail later in this chapter. For now, the only required change is to check the Enable IP Routing check box, as shown in the figure. (The Enable IP Routing option is disabled unless at least two network adapters have been installed.) Click on OK when the setting has been made.

11. Click on OK in the TCP/IP Configuration dialog box.

12. Respond Yes to the warning that WINS is not configured.
13. When you return to the Network Settings dialog box, click on OK.
14. Restart the computer.

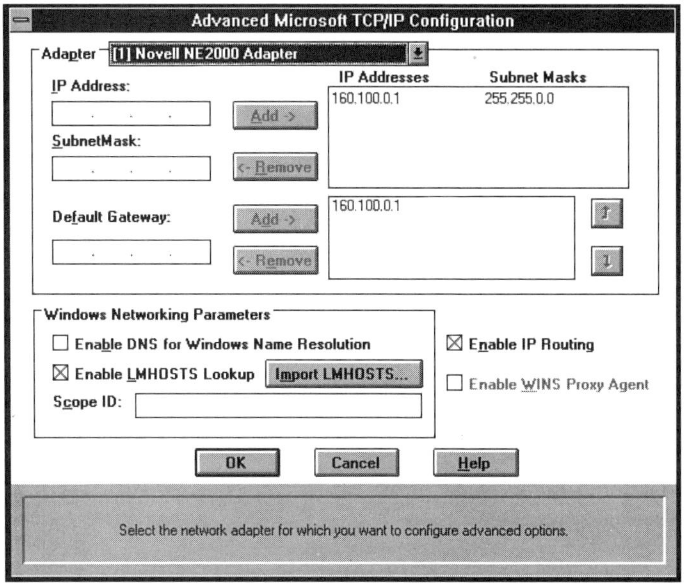

Figure 15.20
Advanced TCP/IP configuration.

After host 160.101.0.100 has been configured, ping can be used to test out the gateway's routing capabilities. It should be possible to ping 160.100.0.100 from either subnet, for example. If that doesn't work, it is necessary to double-check addressing on the adapters in the router and to ensure that IP routing has been enabled.

Note Another example would be to ping 160.100.0.100 from machine 160.101.0.100, which would show that the NT box is routing IP packets.

Configuring Clients for DNS

If a DNS server is available, you should configure TCP/IP hosts with the name of your DNS domain and the address of the DNS server. Figure 15.21 shows a DNS configuration screen with purely fictitious information.

1. In the TCP/IP Configuration dialog box, click on the DNS button.

2. Enter your domain name in the Domain Name box. This name is combined with the host name to create a fully qualified domain name (FQDN) for the computer.

3. To add a DNS server address, enter the address in the Domain Name Service (DNS) Search Order address box and choose Add.

4. Add up to three DNS addresses if required. DNS servers are searched in the order they appear in this list.

5. Add up to six DNS suffixes to the Domain Suffix Search Order list. These suffixes are appended to host names during name resolution and are used in the order they appear in the list.

6. Click on OK when all DNS servers have been specified.

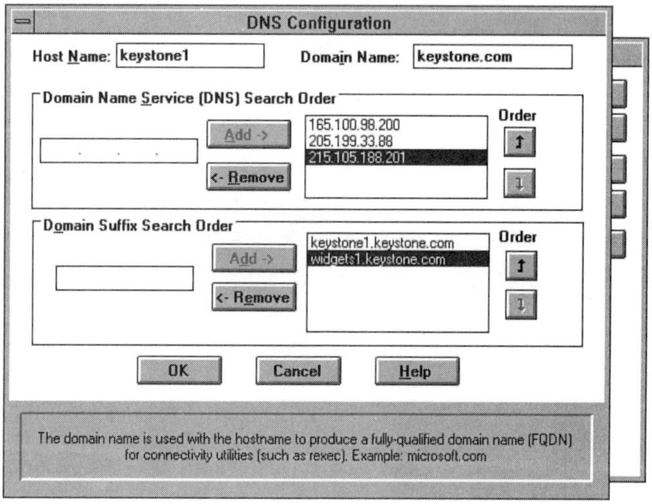

Figure 15.21
Specifying a DNS configuration.

To adjust the order of items in the DNS Search Order or Domain Suffix Search Order lists, select an item to be moved. Then click on the up- and down-arrow buttons to move the item to a new position in the list.

Setting Up Additional Segments

Windows NT computers can function as routers but are limited in a fundamental way. Because Windows NT does not include a protocol such as RIP or OSPF, routing tables must be manually configured whenever segments are separated by more than one hop.

Figure 15.22 illustrates such a network. Two routers are used to internetwork three network segments. As installed, the routers can handle the following routing:

- Router A can route frames between segment 160.100 and 160.101.
- Router B can route frames between segment 160.101 and 160.102

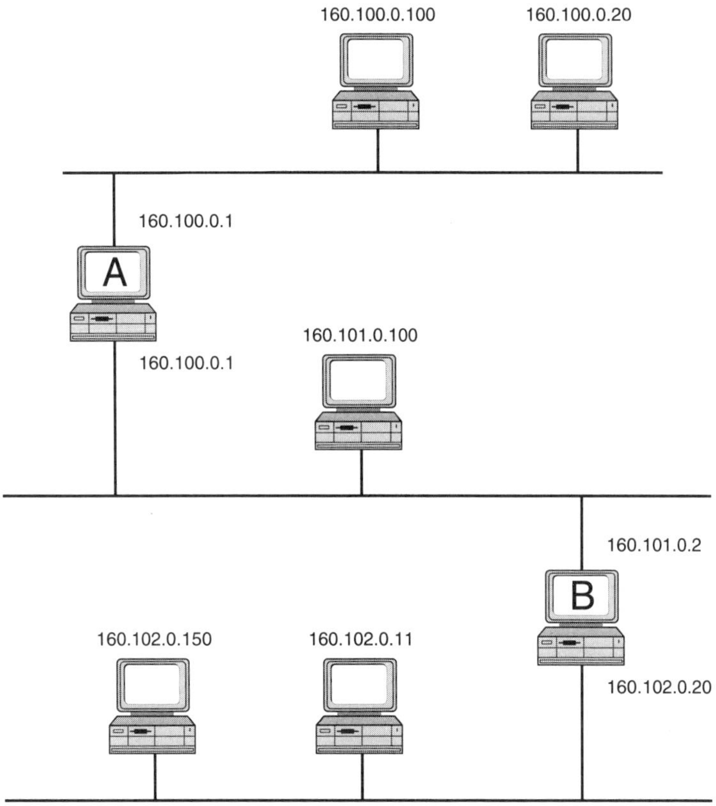

Figure 15.22
A three-segment network.

If a host on segment 160.100 attempts to send a frame to 160.102.0.100, however, router A is unaware of the existence of subnet 160.102 and is unable to route the frame.

Earlier the "route" command was mentioned. route is used to manually maintain routing tables and can add the routes that are required on this network.

route takes two arguments: the segment address of the destination and the address of a gateway that the router can reach. This gateway will perform the next step in routing frames from the specified segment.

On router A, the following command would be entered:

```
route add 160.102    160.101.0.2
```

The command states, "If this router receives a frame addressed to subnet 160.102, the frame will be routed to 160.101.0.2."

Similarly, this command would be entered on router B:

```
route add 160.100 160.101.0.1
```

If more than three segments are used, the route command must be used at each router to ensure that frames are forwarded from router-to-router and segment-to-segment. If you configure such a network, be sure to ping it out thoroughly to ensure that all of the routing tables have been configured properly.

Obviously, you could spend considerable time managing routing tables on a network that changed frequently. That's why most large networks use commercial routers that support a routing protocol. Nevertheless, it is reassuring to know that the basic routing capabilities of Windows NT are adequate to handle many network requirements without the added cost of commercial routers.

Adding Default Gateways

Windows NT computers can specify additional gateways to be used when the default gateway is not available or when the default gateway does not have routing information for a segment. Figure 15.23 shows the three-segment network with an additional router. If desired, hosts on the various subnets can be configured with alternative gateways.

A network that is configured in this way with extra routers is more reliable because any one router can fail without disrupting the network.

To add a default gateway to a computer, follow these steps:

1. In the Network Settings dialog box, select TCP/IP Protocol in the Installed Network Software list.

2. Click on Configure. Then click on Advanced in the TCP/IP Configuration dialog box.

3. Enter a gateway IP address in the Default Gateway box and click on Add to copy it to the list of default gateways. Figure 15.24 shows the result of adding a second default gateway to a computer.

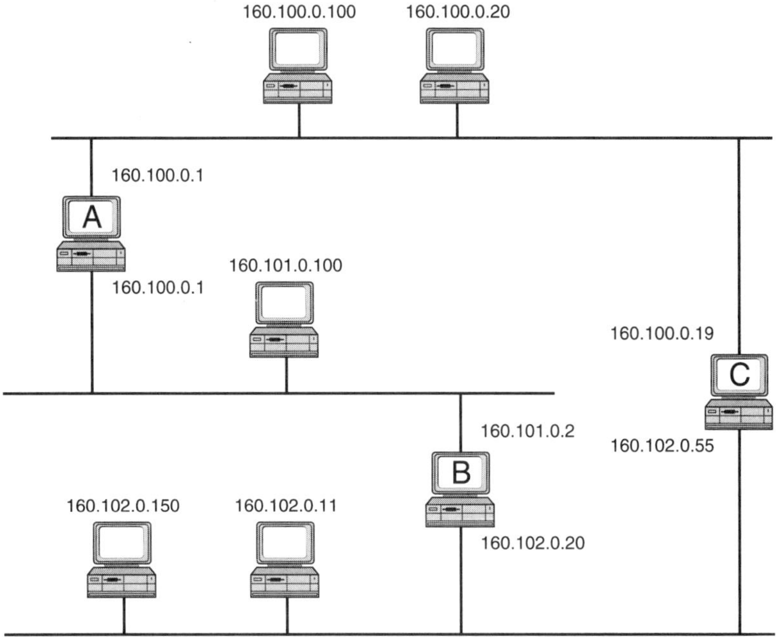

Figure 15.23

A three-segment network with three routers.

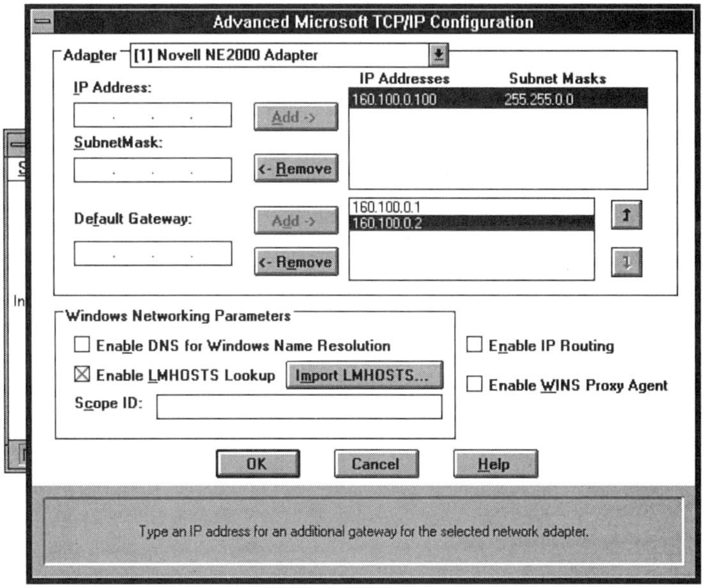

Figure 15.24

Adding multiple default gateways to a computer.

Installing TCP/IP Client Software on Windows for Workgroups 3.11

Windows NT includes TCP/IP client software for Windows for Workgroups 3.11, Windows 3.1, and MS-DOS.

TCP/IP software for Windows for Workgroups 3.11 is included in "TCP/IP 32 for Windows for Workgroups 3.11." This client software is available in the Windows NT Server Workgroup Administrator, which is described in Chapter 19, "Monitoring and Managing the Network."

To install TCP/IP on Windows for Workgroups 3.11, follow these steps:

1. Prepare the client installation disk using Workgroup Administrator.
2. Run the Windows Setup utility in the Main program group.
3. Choose Change Network Settings in the Options menu.
4. Choose Drivers in the Network Setup box.
5. Choose Add Protocol in the Network Drivers dialog box.
6. Select Unlisted or Updated Protocol in the Add Network Protocol list and choose OK.
7. Insert the TCP/IP client diskette and specify a path to the correct diskette drive.
8. When Microsoft TCP/IP-32 v3.311 is added to the Network Drivers list, select the entry and click on Setup.
9. Enter TCP/IP addresses and other parameters as described previously for Windows NT.
10. Click on OK and close Setup.
11. Restart the computer.

Installing TCP/IP Client Software on MS-DOS and Windows 3.1

TCP/IP software for MS-DOS and Windows 3.1 is included in "Network Client v3.0 for MS-DOS and Windows." This client software is available in the Windows NT Server Workgroup Administrator, which is described in Chapter 19, "Monitoring and Managing the Network."

Procedures for installing the Network Client v3.0 are described in Chapter 13, "Using Windows and DOS Clients." When you install the client kits, you will need to select the TCP/IP protocols for installation. Configure the protocols using the same settings as described the previous sections about configuring TCP/IP on Windows NT.

Using the Dynamic Host Configuration Protocol

The procedures required to manually configure IP addresses on just a few computers has probably made you wonder what it would take to configure large numbers of hosts on a changing network. It doesn't take much thought to realize that managing IP addresses can send you screaming into the night.

With Dynamic Host Configuration Protocol (DHCP), you need to hard code only one IP address. All other addresses may be allocated from a pool when a computer demands TCP/IP access to the network. Network administrators are relieved of the necessity of maintaining logs that record every IP address in the organization and who it is assigned to.

Simplifying assignment of IP addresses is just one reason the Dynamic Host Configuration Protocol (DHCP) was developed. Another reason is that DHCP lets a network support more TCP/IP users than it has TCP/IP addresses. Suppose that you have a class C address on the Internet, which gives you the potential for 253 connections (your router takes one). Unfortunately, your company has 500 employees. Fortunately, only 50 of those employees will stay connected for a significant portion of the day. Others will be on the Net only occasionally. After you dedicate an IP address to each one of your "regulars," you have about 200 addresses that can be shared. Those 450 occasional users can share the 200 address pool thanks to DHCP.

How DHCP Works

Figure 15.25 illustrates a network that is supporting DHCP. A single DHCP server can support the network, although multiple DHCP servers may be installed if desired. Notice in the figure that a single DHCP server can support addressing on multiple subnets.

A DHCP client is a computer that requests IP addresses from a DHCP server. When a DHCP client initiates access to the TCP/IP network, the following events take place:

1. The client broadcasts a discover message that is forwarded to DHCP servers on the network.

2. DHCP servers respond by offering IP addresses.

3. The client selects one of the IP addresses and sends a request to use that address to the DHCP server.

4. The DHCP server acknowledges the request and grants the client a lease to use the address.

5. The client uses the address to bind itself to the network.

Figure 15.25

A network offering DHCP support.

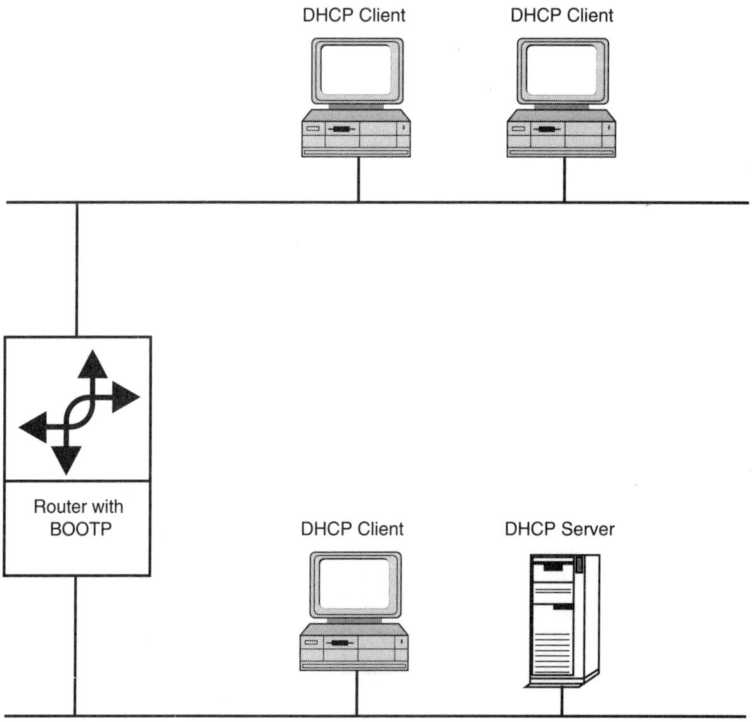

DHCP addresses are leased for a specific duration. When the lease approaches expiration, an active client negotiates to renew the lease. If the current address cannot be reassigned, a new address is assigned to the client. Addresses that are not renewed are returned to the address pool.

Installing a DHCP Server

To support DHCP on a network, at least one Windows NT computer must be configured as a DHCP server. After the DHCP server software is installed, DHCP manager is used to configure and manage the service. After at least one DHCP server has been configured, computers can be configured as DHCP clients.

Because a computer cannot function simultaneously as a DHCP client and a DHCP server, Windows NT computers functioning as DHCP servers must be configured with fixed IP addresses. Before you begin the following procedure, use the techniques described earlier ("IP Addresses") to configure adapters and IP addresses on the computer you'll use as a DHCP server.

To install a DHCP server, follow these steps:

1. Open the Network utility in the Control Panel.
2. Choose Add Software in the Network Settings dialog box.
3. In the Add Network Software box, select TCP/IP Protocol and related components and click on Continue.
4. In the Windows NT TCP/IP Installation Options box (refer to figure 15.12), check DHCP Server Service. Then click on Continue.
5. If this is the first time TCP/IP is being installed on this computer, complete the procedures described in "Installing and Managing TCP/IP Services" earlier in this chapter for configuring TCP/IP with fixed addresses.

   If the DHCP server is multihomed, be sure to configure each adapter with an appropriate IP address.
6. Close Network Settings by choosing OK and restart the computer.

The Microsoft DHCP Server service is a standard Windows NT service that can be managed from the Services utility in the Control Panel. The service is configured to start automatically when Windows NT is started.

Managing DHCP Scopes

Before clients can obtain addresses from DHCP, you must create one or more scopes on each DHCP server. A *scope* is a range of IP addresses that can be leased by clients. DHCP Manager, the utility used to manage DHCP scopes, is installed in the Network Administration program group when DHCP is installed on the computer.

Figure 15.26 shows the main window for DHCP Manager. The left pane lists scopes that have been defined on this server, while the right pane defines options that have been configured.

Figure 15.26

The DHCP Manager main window.

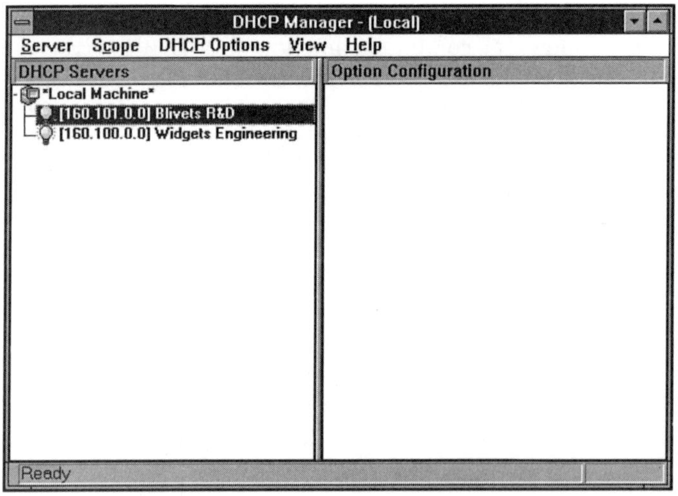

Creating and Modifying a Scope

To create a scope, follow these steps:

1. Open DHCP Manager by double-clicking on the DHCP Manager icon in the Network Administration program group.

2. At least one DHCP server should be displayed in the left DHCP Servers pane. The computer on which DHCP Manager is running will be listed as "Local Machine."

   Select the server on which the scope will be created. Then choose **C**reate in the S**c**ope menu to display the Create Scope dialog box shown in figure 15.27.

3. The address range of a scope is defined by a **S**tart Address and an **E**nd Address. Enter a valid IP address range in these two fields. The IP addresses in the scope include the values you enter.

4. Specify a subnet mask in the Subnet Mas**k** box. Unless you are using address subranges, this entry will be the default mask for the address class you entered in the **S**tart Address and **E**nd Address boxes.

5. If you do not want to have some of the addresses in the scope range assigned to DHCP clients, you can exclude ranges of addresses from the scope.

   To exclude a range, under Exclusion Range, enter a S**t**art Address and an E**n**d Address. Then choose A**d**d.

   To exclude a single address, enter the address in the S**t**art Address box and choose A**d**d.

To remove an excluded address or range, select it in the Excluded Addresses list and click on Remove.

6. Specify the lease duration for this scope.

   If leases should not expire, select Unlimited.

   If leases should expire, select Limited To and specify a lease duration in days, hours, and minutes.

7. Optionally, you can enter a Name and a Comment for this scope. The name you enter will help identify the scope in the DHCP Manager window.
8. When the scope has been defined, click on OK. DHCP Manager will notify you that "The scope has been successfully created, but has not yet been activated. Activate the new scope now?" Choose Yes to activate the scope.
9. When the DHCP Manager window is displayed, the new scope will appear. The light bulb icon will be lit (yellow) indicating that the scope is active.

To modify an existing scope, follow these steps:

1. Select the scope in the DHCP Manager window.
2. Choose Properties in the Scope menu.
3. Make the required changes in the Scope Properties dialog box, which is identical in content to the Create Scope dialog box shown in figure 15.27.
4. Click on OK to save the changes to the scope.

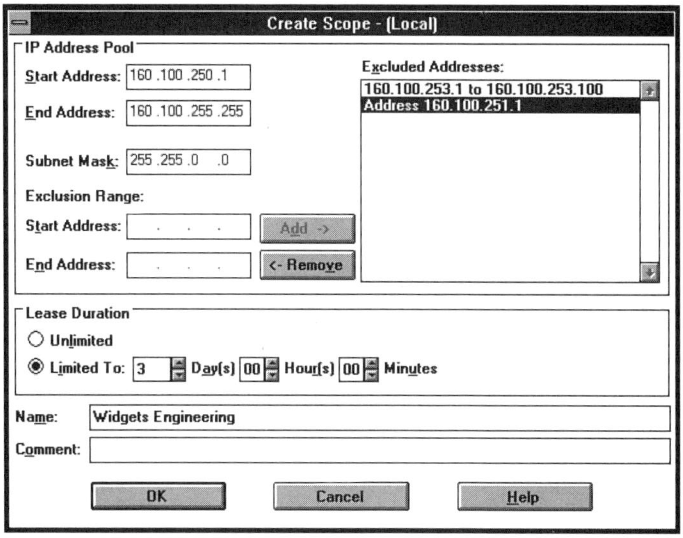

Figure 15.27

Creating a scope.

Note Now that DHCP scopes are active, you can activate DHCP clients. When you configure TCP/IP on the clients, check the Enable Automatic DHCP Configuration box in the Microsoft TCP/IP Configuration dialog box (see fig. 15.13). It is not necessary to specify an IP address or subnet mask.

Restart the client, and it should connect to the DHCP server and lease an address.

Activating, Deactivating, and Deleting Scopes

To activate a deactivated scope, follow these steps:

1. Select the scope in the DHCP Manager window.
2. Choose Activate in the Scope menu.

To deactivate an active scope, follow these steps:

1. Select the scope in the DHCP Manager window.
2. Choose Deactivate in the Scope menu.

Note Deactivating a scope will not disconnect active leases, but will cause DHCP to stop leasing addresses from that scope.

To delete an active scope, use the following steps:

1. Deactivate the scope.
2. Verify that active leases have been released. You can wait for leases to expire or have users disconnect from the DHCP server.
3. Select the scope in the DHCP Manager window.
4. Choose Deactivate in the Scope menu.

Viewing and Managing Active Leases

To view or manage the leases that are active for a scope, do the following:

1. Select the scope in the DHCP Manager window.
2. Choose Active Leases in the Scope menu to display the Active Leases dialog box shown in figure 15.28.

   Information at the top of the dialog box lets you determine how many of the available addresses in the scope are available.

3. To delete a client and terminate the lease, select the lease and click on **D**elete. DHCP Manager knows that this can cause problems and asks you to confirm.

   Delete only entries that are no longer in use. If you delete an active client, deleted addresses can be reassigned to new clients and duplicate IP addresses can be created on the network.

4. To edit the properties for the lease, select the lease and click on **P**roperties. The Client Properties dialog box is shown in figure 15.29.

   You can edit the following items:

   - **Client Name.** This does not necessarily match the user's computer name, and changing the client name will not affect the computer name.
   - **Unique Identifier.** This is the hardware MAC address for the client, and is determined automatically when the lease is established.
   - **Client Comment.** Any comment text you want to add.

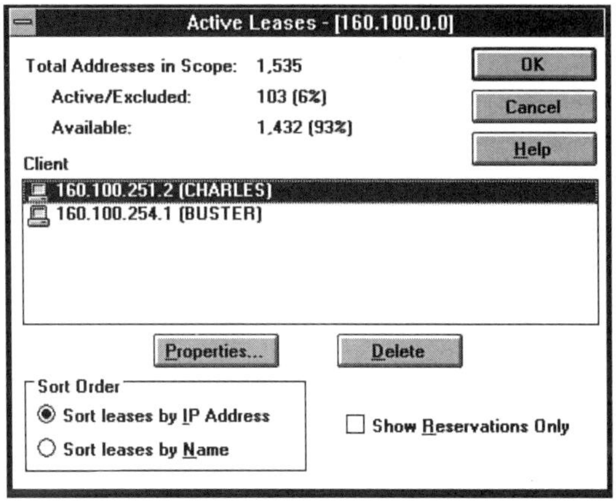

Figure 15.28

Active leases in a DHCP scope.

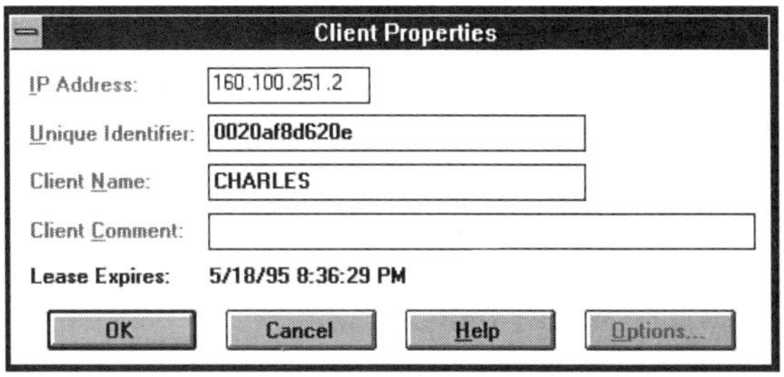

Figure 15.29

Client properties for an active DHCP client.

Tip You can determine the IP address assigned to a DHCP client by entering the command **ipconfig** at a command prompt on the client. The ipconfig utility is installed when you install TCP/IP on a computer.

Note You can install more than one DHCP server on a network. This will improve DHCP responsiveness and also enables DHCP clients to continue to access the network when one DHCP server is down.

The catch is that DHCP servers don't communicate with each other. If two or more DHCP servers are operating with the same address pool, it is possible that more than one client might obtain a lease to the same address from different DHCP servers.

Consequently, when setting up multiple DHCP servers, you should ensure that unique address ranges are assigned to the scopes on each DHCP server on the network.

Reserving DHCP Addresses

It is significantly more convenient to allocate addresses from DHCP than by hard coding them into individual computers. Nevertheless, there will be times when you want to configure a DHCP client to always have the same IP address. You can accomplish this while retaining many of the advantages of DHCP by reserving addresses within DHCP for specific clients.

To reserve an address for a client, follow these steps:

1. Start DHCP Manager.
2. Select a scope and choose Add Reservations in the Scope menu. This will display the Add Reserved Clients dialog box shown in figure 15.30.
3. In the IP Address field, enter an IP address that falls within the range of addresses reserved for this scope.
4. In the Unique Identifier box, enter the hardware address for the client that will use this IP address. You can determine this address by typing the command **net config wksta** at a command prompt at the client. For Ethernet or token ring, this will be a twelve-digit hexadecimal number. The unique identifier, not the client name, is the crucial bit of information that enables a client to access the reserved address. Other information is informational only.
5. Enter a client name in the Client Name box. This doesn't have to match the user's account name and is entered here for informational purposes only.

6. If desired, add a comment in the Client **C**omment box.

7. Choose **A**dd.

If you select this scope and choose Active **L**eases, you will see the reservation listed in the Active Leases box, as shown in figure 15.31.

Note Once a reservation has been created, its properties are managed from the Active Leases dialog box. Select the reservation and click on **P**roperties to display information about the reservation.

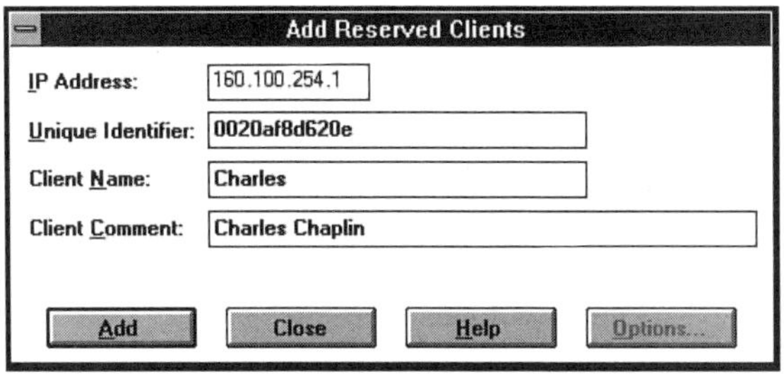

Figure 15.30

Adding a reserved client.

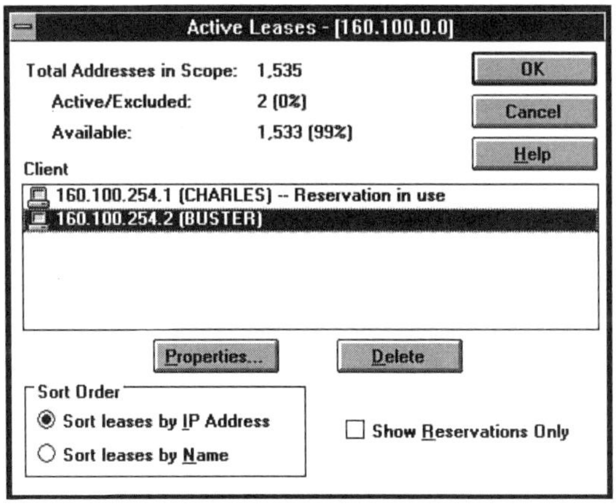

Figure 15.31

An address reservation in the Active Leases list.

Configuring DHCP Options

When DHCP is used to assign IP addresses, the TCP/IP environment of the DHCP client is defined by the options that are assigned to the scope from which the address is obtained. DHCP has about 60 predefined options, only some of which will ever concern you. Among their many functions, you can use options to specify the addresses of default gateways and DNS servers, domain names, and support for WINS.

Options can be assigned at three levels:

- **Defaults.** Options that apply to all scopes unless they are overridden by options assigned globally or to a specific scope.
- **Global.** Options that apply to all scopes and override default options.
- **Scope.** Options that apply only to a specific scope and override global and default options.

The following procedure illustrates how options are added to a scope and configured. The example defines default router addresses for a scope. Since default routers are specific to each network segment, this option would logically be assigned to a specific scope.

To add an option to a specific scope, follow these steps:

1. Select the scope in the DHCP Manager main window.
2. Choose the Scope command in the DHCP Options menu. The DHCP Options dialog box is shown in figure 15.32.
3. Select an option in the Unused Options list and choose Add. The option will be moved to the Active Options list. In figure 15.32, the 003 Router option has been added.
4. For options that must be configured, select the option in the Active Options list and choose Value. An options dialog box will be added to the DHCP Options window, as shown in figure 15.33.

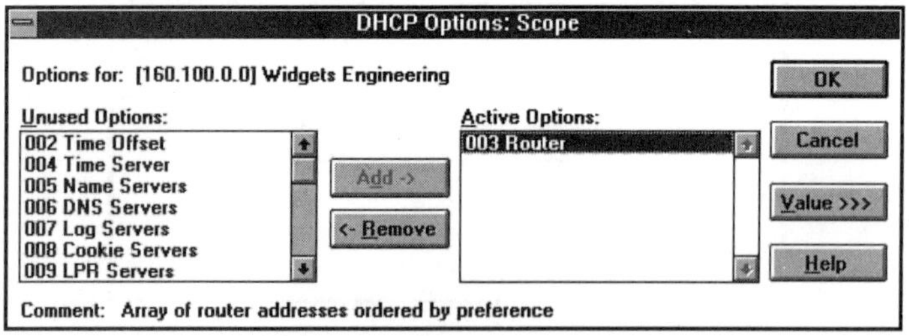

Figure 15.32
Adding a DHCP option to a scope.

5. Some options can be edited directly in this box. Options that accept multiple values require you to display another dialog box by clicking on Edit Array. Figure 15.34 shows the IP Address Array Editor.

   To configure a default router, follow these steps:

- ◆ Remove the initial value of 0.0.0.0 by selecting the entry in the **IP** Addresses list and by clicking on **R**emove.
- ◆ Add a value by entering the default router address in the New **IP** Address box and clicking on **A**dd.

Figure 15.34 shows the dialog box after the initial address of 0.0.0.0 has been removed and an address of 160.100.0.1 has been added.

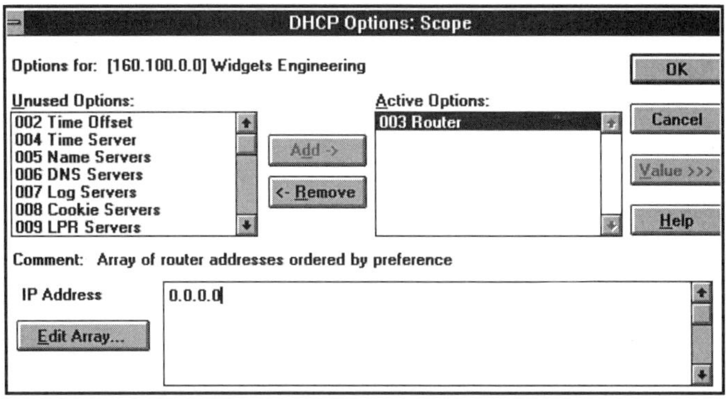

Figure 15.33
Values for a DHCP option.

6. Click on OK twice to save the option and return to the DHCP Manager main menu.

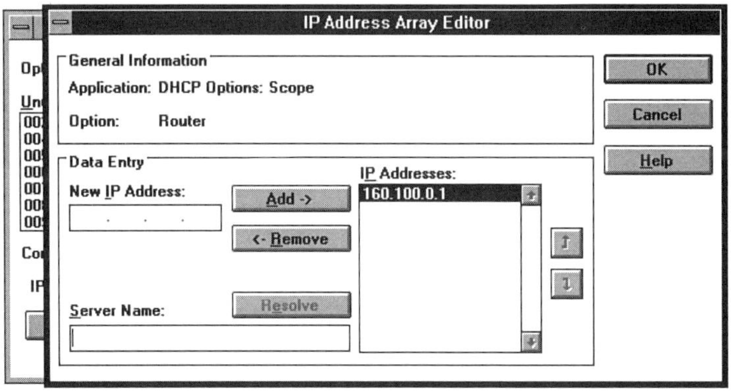

Figure 15.34
Editing an array of values for a DHCP option.

Besides the default router option, here are some options you may require:

- ◆ **006 DNS Servers.** Specifies an address list of available DNS servers.
- ◆ **015 Domain Name.** Specifies the DNS domain name the client should use for DNS host name resolution.

Two other options you can use to relate to WINS are discussed in the next section, "Installing and Managing WINS ."

To manage options for a DHCP reservation, follow these steps:

1. Select the scope that supports the reservation in the DHCP Manager main window.
2. Choose Active Leases in the Scope menu.
3. Select the reservation in the Active Leases box.
4. Click on Properties.
5. Click on Options to display the DHCP Options: Reservation dialog box. This dialog box enables you to manage options for a reservation using the procedures to manage options for a scope.

Installing and Managing WINS

This chapter has been peppered with references to naming services such as Domain Name Service (DNS). Naming services are crucial tools for humanizing access to a network. That's why DNS was invented for the TCP/IP community. Names have another advantage, however: they insulate us from changes in network and host IDs.

Suppose that you're used to referring to a host as 203.95.160.3. One day, the department housing that computer moves to another building on another segment of the network. All of a sudden, the computer has a new address of 199.180.65.43. Lots of other computers probably moved with it, and you have considerable work to do forgetting old numbers and learning new numbers. If you've ever worked for a company that has moved to new quarters, think about the hassle it was getting used to the new phone numbers.

If you think about it, users on a DHCP-managed network face that problem every day. DHCP allocates addresses dynamically, and a given user's TCP/IP address will change from time to time.

The solution to this problem is a name service. Although IP addresses may change, a name service will keep itself up-to-date. Users continue to use familiar network names, regardless of alterations in the network structure.

Naming is one of the problems the Windows Internet Naming Service (WINS) solves by enabling users to use the familiar NetBIOS computer names in a TCP/IP environment. (NetBIOS names are the names that are assigned to a computer when Windows NT or another network client is configured to access the Microsoft network.)

As users connect to the network and as IP addresses change, WINS maintains a database of NetBIOS names and their respective IP addresses. This database is available for reference by Windows and TCP/IP programs on the Microsoft network.

Note Unfortunately, WINS is a Microsoft-only protocol. Only WINS clients on the Microsoft network can use names in the WINS database. Users who are entering your network from the outside cannot use WINS names to identify hosts. For that, you need DNS.

NetBIOS over TCP/IP

Applications running on Windows can use two standard application program interfaces (APIs) for accessing network services:

- *NetBIOS* is the standard API for Windows programs. Essentially, NetBIOS is the native "language" of Microsoft networking.
- *Sockets* is a standard API in the TCP/IP environment. The Windows implementation is called Windows Sockets.

Windows Sockets is fully integrated with TCP/IP networking and interoperates transparently with a TCP/IP network.

NetBIOS, on the other hand, was not developed with large networks in mind. Microsoft enables NetBIOS to operate on the TCP/IP protocol stack, but that isn't enough to enable NetBIOS applications to fully access a TCP/IP network. Without help, NetBIOS cannot operate in a network that incorporates routers, as all large networks must.

The problem is that NetBIOS relies heavily on broadcast messages, messages that are addressed to all other computers on the network. When a Windows computer starts up on the network, it announces itself by broadcasting a message with its name to see if any other computer on the network is already using that name. And when the computer shares resources, broadcast messages are also used to announce the resources that the computer is sharing with the network.

Unfortunately, broadcast messages are not passed over routers, which means that NetBEUI network services are limited to the local subnet. Unless, that is, WINS is enabled on the network.

WINS enables NetBEUI network clients to access name databases using point-to-point communication modes that are routable. Each WINS client is configured with the IP addresses of one or more WINS servers. These IP addresses enable the client to access the WINS server even if client and server are separated by a router.

Figure 15.35 illustrates a routed network that incorporates WINS servers and clients. Three types of computers are shown:

- **WINS servers.** Several WINS servers can be present on a network. They can replicate each other's databases and improve WINS performance.
- **WINS-enabled clients.** Windows NT and Windows for Workgroups 3.11 can interact directly with WINS servers.
- **Non-WINS clients.** Clients that support a feature called *b-node* can interact with WINS clients on their local network segments. The WINS clients will obtain name information from WINS servers on the local or remote segments and provide this information to non-WINS clients. In this way, WINS-enabled clients function as WINS *proxies* for non-WINS computers. A segment can support non-WINS clients provided that at least one computer on the segment is WINS-enabled.

As mentioned at the beginning of this section, two or more WINS servers can be configured on a network. Since these WINS servers can be configured to replicate their databases, multiple WINS servers improves the fault tolerance of WINS services on the network.

Figure 15.35

A multisegment network with WINS servers and clients.

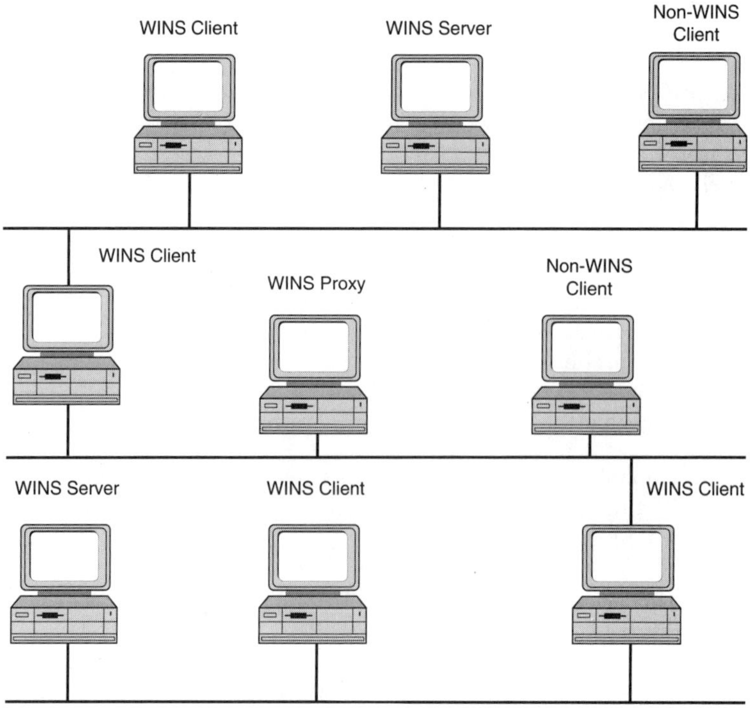

Installing WINS Servers

To install a WINS server, follow these steps:

1. Open the Network utility in the Control Panel.
2. Choose Add Software in the Network Settings dialog box.
3. In the Add Network Software, select TCP/IP Protocol and related components and click on Continue.
4. In the Windows NT TCP/IP Installation Options box, check WINS Server Service (refer to figure 15.12). Then click on Continue.
5. If this is the first time TCP/IP is being installed on this computer, complete the procedures described in "Installing and Managing TCP/IP Services" earlier in this chapter for configuring TCP/IP with fixed addresses.

   If the DHCP server is multihomed, be sure to configure each adapter with an appropriate IP address.
6. Close Network Settings by choosing OK and restart the computer.

WINS is installed as a Windows NT service. It is configured to start automatically when Windows NT starts.

Note A multihomed computer—a computer with more than one network adapter attached to more than one network—cannot be used as a WINS server because a WINS server cannot register its name on more than one network.

Managing WINS Servers

When WINS services are installed, the WINS Manager is added as a program item in the Network Administration program group. The main window for the WINS Manager is shown in figure 15.36. This window lists several statistics that enable you to track the operation of WINS. Since many of these statistics have to do with WINS database replication, you'll return to this screen after replication is discussed.

Several parameters on a WINS server can be adjusted. To configure a WINS server, do the following:

1. Select a server in the WINS Servers pane of the WINS Manager main window.
2. Choose the Configuration command in the Server menu to display the WINS Server Configuration dialog box shown in figure 15.37.

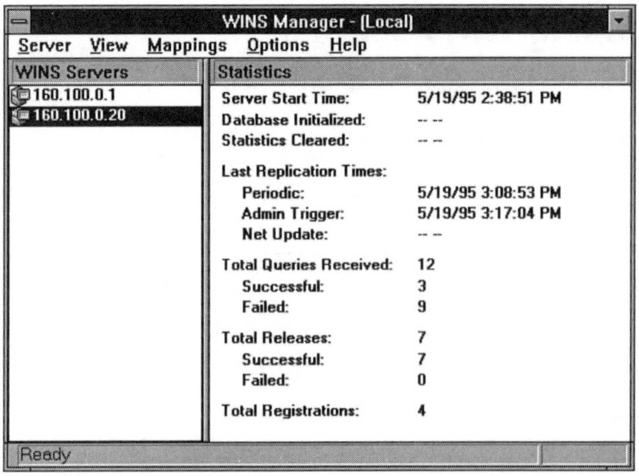

Figure 15.36
Statistics in the WINS Manager main window.

3. Renewal Interval specifies the intervals at which a WINS client must reregister its name. A name that is not reregistered is marked as *released* in the WINS database. The maximum value is 4 days (96 hours). If clients are forced to renew very frequently, network traffic is increased. Try reregistering at 1 to 2 day intervals.

4. Extinction Interval specifies the interval between the time a name is marked *released* and when it is marked *extinct*. Extinct records are eligible to be purged. Try setting this value to 4 times the renewal interval.

5. Extinction Timeout specifies the interval between the time a name is marked extinct and when the name is actually purged from the database. The minimum value is one day.

6. Verify Interval specifies the interval after which a WINS server must verify that names it does not own are still active. The maximum value is 24 days.

7. Pull Parameters and Push Parameters will be discussed in the section about WINS database replication.

8. To access Advanced WINS Server Configuration parameters, click on the Advanced button.

9. Check Logging Enabled if logging to JET.LOG should be turned on.

10. Check Log Detailed Events to turn on detailed logging. Because verbose logging can consume considerable resources, it should be turned on only during performance tuning.

11. Check Replicate Only With Partners if replication should take place only with push and pull partners specifically configured for this server. If this option is not checked, an administrator can force push or pull replication with this server.

12. Check Backup On Termination if the database should be backed up automatically when WINS Manager is stopped (except when the server is shutting down).

13. Database Backup Path accepts a path to a file that is used to back up the database. Backup can be initiated automatically, as discussed in Step 12, or manually by using the Backup Database command in the Mappings menu. Click on the Browse button to browse for a path if desired.

14. Check Migrate On/Off if you are upgrading non-Windows NT systems to Windows NT. This option enables static records to be treated as dynamic and reassigned to eliminate conflicts.

15. Click on OK to save the configuration settings.

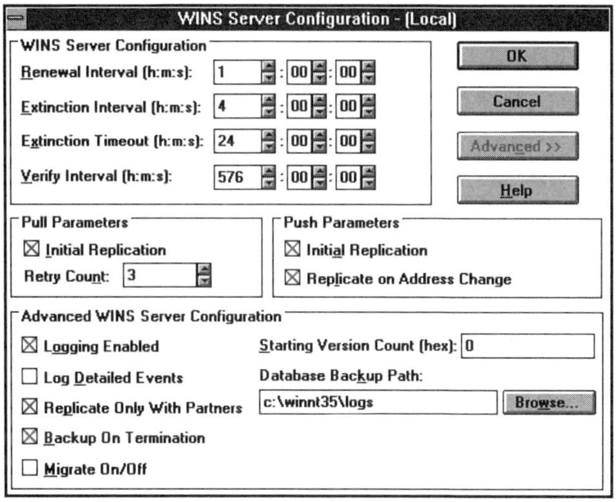

Figure 15.37
Configuring properties of a WINS server.

Configuring WINS Database Replication

Although a single WINS server can service the entire network, ideally you should activate at least two WINS servers to provide a level of fault tolerance. WINS servers can be configured to replicate their databases with one another so that each remains up-to-date with changes on the network. WINS servers can perform two database replication operations: *pushing* and *pulling*.

Because each segment of a network should include either a WINS server or a WINS proxy, the best approach on a multisegment network is to have WINS servers on different network segments. Remember, however, that a multihomed server can't be a WINS server, so you can't add WINS support to two segments with a single computer.

A replication *push partner* is a WINS server that notifies other WINS servers of changes and then sends database replicas upon receiving a request from a pull partner.

A replication *pull partner* is a WINS server that requests replication data from a push partner and then accepts replicas of new database entries.

Figure 15.38 illustrates one manner in which WINS servers might be configured for database replication. A combination of one- and two-way relationships are shown, although I suspect two-way replication by far will be the most common configuration.

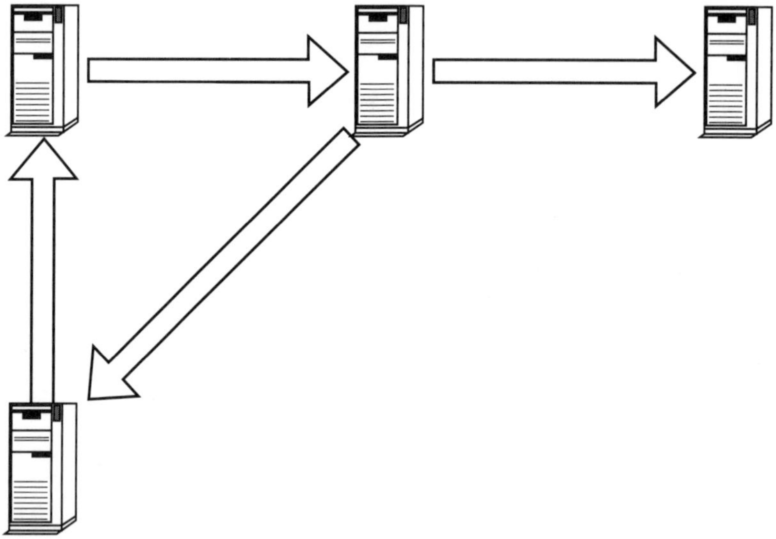

Figure 15.38
Replicating WINS databases.

To configure replication on a WINS server, follow these steps:

1. Select a WINS server in the WINS Manager main window.
2. Choose the **R**eplication Partners command in the **S**erver menu. The Replication Partners dialog box appears, as shown in figure 15.39.
3. Select another WINS server in the Replications Partners dialog box.
4. If the server is to be a push partner:
   - Check the **P**ush Partner box under Replication Options.

- Click on the Configure button to display the Push Partner Properties dialog box shown in figure 15.40. This dialog box has one item: Update Count. Here you specify the number of updates that must take place to the local database before partners will be notified. (Entries pulled from other partners do not count in this context. Only local updates are taken into consideration.)

  Forcing updates to occur too frequently will generate excess network traffic. The minimum value is 5. You can set a default push partner update count in the Preferences window, as described in the next section.

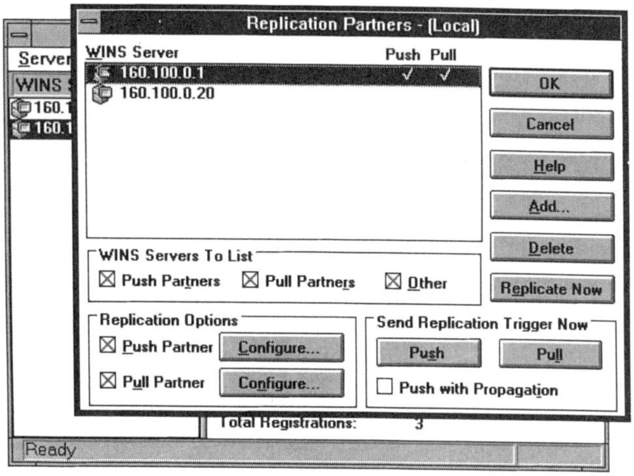

Figure 15.39

Configuring Replication Partners.

5. If the server is to be a pull partner:

   - Check the Pull Partner box under Replication Options.
   - Click on the Configure button to display the Pull Partner Properties dialog box shown in figure 15.41. In this box you can specify an hour in the day when replication should begin and the intervals at which scheduled replications should occur.

6. Choose OK to save the replication configuration.

Note You must configure both sides of a push-pull pair.

- If you have specified server A as a pull partner of server B, be sure to use WINS Manager to make server B a push partner of server A.
- If you have specified server C as a push partner of server D, be sure to use WINS Manager to make server D a pull partner of server C.

Figure 15.40

Configuring a push partner.

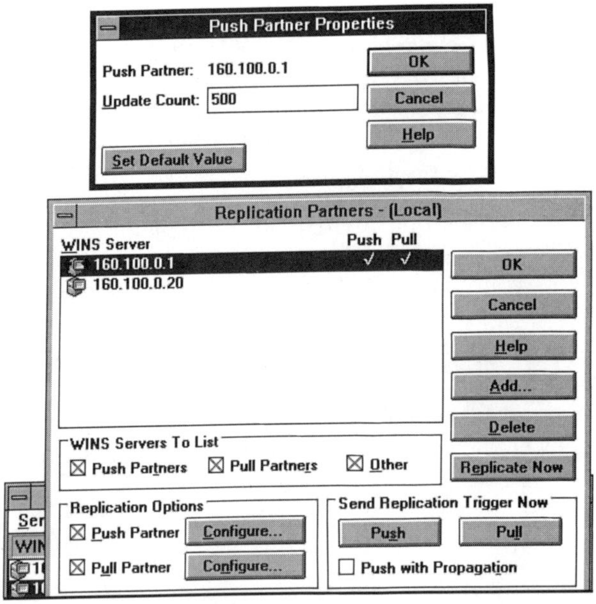

Note You are walking a tightrope when setting push and pull configurations. Changes can only propagate through the network as rapidly as you specify, and the ideal case would be to propagate all changes immediately. Doing so, however, could slow down the network, so you need to make a compromise.

Figure 15.41

Configuring a pull partner.

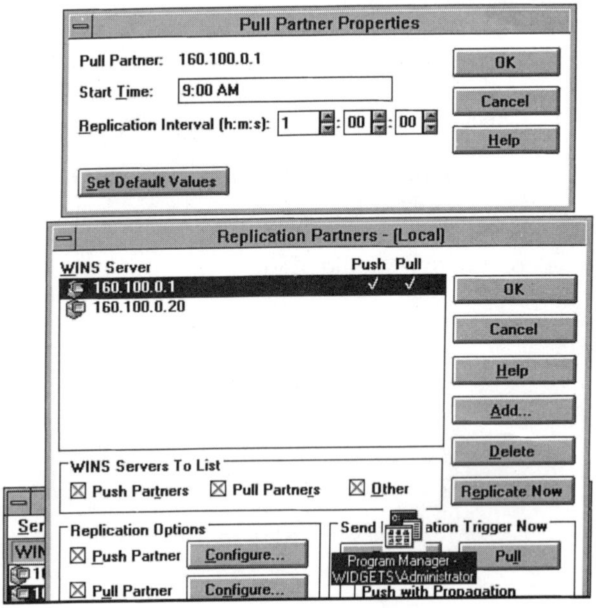

Forcing Database Replication

There are times when you might want to force database replication to occur. You can initiate replication by sending replication triggers, or you can force an immediate replication.

To send a push replication trigger to a pull partner, follow these steps:

1. Select a pull replication partner in the Replication Partners dialog box.
2. Check the Push with Propagation box if the selected server should send a push trigger to its pull partners after it has pulled replicas from the source server.

   Leave the button unchecked if the selected pull partner should not send.
3. Click on the Push button in the Send Replication Trigger Now box to send a replication trigger to the server's pull partners. This trigger takes effect only for other servers that have been configured as pull partners.

To send a pull replication trigger:

1. Select a replication partner in the Replication Partners dialog box.
2. Click on the Pull button in the Send Replication Trigger Now box to send a replication trigger to the server's push partners. This trigger takes effect only for other servers that have been configured as push partners.

To start immediate replication choose Replicate Now.

Setting WINS Preferences

You can configure several WINS preferences by choosing the Preferences command in the WINS Manager Options menu. The Preferences dialog box is shown in figure 15.42. The figure shows how the window appears after the Partners box has been checked to display options for configuring new pull and push partners. Following are the options:

- Options in the Address Display box specify whether the address should be displayed in the main window by IP address, computer name, or both.
- Check Auto Refresh to specify that statistics should be updated automatically at the interval specified.
- Under Computer Names, The LAN Manager-Compatible box should always be checked unless your network will be receiving NetBIOS names from sources other than Microsoft networks. (All Microsoft network clients use LAN Manager compatible names.)

- Check **V**alidate Cache of Known WINS Servers at Startup Time if this server should query its list of known WINS servers each time Windows NT Server starts up. Ordinarily, this option is not required.
- Check Confirm **D**eletion of Static Mappings & Cached WINS servers if warnings should be displayed when you delete a static mapping or the cached name of a WINS server. This option is recommended.
- Specify default options for pull partners in the New Pull Partner Default Configuration box.
- Specify default options for push partners in the New Push Partner Default Configuration box.

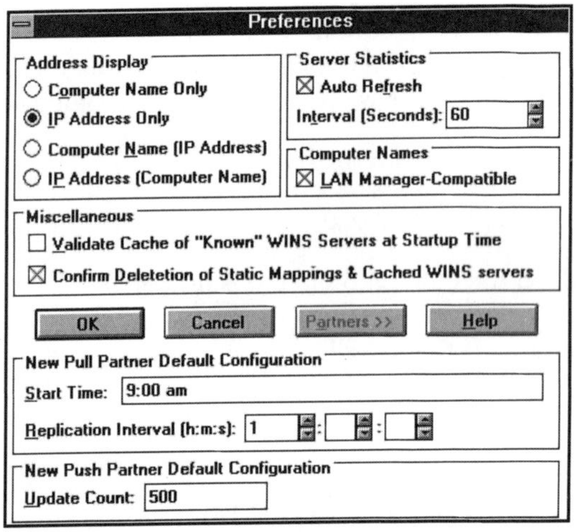

Figure 15.42
Configuring WINS Manager preferences.

Managing Static Mappings

When WINS maps a name to an IP address, the mapping is dynamic. It must be periodically renewed, or it is subject to removal. In most cases, dynamic mapping is in keeping with the nature of a name service, which should adapt to changes in the network without the need for frequent intervention by network administrators.

A *static mapping* is a permanent mapping of a computer name to an IP address. Static mappings cannot be challenged and are removed only when they are explicitly deleted by the network administrator.

If DHCP is run on the network with WINS, reserved IP addresses assigned in DHCP will override static mappings assigned in WINS.

Static WINS mappings permit you to post names and addresses in the WINS database computers that are not WINS-enabled. Static WINS mappings should not be assigned to WINS-enabled computers.

Adding Static Mappings

To add a static mapping, follow these steps:

1. Choose Static Mappings in the Mappings menu. The Static Mappings dialog box is shown in figure 15.43.
2. Click on the Add Mappings button to display the Add Static Mappings dialog box shown in figure 15.44.
3. Type the computer name in the Name box. (WINS Manager will add the leading \\s if you forget them.)
4. Type the address for the computer in the IP Address box.
5. Choose a button in the Type box. Here are the choices:
   - **Unique.** A unique name in the database with a single address per name.
   - **Group.** No address is associated with a group, and addresses of individuals are not stored. The client broadcasts name packets to normal groups.
   - **Internet Group.** A group on an internet that stores up to 25 addresses for members.
   - **Multihomed.** A name that maps from 1 to 25 addresses. This corresponds to adding multiple IP addresses in the Advanced dialog box for TCP/IP settings.
6. Choose Add.

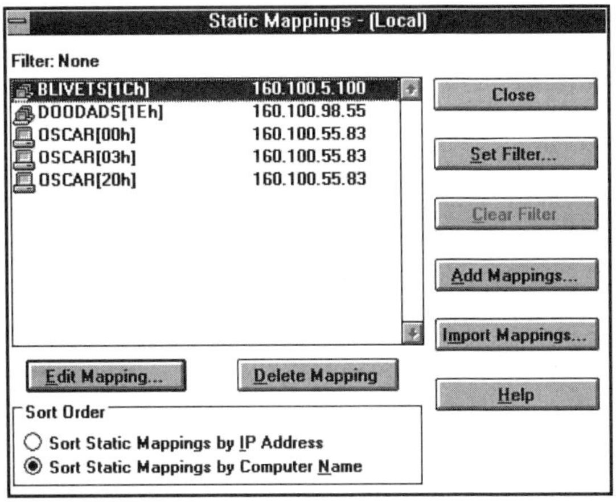

Figure 15.43

Static mappings.

Figure 15.44

Adding a static mapping.

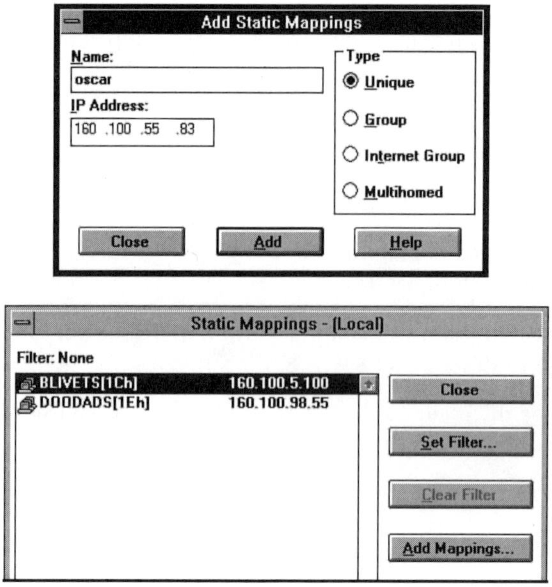

Static mappings are added to the database immediately when you click on Add. Modification of added static mappings is limited, and you will need to delete the static mapping if you want to cancel it.

Editing a Static Mapping

The IP address of a static mapping can be modified as follows:

1. Choose **S**tatic Mappings in the **M**appings menu.
2. Select the mapping to be modified in the Static Mappings dialog box.
3. In the Edit Static Mapping dialog box, enter a new IP address in the **I**P Address box.
4. Click on OK. The change is saved to the WINS database immediately.

Managing the WINS Database

Several operations should be performed periodically to maintain the WINS database. The database consists of four files, which are stored by default in the C:\WINNT35\SYSTEM32\WINS directory:

- *JET.LOG* is the database transaction log, used to recover the database in the event of error.

- *SYSTEM.MDB* stores information about the structure of the WINS database.
- *WINS.MDB* is the actual WINS database file.
- *WINSTMP.MDB* is a temporary file created while WINS is operating.

These files should not be deleted or modified. They should be backed up when the WINS server is backed up, and they should be managed only by utilities in the WINS manager. I suggest that you set up a schedule for performing these duties on a weekly basis.

Scavenging the WINS Database

Extinct and old entries in the database should be removed periodically by choosing the **Initiate Scavenging** command in the **Mappings** menu.

Owned active names for which the renewal interval has expired are marked *released.*

Owned released names for which the extinct interval has expired are marked *extinct.*

Owned extinct names for which the extinct timeout has expired are deleted, as are replicas of extinct and deleted names.

Compacting the WINS Database

After entries have been scavenged, holes in the database will reduce WINS performance. Therefore, the database should be compacted. This must be performed when users will not be accessing WINS.

To compact the WINS database, follow these steps:

1. Use the Services utility in the Control Panel to stop the WINS Internet Name Service service.

   Alternatively, you can stop the service from the command line by typing the command **net stop wins** at the command prompt.

2. Run JETPACK.EXE (which is installed by default in \WINNT35\SYSTEM32).

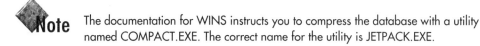

> **Note** The documentation for WINS instructs you to compress the database with a utility named COMPACT.EXE. The correct name for the utility is JETPACK.EXE.

3. Restart WINS with the Services utility or by entering the command **net start wins**.

Tip

Because WINS must be shut down to compact the database, consider putting these commands in your nightly backup batch file, prior to running the backup jobs. Presumably, this batch file runs at a time when users have been logged out of the network. *See Chapter 17, "Backing Up Files," for more information about scheduling batch files for overnight execution.*

Viewing the WINS Database

The Show **D**atabase command in the **M**appings menu displays the Show Database window, which can be used to examine the contents of the WINS database. An example is shown in figure 15.45.

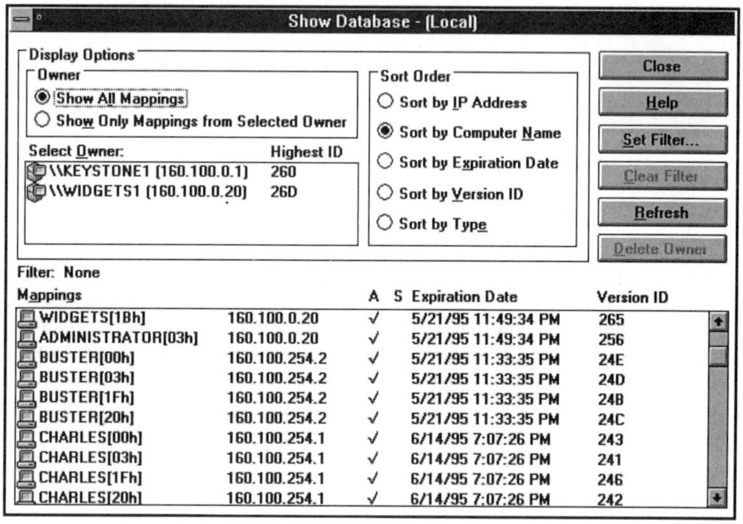

Figure 15.45

Contents of a WINS database.

With WINS, the owner of a mapping is the WINS server that originated the mapping, not a particular user account. To view mappings owned by a particular server, do the following:

1. Select Sho**w** Only Mappings from Selected Owner in the Owner box.
2. Select a WINS server in the Select **O**wner list.

If you want to view all mappings in the database, select Show A**l**l Mappings.

If you want to view only mappings for a particular computer, follow these steps:

1. Choose Set Filter.
2. In the Set Filter dialog box, specify a Computer Name or an IP Address.
3. Choose OK.

To delete all mappings owned by a particular WINS server, follow these steps:

1. Select a WINS server in the Select Owner list.
2. Click on the Delete Owner button.

Backing Up and Restoring the WINS Database

In the earlier section "Managing WINS Servers," you were introduced to options that specify the WINS backup path and whether the WINS database should be backed up when exiting WINS Manager. You can also force a backup of the WINS database.

To back up the WINS database, follow these steps:

1. Choose the Backup Database command in the Mappings menu.
2. In the Select Backup Directory dialog box, browse for a backup directory. You must back up to a local hard drive because the WINS database cannot be restored from a network drive.
3. Check Perform Incremental Backup to back up only records that were created since the most recent backup.
4. Click on OK.

To restore a WINS database, follow these steps:

1. Choose the Restore Local Database command in the Mappings menu.
2. Browse for the directory to be restored from.
3. Click on OK.

Configuring WINS Clients

From the client side, WINS configuration could hardly be easier. All that is necessary is to specify WINS server addresses in the TCP/IP Configuration dialog box. Figure 15.46 shows an example taken from Windows for Workgroups 3.11.

Figure 15.46

Configuring a client for WINS.

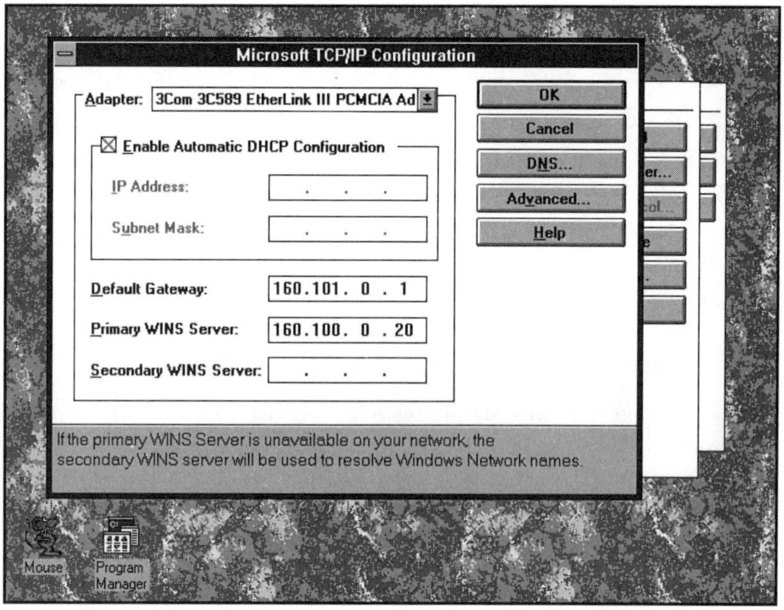

If the WINS client is also using DHCP, you will need to configure the client using DHCP options. If all clients use the same WINS servers, these can be global options. Otherwise, they should be added as scope options.

The required options are

- **044 WINS/NBNS Servers.** As values for this option, specify the IP address(es) of WINS servers to be used by the client.
- **046 WINS/NBT Node Type.** Enter a value of 0x8 for this option, which configures the client for h-node mode. See the following note for a brief explanation of client modes.

Note Clients can be configured to perform registration in four modes:

- **b-node.** The client uses broadcasts, which are restricted to the local subnet. This mode is supported by older Microsoft network clients.
- **p-node.** Clients neither create nor respond to broadcasts. Computers register with a WINS server using point-to-point communication. If a WINS server is unavailable, the client is unable to register with the network.
- **m-node.** The client first attempts to register with b-node mode. If successful, it attempts to switch to p-node. The initial registration in b-node generates

high levels of broadcast traffic and does not achieve the goal of connecting to a WINS server.

- **h-node.** This is the most recently developed mode, supported by Windows NT 3.5 and Windows for Workgroups 3.11. The client first attempts to register with a WINS server using p-node. If registration fails, the client attempts to register on the local subnet with b-node.

Configuring WINS Proxies

If some network clients support only b-node operation, you should ensure that at least one computer on each network segment is either a WINS server or a WINS proxy. Any Windows NT 3.5 or Windows for Workgroups 3.11 client can be configured as a WINS proxy. To configure a WINS proxy, follow these steps:

1. Display the TCP/IP Configuration dialog box for the client.
2. Click on the Advanced button to display the Advanced Microsoft TCP/IP Configuration dialog box.
3. Check Enable WINS Proxy Agent.
4. Click on OK.

Other TCP/IP Options

The Windows NT TCP/IP Installation Options dialog box (refer to fig. 15.12) was used earlier in this chapter to install basic TCP/IP services, DHCP, and WINS. Several other options are available that should be discussed briefly.

Connectivity Utilities

The Connectivity Utilities option installs several standard TCP/IP utilities. The ones you are most likely to use include:

- **ftp.** File transfer protocol is an interactive, command-line utility used to transfer files between ftp-enabled hosts.
- **finger.** Finger is a command-line utility can be used to display information about a host that is running the finger service.

- **telnet.** Telnet supports terminal-emulation access with remote hosts running a Telnet service. Telnet is a graphic utility that is added as a program item to the Accessories program group.
- **tftp.** Tftp is similar to ftp but does not provide user authentication.

Experienced Unix users will be comfortable with the command-line interfaces of ftp, finger, and tftp and will probably not balk at the large command set for ftp. They are, however, a bit out of place in a graphic environment such as Windows NT. I suggest that you obtain Windows versions of ftp and finger. Shareware versions are readily available from Internet providers, information services, and ftp servers.

SNMP Service

The SNMP Service installation option installs support for the Simple Network Management Protocol, the standard network management protocol in the TCP/IP environment. SNMP enables the computer to be managed by network management consoles such as Sun NetManager or Hewlett-Packard Open View. SNMP services are also required to enable the Windows NT Performance Monitor utility to receive statistics from the computer.

TCP/IP Network Printing Support

This option enables Windows NT to support printing over the network using TCP/IP. Choose this option to enable printing to Unix print queues or TCP/IP printers on the network.

FTP Server Service

Choose the FTP Server Service to enable this computer to share files with remote ftp users. The Windows NT FTP Service is integrated into Windows NT security, and users are authenticated based on their Windows NT accounts.

Windows NT FTP Service supports only commands that are included in the Windows NT ftp program. Some commands in other ftp versions might not be supported.

Stop Ftp does not encrypt passwords on the network. If your network is connected to an internetwork with ftp enabled, users' account names and passwords will pass through the network in a form that can be read by any user with physical access to the network.

Part IV

Management

CHAPTER 16

Managing Disk Storage

When you get right down to it, file storage is the heart and soul of a network server. Users need to store their data, often in large quantities, share it, and know that it still will be intact tomorrow.

The typical server has a considerably more sophisticated hard drive system than the typical workstation. At the very least, server drives are likely to be considerably larger. Server drives also tend to be faster. And a premium tends to be placed on reliability.

In this chapter, you will encounter the capabilities Windows NT Server brings to hard drive management. A wide variety of hard drive configurations are available that meet different sets of cost, performance, and reliability needs. In particular, Windows NT Server has the capability to create groups of disks called redundant arrays of inexpensive disks (RAID) using only Windows NT Server software, standard SCSI adapters, and off-the-shelf hard drives. Making RAID technology available to budget-conscious LAN users is one of Microsoft's most significant achievements with Windows NT Server.

How Hard Drives Are Organized

As you read through this chapter, you will notice that the hard drives you hold in your hand often have no direct relation to the drive letters that you actually use to manipulate file systems. You might have two hard drives but only one drive letter. Or, you might have one hard drive but four or more drive letters. Before you learn how to configure hard drives, you need to know something about how hard drives and software drive letters are associated.

Physical Hard Drives

The basic storage unit is the physical hard drive, commonly available with capacities of about 200 megabytes up to almost 10 gigabytes. The individual hard drive has the advantage of simplicity, and it's the most common way to organize hard drive storage. You will see, however, that it is worthwhile to evaluate the alternative of using *arrays*—two or more hard drives that work in association.

Physical hard drives must be low-level formatted, a task that generally is performed by the manufacturer. SCSI hard drives can be low-level formatted in the field using utilities that accompany the SCSI adapter card. IDE and ESDI hard drives cannot be low-level formatted by the user.

As you learned in Chapters 5 and 6, SCSI hard drive subsystems are by far the most appropriate for LAN file storage. Performance is high and they are the only systems that can be productively organized into arrays. Windows NT Server enables you to configure arrays of other drives such as IDE, but you will not gain the fault-tolerance advantage that is possible with an array of SCSI drives.

Each hard drive in a system is assigned a logical number. Drives on the primary drive controller are numbered starting with 0. Logical numbers are assigned differently for SCSI, IDE, and ESDI drives.

- For SCSI, hard drives on the primary controller are numbered from 0 to as high as 6 (one of the eight possible addresses on a SCSI bus, almost always address 7, is reserved for the bus adapter). Drives on the secondary bus adapter start numbering where the first adapter leaves off. As many as four host bus adapters and 28 drives theoretically can be accommodated.

- For IDE and ESDI, hard drives on the primary controller are numbered 0 and 1 (if a second drive is present). A second hard drive controller can support drives numbered starting where the first controller leaves off—usually 2 and 3.

Partitions

Before data can be stored on a hard drive, the hard drive must be partitioned. A *partition* is a designated portion of a hard drive that functions as a separate unit. Partitions can be formatted to create storage volumes. Each hard drive can be configured with as many as four partitions in one of two configurations:

- One to four primary partitions
- One to three primary partitions and one extended partition

A primary partition can be configured to enable an operating system to boot in the partition.

An extended partition is not directly usable for file storage. Extended partitions must be configured with one or more logical drives that are used to store files. Extended partitions are used when it is necessary to have more than four logical drives on a hard drive.

Note MS-DOS is capable of recognizing only a single primary partition—the partition from which it is booted. If there is a chance that you will want to boot your Windows NT computer under MS-DOS, you should restrict each hard drive to a single primary partition and create additional logical drives in extended partitions.

Logical Drives

Before files actually can be stored, partitions must be formatted to establish drive letters. You are familiar with drives as the C, D, E, and other lettered drives that you use to organize the file system on a DOS or Windows NT computer. Drive letters are assigned differently to primary and extended partitions:

- A primary partition may be formatted with a single drive. Therefore, each primary partition will be represented by a single drive letter.
- Extended partitions may be formatted with one or more logical drives.

Figure 16.1 illustrates primary and extended partitions, as shown by the Windows NT Disk Manager.

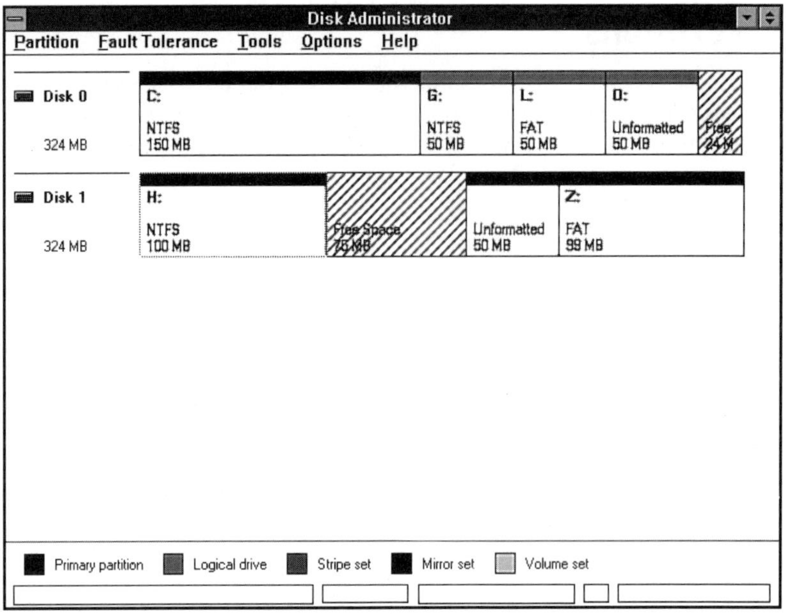

Figure 16.1

Examples of partitions and drives.

Disk 0 has one primary partition, which has been formatted as drive C. This partition has been formatted with the NTFS file system. Disk 0 also has one extended partition, which has been formatted into three logical drives: G, L, and O.

Disk 1 has three primary partitions, formatted as drives H, Z, and one that has not been assigned a drive letter.

Several features should be noted in this figure. If you are familiar with DOS, you might have been surprised that drive lettering did not follow DOS conventions. DOS assigns letters automatically, and letters hard drives continuously starting with drive C. This approach often causes havoc when partitions are deleted or added and drive letters change.

Windows NT enables you to specify the drive letter for each drive. You always can use letters C through Z. The letter B might be available if the system does not have a second floppy drive. A drive letter must be set aside for each CD-ROM drive on the computer.

If the server has more than 25 hard drives, you can create partitions that do not have drive letters.

Some of the partitions in the figure have been formatted with the FAT or NTFS file systems. Others have not been formatted and are labeled `Unformatted`.

Any area that has not been assigned to a partition is marked as `Free Space`. This space is unusable for storage until it has been partitioned and formatted.

Note Each type of drive is designated by a color in the Disk Manager display. A color key appears at the bottom of the Disk Manager window.

I'm not telling you what the colors are, since they are user-definable. To change the colors, choose Colors and Patterns from the Options menu.

Drive Sets

In many cases, volumes will be configured to occupy more than one partition on more than one hard drive. This might be done to create volumes larger than the capacity of a single hard drive, or to enhance the fault tolerance of the volume. Windows NT supports the following types of drive sets:

- **Volume sets.** A volume is extended by using two or more partitions, which can be on multiple hard drives.
- **Stripe sets.** A volume is extended by using two or more partitions, each on a separate drive. A special technique called *striping* is used to write data on all the volume segments.
- **Stripe sets with parity.** Similar to a stripe set, a stripe set with parity uses parity error checking to create a fault-tolerant drive array. Any one drive in the set can fail without causing a loss of data.
- **Mirror sets.** Two partitions on two drives are configured so that each will contain the exact same data. If one drive fails, the mirror contains a replica of the data so that no data is lost and processing can continue.

Now that you have learned how to create partitions and standard drives, the remainder of this chapter shows you more about the types of drive sets and how to create and delete them.

Creating and Deleting Partitions and Drives

All operations required to create, manage, and delete hard drives can be performed with the Disk Manager utility. In this section, you will learn the basics of creating and managing partitions and standard logical drives.

Creating Primary Partitions

A primary partition can be as small as 1 MB or as large as the free space on the hard drive. Up to four primary partitions can be created on a given hard drive.

To create a primary partition in Disk Manager, follow these steps:

1. Select an area marked `Free Space`. The area you select is marked with a wider, black border.
2. Choose Create from the **P**artition menu. The Create Primary Partition dialog box shown in figure 16.2 appears. This box indicates the maximum and minimum sizes allowed for the partition.
3. Enter the desired size in the Create partition of size box.
4. Click on **O**K. Figure 16.3 shows the new, unformatted partition that appears. The designation `New Unformatted` means that the partition has been specified but has not actually been created.
5. To create the partition, choose C**o**mmit Changes Now from the **P**artition menu. After the partition is committed, it is marked as `Unformatted`.

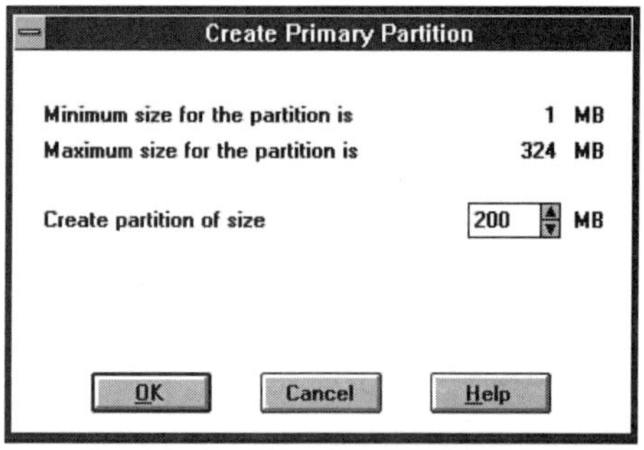

Figure 16.2
Designating the size of a primary partition.

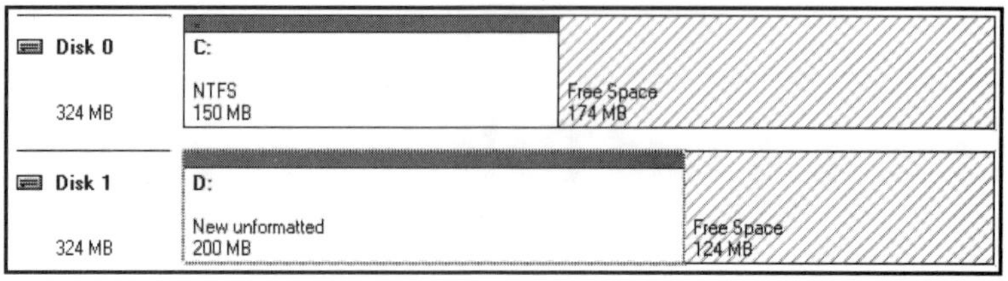

Figure 16.3
An unformatted primary partition.

Note

Many changes made in Disk Administrator do not take effect until they are committed. This feature enables you to quit Disk Administrator and discard any changes you made since changes were committed last. It's a lot like having to save a file after you have edited it in the word processor. You can get the old version back simply by not saving your changes.

Before you can work with a partition, changes must be committed. You cannot format a New Unformatted partition, because the partition is not really created until changes are committed.

When you quit Disk Administrator, you might see the following message: `Changes have been made to your disk configuration. Do you want to save the changes?` Choose Yes to save the changes or No to cancel.

You also can commit changes without leaving Disk Administrator by choosing the Commit Changes Now command from the Partition menu.

Note

MS-DOS can access only one primary partition on a hard drive. Ordinarily, this is not a concern, because you seldom will be booting a Windows NT Server under DOS.

If you begin to create more than one primary partition on a hard drive, the warning shown in figure 16.4 appears.

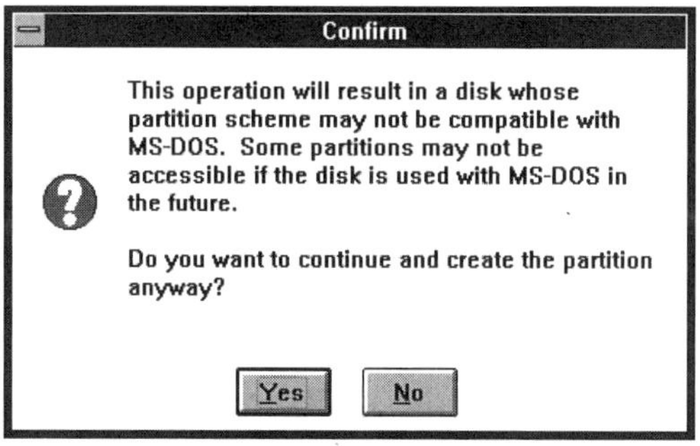

Figure 16.4

The warning you see when creating additional primary partitions on a hard drive.

Designating the Active Partition

Windows NT designates two special partitions, which may or not be the same physical partition:

- The system partition contains hardware-specific files that are used to load Windows NT. On Intel x86 computers, the system partition must be a primary partition that has been marked as active. On RISC computers, the system partition is configured by setup software provided by the manufacturer.

On RISC computers, the system partition must be formatted with the FAT file system. On Intel x86 computers, the system partition may be formatted for FAT or NTFS files.

- The boot partition contains the Windows NT operating system. It may be formatted for the FAT, NTFS, or HPFS file system. The boot partition is generally the same as the system partition.

The hard drive that will boot the system must have one partition designated as the active partition. On an Intel x86 system, an active partition is created when Windows NT is installed. However, you might need to change the active partition if you have created other primary partitions to support other operating systems. You would change the active partition to a Unix partition, for example, if you will be rebooting the computer and want it to start up with the Unix operating system.

Operating systems can boot only from an active primary partition on Disk 0. You cannot designate a partition on another drive as the active partition. The active partition on drive 0 is marked by an asterisk (*) in the colored bar above the partition box.

To mark the active partition on an Intel x86 computer, follow these steps:

1. Select the primary partition on Disk 0 that contains the start-up files for the desired operating system. The selected partition is outlined with a bold black border.
2. Choose the Mark Active command from the Partition menu.
3. Click on OK in the Disk Administrator information box.

Creating Extended Partitions and Logical Drives

You can create a single extended partition on a hard drive, which can range in size from 1 MB to the size of the free space available on the drive. If you create an extended partition, the maximum number of primary partitions on the drive is reduced to three.

To create an extended partition, follow these steps:

1. Select an area marked `Free Space`. The area you select is marked with a wider, black border.

2. Choose Create Extended from the Partition menu. The Create Extended Partition dialog box shown in figure 16.5 appears. This box indicates the maximum and minimum sizes allowed for the partition.

3. Enter the desired size in the Create partition of size box.

4. Click on OK. Figure 16.6 shows the new extended partition that appears. No drives have been created. The area simply is designated as `Free Space`, with cross hatching in a different direction. In figure 16.6, the Free Space with 200 MB is the newly created extended partition.

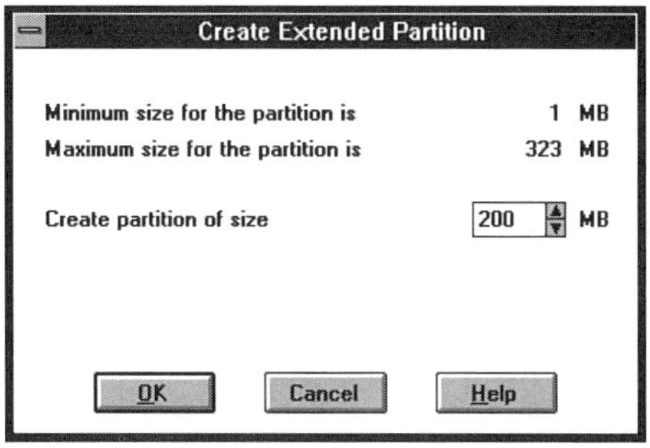

Figure 16.5

Designating the size of an extended partition.

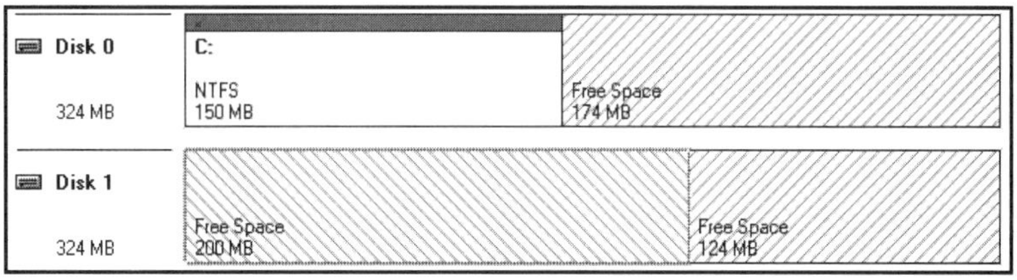

Figure 16.6

A new extended partition.

To create a logical drive in an extended partition, follow these steps:

1. Select an area marked `Free Space` that is cross hatched to indicate that it is an extended partition. The area you select is marked with a wider, black border.

2. Choose Create from the Partition menu. The Create Logical Drive dialog box appears. This box indicates the maximum and minimum sizes allowed for the partition.

3. Enter the desired size in the Create logical drive of size box.

4. Click on OK. Figure 16.7 shows the new, unformatted logical drive that appears.

5. To create the partition, choose Commit Changes Now from the Partition menu. After committing changes, the logical drive is labeled as `Unformatted`.

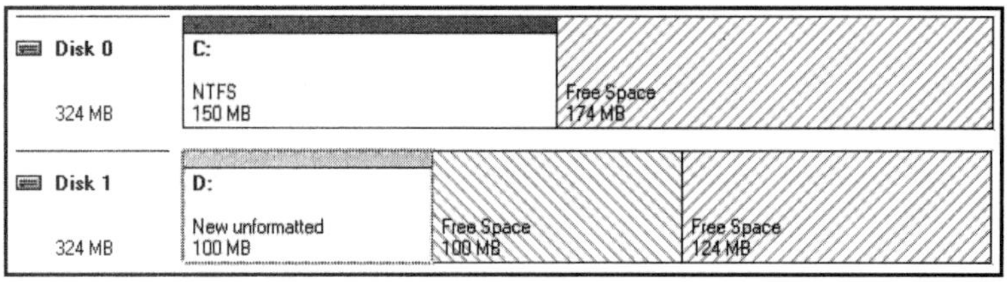

Figure 16.7

A new, unformatted logical drive.

Committing Changes

Partitions and drives are not actually created by the procedures described up to this point. Changes must be committed before they are written to disk. Until you commit changes, you can cancel any changes you have made since the last time changes were committed.

To have the changes you make written to the disks, choose the Commit Changes Now option in the Partitions menu. To cancel changes made since the last commit, quit Disk Administrator and respond No to the prompt `Changes have been made to your disk configuration. Do you want to save the changes?`.

Formatting Partitions and Logical Drives

To format a partition, follow these steps:

1. If the partition is marked `New Unformatted`, it has not been physically created. Choose Commit Changes Now from the Partition menu. After changes are committed, the drive is designated as `Unformatted`.

2. Select the partition. You can click on the partition's box in the Disk Administrator window or press the Tab key until the desired partition is selected. The selected partition is outlined with a bold line.

3. Choose Format from the Tools menu. The Formatting dialog box appears, as shown in figure 16.8.

4. Select the file system type (NTFS or FAT are available) in the File System box.

5. In the Label box, enter a volume label if desired.

6. Click in the Quick Format check box if you want the partition formatted without checking for errors. (Quick Format is not available with mirror sets or stripe sets with parity.)

7. When asked to confirm that you want data in the partition overwritten, choose Yes. As the partition is formatted, progress is displayed on a bar graph.

Normal formatting might be slower than you would like because Disk Administrator is ordinarily very thorough about identifying and locking out bad spots on the disk.

8. When the `Format Complete` message is displayed, click on OK. Figure 16.9 shows a logical drive after it has been formatted.

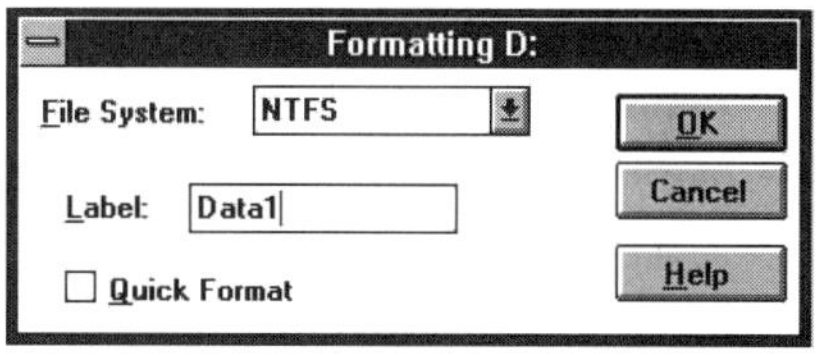

Figure 16.8
Specifying format parameters.

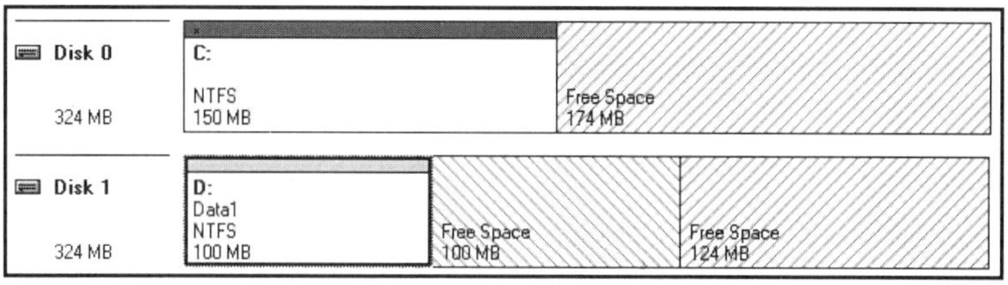

Figure 16.9
A formatted logical drive.

Reformatting a Volume

When you reformat a volume that contains data, all data stored on that volume is lost. Be sure that you back up any files you want to save.

You cannot make any changes to the Windows NT system partition using Windows NT. To modify this partition, back up all data you want to retain. Then reinstall Windows NT, using a Custom installation. You can request that Setup delete, re-create, or reformat the partition.

Changing and Deleting a Volume Label

A label can be assigned to any volume. This label may describe the function or the contents of the volume and is reproduced in a variety of situations when the volume contents are displayed. To change or delete a volume label, follow these steps:

1. Select the formatted volume.

2. Choose Label from the Tools menu. The Label dialog box appears.

3. Enter the new volume name or delete the name that is shown.

4. Click on OK.

Converting a Volume to NTFS

You can convert a FAT or HPFS volume to NTFS with the CONVERT.EXE utility. To convert a volume, follow these steps:

1. Open a command prompt by double-clicking the Command Prompt icon in the Main program group.

2. To convert drive D to NTFS, enter the following command:

   ```
   CONVERT D: /FS:NTFS
   ```

Note The boot partition cannot be converted while Windows NT is running. If you specify that CONVERT should process the active partition, you will see this message:

```
Convert cannot gain exclusive access to the C: drive, so it cannot
convert it now. Would you schedule it to be converted the next time
the system restarts?
```

If you respond **Y**es, you then can shut down Windows NT and restart it. The partition is converted when the system starts back up. The system must boot several times in order to complete the conversion. Be patient. Everything will work fine in the end.

Assigning Drive Letters

Unlike DOS, Windows NT enables you to assign specific drive letters to volumes. This is called *static assignment* of drive letters.

Prior to assigning static drive letters with Disk Administrator, drive letters are assigned automatically using DOS rules. Adding drives or changing partitions can change drive letters for other volumes.

To assign a drive letter to a volume, follow these steps:

1. Select a drive.

2. Choose Drive Letter from the Tools menu. The Assign Drive Letter dialog box appears, as shown in figure 16.10.

3. To assign a drive letter, choose Assign drive letter and select an available letter in the box.

4. To create a drive without a drive letter, choose Do not assign a drive letter.

5. Click on OK.

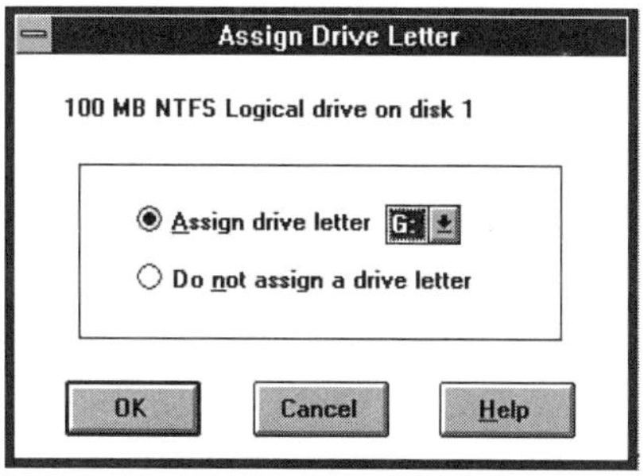

Figure 16.10

Assigning a drive letter.

Note The CD-ROM Drive Letters option on the Tools menu enables you to specify the drive letters for your CD-ROM drives.

Deleting Partitions and Drives

From time to time, you will need to reorganize your disks and will need to delete partitions and drives. To delete a partition or drive, follow these steps:

1. Select the partition or drive.
2. Choose Delete from the Partition menu.
3. In the confirmation box that is displayed, confirm that the partition should be deleted by choosing Yes.
4. Commit the change by choosing Commit Changes Now from the Partition menu or by quitting Disk Manager and choosing Yes.

Note To delete an extended partition, you first must delete each logical drive in the partition.

Volume Sets

A *volume set* is a volume that is made up of several free space segments from as many as 32 disk drives. Later, you will be introduced to striped sets, which might seem similar to volume sets. Volume sets and striped sets are significantly different, however.

Figure 16.11 shows two disk drives. Three areas on the two drives are designated as Free Space. These Free Space areas can be combined into a volume set. Figure 16.12 shows volume D—a volume set that occupies three of those areas.

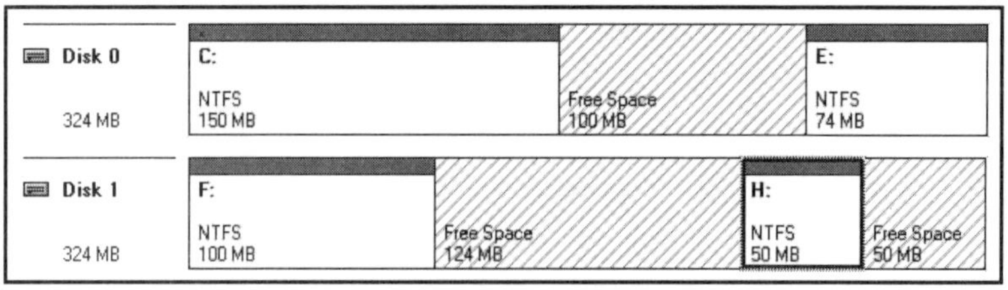

Figure 16.11
Drives prior to creation of a volume set.

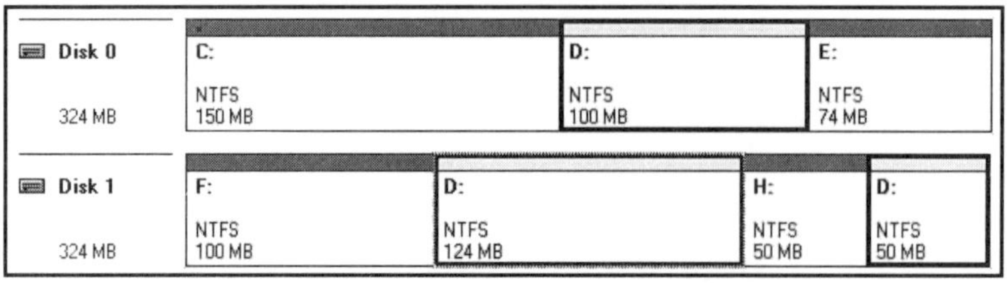

Figure 16.12
Drives after creation of a volume set.

Even though they are constructed from bits and pieces, volume sets function much like standard hard drives. Figure 16.13 illustrates the hard drives in a volume set. As files are stored in the volume set, they are stored first at the beginning of the first segment in the volume set. After the first segment is filled, the second segment is used, then the third, and finally the fourth.

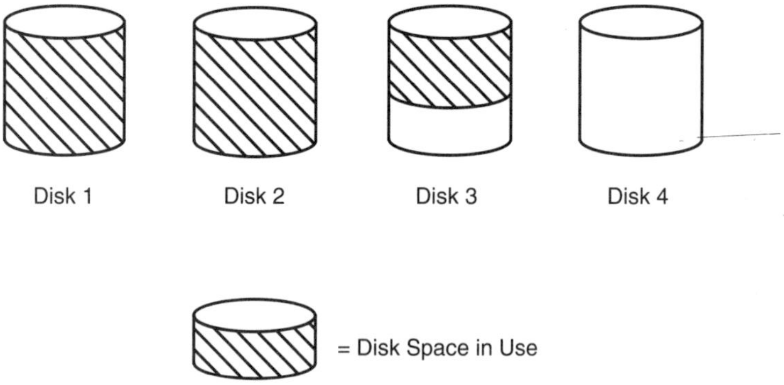

Figure 16.13
How volume sets store files.

Creating a Volume Set

To create a volume set, follow these steps:

1. Select the first area of free space.
2. Select additional areas while holding down the Ctrl key.
3. Choose Create Volume Set from the Partition menu.

4. The Create Volume Set dialog box appears, as shown in figure 16.14. You use this box to specify the size the volume set will be. The maximum size is the total of the sizes of all Free Space partitions that were selected.

5. Click on OK to create the volume set.

6. Choose Commit Changes Now from the Partition menu to create the volume set.

7. Restart the system so that the changes will take effect.

If, in step 4, you select a size that is smaller than the maximum allowed, as was done in figure 16.14, space is deallocated from each of the free space areas. This can create many small, free space gaps in the hard drives, as shown in figure 16.15.

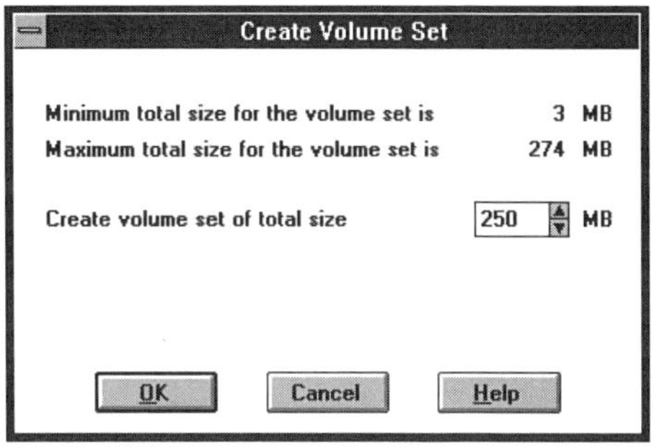

Figure 16.14

Designating the size of a volume set.

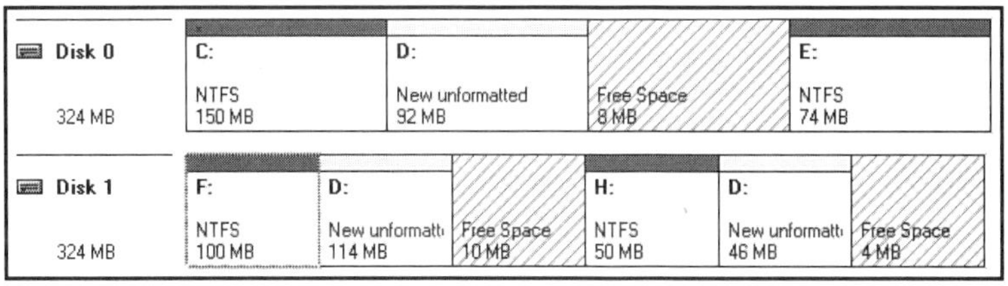

Figure 16.15

Unused free space after a volume set was created with less than the maximum size.

Formatting a Volume Set

To format the volume set, select any segment of the volume set. Notice that all the segments are selected. Then format it as you would a standard partition or hard drive. After the volume set is formatted, all the segments are identified with the same drive letter, as was shown in figure 16.12, where the volume set is drive D.

Extending a Volume Set

Individual volumes and volume sets can be extended by adding free space. Extending an individual volume turns it into a volume set.

Note Stripe sets and mirror sets cannot be extended.

To extend a volume or a volume set, follow these steps:

1. Select the volume or volume set.
2. While holding down the Ctrl key, select a free space area to be added to the volume set.
3. Choose Extend Volume Set from the Partition menu. The Extend Volume Set dialog box appears, as shown in figure 16.16. The "Minimum total size for the volume set is" setting is the size of the existing volume or volume set.
4. Specify the new size for the volume set.
5. Click on OK.

There is no need to commit the changes or to format the new segment of the volume set.

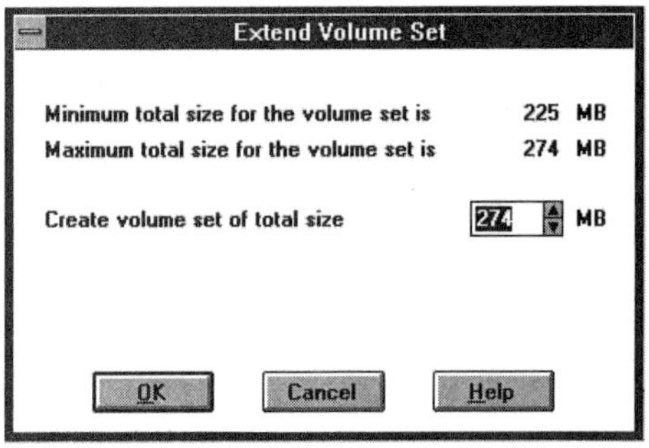

Figure 16.16
Extending a volume set.

Note After free space is used to extend a volume set, the free space cannot be removed. To reduce the space of a volume set, back up the data, delete the volume set, create a new volume set of the desired size, and restore the data.

Considering the Pros and Cons of Volume Sets

Volume sets have two significant advantages:

- They enable you to use small, free space segments in volumes of useful size. The segments used can be of virtually any size.

- They enable you to create volumes that are larger than your largest hard drive. Because a volume set can incorporate free space from up to 32 hard drives, truly huge volumes are possible.

Nothing is free, however, and a cost is associated with volume segments. The cost is an increased risk that a drive failure will result in loss of data on the volume. If any hard drive in the volume set fails, all data in the volume set is lost.

Note The reliability of hardware is rated in a statistic called mean time between failure (MTBF)—the average number of hours the equipment is expected to operate without failure. When volume sets are created with two or more hard drives, the MTBF for the volume set is significantly less than the MTBF for the individual drives. The formula Microsoft provides follows:

$MTBF_{set}–MTBF_{disk}/N$

Where

$MTBF_{set}$ is the MTBF for the volume set

$MTBF_{disk}$ is the average MTBF for an individual disk

N is the number of disks in the set

As you can see, a four-drive set has one-quarter the MTBF of an individual drive.

Using Stripe Sets

Like volume sets, *stripe sets* enable you to build hard volumes with multiple hard drives. However, stripe sets store data in a significantly different way using a technique called *striping*. Figure 16.17 shows how striping works.

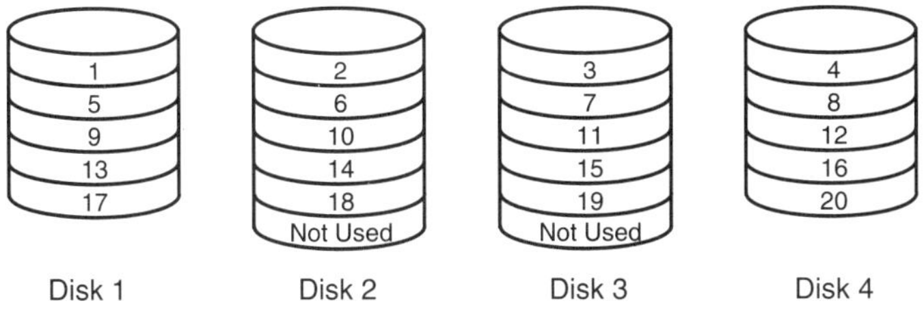

Figure 16.17
Storing data on a stripe set.

When files are written to stripe sets, the written data is broken into stripes, which are written sequentially to all drives in the stripe set. As a result, a file is actually spread out across all the drives in the stripe set.

"Why," you might ask, "would anyone want to split files up in that way? I can build large volumes with volume sets, so what does striping buy me?" The answer is *performance*. Hard drives spend a great deal of time just moving their heads around to seek out the right track. When these head seeks are spread across multiple drives, the time required to retrieve a file is reduced nearly by a factor of the number of drives. The performance improvement is particularly apparent with applications that frequently read data from the disk.

Because data is striped across disks, the disk segments on the various disks must be of roughly the same size. Figure 16.17 shows what happens when some segments are larger than others: portions of some segments are not used. Because space would be wasted otherwise, Disk Administrator always ensures that the segments that are added to a stripe set are the same size.

Disk striping has the same disadvantage as volume sets: the reliability of a stripe set is less than the reliability of an individual drive. Also, if a single drive fails, all data on the stripe set is lost.

Using Stripe Sets with Parity

A technique called *parity* can make a stripe set considerably more reliable. Figure 16.18 shows how data is recorded on a stripe set with parity. With each set of stripes, a parity record is created on one of the drives in the set. This parity record is created by performing a set of calculations on all the stripes in that "row." If a drive fails, the information on that drive can be reverse engineered by combining all the stripes in that row with the parity record. Therefore, a stripe set with parity can continue to function with one drive failure.

Figure 16.18

How data is stored on a stripe set with parity.

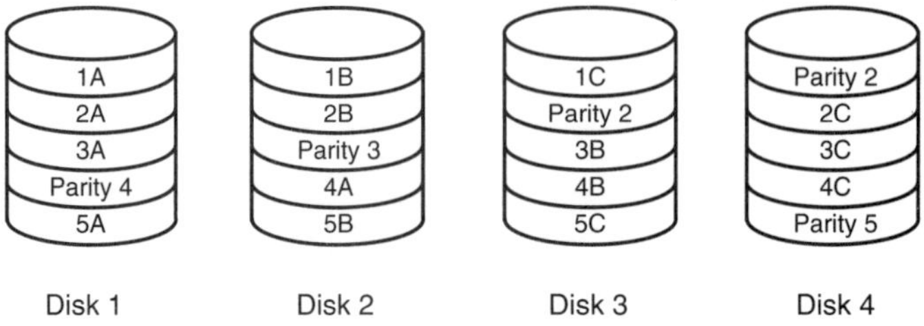

Disk striping with parity produces a fault-tolerant disk array with less drive overhead than mirroring. A pair of mirrored drives loses 50 percent of total drive capacity to achieve fault tolerance. A disk stripe with parity set consisting of four drives loses just

25 percent of total capacity to create the parity records. A set with five drives loses just 20 percent of total capacity to produce a fault-tolerant configuration. Stripe sets can be constructed from free space on as many as 32 disks.

Disk striping with parity generally has better read performance than mirroring when all drives in the set are functioning. When one drive has failed, performance suffers due to the need to recover stripe contents using the parity information. Microsoft recommends disk striping with parity for all read-intensive systems.

Tip The need to create the parity records reduces write performance and requires additional memory. Microsoft recommends 25 percent additional memory to support disk striping with parity. Windows NT Server can perform most tasks with 12 MB of memory, but 16 MB is recommended when using disk striping with parity.

Note Redundant arrays of inexpensive disks (RAID) describes several methods of using multiple disks to improve performance, enhance reliability, or both. Several types of RAID configurations, called *levels*, have been developed, of which only three are of interest to microcomputer LAN users:

- **RAID 0.** Microsoft calls RAID0 stripe sets.
- **RAID 1.** Mirror sets.
- **RAID 5.** Stripe sets with parity.

It is important to realize that RAID is not a hierarchy. RAID 5 is not inherently better than RAID 1. Both meet different needs, and have different advantages and disadvantages. You need to choose the RAID technology that is right for your network.

Windows NT makes it possible to implement RAID systems using only standard microcomputer hardware. When you don't use special RAID hardware, you give up several advantages:

- More robust hardware, possibly with fault-tolerant power supplies.
- The capability to replace failed hard drives without shutting down the server (*hot swapping*).

Microsoft also admits that a hardware-based RAID system should yield greater performance than the Windows NT Server software-based approach.

If RAID 5 meets your needs, you therefore might want to consider a commercial RAID subsystem to obtain some extra fault tolerance and reduce the likelihood of down time.

Creating a Stripe Set (RAID 0)

To create a stripe set, follow these steps:

1. Select an area of free space.
2. Hold down the Ctrl key and select additional areas—up to one each on a total of up to 32 hard drives.
3. Choose Create Stripe Set from the Partition menu.
4. In the Create Stripe Set dialog box, the size Disk Administrator displays takes all of the selected free space areas into account (see fig. 16.19). If you reduce the size, space is removed from each of the drives on which you have selected free space. This size is selected based on the creation of equal-sized segments on all disks.
5. Choose OK. Disk administrator creates a disk stripe with parity logical volume and assigns a single drive letter to the set.
6. Choose Commit Changes Now from the Partition menu.
7. Select the partition.
8. Choose the Format command from the Tools menu to format the partition.

As you can see in figure 16.20, Disk Administrator creates equal-sized unformatted partitions on each of the drives in the stripe set. If you choose a stripe set capacity that cannot be distributed evenly on the disks, Disk Administrator rounds up to the next acceptable value.

Figure 16.19

Specifying the size of a stripe set.

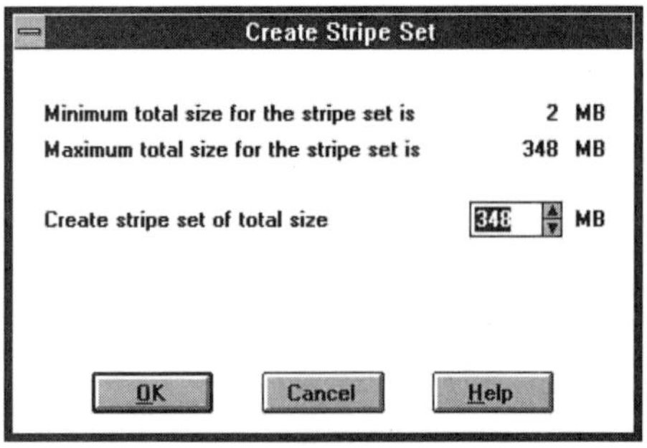

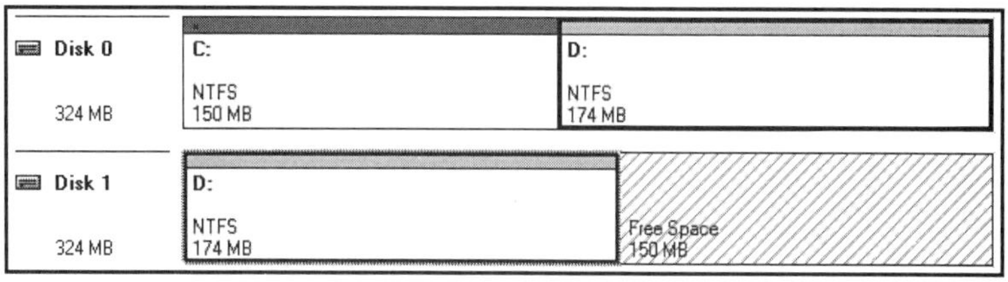

Figure 16.20

A stripe set on two disks.

Creating a Stripe Set with Parity

At least three hard drives are required to create a stripe set with parity: two to store data and one for the parity stripe. To create a stripe set with parity, follow these steps:

1. Select an area of free space on one hard drive.
2. Hold down the Ctrl key and select two or more additional areas—one each on a total of up to 32 hard drives.
3. Choose Create Stripe Set with Parity from the Fault Tolerance menu.
4. In the Create Stripe Set with Parity dialog box that appears, the size that Disk Administrator displays takes all of the selected free space areas into account. If you reduce the size, space is removed from each of the drives on which you have selected free space.
5. Click on OK.
6. Format the partition.

Disk Administrator creates equal-sized, unformatted partitions on each of the drives in the stripe set. If you choose a stripe set capacity that cannot be distributed evenly on the disks, Disk Administrator rounds up to the next acceptable value.

Deleting a Stripe Set

In the event of a drive failure, a stripe set is invalidated and must be deleted.

A stripe set with parity can be recovered from a single drive failure and should not be deleted unless you are through using it.

To delete a stripe set, select any of the segments of the stripe set and choose the Delete command from the Partition menu.

Using Mirror Sets

Mirror sets consist of two drives that are maintained as mirror images. All data on the two drives is identical. Two different hardware configurations are possible:

- Both drives are connected to the same disk controller. In this case, failure of the disk controller halts both drives and the mirrored set is unavailable.
- Each drive is connected to a separate disk controller. If one disk controller fails, the disk drive on the other controller continues to function and the mirror set remains functional. This configuration frequently is called *disk duplexing*.

Mirror sets and disk stripe with parity sets are equally fault tolerant. Mirror sets tend to perform better when writing data, because the parity stripe does not have to be created. Disk stripe with parity sets tend to perform better when reading data, because drive seeks are spread out over a greater number of drives.

Note Mirror sets are the only form of fault tolerance that can be used with the system partition of a server. Stripe sets cannot be booted.

Creating a Mirror Set

Creating a mirror set consists of creating a new partition that duplicates an existing partition on another drive. The same drive letter will be assigned to both disks.

To create a mirror set, follow these steps:

1. Create and format a standard volume.
2. Select the volume.
3. While holding down the Ctrl key, select an area of free space on another disk that is at least as large as the volume created in step 1.
4. Choose Establish Mirror from the Fault Tolerance menu.
5. Choose Commit Changes Now from the Partition menu to create the mirror set.

The new mirrored partition is displayed with the status of `Unformatted`. That status remains until the two partitions are synchronized. Figure 16.21 shows hard drives with a mirror set for drive C.

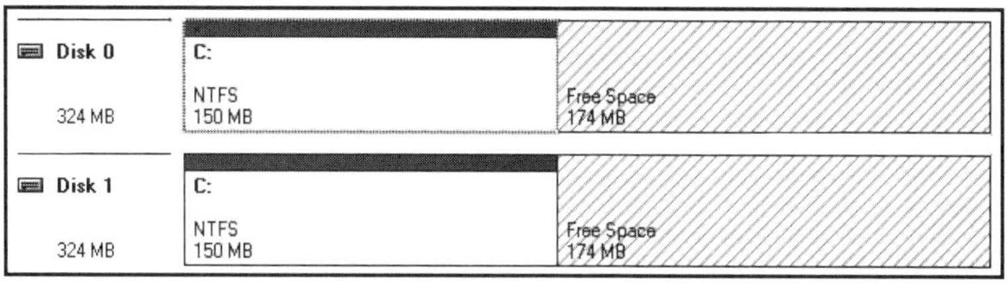

Figure 16.21
A mirrored set for drive C.

Note If the partitions in a mirrored set ever get out of synchronization, Windows NT automatically resynchronizes them. If you look at Disk Administrator while resynchronization is occurring, the drive that is catching up is displayed with its description in red text.

Breaking a Mirror Set

To break a mirror set, follow these steps:

1. Select the mirror set.
2. Choose Break Mirror from the **F**ault Tolerance menu.
3. Disk Administrator presents the message:

   ```
   This will end mirroring and create two independent partitions. Are you
   sure you want to break the selected mirror?
   ```

   Choose **Y**es to confirm.
4. Choose **Y**es after you see the message:

   ```
   Do you wish to continue with this operation?
   ```
5. Choose C**o**mmit Changes Now from the **P**artition menu to break the mirror set.
6. Click on OK after you see the message:

   ```
   Changes have been made which require you to restart your computer.
   ```

After the computer restarts, Disk Administrator displays two independent partitions where the mirror set was formerly. You can delete the unmirrored portion if desired.

Note After you break a mirror set for the system partition, you must reboot the system.

Fixing Mirror Sets and Stripe Sets with Parity

When a drive fails in a mirror set or a stripe set with parity, the failed drive is known as an *orphan.* The action you must take to repair the set depends on the set type.

Repairing a Mirror Set

When a drive of a mirror set fails, you must break the mirror set. This exposes the working drive of the mirror set so that it can resume working as a standard volume. The working member of the mirror set retains the drive letter that was assigned to the set. You then can establish a new mirror set relationship with a replacement hard drive or with another hard drive on the system.

Creating an Emergency Boot Disk

If the system partition is protected by a mirror set and the primary drive fails, you can use an emergency boot disk to start the server by using the mirror copy. First, you need to create a boot disk with the proper files. Then, you need to edit the BOOT.INI file so that it boots from another disk.

To create the boot disk, copy the following files from the root of the system partition to a floppy disk that you have formatted with Windows NT File Manager:

- NTLDR
- NTDETECT.COM
- NTBOOTDD.SYS (if present on your system)
- BOOT.INI

Editing BOOT.INI

Use File Manager to edit the properties of the BOOT.INI file on the floppy disk. Remove the System and Read Only properties from the file so that it can be edited.

Your BOOT.INI file will resemble this one:

```
[boot loader]
timeout=30
```

```
default=multi(0)disk(0)rdisk(0)partition(1)\WINNT35
[operating systems]
multi(0)disk(0)rdisk(0)partition(1)\WINNT35="Windows NT Server Version 3.5"
multi(0)disk(0)rdisk(0)partition(1)\WINNT35="Windows NT Server Version 3.5 [VGA
mode]" /basevideo
```

The BOOT.INI file contains information that helps NTLDR find the system partition. The information is found in entries like this:

```
multi(0)disk(0)rdisk(0)partition(1)
```

This is called an *ARC Name*—a format that is borrowed from Advanced RISC Computers. Each field in the ARC name defines a characteristic of the system partition:

- **multi(n).** This field is multi(*n*) for non-SCSI systems and scsi(*n*) for most SCSI systems. If the server has only one hard drive controller, then *n* will be 0. Additional hard drive controllers will be numbered 1 through 3. Edit this field if the mirror partition is attached to a different disk controller.

- **disk(*o*).** For scsi, *o* is the SCSI bus number for multiple-bus SCSI adapters. Edit *o* to reflect the SCSI address of the drive with the mirror partition. For multi, *o* is always 0.

- **rdisk(*p*).** For scsi, *p* is always 0. For multi, *p* is the ordinal number of the disk on the adapter. Because IDE and ESDI adapters support only two drives, *p* will be 0 or 1.

- **partition(*q*).** Edit *q* to indicate the primary partition number on the drive that contains the mirror of the system partition. Partitions are numbered 0 through 3. Extended partitions and unused partitions are not numbered.

When I was testing, the address for the mirror on disk 1 was as follows:

```
multi(0)disk(0)rdisk(1)partition(1)
```

After you edit the BOOT.INI file on the emergency boot floppy disk, use it to boot the system. It should fail, fill the screen with numbers, and include the following message:

```
***STOP 0x000006B (0xC00000D,0X0000002,0X00000000,0X00000000)
PROCESS1_INITIALIZATION_FAILED
```

If this message fails to appear, your floppy disk is not properly configured to boot your system.

Note I know that an error message is a roundabout way to tell you things are working as they should, but trust me, this error shows that everything is working fine. I tried it by replacing my disk 0 with an unformatted drive. The mirror of the system partition on disk 1 started up without a hitch.

Recovering a Failed System Partition Mirror Set

If the primary drive of the mirror set fails, follow these steps to recover the system:

1. Boot the system with the emergency boot floppy disk.
2. Use Disk Administrator to break the mirror. Because you are breaking the mirror of the system partition, you must reboot the server.
3. Reestablish the mirror between disk 0 and the mirror partition, and exit Disk Administrator.
4. Boot again using the emergency boot floppy disk. The disk 0 mirror partition is rebuilt from the working mirror partition.
5. Use Disk Administrator again to break the mirror.
6. Change the drive letters of the partitions that were part of the mirror set so that the partition on disk 0 is drive C and the other partition from the mirror set is some other drive letter.
7. Exit Disk Administrator.
8. Remove the emergency boot floppy disk and reboot the system.

Note The BOOT.INI file on the emergency boot floppy disk must be updated each time changes in partitions affect the ARC path of the partition that is mirroring the system partition.

Microsoft notes that this procedure works best when the drives in the mirror set have the same disk geometry: the same heads, cylinders, and sectors per track.

Note If you add a new hard drive to the system, you might see a message similar to the one shown in figure 16.22. Choose **Y**es to have the drive signature written.

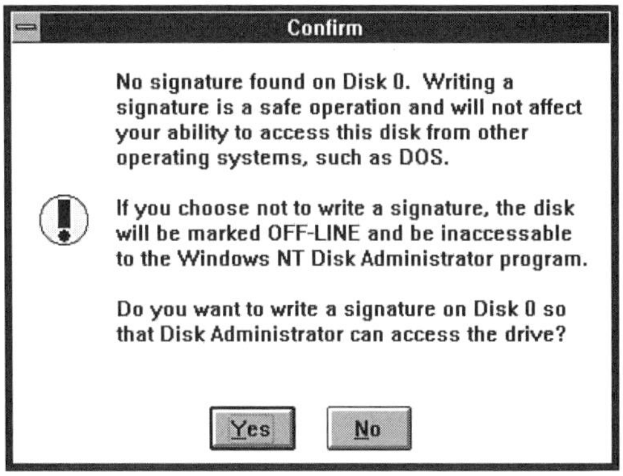

Figure 16.22

Warning that a new disk requires a signature.

Repairing a Stripe Set with Parity

If a member of a parity stripe set fails, you see the message `A disk that is part of a fault-tolerant volume can no longer be accessed.`

After you identify the failed hardware item and replace it, run Disk Administrator and do the following:

1. Select the stripe set with parity that experienced the drive failure.
2. Hold down the Ctrl key and select an area of free space at least as large as the partitions that are members of the stripe set.
3. Choose Regenerate from the Fault Tolerance menu.
4. Restart the server. The stripe set with parity regenerates the image for the new partition.
5. Use Disk Administrator to assign a drive letter to the parity stripe set.

Updating the Emergency Repair Disk

When you change the partitioning on Windows NT, you see a message advising you to update the Emergency Repair disk that you created when the system was installed.

The emergency repair disk is updated with the RDISK.EXE utility. You can access RDISK by using the Run command from the File menu of the Program Manager. The command window for RDISK is shown in figure 16.23. Just select an option and follow the prompts to create or update an emergency repair disk.

If you will be frequently changing the partitions on your system, you probably will want to add an RDISK program item to your desktop using the **N**ew command from the Program Manager **F**ile menu.

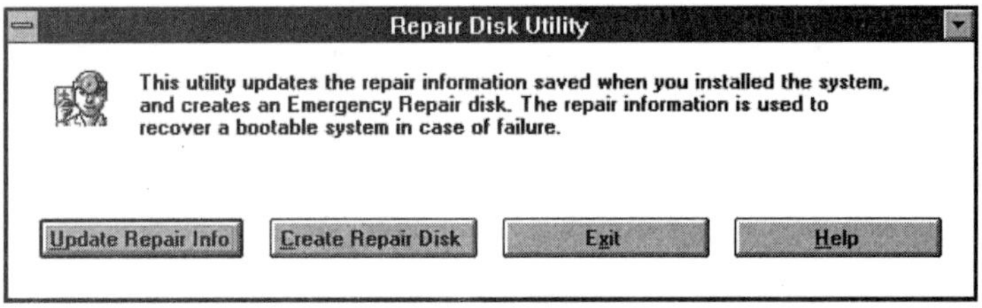

Figure 16.23
The command window for RDISK.

CHAPTER 17

Backing Up Files

Backing up the files on your LAN is among your most important responsibilities as a LAN administrator. File backups are your front-line defense against everything from users losing files to total disasters. Unfortunately, having good, reliable backups is something most organizations fail to think about until disaster already has struck.

Today's computer hardware is pretty reliable. Few users experience hard drive failures, and many PCs run for years without problems. Also, few users take the time to back up their personal hard drives, and this thinking often spills over into LAN administration. Here are some reasons to take the situation seriously:

- Most LANs store many more times the files than individual users store on their PCs.
- Most LANs have more mission-critical data than is found on personal PCs. Ask your users what the impact would be of totally losing the data that is stored on the LAN.
- Multiple hard drives are common on LAN servers, and the chances of a piece of equipment failing are multiplied.

Planning for Disasters

Think the worst. An earthquake has just struck and the building that houses your LAN is now rubble. How soon could you restore basic LAN services and have critical data available for your company?

Just order up backup tapes from the off-site storage, go buy a new server, and restore the data. Sounds simple, right? But have you actually tried it? Where are the master software disks for your server? You need to restore Windows NT Server before you can restore any data, and you can't restore Windows NT Server if your installation disks are under a ton of rubble.

I had a situation that was nearly as bad as an earthquake. A pipe in the ceiling of my LAN room burst. When I arrived at work, water was pouring down right on my server, soaking my manuals, and threatening to flood the drawer that held my on-site backup tapes. Luckily, the pipe had broken only a few minutes before I arrived. A few more minutes and I probably would have found a dysfunctional server and ruined tapes.

If you think about the situation of a real disaster in terms of doing business for a few days without your LAN and re-creating all your data from scratch, it will become clear why managers of corporate mainframe computers take disaster recovery very seriously. The biggest corporations actually maintain duplicate mainframes at a *hot site* that can take over in short order if the main data processing site is down. Smaller companies often have agreements with other companies to serve as hot sites for each other in the event of a disaster.

It therefore is not unreasonable for your company to maintain a basic backup LAN at another site—a LAN hot site. The hot site should be supplied with everything needed to quickly take over your essential computing needs and should, as much as possible, use the same hardware and software as the main site.

Identical hardware and software are especially important with tape backups, which seem to be a bit finicky about being restored on the same type of system on which they were created. There are relatively few standards that ensure portability of data tapes between different hardware systems. The only way to be sure that you can restore the tapes you create is to eliminate software and hardware differences between the source and target systems.

So, don't store only your backup tapes off site. Be sure that your off-site archives include copies of the same release of Windows NT Server as your server is running, along with any patches you might have obtained and copies of any drivers you are using that didn't come on the Windows NT Server distribution disks.

The only way you can be sure that your backup and recovery plan works is to test it—not just once, but periodically. Before you know things work, you're going to have to blow away your server files and try to restore the server. There is no other way. Ideally, such a test should be performed before your server goes into service.

Storing Data Long Term

There is a tendency to forget about data after it is backed up and in the vault. But magnetic tapes are living things, and they are deteriorating from the moment they are recorded. The data on a magnetic tape can be trusted only for three to five years.

How far back do you need to be able to recover any given file on your LAN? You would be surprised how many managers would answer that question, "Forever!" The need for reliable, long-term data archives increases as more and more company documentation is stored in electronic form. Many companies are rapidly eliminating paper forms.

As a result, a need exists for reliable ways of storing large amounts of data affordably but reliably. Magnetic tape can meet these needs, provided that you periodically retrieve tapes from storage and copy them. Three years should be the most you should rely on a tape without refreshing it with a new copy.

You might want to consider various types of write-once optical media. *Write-once optical media* record data by using a laser to burn pits in the plastic surface of the disk. Data recorded in this way should be reliable for about 20 years. Optical media are fairly delicate, however, and you should make at least two copies of any vital files.

Backup Hardware

As the need for volume and speed have increased, backup technologies have evolved. Interfaces have become faster, and new tape formats have evolved as engineers have tried different approaches to solving the data-storage problem. This section will help you select hardware to meet your needs.

Data Backup Formats

You will encounter four major standards for tape media. They differ significantly in terms of cost, capacity, and performance, and you should choose carefully because it is very difficult to convert a tape archive to another format. Consequently, it makes sense to overbuy, obtaining tape equipment that will meet your needs for a number of years.

I strongly feel that it should be your goal to back up your entire LAN every night. Doing so requires you to obtain equipment that has not only the capacity to hold your data, but the speed to back up that data in the time you can allot. As more and more LANs are called on to function 24 hours a day, 7 days a week, the time available for backing up files increasingly is scarce.

The following sections discuss the most common tape formats used on LANs.

The DC-6000 Tape Format

DC-6000 is the latest in a long evolution of tape formats based on technology originated by 3M in 1971. *Quarter-inch cartridge* technology was developed specifically for recording data. With the DC-6000 format, 600 feet of quarter-inch wide magnetic tapes are housed in a fairly large shell—4×6×0.665 inches—that is reinforced by a thick metal bottom plate. The cartridges were designed to be extremely gentle to tape. An elastic drive belt moves the tape, designed to avoid stretching the tape medium. The cartridge is designed so that nothing touches the delicate magnetic surface of the tape.

Data is stored on quarter-inch cartridges using a system called *serpentine recording*, which is illustrated in figure 17.1. The tape is divided into parallel tracks, and the tape head moves up and down to select a particular track. The tape is streamed in one direction and then reverses direction to record the next track.

Figure 17.1

Serpentine recording.

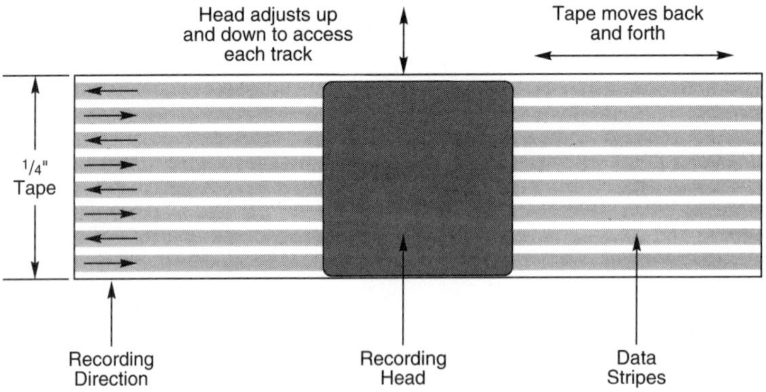

The capacity of quarter-inch cartridges can be increased by extending three parameters: the length of the tape, the bits recorded per inch of tape, and the number of tracks. The practical limit for tape that can fit in the cartridge and yet be stable enough to be reliable is about 600 feet. Therefore, the remaining tools for increasing capacity are to increase data density and to add tracks. The largest technologies, with capacities of up to about 2.1 GB, use 30 tracks and a density of 68 kilobits per inch.

Standards have been proposed that could record up to 35 GB per data cartridge if engineers can solve the problem of recording 216 tracks on a quarter-inch tape.

Standards for quarter-inch cartridges are established by a consortium of equipment manufacturers generally called the QIC Committee. Standards developed for DC-6000 cartridges are named after the capacities they support. For example, QIC-525 supports capacities of 525 MB per cartridge.

In my experience, the quarter-inch cartridge is reliable but slow. Data throughput is slower than other formats—about 5 MB per minute seems typical. Another problem is that locating files involves a sequential search to the entire serpentine track path, resulting in long file searches. Another disadvantage is that the cartridges are mechanically complex and tend to be somewhat more expensive than cartridges for other formats.

The DC-2000 Tape Format

The minicartridge was designed to lower the cost of tape backup using quarter-inch cartridges. This format has become popular for backing up personal computers. Also invented by 3M, DC-2000 uses a smaller shell (2.4×3.2×0.57 inches) to house 205 feet of quarter-inch magnetic tape. Until fairly recently, capacities have been fairly limited for this format, but manufacturers have recently introduced systems that can store 850 MB of data in compressed form.

To reduce hardware costs, the tape format was designed to enable the drives to be managed by a floppy-disk controller. However, high-density floppy disk controllers are capable of supporting data-transfer rates of only about 500 kilobits per second.

Two significant problems limit the usefulness of DC-2000 media on LANs:

- Media must be formatted. This is a time-consuming process that can take about one hour for 40 MB. Formatting has the advantage of identifying and locking out bad spots on the tape. Preformatted tapes are available.

- Data-transfer rates are far too low to back up large hard drives in short time intervals. Performance can be improved by using a dedicated tape controller interface instead of a floppy-disk controller, although manufacturers claims of data throughput rates are notoriously optimistic.

A significant advantage of DC-2000 is that tapes are fairly portable between drives from different manufacturers. The most important formats follow:

- **QIC-40.** Uses 20 tracks and supports up to 40 MB of uncompressed data on a single DC-2000 data cartridge.

- **QIC-80.** Uses 32 tracks to record up to 80 MB of uncompressed data on a DC-2120 data cartridge. Recently introduced extended-length cartridges can record up to 120 MB of uncompressed data. Data-compression techniques frequently are employed to double this capacity to about 250 MB.

- **QIC-3010.** A new format that records 340 MB of uncompressed data (700 MB compressed).
- **QIC-Wide.** Another recently introduced format that records 420 MB of uncompressed data (850 MB compressed).

I feel that minicartridges are most appropriate for workstations, although they might be sufficient for small LANs. Because tapes are usable on many brands of equipment, minicartridges can be an effective means of exchanging large amounts of data with other systems.

8mm Cartridges

This format was developed by Exabyte, which is still the only manufacturer of OEM drive hardware. The format is based on the 8mm tape format developed by Sony for its Betamax video recorders and cameras. The 8mm format became popular when it was the only format that could back up more than 1 GB of data to a cartridge. Most units back up 2.2 GB of uncompressed data, with larger capacities available.

The 8mm and 4mm data cartridges use a technique called *helical-scan recording*, borrowed from the videotape industry, to increase data density on tapes. Figure 17.2 illustrates the way in which helical-scan recording works. The tape moves at a relatively slow speed past a drum that contains the recording head and revolves at high speed. The drum is tilted, and the recording head records data in diagonal stripes on the tape.

Figure 17.2
Helical-scan recording.

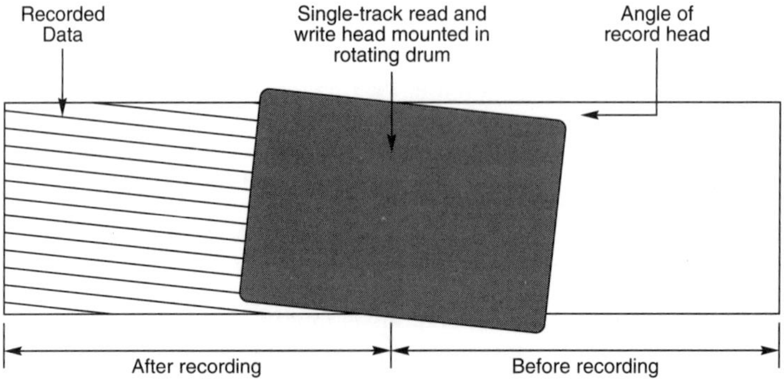

Serpentine recording methods increase the amount of data that can be recorded on a track by moving tape more rapidly past the recording head. Eventually, a limit is reached at which increasing speed would place too much stress on the fragile magnetic tape.

Helical-scan recording increases data density by revolving the recording head more rapidly. Tape speeds are low and tape stress is minimized. However, the tape-drive mechanics are significantly more complicated than DC-6000 drives, and costs of helical scan tape drives have been reduced only recently to the level of less than $1,000.

Although 8mm drives use the same cartridge shells as 8mm video tapes, the magnetic media must be of much higher quality. A lost flake of metal oxide might cause only a white streak in a video picture, but it can invalidate an entire file on a data cartridge.

You can get 8mm data-recording equipment with capacities of 2.2 GB and 5 GB per tape, with data-compression enabling capacities of 10 GB per data cartridge. The 8mm option is an excellent format for backing up LAN data, but it is less popular than other formats, and the basic hardware is manufactured by only one company: Exabyte. Many LAN administrators prefer to select equipment standards that have a broader manufacturer base.

4mm Cartridges

The 4mm data-cartridge format is derived from the Digital Audio Tape (DAT) format developed by Sony. The 4mm format uses helical-scan recording to store 1.3 GB of uncompressed data on a 60-meter tape. Compression techniques have raised capacity per tape to the neighborhood of 9 GB.

Data-recording densities are extremely high, and tape speeds are only about 3 seconds per inch. The tape drum rotates at 2,000 revolutions per minute and records 1,869 tracks per inch of tape. Data-transfer rates are extremely high, and I have observed rates of 30 MB per second with low-end 4mm hardware.

One consequence of these slow tape speeds is that 4mm tapes can be searched extremely rapidly. Typically, the tape can be positioned to any file on its length in 15 seconds or less.

The 4mm format is the hot tape format these days, and manufacturers are competing to raise capacities and lower costs. I just purchased a 2 GB capacity unit for under $800. Units with capacities of up to 16 MB are available at costs of just over $2,000. Because many manufacturers are competing in this format, you have a wide range of options for cost and features.

Because 4mm is a digital format, an innovative approach to increasing data throughput is to operate two tape drives in tandem, writing data to both simultaneously. Now, two data cartridges are required to store data, but throughput is effectively doubled. On LANs that have limited backup windows, this might be the most effective way to back up large amounts of data in a short time.

The 4mm format gets my vote as the best format for backing up most LANs. Costs are low and getting lower, capacities are high and getting higher, and data-transfer rates are as high as they get for tape media.

Optical Disks

Three types of optical media generally are available:

- Compact disc read-only media (CD-ROM)
- Write once read many (WORM)
- Magnetic optical (MO) read/write

CD-ROM is primarily a read-only medium, although recordable CD-ROM (CD-R) technology is becoming more readily available. CD-R is intended primarily for mastering CD-ROM discs, however, not for backing up LANs.

WORM systems are available with large capacities, and are intended primarily for archiving large amounts of data. WORM systems record data by using a laser to burn pits in a plastic medium, as shown in figure 17.3. Recorded media are insensitive to magnetic fields and have a storage life of about 20 years, making WORM an effective archive medium. However, high costs and the inability to reuse recorded media make WORM unsuitable for daily backups.

Figure 17.3
WORM data recording.

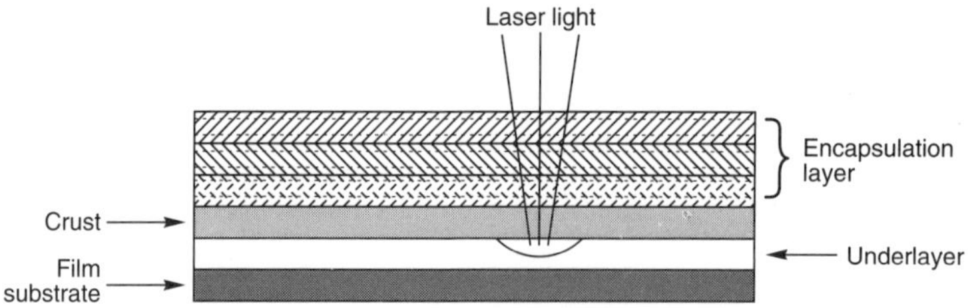

Magnetic optical drives use a combination of lasers and sophisticated magnetic recording technology to store high data densities on a read/write medium. A laser is used to heat small areas of a magnetic medium so that a magnetic field can change the polarization of the area. Figure 17.4 shows how the process works.

Shrinking costs of high-capacity, read/write optical disks have made this medium a contender as a backup medium in certain critical situations. Data throughput generally is higher than tape, and file random access is much higher, making optical disks an excellent place to store seldom-used files that must remain available on short notice.

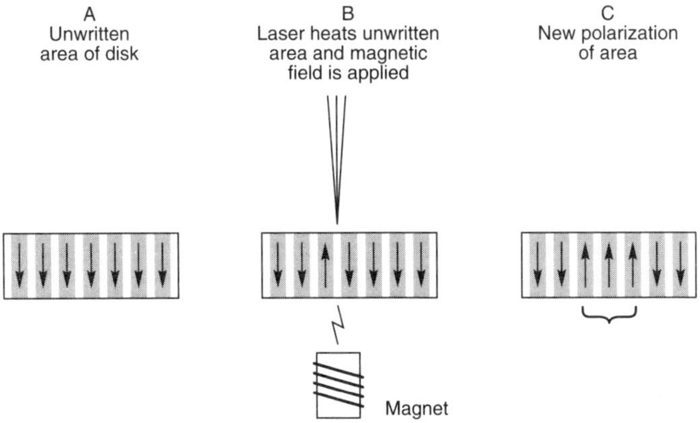

Figure 17.4

Magnetic optical recording.

Some vendors are promoting optical storage as an alternative to tape. Unfortunately, standards are lacking and optical cartridges from one manufacturer seldom are usable on another vendor's equipment. If you are seeking to avoid proprietary technologies in your backup equipment, this can be an important concern.

Costs of optical storage are significantly higher than tape, in part due to the relative newness of optical technology compared to tape. If your network is running 24 hours a day, 7 days a week, however, optical storage might be the best way to make the most of limited backup intervals.

Selecting Backup Hardware

File backup is complicated by the fact that open files cannot be backed up reliably or, in most cases, at all. Therefore, getting good backups means forcing all users to log out. You can do this by using User Manager for Domains to limit the logon hours for user accounts, although this works only for users of Windows NT computers.

In some organizations, the staff leaves at 5:00 p.m. and doesn't return until 8:00 the next morning. This backup situation is easy, and even slow equipment can cope. In most offices, however, there's always someone who *must* use the LAN at any time of the day or night. The best you might be able to ask for is about a two-hour window starting at 3:00 a.m. If you have a couple of hours, you probably can get the job done if you are permitted to obtain the right backup hardware.

Unfortunately, as LANs mature, the available backup window shrinks even as the volume of data to be backed up grows. If you are hard pressed to back up your data, there are four strategies you can examine:

- *Back up data by copying it to other hard drives, then back up the auxiliary hard drives at your leisure.* Hard drives on a fast SCSI subsystem are among the fastest backup systems you can obtain—expensive, but often the only way.

- *Use faster tape drives.* Speeds as high as 60 MB per minute are possible with some DAT systems.
- *Make use of faster file access.* Fast-wide SCSI on a PCI bus can deliver extremely fast data transfers. Remember, however, that bus speed only affects backup of data on the local server. If you are backing up data on other servers, you are limited by the speed of the medium that connects the servers. You need to install a tape drive on each server or install a high-speed link between your servers, such as FDDI or dedicated 100 Mbps Ethernet links.
- *Use more tape drives.* The fastest way of backing up multiple servers might be to simply add a tape drive to each server. Yes, you need to manage more tapes, but all the drives can operate simultaneously.

I strongly recommend that you back up your entire LAN every night if possible. Otherwise, two or more tapes are required to restore the LAN in the event of a catastrophic data loss. Although most backup software spans tapes (continues backup jobs on two or more tapes), someone generally must be available to switch tapes after one tape fills up.

You should either purchase a drive that has the capacity for your entire LAN, purchase multiple drives, or get a tape auto-changer that switches tapes automatically.

Incidentally, the only way to copy a data tape is to copy it to another identical tape drive. It's a good idea to purchase two identical drives if possible. You can use the drives to speed backup operations and have them available when a critical tape must be duplicated. Remember that archive tapes should be copied about every three years to refresh the magnetic image.

Note Databases present a special problem where backups are concerned. Files on a database server generally are held open as long as the database engine is running. This prevents you from backing up the files at the same time you back up other files on the LAN. In general, databases must be backed up using software that is included with the database engine.

Issues in Tape Backup

You should consider several issues when planning your LAN backup procedures. These issues are examined in the following sections.

Security Issues

The designers of Windows NT Server showed considerable foresight by creating the Backup Operators group, which enables users to back up all files on the server without having full administrative access to the server.

When a backup is being performed with a Backup Operators account, it is logged in with a level of security that exceeds normal user security. For that reason, computers that will be performing backups should be placed in a secure location. If the system is not under lock and key, install a screen saver that is password protected so that the computer will be locked with a password when it is unattended.

A backup tape can be a complete snapshot of your LAN data. If your data is sensitive, you don't want one of your tapes to get into the wrong hands. Windows Backup enables you to lock tapes so that they can be read only by the tape owner or by members of the Administrators or Backup Operators groups.

Backups of Open Files

Open files are one of the big headaches where backups are concerned. Most backup software does not even attempt to back up open files, because they are moving targets that might be modified in the middle of the backup operation. Windows NT Backup simply tries for a specified period of time and reports an error if the file is not closed.

Some software that runs continuously keeps files open around the clock. Many mail systems fall into this category. You should periodically stop this software to close the files so that they can be backed up.

Backups that Span Multiple Tapes

Almost any tape backup software continues jobs on additional tapes as data cartridges fill up; this procedure is called *spanning*. Unfortunately, spanning usually involves manually changing tapes, which requires an operator's intervention. If your organization does not maintain an overnight operations staff, a spanning feature is of little value to you.

Workstation Backup Capability

Any computer that can share its resources with the domain (it is configured with a domain name as its workgroup setting) can be connected to for backup. Windows NT Backup recognizes connections established through File Manager and can back up connected volumes.

Automation Features

The degree of automation available on tape backup software varies significantly. Windows NT Backup is somewhat in the middle of the spectrum of automation capabilities. You can automate tasks, but it is a bit of a nuisance and the automation isn't tremendously well integrated with the backup software. If your backup needs are more complicated, you might want to investigate third-party software for backing up your LAN.

Backup Activity Reporting

The best backup software does more than merely log messages in files. It ensures that backup operators are notified of problems by e-mail, fax, or pager. Ideally, backup operators should receive a report of each night's backup activity.

This is another area where Windows NT Backup is limited. Operators must remember to check the logs to ensure that errors are detected. Backups usually run fine and, unfortunately, most operators eventually stop checking the details of the log. For that reason, some form of automatic notification of errors is extremely valuable.

Recordkeeping and Storage Rotation

Some of your tapes should be rotated into off-site storage—preferably, the vault of a commercial data-storage service. Unfortunately, doing so is a hassle that requires considerable manual bookkeeping. Windows NT Backup does not have the capability of tracking vault rotations for you, so you have no choice but to set up clear procedures and tracking forms.

If you are tempted to store your off-site tapes anywhere but the vault of a media storage service, be sure that you obtain a fire safe that is rated for computer media. Ordinary fire safes are designed only to keep paper from combusting. Plastic storage media have a much narrower comfort range than paper.

Scheduling Backups

How you schedule backups depends on a number of factors:

- The capacity of the backup system.
- The speed of the backup system.

- The frequency with which files are being modified.
- The importance of the data.

Ultimately, all your decisions hinge on the last factor. If the data is critical enough to your business, you can justify almost any level of expense to obtain reliable backups.

I am strongly in favor of a full backup every day with tapes retained for various lengths of time. In the following sections, various types of backup schedules are discussed.

Types of File Backups

Windows NT Backup can perform five types of backups. To understand how the backup types differ, you need to understand the file *archive bit* (also called the *archive attribute*). The archive bit is a marker on a file that can be turned on and off to indicate whether the file has been backed up since it was last modified.

Whenever a file is modified in Windows NT (or DOS), the archive bit is set. Some backup operations look only for files for which the archive bit has been set.

Backup operations do one of two things to the archive bit when the file has been backed up: they leave the bit in its current state, or they clear the bit to indicate that the file has been backed up.

The five types of backups are discussed in the following sections.

Normal Backups

A *normal* backup does two things:

- Backs up all files that have been selected, regardless of the setting of the archive bit.
- Clears the archive bit to indicate that the files have been backed up.

Obviously, a normal backup performs a thorough backup of the selected files. By clearing the archive bit, a normal backup indicates that all files have been backed up.

Copy Backups

A *copy* backup does the following:

- Backs up all files that have been selected, regardless of the setting of the archive bit.
- Leaves the archive bit in its prebackup state.

In other words, a copy backup does not alter the files that are backed up in any way, including changing the archive bit.

Differential Backups

Differential backups are so named because they record all the differences that have taken place since the last normal backup. A differential backup does the following:

- Backs up only files that have the archive bit set to show that the file has been modified.
- Leaves the archive bit in its prebackup state.

Differential backups often are used in combination with normal backups. A normal backup of all files is performed each weekend to archive all files on the LAN, for example. Then a differential backup is performed each night of the week to back up all files that have been modified since the weekend. Figure 17.5 shows how this schedule would work.

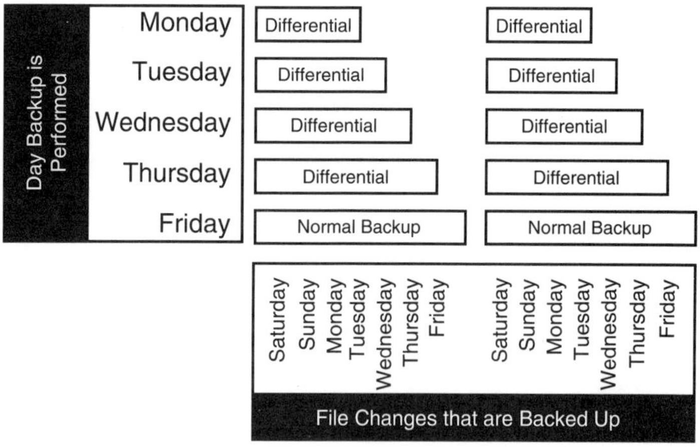

Figure 17.5
Differential backups.

To restore all files on the LAN, you would need to restore two sets of tapes:

- The normal backup for the previous weekend.
- The differential backup for the previous night.

Differential backups commonly are used to reduce the amount of time in which backup jobs must run during the week. If you can schedule a normal (full) backup for the weekend but have limited time during the week, a differential backup still might fit into the weekday backup window.

Incremental Backups

Incremental backups record only the changes that have taken place during a preceding interval of time—often one day. An incremental backup does the following:

- Backs up only files that have the archive bit set to show that the file has been modified.
- Clears the archive bit to indicate that the file has been backed up.

Figure 17.6 shows how a combination of normal and incremental backups would work. The figure assumes that a normal backup is performed during the weekend, while an incremental backup takes place each week night. Notice that each incremental backup only records files that have been modified since the previous backup took place.

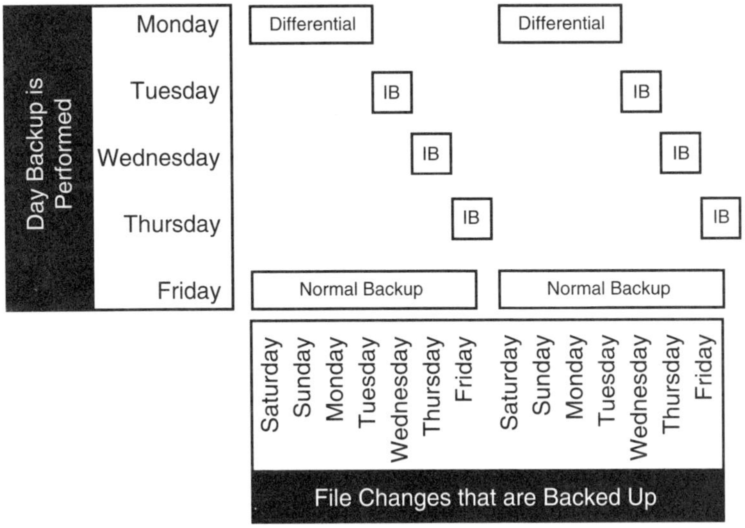

Figure 17.6
Incremental backups.

Incremental backups are used to further reduce the time interval required to back up networks. If your LAN includes critical data, you might want to run incremental backups more than once a day so that an entire day's worth of work cannot be lost.

The disadvantage of incremental backups is that several tapes can be required to restore the network. If the LAN fails on Thursday, you must restore the last normal backup plus the incremental backups for Monday, Tuesday, and Wednesday.

Daily Backups

Daily backups identify files to be backed up by examining the date stamp. If a file has been modified on the same day the backup is being made, the file will be backed up.

Both incremental and daily backups can be used to make checkpoint backups during the working day to capture changes at intervals shorter than 24 hours.

Note Notice that none of these backup types protects you against loss of data in files that have been modified since the most recent backup. What if you cannot afford to lose a single change that is made to any file, regardless of when the last backup was made? If you are running computers for a bank, how do you ensure that not a single transaction is lost?

There is no such thing as continuous backup, and open files can't be backed up. If your data is so critical that nothing may be lost, you need to be looking into one or more of the following options:

- RAID disk storage so that a single hard drive failure will not lose data.
- Fault-tolerant hardware that has redundant power supplies, error-correcting memory, and other goodies that keep you from losing data.
- Fault-tolerant software that can rebuild damaged files. A good database system keeps a log file that can reconstruct all transactions that take place. As long as the hard drives that contain the log file survive a disaster, you can restore last night's backup and roll the log forward to reconstruct the database to the point of failure.

Tape-Rotation Schedules

Your goal in rotating tapes is to have as much of your data as possible both on-site and safely off-site in storage. Ideally, your on-site tapes would be sufficient to rebuild the LAN, and you would need files from the off-site archive only in an emergency. The following sections explain several rotation schemes, each of which has advantages and disadvantages.

Two-Set Rotation

A basic scheme simply uses 10 tapes divided into 2 sets of 5. One set is used one week, and the other set is used the next week. Figure 17.7 illustrates the process.

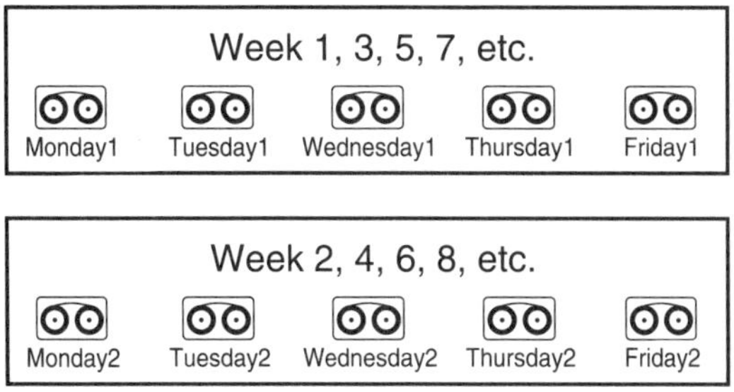

Figure 17.7
Two-set rotation.

This method does not provide for long-term archives and does not enable you to reach back very far in time. Suppose that you find that an unknown virus infected your LAN a month ago. Wouldn't it be nice to be able to restore all your program files (the only ones the virus could infect) from a tape that was made before the virus infection began?

You also may need greater scope in your archive if you have data that must be stored for long periods of time.

Grandfather-Father-Son Rotation

The *grandfather-father-son* (GFS) method is simple to manage and is adequate for most small- to medium-sized LANs. Several GFS tape rotations could be developed, but here is one that works well without being unduly complicated. You need the following tapes:

- Four tapes for each weekday: Monday, Tuesday, Wednesday, and Thursday.
- Five Friday tapes, one for each Friday of the month, labeled Friday1 through Friday5 (the fifth tape is for months with five Fridays).
- Twelve monthly tapes.

The GFS rotation scheme is shown in figure 17.8.

Monday through Thursday, a backup is performed using the appropriate tape. These tapes are reused weekly. Normal, differential, or incremental backups may be performed, depending on your requirements.

Friday1 through Friday4 are used on the first through fourth Friday of the month. These tapes are stored off-site and are retrieved after two weeks. In this way, the two most recent Friday tapes are stored off-site.

On the last day of each month, the appropriate monthly tape is used. These tapes are stored off-site for at least one year. If your organization needs a longer archive period, monthly tapes could be stored off-site indefinitely.

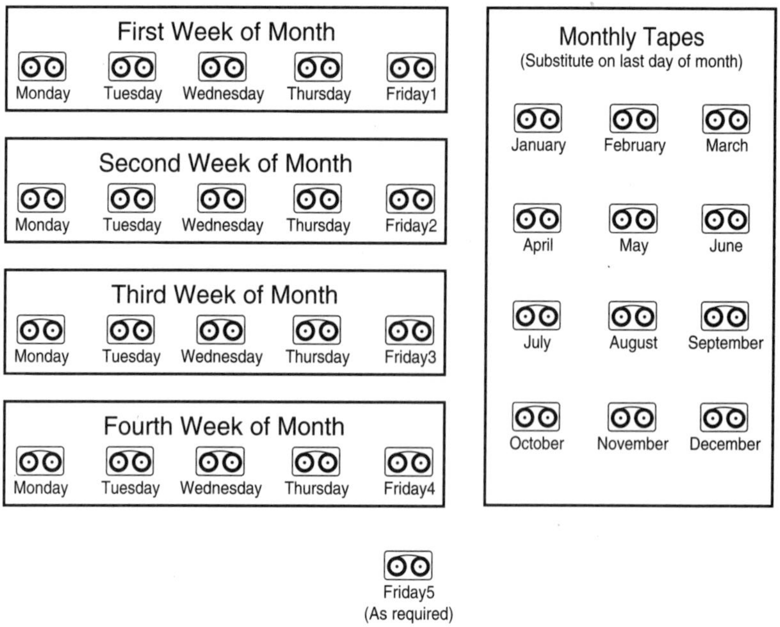

Figure 17.8
Grandfather-father-son tape rotation.

If you own two tape drives, you could make an on-site copy of each tape before it is sent to off-site storage. This ensures that you can locate any file in your archive without the delay of retrieving files from the vault.

Note Of course, if all your files will not fit on a single tape, you will be working with spanned tape volumes. Work out an appropriate labeling scheme to keep related tapes together, such as MONDAYA, MONDAYB, and so on.

Ten-Tape Rotation

The GFS method has many desirable qualities, and is probably the most commonly used approach. However, GFS rotation uses some tapes much more heavily than others. The daily tapes are used 52 times a year, while the monthly tapes are used only one time. A 10-tape rotation spreads the wear on all tapes.

This method uses a series of four-week cycles. During each cycle, the same tapes are used on each Monday, Tuesday, Wednesday, and Thursday. A new tape is rotated in on Friday. Figure 17.9 shows how the process works. As you can see, the rotation begins to repeat after 40 weeks.

The biggest problem with 10-tape rotation is that it is easy to get the schedule confused. Unfortunately, automated scheduling of a 10-tape rotation is beyond the scope of most tape backup software systems, and scheduling becomes a manual affair.

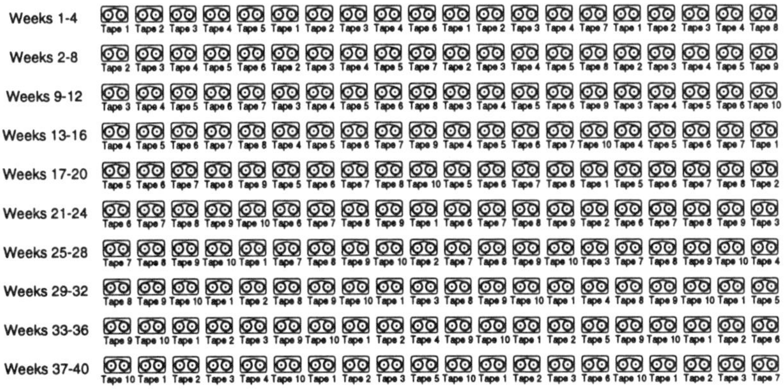

Figure 17.9
Ten-tape rotation.

Using Windows NT Backup

Windows NT Backup is a reasonably capable backup system. Its main deficiency is its lack of a versatile macro language. Scheduling jobs is a bit complicated, due to an involved process of editing batch files and scheduling them with a separate utility. Still, before you invest in third-party backup software, live with Backup for a while. It may be all you need. At the very least, it will help you learn the features you want most in backup software.

Before you can back up files, you need to install tape-device support on the server. First, you will learn how to install these devices, then you will look in detail at using Windows NT Backup to save and restore files.

Note Before you buy a tape device for use with Windows NT, be sure it is on the list of supported hardware. Most SCSI devices should work fine. I have worked with several SCSI tape subsystems and had good results. Even though several models are supported, I have not tried to work with any QIC-40/QIC-80 tape drives, so I can't be sure what configuration issues you might encounter.

Installing Tape Drives

If you have never installed a tape device on your server, you need to install drivers with the Setup program. Run the Windows NT Setup program in the Main program group and follow these steps:

1. Choose the Add/Remove **T**ape Devices command from the **O**ptions menu. The Tape Device Setup dialog box shown in figure 17.10 appears. The figure shows one device installed.

2. To add a device, choose **A**dd to display the Select Tape Device Option dialog box shown in figure 17.11.

3. Pull down the **D**evice list and select one of the available options. Or, choose Other from the list if you have drivers on a floppy disk.

4. Supply the path to the installation files and choose Continue to install the drivers.

5. Choose Close and quit the Windows NT Setup utility.

6. Restart Windows NT Server to activate the software.

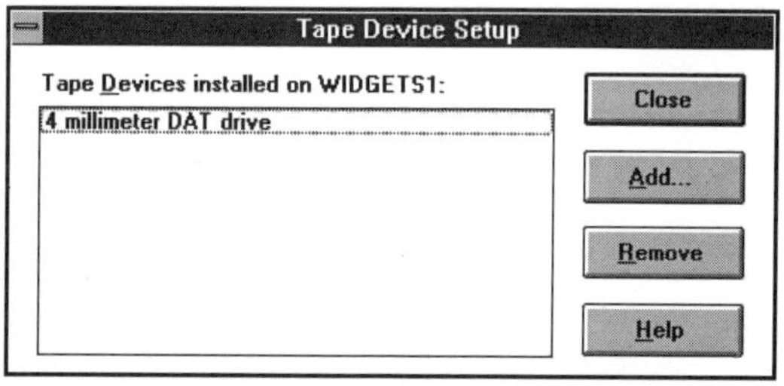

Figure 17.10
The Tape Device Setup dialog box.

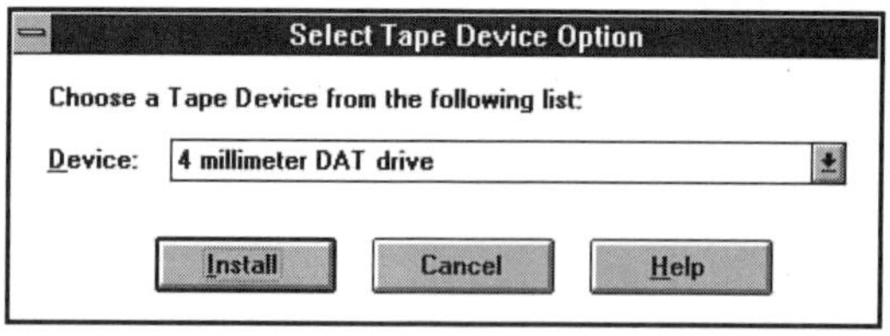

Figure 17.11
Installation of a tape device driver identified by Windows NT.

Backing Up Files

Figure 17.12 shows the Backup utility window and identifies several features. The Drives window normally will be open when you start Backup to display drive letters that currently are connected to the computer. Any drives that have been connected with File Manager are displayed in the Drives window.

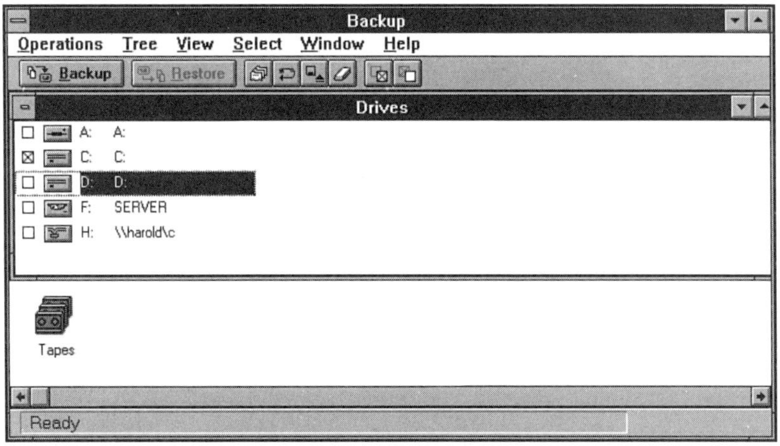

Figure 17.12

The main window in Backup.

Backing up files is a five-step process:

1. Prepare the tape media.
2. Select the files to be backed up.
3. Specify the backup options.
4. Run the backup.
5. Verify the backup.

Note To make backups or restore files, you must be a member of the Administrators or Backup Operators group.

Preparing the Tape Media

In most cases, new tapes require little or no preparation. If tapes have existing data from another backup system, they might need to be erased or formatted. Several tape options are found on the Operations menu.

◆ **Erase Tape.** Choose this operation to erase records of previous backups. You have two choices:

Quick Erase. Simply erases the tape label and makes the tape usable with Windows NT Backup. Existing data remains on the tape and can be accessed.

Secure Erase. Physically erases all data from the tape so that it cannot be accessed.

- **Retension Tape.** DC-6000 and DC-2000 data cartridges should be retensioned prior to first use and every 20 backup operations. *Retensioning* fast forwards and rewinds the tape to equalize tension on the tape medium. The 4mm and 8mm tapes do not require retensioning.

- **Eject Tape.** Ejects a tape if a tape device supports software tape ejection.

Note You should erase any tapes that will be used during unattended operation, because no one will be present to correct errors if Backup is unable to read the tape.

If Backup produces an error message such as `Tape Drive Error Detected` or `Bad Tape`, you might not be able to erase the tape with Backup in normal mode. To erase a tape that causes these errors, start Backup by choosing **R**un from the **F**ile menu and add the /nopoll switch. (The command would be `NTBACKUP /NOPOLL`.)

After you format tapes with the /NOPOLL switch, stop Backup and restart it normally. Do not attempt to execute normal operations with the /NOPOLL switch.

Selecting Files for Backup

To select entire volumes, simply check the check boxes of the desired volumes in the Backup window.

Tip You also can check and uncheck items by using the Check and Uncheck icons on the toolbar or by choosing the **C**heck and **U**ncheck commands from the **S**elect menu.

To select directories or files, follow these steps:

1. Double-click a drive name to open a drive tree window similar to that shown in figure 17.13.

2. This drive tree window works much like the windows in File Manager. You double-click a directory to open a directory, for example.

3. Choose the files or directories to be backed up by checking the associated box. Checking a directory selects all subdirectories of that directory. You can, if you want, open the subdirectories and remove the check marks.

   Notice that a directory check box is filled with gray if any files or subdirectories under that directory are unchecked.

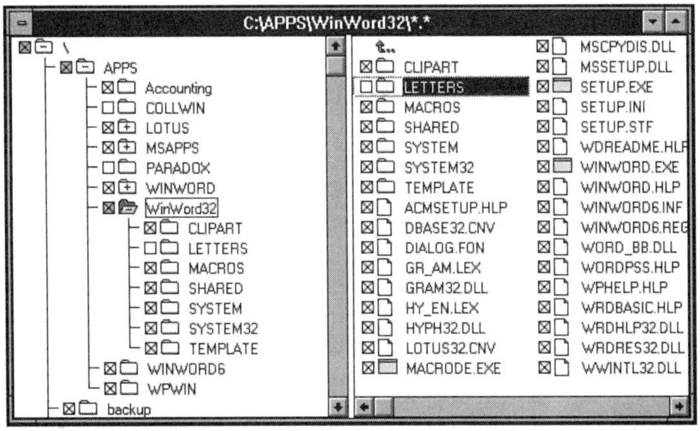

Figure 17.13

Selecting files and directories for backup.

Specifying Backup Options

After you have selected the items to be backed up, begin the backup by choosing the Backup command from the Operations menu, or click the Backup button in the toolbar. This displays the Backup Information dialog box shown in figure 17.14.

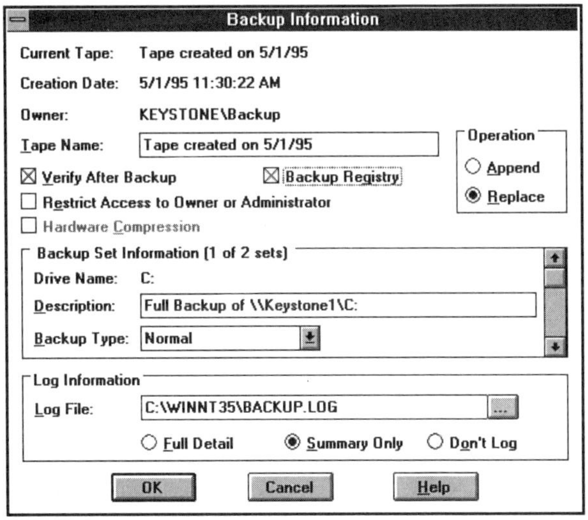

Figure 17.14

Specifying backup job information.

The options in this box follow:

- **Current Tape.** The name of the currently mounted tape, unless the tape is blank or has an unrecognized format.
- **Creation Date.** The date the first backup set on the tape was created.

- **Owner.** The user who placed the first backup set on the tape.
- **Tape Name.** You can specify a tape name or permit Backup to use the default name "Tape created on *date.*" This box is available only when you choose the Replace option.
- **Append.** Select this button to add the new backup set to the end of the tape.
- **Replace.** Select this button to overwrite existing backup sets on the tape with the current backup.
- **Verify After Backup.** Check this item to have Backup compare the tape contents to the original files to ensure that file data was written to tape without error.
- **Backup Registry.** The Registry is the heart and soul of Windows NT, and contains all the system's vital operational data. You should include the Registry in every backup of drive C to ensure that you have a valid, recent copy in case the Registry files are damaged.
- **Restrict Access to Owner or Administrator.** Check this option to make the tape more secure. Data from the tape can be retrieved only by the tape owner, or by a member of the Administrators or Backup Operators group. This box is available only when you choose the Replace option.
- **Hardware Compression.** This option is active only if your tape device supports hardware data compression. Check this box to activate the feature. Be aware, however, that using hardware compression can prevent you from restoring the tape from another brand of drive or from a drive that does not support data compression.
- **Drive Name.** This field displays the name of a drive that you checked in the Backup window. If you checked more than one drive letter, you see a scroll bar that can be used to display each of the drives. For each drive, you can enter a description and select a backup type.
- **Description.** Enter a brief description of the job.
- **Backup Type.** Choose the backup type from the options Normal, Copy, Differential, Incremental, and Daily. Each type was discussed earlier in the chapter.
- **Log File.** Enter a path describing a file where log messages will be recorded.

  Full Detail. Logs all operations, including the files and directories that are backed up.

  Summary Only. Logs only major operations, such as starting and completing the backup and backup errors.

Stop Windows NT Backup does not back up Registries on remote computers.

Running the Backup

When you have completed entries in the dialog box, choose OK to continue with the backup.

If the tape in the drive already contains data and you have specified **R**eplace as the backup operation, you will see an error message. Be sure that you don't mind whether the files on the tape will be destroyed before you choose **Y**es to continue.

Verifying the Backup

As the backup proceeds, the Backup Status box updates you on events (see fig. 17.15). Pay particular attention to two statistics:

- **Corrupt files.** High or increasing numbers of corrupt files might indicate hardware problems.
- **Skipped files.** These files were, of course, not backed up. If you see skipped files, check the log to ensure that missing these files is not a critical omission. You might need to force a user to log out to close the files.

It is always a good idea to check the backup log, which is a text file you can print or review with NOTEPAD.

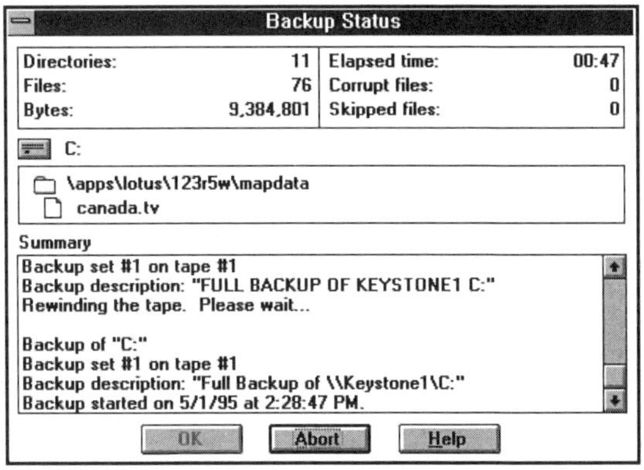

Figure 17.15

The Backup Status dialog box.

Restoring Files

To restore files, first review your logs to identify the appropriate tape. If you are restoring a complete volume from a combination of several backup sets, be sure to restore the backup sets in the order they were made so that newer copies of files overwrite older copies.

Selecting Files to Restore

Prior to a restore, you must select the files to be restored. Backup enables you to restore entire tapes, specific backup sets, or individual files or directories. To select files to restore, follow these steps:

1. Open the Tapes window by double-clicking the Tapes icon.

2. Insert the desired tape. After you insert a tape, Backup reads a catalog of items on the tape and creates an icon for the tape in the Tapes window. Figure 17.16 shows a Tapes window with two tape catalogs loaded.

   You can request loading of a tape catalog by selecting the tape icon and choosing Catalog from the Operations menu.

3. You can restore entire tapes, specific backup sets, or individual directories or files by selecting the items you want in the Tapes window. You can open folders to locate subdirectories and files on a drive. Check all items that are to be restored.

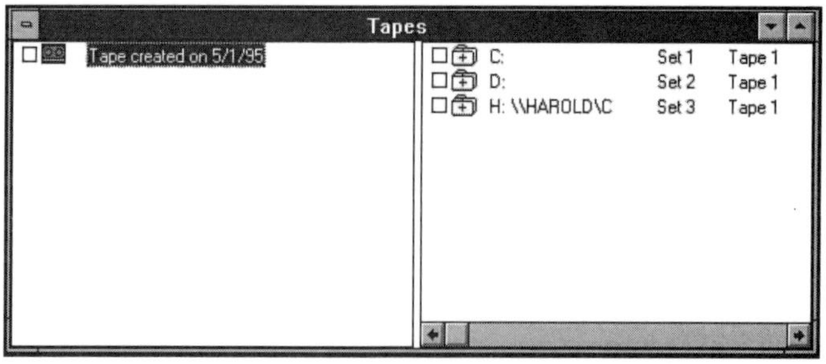

Figure 17.16
Selecting a tape to restore.

Note Creating catalogs is a time when you will really appreciate the fast seek times that are possible with 4mm data cartridges. The catalog is stored as the last item on the tape, and Backup must search the entire tape. This can take considerable time with QIC cartridges, but takes less than a minute with a 4mm drive.

Specifying Restore Options

After selecting items to be restored, choose the Restore icon in the toolbar or choose Restore from the Operations menu. The Restore Information dialog box appears, as shown in figure 17.17.

If you have selected two or more tape sets to restore, a scroll bar will be included in the Restore Information dialog box. You can select each set by moving the scroll handle.

For each tape set being restored, the following information and options are displayed:

- **Tape Name.** The name of the tape from which files are being restored for this set.
- **Backup Set.** The name you assigned to the backup set.
- **Creation Date.** The date the backup set was created.
- **Owner.** The user who created the backup set.
- **Restore to Drive.** Specify a different destination drive by entering the drive path here. This path can include local hard drives or drives that are created by network connections.
- **Alternate Path.** If files will not be restored to their original directories, specify the base directory to which the directory tree should be restored.
- **Verify After Restore.** Check this option to have restored files compared to the image on tape to ensure that errors have not occurred.
- **Restore File Permissions.** Check this box if you want to retain file permissions that originally were assigned to the directories and files. This option is available only if you are restoring to an NTFS volume.
- **Restore Local Registry.** Check this box to restore the server Registry. This option is active only if the Registry was backed up to the tape set and if it would be restored to the same volume on which it originally was located.
- **Log File.** Enables you to specify where messages should be logged. Options are the same as the options available in the Backup Information dialog box.

Restoring Files

After you have completed the Restore Information dialog box, begin the restore operation by choosing OK. A Restore Status box similar to figure 17.18 displays the progress of the file restoration.

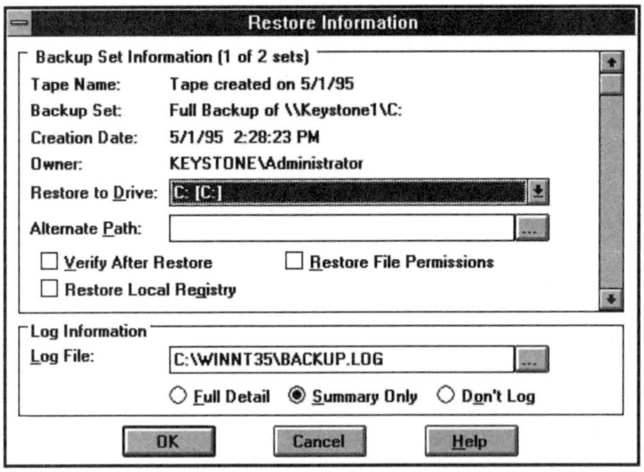

Figure 17.17

Specifying restore options.

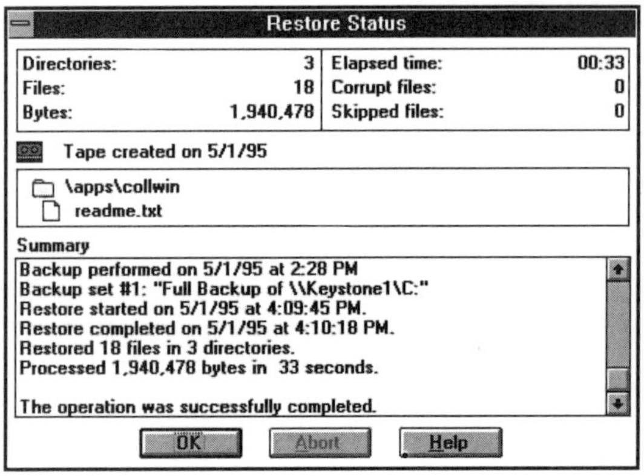

Figure 17.18

The Restore Status dialog box.

Restoring from Spanned Tape Sets

If the tape set you are restoring spans more than one physical tape, the catalog will be on the last tape on the set. Backup asks you to mount the appropriate tape so that it can read the catalog.

If a tape from the spanned set is missing or damaged, you might need to force Backup to rebuild a catalog by scanning each tape. To do this, start Backup by choosing Run from the File menu and typing the command **NTBACKUP /MISSINGTAPE**. Backup then scans each tape to build a catalog—a lengthy process, but one that is preferable to losing your data.

Restoring a Registry

You can restore only the Registry files to the volume from which they were archived, if you prefer. With the Windows Backup utility, you must select at least one file to activate the Restore button. Then you can check the Restore Local Registry box in the Restore Information dialog box.

To restore from the command line, specify the following directory

\WINNT35\SYSTEM32\CONFIG

to restore. You cannot restore this directory to any disk other than the disk from which it was backed up.

Note If you need to restore files to a newly installed server, be sure that the software on the new server is identical to the software on the old server. If any patches or upgraded drivers were installed on the old server, be sure that they go on the new server before you try to restore the files. Otherwise, the backup software might not be able to read your tapes.

Backing Up from the Command Line

A command-line interface is available for Backup. The primary use for the command-line interface is to build batch files that can be executed manually or using the Windows NT command scheduler.

The syntax for the NTBACKUP command follows:

```
NTBACKUP operation path [/A][/B][/D "text"][/E][/HC:[ON¦OFF]]
     [/L "filename"][/R][/T option][/TAPE:n][/V]
```

The command recognizes several options (square brackets indicate that a parameter is not required in Microsoft syntax diagrams). The parameters and options for NTBACKUP follow:

operation	Always specify BACKUP.
path	Enter one or more path specifications of directories to be backed up.
/A	Include this option to have Backup append this job to tape. Omitting this option instructs Backup to replace the tape contents with the current job.
/B	Include this option to back up the local Registry.
/D "*text*"	Use this option to specify a description of the backup set. Place the description in quotation marks.

/E	If this option is used, the backup log includes exceptions only. Without this option, a full backup log is created.
/HC:[ON|OFF]	Use this option to force a backup device to operate with hardware compression on or off. Specify the option as /hc:on or /hc:off. This option is effective only when the /A option is omitted, because the compression mode of the tape is determined by the mode used for the first set on the tape.
/L "filename"	This option specifies the name of the backup log. Include the file name and path in quotation marks.
/R	Secures the backup set by restricting access to the tape owner and to members of the Administrators or Backup Operators group. This option is effective only when the /A option is omitted.
/T *option*	Specify the backup type. Replace *option* with normal, copy, incremental, differential, or daily.
/TAPE:*n*	If the server has more than one tape drive, specify the drive to be used with a number *n* from 0 through 9 to reference the drive's number as listed in the Registry.
/V	Include this option to have Backup verify the tape.

Now look at some examples. Following is a command that backs up the APPS directory of drive C:

```
ntbackup backup c:\apps /a/e/v /l "c:\winnt35\backup.log"
/t differential
```

Notice that the order of the options does not matter. This command accomplishes the following:

- Backs up all files and subdirectories of C:\APPS
- Appends the tape set to the current tape
- Restricts tape log entries to exceptions only
- Verifies the backup
- Places the log in the file C:\WINNT35\BACKUP.LOG
- Performs a differential backup

Here is another example:

```
ntbackup backup c: d: h: /r/b /t normal /l:c:\tape.log
```

This example does the following:

- Backs up drives C, D, and H
- Backs up the Registry on local drives
- Replaces contents of the tape (no /a option)
- Restricts access to the backup set
- Performs a normal backup
- Records a full detail log (no /e flag) in C:\TAPE.LOG

Because the interactive Backup utility is so quick and easy to use, you probably will use the command-line format primarily to create batch files. However, because Backup does not support a macro language, the command-line approach is the only way to store backup procedures for repeated execution.

In the next section, you will see how backup batch files can be scheduled for delayed or repeated execution. Here is a batch file that backs up drives on several servers:

```
net use g:\\widgets1\c$ /yes
net use h:\\widgets2\c$ /yes
net use i: \\acct\c$ /yes
ntbackup backup c: d: g: h: i: /e/v /l "c:\winnt35\backup.log"
/t normal /d "Complete backup of KEYSTONE, WIDGETS, and ACCT domains"
```

Of course, a backup operator must be trusted on other domains before being permitted to back up his or her data in those other domains.

Note The administrative shares such as C$ and D$ are available only to members of the Administrators local group. If members of Backup Operators will be backing up remote servers, you need to create shares that can be accessed by them.

Scheduling Backup Jobs

Windows NT has a Schedule service that can be used to schedule execution of commands. The Schedule enables you to schedule jobs to execute overnight or over the weekend, and to execute repeatedly without the need for rescheduling. This section shows you how to set up and use the Schedule to make tape backups. You will learn more about managing services in Chapter 18, "Managing the Server."

Starting the Schedule Service

The Schedule service can run in two modes:

- As a system account. In this mode, Schedule operates in the current logon session, using the permissions assigned to the logged on user account. Schedule cannot operate when no user is logged on.
- In its own logon session, using permissions assigned to its own user account. Schedule can operate whenever the server is active and can function in the background when users are logged on to the server.

The first choice is useful when you are scheduling tasks that will take place while you are logged on.

In many cases, however, you will want to use the second approach with tape backups. By assigning a user account to the Schedule, you make it possible for backups to take place even when no one is logged on to the backup server.

Starting the Schedule Service as a System Account

Services are managed using the Service utility in the Control Panel. Open the Service utility to see a list of services, as shown in figure 17.19. Notice that the Schedule service status is not started and its Startup mode is Manual. Services that are configured with an Automatic Startup mode are started when Windows NT Server is booted.

To set up the Schedule service as a system account, follow these steps:

1. Open the Service utility in the Control Panel.
2. Select the Schedule service in the Service box.
3. Choose Startup to display the Service dialog box shown in figure 17.20.
4. Select **A**utomatic so that Schedule service will be started automatically.
5. Select **S**ystem Account.
6. Select Allow Service to Interact with Desktop if you want to monitor backup jobs as they run. I recommend using this option when you are learning to schedule backups.
7. Click on OK. You will be returned to the Services window.

8. Choose **S**tart to start the Schedule service. It restarts automatically each time the server is booted.

9. Exit the Service utility.

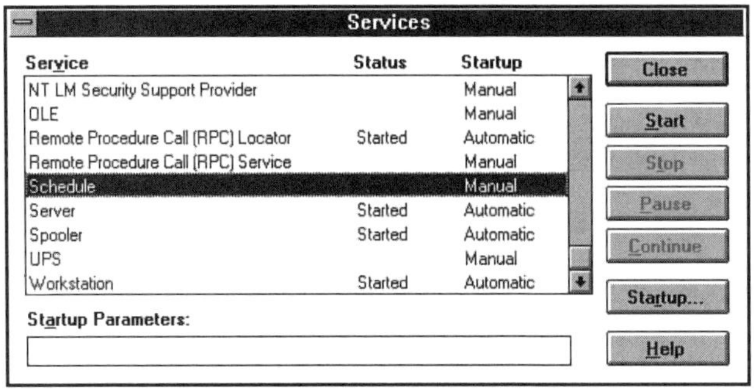

Figure 17.19

Services in the Services utility.

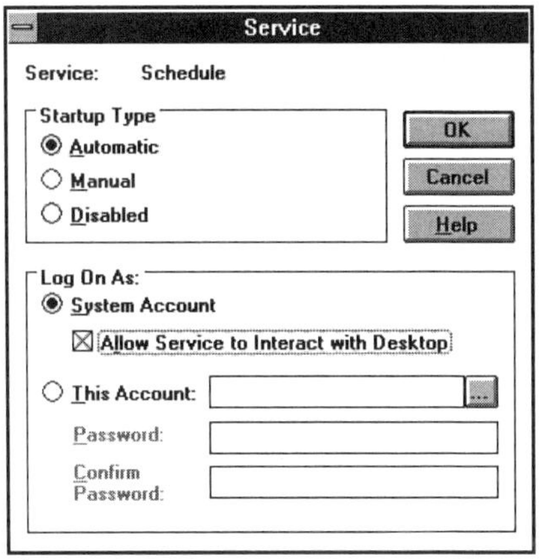

Figure 17.20

Setting Service options.

Note When you are experimenting, set up the Schedule service as a System service. You will find it much easier to learn the ropes and to set up your regular backup jobs.

Note Any time you change the settings for the Schedule service, you must stop and restart the service to have the changes take effect.

Starting the Schedule Service with Its Own User Account

Create a user account that will be used by the scheduler. The user ID also must be a member of the Backup Operators local group of any domain that it will be responsible for backing up. Of course, proper trust relationships must be set up between domains before cross-domain memberships can be assigned.

Because the Schedule service will be running backup jobs, the user account must be made a member of the Backup Operators local group. Other group memberships might be required as well.

Before you go further, log on with the user account you have created and be sure you can perform the required functions.

To set up the Schedule service to log on with the user account you have created, follow these steps:

1. Open the Service utility in the Control Panel.
2. Select the desired service in the Service box.
3. Choose Startup to display the Service dialog box.
4. Select **A**utomatic so that Schedule service will be started automatically.
5. As shown in figure 17.21, select **T**his Account and enter the user account name you have created for backups. You can click the Browse (...) button to browse the network and select the user name.
6. Enter the password for the user account in the two password fields.
7. Choose OK. You will be returned to the Service dialog box.
8. Stop the service if it is running. Then choose **S**tart to activate the service with the changes you have made.
9. Exit the Service utility.

Figure 17.21

Configuring a service to log on with a user account.

Note You only need to set up the Schedule service to log on with a user account if you are planning to have it run jobs in the background or when a user is not logged on. If the backup computer is located in a secure, locked area, you can do just as well by configuring Schedule as a system service and leaving it logged on with appropriate privileges. If you are concerned about security, install a password-protected screen saver so that the computer will be locked with a password when it is unattended.

Scheduling Jobs with the AT Command

Now that the Schedule service is started, you can enter scheduled jobs with the AT command. AT commands are entered at a command prompt. The syntax of the AT command follows:

```
AT [\\computer] [[id][/DELETE] ¦ /DELETE [/YES]]
```

or

```
AT [\\computer] time [/INTERACTIVE][/EVERY:date[,...] "command"
```

or

```
AT [\\computer] time [/INTERACTIVE][/NEXT:date[,...] "command"
```

The AT command typed alone lists all currently scheduled jobs.

The command recognizes several options (square brackets indicate that a parameter is not required in Microsoft syntax diagrams). The parameters and options for AT follow:

`\\computer`	Specify the name of a Windows NT computer on which the command will execute. If this command is omitted, the current computer is assumed.
`id`	The identification number that is assigned to a scheduled command.
`/DELETE`	Include this option to cancel a schedule command. If an *id* is specified, only the jobs associated with that *id* are deleted. Otherwise, all scheduled commands are deleted.
`/YES`	When used to cancel all jobs, /YES eliminates the need to confirm the request.
`time`	Specifies the time in 24-hour format when the job should be scheduled.

`/INTERACTIVE`	Include this option to enable the current user to interact with the job. Without this flag, the job operates in the background.
`/EVERY:`*`date`*	Use this option to schedule repeating jobs. Specify one or more dates, where *date* is a day of the week (Monday, Tuesday, and so on) or a day of the month (1 through 31). If *date* is omitted, the current day of the month is assumed.
`/NEXT:`*`date`*	Use this option to schedule a job the next time *date* occurs. Specify one or more dates, where *date* is a day of the week (Monday, Tuesday, and so on) or a day of the month (1 through 31). If *date* is omitted, the current day of the month is assumed.
`"`*`command`*	The command to be executed.

Assuming that BACKUP.BAT is a batch file, here are some examples of scheduling jobs with the AT command. This first example schedules the job once at 3:00 a.m. If it is later than 3:00 a.m., the job is scheduled for the morning of the next day.

```
AT 3:00 "backup"
```

To schedule a job to happen regularly on Wednesdays at midnight, use the /EVERY option:

```
AT 0:00 /every:Wednesday "backup"
```

If you want the job to happen every weekday, just add the extra days:

```
AT 0:00 /every:Monday,Tuesday,Wednesday,Thursday "backup"
```

Particularly when you are debugging backup procedures, you might want to have the job operate in interactive mode. Here is an example:

```
AT 15:00 "backup" /interactive
```

After each job is scheduled, you see this message:

```
Added a new job ID=n
```

where *n* is the job number. To delete a job, use the job ID with the /DELETE command.

Stop Do not use the /INTERACTIVE option with backup jobs that will run overnight without a user logged on to the desktop. Interactive jobs will attempt to connect with an active desktop and will fail.

New Riders Publishing INSIDE SERIES

Scheduling Jobs with Command Scheduler

The Windows NT Resource Kit includes a useful utility called Command Scheduler that enables you to schedule and manage jobs in an interactive windows-based environment. Figure 17.22 shows the main window of Command Scheduler with three jobs scheduled.

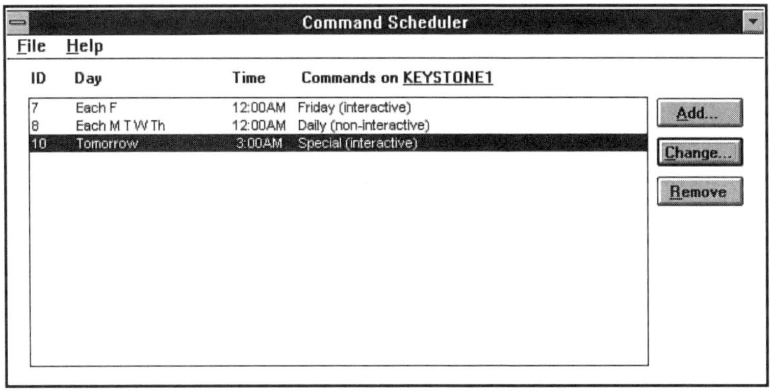

Figure 17.22
The main window of Command Scheduler.

If you start the Command Scheduler and the Schedule service is not started, Command Scheduler asks whether you want to start the service.

From the main window, choose Add to add a new command using the dialog box shown in figure 17.23. The fields in the Change Command dialog box follow:

- **Command.** Enter the command to be executed.
- **This Occurs.** Specify whether the job should occur:

  Today

  Tomorrow

  Every—Day(s) specified in the Days box

  Next—Day(s) specified in the Days box
- **Days.** If Every or Next is selected, select one or more days in this box.
- **Time.** Enter the time. You can tab to each time field and enter a number, or select each field in turn and change the value with the arrow buttons.
- **Interactive.** Check this box if the job should be available on the desktop of the currently logged-on user. (See the earlier warning about interactive jobs.)

After you have completed the dialog box, choose OK to add the job and return to the Command Scheduler main window.

To change or remove a job, select the job and choose **C**hange or **R**emove in the Command Scheduler main window.

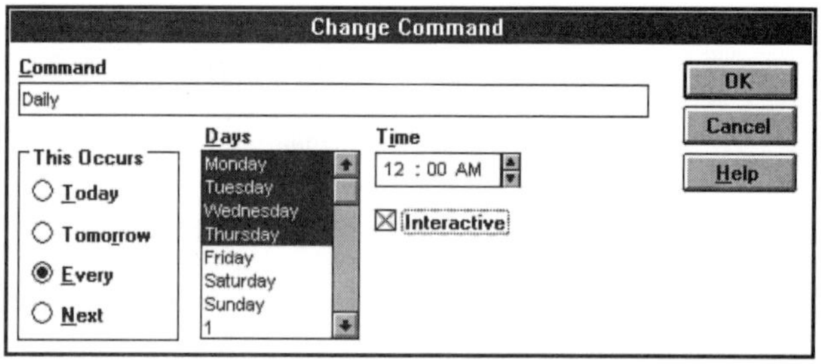

Figure 17.23
Adding a job in Command Scheduler.

Recovering a Server

If you experience total failure of a server's boot hard drive, Microsoft recommends the following procedure for recovering the drive:

1. After replacing the drive, reinstall Windows NT Server on the boot partition. Use the Repair option and the server's Emergency Repair Disk to recover the BOOT.INI file and critical portions of the Registry.

2. Restart the server.

3. Use a tape drive attached to the server to restore the system partition. Start with the last normal backup, and then restore any incremental or differential backups that are required.

4. Restart the server.

Tip

To shorten the time a boot drive failure puts a server out of service, I suggest that you create an emergency hard drive that is preconfigured with Windows NT Server. In the event of failure, disable the current boot drive, attach the emergency drive to the SCSI bus, and use it to boot the server. Finally, recover your backups to the emergency hard drive and restart the server. Your server will be up and running without the delay of reinstalling Windows NT Server. You can swap the hard drives and reinstall a new boot drive during a scheduled maintenance period.

CHAPTER 18

Managing the Server

This chapter explores the tools that are provided to manage Windows NT Server. Some of these tools you have encountered in earlier chapters, but some features still require discussion. You will examine a few tools in this chapter for the first time.

The following utilities are covered in this chapter:

- **Control Panel.** Actually a collection of tools for managing Windows NT hardware and software.
- **Server Manager.** The primary tool for managing server resources. You examined this tool extensively when domains and workstations were discussed. This chapter examines the remainder of the features of Server Manager.
- **Service Manager.** The utility for starting, stopping, and configuring services.
- **UPS.** A utility for monitoring the status of an uninterruptible power supply.
- **Network Client Administrator.** A tool for creating client installation disks and for installing client software through the network.

- **Registry Editor.** The tool that enables you to directly manipulate the contents of the Windows NT Server Registry database.
- **File Manager.** This chapter covers use of File Manager to audit network file activities.
- **Print Manager.** This chapter covers use of Print Manager to audit network printing activities.

Using the Control Panel

Anyone who has used Windows will be familiar with the Control Panel. Because this book isn't a basic tutorial on Windows, not much attention is lavished on the Control Panel, but a few of the tools are discussed. (If you want to change your cursor to a walking dinosaur using the Cursors utility, you'll just have to get curious and figure it out for yourself.) Figure 18.1 shows the Control Panel window. The exact tools you have vary a bit depending on the features that are installed.

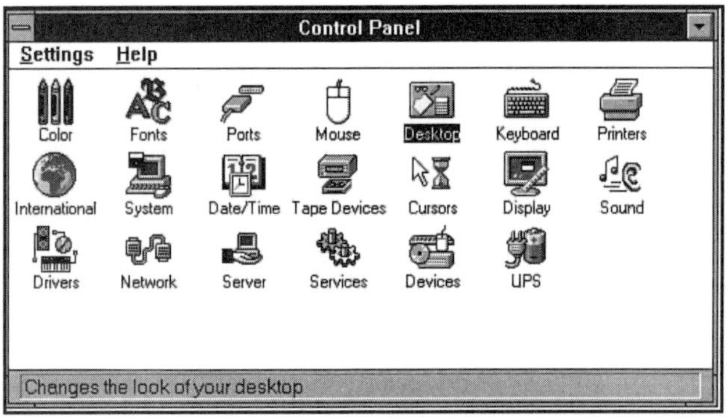

Figure 18.1
The Control Panel.

I will mention here only the tools that relate closely to server management:

- **Date/Time.** Computer clocks drift, and you occasionally should use this utility to keep your computers' clocks in reasonable agreement.
- **International.** A tool for defining language, time, date, currency, and other characteristics. You must select international characteristics during installation and seldom should need to change them.
- **Network.** Following installation, this is the tool used to add and remove network card drivers and protocols.

- **Ports.** A tool for adding, configuring, and deleting communication ports. The Ports tool was discussed in detail in Chapter 12, "Managing Printing Services."
- **Printers.** This icon is an alternative way to start the Print Manager, which has its own icon in the Administrative Tools program group. Print Manager also was discussed in Chapter 12.
- **Services.** The tool that configures, activates, and deactivates services. The Services tool is discussed in this chapter.
- **System.** A utility for configuring several characteristics of the Windows NT operating system environment. The System tool is discussed later in this chapter.
- **UPS.** The utility that monitors an uninterruptible power supply and takes action during power failures. UPS is described later in this chapter.

Server Manager

Figure 18.2 shows the main window of Server Manager, which is used to manage Windows NT Servers and Workstations. Chapter 9, "Managing Domains and Trust Relationships," demonstrates how Server Manager is used to add and remove network servers and computers.

Server Manager has three command menus, each of which has a few features that still require further discussion. Each menu is described in the following sections.

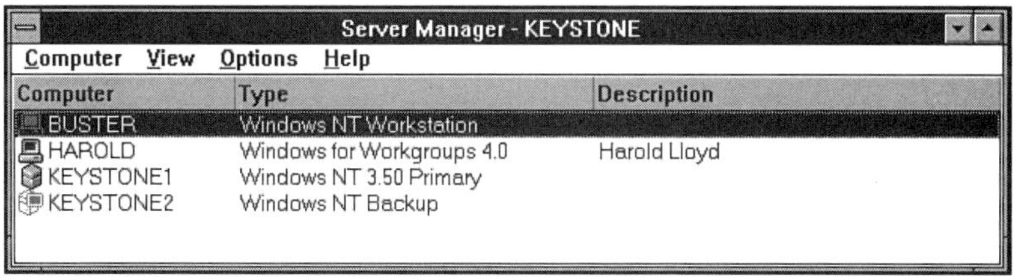

Figure 18.2

The Server Manager main window.

The Computer Menu

The Computer menu contains commands that enable you to manage Windows NT computers on the network. Some commands are discussed more fully in other chapters, particularly Chapter 9, but they are reviewed here for the sake of completeness. To manage a server with commands in the Computer menu, first select the computer in the Server Manager window.

Managing Windows NT Computer Properties

The Properties command displays the computer Properties box shown in figure 18.3. This box is used both to view and to manage properties of computers. The Properties dialog box has one input box that enables you to enter a description of the server. It also has five buttons you can use to manage specific categories of computer properties.

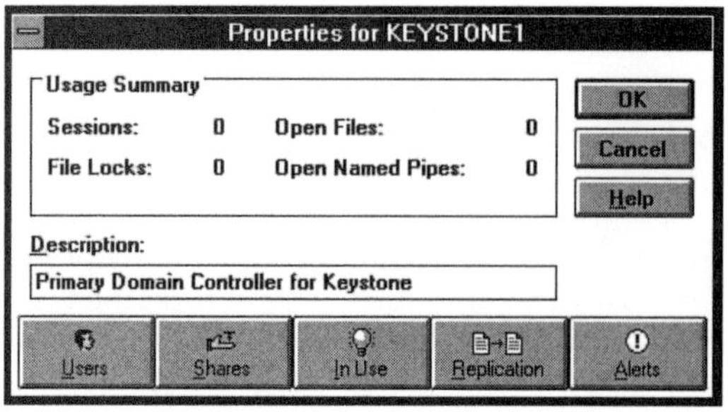

Figure 18.3

The computer Properties dialog box.

Viewing and Disconnecting Users Connected to a Server

The Users button calls up the User Sessions window shown in figure 18.4. Each user who is connected to the computer is listed in the Connected Users box. When you select a user, any shares that user has connected are listed in the Resource box.

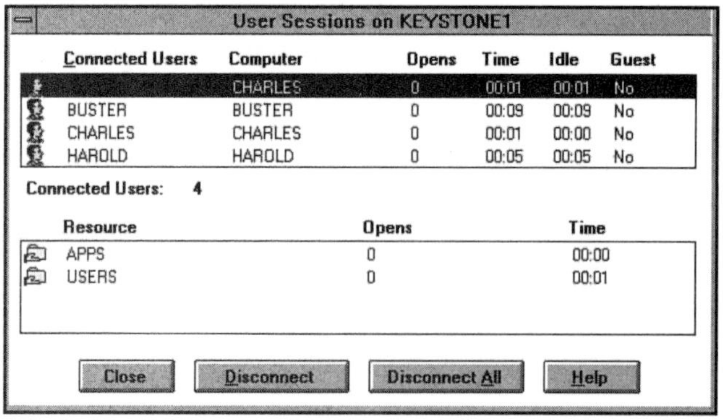

Figure 18.4

The User Sessions dialog box.

For each user, the following information is displayed:

- **Opens.** The number of files the user has open.
- **Time.** The time that has elapsed since the connection was established.
- **Idle.** The time that has elapsed since the user accessed this connection.
- **Guest.** Whether the user is logged on as Guest.
- **Resource.** Shares to which the user is connected.

Note It is important not to confuse being logged on to a domain with being connected to a computer. Simply being logged on to the domain does not guarantee that a user will appear in this list. The user must be actively connected to a share on this computer to be listed.

It is common for users to create persistent connections to a server. Persistent connections are easily reused each time the user logs on, but in most cases, persistent connections are reestablished in a disconnected state. Until the user actually uses a directory in the connected share (by displaying the directory in File Manager, for example), the connection does not go active and the user doesn't appear in the User Sessions list.

Administrators and Server Managers can take the following actions with connected users displayed in this window:

- To disconnect a single user from this computer, select the user in the Connected Users box and click the Disconnect button. You will need to confirm this action.
- To disconnect all users from this computer, click the Disconnect All button

Disconnecting a user does not log the user out. Disconnecting simply closes any resources to which the user is connected.

Viewing and Disconnecting Users Connected to a Share

The Shares button reveals the Shared Resources box shown in figure 18.5. In many ways, the Shared Resources dialog box does the opposite duty of the User Sessions dialog box. Instead of displaying users first and their shares after a user is selected, the Shared Resources box enables you to select a share and see who is connected to the share. For each share, you see how many users are attached and the path to which the share is assigned.

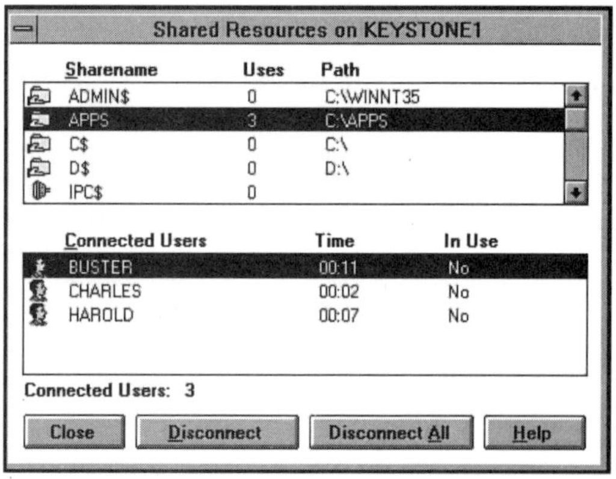

Figure 18.5
The Shared Resources dialog box for a server.

Administrators and Server Managers can take the following actions with connected users displayed in this window:

- To disconnect a single user from all connected resources, select the user in the Connected Users box and click the Disconnect button. You will need to confirm this action.

- To disconnect all users from a share, select the share in the Sharename box and click the Disconnect All button

Disconnecting a user does not log out the user. Disconnecting simply closes any resources to which the user is connected.

Viewing and Closing Open Resources

After a user opens a shared resource, it is listed in the Open Resources dialog box that is displayed by clicking the In Use button in the computer Properties box (see fig. 18.6).

Unlike the User Sessions and Shared Resources dialog boxes, the Open Resources dialog box only displays resources that actually are opened by users. This information is especially useful when you are attempting to manage an open resource, because open resources cannot be copied, deleted, or modified. With the Open Resources dialog box, you can identify users who are holding a resource open so that you can ask them to release it.

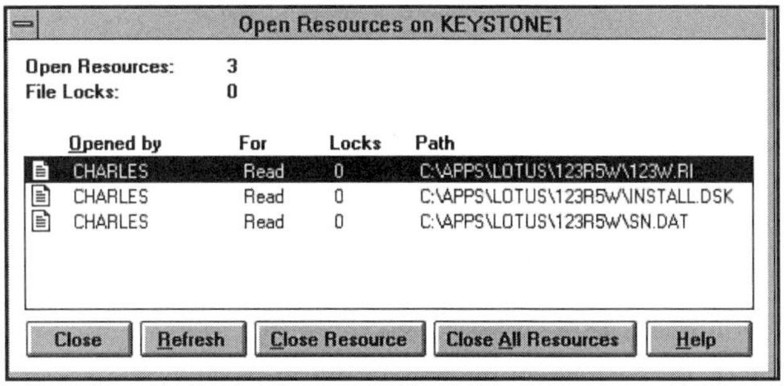

Figure 18.6

The Open Resources dialog box.

If you must force users off a resource, you have two choices:

- **Close Resource.** Closes a single, selected resource.
- **Close All Resources.** Forces all resources on the server to close.

Managing Directory Replication

The directory-replication feature accessed by the **R**eplication button in the computer Properties dialog box brings up the Directory Replication dialog box. This feature is thoroughly explained in Chapter 21, "Managing Directory Replication."

Configuring Computer Alerts

The Alerts button in the computer Properties dialog box reveals the Alerts dialog box shown in figure 18.7. In this box, you determine which users and computers receive administrative alerts that are generated by this computer.

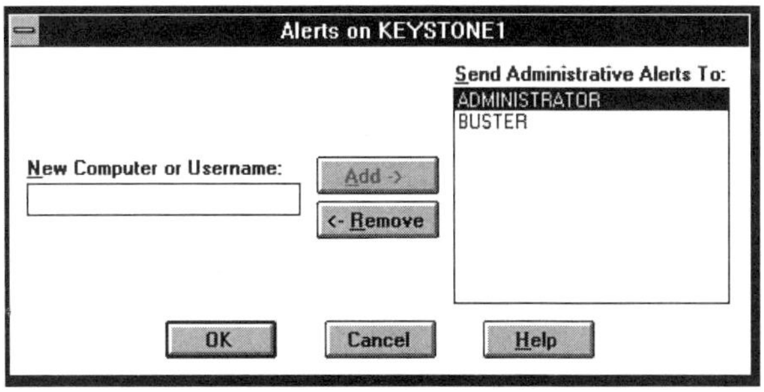

Figure 18.7

The Alerts dialog box.

- To have a user or computer receive alerts from this computer, type the user or computer name in the New Computer or Username box and choose Add.
- To disable alerts for a user or computer, select the user or computer in the Send Administrative Alerts To box and choose Remove.

Note The Alerter service must be running for alerts to be sent.

Managing Shared Directories

Shared directories can be managed with File Manager or with the Shared Directories dialog box which is accessed by choosing the Shared Directories command from the Computer menu of Server Manager. The Shared Directories dialog box is shown in figure 18.8.

This is the place where you can see *all* the shares on a server. Each share type has a distinctive symbol, as you can see in figure 18.9. You can manage these shares using techniques similar to those used with File Manager and Print Manager.

Figure 18.8

The Server Manager Shared Directories dialog box.

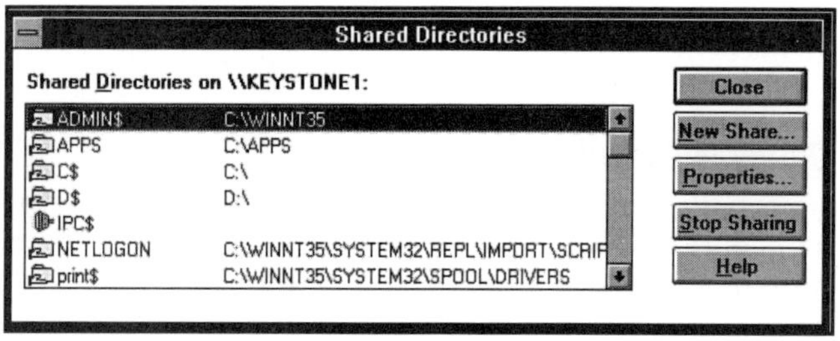

Managing Computer Services

You can start the Service Manager by choosing the Services command from the Computer menu. The Service Manager is described later in this chapter in the "Service Manager" section.

Sending Messages to Users

You can choose the Send Message command from the Computer menu to communicate with users on the network. Simply enter the text of the message in the Send Message dialog box, as shown in figure 18.9, and click OK to send the message to all users who are connected to the server. Only connected users receive the message—not all users in the domain.

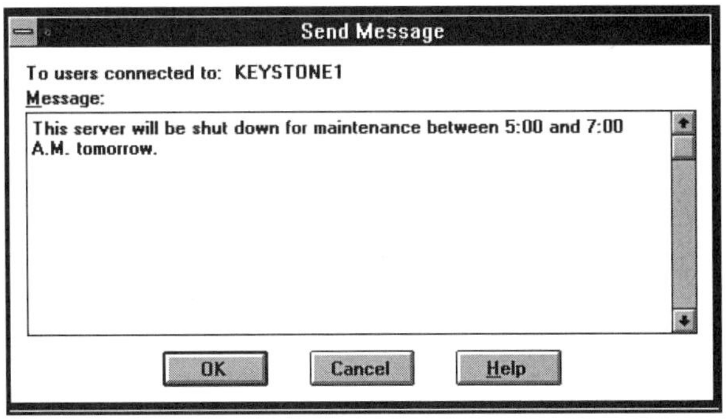

Figure 18.9
Sending a message to connected users.

Users of Windows 3.*x* must be running the Windows Popup program. See Chapter 13, "Using Windows and DOS Clients," for information on configuring this option.

Promoting a Domain Controller

The next option on the Computers menu is Promote to Primary Domain Controller. Chapter 9 explains how this option is used to promote a backup domain controller to enable it to be a primary domain controller.

Synchronizing the Domain Database

On rare occasions, the copies of the domain database on the various backup domain controllers can get out of synchronization with the database on the primary domain controller. Synchronization is performed automatically, but also can be initiated manually.

To resynchronize the database of a single BDC, follow these steps:

- Select the computer name of the BDC in the Server Manager window.
- Choose Synchronize with Primary Domain Controller from the Computer menu.

The database on the BDC is resynchronized with the database on the domain PDC.

To resynchronize all BDCs in the domain, follow these steps:

1. Select the computer name of the domain PDC in the Server Manager window.
2. Choose Synchronize Entire Domain from the Computer menu.

The database is copied from the PDC to all BDCs in the domain, which can be a time-consuming process.

Adding and Removing Domain Computers

Chapter 9 explains how the Add to Domain and Remove from Domain commands on the Computer menu are used.

Selecting a Domain to Manage

By default, Server Manager selects your logon domain to manage. You can change to another trusting domain by choosing the Select Domain command from the Computer menu.

The View Menu

Use options in the View menu to determine which computers are displayed in the Server Manager window. You have the following choices:

- **Servers.** Choose to display only Windows NT Servers.
- **Workstations.** Choose to display only Windows NT Workstations.
- **All.** Choose to display all Windows NT computers.
- **Show Domain Members Only.** Check this option to limit displayed computers to computers that are members of the current domain.

The Options Menu

Commands in the Options menu enable you to configure the operation of Server Manager. Two of the commands on this menu follow:

- **Save Settings on Exit.** If you want Server Manager to retain your current setup each time you quit, check this option. If you want to have Server Manager restore default settings or savings you saved at an earlier time, remove the check from this option.
- **Font.** Use this option to select a new font to be used in Server Manager. A good use of this option is to select an enlarged font for an administrator who has a vision impairment.

Service Manager

The Service Manager can be started in two ways:

- Choosing the Services command from the Server Manager Computers menu
- Double-clicking on the Services icon in the Control Panel

Starting Service Manager displays the Services dialog box, shown in figure 18.10.

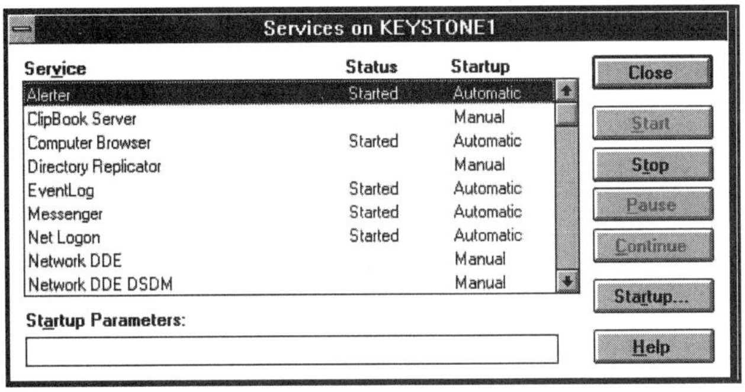

Figure 18.10
The Services dialog box in Server Manager.

Table 18.1 lists the services this utility offers.

TABLE 18.1
Service Manager Utilities

Service	Function
Alerter	Sends alert messages to designated recipients, as declared in the Alerts dialog box of Server Properties. Requires the Messenger service.
ClipBook Server	Supports Clipbook Viewer, and enables remote Clipbooks to see local pages.
Computer Browser	Maintains resource lists used by applications when browsing the network.
Directory Replicator	Supports directory and file replication between computers.
EventLog	Writes application, security, and system events in the Event log.

continues

Table 18.1, Continued
Service Manager Utilities

Service	Function
Messenger	Transmits and receives messages sent by the Alerter service or by Administrators.
Net Logon	Authenticates user logons. Synchronizes the domain database among domain controllers in a domain.
Network DDE	Transports and provides security for network DDE conversations.
Network DDE DSDM	The DDE share database manager (DDSM) supervises shared DDE conversations.
NT LM Security Support Provider	Provides security to RPC applications using transports other than named pipes.
Remote Procedure Call Locator	Provides RPC name service to distributed applications. RPC servers register names with the RPC Locator Service. RPC clients query the RPC Locator Service for server applications.
Remote Procedure Call Service	The RPC subsystem for Windows NT.
Schedule	Enables delayed jobs to be scheduled and supports their execution.
Server	Remote procedure call (RPC) support for file, print, and named pipes sharing.
Spooler	Supports print spooler.
UPS	Monitors uninterruptible power supply and responds to UPC conditions.
Workstation	Provides workstation network connectivity.

Starting, Stopping, and Pausing Services

Select a service and choose the Start, Stop, or Pause button to change the status of the service.

To pass arguments to a service, type them in the Startup Parameter box before clicking the Start button.

Note The Server service supports all remote user connections. Stopping the Server service disconnects all users, including Administrators. Therefore, remote Administrators cannot stop and restart this service; it must be restarted locally.

Before stopping the Server service, use the Send Message command to alert users so that they can close open files and prepare to be disconnected.

When the Server service is paused, members of the Administrators and Server Operators groups can establish new connections with the server, but other users cannot.

Configuring Services

Follow these steps to define the characteristics of a service:

1. Select a service in the Services window.
2. Choose the Startup button to display the service startup dialog box shown in figure 18.11.
3. Choose the service startup type from the following:
   - **Automatic.** The service starts when the server is booted.
   - **Manual.** The service must be started manually from the Services dialog box.
   - **Disabled.** The service cannot be started.
4. Choose System Account if the service should log on using the system account. This setting is used for almost all services.
5. Choose This Account to have the service log on with a user account. Only the Directory Replicator and Schedule services log on using other accounts. See Chapter 17, "Backing Up Files," for information about setting up the Schedule service. See Chapter 21, "Managing Directory Replication," for information about setting up the Directory Replicator service.

   If This Account has been chosen, enter a user account and passwords in the appropriate boxes.
6. Click on OK.
7. Start the service.

Service startup settings take effect only when the service is started. A running service must be stopped and restarted if start-up settings change.

Figure 18.11

The Service Startup dialog box.

The System Utility

Double-clicking on the System icon in the Control Panel reveals the System dialog box shown in figure 18.12. This dialog box is used to configure several Windows NT settings.

Figure 18.12

The System dialog box.

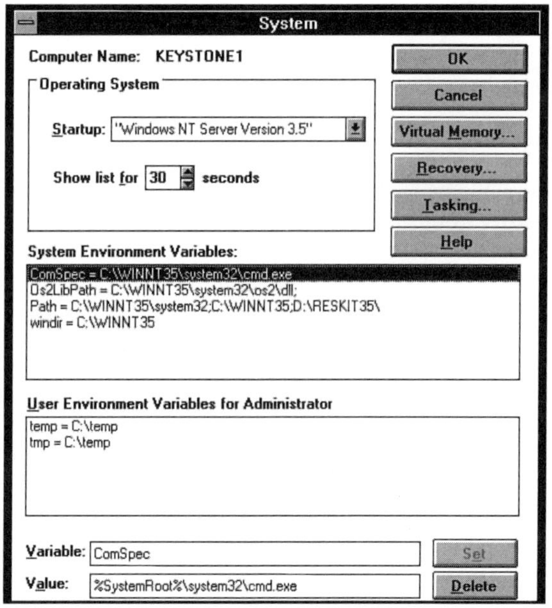

Configuring the Server Bootup Selections

Windows NT always makes two options available during bootup:

- Booting with your custom settings
- Booting with default settings, including VGA video

These options are defined in the BOOT.INI file, which typically looks like this:

```
[boot loader]
timeout=30
default=multi(0)disk(0)rdisk(0)partition(1)\WINNT35

[operating systems]
multi(0)disk(0)rdisk(0)partition(1)\WINNT35="Windows NT Server Version 3.5"
multi(0)disk(0)rdisk(0)partition(1)\WINNT35="Windows NT Server Version 3.5 [VGA
mode]" /basevideo
```

The `[operating systems]` section defines start-up options for the computer. More than two start-up options can be configured, but generally you will see only the two default options.

The path to each start-up option is described by an Advanced RISC Computer (ARC) path convention, which is described in Chapter 16, "Managing Disk Storage."

The System dialog box displays the names of the options, such as Windows NT Server Version 3.5 (VGA mode). You can configure the start-up defaults by editing the `[boot loader]` section of BOOT.INI, but it is better to make the changes in System. It seldom is necessary to directly manipulate Windows NT configuration files, and doing so can be hazardous to your system.

To select the startup configuration, choose a configuration in the **S**tartup box.

To specify the time that the start-up configuration menu is displayed, edit the time in the Show list for box. I don't recommend that you set this value to 0, because that will make it difficult to start the computer in default VGA mode.

Managing Environment Variables

Windows NT is much less dependent on environment variables than is Windows 3.*x* or DOS. Nevertheless, a few environment variables are maintained. In fact, two sets are available:

- **System environment variables.** Used by the system regardless of the user who is logged on.
- **User environment variables.** Can be customized for each user.

To delete a variable, select the variable and choose the Delete button.

To add an environment variable, follow these steps:

1. Select the System Environment Variables or the User Environment Variables box.
2. Enter the variable name in the Variable box.
3. Enter a value for the variable in the Value box
4. Choose Set.

To edit an environment variable, follow these steps:

1. Select the variable.
2. Change the value in the Value box.
3. Choose Set.

Changes made to system environment variables take effect the next time the computer is started.

Changes made to user environment variables take effect the next time the user logs on to the computer.

Note It is instructive to select a system environment variable and observe the value in the Value box. Notice that the values make extensive use of Windows NT variables such as %SystemRoot%.

Use extreme caution when changing system environment variables. Most are vital to the proper functioning of Windows NT.

Configuring Virtual Memory

Windows NT uses the virtual memory capability of Intel 386 and later processors to significantly increase the memory that is available to the operating system. Virtual memory uses disk storage to simulate RAM—a process called *paging*, which uses a *paging file* to create virtual memory. Although virtual memory is much slower than RAM, it is much better to have slow memory than to run out.

Microsoft recommends that you create a paging file for each volume. Depending on the capabilities of the computer hard drive controller, multiple paging files can enhance virtual memory performance.

A paging file is created automatically when the system disk is created. Paging files for other disks must be created manually. A minimum and maximum size is declared for each paging file. With NTFS volumes, Windows NT will automatically increase the sizes of paging files as required. If multiple paging files exist, size increases will distributed across all paging files.

Administrators can change the values in the Virtual Memory dialog box, which is accessed by clicking the Virtual **M**emory button in the System dialog box. The Virtual Memory dialog box is shown in figure 18.13.

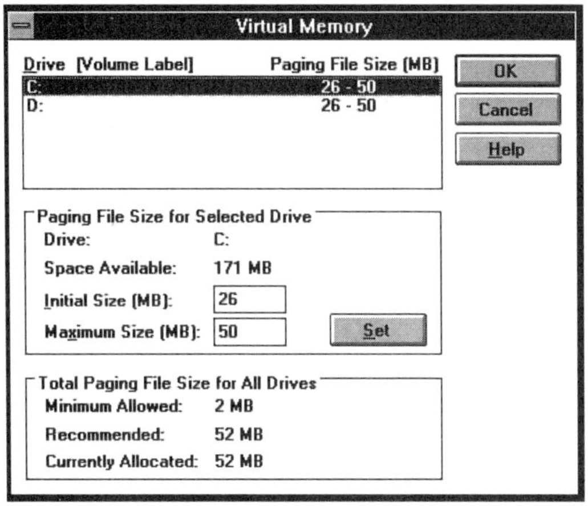

Figure 18.13

Configuring Windows NT virtual memory.

To create or modify the paging file for a volume, follow these steps:

1. Select a volume in the **D**rive box.
2. Enter the paging file parameters in the Paging File Size for Selected Drive box. A recommended total value is displayed in the Total Paging File Size for All Drives box.
3. Click on OK to save the changes.
4. Restart the system to have changes go into effect.

Note Virtual memory is stored in a file named PAGEFILE.SYS, which cannot be deleted under Windows NT. If the file is deleted under another operating system, it is re-created when Windows NT is restarted.

Configuring System Recovery Options

When Windows NT Server encounters a critical error, called a *STOP error* or a *fatal system error*, the system records an event in the System log, transmits an Administrator alert, and optionally reboots itself. Because Windows NT Server reboots itself without waiting for an Administrator to intervene, downtime is reduced.

The **R**ecovery button in the System dialog box enables you to control the behavior of Windows NT Server when STOP errors are encountered. The options are shown in figure 18.14. The primary reason for disabling options in this box is to save memory. Up to about 70 KB of memory can be saved, because recovery drivers do not need to be kept in memory.

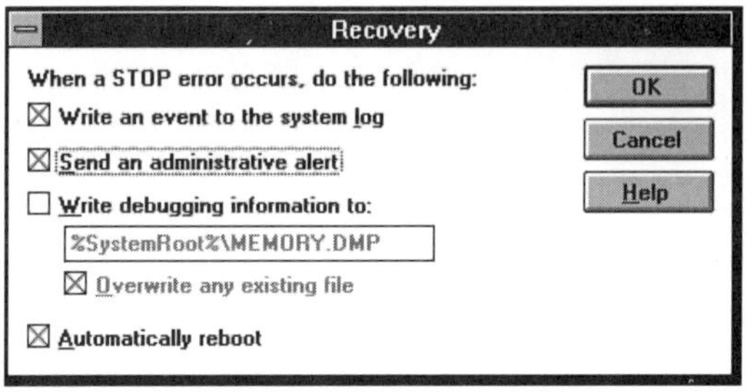

Figure 18.14
Windows NT Server recovery options.

Options in the Recovery dialog box follow:

- **Write an event in the system log.** You probably will not want to disable this option, because it's your second best clue about the error event that occurred.
- **Send an administrative alert.** Again, when an error occurs, you really want to know about it. So you probably don't want to disable this option either.
- **Write debugging information to.** By default, Windows NT Server writes the contents of system memory to a file. This file can be used by Microsoft Product Support to diagnose problems, because it is a complete snapshot of memory at the time of the error. The box associated with this option declares the name of the log file.
- **Overwrite any existing file.** If this box is checked, a new memory dump overwrites any previous dump that is recorded in the log file. I recommend that you leave this option enabled and make a copy of the dump file when a fatal error occurs.
- **Automatically reboot.** Disable this option to prevent the automatic reboot.

Configuring Windows NT Multitasking Behavior

The Tasking button in the System dialog box brings up the Tasking dialog box shown in figure 18.15. For a dedicated server, you should de-emphasize foreground tasks and select the option Foreground and Background Applications **E**qually Responsive.

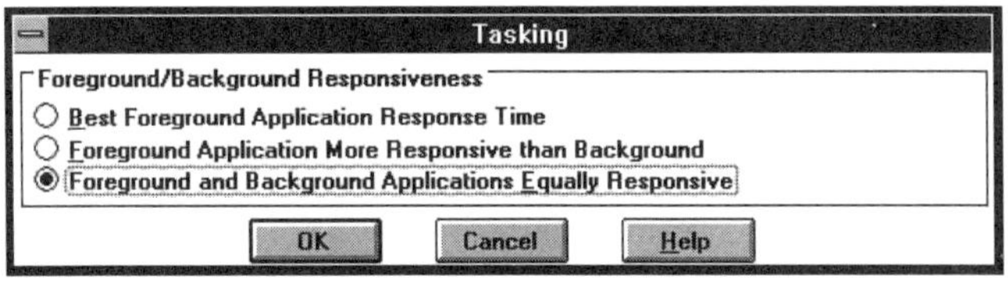

Figure 18.15

The Windows NT Tasking dialog box.

Using Windows NT Diagnostics

The Windows NT Diagnostics (WINMSD) program enables you to observe configuration information for some features of the server hardware and software. It isn't a full-blown diagnostics program. In particular, Windows NT Diagnostics is not capable of testing hardware. For that, you should obtain a third-party program. However, third party-programs generally are oriented around DOS, so you would need to bring the server down to perform any diagnostics. Windows NT Diagnostics is a Windows NT program that can be run while the server is operating and, of course, it is free.

The Windows NT Diagnostics icon is installed in the Administrative Tools program group. When you run the utility, you see the window shown in figure 18.16. All the information options of Windows NT Diagnostics are reached through this function menu.

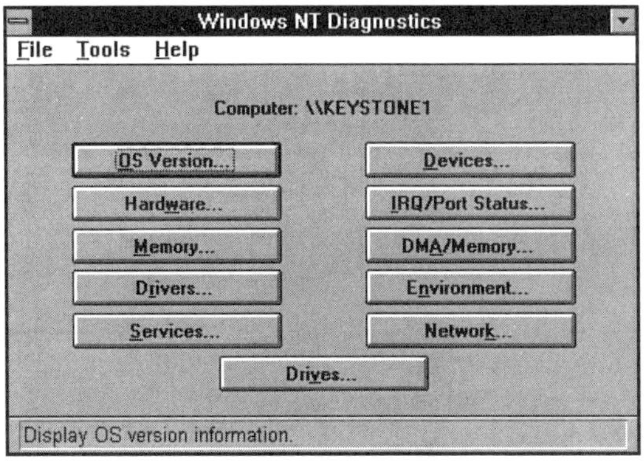

Figure 18.16

The main function menu of Windows NT Diagnostics.

The following sections cover the various options.

The File menu enables you to save or print a WINMSD report.

The Tools menu has options for starting Event Viewer, Registry Editor, and Disk Administrator.

Note As you click each button, a brief description appears in the bottom box of the option menu. There is no help for this utility, and that message is about all the assistance Microsoft gives you. Fortunately, most of the information is self-explanatory.

OS Version

OS Version information is shown in figure 18.17.

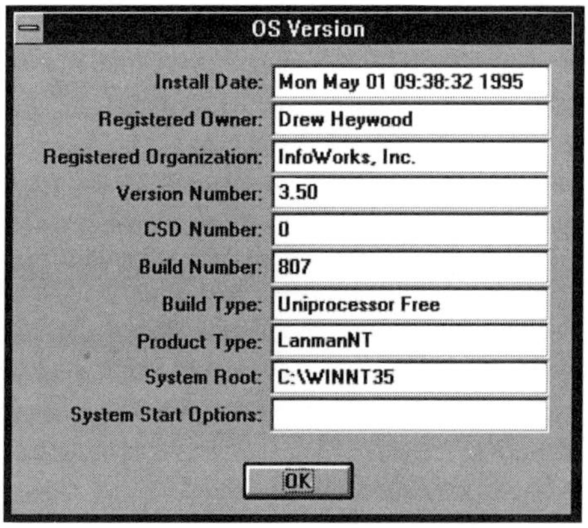

Figure 18.17
OS version information.

Most of the information is self-explanatory. A few, however, require further explanation:

- **CSD Number.** This entry refers to *Corrective Service Diskettes*—corrective disks issued from time to time to fix bugs. If a CSD is installed on the server, it is identified here.
- **Build Number.** When a complex software product is being developed, the programmers periodically collect all the modules and build a complete copy of the operating system at that point. Microsoft calls these "snapshots" *builds.* As

beta programs progress, different builds are issued—some for internal use, and some for use by outside beta testers. After a product ships, the build number generally does not change, and Microsoft relies on CSDs and other patches to add or modify features.

Most of the information on this screen is changed with the installation program.

Note When you display an information box, your cursor turns into an insertion point. You can select text with the mouse. This feature enables you to copy information in WINMSD that can be pasted into other programs, including the Registry in some cases.

Unfortunately, despite the text cursors, all you can do is look. You can't even change your name. To change information, you need to use other utilities such as the Control Panel or the Registry Editor.

Hardware

An example of the Hardware screen is shown in figure 18.18. This screen gives you a pretty good look at your server's hardware environment. It's handy to have if you need to report a problem to Microsoft.

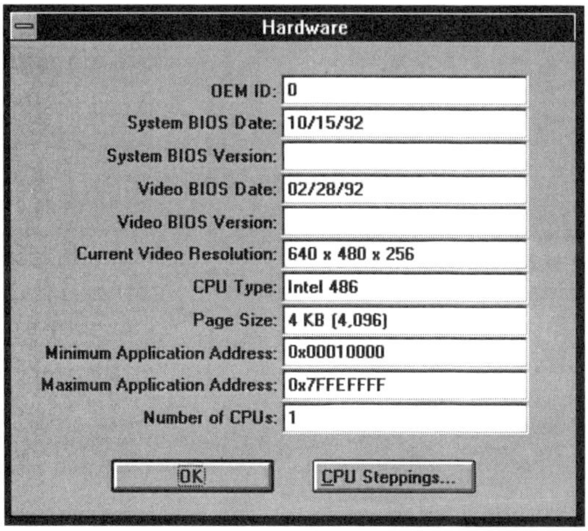

Figure 18.18
Hardware information.

Some of the options on this screen follow:

- **Page Size.** This entry refers to the amount of memory that is swapped between main memory and the virtual memory paging file, which was described earlier in the chapter.
- **Minimum Application Address and Maximum Application Address.** These entries define the range of memory that is available for use by applications.
- **CPU Steppings.** This button brings up the screen shown in figure 18.19. Windows NT can support up to 32 processors. The numbers on this screen describe the capabilities of different brands and models of processors.

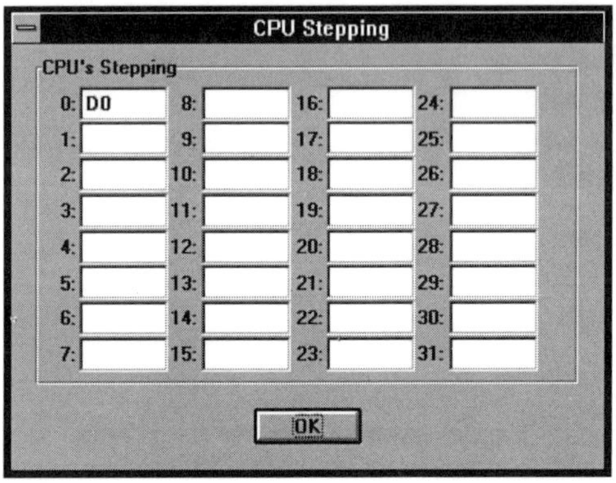

Figure 18.19
CPU steppings.

Memory

Figure 18.20 shows the information Windows NT Diagnostics can display about memory. The Memory Load Index field indicates the amount of memory that is currently in use. A bar graph in this box shows green from 0 percent to 50 percent, yellow from 50 percent to 75 percent, and red at higher values. This is the best way to find out whether you need to add memory.

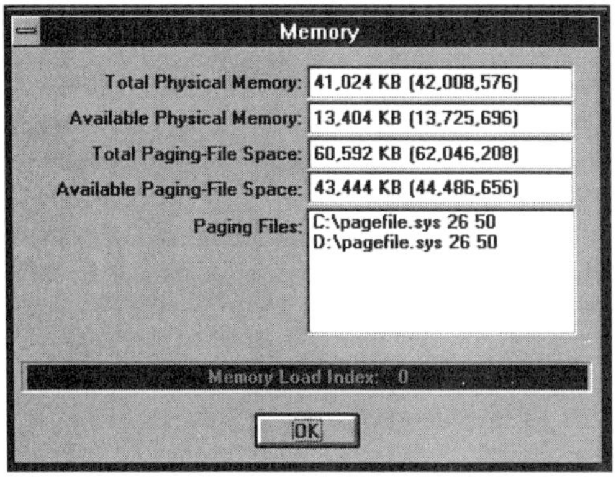

Figure 18.20
Memory information.

Drivers

The drivers that are running on Windows NT are listed in the Driver List dialog box shown in figure 18.21. Drivers that are subject to administrative control are installed, activated, and deactivated from tools in the Control Panel, including the Services utility.

You can display more detail for each driver by selecting the driver and clicking the **Driver Details** button. The detailed information for one driver is shown in figure 18.22.

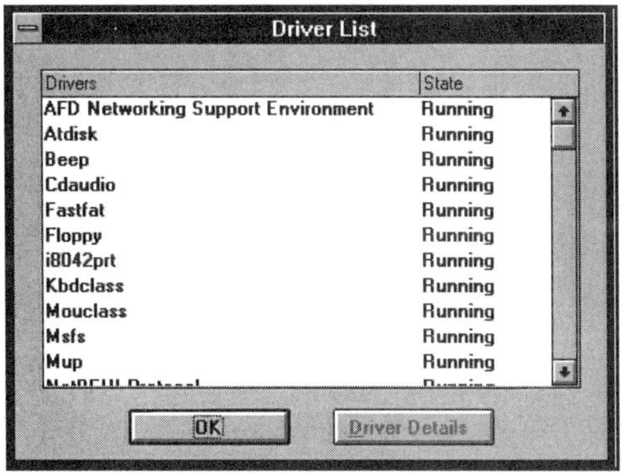

Figure 18.21
Driver information.

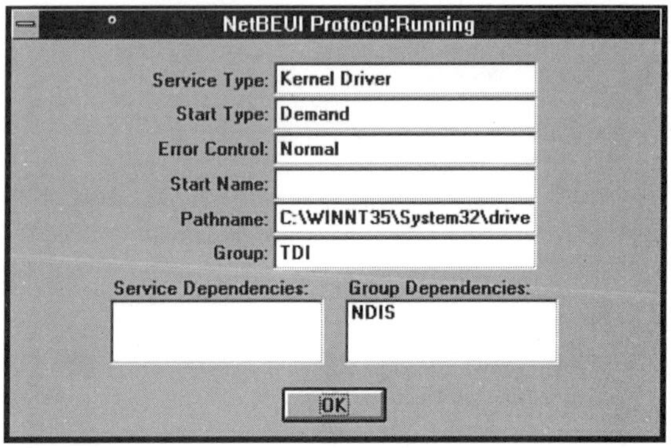

Figure 18.22

Details about the NetBEUI Protocol driver.

Services

The display shown in figure 18.23 contains information about the services that are managed with the Control Panel Services utility. Details about each service can be displayed by selecting the service and choosing **D**isplay Service. An example of a detailed display is shown in figure 18.24. Many features should be familiar to you if you have used the Services utility to configure services. See the discussion about the Service Manager earlier in this chapter for more information.

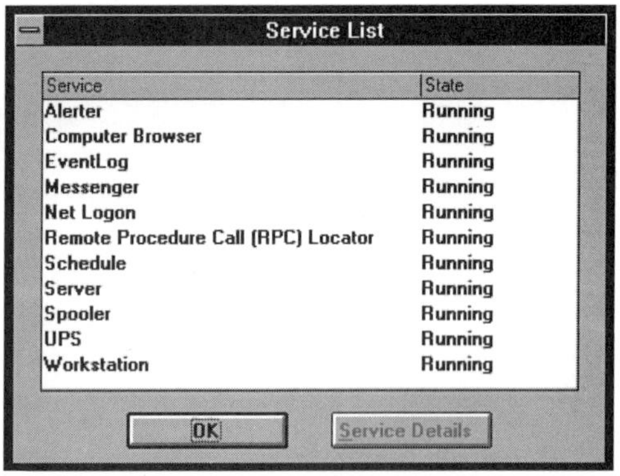

Figure 18.23

Service information.

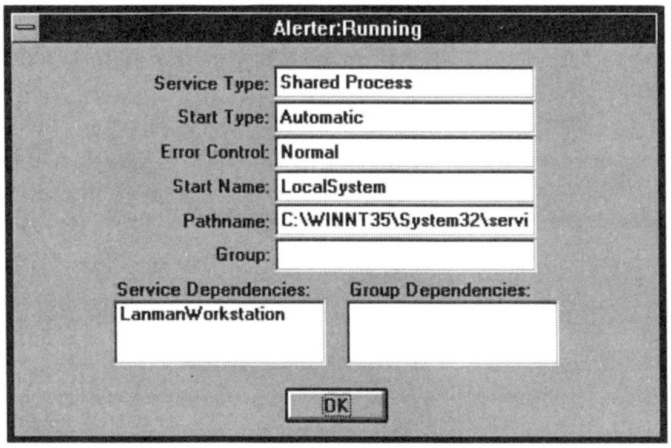

Figure 18.24

Details about a service.

Devices

The devices information shown in figure 18.25 puts some of the information in the Registry in human-readable form. Later in the chapter, you see how this information is related to the Registry. You can access a detailed display about each device by selecting the device and choosing Device Details. An example is shown in figure 18.26.

The detailed display shows the settings of the device. This information is useful when new hardware is being added and you need to determine available settings.

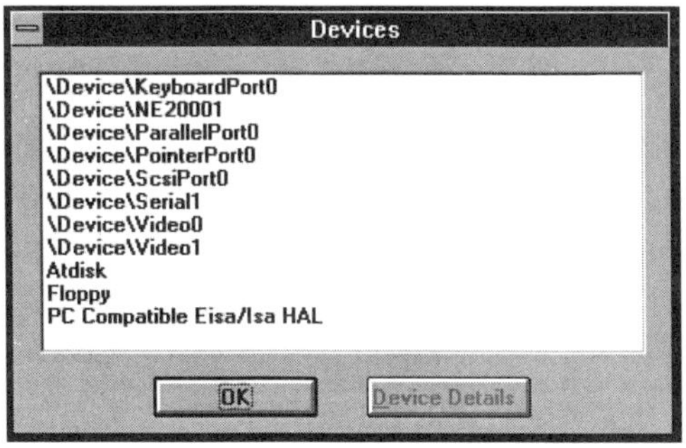

Figure 18.25

Devices information.

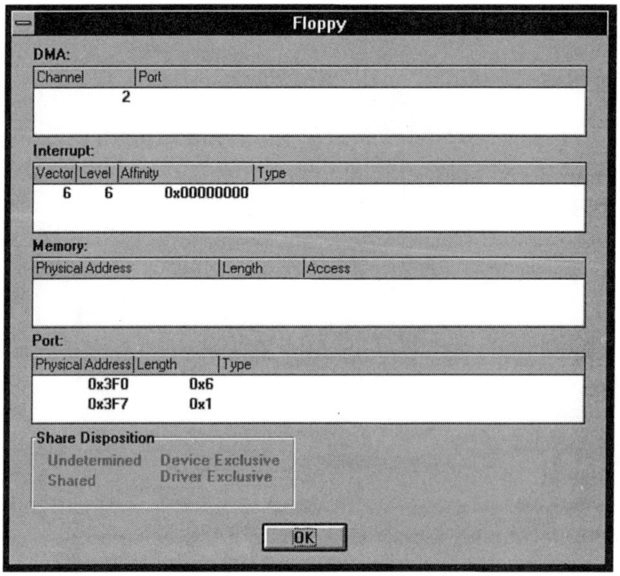

Figure 18.26

Detailed information about a device.

IRQ/Port Status

The Interrupts/Ports screen summarizes the interrupts and ports that are in use on the computer (see fig. 18.27). Like the information on the Devices screen, this screen is useful for identifying free interrupts and ports that can be used to add new hardware.

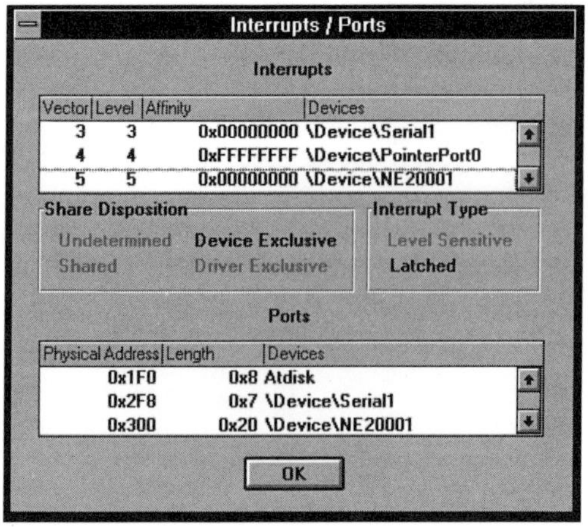

Figure 18.27

Interrupt and port information.

DMA/Memory

The DMA box of the DMA/Memory dialog box lists dynamic memory access (DMA) addresses that have been assigned to equipment (see fig. 18.28). Relatively few devices use DMA, and only the Floppy device is listed for this computer.

The Memory box lists memory blocks that are reserved for hardware devices. The block starting at 0×A0000 is reserved for the VGA video display adapter.

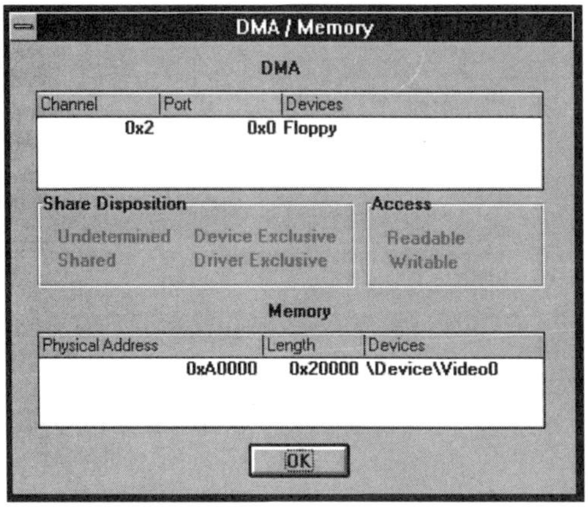

Figure 18.28
DMA and memory information.

Environment

Earlier in this chapter, the System utility was examined along with its role of defining the computer environment. The Environment screen in WINMSD displays this same information in non-editable form (see fig. 18.29).

Network

The Network screen displays information that is not readily available elsewhere (see fig. 18.30). It is extremely useful for you to examine this screen as you configure and reconfigure your server. If you are running a service in the background with its own logon name, it appears as a logon count in the Network Info for box, for example.

Figure 18.29

Environment information.

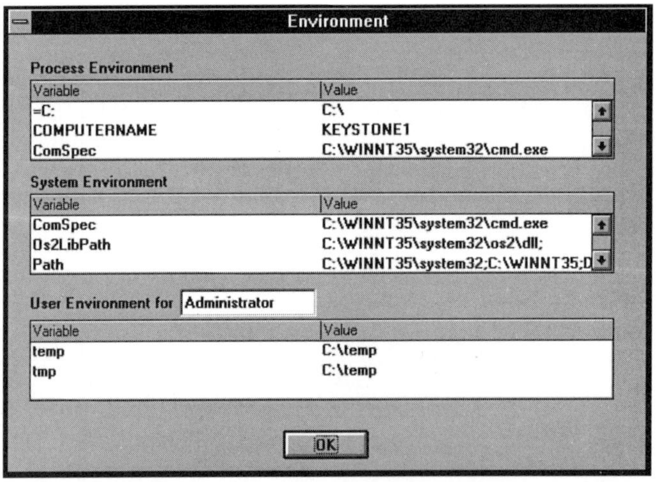

Figure 18.30

Network information.

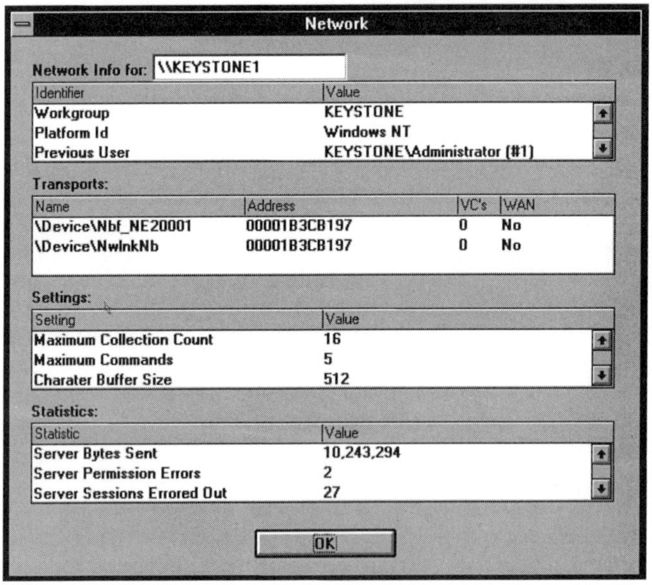

The sections in the Network screen follow:

- **Network Info for.** This box lists information about the computer's network configuration and currently logged-on users.
- **Transports.** This box describes the transport protocol layers that are installed along with configuration information.
- **Settings.** Shows the current values of numerous Windows NT Server settings.
- **Statistics.** WINMSD keeps a running total of dozens of events that occur as the server operates. Of particular interest are various reports of errors. If you see that the Network Errors statistic is climbing, for example, you might suspect a problem in your network hardware or cabling.

Drives

The Drive Information screen lists all the drives that are configured on your system (see fig. 18.31). You see information about every disk you have configured in Disk Administrator (see Chapter 16), so you will not necessarily see one drive for each physical hard drive.

To see details about a drive, select it and choose Details. An example of a detailed display is shown in figure 18.32. Besides the physical characteristics of the drive, the display describes the file system used to format the disk along with significant characteristics of that file system.

NTFS is the only file system for which you see `Unicode Stored on Disk`. *Unicode* is a means of representing many different character sets so that applications can be written to support languages that could not be comprehended by ASCII.

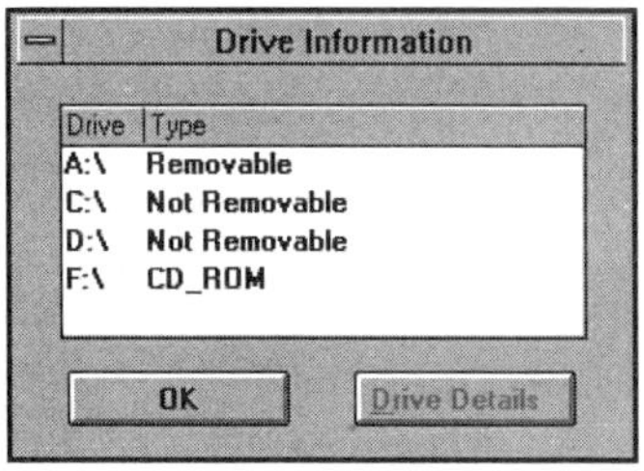

Figure 18.31

Drive information.

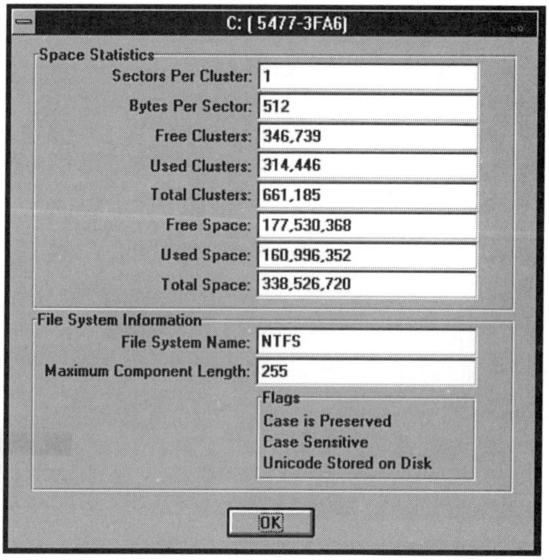

Figure 18.32
Details about a drive.

Auditing Files and Printers

Auditing is a useful function in any large LAN. Auditing is a way of gathering statistics about how resources are being used. More important, auditing is a way to determine who is responsible if resources are being misused. As LANs take on increasingly critical tasks, it becomes more desirable to implement auditing.

Windows NT Server enables you to audit the use of domains, files, directories, and printers.

Note You must be logged on as a member of the Administrators group to audit files and directories.

Auditing Domains

Domain auditing is configured by using User Manager for Domains. In some ways, domain auditing is the most important auditing category, particularly if your network is part of a wide area network. WANs—particularly when they participate in the Internet—are more vulnerable to intruders than networks that are confined to a company's own buildings. Domain auditing can tell you whether large numbers of attempted security breeches are taking place, which might indicate that someone is trying to break into your system.

To define the audit policy for a domain, follow these steps:

1. Open User Manager for Domains.
2. Choose the Select Domain command from the User menu to select the domain to be audited.
3. Choose Audit These Events to activate auditing for the domain.
4. Choose the Audit command from the Policies menu to display the Audit Policy dialog box shown in figure 18.33. Check the events to be audited.
5. Click on OK to save the auditing policy.

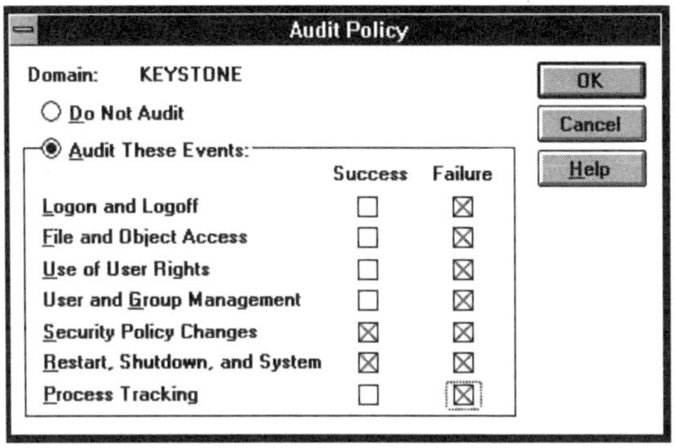

Figure 18.33
Setting the domain audit policy.

The following domain events can be audited:

- **Logon and Logoff.** A user logs on, logs off, or makes a connection through the network.
- **File and Object Access.** A directory or file was accessed that had been configured for auditing in File Manager. A print job was sent to a printer that was configured for auditing in Print Manager.
- **Use of User Rights.** Use of a user right apart from rights related to logging on or off.
- **User and Group Management.** The following activities are audited with respect to user accounts or groups: creation, changing, deleting, renaming, disabling or enabling, and password changes.
- **Security Policy Changes.** Any change to user rights, audit, or trust relationships policies.

- **Restart, Shutdown, and System.** Shutting down or restarting the server. Any action that affects system security or the security log.
- **Process Tracking.** Program activation, process exit, handle duplication, and indirect object access.

Tip

When you are setting up auditing, audit the success and failure of everything. That makes it easy to determine that you have set up your auditing to track the resources you want. When you are confident that you are tracking the correct resources, pare back the audited events to the events you really want to know about.

Auditing Directories and Files

The auditing of directories and files is managed through File Manager. Setting up auditing is a simple matter of declaring the groups or users whose use of a file or directory will be audited along with the events to be audited. Auditing is available only for NTFS volumes.

To view or change auditing for a directory or file, follow these steps:

1. Select the directory or file to be audited in File Manager.
2. Choose Auditing from the Security menu to display the Directory Auditing dialog box shown in figure 18.34.
3. Check Replace Auditing on Subdirectories if all subdirectories of this directory are to be audited in the same fashion.
4. Check Replace Auditing on Existing Files if existing files should be audited in the same fashion. If this box is not checked, auditing affects the directory only.
5. To add a user or group, choose Add to display a Browse list. Select each name to be added in the Browse list and click the Add button. Click OK when all desired names have been added. When you return to the Auditing window, the names are listed in the Name box.
6. To remove a user or group, select the entry in the Name box and choose Remove.
7. For each event that is to be audited, check the appropriate box in the Events to Audit box.
8. Choose OK to save the auditing information.

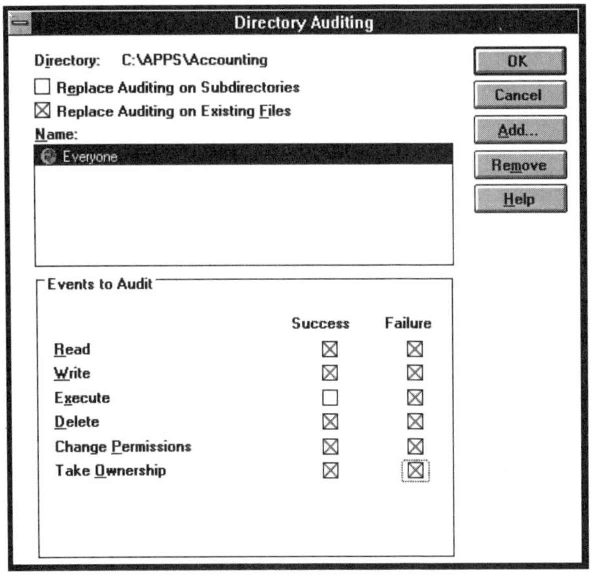

Figure 18.34

Auditing a directory.

Tables 18.2 and 18.3 summarize the actions that are audited by each event that can be checked in the Auditing dialog box.

Table 18.2

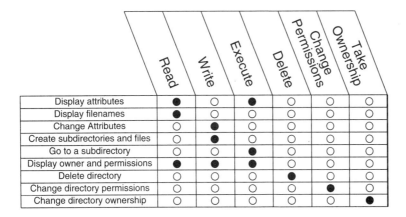

Actions audited by directory audit events.

	Read	Write	Execute	Delete	Change Permissions	Take Ownership
Display attributes	●	○	●	○	○	○
Display filenames	●	○	○	○	○	○
Change Attributes	○	●	○	○	○	○
Create subdirectories and files	○	●	○	○	○	○
Go to a subdirectory	○	○	●	○	○	○
Display owner and permissions	●	●	●	○	○	○
Delete directory	○	○	○	●	○	○
Change directory permissions	○	○	○	○	●	○
Change directory ownership	○	○	○	○	○	●

Note Directory and file events are audited only if you have activated **F**ile and Object Access auditing in the Audit Policy for the domain. The procedure for setting the domain audit policy is described in the preceding section.

Table 18.3

Actions audited by file audit events.

	Read	Write	Execute	Delete	Change Permissions	Take Ownership
Display file attributes	●	○	●	○	○	○
Read file data	●	○	○	○	○	○
Display owner and permissions	●	●	●	○	○	○
Change file attributes	○	●	○	○	○	○
Change file attributes	○	●	○	○	○	○
Change file data	○	○	●	○	○	○
Execute program file	○	○	○	●	○	○
Change file permissions	○	○	○	○	●	○
Change file ownership	○	○	○	○	○	●

Auditing Printers

Printing is a service that often is abused. If you don't want users printing football pools on the $10,000 color printer, or if you want to know which user is going though all those reams of paper, printer auditing might give you the support you need.

Printer auditing is configured with Print Manager. To configure auditing for a printer, follow these steps:

1. Select the printer or window or icon for the printer to be audited.
2. Choose Auditing from the Security menu. The Printer Auditing dialog box appears, as shown in figure 18.35.
3. To add a user or group, choose Add to display a Browse list. Select each name to be added in the Browse list and choose the Add button. Click OK when all desired names have been added. When you return to the Auditing window, the names are listed in the Name box.
4. To remove a user or group, select the entry in the Name box and choose Remove.
5. For each event that is to be audited, check the appropriate box in the Events to Audit box.
6. Click on OK to save the auditing information.

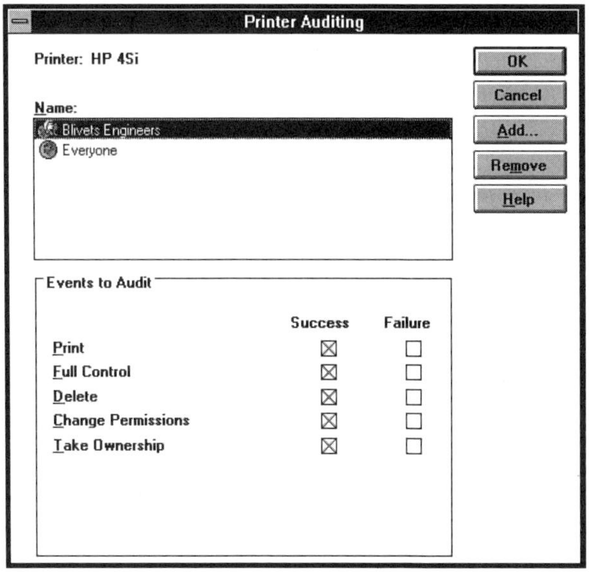

Figure 18.35
Configuring printer auditing.

The printer events that can be audited follow:

- **Print.** Printing documents.
- **Full Control.** Changing document job settings. Pausing, restarting, moving, and deleting documents.
- **Delete.** Deleting a printer.
- **Change Permissions.** Changing printer permissions.
- **Take Ownership.** Taking ownership of a printer.

Note Printer events are audited only if you have activated File and Object Access auditing in the Audit Policy for the domain. The procedure for setting the domain audit policy is described in the preceding section.

Reviewing the Security Log

All the auditing facilities record their messages in the Security log, which is examined by using the Event Viewer. Figure 18.36 shows an example of Security log entries. Using the Event Viewer is described in the following section.

Security log entries are identified with two icons. A key designates a successful action, and a lock designates an unsuccessful action.

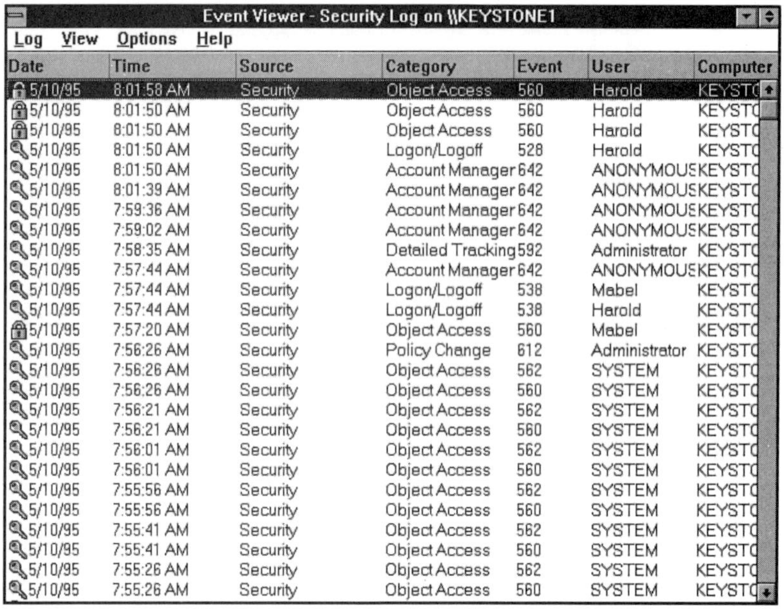

Event Viewer - Security Log on \\KEYSTONE1

Log View Options Help

Date	Time	Source	Category	Event	User	Computer
5/10/95	8:01:58 AM	Security	Object Access	560	Harold	KEYSTC
5/10/95	8:01:50 AM	Security	Object Access	560	Harold	KEYSTC
5/10/95	8:01:50 AM	Security	Object Access	560	Harold	KEYSTC
5/10/95	8:01:50 AM	Security	Logon/Logoff	528	Harold	KEYSTC
5/10/95	8:01:50 AM	Security	Account Manager	642	ANONYMOUS	KEYSTC
5/10/95	8:01:39 AM	Security	Account Manager	642	ANONYMOUS	KEYSTC
5/10/95	7:59:36 AM	Security	Account Manager	642	ANONYMOUS	KEYSTC
5/10/95	7:59:02 AM	Security	Account Manager	642	ANONYMOUS	KEYSTC
5/10/95	7:58:35 AM	Security	Detailed Tracking	592	Administrator	KEYSTC
5/10/95	7:57:44 AM	Security	Account Manager	642	ANONYMOUS	KEYSTC
5/10/95	7:57:44 AM	Security	Logon/Logoff	538	Mabel	KEYSTC
5/10/95	7:57:44 AM	Security	Logon/Logoff	538	Harold	KEYSTC
5/10/95	7:57:20 AM	Security	Object Access	560	Mabel	KEYSTC
5/10/95	7:56:26 AM	Security	Policy Change	612	Administrator	KEYSTC
5/10/95	7:56:26 AM	Security	Object Access	562	SYSTEM	KEYSTC
5/10/95	7:56:26 AM	Security	Object Access	560	SYSTEM	KEYSTC
5/10/95	7:56:21 AM	Security	Object Access	562	SYSTEM	KEYSTC
5/10/95	7:56:21 AM	Security	Object Access	560	SYSTEM	KEYSTC
5/10/95	7:56:01 AM	Security	Object Access	562	SYSTEM	KEYSTC
5/10/95	7:56:01 AM	Security	Object Access	560	SYSTEM	KEYSTC
5/10/95	7:55:56 AM	Security	Object Access	562	SYSTEM	KEYSTC
5/10/95	7:55:56 AM	Security	Object Access	560	SYSTEM	KEYSTC
5/10/95	7:55:41 AM	Security	Object Access	562	SYSTEM	KEYSTC
5/10/95	7:55:41 AM	Security	Object Access	560	SYSTEM	KEYSTC
5/10/95	7:55:26 AM	Security	Object Access	562	SYSTEM	KEYSTC
5/10/95	7:55:26 AM	Security	Object Access	560	SYSTEM	KEYSTC

Figure 18.36

Viewing the Security Log on Event Viewer.

Event Viewer

The Event Viewer is used to examine three Windows NT Server logs:

- **System log.** Records events logged by the Windows NT system.
- **Application log.** Records events logged by applications. A Windows NT Server-aware application might log a message when a file error is encountered, for example.
- Records events that have been selected for auditing in User Manager for Domains, File Manager, or Print Manager.

Viewing Event Logs

To view a log, choose Sy̲stem, Sec̲urity, or A̲pplication from the L̲og menu. Figure 18.37 shows an example of a System log.

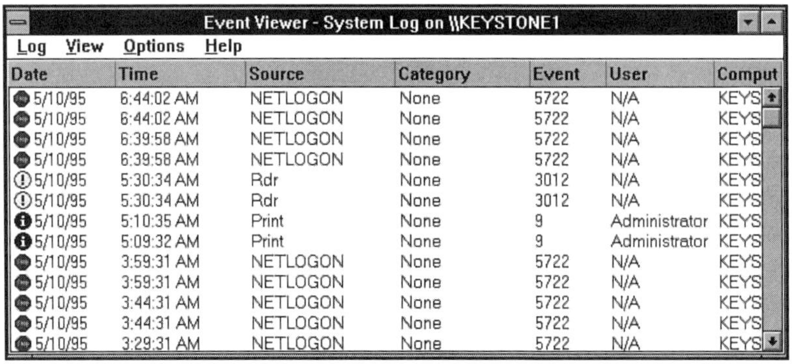
Event Viewer - System Log on \\KEYSTONE1

Log View Options Help

Date	Time	Source	Category	Event	User	Comput
5/10/95	6:44:02 AM	NETLOGON	None	5722	N/A	KEYS
5/10/95	6:44:02 AM	NETLOGON	None	5722	N/A	KEYS
5/10/95	6:39:58 AM	NETLOGON	None	5722	N/A	KEYS
5/10/95	6:39:58 AM	NETLOGON	None	5722	N/A	KEYS
5/10/95	5:30:34 AM	Rdr	None	3012	N/A	KEYS
5/10/95	5:30:34 AM	Rdr	None	3012	N/A	KEYS
5/10/95	5:10:35 AM	Print	None	9	Administrator	KEYS
5/10/95	5:09:32 AM	Print	None	9	Administrator	KEYS
5/10/95	3:59:31 AM	NETLOGON	None	5722	N/A	KEYS
5/10/95	3:59:31 AM	NETLOGON	None	5722	N/A	KEYS
5/10/95	3:44:31 AM	NETLOGON	None	5722	N/A	KEYS
5/10/95	3:44:31 AM	NETLOGON	None	5722	N/A	KEYS
5/10/95	3:29:31 AM	NETLOGON	None	5722	N/A	KEYS

Figure 18.37

Events in the System log.

For each entry, you see the following information in addition to the date and time when the log entry was recorded:

- **Source.** The software that logged the event—either an application name or a component of Windows NT.
- **Category.** An event classification.
- **Event.** Each source is assigned a unique number, which appears in this column.
- **User.** The user name of the account that was logged in when the event was logged.
- **Computer.** The computer name where the event occurred.

To make it easy to visually scan events, each event is labeled with an icon. Figure 18.38 identifies the icons and their meanings.

Figure 18.38

Icons in the Event logs.

Here are more complete descriptions of the events:

- **Information.** Infrequent significant events that describe the successful operation of Windows NT Server services.
- **Warning.** Non-critical errors that may predict future problems.
- **Critical Error.** Data loss or failure of major functions.
- **Success Audit.** Audit events that are associated with the successful execution of an action.
- **Failure Audit.** Audit events that are associated with the unsuccessful execution of an action.

You can display a detailed view of each event by double-clicking the event entry. An example of a detailed display is shown in figure 18.39.

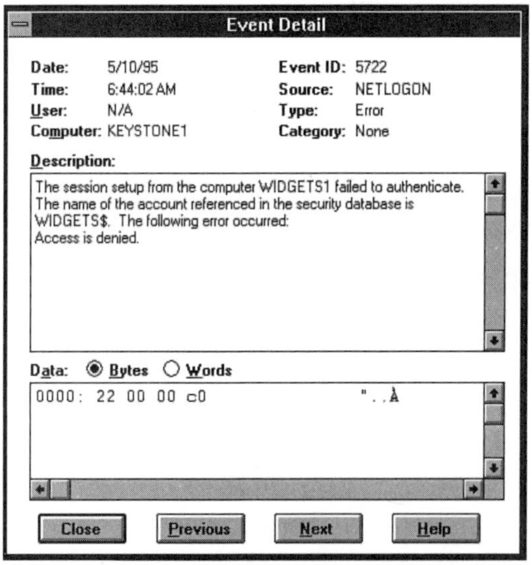

Figure 18.39
Detailed information about an event.

Configuring Event Log Options

The Event Log Settings dialog box enables you to determine how large log files will grow (see fig. 18.40). Unless they are properly controlled, log files can grow to a significant percentage of server file capacity.

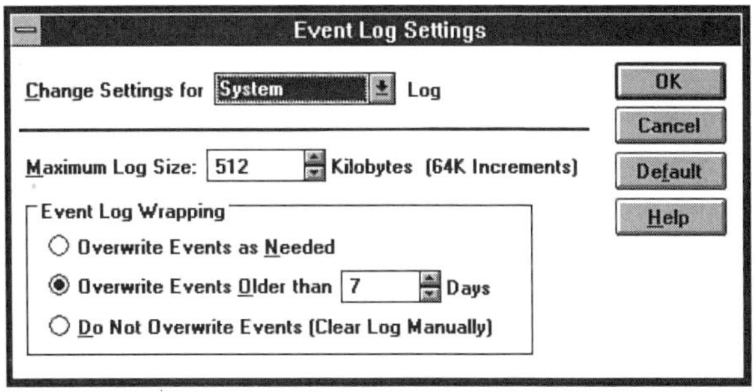

Figure 18.40

The Event Log Settings dialog box.

To configure Event log settings, follow these steps:

1. Choose Log Settings from the Log menu to access the Event Log Settings dialog box.
2. Select a log in the Change Settings for...Log box.
3. Enter a maximum size in the Maximum Log Size box. If the log reaches this size and you have not specified a means of trimming old records, event logging ceases.
4. To have new events overwrite old events after the log is full, choose Overwrite Events as Needed.
5. To limit the log by discarding old records, choose Overwrite Events Older than Days and specify a number in the box. If logs will be archived weekly, a good choice is 7 days.
6. To clear the log manually, choose Do Not Overwrite Events (Clear Log Manually). Avoid using this option unless there are events you cannot afford to miss. Security on a critical server might be an example of such information.
7. Click on OK after the Event log settings are entered.

Clearing a Log

To clear an Event log, follow these steps:

1. Select the log to be cleared from the Log menu.
2. Choose Clear All Events from the Log menu. You are asked to verify your decision to clear the log.

Viewing Specific Events

Event Viewer has several tools that enable you to more easily identify specific events. You can change the order for sorting events and add filters to determine which events are displayed.

Sorting Events

To change the sorting order for events, choose Newest First or Oldest First from the View menu.

Filtering Events

Event logs can grow to be quite large, and you might find yourself wanting to limit the events that are displayed, or limiting yourself to only a specific type of event to enable you to focus on a problem. Event Viewer enables you to filter events in a wide variety of ways.

To filter events, follow these steps:

1. Choose Filter Events from the View menu to display the Filter dialog box shown in figure 18.41.
2. To restore default filters, click the Clear button.
3. Specify the filters to be used. The various filters are discussed below.
4. Choose OK to activate the filters.

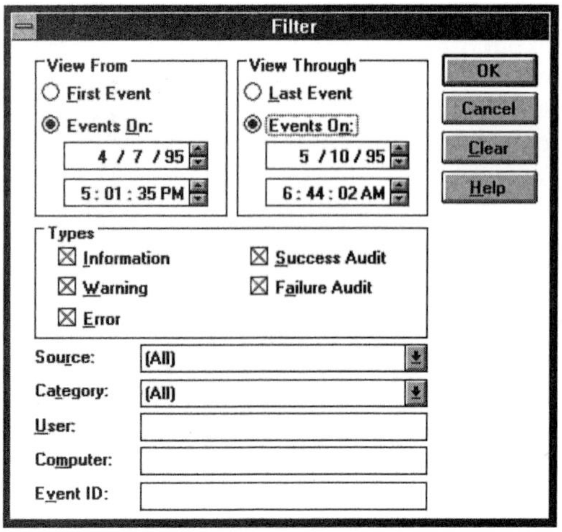

Figure 18.41
Filtering Event Viewer events.

The following event filters can be selected:

- **View From.** Specifies a date of the oldest records that should be displayed.
- **View Through.** Specifies a date of the newest records that should be displayed.
- **Information.** Infrequent significant events that describe successful operation of Windows NT Server services.
- **Warning.** Non-critical errors that may predict future problems.
- **Error.** Critical errors. Data loss or failure of major functions.
- **Success Audit.** Audit events that are associated with the successful execution of an action.
- **Failure Audit.** Audit events that are associated with the unsuccessful execution of an action.
- **Source.** The application, computer, or driver that originated the log entry.
- **Category.** Event categories specific to the log source.
- **User.** User name of the account that was logged on when the log entry was generated (not case sensitive).
- **Computer.** Computer from which the log message originated (not case sensitive).
- **Event ID.** The number that corresponds to the specific type of event.

To disable event filtering, choose All Events from the View menu.

Searching for Events

You can search for specific events. This capability is useful when it is necessary to locate specific events in large log files.

To search for specific events, follow these steps:

1. Choose Find from the View menu to display the Find dialog box shown in figure 18.42.
2. Choose Clear to restore default values to the dialog box.
3. Enter the criteria of the events to be found.

4. Select Up or Down to specify the search direction.
5. Choose Find Next to locate successive records that meet the criteria.
6. Click on Cancel to exit the dialog box.

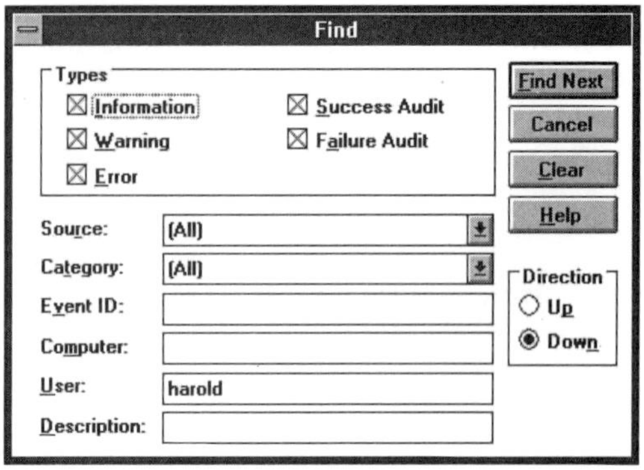

Figure 18.42
Finding events in Event Viewer.

Archiving Event Logs

Logs can be archived in three forms:

- Event log format that you can review later in the Event log.
- Text Files, which may be read by any text editor.
- Comma-delimited format that can be read by many other programs for analysis of the data.

To archive a log, follow these steps:

1. Select the log in the Log menu.
2. Choose Save As from the Log menu.
3. In the Save As dialog box, select a directory and a log file name (see fig. 18.43).
4. Select the file format in the Save File as Type box.
5. Click on OK to save the file.

To view an archived log, follow these steps:

1. Choose Open from the Log menu.
2. Select the directory and file name in the File Name list dialog box.

3. Click on OK to retrieve the archive file.

4. In the Open File Type dialog box, specify the type of log you are retrieving: System, Security, or Application.

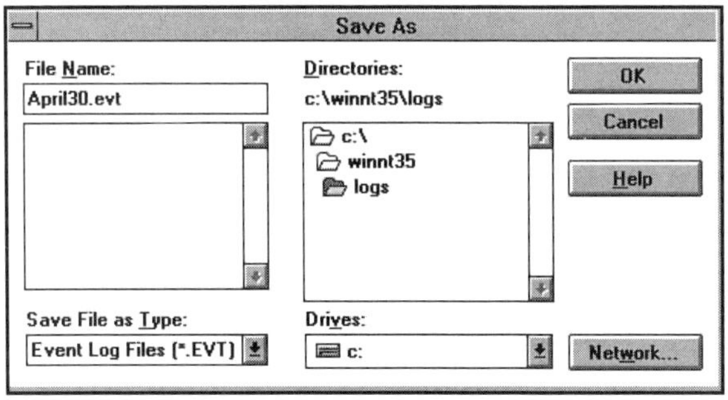

Figure 18.43

Specifying the file name and directory for an archive log file.

Note Logs that are archived in text file or comma-delimited format include data in the following fields:

1. Date
2. Time
3. Source
4. Type
5. Category
6. Event
7. User
8. Computer
9. Description

Comma-delimited files can be imported by most spreadsheet and database applications.

Registry Editor

The *Registry* is the database that serves as the central repository for configuration data on a Windows NT computer. If you are familiar with Windows and DOS, you will find that the functions of many files are brought together in the Registry, including the following:

- CONFIG.SYS
- AUTOEXEC.BAT
- SYSTEM.INI
- WIN.INI
- PROTOCOL.INI

Although Windows NT still supports INI files for the sake of compatibility with applications not written with Windows NT in mind, the Registry is a significantly improved means of storing configuration data.

The Registry is configured as a fault-tolerant database that is nearly impossible to crash. If a system failure occurs when entries are being written to the database, log files enable Windows NT to recover the database and fix any damage.

A considerable amount of data is stored in the Registry. Some is of little concern to users or administrators, and much of the information is stored in a binary form that cannot be easily interpreted or modified. In the vast majority of cases, you will make modifications to the Registry by means of utilities such as the Control Panel or Setup.

On rare occasions, however, you might be instructed to make a change directly to the Registry. Or you might find it useful to examine the Registry contents directly. At those times, it is handy for you to understand the structure of the Registry and the use of the Registry Editor.

Note I can't possibly tell you everything there is to know about the Registry. The most thorough description of the Registry—more than 150 pages—is found in the *Windows NT Resource Guide,* a volume in the Windows NT Resource Kit.

Viewing the Registry

An icon is not assigned to the Registry Editor when Windows NT is installed. You can run the Registry Editor by entering the command **REGEDT32** after choosing Run from the Program Manager File menu. Or, you can choose the New command from the File menu to add the REGEDT32.EXE command as a new program item to the desktop.

Tip After you run the Registry Editor, convert the editor to read-only mode by choosing the Read Only Mode command from the Options menu. When this option is checked, you can browse the Registry all you want without fear of damaging critical data.

When you start the Registry Editor, four windows are available, as shown in figure 18.44. The Registry is organized in a tree, and you navigate the Registry tree just as you navigate directory trees in File Manager. The windows in figure 18.44 have been arranged so that you can see the information in the topmost level of each tree.

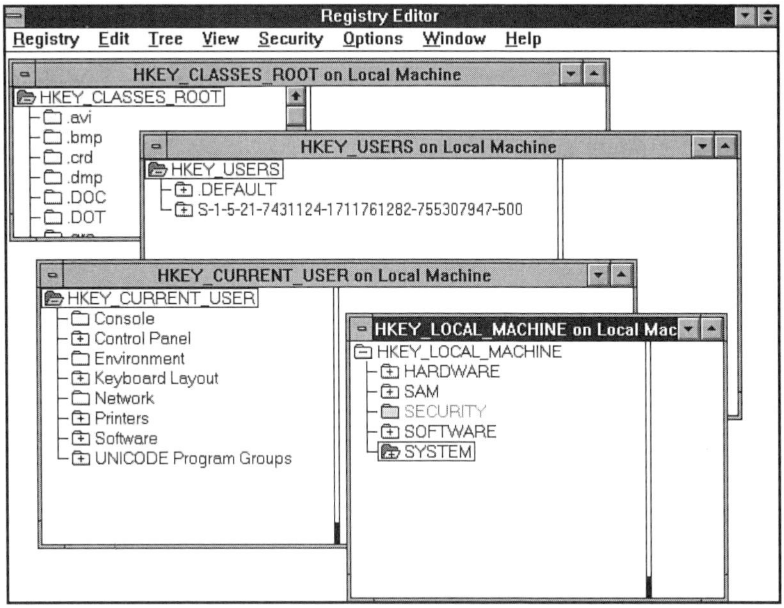

Figure 18.44

The Registry Editor window.

The organization of the Registry database is shown in figure 18.45. As you can see, the database has four subtrees. Close examination reveals that the name of each subtree corresponds to a window in the Registry Editor. Each entry in the tree is called a *key*, and each key can have *subkeys*.

The four subtrees in the Registry follow:

- **HKEY_LOCAL_MACHINE.** Contains computer hardware information. Part of this subtree is reconstructed each time the computer is started to reflect the current hardware configuration.
- **HKEY_CLASSES_ROOT.** Contains object linking and embedding (OLE) and file-class association data.
- **HKEY_CURRENT_USER.** Contains user-profile data for the currently logged-on user.
- **HKEY_USERS.** Contains all actively loaded user profiles, including the default profile and a duplicate of information in HKEY_CURRENT_USER. Profiles for remotely logged-on users are stored in the Registries of their local computers.

Figure 18.45

Organization of the Registry database.

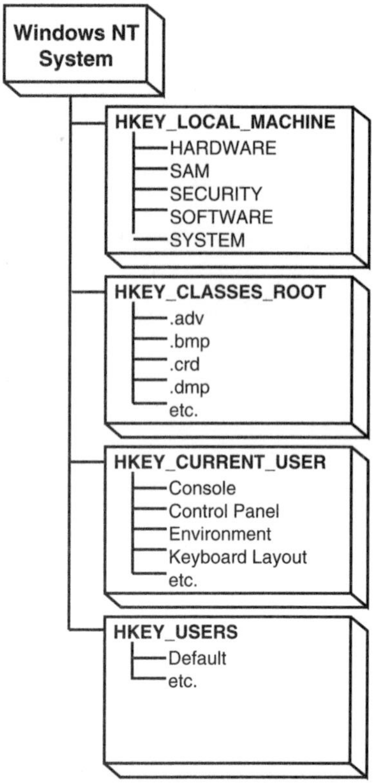

Much of the information that concerns you is stored in HKEY_LOCAL_MACHINE, which makes a good starting point for examining the structure of the Registry. The symbol for a key is a folder, and open keys are represented by open folders. To open subkeys in a window, double-click any folder that shows a plus sign (+). To close a subkey, double-click the open folder.

Looking at the Structure of Registry Values

Figure 18.46 shows the HKEY_LOCAL_MACHINE window after taking the following actions:

1. Double-clicking on the SYSTEM key to open the SYSTEM subtree.
2. Double-clicking on the CurrentControlSet key to open the subtree that describes the current state of the computer.
3. Double-clicking on the Control key.
4. Double-clicking on the ComputerName key.

5. Clicking on the ActiveComputer key. Notice that this key is not flagged with a plus sign (+), indicating that it is the final key in the branch.

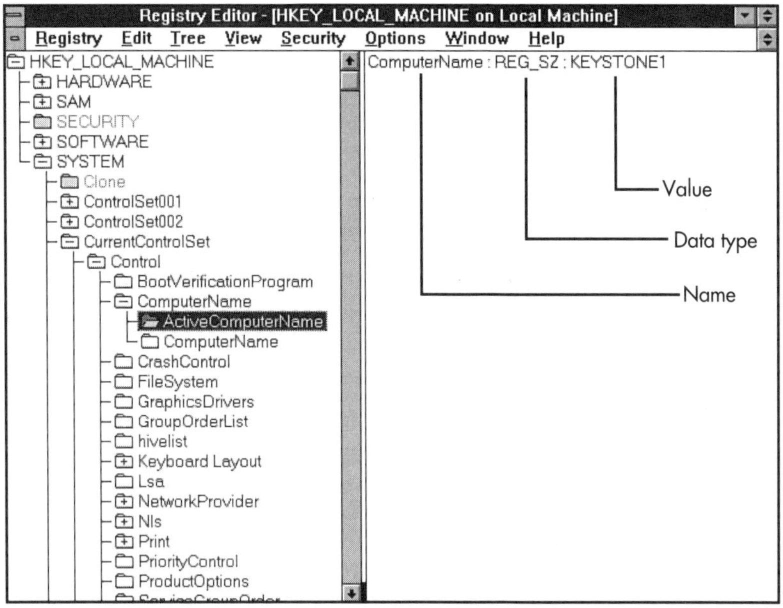

Figure 18.46

Opening keys in HKEY_LOCAL_MACHINE.

Note To describe the complete path to a file, the same convention is used as for files in subdirectories: each level of the tree is represented by a backslash. The path that was opened in figure 18.47 is

HKEY_LOCAL_MACHINE\SYSTEM\CurrentControlSet\Control\ComputerName\ActiveComputer.

Each key and subkey can be assigned one or more *values*, which are displayed in the right-hand pane of the window. These values have a specific structure. ActiveComputer key has only one value, but you will see examples of keys that have many values. A value has three fields:

- **Name.** The name of the value.
- **Data type.** Programmers are familiar with the concept that data has a type that restricts the information that the data can display. Each data type is discussed in this section.
- **Value.** The actual data. The type of value stored depends on the data type.

Each value is classified by a data type that describes the types of values that can be stored. You encounter some other data types if you browse around, but these five types are the ones that most concern you:

- **REG_BINARY.** This data type describes raw binary data, the form used to store most hardware data, which can be viewed in more readable form in WINMSD. An example of such an entry follows:

```
Video:REG_BINARY:00 00 00 00
```

- **REG_DWORD.** Data represented by a number up to 4 bytes long. This data can be displayed in binary, hexadecimal, or decimal form. An example follows:

```
ErrorMode:REG_DWORD:0
```

- **REG_EXPAND_SZ.** Data represented in an expandable data string, which contains a system variable. The following example makes use of the %SystemRoot% variable:

```
SystemDirectory:REG_EXPAND_SZ:%SystemRoot%\system32
```

- **REG_MULTI_SZ.** Data represented in a multiple string consisting of lists or multiple values. Most human-readable text is of this type. Here is an example that has three values (autocheck, autochk, and *):

```
BootExecute:REG_MULTI_SZ:autocheck autochk *
```

- **REG_SZ.** Character data used to store human-readable text. For example:

```
DaylightName:REG_SZ:US Eastern Standard Time
```

Hives, Files, and Subtrees

The data in the four Registry subtrees is derived from six or more sets of files called *hives*. The term *hive* was coined by a Microsoft systems programmer to reflect the way Registry data is stored in compartmentalized forms. Each hive consists of two files: a data file and a log file. The log file is responsible for the fault tolerance of the Registry, and is described in greater detail later.

Each hive represents a group of keys, subkeys, and values that is rooted at the top of the Registry tree; it is easy to identify the keys in the Registry that are associated with each hive. Figure 18.47 shows a composite of two windows: the HKEY_LOCAL_MACHINE window from Registry Editor, and a File Manager window that shows the C:\WINNT35\SYSTEM32\CONFIG subdirectory.

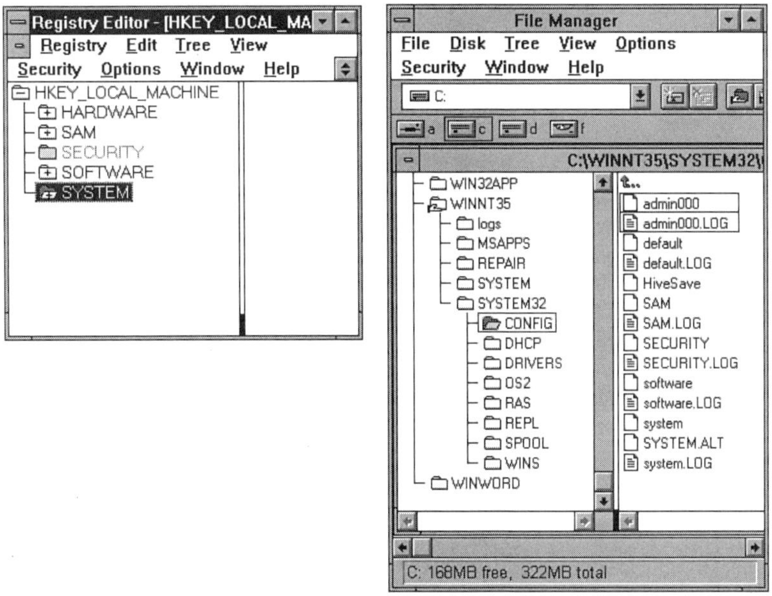

Figure 18.47
Relationship of Registry hives to files in the CONFIG subdirectory.

You easily can identify files in the directory that are related to keys in the Registry. The SOFTWARE key, for example, is associated with the files SOFTWARE and SOFTWARE.LOG.

The registry hives and files are summarized in table 18.4.

TABLE 18.4
Registry Hives and Associated Files

Registry Hive	Associated Files
HKEY_LOCAL_MACHINE\SAM	SAM and SAM.LOG
HKEY_LOCAL_MACHINE\SECURITY	SECURITY and SECURITY.LOG
HKEY_LOCAL_MACHINE\SOFTWARE	SOFTWARE and SOFTWARE.LOG
HKEY_LOCAL_MACHINE\SYSTEM	SYSTEM, SYSTEM.LOG and SYSTEM.ALT
HKEY_USERS\DEFAULT	DEFAULT and DEFAULT.LOG
HKEY_CURRENT_USER	USER*nnn* and USER*nnn*.LOG or ADMIN*nnn* and ADMIN*nnn*.LOG

Notice that in figure 18.47, hives are associated with all the subtrees in HKEY_LOCAL_MACHINE except HARDWARE. The information in the HARDWARE subtree is regenerated each time the computer is booted and therefore is not stored permanently in hives. On Intel x86 computers, the information is gathered by the NTDETECT program. On Advanced RISC computers, the information is gathered by the ARC configuration database.

The hives are responsible for storing different categories of information:

- **HKEY_LOCAL_MACHINE\SAM.** Stores security information for user and group accounts. This information is used by the Windows NT Server Security Access Account Manager (SAM).
- **HKEY_LOCAL_MACHINE\SECURITY.** Security information regarding local account policy, used by the Windows NT security subsystem.
- **HKEY_LOCAL_MACHINE\SOFTWARE.** The configuration database for locally installed software. Serves the same purpose as application INI files for Windows NT applications.
- **HKEY_LOCAL_MACHINE\SYSTEM.** The system start-up database. Data is configured during installation and when the computer is reconfigured. The computer cannot start without this information.
- **HKEY_USERS\DEFAULT.** The default user profile.
- **HKEY_CURRENT_USER.** The profile for the current user of the computer. This information is duplicated in the HKEY_LOCAL_MACHINE\SYSTEM hive. If entries in the hives disagree, HKEY_CURRENT_USER takes precedence.

Editing Values in the Registry

You will seldom, and may never, need to directly edit values in the Registry. However, there are a few features in Windows NT that can be configured only in Registry Editor.

An example is the behavior of Windows NT computers that function as browsers on the network. A *browser* is a computer that maintains a network Browse list of all domains and servers that are available. It isn't my intention to explain the details of browsers. The point is that a computer functions as a browser depending on the value of its HKEY_LOCAL_MACHINE\SYSTEM\CurrentControlSet\Services\Browser\Parameters key. To change a computer's behavior as a browser, you must edit the value of this key, which can be No (never a browser), Yes (always a browser), or Auto (potentially a browser).

Here is a harmless example of using the Registry Editor. It edits the Registry value that describes the wallpaper file that is used on the computer desktop. (The example will work for you only if you installed wallpaper files on your computer.)

The current user's working environment is defined in the HKEY_CURRENT_USER subtree of the Registry. The window associated with this subtree is shown in figure 18.48.

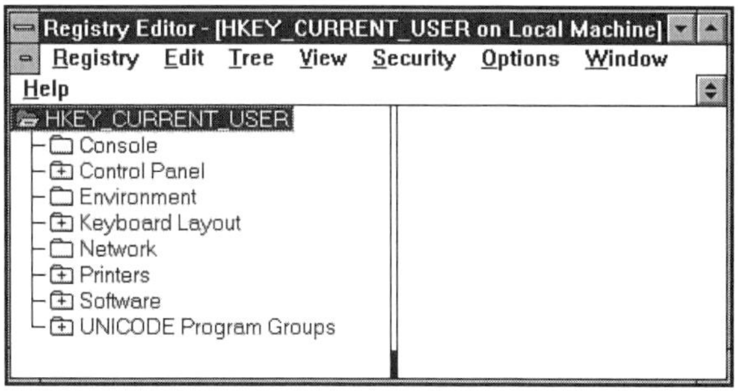

Figure 18.48
The HKEY_CURRENT_USER subtree.

Much of the information in this subtree will be quite familiar, and you might want to browse around to see what you can find. Then, you might want to try a little experiment to see what editing the Registry is like:

1. Start the Registry Editor. If you have not created a program item, choose the **R**un command from the **F**ile menu of the Program Manager. Enter **REGEDT32** in the Command Line box and press Enter.

2. After Registry Editor starts, check the **O**ptions menu. If the **R**ead Only Mode option is checked, remove the check mark. Otherwise, you will be unable to save changes.

3. If the HKEY_CURRENT_USER window is not open, open it by doing one of the following:

   ◆ Choosing HKEY_CURRENT_USER in the **W**indow menu.

   ◆ Double-clicking on the HKEY_CURRENT_USER icon.

4. Double-click the Control Panel key. After this key opens, you see the subkeys shown in figure 18.49. In the figure, the Desktop subkey has been selected, which contains the field you will be editing.

5. Double-click the Desktop key to display its values.

6. Double-click the entry named Wallpaper. A dialog box opens that contains the value of the current Wallpaper file. Edit this entry to read `winlogo.bmp`. (The change already has been made in fig. 18.49.)

You also might want to change the value of TileWallpaper to 1, if it is not 1 already. This turns on tiling. Generally, a 0 value turns off a feature and a 1 turns on a feature.

7. Click on OK to save the entry.

8. Quit Registry Editor and restart Windows. When Windows restarts, the wallpaper will be changed.

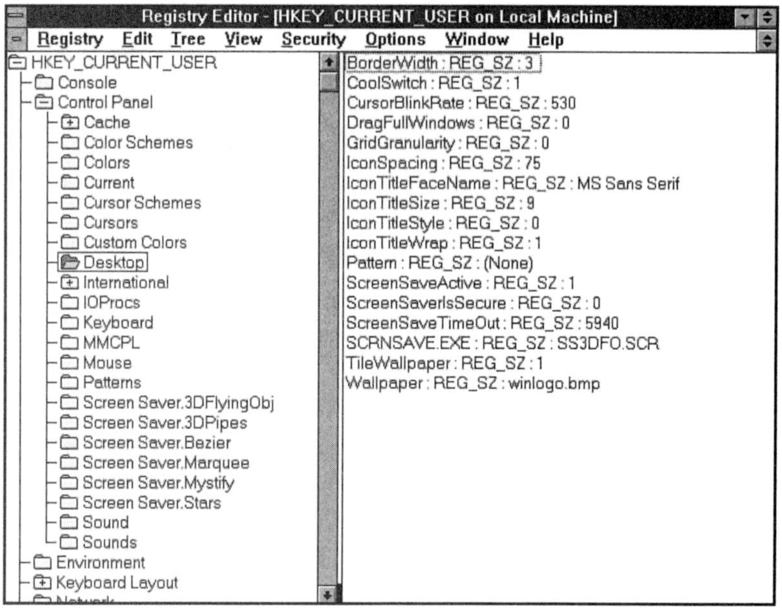

Figure 18.49
Subkeys for the Control Panels key.

Note If you have Administrative access, you can use the Registry Editor to edit hives on remote PCs. The Load Hive command on the Registry menu can be used to load a hive through a connected drive. After you are through with the hive, use the Unload Hive command to save the files back to the remote computer.

Examining User Profiles in the Registry

User profile information is duplicated in two subtrees: HKEY_CURRENT_USER and HKEY_USERS. If information conflicts in these two subtrees, Windows NT uses the values in HKEY_CURRENT_USER.

If you open the HKEY_USERS subtree, you see two keys, as shown in figure 18.50. One key is named DEFAULT. The subtree under the DEFAULT key stores the default profile that is accessed by users who do not have an assigned profile. The other key is labeled by a longer number that begins with an S. This is a copy of the Registry profile for the current user of the computer.

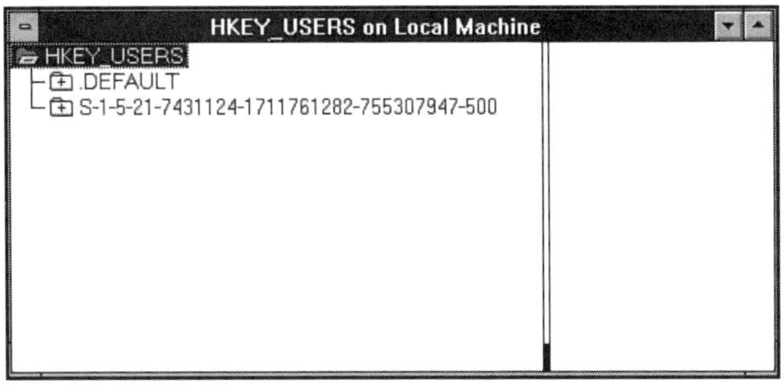

Figure 18.50

Subtrees in the HKEY_USERS window.

The number is the user security ID (SID) that was assigned to the user account when it was created. Different users result in different numbers in the name of this key.

User profiles are associated with hive files, which are located with other hive files in C:\WINNT35\SYSTEM32\Config. If you look in that directory, you see a hive profile file for each user who has logged on locally on the computer. The file is based on the first five characters of the user name plus the number 000. The file for the user Buster would be named BUSTE000, for example. The currently logged-on user also will have a file with a LOG extension—for example, BUSTE000.LOG.

You can examine the SIDs and profile file information for user accounts by opening HKEY_LOCAL_MACHINE\SOFTWARE\Microsoft\Windows NT\ProfileList. Although you could, don't be tempted to edit the SIDs. Doing so prevents the user from accessing any resources for which the user account has been given permissions.

Finding Registry Keys

The Registry is a big place, and you might be wondering how to locate specific keys. Once you become familiar with the Registry structure, you can find a great deal by browsing, but Registry Editor does have a Find Key command. The catch is that you need to know which subtree to look in. After that, it's pretty straightforward.

As an example, look for entries regarding installed printers. Because this is hardware, the keys appear in the HKEY_LOCAL_MACHINE subtree. To search for the information, follow these steps:

1. Open the HKEY_LOCAL_MACHINE window.
2. Select the root key of the tree HKEY_LOCAL_MACHINE.
3. Choose the <u>F</u>ind Key command from the <u>V</u>iew menu.
4. Type **printer** in the Fi<u>n</u>d What box.
5. Do not check the Match <u>W</u>hole Word Only box because many of the names of keys are compound words, and *printer* might be only part of the key name.
6. Do not check Match <u>C</u>ase unless you are trying to find a specific entry for which the case of the letters is known.
7. Select <u>D</u>own if it is not already selected.
8. Choose <u>F</u>ind Next to initiate the search.
9. The search result is shown in figure 18.51. (I opened the Printers key after it was found that it held the information I wanted.) The specific printer information probably differs on your computer, but the key under which the information is located should be found without trouble.

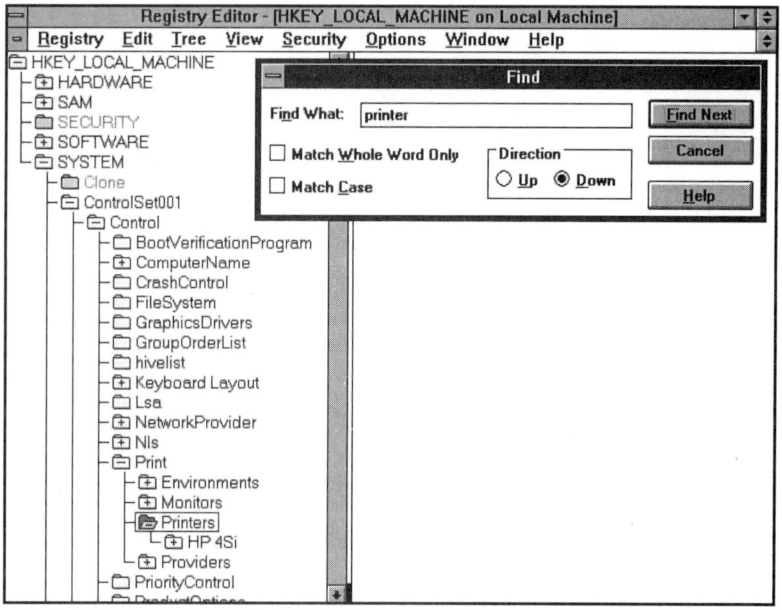

Figure 18.51

Results of finding a key in the Registry.

Registry Fault Tolerance

The Registry is an extremely robust database that can survive even critical system failures in the middle of writing data. This capability to shrug off faults results from the use of a technique borrowed from databases. When a key value is saved to a hive in the Registry, the following events take place:

1. The change is written to the LOG file associated with the hive.
2. File buffers are flushed to force data to be physically written out to the LOG file. Normally, file writes are stored in buffers until Windows NT has some spare time to write data to files. Flushing the buffers ensures that the change is stored safely in the LOG file.
3. The information in the LOG file is used to update the hive file.

Suppose the server crashes while the change is half written to the hive file. A half-written change is a corrupt change, and the hive file would be unreliable. Fortunately, when the system restarts, information in the LOG file can be used to roll back the hive file to a stable state.

In one case, the Registry goes even further to ensure reliability and data integrity. The System hive is stored in two files: system and SYSTEM.ALT. If the server cannot boot with the primary copy, the alternate copy can be used.

Using the Last Known Good Configuration

The control settings most recently used on the computer are stored in the Registry in the key HKEY_LOCAL_MACHINE\SYSTEM\CurrentControlSet. Information in this key is accessed when the computer is started.

The CurrentControlSet can be damaged in a number of ways that can prevent the system from being able to start. Installing bad drivers or options with conflicting settings might have this effect. Or, you accidentally might configure the video adapter so that you simply cannot see data on-screen.

Besides the current control set, Windows NT keeps a copy of the last control set that was used successfully to start the computer. If, for any reason, the computer does not start with the current control set, you can invoke the last known good control set by pressing the spacebar when you see the message `Press spacebar NOW to invoke Last Known Good Menu`.

After you invoke the Last Known Good Menu, you lose any changes that were made to the system configuration since the last time the computer was started.

The UPS Utility

An uninterruptible power supply is essential equipment for any network server. You simply cannot have servers crashing with every power outage. Files get damaged and user productivity is interrupted. There are actually several electrical conditions from which you want to protect your server:

- **Power outages.** Complete losses of power.
- **Voltage variations.** You know how the lights in your house dim when you start the vacuum cleaner? Power-hungry systems can cause the voltage at an AC outlet to vary by a surprising degree. I've seen more than one server problem caused by periodic brownouts.
- **Voltage spikes and surges.** Equipment can be damaged by a voltage spike so short that you might not even notice it. Lightning is a prime cause of voltage spikes.
- **Noise.** Radio frequency noise on the AC line might get past the filtering in your computer power supply, which is really only designed to cope with the 50Hz to 60Hz frequency of line current. Noise also can cause computers to act erratically.

Equipment for Surges, Spikes, Noise, and Power Fluctuations

Depending on your equipment, you might need more than one device to deal with all these problems. Many UPS units don't provide spike protection or filtering, and most cannot protect against voltage variations in the AC line.

At a minimum, every computer should be plugged into a surge and spike protector, and you need to plug your UPS into one unless the UPS provides surge and spike protection. Don't even think about using a $10 special. Expect to spend at least $50 for a spike and surge suppressor—particularly one that also filters out high-frequency noise. This device is a must.

A surge and spike suppressor is designed to eliminate relatively short voltage changes. If your power line experiences periodic brownouts or overvoltages, the device you need is the power-line conditioner. These devices are capable of leveling off low and high voltages, maintaining a constant output voltage within a reasonable range of line fluctuations. Expect to spend about $300 for a power-line conditioner. If you have an electrician install a dedicated power line for your server, however, chances are you won't need a power conditioner.

Uninterruptible Power Supplies

All UPS devices work by charging a battery during normal operation. The power in the battery can be converted to AC current that can be used to power a computer. A UPS can be designed in two ways: to operate with the battery online or offline. Figure 18.52 shows how the two types of UPS devices work.

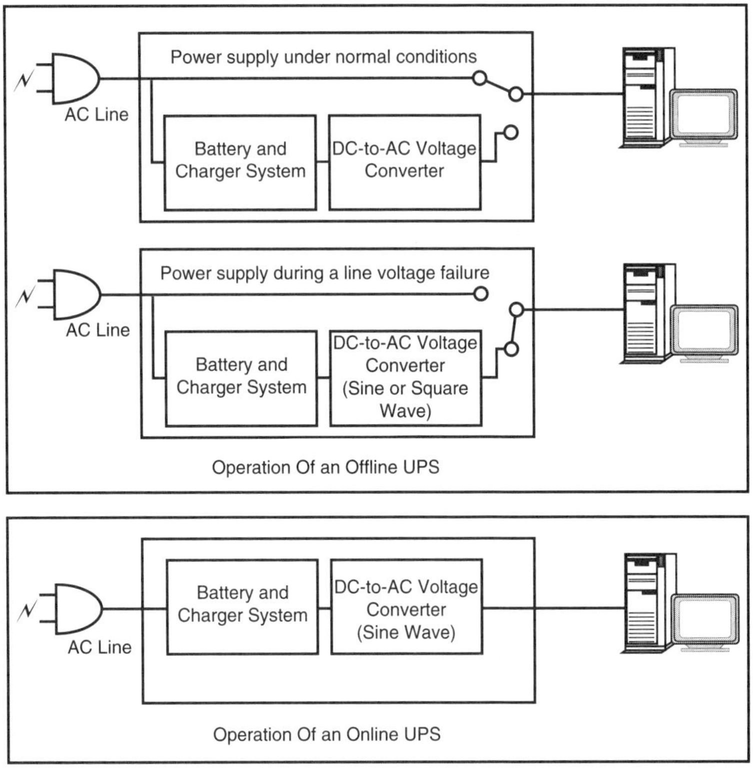

Figure 18.52
Offline and online UPS systems.

The majority of UPSs use the offline approach. Under normal conditions, the AC line is switched directly to the outlets that service the computer. AC power also is directed to the battery system, which is kept constantly charged. When power fails, an electronic switch connects the UPS outlets to the inverter circuits that convert DC power from the battery into AC power that can run the computer.

The most significant problem with an offline UPS is the period of time that is required to switch from direct AC power to the inverter. Most UPS devices now are designed to make the switch rapidly enough that few computers are bothered, but this was once a common problem.

The online UPS makes it unnecessary to switch power because the computer always is connected to the battery/inverter system. The outside AC power runs the charging circuits that keep the battery topped off, but it is never directly connected to the computer. Because there is no switch-over, a power outage is handled much more smoothly. Because the AC line voltages are never connected to the computer, an offline UPS inherently functions as a surge, spike, and power-line conditioner.

Every battery-powered UPS must be capable of converting battery direct current (DC) into the alternating current (AC) required by the protected computer. In the majority of UPS devices, the AC voltage produced is not a true sine wave, like the AC current you get from the wall. Most UPS devices produce a square wave that can cause problems with some computer equipment. Some manufacturers design their equipment to produce a simulated sine wave, which is a stepped-square wave. Simulated sine waves are acceptable to most equipment. Figure 18.53 illustrates the various waveforms.

Because an online UPS is constantly supplying the computer with remanufactured AC, it must produce a true sine wave. Equipment operating on a square wave AC for long periods of time will be damaged.

Most offline UPS systems produce square-wave voltages, which can be used to operate the majority of computers for relatively short periods of time, such as the few minutes it takes to shut down the server properly in the event of a long power failure.

UPS systems can power a server only for a limited time before their batteries are depleted. Therefore, it is desirable to have a means of automatically monitoring the UPS and shutting down the server before the UPS no longer can sustain the required operating voltage. Windows NT includes a UPS service that can provide UPS monitoring with many UPS systems.

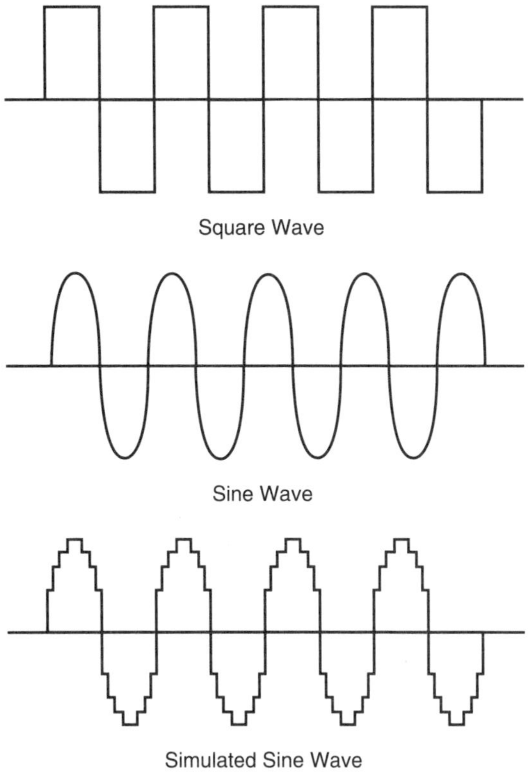

Figure 18.53
Wave forms produced by UPS systems.

Connecting the UPS to the Server

To use the UPS service, your UPS must be equipped with a monitoring interface—usually a DB-9 connector that uses RS-232 serial interface signaling. A cable is used to connect the UPS to a serial port on the computer.

Unfortunately, there are no standards for how UPS monitoring should be done, and every manufacturer seems to have a different way of configuring the monitoring port. It always is best, therefore, to obtain a cable from the manufacturer of your UPS that is designed for Windows NT Server. At the very least, contact the manufacturer for cabling recommendations.

You might, in a pinch, be able to reverse-engineer the hardware and build a cable yourself. Be aware, however, that this might not be straightforward or even possible. The cable for my UPS requires a CMOS integrated circuit to support Windows NT Server, for example. In case you want to make the attempt, table 18.5 shows the pin requirements for Windows NT Server.

Table 18.5
Pin Requirements for Windows NT Server

Signal	DB25	DB9	Purpose
CTS	5	8	The UPS can supply a positive or negative voltage at this pin to signal the UPS service that a power failure has occurred.
DCD	8	1	The UPS can supply a positive or negative voltage at this pin to signal the UPS service that a low-battery condition exists.
DTR	20	4	Windows NT can send a positive voltage at this pin to signal the UPS that it can shut itself off.
TXD	2	3	Windows NT maintains a negative voltage at this pin for use with contact-closure signaling from some UPSs.
RTS	4	7	Windows NT maintains a positive voltage at this pin for use with contact-closure signaling from some UPSs.

Before you can configure the UPS service, you most know whether your UPS will generate a positive or a negative signal at the CTS and DCD pins.

After you connect the UPS to your server with a suitable cable, you can configure the UPS service.

Configuring the UPS Service

You access the configuration dialog box from the UPS icon in the Control Panel. The UPS window is shown in figure 18.54.

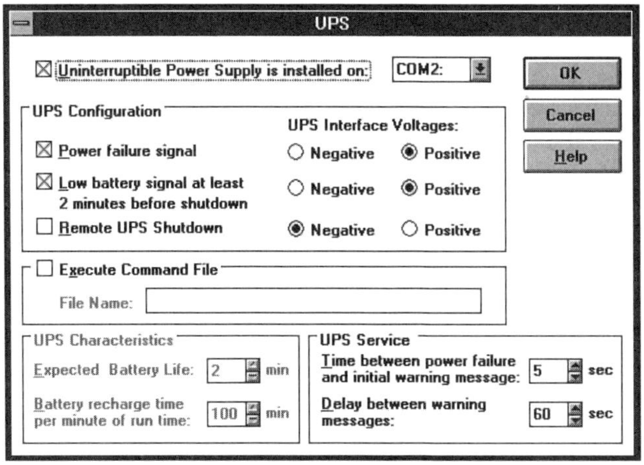

Figure 18.54

Configuring the UPS service.

Configure the UPS settings as follows:

1. Open the UPS utility in the Control Panel.
2. Check the "**U**ninterruptible Power Supply is installed on" box to activate the other options in the window.
3. Select a COM port. You might need to use the Ports utility in the Control Panel to activate the port you need.
4. If your UPS can send a signal indicating that a power failure has taken place, check the **P**ower failure signal box. Then indicate whether the signal will consist of a Negative or a Positive voltage.
5. If your UPS can send a signal indicating that its battery is low, check the "**L**ow battery signal at least 2 minutes before shutdown" box. Then indicate whether the signal will consist of a Negative or a Positive voltage.
6. If your UPS can accept a signal that orders it to shut itself off, check the **R**emote UPS Shutdown box. Then indicate whether the signal will consist of a Negative or a Positive voltage.
7. If you did not check the "**L**ow battery signal at least 2 minutes before shutdown" box, options in the UPS Characteristics box will be active.

- Enter a conservative estimate of the time the UPS can power the server in the Expected Battery Life box.
- Enter a conservative estimate of the time required to recharge the UPS battery in the "Battery recharge time per minute of run time" box.

The manufacturer of your UPS is the best source of information for the values to put in these fields. Because the UPS cannot signal a low-battery condition, the UPS service uses these values to estimate when a low battery condition is likely.

8. Most UPSs send a power failure warning immediately, even for a very short loss of service. If the UPS service interpreted such a short loss as the start of a serious outage, it would often notify network users to log off when logging off was unnecessary.

   You can specify a delay between the signaling of a power failure by entering a value in seconds in the "Time between power failure and initial warning message" box. If power is restored within this time period, no message is sent.

9. UPS sends periodic messages as long as the power outage continues. You can specify the delay between these messages by entering a value in seconds in the "Delay between warning messages" box.

10. You can instruct the UPS service to execute a command file when a low-battery condition exists. This command file could be a batch file that shuts down special applications such as a database server. The UPS service will shut down most server functions normally, so a command file is required only in special instances.

    To activate the feature, follow these steps:

    - Check the Execute Command File box
    - Enter a command file name in the File Name box

11. When you have configured the service, click on OK.

When you activate the UPS service, it automatically configures its own startup parameters so that it will start automatically. It also ensures that the Alerter, Messenger, and EventLog services are started.

When the UPS service starts up, it tests the interface to the UPS hardware by assuming that normal power conditions prevail. If you have specified a positive voltage at the CTS pin to signal a power failure, the UPS service assumes that a negative voltage will be found at the pin. Each pin you have activated in the UPS Control Panel will be tested. If the expected voltages are not found, the UPS service will not start.

Testing the UPS

Never assume that your UPS will work. After you have configured the UPS service, plan on a test. If the server is being used, schedule the test for after hours. You can use the Send Message command in Server Manager to notify users that a test will take place. Users should log out for the duration of the test.

Testing is simple. Pull the plug on your UPS and see what happens.

After the delay you specified (in the "Time between power failure and initial warning message" box), a message is broadcast to the domain stating that `A power failure has occurred at` *`server name`*`. Please terminate all activity with this server.` This message repeats at the intervals you specified. During this period, new users cannot attach to the server.

At this time, the server can resume normal function if power is restored. When power comes back up and the UPS hardware clears the power failure signal to the UPS service, a message is sent to users stating that `Power has been restored at` *`server name`*`. Normal operations have resumed.` Users can reconnect to the server and resume their work.

The next step is initiated in one of two ways:

- If you configured the UPS service to expect a low battery signal, the UPS initiates the next phase of the shutdown.
- If you configured the UPS service to use a timed shutdown (Expected battery life), the next phase starts when the shutdown timer expires.

After a low-battery condition occurs, UPS executes any command you specified in the UPS command screen. This command must execute in 30 seconds or less if the server is to be shut down smoothly within two minutes.

After executing the command, the UPS service starts a controlled shutdown of the server. Once it begins, the shutdown process cannot be aborted.

You should let your test continue until the UPS service shuts down the server.

CHAPTER 19

Monitoring and Managing the Network

A network is a dynamic, almost living thing. It has a heartbeat, a pulse, and a health that can be measured. That is yet another of your many jobs as a LAN administrator: monitoring the network, so you can anticipate when it is healthy and when its health is in decline.

This chapter covers several tools that focus on monitoring and managing the network and network clients.

Network Client Administrator

Network Client Administrator is a central resource for managing client installation.

Five different sets of client software installation disks can be made. These disk sets contain all files required to install client software on the following clients:

- Network Client 3.0 for MS-DOS and Windows (covered in Chapter 13, "Using Windows and DOS Clients")
- Remote Access v1.1a for MS-DOS (discussed in Chapter 20, "Using the Remote Access Server")
- TCP/IP 32 for Windows for Workgroups 3.11 (covered in Chapter 15, "Using TCP/IP")
- LAN Manager 2.2c for MS-DOS (not covered in this book)
- LAN Manager 2.2c for OS/2 (also not covered)

Network Client Administrator also can build network installation startup disks. Network installation startup disks contain only the files required to enable a client to access the network and connect to installation files on a server. The actual client files are then installed to the client from a shared network directory. Network installation is supported for two clients:

- Windows for Workgroups 3.11
- Network Client for MS-DOS and Windows

Creating Client Installation Disk Sets

A client installation disk set contains all the files required to install client software on a computer. In general, installing from a client installation set is the most successful method of installing client software. Clients can vary in their hardware configurations without requiring you to rebuild the installation disks.

To create a client installation disk set, perform the following steps:

1. Start Network Client Administrator. The program icon is installed in the Network Administration program group. When the program starts, the Network Client Administrator window appears (see fig. 19.1).
2. Choose Make Installation Disk Set and choose Continue. The Share Network Client Installation Files dialog box appears (see fig. 19.2).

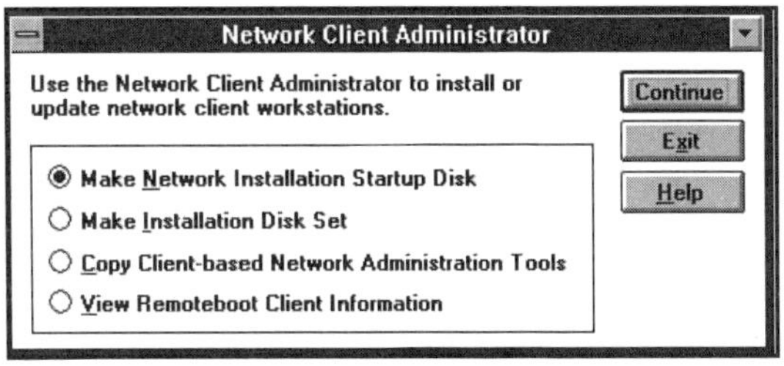

Figure 19.1
The Network Client Administrator main window.

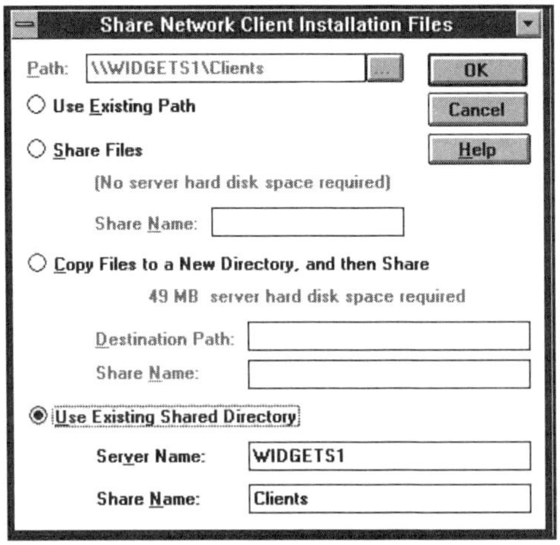

Figure 19.2
The Share Network Client Installation Files dialog box.

3. Specify the location of the installation disk files.

   - If the installation files are on CD-ROM or in an unshared directory, choose Use Existing Path and specify the path in the Path box. If desired, click on the ... button and browse for the file path. The required files are in the \CLIENTS subdirectory of the CD-ROM.
   - To share installation files on a CD-ROM, choose Share Files, specify a path in the Path Box, and enter a share name in the Share Name box. This option is more applicable to the network installation method.
   - If you want to copy the files to a hard disk and share them, choose Copy Files to a New Directory, and select Share. Specify a Destination Path and Share Name. Although 49 MB of hard disk space are initially required, you can delete client software you don't require after the files are copied.
   - If files are already copied and shared, choose Use Existing Shared Directory. Supply the Server Name and the Share Name.

4. Choose OK to continue.

   If you chose Copy Files to a New Directory and then selected Share, files will be copied. This process is a rather lengthy one, so take a break.

   When ready to proceed, Network Client Administrator displays the Make Installation Disk Set menu shown in figure 19.3.

5. Select the Network Client or Service you want to create. The dialog box tells you how many disks will be required.

6. Select the Destination Drive.

7. Choose Format Disks if the disks are unformatted or already contain files.

8. Click on OK. Supply disks as requested. Be sure to label the disks as specified in the prompts.

The procedure for using the installation disks depends on the operating system being used. Chapter 13 covers the installation of client software for MS-DOS and Windows 3.1. Chapter 15 discusses installation of the TCP/IP client software for MS-DOS and Windows for Workgroups 3.11.

Figure 19.3
Specifying which client software disks to make.

Creating a Network Installation Startup Disk

To create a network installation startup disk, perform the following steps:

1. Format a bootable disk for the target computer. Ideally, all computers on which you will be using network installation will be configured with the same version of MS-DOS.

2. Start Network Client Administrator. The program icon is installed in the Network Administration program group. When the program starts, the Network Client Administrator window appears (refer to fig. 19.1).

3. Choose Make Network Installation Startup Disk and choose Continue. The Share Network Client Installation Files dialog box appears (refer to fig. 19.2).

4. Network installation must be performed from a shared directory. In the Share Network Client Installation Files dialog box, you can use all options except Use Existing Path.

   - To share installation files on a CD-ROM, choose Share Files, specify a path in the Path box, and enter a share name in the Share Name box. This option is particularly useful for network client installation because you can share the CD-ROM during installation and no hard drive space is required.

   - If you want to copy the files to a hard disk and share them, choose Copy Files to a New Directory, and select Share. Specify a Destination Path and Share Name. Although 49 MB of hard disk space are initially required, you can delete client software you don't require after the files are copied.

   - If files are already copied and shared, choose Use Existing Shared Directory. Supply the Server Name and the Share Name.

5. Click on OK to continue. Network Client Administrator displays the Target Workstation Configuration dialog box (see fig. 19.4).

6. Select the Network Client you want to create. Only one disk is required for each client.

7. Select the Destination Drive.

8. Installation must be made to a disk in Drive A. In the Floppy Drive box, choose Drive A: is 3.5" or Drive A: is 5.25".

9. Select a network adapter card in Network Adapter Card. If your network uses more than one model of network adapter, you must create a network installation startup disk for each card model.

10. Click on OK. A license warning appears. Choose OK again.

11. The Network Startup Disk Configuration dialog box appears (see fig. 19.5). This box configures the client that is to be used when the startup disk connects to the server containing the installation files.

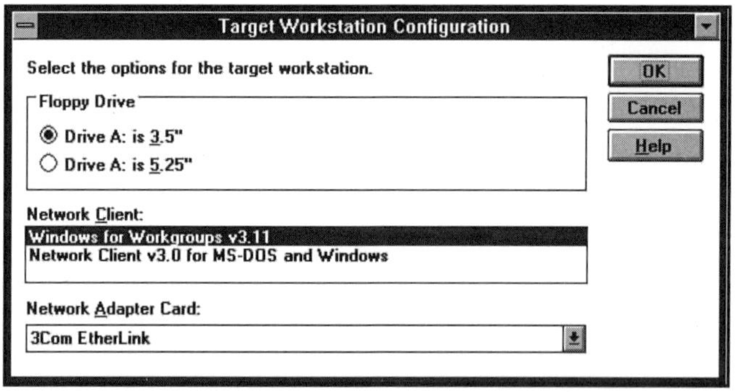

Figure 19.4
Building a network installation startup disk.

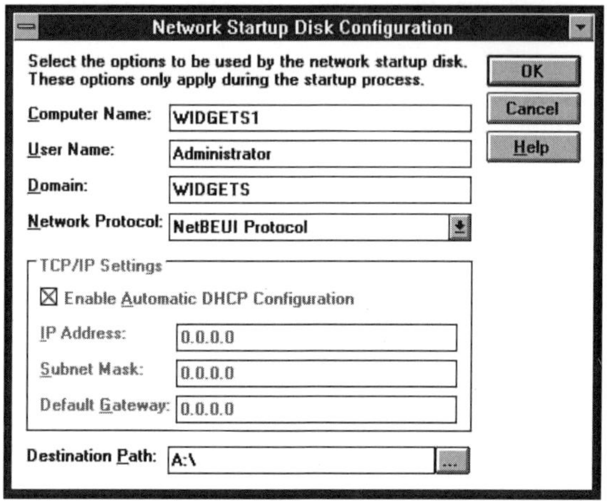

Figure 19.5
Configuring the network installation startup disk.

- Enter the **C**omputer Name to be used while the network installing is taking place. This computer name should not be in use by any other computer. Designate a computer name that is reserved for use during network client installation.

- Enter a **U**ser Name for an account that can access the shared directory. An administrator account is often best here.

- Enter the **D**omain in which the computer resides.

- Select a protocol in the **N**etwork Protocol dialog box. NetBEUI is installed by default on all Windows NT Servers. NetBEUI can only be used if the client is attached to the same network segment as the server.

If TCP/IP is installed on the server, TCP/IP can be used to install clients through the internetwork. If TCP/IP is selected, enter the required TCP/IP settings. *See Chapter 15 for guidance.*

12. The Destination Path is almost always the disk drive on which you are installing the startup files.

13. Insert the formatted system disk in Drive A and click on OK after entering the required information. Files are copied to the disk.

To use the network installation startup disk, perform the following steps:

1. Install the appropriate client operating system on the new client computer.

2. Make sure the source server is active and the share containing the files is available.

3. Boot the network client computer with the network startup disk.

4. Install the client software. Procedures are similar to those described in Chapter 13. Be sure to verify the settings for the network adapter card. The network setup disk was configured with default settings.

Monitoring Computer Performance

The Windows NT Performance Monitor is capable of monitoring quite a few performance characteristics of Windows NT computers. The resulting data can be displayed in the form of charts, can be used to generate alerts, or can be captured into data files for statistical analysis.

Performance Monitor is actually four related utilities. Each has its own screen and command set. This section doesn't attempt to tell you everything there is to know about Performance Monitor. It does, however, show you some of its most useful features.

Charting Performance Statistics

Figure 19.6 shows an example of a chart produced by Performance Monitor. This chart displays a line graph, although bar charts (histograms) are also available and are more appropriate for some types of data. This particular example is tracking processor utilization on two computers. The two lines at the bottom of the window describe the collected statistics.

The statistics are summarized in the *value bar* below the chart:

- **Last.** Shows the most recent reading taken.

- **Average.** Shows the average of all readings since the chart was created.

- **Min** and **Max.** Show the lowest and highest readings recorded.
- **Time.** Shows the time in seconds displayed on one screen of the graph.

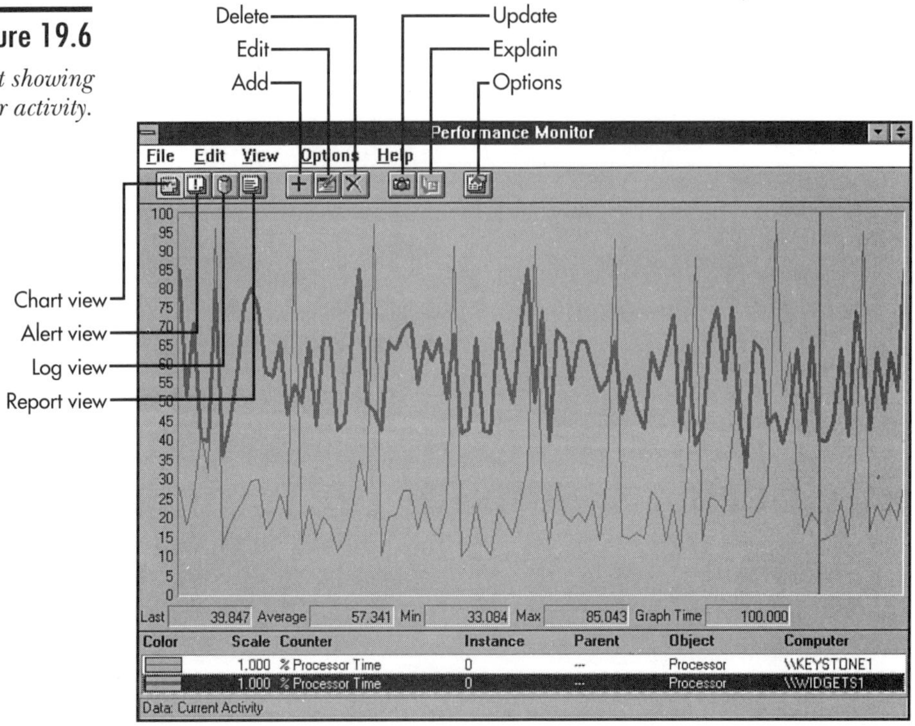

Figure 19.6

A chart showing processor activity.

The callouts in figure 19.6 identify the toolbar buttons. Performance Manager consists of four related tools (Chart, Alert, Log, and Report) with differing commands in their menus, but these four buttons are consistently available.

The easiest way to understand how a chart works is to create one. To create a performance chart, perform the following steps:

1. Select chart view by choosing the Chart command in the View menu or by clicking on the Chart icon in the toolbar.
2. If you want to clear an existing chart, choose New Chart in the File menu.
3. To create a new chart line, choose Add to Chart in the Edit menu or click on the Add button in the toolbar. The Add to Chart dialog box appears (see fig. 19.7).

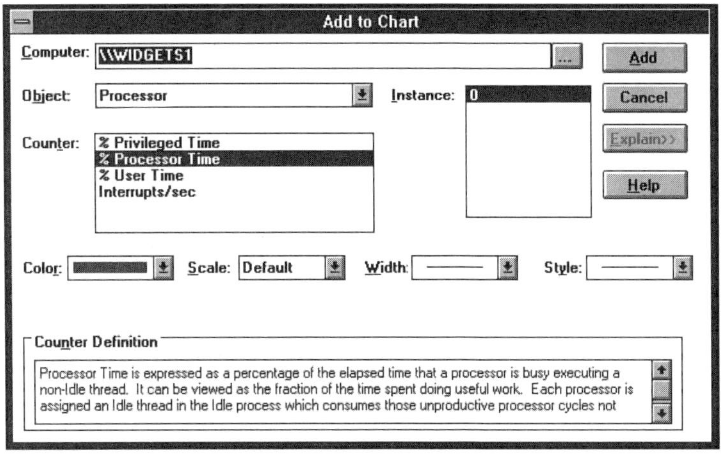

Add to Chart
Computer: \\WIDGETS1
Add
Object: Processor
Instance: 0
Cancel
Counter: % Privileged Time
% Processor Time
% User Time
Interrupts/sec
Explain>>
Help
Color:
Scale: Default
Width:
Style:
Counter Definition
Processor Time is expressed as a percentage of the elapsed time that a processor is busy executing a non-Idle thread. It can be viewed as the fraction of the time spent doing useful work. Each processor is assigned an Idle thread in the Idle process which consumes those unproductive processor cycles not

Figure 19.7

Adding an item to a chart.

4. Enter the computer to be monitored in the Computer box. If you want, click on the Browse button (...) to browse for a computer.

5. Pull down the Object list and select an object to be monitored. Objects are processes running on the computer. Each object has a number of different counters that you can select. The objects displayed in the Object list are different depending on the operating system, and on the services, protocols, and programs that are installed.

6. Select an Instance if more than one is listed. If the example had been created on a multiprocessor server, there would have been more than one instance of a processor. You also would see multiple instances for disk drives in a multi-drive computer.

   If you choose Explain, as was done in figure 19.7, each counter is described briefly in the Counter Definition box at the bottom of the window.

7. Select a Counter to be monitored.

8. Select the Color, Scale, Width, and Style for the line associated with this object. Line width and style are probably more useful than color if you want to print these graphs on a monochrome printer.

   The Scale factor determines how the data is to be scaled on the chart. The default scale is generally 1.000, which is especially appropriate for percentages because the chart scale runs from 0 to 100. Change this factor to increase or reduce the height of the graph as required.

9. Choose Add when you have defined the chart line to your satisfaction.

10. Define and add other chart lines if desired.
11. When all chart lines are defined, choose **D**one. You return to the Chart screen, and the data is displayed.

Tip If you plan to run Performance Monitor for an extended period of time, I suggest you turn off any screen savers you might have configured, or choose a screen saver that simply blanks the screen. Animated screen savers typically peg the processor at 100 percent and probably distort other readings as well. You are attempting to monitor the actual work the computer is performing, not the effort that goes into putting on a show.

To edit the characteristics of any chart line, perform the following steps:

1. Select the legend at the bottom for the chart line to be modified.
2. Choose the **E**dit Chart Line command in the **E**dit menu, or click on the Edit icon in the toolbar. The Edit Chart Line window has the same dialog items as the Add to Chart dialog box. (You also can double-click on the legend to display the Edit Chart Line window.)
3. After making the desired changes, click on OK.

To delete a chart line, perform the following steps:

1. Select the legend at the bottom for the chart line to be deleted.
2. Choose **D**elete From Chart in the **E**dit menu or press the Delete key.

Note Disk performance counters are not ordinarily active because they typically slow disk access time. Although any user can run Performance Monitor, only an administrator can turn on the disk performance counters.

To activate or deactivate disk performance counters, execute the command **diskperf** at a command prompt. Answer **Y** to turn counters on and **N** to turn counters off. (-Y and -N also can be included as command line parameters, as can a computer name in the format *computername*.) The computer must be restarted to put the change into effect.

Setting Chart Options

Several options are available for customizing the chart display. The Chart Options dialog box, shown in figure 19.8, controls these options:

- **Legend.** Check this box to display the chart legends at the bottom of the chart window. Remove the check to hide the legends.
- **Value Bar.** Check this box to display the value bar. Remove the check to hide the value bar.
- **Gallery.** These choices determine whether the data is to be displayed as a Graph (line chart) or as a Histogram (bar chart). A graph displays each item as a line that is tracked by time. A histogram displays a single bar for each item, which is updated at each update time. The graphs are more useful in most circumstances.
- **Update Time.** Choose Periodic Update if you want the data to be updated at regular intervals; the interval in seconds is specified in the Interval box. Choose Manual Update if you want to trigger updates yourself.
- **Vertical Grid** and **Horizontal Grid.** Check these options to display grid lines. Remove the checks to suppress grid lines.
- **Vertical Labels.** Check this option to display labels on the Y (vertical) axis. Remove the check if you do not want the vertical axis to be labeled.
- **Vertical Maximum.** This value specifies the maximum value on the Y (vertical) axis. For percentages, 100 is good, but Performance Monitor also tracks many characteristics that are not percentages. To track megabytes in use on a 512 MB drive, for example, you might set this value to 512.

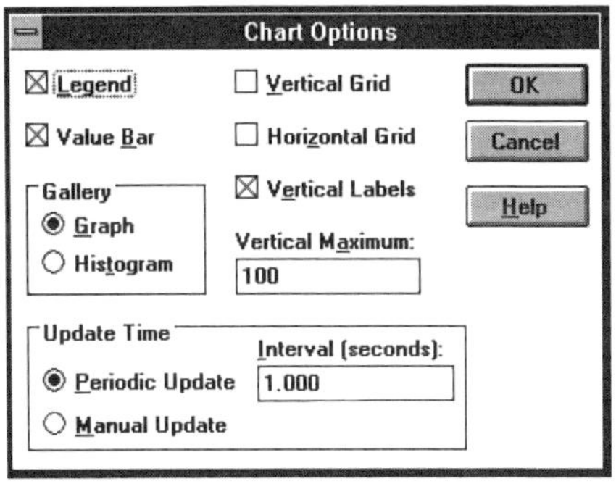

Figure 19.8
Configuring chart options.

Tip Performance Monitor does not have a provision for printing data directly. Any screen can be copied to the clipboard, however, by pressing Alt+Print Screen. Then you can open Paintbrush, paste the image there, and print it.

Setting Alerts

Performance Monitor enables you to set alerts that can monitor any of its counters. Alerts log and can notify administrators when counters rise above or fall below specified values. You might, for example, set an alert on each disk drive so that you are notified when the percent in use rises above 90 percent. Figure 19.9 shows such an alert.

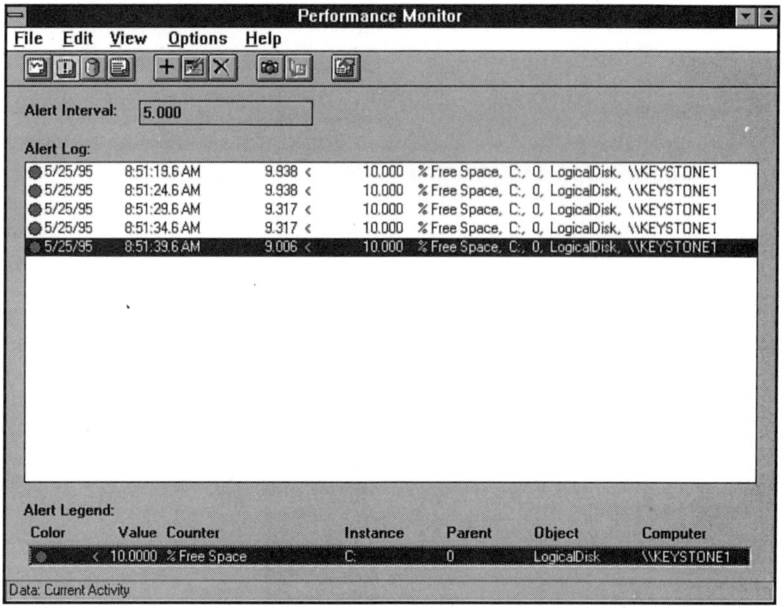

Figure 19.9

An alert in Performance Manager.

Optionally, you can arrange to send network messages when alerts occur (see fig. 19.10).

To add an alert, perform the following steps:

1. Select alert view by choosing the **A**lert command in the **V**iew menu or by clicking on the Alert icon in the toolbar.

2. Choose **A**dd To Alert in the **E**dit menu, or click on the Add icon in the toolbar. The Add to Alert dialog box appears (see fig. 19.11). This screen shot was taken after the **E**xplain button had been clicked on, so explanations of the options appear at the bottom of the window.

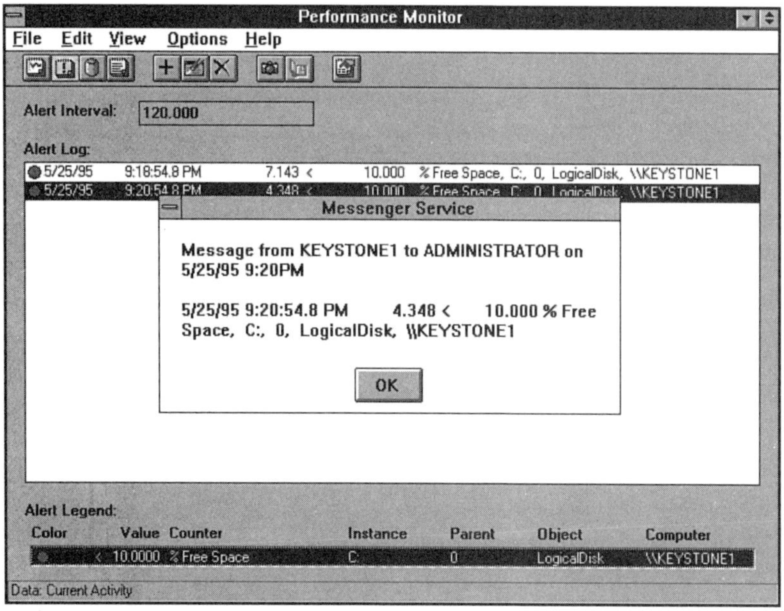

Figure 19.10

A Monitor alert message.

3. Enter the computer to be monitored in the Computer box. If you want, click ... to browse for a computer.
4. Select an Object to be monitored.
5. Select an Instance if more than one is listed.
6. Select a Counter to be monitored.
7. Select the Color to be associated with the alert.
8. In the Alert If box, choose Over or Under and specify a value that is to be used as the alert threshold.
9. If a program is to be run when an alert occurs, enter the program name in the Run Program on Alert box. Then choose whether the program should run the First Time the alert occurs or Every Time the alert occurs.
10. When the alert has been configured, choose Add.

Figure 19.11

Adding an alert.

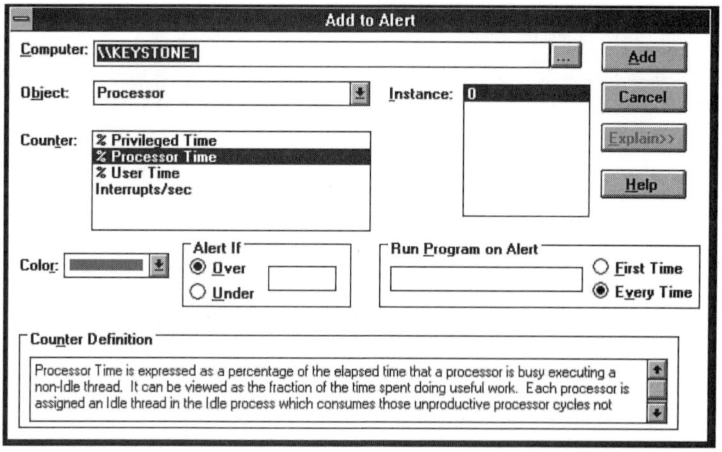
Add to Alert
Computer: \\KEYSTONE1
Add
Object: Processor
Instance: 0
Cancel
Explain>>
Counter: % Privileged Time
% Processor Time
% User Time
Interrupts/sec
Help
Color:
Alert If
Over
Under
Run Program on Alert
First Time
Every Time
Counter Definition
Processor Time is expressed as a percentage of the elapsed time that a processor is busy executing a non-Idle thread. It can be viewed as the fraction of the time spent doing useful work. Each processor is assigned an Idle thread in the Idle process which consumes those unproductive processor cycles not

Setting Alert Options

You can configure options by choosing the Alert command in the Options menu when the alert view is displayed, or by clicking on the Options icon in the toolbar when the alert view is displayed. Figure 19.12 shows the Alert Options dialog box. The available options are the following:

- **Switch to Alert View.** Check this option if you want Performance Monitor to switch to alert view when an alert condition is detected.
- **Log Event in Application Log.** Check this option if you want the event logged. Logged events can be viewed in the Event Monitor.
- **Send Network Message.** Check Send Network Message and enter the user name in the Net Name box, if a network message should be sent to notify users of the alert.
- **Periodic Update.** Check this option if you want to display alerts at regular intervals. Specify the Interval in seconds. (Don't specify an interval too short, or you'll find yourself doing nothing but clearing messages during a crisis.) Check Manual Update if you want to display alerts on demand.

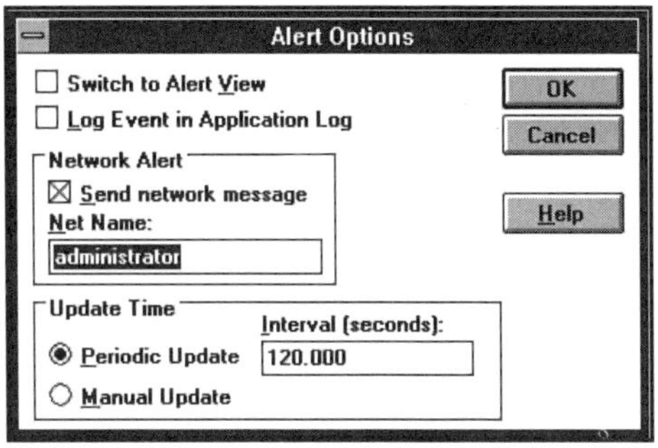

Figure 19.12
The Alert Options dialog box.

Note The messages generated by Performance Monitor are NetBIOS messages, and you need to make sure that the NetBIOS messenger service is running and that it has been alerted of your message recipients. To set up messaging, enter the following commands at a command prompt:

```
net start messenger
net name username add
```

The *username* should match the name you entered in the **N**et Name box in the Alert Options dialog box.

Using Log Files

One task you should perform consistently with Performance Monitor is recording periodic logs of the status of the network. If you record logs when the network is functioning well, the data can help you spot what's wrong when the network starts to falter. You can, for example, record a log for the entire day every Monday, sampling the network at five-minute intervals, then archive these logs for future review.

Recording a Log File

To record a log file, perform the following steps:

1. Select the log view by choosing the **L**og command in the **V**iew menu or by clicking on the Log icon in the toolbar.

2. Choose **N**ew Log Settings in the **F**ile menu to clear out existing log settings.

3. Choose Add To Log in the Edit menu. The Add To Log dialog box appears (see fig. 19.13). This screen shot was taken after the Explain button had been clicked, so explanations of the options appear at the bottom of the window.

4. Enter the computer to be monitored in the Computer box. If you want, click the Browse button (...) to browse for a computer.

5. Select an Object to be logged. All the instances for the objects you select are logged.

6. Choose Add to add the object to the log.

7. Repeat steps 5 and 6 for any other objects you want recorded in the log.

8. Choose Done when all objects have been added. You return to the log view, which specifies the objects to be monitored.

9. Next, specify a log file and turn on logging. Choose Log in the Options menu, or click on the Options button in the toolbar. The Log Options dialog box appears (see fig. 19.14).

Figure 19.13
Adding to a log.

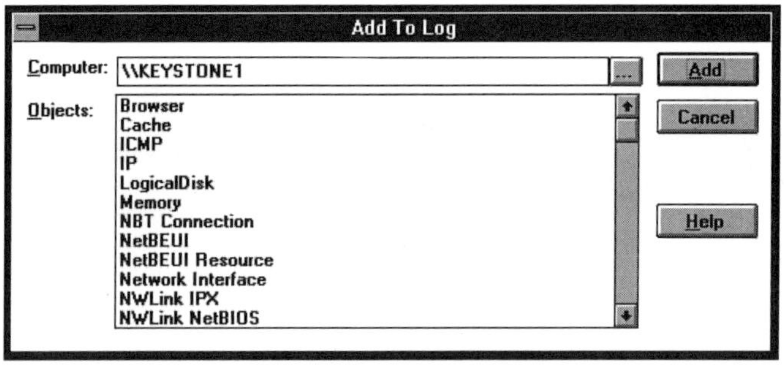

10. In the Directories box, browse for the directory in which log files are to be stored. Choose the Network if you want to browse for a shared network directory.

11. Specify a file name for the log file in the File Name box. Performance Manager supplies the default LOG file name extension.

    Alternatively, select an existing log file.

12. In the Update Time box, specify the log updates desired. Choose Periodic Update and specify an update Interval if updates should take place at automatic intervals. Choose Manual Update if you want to record updates only on demand.

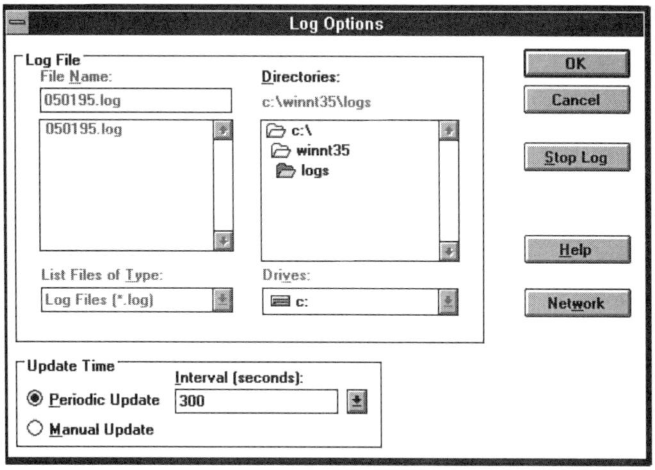

Figure 19.14

Specifying log options.

13. Turn on logging by choosing <u>S</u>tart Log. Then click on OK to return to the log view. The log view in figure 19.15 shows a log that has been configured and started.

14. When you want to stop logging, open the Log Options dialog box and choose <u>S</u>top Log.

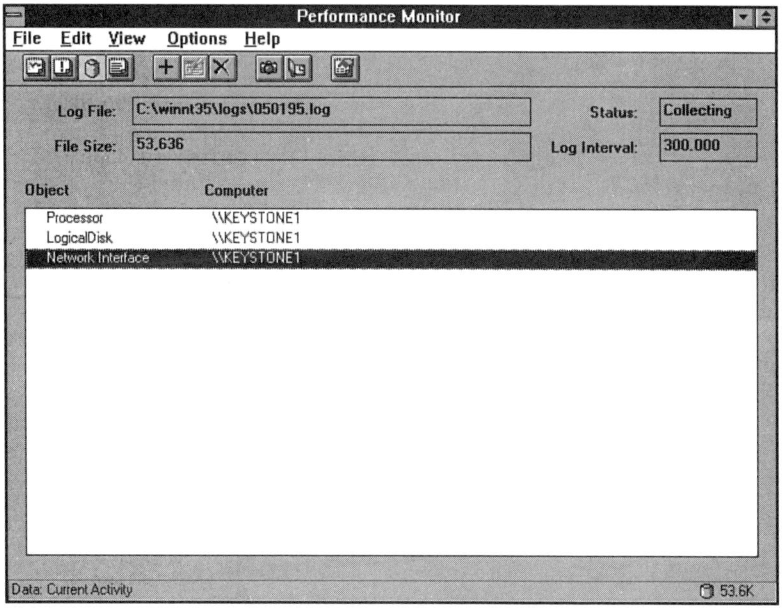

Figure 19.15

A log being recorded.

Using a Log File

After recording a log file, it can be opened for analysis. To open a log file, perform the following steps:

1. If the log file is still collecting data, it must be closed. Select the log view by choosing the **Log** command in the **View** menu or by clicking on the Log icon in the toolbar.

   Open the Log Options window and choose **Stop** Log.

2. Up to this exercise, Performance Monitor has been using data from the current activity. To display data from a log file, do the following:

   - Choose the Data **From** command in the **Options** menu. The Data From dialog box appears (see fig. 19.16).
   - Select **Log** File.
   - Specify the path and file name in the Log File box. Click on ... to browse for a directory and file.
   - Click on OK.

3. If desired, you can specify a time window within the log file.

   - Choose the **Time** Window command in the **Edit** menu. This command is active only when data is coming from a log file. The Input Log File Timeframe appears, as shown in figure 19.17.

   The bar above the **Bookmarks** box graphically indicates the time line in the log file.

   The **Bookmarks** box lists events when data were logged.

   - To select a start time for the data window, do the following:

     Select a bookmark in the **Bookmarks** box and choose Set as **Start**

     or

     Drag the start time handle of the timeline to the desired start time.

- To select a stop time for the data window, do the following:

  Select a bookmark in the **B**ookmarks box and choose Set as Stop.

  or

  Drag the stop time handle of the timeline to the desired stop time.

4. Click on OK.

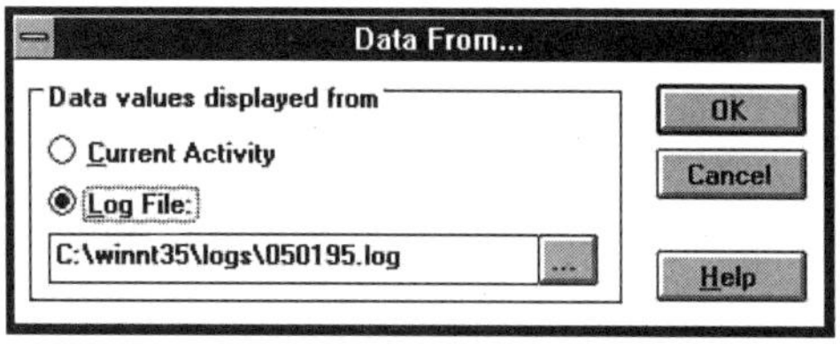

Figure 19.16

Selecting where data is to be taken from.

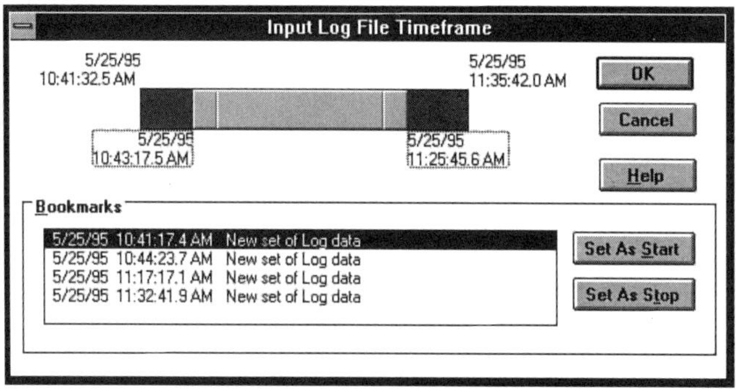

Figure 19.17

Specifying an input log file time frame.

Now, you can enter the chart, alert, or report views and examine the data. You can chart old data, set alert parameters to see if any thresholds were exceeded, or generate reports, just as if data were being actively collected. The only restriction is that you can only include those objects you added to the log.

To resume real-time data analysis, be sure to reset the Data **F**rom command to **C**urrent Activity.

Creating Reports

Reports enable you to capture data in a tabular format. Reports represent a snapshot of the current activity data, and are most valuable when prepared using a log file, because you can scan through the log file to find the data on which you want to report. Reports are configured in a similar manner as charts and alerts. Perform the following steps:

1. Select the report view by choosing the Report command in the View menu or by clicking on the Report icon in the toolbar.
2. If you want to clear a displayed report, choose New Report Settings in the File menu.
3. To create a new report item, choose Add to Report in the Edit menu. The Add to Report dialog box appears, from which you can select the objects and counters to be reported.
4. When all desired objects and counters have been added to the report, choose Done. The report is displayed in the report view.

Exporting Reports

Reports can be exported in tab- or comma-delimited format, enabling report data to be transferred to spreadsheet and database programs for more detailed analysis.

To export a report, perform the following steps:

1. Select the report view.
2. Define the report.
3. Choose Export Report in File menu.
4. In the Performance Monitor—Export As dialog box, specify the directory and file name for the export report file.
5. Select the file format in the List Files of Type box.
    - ◆ TSV files delimit data fields with tab characters.
    - ◆ CSV files delimit data fields with commas.
6. Click on OK to export the file.

Filing Performance Monitor Settings

You may spend quite awhile defining the settings for a view to meet your needs. You can save the settings you have created for any view and retrieve them for use at another time.

To save settings for a view:

1. Select the desired view.
2. Choose Save ... Settings in the File menu. If you have not previously saved the settings, a Save As dialog box appears.

   Or choose Save ... Settings As
3. In the Save As dialog box, specify the Directory and File for the saved settings. The following default file name extensions are used:
   - Chart: .PMC
   - Alerts: .PMA
   - Log: .PML
   - Reports: .PMR

Save As saves only the view settings, not the data. To save data in a file, you must create a log.

To save all settings for all four windows choosing the Save Workspace command in the File menu. You prompted for a file name that is used to store the workspace data.

Tips on Using Performance Monitor

The number of objects and counters available in Performance Manager might overwhelm you. Fortunately, you probably won't need too many of them.

Most problems are manifested in terms of system throughput, and you can focus on several areas when the system seems to be slowing down:

- The processor(s)
- Memory

- Hard drive performance
- Network hardware and software

A good indicator of whether or not the processor is overloaded is %Processor Time, which indicates the percentage of time the processor is busy.

A good way to check memory is to examine cache performance. If the cache is working smoothly, your system probably has enough memory. Monitor the Memory object for Cache Faults/sec and Page Faults/sec. Increasing numbers of errors in these areas indicates that the system is finding data less frequently in memory and must increase the frequency with which data is retrieved from disk. Eventually, a phenomenon called *thrashing* occurs, which means virtually all data accesses require data to be swapped between memory and the hard drive. Thrashing is death to system performance.

Virtual memory makes use of a file named PAGEFILE.SYS. The Paging File object has two counters that can help indicate whether PAGEFILE.SYS is large enough. If %Usage Peak approaches the maximum size you have specified for the paging file, reconfigure virtual memory so that the paging file has a larger maximum size.

Check several statistics for the Logical Disk object. %Disk Time indicates the percentage of time the disk is active. If this value is high, check the Disk Queue Length counter, which indicates the number of pending I/O requests. Microsoft recommends that the Disk Queue Length value not exceed 1.5 to 2 times the number of physical drives that comprise the logical drive.

Avg. Disk sec/Transfer is a good indicator of how rapidly data can be transferred to and from the disk. An increasing value for this counter might indicate a pending hardware failure that is slowing disk throughput.

Network counters are organized by protocol. Select the protocols used most heavily on your network and check a few counters. Monitor the Failures Adapter, which might predict impending failure of a network adapter. Also check Frame Bytes Re-Sent/sec, because frame bytes are resent due to errors. Always expect to see some errors on a network, but be concerned if the number of errors begins to increase.

The absolute number of errors on a network is often less important than changes in the error rates. You should periodically log critical counters on your network and save the log files. Logging statistics when the network is performing well is called *baselining*. Your baseline measurements can serve as basis for comparison when the network slows down. Differences in the statistics help isolate the system that is having problems.

You also can use Performance Monitor to compare statistics on several servers. If one server is working harder than another, move applications or other shared files to the less busy server.

The Process object has an instance for every process running on the computer. It is time consuming, but if you suspect that a particular process is dominating a computer, add a chart line for each process. Track the %Processing Time counter for each process to see if any of the processes is consuming an excessive amount of processor time. (Another option is to use the Process Viewer described at the end of this chapter.)

Managing Browsers

You have seen many instances of using browsing to locate resources on the network. Browsing is yet another service that is supported on the network, and you should be aware of how browsing works in case your users have trouble browsing.

Each domain has a *master browser,* which is usually the primary domain controller. If a master browser announces that it is shutting down, other computers hold an election to determine which is best able to become the domain master browser. If a client cannot find a browser, it can force an election of a new master browser.

As additional computers are added to the network, they may become backup browsers. By default, Windows NT computers become backup browsers, although computers can be configured as standby browsers. The master browser can instruct standby browsers to become backup browsers, attempting to maintain about one backup browser per fifteen computers. Backup browsers spread the work of browsing around. Backup browsers check in every 15 minutes with the master browser to update their databases.

When a server comes onto the network, it announces itself to the master browser. Periodically, the server checks in with the master browser, decreasing the frequency until it is checking in about every 12 minutes.

When a master browser fails, it might be 15 minutes before backup browsers detect the failure. The first backup browser to detect the failure forces an election to select a new master browser.

When clients browse the network, they use a browser API call to identify browsers on the network, to select a browser, and to browse the database in the browser.

A computer's browser behavior is determined by a key in the Registry: HKEY_LOCAL_MACHINE\SYSTEM\CurrentControlSet\Services\Browser\Parameters. The MaintainServerList value entry for this key can have three values:

- **No.** Indicates that the computer will never be a browser.
- **Yes.** Indicates that the computer will be a browser. It will attempt to contact the master browser and become a backup browser. If no master browser is found, the computer forces an election for a master browser. This value is the default value for Windows NT computers.
- **Auto.** Indicates that the computer is a standby browser and can become a backup browser if a master browser notifies it do so.

With a Windows for Workgroups computer, you can control the computer's browser behavior by adding a line to the `[network]` section of the SYSTEM.INI file. To prevent the computer from functioning as a browser, add the following line:

```
MaintainServerList=No
```

Note The list of servers maintained by a master browser is limited to 64 KB of data. As a result, a domain or workgroup is limited to about 2,000–3,000 computers.

Monitoring Browser Status

The Windows NT Resource Kit includes a Browser Monitor that can be used to monitor the status of browsers on a network. The icon for this program is installed in the Resource Kit program group.

When you start the Browser Monitor utility, you must tell it which domain or domains to display. Choose the Add Domain command in the Domain menu. Then select a domain from the Select Domain list. Workgroups count as well as Windows NT domains; you can add either or both. After you have added domains, you should have a list similar to the one in figure 19.18.

Each protocol that supports browsing should show a master browser. This figure shows a master browser for the Keystone domain, for the *NWLinkNB* (NetBIOS over NWLink) protocol, and for *Nbf* (NetBIOS Frame Protocol, Microsoft's name for TDI-compliant NetBEUI).

You can determine from this window which computer is functioning as the master browser for each domain. KEYSTONE1 is the master browser for the KEYSTONE domain, which isn't surprising as it is the primary domain controller. The Windows for Workgroups computer named BUSTER is the master browser for Workgroup.

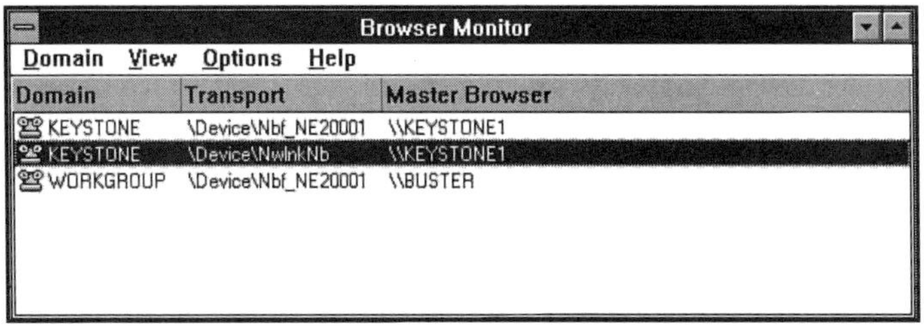

Figure 19.18

A master browser list.

Each of these entries can be used to access a separate browser status window, which you can examine by selecting an entry and choosing the **P**roperties command in the **D**omain menu. Figure 19.19 shows the browser status display for the KEYSTONE domain NBF protocol. From this window, you can determine that KEYSTONE1 and KEYSTONE2 servers are both functioning as browsers for the KEYSTONE domain. They are also backup browsers for WORKGROUP.

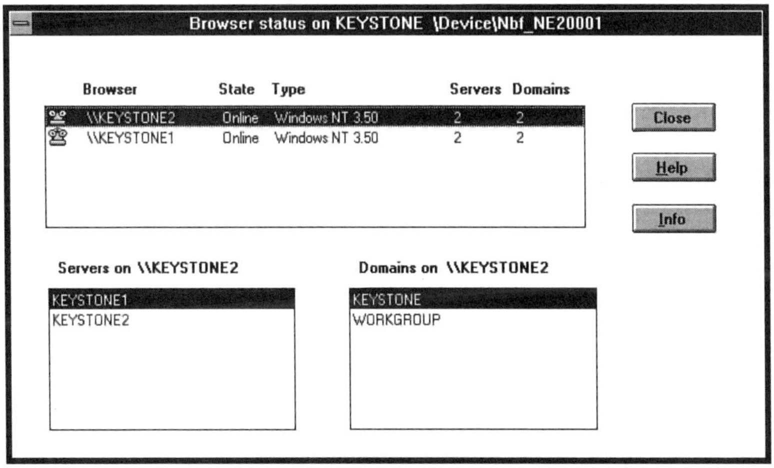

Figure 19.19

Browser status for a domain.

Remember that it takes some time for backup browsers and servers to register their presence with the master browser. If you are running Browser Manager immediately after starting computers on the network, it might take awhile before the data catches up with your expectations.

If you want to see details about one of the browsers, double-click on its entry in the Browser list. You are rewarded with a list containing more statistics than you care to have. Figure 19.20 offers an example.

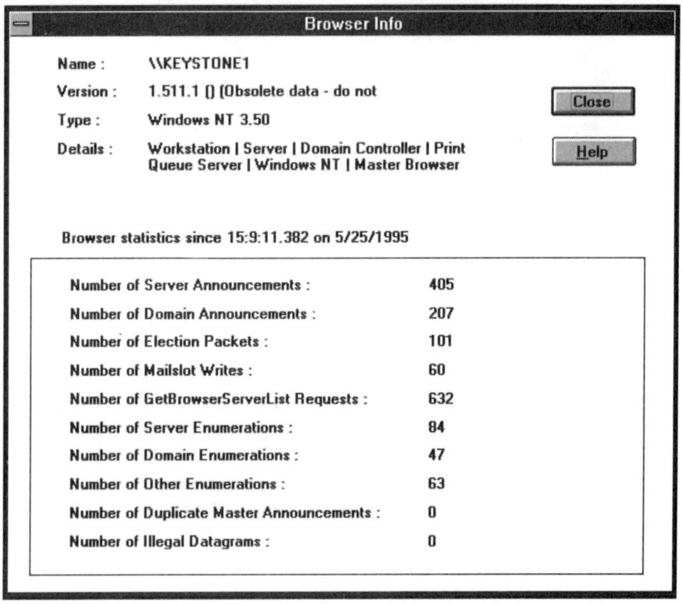

Figure 19.20
Detailed information about a browser.

Other Mini Network Utilities

The Windows NT Resource Kit includes some other simple utilities that you might find useful for network monitoring.

Domain Manager

After you use the Add Domain in the Domain menu to add a domain to Domain Manager, double-click on the domain in the main window to display an information box similar to the one in figure 19.21. This Domain Controller Status window offers a quick way to find out about the domain controllers and trust relationships for a domain.

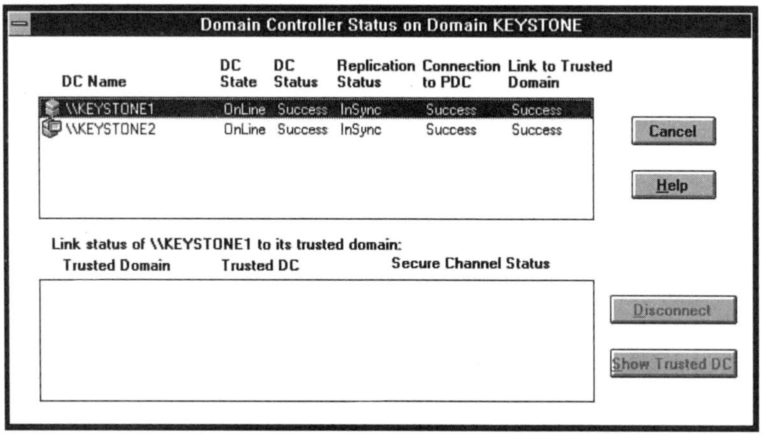

Figure 19.21

The status of a domain in Domain Manager.

Net Watcher

Net Watcher displays a browseable list of shares and users in the domain, an example of which is shown in figure 19.22. You can double-click on any of these items for more detail.

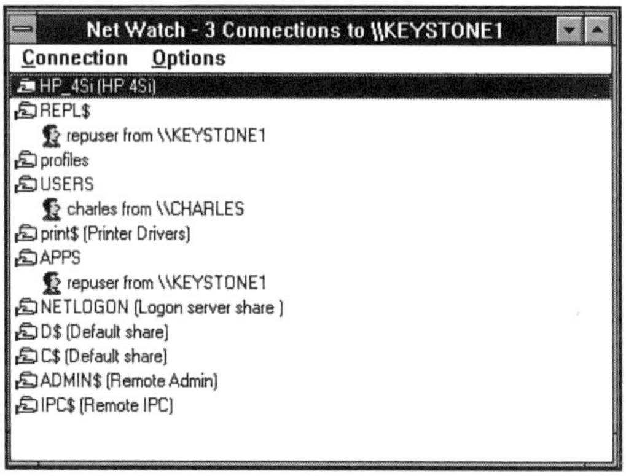

Figure 19.22

You can double-click on shares and users to see more information about them.

Shares and Users Displayed in Net Watcher.Process Viewer

This utility shows you detailed information about every process running on a computer. Figure 19.24 offers an example of a Process Viewer display. You need to dig in to the Windows NT Resource Kit to find out what all the statistics are, but that is true of Performance Monitor as well. The **M**emory Detail button in Performance Viewer enables you to examine the detailed memory usage of a process. You also can kill processes with the **K**ill Process button, so Process Viewer can make you very dangerous.

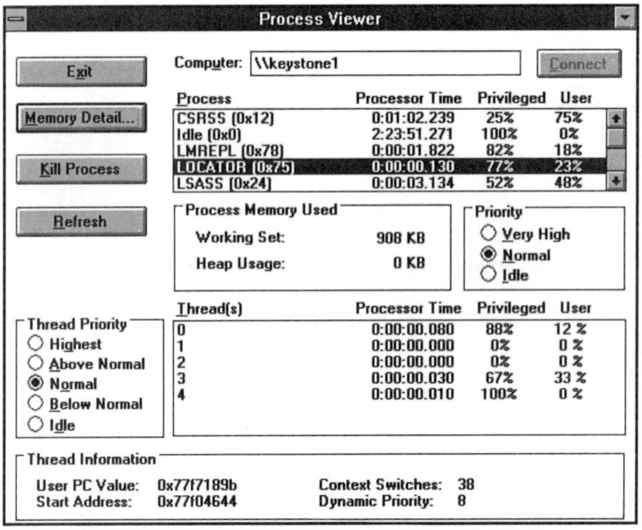

Figure 19.24

The Process Viewer.

CHAPTER 20

Using the Remote Access Server

Executives, sales, and marketing staffs are used to traveling, but increasingly other categories of staff members are finding themselves working away from the office. A few companies have even closed entire offices, given their employees a desk and a business telephone, and sent them home to work. When users travel, or when they work at home, they still expect to maintain contact with the central office. Increasingly, that means that users are demanding remote access to their company LANs.

Offices that can be anywhere have come to be called *virtual offices*, and we can expect to see a lot more virtual offices as portable computers become less expensive and telecommuting becomes easier. Consequently, it is extremely likely that users will be demanding remote access to your LAN to send e-mail, to access central databases, or to exchange files with their co-workers.

Remote LAN access has been possible for several years, thanks to programs such as PC Anywhere and Carbon Copy. But adding dial-up capability has generally meant buying additional products, integrating them, and training your users to use them and live with the quirks.

Microsoft has simplified remote LAN access considerably by building a Remote Access Server (RAS) into Windows NT and into Windows for Workgroups. RAS integrates smoothly with Windows and doesn't require users to learn a new method of using LAN resources. The only difference between a remote user and a local user is the initial dial-in step. Once the dial-in is set up, everything works as though the computer were directly attached to the LAN cable.

RAS isn't a telecommunication program, and it can't be used for accessing, say, CompuServe or a BBS. But it is easy to integrate TCP/IP with RAS, and RAS can be used as a way to access the Internet.

This chapter will teach you how remote access works with an emphasis on RAS. You will learn how to add remote access capability to your LAN, how to connect to the LAN from a remote location, and how to use RAS to access the Internet.

Styles of Remote Access

Remote access wasn't a big problem when applications and terminals were based on text and when all controls were typed commands. But PCs eliminated that simplicity long ago by introducing graphic interfaces and non-keyboard input devices. Windows users want to be able to use their mice, they don't want to give up their graphic interfaces, and they certainly don't want to learn a complicated command language for transferring files or using central computer resources. Therefore, a successful remote access strategy must enable users to carry their desktop graphic environments with them.

There are two approaches to remote network access that meet the needs of a graphic environment: remote control and remote node. You need to comprehend the differences to understand when RAS is appropriate and when you should examine another approach.

Remote Access Using Remote Control

Remote control is the older and better-established of the two approaches. It was pioneered by programs such as Carbon Copy and PC Anywhere, and works as shown in figure 20.1. For every remote user, you need two computers: one remote and one with a local LAN attachment.

The local PC operates just like a normal PC. It connects to the LAN, runs applications, reads and writes network files, and prints as if it were a stand-alone PC. The trick with remote control is that special software enables a remote computer to clone the local computer's screen, keyboard, and mouse. When the remote user types a key, the keystroke is transferred to the local computer that treats the keystroke as its own. When the screen on the local computer is updated, data describing the change is sent to the remote computer which also updates its screen.

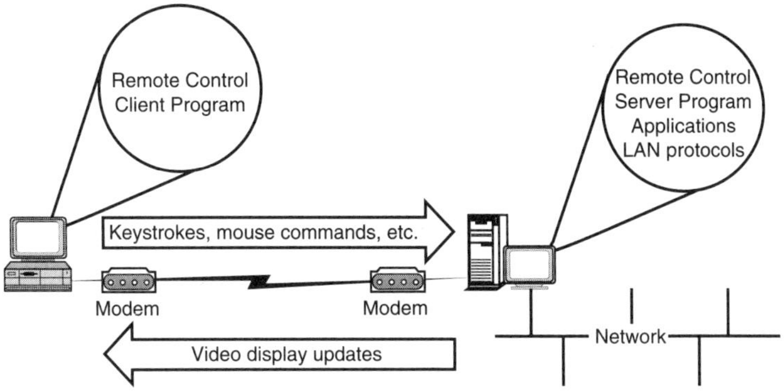

Figure 20.1

Remote computer access using remote control.

The only thing running in the remote computer is the remote control software. When the user runs Lotus 1-2-3, the program is loaded in the local computer. Files are opened and calculations take place all on the local computer. The only things that travel between the remote and the local computer are control codes: keystrokes, screen updates, and mouse commands.

The remote control approach was not developed for LANs but works fine in a LAN environment. A user might leave Carbon Copy running on his desktop PC when leaving for the night, enabling him to dial in from his home PC. Or a department might install a bank of PCs strictly for dial-in support, leaving PC Anywhere running on those computers full time.

Remote control works well, but often not as well as we would like. Graphics screen data in particular can fill up a 14.4 Kbps modem line. You can buy a faster computer, but unless you have ISDN—and what hotel rooms do—you are lucky to be able to push more that 1400–2800 characters through a phone line in a second. When the display is a 640×480 color VGA display, modem bandwidth gets bogged down in a hurry. Consequently, users often complain that remote control access is too painfully slow to work with.

Another problem with remote control is that users need to learn how to use the remote control software. If they want to copy a file from their remote computer to the LAN, they can't use File Manager. Instead, they must use the copy utility that is built into the remote control software. As a result, remote control is not as natural as using a local computer.

Remote Access with Remote Nodes

Remote node technology was developed with LANs in mind. The basic idea is that, instead of connecting to the LAN through a network adapter card, a remote computer connects through a modem and a network access server. Yes, the modem connection is slower than a LAN card, but many LAN operations don't transfer a lot of data and a modem can often keep up just fine.

Figure 20.2 shows how remote node operation works. A big difference is that applications are now running on the remote computer. All the local computer is doing is running a modem program that enables the user to dial in and access the LAN. Since the local computer doesn't have to run applications for the dial-in user, it can often support several users. Windows NT RAS can theoretically support up to 256 remote users.

Figure 20.2

Remote access using a remote node.

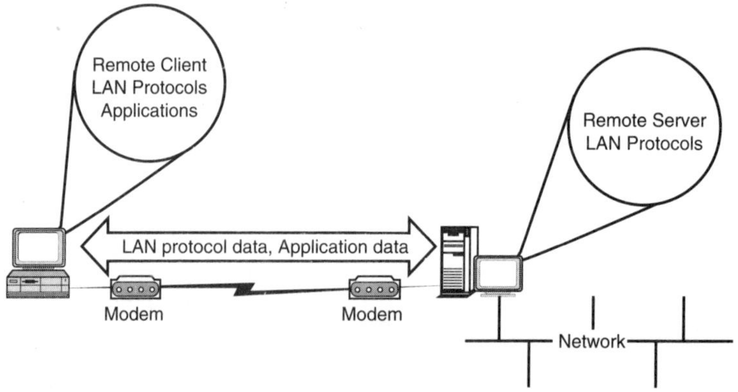

So what's passing through the modems? Data, of course. If a user copies a file, it is transferred through the phone line. Also going through the remote node is LAN protocol traffic. In fact, the remote computer is running almost exactly the same software it would be running if it were directly attached to the LAN. If the LAN runs on NetBEUI, the remote computer must load a NetBEUI protocol stack. The difference is that traffic to and from the protocol stack is routed through the phone line.

After a user achieves a dial-up connection, the remote computer is used as though it is locally attached. Users don't need to learn a new software package. File Manager copies files to the LAN just as it would if the user were directly attached.

The down side to remote node is that it doesn't work well in a lot of situations. Suppose a remote user needs to edit an Excel spreadsheet that is stored on the LAN. Excel spreadsheet files are big! If the user opens a 546 KB file, nothing happens until 546 KB of file data are transferred through the modem connection and into the users PC, which can take about ten minutes. When the file needs to be saved, the process is reversed. To make matters worse, what if the Excel program itself is being run from the LAN. Excel makes use of several megabytes of files, swapping file data in and out of memory almost constantly. A LAN can handle that much data transfer, but a modem can't.

Remote control works better with large files and applications being run from the LAN because the files and the applications are never transferred through the modem; they only need to get as far as the local PC that is functioning as a remote control host. Only screen, keyboard, and mouse data go through the modem, and they constitute a much smaller volume of data than an Excel spreadsheet.

Remote node access is preferred when:

- All applications required by the user are loaded on the remote PC.
- Data transfer volumes when running applications are relatively low.
- Users don't want to learn a new procedure.

Remote control is the preferred approach when:

- Users must access applications that are only stored on the LAN. A custom database application is a good example.
- Users must interact with large files.

Eventually, ISDN will do away with the need to make this distinction. When users have access to over 100 Kbps of data bandwidth, remote node becomes a viable technology even when large data transfers are required. Until that time, however, planning a remote access strategy requires some strategy and analysis of tradeoffs.

Introduction to Remote Access Service

RAS is both a dial-in and a dial-out utility. As a dial-in utility, RAS can be configured to support modems on as many as 256 serial ports which can be configured into a modem pool.

Dial-out capability enables the user of the RAS computer to dial out to remote RAS hosts. Unfortunately, RAS does not support a dial-out modem pool that can be accessed by users on the local LAN.

Before looking at installation, management, and use of RAS, we need to examine Remote Access Service features so that you can plan your RAS installation.

Security

Security is a significant concern for any LAN with dial-in capabilities. Unfortunately, the world is full of people who have made breaking into computers a hobby or a profession, and a modem tone on a phone line is a challenge to too many people.

RAS can support a very high level of security. Dial-in users are authenticated by Windows NT Server standard security, which can be enough for many organizations. If added security is desired, RAS can be configured to operate in dial-back mode. When a user calls in dial-back mode, RAS hangs up and calls the user at a specific telephone number. That way, it isn't enough for an intruder to have a valid user name and password, the intruder must also be calling from a specific telephone to get in. Dial-back makes dial-in access extremely secure.

Dial-back operation has another benefit because the bulk of long-distance calling charges will be born by the organization's company lines, which probably have a better cost structure than telephone credit cards.

When the tightest dial-in control is desired, RAS can interface with a separate security access system. These systems typically require users to carry a calculator-like security card that incorporates a security algorithm. The dial-in security host issues a challenge to the user in the form of a numeric code. The user's security card is used to generate a secure response that the user enters into the terminal. Only if the response matches the anticipated result is the user granted access.

Communication security between RAS computers is maintained through support for data encryption using the RC4 algorithm licensed from RSA Data Security Incorporated.

Another security feature available with RAS is the ability to configure each user's dial-in restrictions to determine whether the user will be permitted to access the entire LAN or will be limited to accessing files on the RAS server itself.

RAS Communication Methods

RAS is equally versatile in terms of available communication methods. Users can connect through conventional analog modems, Integrated Services Digital Network (ISDN), or widely-available X.25 networks. Null Modem connections are also supported for local access.

Analog Modems

RAS supports a wide variety of modems. Windows NT supports up to 256 modems, which can be configured in modem pools that support dial-in and dial-out traffic.

RAS supports three modem protocols: PPP, SLIP, and a proprietary RAS protocol, enabling a variety of clients to dial into and out of a RAS server. To support more than four modems on an Intel *x*86 PC, you will need to install multi-port serial adapters. Consult the Hardware Compatibility List for supported multi-port adapters.

Note Microsoft recommends using the same brand and model of modem on both ends of communication, because mixing models can result in difficult-to-troubleshoot problems. Of course, unless you are starting from scratch, you will seldom have a single-model modem pool, so be prepared to experiment.

The following list describes the modem protocols that RAS supports:

- **SLIP.** The Serial-Line Internet Protocol (SLIP) is an extremely basic protocol developed for the Unix environment. SLIP operates without error checking, flow control, or security. However SLIP remains popular because it operates with little overhead and provides good performance. RAS supports SLIP for dial-out operating, enabling RAS clients to access Unix computers and many Internet providers.

- **PPP.** The Point-to-Point (PPP) protocol is sometimes referred to as "SLIP done right." PPP performs error checking and recovery and can cope with noisier lines than SLIP. Although PPP has slightly higher overhead than SLIP, PPP is becoming the preferred protocol for remote access. RAS supports PPP for dial-in and dial-out operation.

- **RAS Protocol.** The RAS protocol is a Microsoft proprietary protocol that supports NetBIOS, and is supported by all versions of RAS. The RAS protocol is required to use the NetBEUI protocol.

RS-232C Null Modem

A *null modem* is a cable that crosses wires to enable two RS-232 ports to connect as though there were modems between. This setting can be used for local testing of the RAS server. It also enables a PC to attach through a serial connection to a local network when it is not equipped with a network adapter on that network. Wiring of null modem cables is described in the last section of this chapter.

X.25

X.25 is an old and clunky but reliable and widely available wide area network service that is based on packet switching. In most cases, companies lease the use of a commercial X.25 network, gaining access through a dedicated phone line or a dial-up port. Several commercial X.25 networks are available, and a company could easily plan an affordable WAN strategy using X.25.

Figure 20.3 illustrates how X.25 might be used with RAS. X.25 networks are typically drawn as clouds, because the operation of the X.25 network is invisible to users. A customer simply sends a packet into a cloud at one point, and the packet emerges from the cloud at the destination. The route the packet took through the network is not the customer's concern.

Computers can access an X.25 network in two ways:

- Through a direct connection, using a device like an X.25 smart card.
- Through a modem using a device called a packet assembler-disassembler (PAD), which performs the task of formatting user messages into packets that can travel through the network and reassembling messages from received packets.

For organizations with large volumes of remote access, X.25 might be preferable to relying on long-distance modem access. Performance is potentially better, and costs will be lower for high-volume users.

Figure 20.3

Features of an X.25 network.

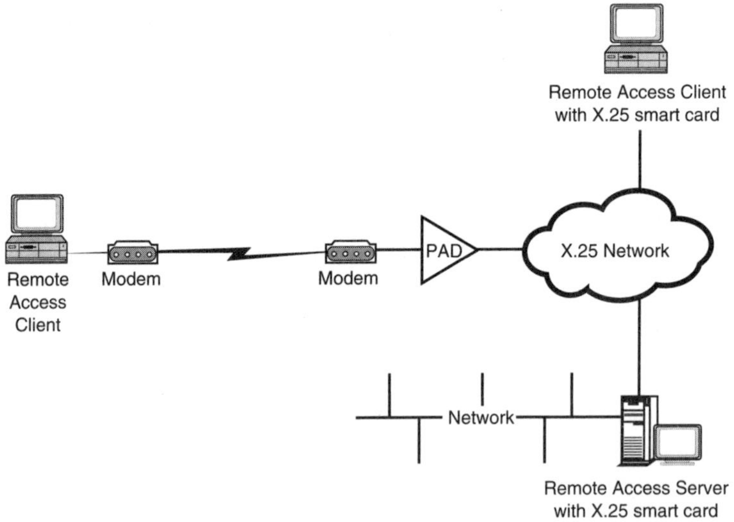

ISDN

Integrated Services Digital Network (ISDN) is the state-of-the-art for dial-up digital communications. Modems working with voice telephone lines must convert digital signals to analog, a process that limits bandwidth typically to 14,400 bps, although higher rates can be achieved using data compression. Unfortunately, much of the data that is transmitted between computers is already compressed, and compression of the data communication channel yields little improvement in bandwidth. Although speeds higher than 14,400 bps are practical, even the slightest degradation of line performance can cause modems to shift down to a lower speed.

ISDN is digital all the way. Several levels of service are available and multi-megabit speeds are possible. Service is offered in several channel configurations that are assigned an identifying letter. A basic rate ISDN line for a customer is configured with two B channels that operate at 64 kilobits per second (Kbps). A D channel is included to support 16 kilobits per second.

Ordinarily, the two B channels provide separate routes of communication. Some ISDN interface devices and drivers have the capability of aggregating the B channels to provide 128 Kbps of channel bandwidth.

ISDN requires use of ISDN cards in place of modems. Both ends of the communication must be equipped with ISDN, which can be a significant problem. Local telephone companies have been inconsistent in their eagerness to offer ISDN to their customers. While some providers have committed to offering ISDN to all their customers, others have dragged their feet. As a result, you might have ISDN service, but the place you are calling might not.

RAS Clients

RAS supports a variety of remote clients. Windows NT and Windows for Workgroups include RAS. RAS software is also available for MS-DOS. Additionally, clients that communicate with the PPP protocol (described later) can connect with RAS.

Windows NT Clients

Windows NT 3.5 Workstation and Server includes RAS and introduces support for the PPP protocol. Windows NT 3.5 clients can dial into and negotiate security with RAS servers using the RAS, PPP, or SLIP protocols. They can also access other remote services, such as Unix or the Internet, using PPP or SLIP.

Windows NT 3.1 is compatible with RAS with the exception that version 3.1 lacks support for the PPP protocol. Users of Windows NT 3.1 must use the proprietary RAS protocol to call a RAS server.

Windows for Workgroups Clients

WfW includes RAS. If you are not using WfW version 3.11, you might want to upgrade the network client software using the WfW client that is included with Windows NT Server 3.5. *See Chapter 13, "Using Windows and DOS Clients," for information about the WfW client.*

MS-DOS and Windows 3.1 Clients

The Microsoft Network Client version 3.0 for MS-DOS and Windows provides RAS support. You must install the full redirector and access RAS using the **rasphone** command.

RAS for MS-DOS supports only NetBEUI applications and does not support client applications that require TCP/IP or IPX.

PPP Clients

Terminal-mode PPP clients can access RAS. The RAS server will automatically initiate an authentication dialog. This mode enables Unix and other non-Microsoft clients to access files on the RAS server or the Windows NT Server network.

Installing and Configuring RAS

RAS is configured as a network service. In many ways, installation and configuration procedures resemble the procedures used with a network adapter card, and much of the material in this chapter will be familiar to you from earlier chapters.

The RAS installation and configuration procedure has these major stages:

1. Hardware installation
2. Configuration of serial ports
3. Installation of the RAS software
4. Configuration of RAS LAN protocols
5. Configuration of RAS user accounts

Because hardware installation is highly varied, it won't be addressed here; it is beyond the scope of this book.

Serial port configuration is performed with the Ports utility in the control panel. This tool was described in Chapter 12, "Managing Printing Services." Only serial ports that have been configured with the Ports utility can be configured to support RAS.

X.25 PADs are installed as serial devices on RS-232C ports.

ISDN adapters should be installed according to the manufacturer's instructions. Installation of this hardware is beyond the scope of this book.

Installing RAS Software

As with all network services, RAS is installed and its protocols are configured using the Network utility in the Control Panel. This tool has been encountered several times in this book, most notably in Chapter 7, "Installing Windows NT Server." This chapter will only dwell on procedures that are specific to RAS.

To install the RAS software:

1. Start the Network utility in the Control panel.

2. Click on the Add Software button.

3. In the Add Network Software dialog box, pull down the Network Software box and select Remote Access Server from the list.

4. Click on Continue.

5. In the Windows NT Setup dialog box, supply the path name for the installation files and choose Continue. Files will be copied to the server.

6. After the software is installed, the Remote Access Setup dialog box is produced. (See figure 20.4, which shows the box after a port has been configured.) At first, no ports or devices will be defined.

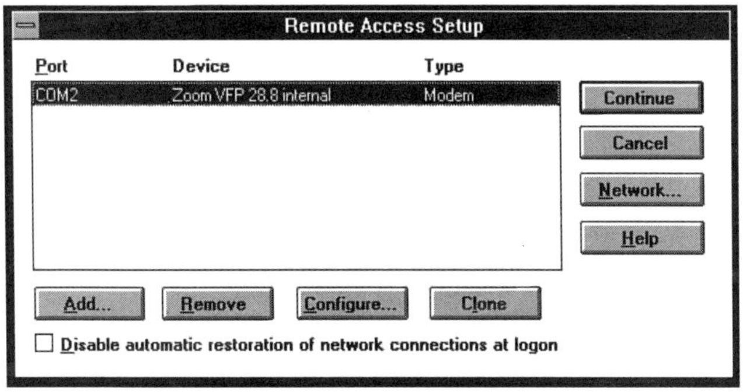

Figure 20.4

Adding ports and modems to RAS.

7. Check Disable automatic restoration of network connections at logon option if previous connections should be restored when a user logs on remotely. Since restoring connections over a remote link can be time-consuming, this option is checked by default.

8. To begin adding a port and device, click on Add to display the Add Port dialog box shown in figure 20.5. Only ports you have configured with the Ports utility in the Control Panel will be available in this dialog box.

Figure 20.5

Adding a port to RAS.

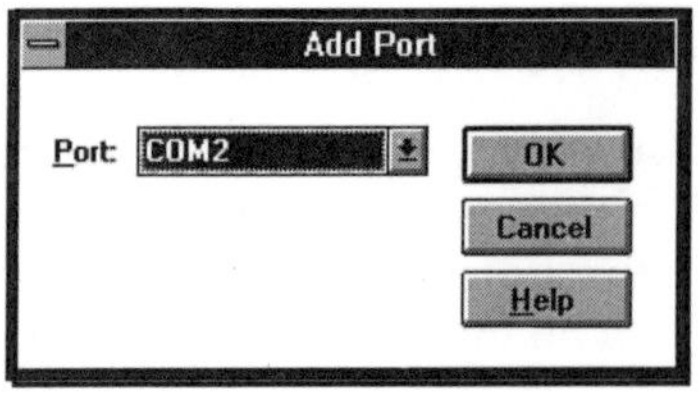

9. Pull down the **P**ort box, and select the port that supports your communication device. Click on OK to continue.

10. Next you will see the message shown in figure 20.6. RAS setup can attempt to discover your modem brand and model. If you want to choose a modem from a list, click on Cancel. Otherwise click on OK to start automatic modem detection.

Figure 20.6

Message displayed prior to modem detection.

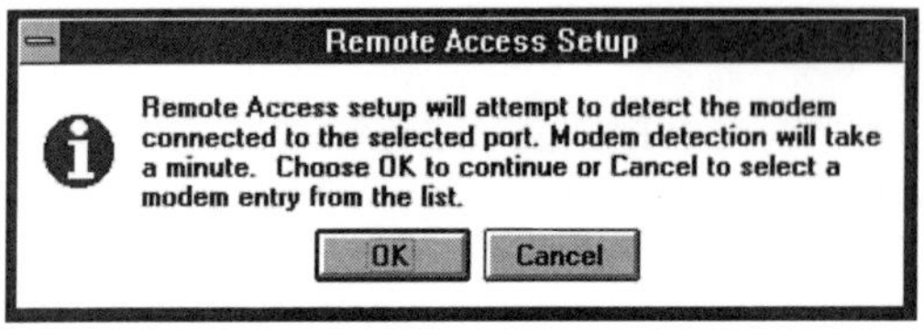

11. When the search is complete, one or more candidate modem models should be listed in the Detect Modem dialog box shown in figure 20.7. Select a modem and click on OK. You will be directed to the Configure Port dialog box shown in figure 20.8, with the modem you selected highlighted.

Figure 20.7

Selecting a modem after modem detection.

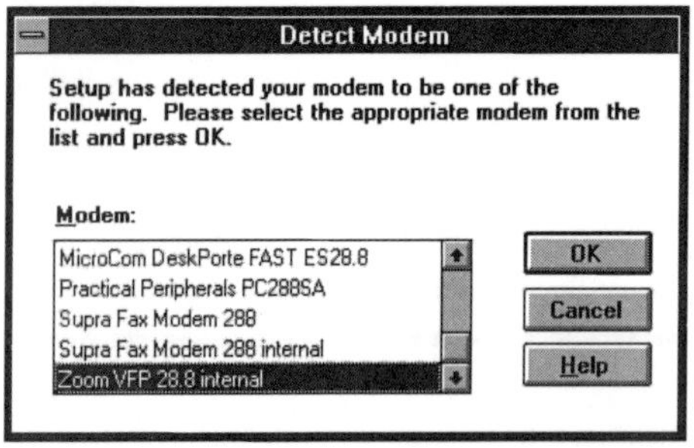

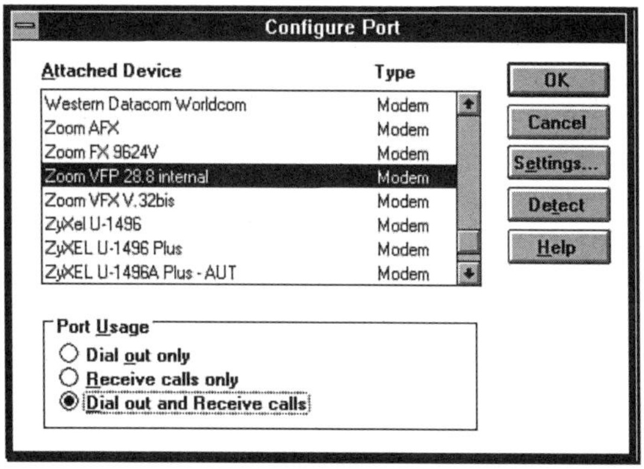

Figure 20.8

Configuration settings for a port.

Note Not only modems appear in the **A**ttached Device list, and it's worth scrolling through it to familiarize yourself with the choices. You will find:

- Several X.25 PADs
- Null modems with settings of 4,800, 9,600, 19,200, and 38,400 bps. Only high-speed serial ports will support the higher data rates.

12. The Port Usage box offers three settings that determine how this modem can be used:

    - Dial out only
    - Receive calls only
    - Dial out and Receive calls

    Select the desired setting for this port.

13. The Settings button reveals a modem Settings dialog box, shown in figure 20.9. Four settings can be selected or deselected for the modem. These settings apply only when receiving calls:

    - Enable Modem Speaker. Select this setting to enable the modem speaker when a call is coming in. This is useful when troubleshooting, but a real noisemaker if several modems are in operation at once.

- Enable Hardware **F**low Control (RTS/CTS). In almost all cases, you want to enable hardware flow control, which uses the RTS/CTS (Request to Send/Clear to Send) wire pairs in a conventional serial cable to provide flow control between the computer and modem.

- Enable **E**rror Control. Enable this setting to have the modem perform cyclic redundancy checks (CRCs) on blocks of data. This setting reduces communication overhead by eliminating the use of start and stop bits.

- Enable Modem **C**ompression. If modems at both ends of the communication can perform data compression, this setting will improve data throughput. Be sure that the modems conform to the same data compression standards. Microsoft does not recommend the use of hardware data compression. Software compression has better performance because a larger pattern buffer is available.

Note NT 3.5 service pack #2 from Microsoft provides software compression for WFN6 3.11 clients. Contact MS about receiving SP #2 for this update.

After selecting the desired settings, click on OK to return to the Configure Port dialog box. Click on OK in the Configure Port dialog box when this port is configured as desired. You will return to the Remote Access Setup dialog box.

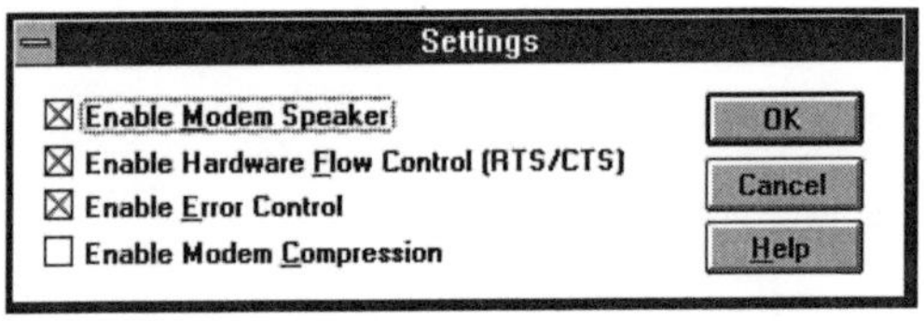

Figure 20.9
Selecting modem settings.

14. The **N**etwork button in the Remote Access Setup dialog box is used to configure the protocols that RAS will support. Click on this button to display the dialog box shown in figure 20.10.

    Check the protocols that will be supported for dial-in and dial-out operation.

Note Windows 3.*x* clients can use only NetBEUI with RAS.

Windows NT clients can use NetBEUI, NWLink, and TCPIP over RAS.

Windows 95 will also support all protocols over RAS.

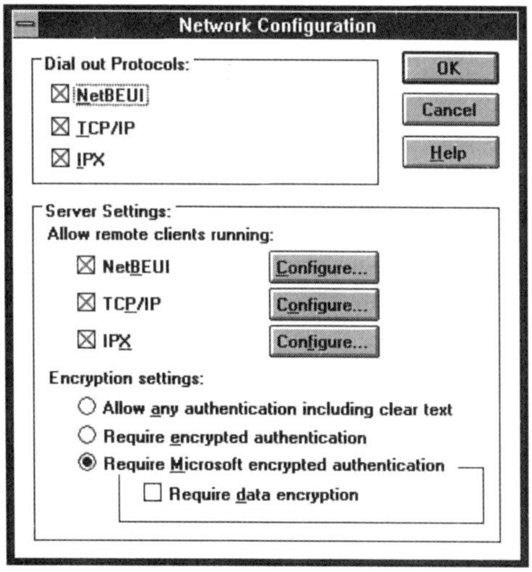

Figure 20.10
RAS network configuration.

15. Select the encryption setting:

   - Require **M**icrosoft encrypted authentication. For clients that support Microsoft encryption (MS-CHAP), this is the preferred setting. If you check the box Require **d**ata encryption, all data transferred between the client and server are encrypted using the RSA Data Security Incorporated RC4 algorithm.

   - Require **e**ncrypted authentication enables users to connect with MS-CHAP, MD5-CHAP, and SPAP.

   - Allow **a**ny authentication permits clear text authentication as well as encrypted authentication using MS-CHAP, MD5-CHAP, SPAP, and PAP. This setting is useful with clients that do not support data encryption.

   Choose OK when Network Configuration settings are complete.

16. When you exit the Network Configuration settings dialog box, you will be shown a dialog box to configure each of the protocols you have selected. Network configuration for NetBEUI, TCP/IP, and IPX are described in their own sections.

17. After RAS has been configured, you will be returned to the Network utility. You will need to supply a path for additional software installation. After the RAS program icons are created, you will be warned that you need to use the Remote Access Admin program to assign RAS permissions to users. Click on OK to continue.

18. Click on OK in the Network Settings dialog box to complete installation. After RAS is configured, you might see further dialog boxes for protocol configuration.

    - Complete the IPX/SPX protocol configuration as described in Chapter 7, "Installing Windows NT Server." Be sure that your installation supports all frame types that may be used by your dial-in users.

    - Complete TCP/IP protocol configuration as described in Chapter 15, "Using TCP/IP." These settings affect this computer only, not dial-in users, who receive their settings from RAS.

19. You will need to restart the computer to activate RAS.

Configuring RAS LAN Protocols

When you are installing RAS, you will need to configure the protocols that RAS will support. It is important to remember that RAS clients must be running a network protocol stack that is supported by RAS: NetBEUI, IPX, or TCP/IP. If you accept the default values, little protocol configuration is required. RAS will do most of the work of making address assignments.

If you do need to reconfigure RAS LAN protocol support, return to the Network Configuration dialog box and click on the appropriate Configure button to access the protocol configuration box.

RAS Server Configuration for NetBEUI

The RAS Server NetBEUI Configuration box is shown in figure 20.11. Use this box to choose the network access that will be granted to RAS users. Your choices are:

- Entire network
- This computer only

After you make your choice, click on OK.

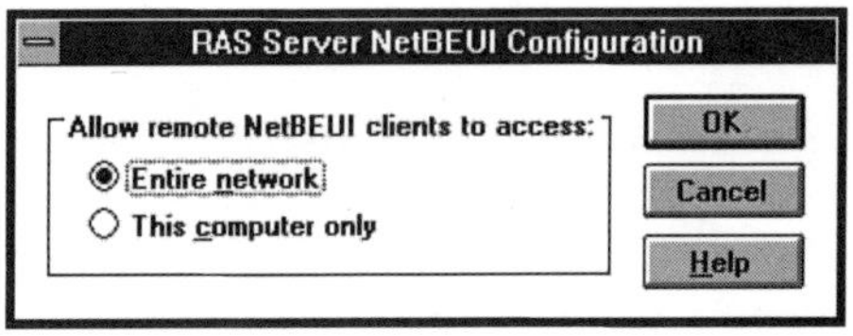

Figure 20.11
RAS server NetBEUI configuration.

RAS Server Configuration for TCP/IP

The RAS Server TCP/IP Configuration dialog box is shown in figure 20.12. Issues such as TCP/IP addressing are discussed in detail in Chapter 15, "Using TCP/IP."

As with NetBEUI, you can determine whether TCP/IP clients will be given access to the Entire network or to This computer only.

Three approaches are available to determine IP addresses that will be assigned to dial-up users:

- **Use DHCP to assign remote TCP/IP client addresses.** If the Dynamic Host Configuration Protocol (DHCP) is running on your network, this is the most satisfactory approach because no further address configuration is required.
- **Use static address pool.** You can select a range of addresses from which an address will be assigned to dial-in users. You will need to specify the address where the range will Begin and End.

  If you want, you can add ranges of addresses that fall between Begin and End that are to be excluded from the address pool. The exclusion range From the beginning address To the last excluded address and choose Add.
- **Allow remote users to request a predetermined IP address.** Use this option only if users must have control over their IP address.

When TCP/IP has been configured, click on OK.

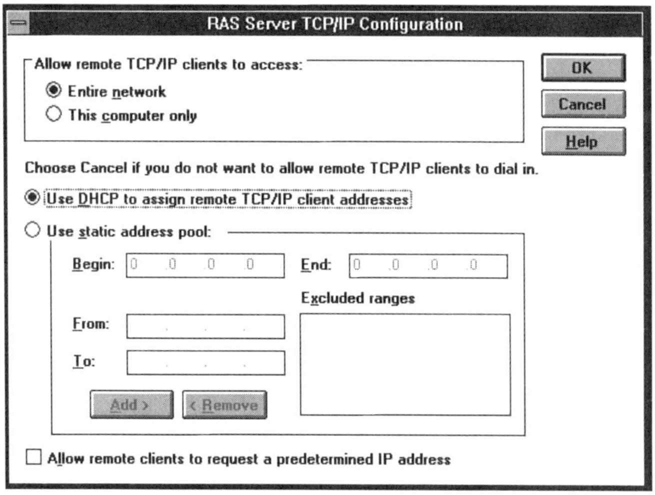

Figure 20.12

RAS server TCP/IP configuration.

RAS Server Configuration for IPX

The RAS Server IPX Configuration dialog box is shown in figure 20.13.

As with the other protocols, you determine whether IPX clients will be given access to the Entire network or to This computer only.

If you configure network and node number settings as shown in figure 20.13 (the default setting) no further IPX configuration is required.

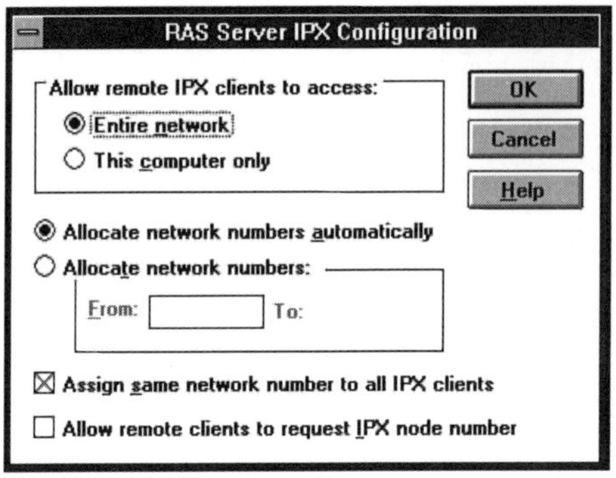

Figure 20.13
RAS Server IPX Configuration.

Assigning IPX Network Numbers

IPX requires all clients to be associated with a network number for routing purposes. In most cases, a given network segment is assigned a single network ID for each protocol and frame type that the segment supports. An IPX network number is a hexadecimal number up to 8 digits.

Routing Information Protocol (RIP, similar in principle to TCP/IP RIP) advertises network numbers by having routers announce them at one minute intervals. As the quantity of network numbers increases, RIP traffic increases rapidly. It is desirable to minimize the number of network numbers whenever possible.

Therefore, the default setting is to check Assign same network number to all IPX clients.

You can choose two methods of assigning network numbers:

- **Allocate network numbers automatically.** RAS will assign a network number that does not conflict with existing network numbers.
- **Allocate network numbers.** Use this option to specify a range of addresses from which network numbers will be assigned.

Assigning IPX Node Numbers

Each device on a network has a node number, a hexadecimal number up to 16 digits. For clients that are attached to the network, this number is usually derived from the hardware address of the Ethernet or token ring card.

You can, if you want, enable users to specify their own IPX node address by checking Allow remote clients to request IPX node number. This is a risky option because it can permit users to impersonate other users by using their node numbers.

Configuration of RAS User Accounts

When RAS is installed, a new program group is created. In the Remote Access Service group, you will find the following icons:

- **Remote Access.** This is RAS dial-out program.
- **Remote Access Monitor.** This utility echoes status lights for several of the modem's most critical lines. It is especially useful with internal modems.
- **Remote Access Admin.** This is the utility you use for configuring a RAS server. It is also used to start a RAS server.
- **Read Me.** A Write document containing RAS information.
- **Remote Access Help.** A help document for RAS.
- **Remote Access and the Internet.** A help document with much of information about using RAS to access the Internet.

Before users can make use of a RAS server, you must use Remote Access Admin to set up user permissions. The main window for Remote Access Admin is shown in figure 20.14. This window displays the status of each RAS communication channel and is used to access RAS administration functions.

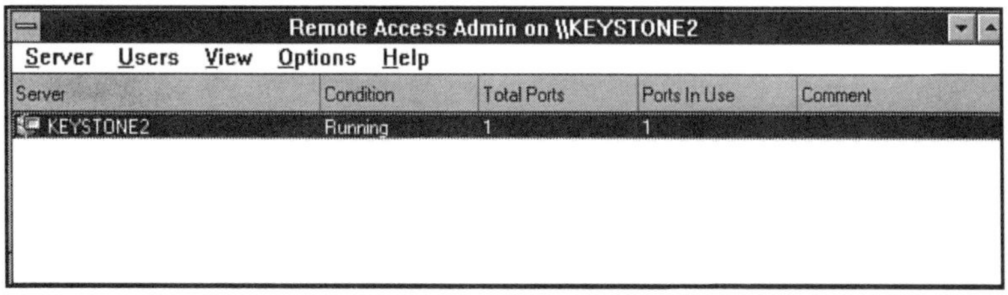

Figure 20.14

The main window for Remote Access Admin.

To administer RAS user permissions, choose the Permissions command in the Users menu to open the Remote Access Permissions box shown in figure 20.15. This dialog box can be used to administer remote access permissions for individuals or for all network users.

To revoke RAS permissions from all users, click on Revoke All.

To grant the same permissions to all users, set the permissions and click on Grant All.

To grant permissions to an individual user, select the user account name in the Users box. Then set the permissions to apply to that user.

Check the Grant dialin permission to user box to grant RAS dial-in access.

Three options are available in the Call Back box:

- **No Call Back.** This option enables users to call in and connect with the network on the same call.
- **Set By Caller.** With this option, the caller will be asked to enter a telephone number. RAS will disconnect, call the user at the number specified, and connect the user to the network.
- **Preset To.** This option requires you to specify a number that RAS will call to connect the user. Using a specified number enhances security because a user must have physical access to a particular telephone to enter a remote session.

After making the required settings, click on OK.

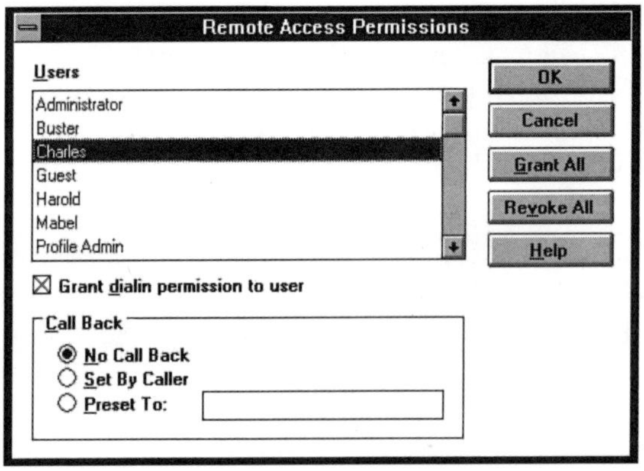

Figure 20.15

Granting remote access permissions.

Stop Because the Guest account does not ordinarily have a password, you should avoid giving this account dial-in permissions. If you intend to grant guests dial-in access, either strictly restrict permissions assigned to this account or assign a password.

Managing the Remote Access Server

The Remote Access Admin utility can be left active to monitor RAS operation. The main window (figure 20.14) lists the status of active RAS servers in the current domain. The status indicates the number of ports that are configured for each server, as well as the number of active connections.

Note Remote Access Admin can manage RAS servers in any domain on the network. Use the Select Domain or Server command in the Server menu to change domains.

If you are managing another domain through a modem or other slow connection, choose the Low Speed Connection option in the Options menu to reduce the amount of data that will be transmitted through the communication link.

Starting and Stopping the Server

After RAS has been installed and the server has been restarted, the Remote Access Service should be started. The Server menu in Remote Access Admin has four options for starting, stopping, and pausing the RAS server:

- **Start Remote Access Service.** Starts the Remote Access Service.
- **Stop Remote Access Service.** Stops the Remote Access Service.
- **Pause Remote Access Service.** This action prevents users from accessing the service, but leaves it enabled for administrators and server operators.
- **Continue Remote Access Service.** Changes the status of the service from Paused to Started.

All of these actions can be performed using the Services utility in the Control Panel, as described in Chapter 18, "Managing the Server." When the RAS software is installed, the Remote Access Service is configured to start automatically when Windows NT Server is restarted.

Managing Server Ports

To obtain details about server ports, double-click on the entry in the main window, or select the server and choose the Communication Ports command in the Server menu. Figure 20.16 shows an example of a Communication Ports display. Four buttons can be used to access port management features:

- **Port Status.** This button displays a detailed status report for the selected port. An example is shown in figure 20.17. Click on the Reset button to zero out the statistics. This display is extremely useful for troubleshooting RAS connections.
- **Disconnect User.** Select a user and click on this button to break a remote connection.
- **Send Message.** Use this option to send a message to the selected port.
- **Send to All.** Use this option to send a message to all users connected to this server.

A similar display is available organized by connected users. Choose the Active Users command in the Users menu to display the Remote Access Users dialog box shown in figured 20.18. Options are similar to the detailed port status display with the exception of the User Account button, which displays information about the user's account.

Figure 20.16

Port information for a RAS server.

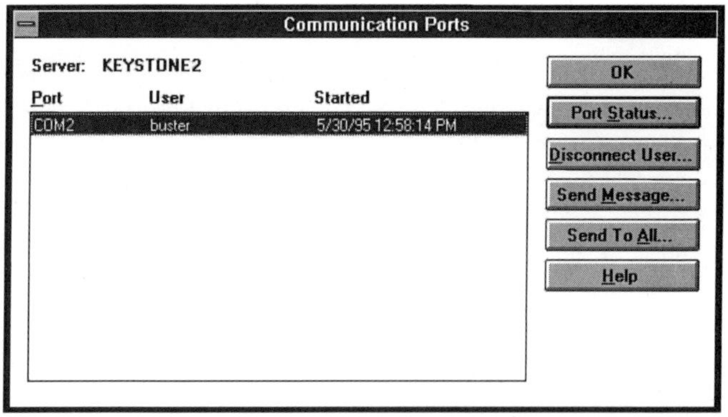

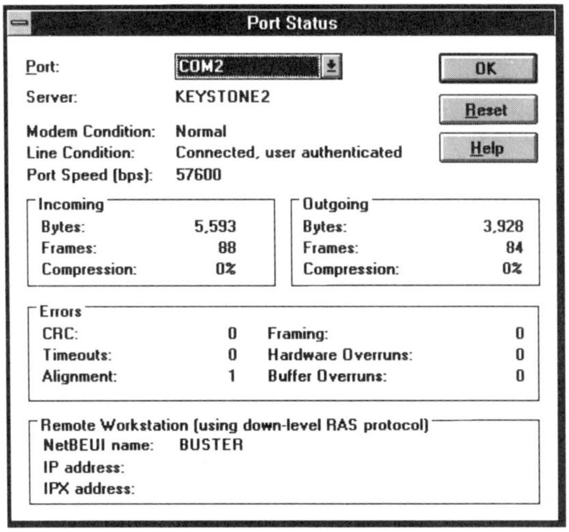

Figure 20.17
Detailed port status.

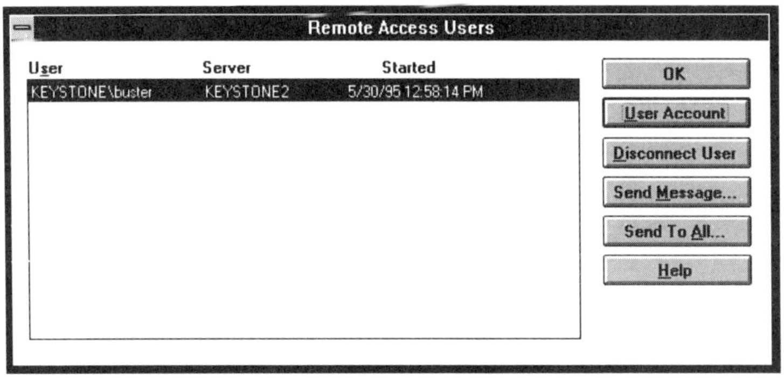

Figure 20.18
The active RAS users list.

Installing the RAS Clients for Windows for Workgroups

RAS client software is included with Windows for Workgroups. As with Windows NT RAS is considered a network service. To install RAS on WfW, use the following steps:

1. Start the Windows Setup utility.
2. Choose Change Network Settings in the Options menu.
3. In the Network Settings dialog box, click on the Drivers button.
4. In the Network Drivers dialog box, click on Add Adapter.
5. In the Add Network Adapter box, scroll the adapters in the Select a Network Adapter to Install list until you find Remote Access Service. Select that option and click on OK.
6. When installation begins, supply the path name for files and change disks as requested.
7. In the Remote Access Configuration dialog box, select a COM port in the Port box. Then pull down the Device list and select a communication device. Then click on OK.
8. Choose Close in the Network Drivers box. Then click on OK to close Network Setup.
9. In the Microsoft Windows Network Names box, specify:
    - **User Name.** The user name to be used to access the network.
    - **Workgroup.** The workgroup or domain to be accessed.
    - **Computer Name.** A name for this computer that is not in use on the network to be accessed.

    Choose OK when this information has been entered. Remote Access files will be copied to the computer.
10. Restart the computer when prompted.

The Remote Access program icon will be installed in the Network program group.

Dialing Out with RAS

For Windows NT, the Remote Access dial-out program is installed in the Remote Access Service program group when the RAS software is installed. In many ways Remote Access is similar to any modem communication program, and you will probably find most of the features at least a bit familiar.

When you run the Remote Access program, shown in figure 20.19, the Remote Access Monitor is also run by default. Lights in this utility indicate the following conditions:

- Data being transmitted (TX)
- Data being received (RX)
- Errors
- Carrier Detect (CD, the modem is on-line)

Before you can connect with Remote Access, you must define one or more phone book entries.

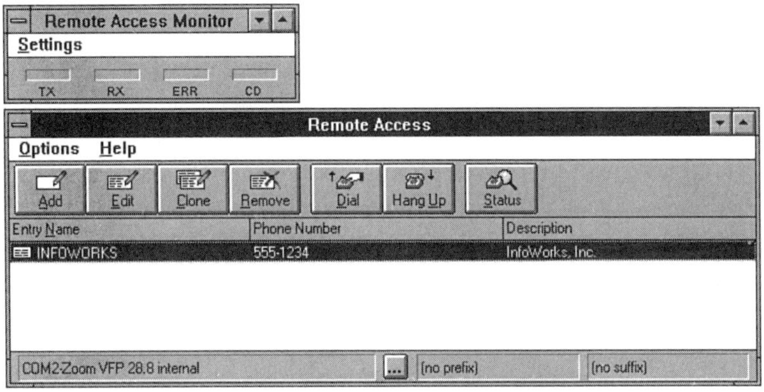

Figure 20.19

The main window for the Remote Access program.

Adding Phone Book Entries to Remote Access

A phone book entry consists of the telephone number, protocols, and other configuration information for a RAS or TCP/IP computer you will be dialing into. To create a phone book entry:

1. Click on Add in the Remote Access main window to display the Add Phone Book Entry dialog box shown in figure 20.20.
2. In Entry Name, enter a label by which the entry will be identified in your phone book. The entry can consist of up to 20 characters, and commas are not permitted.

Figure 20.20
A completed new phone book entry.

3. The Phone **N**umber box will accept one or more telephone numbers to be used. If the service being called has several numbers, Remote Access will try all of the numbers you enter until one is found that completes a connection.

4. The **D**escription box can be used to enter a more detailed description of the service.

5. Remote Access retains the user name and domain that were last used to log in. This information is used to connect when dialing if you check the box Authenticate using **c**urrent user name and password.

   If you want to connect to a new domain or user account, do not check this box.

6. To configure communication details, click on the **A**dvanced button to expand the Add Phone Book Entry dialog box as shown in figure 20.21.

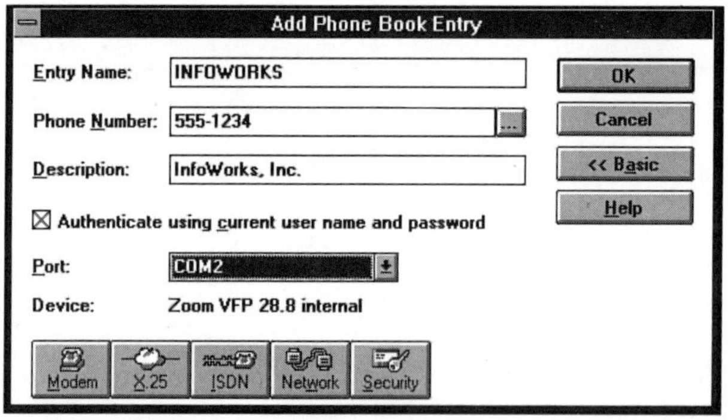

Figure 20.21
Configuring advanced features for a phone book entry.

7. The procedure for configuring a connection type depends on whether you are configuring a modem, X.25, or ISDN.

7a. To configure a modem, select the COM port or the Any modem port entry in the **P**ort box, then click on the **M**odem button to display the Modem Settings dialog box shown in figure 20.22. This box can be used to set the following modem options:

- **Initial speed (bps).** When modems connect, they will negotiate the fastest speed that they both support and that is compatible with the quality of the connection. Set this entry to the fastest speed supported by your modem.

- **Enable hardware flow control.** This option should usually be checked so that the computer and modem can perform flow control using the RTS/CTS lines.

- **Enable modem error control.** If modems at both ends can perform error control using either the MNP4 or the V.42 standard, check this box.

- **Enable modem compression.** Although most modems can perform compression, Microsoft does not recommend that you enable hardware data compression. Software compress performs better because it supports a larger pattern buffer than is available in the modem hardware. If you choose to enable hardware compression, disable RAS data compression.

- **Enter modem commands manually.** If you are troubleshooting a connection and are familiar with the error codes for your modem, you can enter all session commands manually if you check this box.

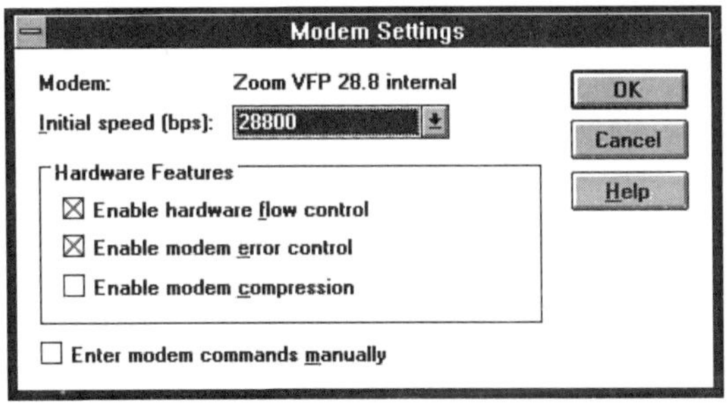

Figure 20.22
Configuring modem settings.

Click on OK when done configuring the modem.

7b. To configure an X.25 connection, choose the Any X.25 port entry in the Port box. Then click on the X.25 button if you are configuring an X.25 connection. The X.25 Settings dialog box is shown in figure 20.23. The values you enter must be obtained from your X.25 service provider.

- **PAD Type.** Select the entry that matches your PAD hardware.

- **X.121 Address.** This entry is the equivalent of an X.25 phone number.

- **User Data.** This field can be left blank unless required by the system administrator.

- **Facilities.** This box accepts any parameters required by the X.25 provider.

Click on OK when done configuring the X.25 information.

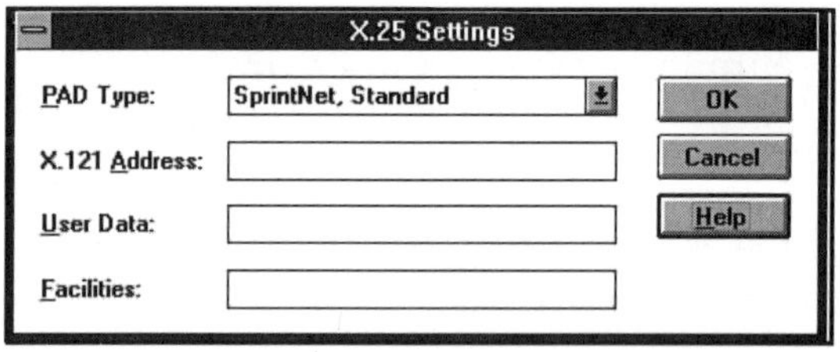

Figure 20.23
Configuring X.25 settings.

7c. To configure an ISDN port, choose Any ISDN port in the Port box. Then click on the ISDN button to display the ISDN Settings dialog box shown in figure 20.24. This box has the following entries:

- **Line type.** Select the line type that matches your service. Line types are listed from best to worst quality, starting with 64K Digital.
- **Negotiate line type.** Check this setting to negotiate with the carrier for the best available line type.
- **Enable hardware compression.** Check this option only if the ISDN card being used supports compression.
- **Channels to use.** ISDN services generally provide two or more 64 KB channels. If your ISDN hardware can aggregate multiple 64 KB channels into one effective channel, enter the number of channels here.

Click on OK when finished.

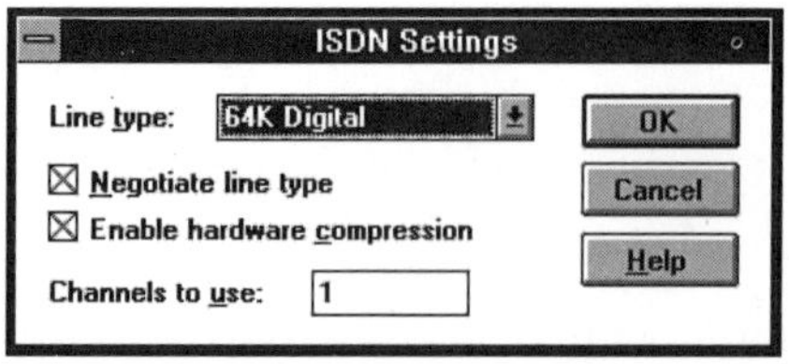

Figure 20.24
Configuring ISDN settings.

8. Click on the Network button to display the Network Protocol Settings dialog box shown in figure 20.25. This box is used to determine the protocol settings that will be used.

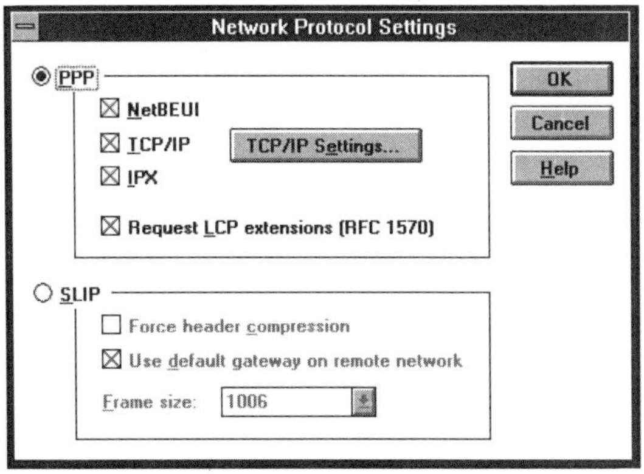

Figure 20.25

Configuring dial-out protocols.

8a. PPP is the default protocol for RAS and should be selected if you are calling a RAS server. PPP is supported for most Internet dial-in services. If you will be connecting using the PPP protocol do the following:

- Select **P**PP.
- Check the protocols that will be supported. NetBEUI, IPX, and TCP/IP are available.
- If you checked TCP/IP, click on the TCP/IP S**e**ttings button and use the PPP TCP/IP Settings dialog box (figure 20.26) to configure dial-in settings.

The entries you make are determined by the administrator of the system you are dialing. Figure 20.26 shows settings that are appropriate for RAS if the dial-in server is configured to assign IP addresses.

Internet access providers will typically assign specific IP addresses that should be entered in the **R**equire specific IP address box. The address for the DNS server specified by the provider should also be specified.

Check Use **V**J header compression if the host you are dialing supports Van Jacobson IP header compression during login. VJ header compression is supported by RAS for Windows NT 3.5. Clear this box only when you cannot connect successfully.

The Use de**f**ault gateway on remote network option applies to computers that are connected to local networks at the same time they are dialing remotely. When this option is checked, packets that cannot be routed to the local network are routed to the default gateway on the remote network.

Check Request LCP Extensions if calling a newer PPP server that supports the LCP extensions described in RFC 1570. Do not check this box if calling a PPP server that does not support these extensions. This box can be checked for Windows NT 3.5 RAS servers.

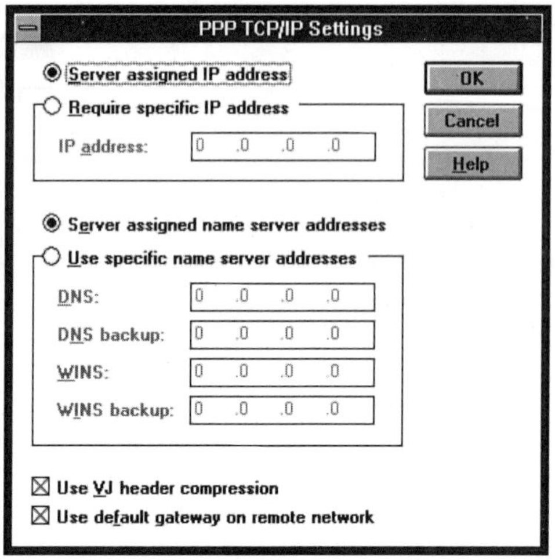

Figure 20.26
TCP/IP protocol settings.

8b. SLIP is the secondary TCP/IP dial-up protocol supported by RAS. If you are calling a dial-up host that does not support PPP, select SLIP.

- Check Force header compression if the host supports Van Jacobson packet header compression.
- The Use default gateway on remote network option applies to computers that are connected to local networks at the same time they are dialing remotely. When this option is checked, packets that cannot be routed to the local network are routed to the default gateway on the remote network.
- For Frame Size, specify a frame size that is supported by the dial-in host. Frame sizes of 1006 and 1500 can be selected.

9. Click on the Security button to enter the Security Settings dialog box shown in figure 20.27.

- The various authentication options were described in the section about RAS installation. When dialing a RAS server, you should select Require Microsoft encrypted authentication and check the Require data encryption box.
- Before dialing enables you to specify the path for a script file to be executed before dialing. Alternatively, you can choose Terminal, in which

case you will enter a terminal interface before dialing from which you can enter commands.

- After dialing is similar to Before dialing except that the script or terminal dialog take place after dialing has been completed.

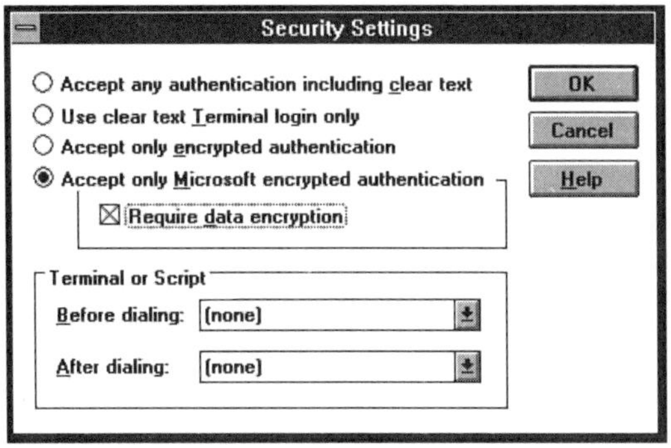

Figure 20.27

RAS dial-out security settings.

Dialing with a Phone Book Entry

Once a phone book entry has been completed, making a connection is simple. The exact steps will differ depending on the following factors:

- Whether the host is a RAS server or a TCP/IP network.
- Whether the host is configured for dial-back operation.

Here is the sequence of events when a RAS client calls a RAS server:

1. You might need to specify a dialing prefix or suffix. A prefix might be required to access an outside line from your office phone network or to access a long-distance service. A suffix might be required to enter long distance calling card information or to access a line at the receiving end of your call.

   The Remote Access main screen enables you select a prefix and a suffix for the call by clicking on the ... button. Select a prefix from the list, or add one of your own.

2. Dial a host by selecting an entry in the phone book and clicking on **Dial**.
3. The client dials and enters a conversation with the server.
4. The server sends a challenge to the client.
5. The client sends an encrypted response.

6. The server checks the response against its database.
7. If the response is valid, the server checks for remote access permission.
8. If the user has been given remote access permission, the client is connected.
9. If callback is enabled, the server disconnects, calls the client, and completes steps 3 through 8 again.

Once the connection is completed, the user of the client computer can minimize the Remote Access icon and work as if directly attached to the LAN.

When the session is completed, the user disconnects by opening the Remote Access program and clicking on the Hang Up button.

RAS Serial Cable Requirements

Table 20.1 summarizes the pin connection requirements RAS expects in a cable that is used to connect a RAS computer to a modem. If you purchase a commercial cable, be sure it supports these wiring configurations.

Table 20.1
Pin Connection Requirements

Computer 25-pin connector	Computer 9-pin connector	Modem 25-pin connector	Modem 9-pin connector	Signal
1		1		Ground
2	3	2	3	Transmit Data
3	2	3	2	Receive Data
4	7	4	7	Request to Send
5	8	5	8	Clear to Send
6	6	6	6	Data Set Ready
7	5	7	5	Signal Ground
8	1	8	1	Carrier Detect
20	4	20	4	Data Terminal Ready

Table 20.2 lists the RAS cable requirements for a null modem cable.

Table 20.2
Cable Requirements for a Null Modem Cable

Server 25-pin connector	Server 9-pin connector	Client 25-pin connector	Client 9-pin connector	Signal
1		1		Ground
2	3	3	2	Transmit Data
3	2	2	3	Receive Data
4	7	5	8	Request to Send
5	8	4	7	Clear to Send
6,8	6,1	20	4	Data Set Ready, Carrier Detect
7	5	7	5	Signal Ground
20	4	6,8	6,1	Data Terminal Ready

Troubleshooting RAS

By far the most common problems you will have, at least while you are learning RAS, will result from misconfiguration of the client or the server. Start with a basic setup, get everything working, then add modem pools, and other fancy features.

If possible, do your initial testing with two identical modems. If that works and other modems don't, you can be pretty sure the modems are incompatible with RAS.

The Port Status box (see figure 20.16) is an extremely useful tool for testing flakey connections. Look especially for high error rates that might be causing lost connections.

Logging RAS Events

You can enable two RAS logs by changing Registry entries. The PPP log can be used to troubleshoot problems with PPP connections. To enable the PPP log, change the following Logging parameter to 0×1 in the key HKEY_LOCAL_MACHINE\SYSTEM\CurrentControlSet\Services\RasMan\PPP.

The device log records all communication from serial ports to connected devices when modem commands are being executed. To enable the device log, change the Logging parameter to 0×1 in the key HKEY_LOCAL_MACHINE\SYSTEM\CurrentControlSet\Services\RasMan\Parameters. Log data is stored in the file DEVICE.LOG in the C:\WINNT35\SYSTEM32\RAS directory.

See Chapter 18, "Managing the Server," for information about changing values in the Registry.

By default, the logs are stored in the directory C:\WINNT35\SYSTEM32\RAS. The PPP log file is named PPP.LOG and the device log is named DEVICE.LOG. You can view these files using the Windows Write program.

CHAPTER 21

Managing Directory Replication

Directory replication is one of the surprise bonus features of Windows NT Server. Many times in my career as a LAN administrator, I have needed to duplicate data between servers. To accomplish this I have had to rely on indirect approaches involving job schedulers and copy procedures. Between the times I scheduled the copy jobs to run, the directories gradually went out of synchronization. So I appreciate the ease with which Windows NT Server directory replication works.

The most common use of directory replication is probably to copy logon scripts from one domain controller to other DCs. This enables users to log on through any DC and access a copy of their logon script on the local computer. Since the logon script is local, it need not be retrieved from another server, and both network traffic and server demand are reduced.

Directory replication can be used with any data that is shared on multiple computers or domains. Suppose, for example, that your company maintains an employee directory or a newsletter online. Rather than having everyone in the enterprise hit on the same server, you can replicate the files to as many computers as you like.

Directory replication does not merely perform "one time" copies. It is a dynamic service that continuously identifies changes and new files and replicates them to other computers, all without the need for administrator intervention. Essentially, directory replication keeps directory trees on different computers synchronized. It does not merely copy files, but will remove files and create subdirectories (it does not delete subdirectories) as well to keep the two directories identical.

How Directory Replication Works

Directory replication copies files from computers called *export servers* to computers called *import computers*. Although only Windows NT Server computers can be configured as an export server, both Windows NT Workstations and Servers can be import computers.

When you configure an export server, you designate two things:

- **An export directory.** All subdirectories and files created in the export directory are eligible for export.
- **An "export to" list of computers and domains to which files will be exported.** If an export server exports to a domain, every computer that is configured to import files will receive the import.

When you configure an import computer, you designate similar properties:

- An import directory to receive imported files.
- An "import from" list of computers and domains from which import files will be accepted.

Figure 21.1 illustrates directory trees on an export server and an import computer. The figure is based on the default export and import directories that are established when Windows NT is installed. The default export directory is \WINNT35\SYSTEM32\REPL\EXPORT, and the default import directory is \WINNT35\SYSTEM32\REPL\IMPORT. The result of directory replication is that subdirectories and files in the IMPORT subdirectory will be mirror images of subdirectories and files in the EXPORT directory.

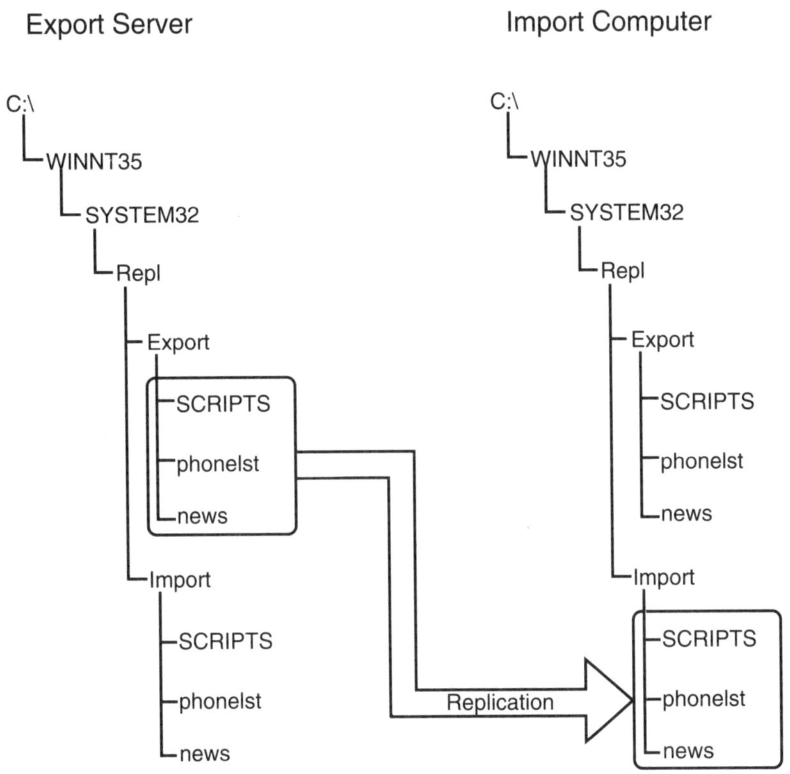

Figure 21.1

Export and import directories.

The same computer can function as an export server and as an import computer. In fact, an export server can replicate files to its own import directory. Figure 21.2 shows some of the possibilities.

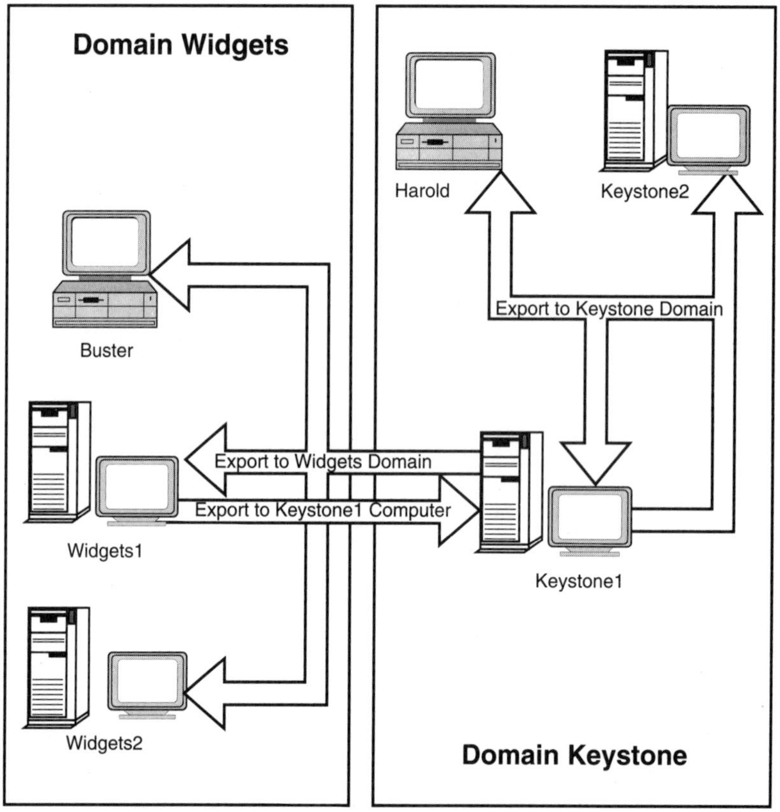

Figure 21.2
Examples of export servers and import computers.

Starting the Directory Replicator Service

Every export server and import computer must be running the Directory Replicator service. This service is configured to log on with a user account that has the privileges needed to replicate files. First you need to create the user account and then you must configure and start the Directory Replicator service.

Creating the Directory Replicator User Account

In each domain that will be importing or exporting files, create a user account with the following properties:

- Password Never Expires has been checked.
- The account Logon Hours enable it to log on 24 hours a day, 7 days a week.
- The account is a member of the Backup Operators local group.

You won't be able to name this user account Replicator because a built-in local group already exists with that name. I called my user RepUser in the examples.

Starting the Directory Replicator Service

After you have created the user account, you can configure and start the Directory Replicator service. Services are managed with the Service Manager, which is accessible through the Control Panel Services utility or through the Server Manager. This section will use the Server Manager.

1. Open the Services dialog box for the server using one of the following methods:
   - Run the Servers utility in the Control Panel.
   - Select the server in Server Manager and choose Services from the Computer menu. The Services dialog box is shown in figure 21.3.

   If you have not replicated directories, the Directory Replicator service will not show an entry in the Status column and will be configured as Manual in the Startup column.

2. Select the Directory Replicator service and choose Startup to configure the startup options for the service. Figure 21.4 shows how this box will appear when the Directory Replicator service has been properly configured.

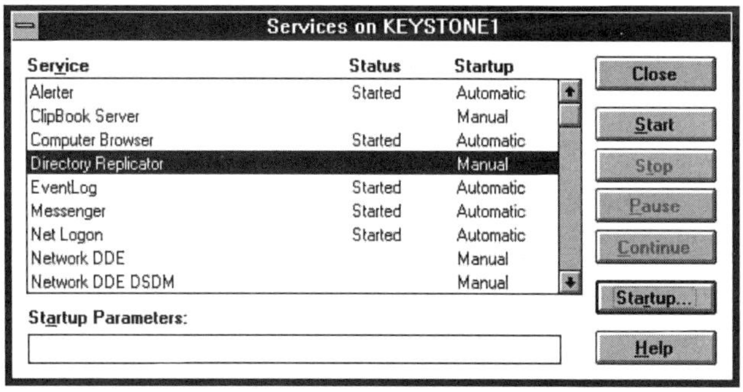

Figure 21.3
The Services list.

Figure 21.4

Configuring startup options for the Directory Replicator service.

3. Choose the **A**utomatic option in the Startup Type box.
4. Select the **T**his Account button and enter the user name of the replicator account you created. You can click on the ... button next to the **T**his Account button to choose the account from a browse menu.
5. Enter the password in the **P**assword and **C**onfirm Password boxes.
6. Click on OK to return to the services list. You will see the message shown in figure 21.5. As you can see, the user account used by the Directory Replicator service is granted some special permissions.
7. Select the Directory Replicator service and click on **S**tart. You will see a message `Attempting to Start the Directory Replicator service`. If the service starts successfully, the confirmation message shown in figure 21.5 is presented.

   The Directory Replicator service should show as Started in the Status column and as Automatic in the Startup column.

8. Choose Close to return to Server Manager.

Repeat this procedure on each computer that will be an export server or an import computer.

Figure 21.5

Message verifying setup of the Directory Replicator user account.

Configuring Trust Relationships

Every domain that will be importing files from another domain must trust the export domain. The procedures for configuring trust relationships were described in Chapter 9, "Managing Domains and Trust Relationships."

Be sure that each exporting domain permits the importing domain to trust it. Then configure each importing domain to trust the exporting domain.

If directories will be replicated in both directions, two-way trust relationships must be established.

Configuring the Export Server

Any Windows NT Server can be configured as an export server. Recall that setup configures the server with a default export directory. I don't recommend that you change the default export directory. If you want to do so, however, create the directory and assign Full Control permissions for the directory to the Replicator local group.

The permissions you give to other users and groups depend on how the directories and files are used. You can enable users to create files in the export directory tree if desired.

Follow these steps to configure the export server:

1. Open the Properties dialog box (shown in figure 21.6) for the server using one of the following methods:

   - Run the Servers utility in the Control Panel.

   - Select the server in Server Manager and choose Properties from the Computer menu.

2. In the Properties box, choose **R**eplication to display the Directory Replication dialog box shown in figure 21.7. By default, the Do Not E**x**port and Do Not I**m**port options will be selected. The example in the figure has already been set up as an export server that will export to the domains KEYSTONE (its own domain) and WIDGETS.

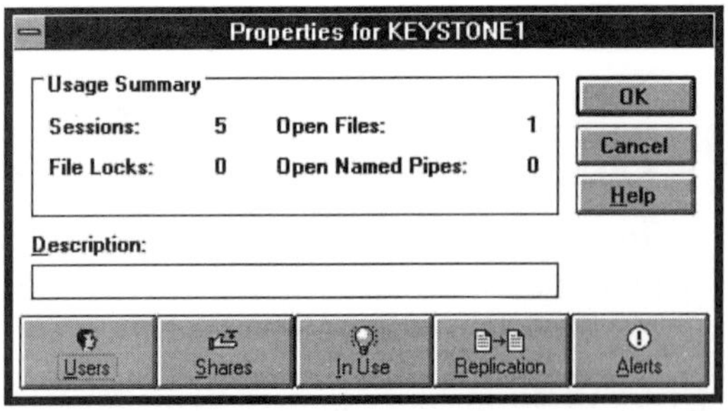

Figure 21.6

The server Properties box.

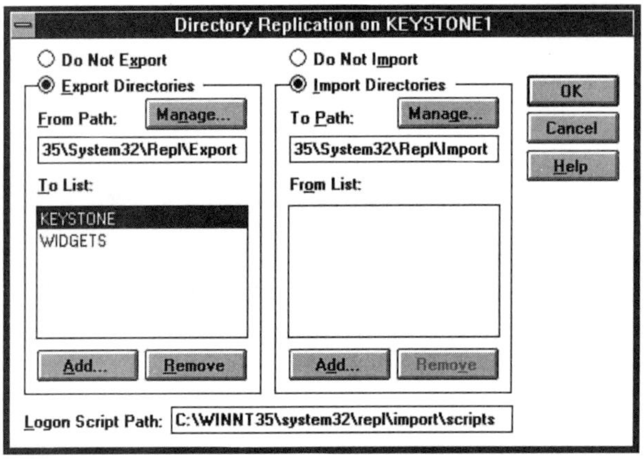

Figure 21.7

Directory replication configuration for an export server.

3. Choose **E**xport Directories.

4. If you are not using the default export directory, edit the entry in the **F**rom Path box.

5. At least one import computer or import domain must be specified in the **T**o List box. To add an import destination, choose **A**dd to display the Select Domain dialog box shown in figure 21.8. Only the current domain and domains that trust this domain will be shown in the Select Domain box.

6. If the domain you want to add is shown, you may browse the **S**elect Domain box and select a domain or a computer. If the domain is not shown, type the domain or computer name in the **D**omain box.

7. Choose OK to save the entry and return to the Directory Replication dialog box.

8. Add any other desired destinations to the To List.

9. Click on OK to save the server properties.

Note Directory replication to a domain may fail if the export and import domains are connected through a wide area network connection. With a WAN connection, you should export to individual computers in the import domain.

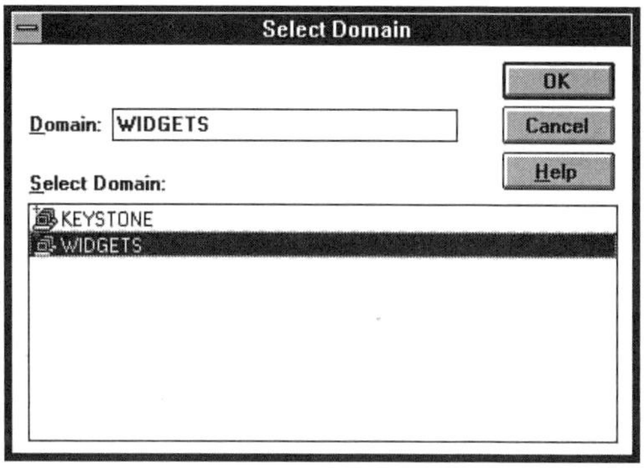

Figure 21.8
Selecting an import domain.

Configuring the Import Computer

Import computers can be Windows NT workstations or servers. They are also configured with the server Properties dialog box:

1. Open the Properties dialog box for the server using one of the following methods:

   - Run the Servers utility in the Control Panel.

   - Select the server in Server Manager and choose Properties from the Computer menu.

2. In the Properties dialog box, choose Replication to display the Directory Replication dialog box shown in figure 21.9. By default, the Do Not Export and Do Not Import options will be selected. The example in the figure has already been set up as an import server.

3. Choose Import Directories.

4. If you are not using the default import directory, edit the entry in the To Path box.

5. At least one export computer or export domain must be specified in the From List box. To add an export source, choose Add to display the Select Domain dialog box.

6. If the domain you want to add is shown, you may browse the **S**elect Domain dialog box and select a domain or a computer. If the domain is not shown, type the domain or computer name in the **D**omain dialog box.

7. Choose OK to save the entry and return to the Directory Replication dialog box.

8. Add any other desired sources to the From List.

9. Click on OK to save the server properties.

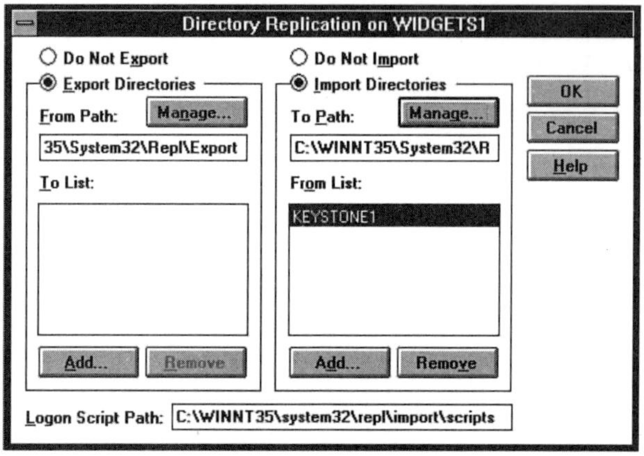

Figure 21.9

The Directory Replication properties box for an import computer.

Testing Directory Replication

Now that you have started the Directory Replication services and configured the export and import servers, directory replication should commence. Some delay is always present in the directory replication process, so don't expect things to happen immediately.

To verify that directory replication is working, do the following:

1. Open a window in File Manager to view the export directory.

2. Open another window in File Manager to view the import directory.

3. Create a file in the export directory. You can copy a file to the directory or use Notepad to create a text file.

4. Create a subdirectory in the export directory.

5. Wait. Take a break and check the import directory in a few minutes. It should be a mirror image of the export directory.

Note Replication takes place after a stabilization period has been completed. The length of the stabilization period is determined by the value of the Stabilize option specified for the properties of the export computer. The Stabilize option is described in the section "Managing Export and Import Computers."

Troubleshooting Directory Replication

Directory replication errors are recorded in the applications log, which you may view with the Event Viewer utility, which is installed in the Administrative Tools program group. Choose Applications from the Log menu to view any errors.

If directory replication is not working, check the following items:

- Examine the user account being used by the Directory Replicator service. Is the user account a member of the Backup Operators group?

- Has the Directory Replicator service been configured in each export and import computer with the following?

  Startup Type: Automatic.

  This Account is selected and an account specified that has Backup Operators membership.

  Proper passwords.

- Do all export domains permit themselves to be trusted by the appropriate import domains?

- Do all import domains trust the appropriate export domains?

- Is the Directory Replicator service started on each export and import computer?

- On NTFS volumes, does the directory replicator user account have Full Control permissions in the Export and Import directories, either through direct or group assignments?

- Are files that are not being replicated being held open by a user or an application? Files must be closed to be replicated.
- Are the system clocks on the export and import domains reasonably close in settings?

Managing Export and Import Computers

The Directory Replication properties dialog box (see figure 21.7) enables you to manage several characteristics of export servers and import computers.

Choose the Manage button in the Export Directories box to display the Manage Exported Directories dialog box, shown in figure 21.10. An entry will be listed for each subdirectory that is in the export directory. The following information is displayed for each subdirectory:

- **Locks.** Unless the lock count is 0, this subdirectory will not be exported. Locks are added with the Add Lock button, discussed in the next list.
- **Stabilize.** Indicates whether the Wait Until Stabilized option has been selected. If this field is No, files are eligible to be exported as soon as they are modified. If this field is Yes, modified files will be allowed to stabilize for at least two minutes.
- **Subtree.** Indicates whether the Entire Subtree option has been selected. If this field is No, subdirectories of this directory will not be exported. If this field says Yes, subdirectories will be exported.
- **Locked Since.** For locked subdirectories, indicates the time and date when locks were applied.

To manage a subdirectory, select it and use the following controls:

- **Add Lock.** If a lock is added to a subdirectory, nothing will be exported from it or from its subdirectories. You can add more than one lock (although Microsoft does not explain why you would want to do so). Exporting will not resume until all locks are removed.
- **Remove Lock.** Choose this option to reduce the lock count by one. Exporting resumes when the lock count is 0.

- **Wait Until Stabilized.** Check this box to force Directory Replication to wait at least two minutes after a file is modified before exporting the file. Use this option to help eliminate partial replication. If this box is checked, the Stabilize column will indicate Yes for this subdirectory.
- **Entire Subtree.** If this box is checked, subdirectories of this directory will be exported whenever this directory is exported. If the box is not checked, only this directory will be exported, without its subdirectories.
- **Add.** If a subdirectory in the export directory is not listed in the Manage Export Directories window, choose the Add button to add it to the display. In most cases, subdirectories will be added and removed by the system.
- **Remove.** To remove a subdirectory from the window, select the subdirectory and choose Remove.

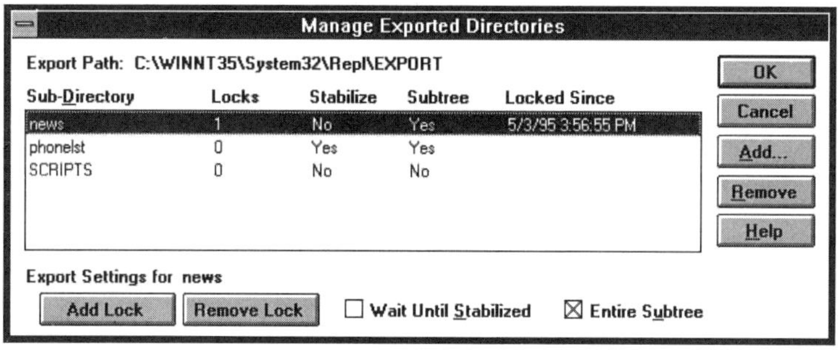

Figure 21.10
Managing exported directories.

The Manage button in the Import Directories box displays a slightly different window, as shown in figure 21.11. The following information is displayed for each subdirectory:

- **Locks.** Unless the lock count is 0, this subdirectory will not be imported. Locks are added with the Add Lock button, discussed in the next list.
- **Status.** This field can have the following values:
  - *OK* indicates that the subdirectory is receiving regular imports.
  - *No Master* indicates that imports are not being received. The export server may not be running or a configuration error may exist.
  - *No Sync* indicates that imports have taken place, but that data is not current. This condition can be due to communication errors or to incorrect permissions at the export server.
  - If the field is blank, replication has not occurred in this subdirectory.

- **Last Update.** The date and time the subdirectory last received an import.
- **Locked Since.** For locked subdirectories, indicates the time and date when locks were applied.

The Manage Imported Directories window has only two controls:

- **Add Lock.** As with export directories, you can place locks on import subdirectories. Files will not be imported to a subdirectory if any locks are applied.
- **Remove Lock.** Select this button to remove a lock from the selected subdirectory.
- **Add.** If a subdirectory in the export directory is not listed in the Manage Export Directories window, choose the Add button to add it to the display. In most cases, subdirectories will be added and removed by the system.
- **Remove.** To remove a subdirectory from the window, select the subdirectory and choose Remove.

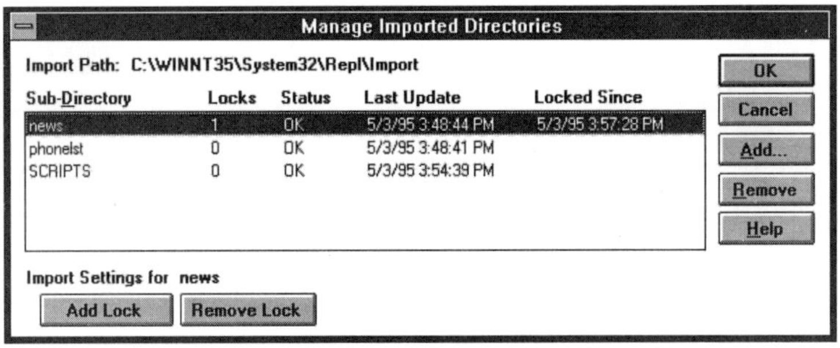

Figure 21.11
Managing imported directories.

Managing Logon Scripts

The Directory Replication dialog box is used to declare the location of logon scripts for the server (see figure 21.7). Directory replication is commonly used to replicate master copies of logon scripts to all domain controllers in a domain or on the entire network.

The logon script path is a subdirectory of the default export directory. By default, the logon scripts path is C:\WINNT35\SYSTEM32\REPL\IMPORT\SCRIPTS. To replicate logon script files, the master copies should be placed in the same subdirectory of the export subdirectory. The default subdirectory for master logon scripts that are to be exported is C:\WINNT35\SYSTEM32\REPL\EXPORT\SCRIPTS.

Users whose logons are replicated by the master export server, must be able to access logon scripts in the IMPORT\SCRIPTS subdirectory. The easiest way to achieve this is to configure the master export server to export to its own domain. This will cause scripts to be replicated to the IMPORT\SCRIPTS directory on the master export server at the same time it is replicated to other import computers in the domain.

CHAPTER 22

Windows NT Server and NetWare

Novell NetWare is found on approximately two-thirds of all network servers in the world. When Microsoft developed Windows NT 3.5, they realized that Windows NT Server had to coexist in a NetWare world. Several technologies promote this coexistence:

- NDIS enables Windows computers to run protocol stacks for both Windows NT and NetWare, enabling users to access data on both server types.
- A NetWare Gateway, new with Windows NT 3.5, enables users on a Windows NT Server network to access files and printers on the NetWare server without the necessity of running a dual protocol stack.
- A NetWare migration tool enables Windows NT Server administrators to move NetWare user accounts to Windows NT Server if desired.

This chapter discusses issues and procedures for all of these technologies. Before starting the how-to, however, you are provided with some background information comparing the use of multiple protocol stacks to gateways.

Technologies for Accessing Different Servers

NetWare and Windows NT Server differ significantly in the protocols they use. As a result, computers that need to access both environments require special configuration.

NetWare servers rely on two key protocols:

- **IPX/SPX.** Provide network and transport layer network functionality.
- **NCP (NetWare Core Protocols).** Are the protocols that enable NetWare clients to request services from NetWare servers.

Windows NT Server, on the other hand, relies on the following protocols:

- **NetBIOS.** (Actually an API that is usually run over NBF, the NetBIOS Frame Protocol, an updated form of NetBEUI.) NetBIOS is also supported over NWLink, Microsoft's implementation of IPX/SPX.
- **SMB (Server Message Blocks).** Provide much the same service for Windows NT Server as NCP messages do for NetWare.

Windows NT supports the IPX/SPX protocols with NWLink, so that aspect doesn't present a problem. However, NCP and SMB are wholly incompatible, and Microsoft had to do some extra work to give a client access to both network service protocols.

In fact, Microsoft has made two approaches available. You can configure clients to access Windows NT Server by installing both protocol stacks on the client, or you can use a NetWare gateway. Both alternatives are examined.

Accessing Different Environments with Multiple Client Protocol Stacks

NDIS was designed with multi-protocol support in mind. You have seen throughout the book how NDIS enables Microsoft network clients to simultaneously support

NetBEUI, NWLink, TCP/IP, and DLC protocols. In fact, you can access both Windows NT and NetWare using NWLink because IPX/SPX is now the default network protocol for Microsoft Windows products. All that remains is to support NCP in addition to SMB messaging.

Windows NT is capable of supporting two network software interfaces. Novell's ODI architecture enables you to support the Novell and Microsoft protocols in the MS-DOS environment by using the ODINSUP program to support NDIS drivers. When the appropriate software is installed and configured, client network communication resembles figure 22.1.

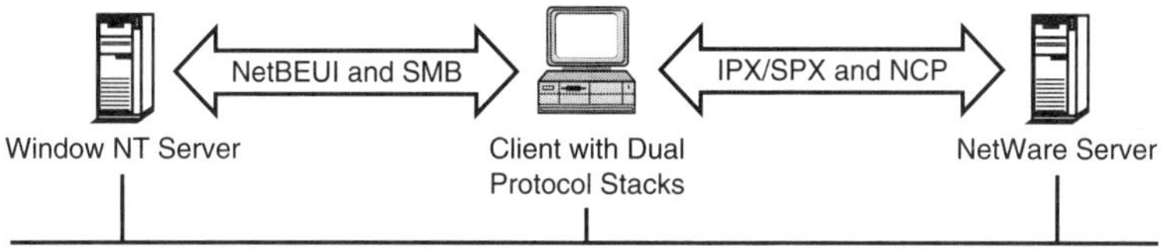

Figure 22.1
Client network access with multiple protocol stacks.

This approach has several advantages:

- Each server environment is accessed in its native environment. All services and security features are in force.
- No performance is lost because protocols do not require translation.

However, the following two disadvantages must be noted:

- Dual protocol stacks require increased client maintenance.
- Dual server environments require separate maintenance.

Two approaches are available for supporting Microsoft and NetWare protocols on DOS and Windows 3.1 computers:

- Microsoft NDIS technology
- Novell's Open Datalink Interface (ODI) technology

Windows for Workgroups 3.11 can support more than one server environment if you install the Novell ODI drivers and use the ODINSUP to support NDIS protocols.

Windows NT supports NetWare as a secondary protocol stack using the Client Services for NetWare, which are installed as part of the Gateway service.

Note At the present time, no Microsoft client software provides support for NetWare Directory Services (NDS) and Microsoft clients are limited to accessing NetWare 4.*x* servers in bindery mode. If your installation includes NetWare 4.*x* servers and NDS support is crucial, you will need to use Novell's ODI drivers.

Accessing Different Environments with a Gateway

A gateway is a heavy-duty translator. While routers translate network protocols at the OSI network layer, above that layer a more powerful approach is required because the environments can differ in fundamental ways. The NetWare NCP command to open a file is nothing like the Microsoft SMB command to do the same thing.

Figure 22.2 shows a network that incorporates a Windows NT NetWare gateway. On the Windows side of the gateway, clients communicate using any supported protocol and server message blocks. The gateway translates client messages into IPX/SPX and NCP format, and communicates with the NetWare server.

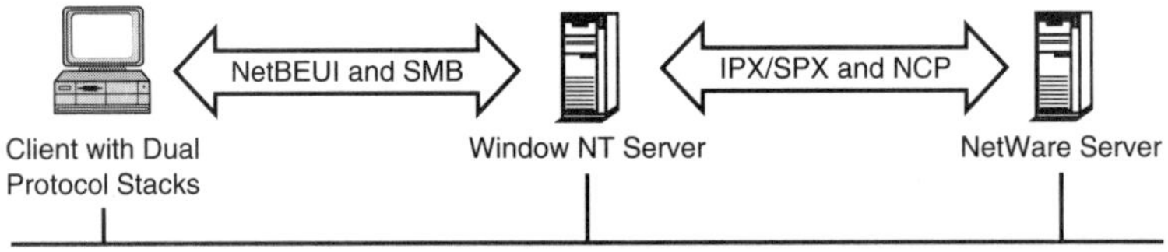

Figure 22.2
A network with a Windows NT Server NetWare gateway.

The interesting thing about the gateway approach is that the NetWare server appears to users as just another shared resource on the Windows NT gateway server. No changes to Windows network clients are required to enable them to access the NetWare server through the gateway.

As you can see, a gateway approach has several advantages:

- Clients do not require multiple protocol stacks, and client maintenance is simplified.
- Users access all resources in the same way.
- Very little additional maintenance is required on the NetWare side. A gateway is a great way for a NetWare-based department to share files with Windows NT Server users in another department without maintaining a NetWare user account for each user.
- Administration can be simplified because access to resources is controlled by the gateway.

However, a gateway may not be an ideal solution for the following two reasons:

- The translations the gateway must perform are extensive, and performance is generally slower than a connection with the proper protocol stack.
- Some features on the NetWare host might not be available. In particular, the NetWare gateway cannot access NetWare 4.*x* NetWare Directory Services, and users must access NetWare 4.*x* servers in bindery mode.

Note Opinions on gateways differ. I'll give you mine, but you'll need to study the pros and cons in light of your organization's needs.

I've operated Windows networks with multiple protocol stacks with no real trouble. It is extremely easy to add support for a second network with Windows for Workgroups. Performance doesn't take a hit with multiple protocols, and I haven't seen a user yet who wasn't performance-conscious. I also prefer native NetWare security to the share-level security that is available with the Windows NT Gateway. Yes, it means extra administration, but good security is worth the effort.

If NetWare 4 is in your future, a gateway won't meet your needs because you don't want to give up NDS. Dual protocols with Novell drivers is the way to go.

Consider using a gateway if your users require fairly casual access to NetWare, particularly if they need to access printers on the NetWare network because printing performance isn't as critical to most users as application performance. A gateway also is an easy way to enable users to pass files between the two networks.

Setting Up a Gateway

Configuring a gateway has four major steps:

1. Preparing NetWare to support the gateway
2. Installing the gateway
3. Activating the gateway and sharing NetWare files with users
4. Sharing NetWare printers with users

Each step is covered. Throughout this discussion, it is assumed that you are familiar with NetWare administration so that I don't have to write a book within a book. If you need to know more about NetWare, please allow me to recommend my book *Inside NetWare 3.12, Fourth Edition,* also from NRP.

Preparing the NetWare Server to Support a Gateway

Very little setup is required on the NetWare side. Essentially, all you need to do is add accounts that let the gateway into the NetWare LAN.

Gateway Services for NetWare consists of two components:

- A client service that enables the user of the gateway computer to log directly into the NetWare server.
- A gateway service that enables Microsoft network users to access shared NetWare resources.

Each of these services can be configured to access the NetWare server through a separate NetWare user account. I do not recommend using the same account for both purposes. You might be using the client service account as a NetWare supervisor account, with privileges you don't want to make available to gateway users.

For smoothest operation, users should log on to the Windows and NetWare networks with the same user name, which should have the same password on each server. After this is done, Windows can automatically log the user on to each service environment when the user name and password are specified.

To set up the NetWare server to support Gateway Services for NetWare, use SYSCON to create the following entities:

- A group named NTGATEWAY. Grant this group the rights that should be available to users who access the server through the gateway.
- A user account with the same user name that is used to log on to the Windows NT network from the gateway computer. Give this user the appropriate rights. because I'm logging in as the Windows NT Administrator user, I created a user account named ADMINISTRATOR on the NetWare server. Configure passwords so that they are the same on the Windows NT Server and the NetWare server. (Several accounts might be necessary if the gateway computer is shared.)
- A user account that will be used by the gateway service. I named my user account GATEWAY. Make this user account a member of the NTGATEWAY group. To create other gateways, create a user account for each gateway and add each account to the NTGATEWAY group.

Installing the Gateway Service

The Gateway Service is installed from the Network utility in the Windows NT Server Control Panel. To install the service, use the following steps:

1. Start the Network utility.

2. In the Network Settings dialog box, click on the Add Software button.

3. In the Add Network Software dialog box, pull down the Network Software box and select the entry Gateway Service for NetWare. Then click on Continue.

4. Supply a file path name when one is requested and choose Continue to install the software.

5. When you return to the Network Settings dialog box, click on OK. The Network utility will proceed to configure the network.

6. If NWLink was not previously installed on the computer, it will be added, and you will be shown the NWLink IPX/SPX Protocol Configuration dialog box. Unless your network has specific protocol requirements, no configuration should be needed. *Consult Chapter 7, "Installing Windows NT Server," for information about configuring NWLink.*

7. Restart the computer to activate the changes.

Activating the Gateway Server and Adding Shares

After the server reboots and you log on within the Welcome box, you are shown a new dialog box: Select Preferred Server for NetWare.

A preferred server is the first NetWare server that the login process attempts to connect you with. The server you select will be the preferred server for your personal NetWare user ID, as well as the NetWare gateway user ID. Click on OK when you have entered a preferred server.

Windows NT will attempt to authenticate you on the NetWare server using your Windows NT account name and password. If the login fails, you will be asked to enter a user name and password for NetWare.

When Gateway Service for NetWare is installed, a new GSNW icon is added to the Control Panel. This tool is used to configure NetWare services on the computer (see fig. 22.3).

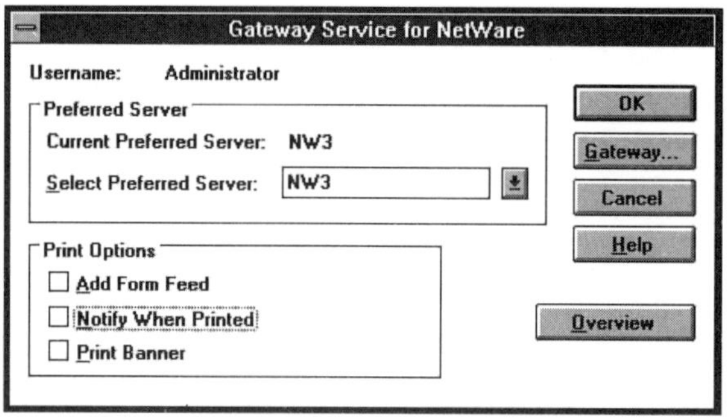

Figure 22.3
User account information for Gateway Service for NetWare.

Configuring the User Account Information

Information in the Gateway Service for NetWare box pertains to the user whose name is shown after `Username`. This information is used to configure this user's NetWare environment.

If you want to change your preferred server, change the entry in the Select Preferred Server box.

Print options for printing to NetWare printers can be set as follows:

- **Add Form Feed.** Check this box if NetWare should force a form feed at the end of print jobs. Most software sends a form feed, and this option should not be checked in most cases.
- **Notify When Printed.** Check this box if you want to receive a message when a job has been sent to a printer.
- **Print Banner.** When this option is checked, NetWare prints a banner page before each job. Do not check this option if printing to a Postscript printer. Most organizations do not find it necessary to activate banners.

At this point, you have configured the computer so that locally logged on users can log on to NetWare. If you will not be configuring a gateway, click on OK to exit the utility.

Note

When the NetWare account was set up for the locally logged on user, the password was probably not synchronized to the user's password on the Windows network. As a result, the user is asked to enter a password each time a connection is established with the NetWare server.

To change the password on the NetWare server, follow these steps:

1. Open a command prompt.
2. Use the `net use` command to connect a drive to the NetWare SYS volume. For example, enter the command:

   `net use s: \\nw3\sys`

3. Change to the connected drive.
4. CD to the \PUBLIC directory.
5. Enter the command **SETPASS**. Follow the prompts to change the NetWare password.

After passwords match in Windows NT and NetWare, you will need to enter your password only once while logging on to the network.

Configuring the NetWare Gateway and Sharing Directories

To configure the gateway, click on the **G**ateway button in the Gateway Service for NetWare dialog box (see fig. 22.4). At first, the **A**dd, **R**emove, and **P**ermissions options are not active because the gateway service has not been started.

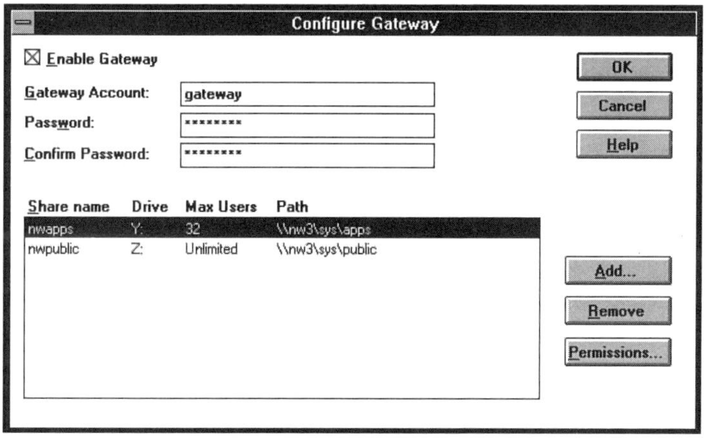

Figure 22.4

Configuring a gateway.

To configure a gateway, use these steps:

1. Check **E**nable Gateway. Checking this option instructs Windows NT Server to start the gateway service when the server starts. You can disable the gateway without removing the software by removing the check mark for this box.

Stop Do not stop the Gateway Service for NetWare service using the Service utility in the Control Panel. Several other vital services are stopped with it. Instead, disable the gateway in the GSNW utility.

2. Enter the NetWare user account name that you created for the gateway server in the Gateway Account box. When an account name has been entered, the Add button is activated.

3. Enter the password for the NetWare user account in the Password and Confirm Password boxes.

4. To make directories on the NetWare server available to gateway users, you must define them as shares. To add a share, click on Add to display the New Share dialog box shown in figure 22.5. Complete the following information for the share you are adding:

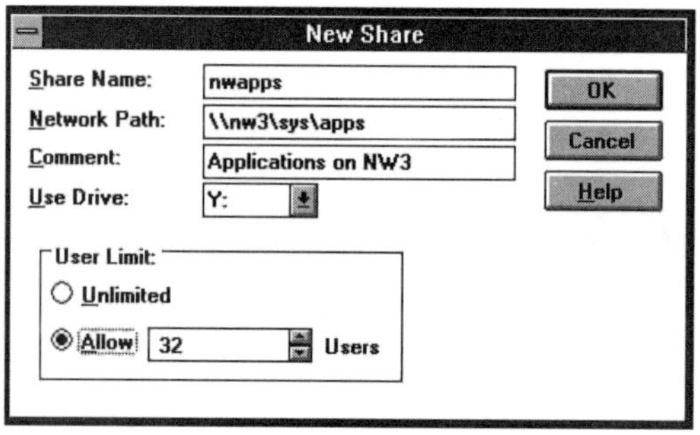

Figure 22.5
Adding a gateway share.

- **Share Name.** Enter the name by which the share will be known to gateway users.

- **Network Path.** Enter the path to the NetWare directory that will be shared. The utility accepts uniform naming convention (UNC) names, which have the following format:

  \\server\volume\directory\subdirectory...

Figure 22.5 shows the UNC name for the APPS directory on the SYS volume of the NW3 server.

- **Comment.** You can add a comment to describe the share if desired. This comment will be shown when the share is listed in users' browse lists.

- **Use Drive.** Select an available drive letter from the list. Drive letters that correspond to physical drives on the computer are not available, and available drives are usually limited to the letters E through Z because a gateway can provide access to at most 22 or 23 directory shares.

- **Unlimited.** Choose this option if you do not want to restrict the number of users who can access the share.
- **Allow.** Choose this option and specify a number to restrict the number of users who can access the share. Because performance will suffer if too many users connect to a given share, a limit is desirable.

Click on OK when you have configured the share. The Gateway service will attempt to locate the shared directory on the specified NetWare server. If the share can be validated, it will be added to the Share Name list in the Configure Gateway dialog box.

Note Unfortunately, you cannot modify a gateway share once it is added. To make changes, you must remove the existing share and add a new share with the desired settings.

5. By default, the group Everyone is given Full Control permissions to a newly created Gateway share. If you want to change the default permissions, select the entry in the Share Name box and click on Permissions. The Access Through Share Permissions dialog box (see fig. 22.6) functions like the share permissions dialog boxes in File Manager. Consult Chapter 11, "Sharing Drives, Directories, and Files," for details about setting share permissions.

6. After you have configured the desired gateway shares click on OK to quit the Gateway Services For NetWare utility.

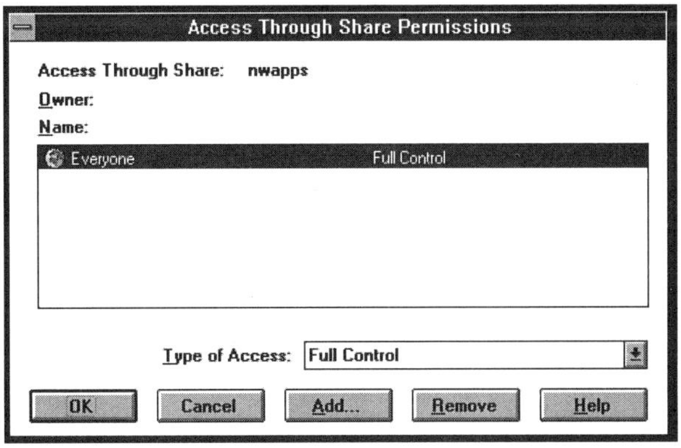

Figure 22.6
Managing permissions for a share.

Note: Gateway Service shares must be created, and their permissions managed, in the Gateway Services For NetWare utility. Gateway file shares cannot be managed in File Manager. As a result, you cannot use File Manager to fine-tune directory and file permissions.

You can, however, assign detailed NetWare rights to the NTGATEWAY group. Directory and file rights will set maximum permissions for all gateway users, regardless of the share permissions that may be assigned by the Gateway Service.

As a result, NetWare directories that are accessed through the gateway should generally be regarded as group directories, not personal directories. You could add a share that would grant permissions to only one user, but because you are restricted to 22 gateway shares, assigning shared directories on the gateway is not very practical.

If any users require personal directories on the NetWare sever, you should assign them individual NetWare accounts and equip their computers with NetWare client software.

Sharing NetWare Printers

NetWare users do not print directly to printers. They print to print queue files, from which jobs are printed by a print server. Gateway Service for NetWare enables users on the Windows network to connect to NetWare print queues and print to NetWare-managed printers.

Although NetWare directory sharing is managed with the GSNW utility instead of File Manager, NetWare printers are shared using fairly standard procedures in the Print Manager.

To share a NetWare-based printer:

1. Log on to the NetWare network from the gateway computer. The account you use must have NetWare rights to use the desired print queue.

2. Start Print Manager

3. Choose the Connect to Printer command in the Printer menu to access the Connect to Printer dialog box (see fig. 22.7). Because this user is directly logged in to NetWare, a NetWare Network icon is included in the browsable list of Shared Printers. The browse list in the figure has been expanded to show shared print queues.

4. Enter a UNC printer name in the Printer dialog box; for example, **NW3\LASERJET** to specify the LASERJET queue on the NW3 server.

   Or you can browse the Shared Printers list. Double-click a NetWare server to observe the available queues. Then double-click on a queue to connect to it.

   When you are done, the printer's UNC name appears in the Printer box, as shown in figure 22.7.

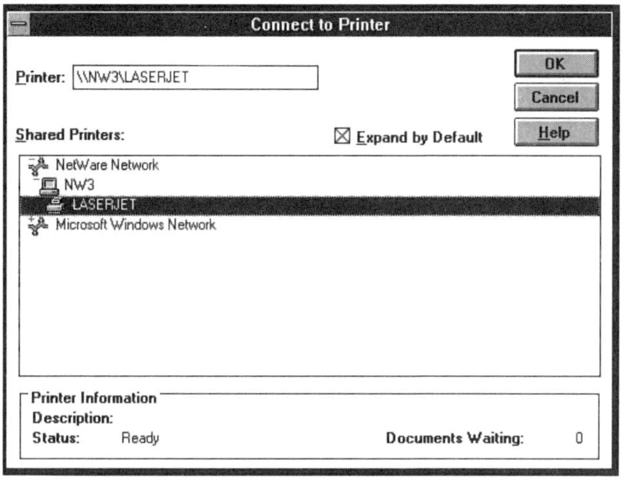

Figure 22.7

Connecting to a NetWare printer.

5. Windows NT ordinarily expects to find a suitable printer driver on the computer to which it is connecting. Because NetWare servers don't come equipped with Windows print drivers, you will see the warning in figure 22.8. Before you can print to the NetWare queue, a suitable printer driver must be added to the local computer. Click on OK in this dialog box and go through the steps of selecting and installing a print driver. *See Chapter 12, "Managing Printing Services," if you want more information.*

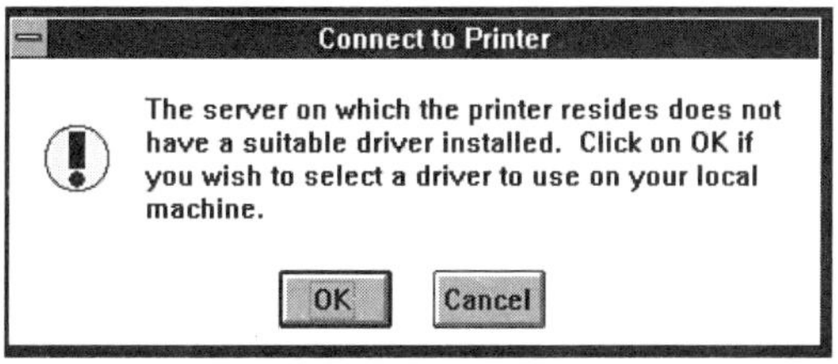

Figure 22.8

Warning to install printer drivers.

6. After the print driver has been installed, the printer is connected and a printer window is created for it in Print Manager. The locally connected user can now print to the printer. Before gateway users can use the printer, however, it must be shared.

7. To share the printer with the gateway, select the printer in the Print Manager main window. Then choose the Properties command in the Printer menu. An example of a Printer Properties dialog box is shown in figure 22.9.

Figure 22.9

Configuring share properties for a gateway printer.

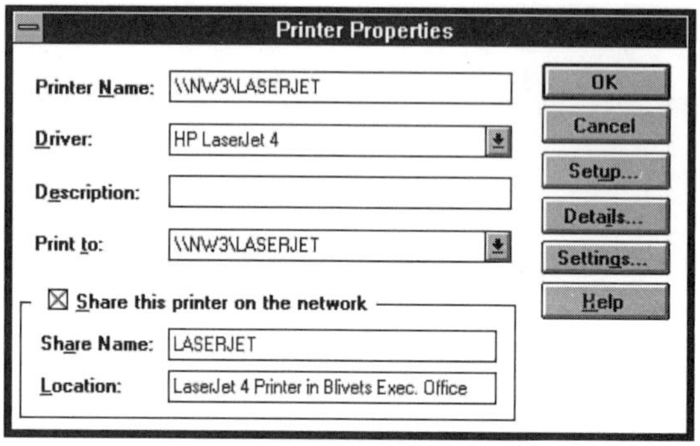

8. To share the printer, check Share this printer on the network. Enter a Share Name and, if desired, a Location description for the printer.

   You can, if desired, configure the Setup, Details, or Settings for the share. *Consult Chapter 12 for thorough coverage of these options.*

9. Click on OK when the share properties are specified.

Windows users can now access this shared printer as though it were directly attached to the gateway computer.

Client Access to Gateway Shares

There really isn't much to say about how clients use shares that are provided by the Gateway Service for NetWare. Shared printers and directories are advertised in the browse list for the gateway computer, just as though they resided physically on that computer. As a result, most of the NetWare gateway mechanism is invisible to network users.

Using NetWare Applications Through the Gateway

A wide variety of NetWare MS-DOS utilities can be run through the gateway:

chkvol	grant	pconsole	rights	slist
colorpal	help	psc	security	syscon
dspace	listdir	pstat	send	tlist
flag	map	rconsole	session	userlist
flagdir	ncopy	remove	setpass	volinfo
fconsole	ndir	revoke	settts	whoami
filer				

NetWare menu utilities such as RCONSOLE require access to files such as SYS$MSG.DAT, which is installed in the SYS:PUBLIC directory. To access these files, either make SYS:PUBLIC your default utility before running the utility, or add SYS:PUBLIC to your search path.

Not all NetWare-aware applications run in a Windows NT gateway environment. Consult your program documentation for information about supported environments. Some applications may require that the NWLink or IPX/SPX protocol stacks be loaded on the client.

Many NetWare-aware applications that are written for 16-bit Windows require DLL files that are provided by Novell. The NWIPXSPX.DLL file is included with the NetWare DOS client software. If the NetWare client software has ever been installed on the client, this file should have been installed. To make this available to gateway clients, obtain NWIPXSPX.DLL and copy it to the directory C:\WINNT35\SYSTEM32.

Some NetWare-aware applications directly send and receive NCP packets. These applications might require one of the file NETWARE.DRV. This file is copied to the C:\WINNT35\SYSTEM32 directory when the Gateway Service is installed; it is used in combination with either NWNETAPI.DLL or NWCALLS.DLL, depending on the version of NetWare being used. Consult the NetWare documentation for the correct file to use. Copy these files to the directory C:\WINNT35\SYSTEM32.

For MIPS and ALPHA AXP clients, the file TBMI2.COM must be copied to the directory C:\WINNT35\SYSTEM32. Also, add the following line to the AUTOEXEC.NT file and restart the computer:

```
lh winnt35\system32\tbmi2.com
```

Applications do not generally perform as well through the gateway as they would with a direct logon connection. This will be the case particularly if large amounts of data must flow through the gateway. Gateway translation takes time.

Stop One particular area of incompatibility is tape backup. You might be tempted to use the backup program from Windows NT Server because it's already included with the product. When backing up NetWare, however, you must use a backup product that is aware of the existence of the NetWare bindery files. Windows NT Backup was written for Windows NT, not for NetWare.

Note Gateway Service for NetWare must translate several file system characteristics when users access NetWare files. Among the features that require translation are file attributes. Following is a comparison of Windows NT file attributes and the way they are translated for NetWare files:

Windows NT Attribute	NetWare Attribute
R (Read Only)	Ro, Di (Delete Inhibit), Ri (Rename Inhibit)
A (Archive)	A
S (System)	Sy
H (Hidden)	H

Note The NetWare Ci (Copy Inhibit), P (Purge),RW (Read Write), S (Shareable), T (Transactional), Ra (Read Audit), and Wa (Write Audit) attributes are not supported by the gateway, although they do restrict the operations that gateway users can perform on NetWare-based files.

Migrating Users from NetWare to Windows NT

If you dislike the idea of maintaining two types of servers and have decided to move all of your servers over to Windows NT Server, you are faced with the big problem of moving user accounts from NetWare to Windows NT. If you have a large number of NetWare users, you might decide that the task of creating new accounts in the Windows NT Server environment is too daunting.

Microsoft includes a Migration Tool for NetWare with Windows NT Server that reduces the pain of moving users to Windows NT networks. The Migration Tool is not installed as an icon, and, because you will probably not be running it frequently, you will probably choose to run it from a Run command.

The server that is running the migration must meet the following conditions:

- Volumes to which NetWare files will be migrated must be formatted with the NTFS file system so that NetWare directory and security information can be migrated.
- The NWLink protocols must be installed.
- The Gateway Service for NetWare must be installed. The Gateway Service enables the Migration Tool to access the NetWare server from which you are migrating.

To start the Migration Tool, choose the Run command in the Program Manager File menu. In the Command Line box, enter the command **nwconv** and click on OK. The first dialog box you see, Select Servers for Migration, is shown in figure 22.10. Specify the names of the NetWare and Windows NT Server computers and click on OK. If you need to log on to either server, you are prompted for a user name and a password. The NetWare user account should be secured as a Supervisor equivalent. The Windows NT user account should have administrator permissions on the target server.

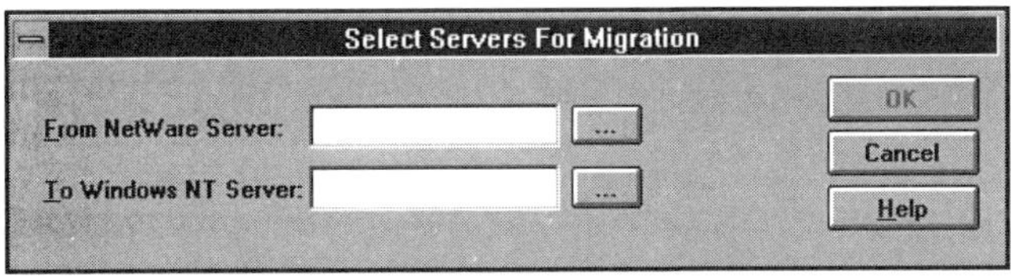

Figure 22.10

Selecting file servers for migration.

After logging on to the source and destination servers, the main Migration Tool window is displayed (see fig. 22.11).

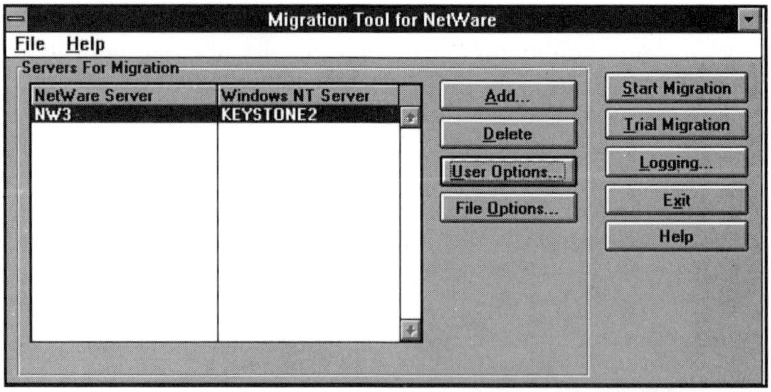

Figure 22.11
Main window for the Migration Tool.

The Add and Delete buttons are used to add and delete source and destination servers.

Setting Migration User Options

The User Options button in the Migration tool is used to access the User and Group Options dialog box (see fig. 22.12). This dialog box has four subboxes that are accessed by clicking tabs: Passwords, Usernames, Group Names, and Defaults. Each of these boxes is covered in turn.

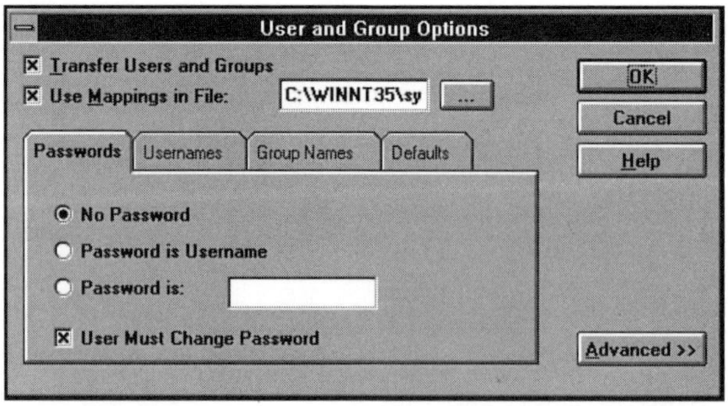

Figure 22.12
User and group options for the Migration Tool.

Selecting the Transfer Option

Check Transfer Users and Groups if you want to migrate NetWare groups and users. If you wish, you can turn this option off to transfer only files.

Using a Mappings File

If you want to control how names of users and groups are handled during the migration, use a mappings file. To use a migration mapping file, do the following:

1. Check Use Mappings in File.

2. Enter a file name in the box or click ... to browse for a directory and name a file. The file the Migration Tool creates is a text file that will have a MAP extension.

3. After you click on OK in the User and Group Options window, you are shown the message `Mapping file created successfully. Do you want to edit it?`. If you choose Yes, Notepad is started up, and the mapping file is loaded for editing. An example is shown in figure 22.13. The example was kept very simple. As you can see, you can map the user's NetWare account name to a new name on the Windows NT server. You can also change user group names and specify an initial user password.

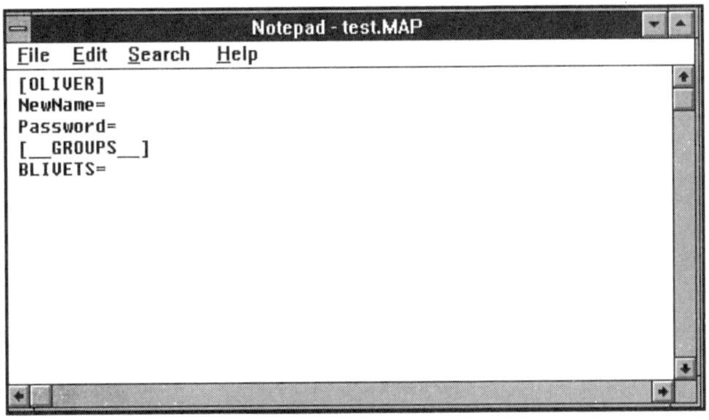

Figure 22.13

Editing a migration mappings file.

Selecting Password Options

Not even a NetWare Supervisor can discover user passwords, so passwords cannot be migrated to Windows NT. The passwords box has three options for creating passwords:

- **No Password.** This option makes it unnecessary for you to distribute passwords to users.

- **Password is Username.** The password for the user account will be the same as the user name.

- **Password is.** The initial password will be the password you specify.

It is recommended that you check User Must Change Password if you use the No Password option, so that users will be forced to change or create a password when they first log on.

Selecting Username Options

Click the Usernames tab in the User and Group Options box to display the Usernames options (see fig. 22.14). Options in this box specify the action that will be taken if a user name on the NetWare server is duplicated by an existing name on the Windows NT Server.

- **Log Error.** This option records conflicts in the ERROR.LOG file that is created during migration.
- **Ignore.** This option ignores accounts on the NetWare server that already exist on the Windows NT Server.
- **Overwrite with new Info.** This option replaces account information on the Windows NT Server with account information from NetWare.
- **Add prefix.** You can specify a prefix that is appended to the NetWare name if a conflict occurs.

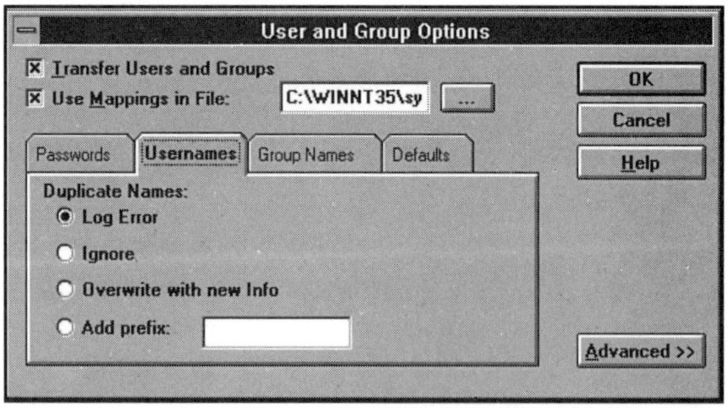

Figure 22.14
Specifying migration action when duplicate user names are encountered.

Selecting Group Name Options

Click on the Group Names tab to display the box shown in figure 22.15. Because these options duplicate options on the Usernames tab, they require no discussion.

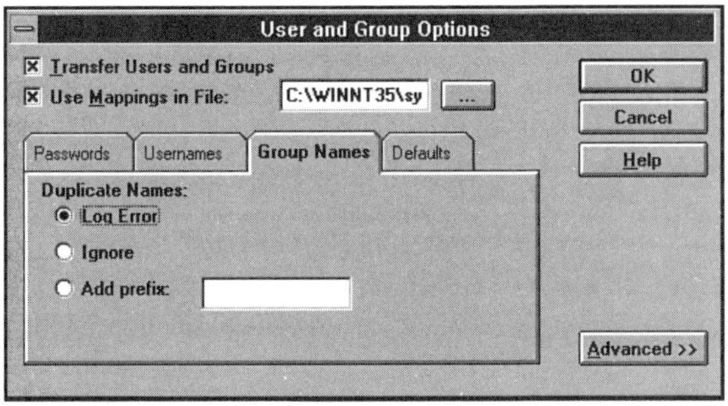

Figure 22.15

Specifying migration action when duplicate group names are encountered.

Selecting Supervisor Defaults

Click on the Defaults tab to determine how supervisor rights will be transferred to the Windows NT Server environment. Options are shown in figure 22.16.

- **Use Supervisor Defaults.** Check this box to transfer account restrictions from NetWare to Windows NT Server. Remove the check mark if Windows NT account policy settings should be used.
- **Add Supervisors to the Administrators Group.** Check this box if users who are user-equivalent to the NetWare Supervisor should be added to the Administrators group. Remove the check mark if supervisor equivalents should not be made administrators of the Windows NT Server.

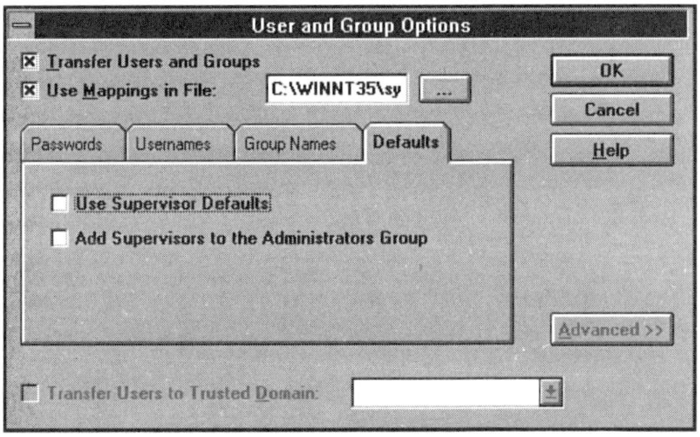

Figure 22.16

Specifying supervisor rights transfer.

Setting Migration File Options

The File **O**ptions button in the Migration Tool main window produces the File Options dialog box shown in figure 22.17. This box enables you to control where files will be placed on the Windows NT Server. The NetWare server used in this example has only one volume, named SYS. All of the volumes on the NetWare server should be listed, and the **A**dd button will only be activated if you delete a volume.

Figure 22.17

Setting file migration options.

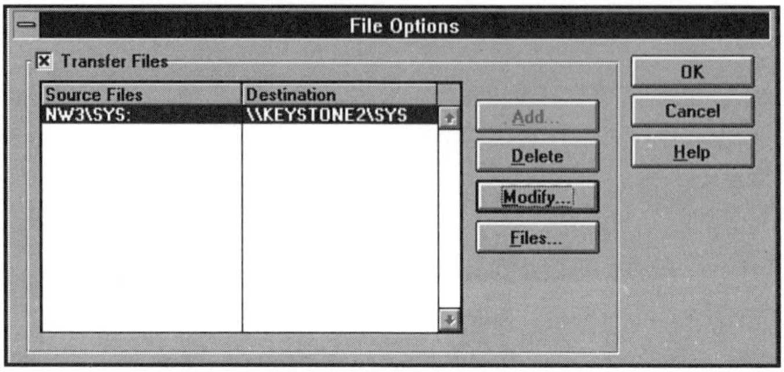

The **M**odify button displays the Modify Destination dialog box shown in figure 22.18. By default, files in a NetWare volume are copied to a directory with the same name as the volume. The share name assigned to the directory will be the same as the original volume name.

You can modify the destination directory and share name in this dialog box. Change the Share entry to specify the share name that is assigned to the directory to which these files are copied. You can also specify a different directory by clicking on Properties.

Figure 22.18

Specifying the file migration destination.

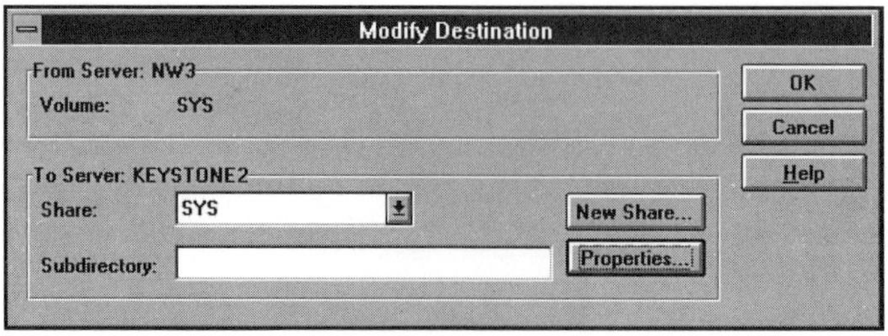

If you want to select specific files and directories to be transferred, click on the Files button in the File Options dialog box to display the Files to Transfer box shown in Figure 22.19. Select directories and files much as you would in File Manager. Double-click a closed folder icon to examine the directory contents. Check the directories and files to be transferred and clear check marks for items that should not be migrated.

In figure 22.19, the SYS volume was opened to reveal the first-level directories. By default, several directories are not checked. It would make no sense to migrate the SYSTEM directory, for example, which contains the NetWare system files. You can go down to the file level if you want to exercise that much control over files that will migrate. You will probably want, for example, to exclude most if not all of the files in the PUBLIC directory.

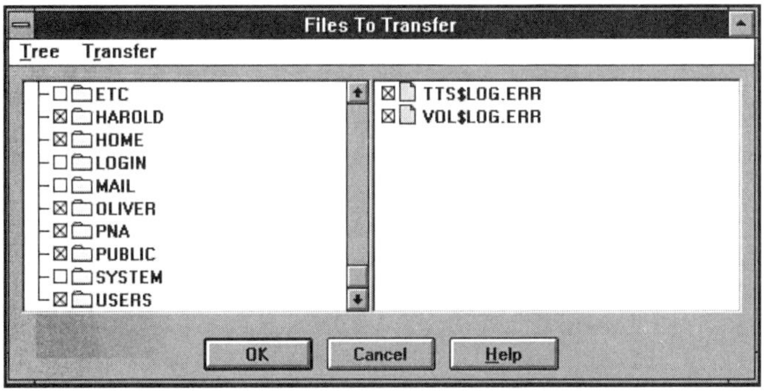

Figure 22.19

Selecting directories and files to migrate.

The Transfer menu in the Files to Transfer dialog box contains two options that determine whether Hidden Files and System files will be transferred.

Setting Migration Logging Options

You can determine the amount of logging that will take place during migration by clicking on the Logging button in the Migration Tool main window. Logging options are shown in figure 22.20.

The View Log Files button is only active if log files have been created.

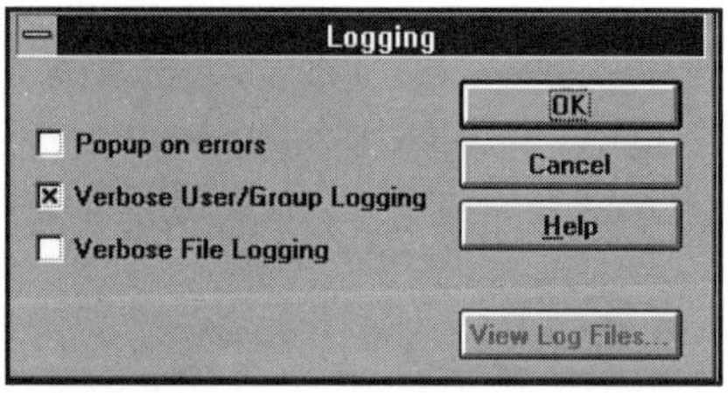

Figure 22.20

Options for logging during migration.

Running a Trial Migration

Before you perform an actual migration, run a trial by clicking on the Trial Migration button in the Migration Tool main window. Your migration settings will be tested without actually migrating anything.

After the trial migration is completed, a summary box reports the results (see fig. 22.21).

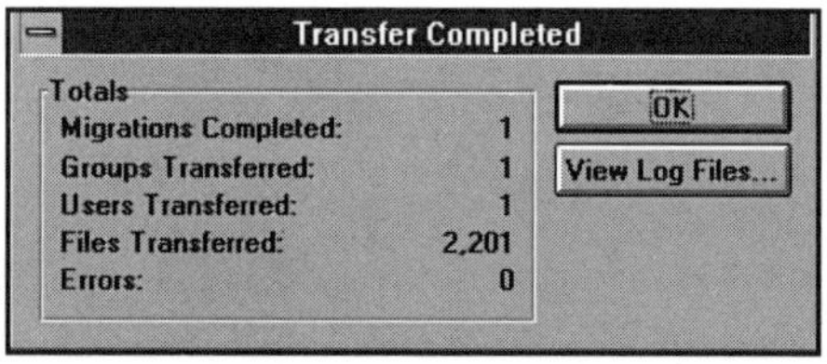

Figure 22.21

The Transfer Completed summary box.

A trial migration creates log files just as would be created by an actual migration. Three log files are created:

- *LOGFILE.LOG* contains information about users, groups, and files.
- *SUMMARY.LOG* contains an overview of the migration process.
- *ERROR.LOG* reports any migration errors that were encountered.

You can view these logs by clicking the View Log Files button in the Transfer Completed box. The LogView utility (see fig. 22.22) that is invoked includes windows for the three migration logs. You can select logs for review as required.

Be especially sure that the ERROR.LOG file does not report critical errors, such as:

- User and group names that did not transfer
- Network errors, such as a failure to access the source server
- System errors, such as insufficient space for transferred files on the destination drives

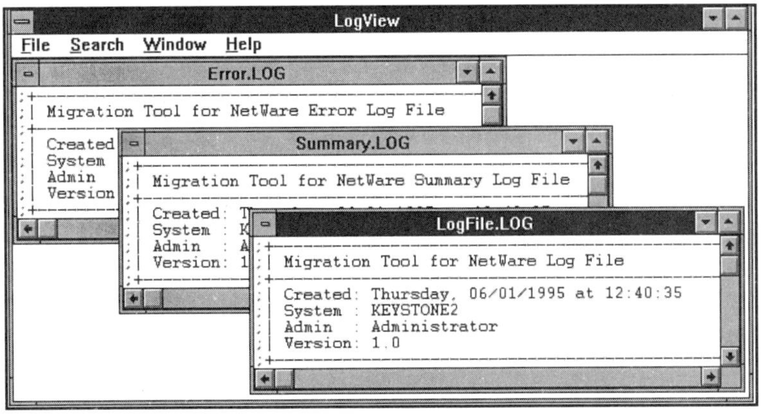

Figure 22.22
Reviewing the migration logs.

The following listing contains part of the LOGFILE.LOG file that is created. This file was created with the Verbose User/Group Logging option and contains a detailed record of the migration.

```
;+-----------------------------------------------------------------------+
;¦ Migration Tool for NetWare Log File                                   ¦
;+-----------------------------------------------------------------------+
;¦ Created: Thursday, 06/01/1995 at 12:40:35                             ¦
;¦ System : KEYSTONE2                                                    ¦
;¦ Admin  : Administrator                                                ¦
;¦ Version: 1.0                                                          ¦
;+-----------------------------------------------------------------------+
Conversion = Trial

Number of Migrations = 1

[Servers]
   From: NW3              To: KEYSTONE2

;+-----------------------------------------------------------------------+
;¦ Server Information                                                    ¦
;+-----------------------------------------------------------------------+

[KEYSTONE2]
   Windows NT(R) Server
   Version: 3.50

   [Drives]
      C: [NTFS]
         Free Space: 166,367,232
```

```
[NW3]
   NetWare(R) Server
   Version: 3.12

   [Shares]
      SYS

;+-------------------------------------------------------------------------+
;¦ Setting User Defaults from Supervisor Defaults                          ¦
;¦ From: NW3                                                               ¦
;¦ To:   KEYSTONE2                                                         ¦
;¦ Converted: Thursday, 06/01/1995 at 12:40:36                             ¦
;+-------------------------------------------------------------------------+

[Transfer Options]
   Convert Users and Groups: Yes

   User Transfer Options:
      Use mapping file: Yes
         Mapping File: C:\WINNT35\system32\test.MAP
      Passwords: 1 - Use NULL
         User must change password: Yes
      Duplicate Names: Log Error
      Duplicate Groups: Log Error
      Use supervisor defaults: No
      Add Supervisors to the Administrators Group: No

[File Options]
   Convert Files: Yes

[New Shares]
   SYS
      Path: C:\SYS

[Users]
   Number of Users = 1

   Users to Transfer
   +---------------------------------------------------+
    OLIVER
```

```
[OLIVER]                                                  (Added)
Original Account Info:
   Name:       Oliver Hardy
   Account disabled: No
   Account expires: (Never)
   Password expires: 07/11/1995
   Grace Logins: 6
   Initial Grace Logins: 6
   Minimum Password Length: 5
   # days to Password Expiration: 40
   Maximum Number of Connections: (Unlimited)
   Restrictions:
      Anyone who knows password can change it
      Unique passwords required: Yes
   Number of login failures: 0
   Max Disk Blocks: (Unlimited)

Login Times:
 Midnight            AM                 Noon               PM
    12 1  2  3  4  5  6  7  8  9  10 11 12 1  2  3  4  5  6  7  8  9  10 11
   +-----------------------------------------------------------------------+
Sun ** ** ** ** ** ** ** ** ** ** ** ** ** ** ** ** ** ** ** ** ** ** ** **
Mon ** ** ** ** ** ** ** ** ** ** ** ** ** ** ** ** ** ** ** ** ** ** ** **
Tue ** ** ** ** ** ** ** ** ** ** ** ** ** ** ** ** ** ** ** ** ** ** ** **
Wed ** ** ** ** ** ** ** ** ** ** ** ** ** ** ** ** ** ** ** ** ** ** ** **
Thu ** ** ** ** ** ** ** ** ** ** ** ** ** ** ** ** ** ** ** ** ** ** ** **
Fri ** ** ** ** ** ** ** ** ** ** ** ** ** ** ** ** ** ** ** ** ** ** ** **
Sat ** ** ** ** ** ** ** ** ** ** ** ** ** ** ** ** ** ** ** ** ** ** ** **

New Account Info:
   Name: Oliver Hardy
   Password:
   Privilege: User
   Home Dir:
   Comment:
   Flags:
      Execute login script: Yes
      Account disabled: No
      Deleting prohibited: No
      Home dir required: No
      Password required: Yes
      User can change password: Yes
```

```
      Script path:
      Full Name: Oliver Hardy
      Logon Server:

   Logon Hours:
    Midnight            AM                    Noon                  PM
       12 1  2  3  4  5  6  7  8  9  10 11 12 1  2  3  4  5  6  7  8  9  10 11
      +-------------------------------------------------------------------+
   Sun ** ** ** ** ** ** ** ** ** ** ** ** ** ** ** ** ** ** ** ** ** ** ** **
   Mon ** ** ** ** ** ** ** ** ** ** ** ** ** ** ** ** ** ** ** ** ** ** ** **
   Tue ** ** ** ** ** ** ** ** ** ** ** ** ** ** ** ** ** ** ** ** ** ** ** **
   Wed ** ** ** ** ** ** ** ** ** ** ** ** ** ** ** ** ** ** ** ** ** ** ** **
   Thu ** ** ** ** ** ** ** ** ** ** ** ** ** ** ** ** ** ** ** ** ** ** ** **
   Fri ** ** ** ** ** ** ** ** ** ** ** ** ** ** ** ** ** ** ** ** ** ** ** **
   Sat ** ** ** ** ** ** ** ** ** ** ** ** ** ** ** ** ** ** ** ** ** ** ** **

[Groups]
   Number Groups = 1
   BLIVETS                                          (Added)

   [BLIVETS]
      OLIVER

[Security Equivalences]
   [OLIVER]
      BLIVETS

[Files]

   Copying Files From Volume: SYS
   To Share: SYS
      [Files]

Conversion Finished: Thursday, 06/01/1995 at 12:40:57
```

Completing the Migration

When the trial migration runs satisfactorily, use the **S**tart Migration button in the Migration Tool main window to start the actual migration.

APPENDIX

Windows NT Server Command Reference

Although the majority of Windows NT functions can be executed using graphic utilities, there are several reasons for using NET commands at the command prompt. In some cases, entering a command at the command prompt is faster than starting a graphic utility and stepping through menus. Of greater significance is that NET commands can be put into batch files, which are useful for building logon scripts, executing commands at schedule times, or performing functions when events are triggered. The UPS command, for example, can be configured to execute a batch file before shutting down Windows NT. Although the NET commands are described in online help displays, they are summarized here for your convenience.

The following conventions are used to indicate command syntax:

- **Bold** letters are used for words that must be typed as shown.
- *lowercase italic* letters are used for items that vary, such as file names.

- The [and] characters surround optional items that can be supplied with the command.
- The { and } characters surround lists of items. You may select one of the items in the list.
- The ¦ character separates items in a list. Only one of the items can be included with the command.

  For example, in the following syntax, you must type NET COMMAND and either OPTION1 or OPTION2. Supplying a name is optional.

  ```
  NET COMMAND [name] {OPTION1 ¦ OPTION2}
  ```

- The [...] characters mean you can repeat the previous item, separating items with spaces.
- The [,...] characters mean you can repeat the previous item, separating items with commas or semicolons, not spaces.
- When service names consist of two or more words, enclose the service name in quotation marks. For example, `NET PAUSE "FTP SERVER"` pauses the FTP server service.

To view a listing of syntax conventions for the online help, type the command **net help syntax**.

NET ACCOUNTS

NET ACCOUNTS is used to maintain the user account database. It can modify password and logon requirements for all user accounts. When entered without options, NET ACCOUNTS displays current settings for the password, logon limitations, and domain information for the logged-on account.

Syntax

```
NET ACCOUNTS   [/FORCELOGOFF:{minutes ¦ NO}]
               [/MINPWLEN:length]
               [/MAXPWAGE:{days ¦ UNLIMITED}]
               [/MINPWAGE:days]
               [/UNIQUEPW:number]
               [/DOMAIN]
NET ACCOUNTS [/SYNC] [/DOMAIN]
```

Options

`/FORCELOGOFF:{minutes ¦ NO}`	*Minutes* specifies the number of minutes a user has before being automatically logged off when an account expires or logon hours expire. NO is the default value and specifies that forced logoff will not occur.
`/MINPWLEN:length`	*Length* specifies the minimum number of characters required for a password. The range is 0–14 characters. The default is 6 characters.
`/MAXPWAGE:{days ¦ UNLIMITED}`	*Days* specifies the maximum number of days a password is valid. The UNLIMITED option specifies that no limit is imposed. /MAXPWAGE cannot be less than /MINPWAGE. The range is 1–49710 and the default is 90 days.
`/MINPWAGE:days`	*Days* specifies the minimum number of days that must pass before a user can change his or her password. A value of 0 specifies no minimum time. The range is 0–49,710; the default is 0 days. /MINPWAGE cannot be greater than /MAXPWAGE.
`/UNIQUEPW:number`	Specifies that the user's passwords must be unique for the number of changes specified by *number*. The maximum value is 8.
`/SYNC`	Synchronizes the account database.
`/DOMAIN`	Include this option to perform the specified action on the entire domain controller instead of the current computer. This option is effective only when executed on Windows NT computers that are members of a domain.

See Also

For a thorough discussion of the options for user accounts, see Chapter 10, "Managing Users and Groups."

Examples

NET ACCOUNTS can be used to make global changes to all user accounts. To change the minimum password length for all user accounts to five days, enter the following command:

```
NET ACCOUNTS /MINPWAGE:5
```

Figure A.1 shows an example of using the NET ACCOUNTS command without options.

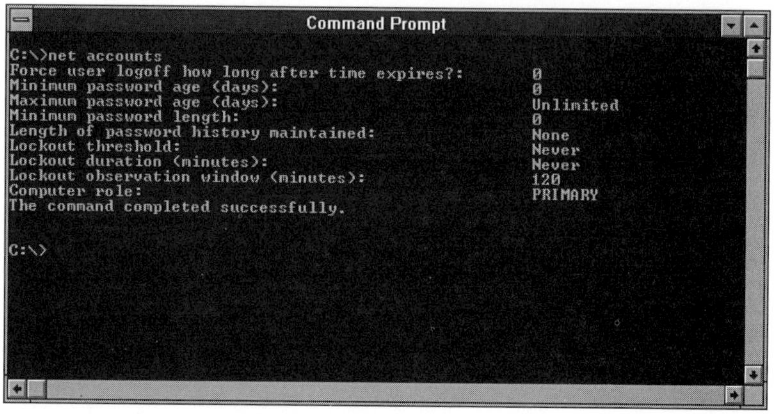
Command Prompt
C:\>net accounts
Force user logoff how long after time expires?: 0
Minimum password age (days): 0
Maximum password age (days): Unlimited
Minimum password length: 0
Length of password history maintained: None
Lockout threshold: Never
Lockout duration (minutes): Never
Lockout observation window (minutes): 120
Computer role: PRIMARY
The command completed successfully.
C:\>

Figure A.1
Displaying account information with the NET ACCOUNTS command.

Notes

For options used with NET ACCOUNTS to take effect the following conditions must be true:

- User accounts must have been set up by the User Manager or the NET USER command
- The Net Logon service must be running on all domain controllers.

NET COMPUTER

Use this command to add or delete computers from the domain database.

Syntax

```
NET COMPUTER \\computername {/ADD ¦ /DEL}
```

Options

computername	The name of the computer to be added or deleted.
/ADD	Adds the computer to the domain.
/DEL	Deletes the computer from the domain.

Example

To add a computer named GEORGE to the domain, enter this command:

```
NET COMPUTER \\GEORGE /ADD
```

Notes

This command is available only with Windows NT Server.

NET CONFIG SERVER

Use this command to display or change settings for the server service. This command affects only the server on which it is executed.

You must be logged on as a member of the Administrators group to configure the server.

Syntax

```
NET CONFIG SERVER   [/AUTODISCONCONNECT:time]
                    [/SRVCOMMENT:"text"]
                    [/HIDDEN:{YES¦NO}]
```

Options

/AUTODISCONNECT:*time*	*Time* specifies the number of minutes an account can be inactive before it is disconnected. Specify -1 to never disconnect. Range is 1–65535 minutes. Default is 15.
/SRVCOMMENT:"*text*"	The message in "*text*" specifies a message that is displayed along with the server in many Windows NT screens. The message can consist of up to 48 characters and must be enclosed in quotation marks.
/HIDDEN:{YES ¦ NO}	Determines whether a computer name is advertised in listings of servers. YES hides the server. NO includes the server name in lists.

Example

To display the current configuration for the Server service, type **NET CONFIG SERVER** without parameters. An example NET CONFIG SERVER display is shown in Figure A.2.

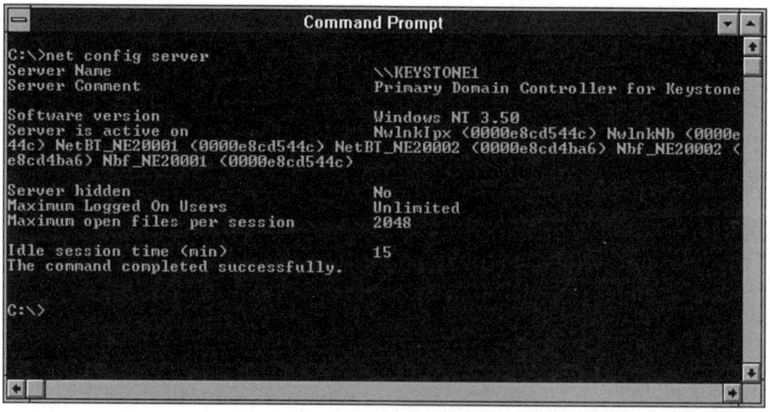
Command Prompt
C:\>net config server
Server Name \\KEYSTONE1
Server Comment Primary Domain Controller for Keystone
Software version Windows NT 3.50
Server is active on NwlnkIpx (0000e8cd544c) NwlnkNb (0000e
44c) NetBT_NE20001 (0000e8cd544c) NetBT_NE20002 (0000e8cd4ba6) Nbf_NE20002 (
e8cd4ba6) Nbf_NE20001 (0000e8cd544c)
Server hidden No
Maximum Logged On Users Unlimited
Maximum open files per session 2048
Idle session time (min) 15
The command completed successfully.
C:\>

Figure A.2
Example NET CONFIG SERVER display.

NET CONFIG WORKSTATION

This command displays and changes settings for the Workstation service.

Syntax

```
NET CONFIG WORKSTATION   [/CHARCOUNT:bytes]
                         [/CHARTIME:msec]
                         [/CHARWAIT:sec]
```

Options

/CHARCOUNT:*bytes*	Specifies the *bytes* of data that are collected before data is sent to a communication device. If /CHARTIME is set, Windows NT relies on the value that is satisfied first. Range is 0–65535 bytes. Default is 16 bytes.
/CHARTIME:*msec*	*msec* specifies the number of milliseconds that Windows NT collects data before sending it to a communication device. If /CHARCOUNT is set, Windows NT relies on the value that is satisfied first. Range is 0–65535000 milliseconds. Default is 250 milliseconds.
/CHARWAIT:*sec*	Specifies the number of seconds Windows NT waits for a communication device to become available. Range is 0–65535 seconds. Default is 3600 seconds.

Notes

To display the current configuration for the Workstation service, type **NET CONFIG WORKSTATION** without parameters.

NET CONTINUE

NET CONTINUE reactivates a Windows NT service that has been suspended by NET PAUSE.

Syntax

NET CONTINUE *service*

Options

`service` Is any of the following paused services:

- FILE SERVER FOR MACINTOSH
- FTP SERVER
- LPDSVC
- NET LOGON
- NETWORK DDE
- NETWORK DDE DSDM
- NT LM SECURITY SUPPORT PROVIDER
- REMOTEBOOT
- REMOTE ACCESS SERVER
- SCHEDULE
- SERVER
- SIMPLE TCP/IP SERVICES
- WORKSTATION

NET FILE

Use this command to list ID numbers of files, to close a shared file, and to remove file locks. When used without options, NET FILE lists the open files on a server along with their IDs, path names, user names, and number of locks.

Syntax

```
NET FILE [id [/CLOSE]]
```

Options

id	The identification number of the file.
/CLOSE	Include this option to close an open file and remove file locks. This command must be typed from the server where the file is shared.

Notes

This command works only on computers running the Server service.

NET GROUP

This command adds, displays, or modifies global groups on servers. Enter the **NET GROUP** command without parameters to display the group names on the server.

Syntax

```
NET GROUP [groupname [/COMMENT:"text"]] [/DOMAIN]
NET GROUP groupname {/ADD [/COMMENT:"text"] ¦ /DELETE} [/DOMAIN]
NET GROUP groupname username [...] {/ADD ¦ /DELETE} [/DOMAIN]
```

Options

groupname	This parameter specifies the name of the group to add, expand, or delete. This parameter is also included when user names are to be added to or deleted from a group. Supply the group name alone to see a list of users in a group.
/COMMENT:"*text*"	This switch adds a comment of up to 48 characters, as specified by *text*. Enclose the text in quotation marks.
/DOMAIN	Include this switch to perform the operation on the primary domain controller of the current domain. Without the /DOMAIN switch the operation is affects only the local computer.
username[...]	Specifies one or more usernames to be added to or removed from a group. Multiple user name entries must be separated with a space.
/ADD	Adds a group to a domain or adds a user name to a group.
/DELETE	Removes a group from a domain or removes a user name from a group.

Examples

To view membership of the local group Server Operators, enter this command:

```
NET GROUP "SERVER OPERATORS"
```

To add a group named Blivet Engineers you would use the following command:

```
NET GROUP "Blivet Engineers" /ADD
```

NET HELP

Use this command to display a help listing of the options available for any NET command.

Syntax

`NET HELP` *`command`*

or

`NET` *`command`* `/HELP`

Options

Help information is available for the following commands:

NET ACCOUNTS
NET COMPUTER
NET CONFIG
NET CONFIG SERVER
NET CONFIG WORKSTATION
NET CONTINUE
NET FILE
NET GROUP
NET HELP
NET HELPMSG
NET LOCALGROUP
NET NAME
NET PAUSE
NET PRINT
NET SEND
NET SESSION
NET SHARE
NET START
NET STATISTICS
NET STOP
NET TIME
NET USE
NET USER
NET VIEW

Notes

`NET HELP` ***`command`*** **`¦ MORE`** displays Help one screen at a time.

`NET HELP SERVICES` lists the network services you can start.

`NET HELP SYNTAX` explains how to read NET HELP syntax lines.

NET HELPMSG

The NET HELPMSG command displays explanations of Windows NT network messages, including errors, warnings, and alerts. Type NET HELPMSG along with the 4-digit number of the Windows NT error. Although network error messages include the word NET (for example NET1234), you do not need to include NET in the message# parameter.

Syntax

```
NET HELPMSG message#
```

Options

message# Is the 4-digit number of the Windows NT message you need help with.

Example

Figure A.3 shows an example of using the NET HELPMSG command.

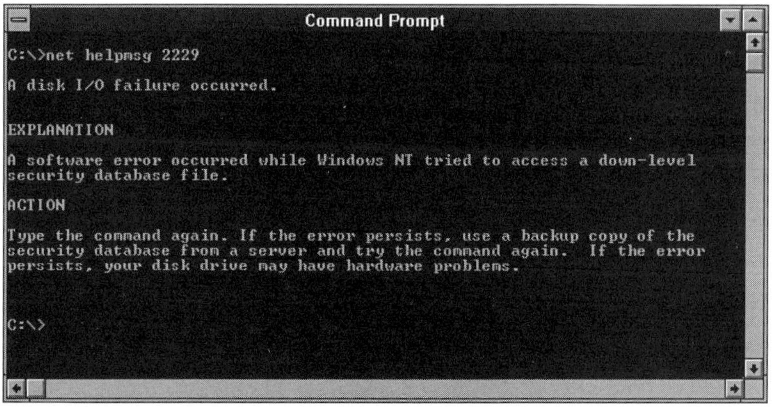

Figure A.3

An example of a NET HELPMSG command.

NET LOCALGROUP

Use this command to modify local groups on computers. Enter the NET LOCALGROUP command without parameters to list the local groups on the computer.

Syntax

```
NET LOCALGROUP [groupname [/COMMENT:"text"]] [/DOMAIN]
NET LOCALGROUP groupname {/ADD [/COMMENT:"text"] ¦ /DELETE} [/DOMAIN]
NET LOCALGROUP groupname name [...] {/ADD ¦ /DELETE} [/DOMAIN]
```

Options

groupname	*groupname* specifies the name of the local group to add, expand, or delete. Supply a group name without parameters to list users or global groups in the local group. If the group name includes spaces, enclose the name in quotation marks.
/COMMENT:"*text*"	This switch adds a comment of up to 48 characters, as specified by *text*. Enclose the text in quotation marks.
/DOMAIN	Include this switch to perform the operation on the primary domain controller of the current domain. Otherwise, the operation is performed on the local computer. By default, Windows NT Server computers perform operations on the domain. This option is effective only when executed on a computer that is a member of a domain.
name [...]	Specifies one or more user names or group names to be added to or removed from the local group. Multiple entries must be separated with a space. Include the domain name if the user is from another domain (Example: WIDGETS\CHARLES).
/ADD	Adds the specified group name or user name to a local group. User and group names to be added must have been created previously.
/DELETE	Removes a group name or user name from a local group.

Examples

To display the membership of the local group "Domain Admins," enter the following command:

```
NET LOCALGROUP "DOMAIN ADMINS"
```

To add the user Harold to the local group Widgets, enter the command:

```
NET LOCALGROUP WIDGETS HAROLD
```

NET NAME

The NET NAME command adds or deletes a messaging name at a computer. A messaging name is a name to which messages are sent. Use the NET NAME command without options to display names accepting messages at this computer.

A computer's list of names comes from three places:

- **Message names**, which are added with NET NAME.
- A **computer name**, which cannot be deleted. The computer name is added as a name when the Workstation service is started.
- A **user name**, which cannot be deleted. Unless the name is already in use on another computer, the user name is added as a name when you log on.

Syntax

NET NAME [*name* [/ADD ¦ /DELETE]]

Options

name	The name of the user account that is to be added to names that will receive messages. The name can have as many as 15 characters.
/ADD	Adds a name to a computer. /ADD is optional and typing **NET NAME** ***name*** works the same way as typing **NET NAME** ***name*** **/ADD**.
/DELETE	Removes a name from a computer.

NET PAUSE

Use the NET PAUSE command to suspend a Windows NT service or resource. Pausing a service puts it on hold. Use the NET CONTINUE command to resume the service.

Syntax

```
NET PAUSE service
```

Options

service	The service to be paused. Please see the NET CONTINUE command for a list of services that can be paused.

Notes

If the Server service is paused, only users who are members of the Administrators or Server Operators groups will be permitted to log on to the network.

NET PRINT

Use this command to list print jobs and shared queues. For each queue, the command lists jobs, showing the size and status of each job, and the queue status.

Syntax

```
NET PRINT \\computername\sharename
        [\\computername] job# [/HOLD ¦ /RELEASE ¦ /DELETE]
```

Options

\\computername	Specifies the name of the computer sharing the printer queue(s).
sharename	Specifies the share name of the printer queue.

job#	Specifies the identification number assigned to a print job. Each job executed on a computer is assigned a unique number.
/HOLD	Assigns a "hold" status to a job so that it will not print. The job remains in the queue until it is released or deleted.
/RELEASE	Removes the "hold" status on a job so that it can be printed.
/DELETE	Removes a job from a queue.

Examples

To display active print jobs on a computer named Blivets, enter the following command:

```
NET PRINT \\BLIVETS
```

To hold job number 234 on the computer Blivets, for example, the command is

```
NET PRINT \\BLIVETS 234 /HOLD
```

NET SEND

This command sends messages to other users, computers, or messaging names on the network.

Syntax

```
NET SEND {name ¦ * ¦ /DOMAIN[:domainname] ¦ /USERS} message
```

Options

name	Specifies the user name, computer name, or messaging name to which the message is sent. If the name contains blank characters, enclose the name in quotation marks.
*	An *, when substituted for *name*, sends the message to all the names in your group.
/DOMAIN[:*domainname*]	Specifies that the message should be sent to all users in the domain. If *domainname* is specified, the message is

	sent to all the names in the specified domain or workgroup.
`/USERS`	Sends the message to all users connected to the server.
`message`	The text to be sent as a message.

Examples

To send a message to everyone in a domain, type a command like the following:

`NET SEND /DOMAIN:WIDGETS A message for everyone in Widgets`

You can also specify a user, in this case, Mabel:

`NET SEND MABEL A message for Mabel`

Notes

The Messenger service must be running on the receiving computer to receive messages.

You can send a message only to a name that is active on the network.

NET SESSION

The NET SESSION command lists or disconnects sessions between the computer and other computers on the network. When used without options, NET SESSION displays information about all sessions running on the computer that currently has the focus.

Syntax

`NET SESSION [\\`*`computername`*`] [/DELETE]`

Options

`\\`*`computername`*	Lists the session information for the named computer.

`/DELETE`	Ends the session between the local computer and *computername*. All open files on the computer are closed. If *computername* is omitted, all sessions are ended.

Notes

This command works only when executed on servers.

NET SHARE

The NET SHARE command is used to share a server's resources with network users. Use the command without options to list information about all resources being shared on the computer. For each shared resource, Windows NT reports the device name(s) or path name(s) for the share along with any descriptive comment that has been associated with the share.

Syntax

```
NET SHARE   sharename
NET SHARE   sharename=drive:path
            [/USERS:number ¦ /UNLIMITED]
            [/REMARK:"text"]
NET SHARE   sharename [/USERS:number ¦ /UNLIMITED] [/REMARK:"text"]
NET SHARE   {sharename ¦ devicename ¦ drive:path} /DELETE
```

Options

sharename	Specifies the network name of the shared resource. Typing NET SHARE with a share name only displays information about that share.
devicename	Specifies one or more printers (LPT1 through LPT9) shared by *sharename*. Use this option when a printer share is being established.
drive:path	Specifies the absolute path of a directory to be shared. Use this option when a directory share is being established.
/USERS:*number*	Specifies the maximum number of users that will be permitted to simultaneously access the shared resource.

/UNLIMITED	Specifies that no limit will be placed on the number of users that will be permitted to simultaneously access the shared resource.
/REMARK:"*text*"	Associates a descriptive comment about the resource with the share definition. Enclose the text in quotation marks.
/DELETE	Stops sharing the resource.

Examples

To share the directory C:\APPLICATIONS with the share name APPS, enter the command:

NET SHARE APPS=C:\APPLICATIONS

You can limit the number of users who can access a share by using the /USERS options. The following example limits users to 10:

NET SHARE APPS=C:\APPLICATIONS /USERS:10

To stop sharing the printer on LPT3, enter the following command:

```
NET SHARE LPT3: /DELETE
```

Notes

Printers must be shared with Print Manager. NET SHARE may be used to stop sharing printers.

NET START

Use the NET START command to start services that have not been started or have been stopped by the NET STOP command. Enter the command **NET START** without options to list running services.

Syntax

NET START [*service*]

Options

service One of the following services to be stopped:

- ALERTER
- CLIENT SERVICE FOR NETWARE
- CLIPBOOK SERVER
- COMPUTER BROWSER
- DHCP CLIENT
- DIRECTORY REPLICATOR
- EVENTLOG
- FTP SERVER
- LPDSVC
- MESSENGER
- NET LOGON
- NETWORK DDE
- NETWORK DDE DSDM
- NETWORK MONITORING AGENT
- NT LM SECURITY SUPPORT PROVIDER
- OLE
- REMOTE ACCESS CONNECTION MANAGER
- REMOTE ACCESS ISNSAP SERVICE
- REMOTE ACCESS SERVER
- REMOTE PROCEDURE CALL (RPC) LOCATOR
- REMOTE PROCEDURE CALL (RPC) SERVICE
- SCHEDULE
- SERVER
- SIMPLE TCP/IP SERVICES
- SNMP
- SPOOLER
- TCPIP NETBIOS HELPER
- UPS
- WORKSTATION

These services are available only on Windows NT Server:

- FILE SERVER FOR MACINTOSH
- GATEWAY SERVICE FOR NETWARE
- MICROSOFT DHCP SERVER
- PRINT SERVER FOR MACINTOSH
- REMOTEBOOT
- WINDOWS INTERNET NAME SERVICE

Notes

To get more help about a specific service, see the online Command Reference (NTCMDS.HLP).

When typed at the command prompt, service names of two words or more must be enclosed in quotation marks. For example, NET START "COMPUTER BROWSER" starts the computer browser service.

NET START can also start network services not provided with Windows NT.

NET STATISTICS

NET STATISTICS displays the statistics log for the local Workstation or Server service. Used without parameters, NET STATISTICS displays the services for which statistics are available.

Syntax

```
NET STATISTICS [WORKSTATION ¦ SERVER]
```

Options

`SERVER`	Displays the Server service statistics.
`WORKSTATION`	Displays the Workstation service statistics.

NET STOP

NET STOP stops Windows NT services.

Syntax

NET STOP *service*

Options

service	Is a Windows NT service that can be stopped. *See the NET START command for a list of eligible services.*

Notes

NET STOP can also stop network services not provided with Windows NT.

Stopping a service cancels any network connections the service is using. Because some services are dependent on others, stopping one service can stop others.

You must have administrative rights to stop the Server service.

The Eventlog service cannot be stopped.

NET TIME

Use the NET TIME command to synchronize the computer's clock with that of another computer or domain. NET TIME can also be used to display the time for a computer or domain. When used without options or a Windows NT Server domain, it displays the current date and time at the computer designated as the time server for the domain.

Syntax

```
NET TIME [\\computername ¦ /DOMAIN[:domainname]] [/SET]
```

Options

`\\computername`	Specifies the name of the computer you want to check or synchronize with.
`/DOMAIN[:domainname]`	Specifies the domain with which to synchronize time.
`/SET`	Synchronizes the computer's time with the time on the specified computer or domain.

NET USE

This command connects a computer to a shared resource or disconnects a computer from a shared resource. NET USE without options lists the computer's connections.

Syntax

```
NET USE [devicename ¦ *]
        [\\computername\sharename[\volume] [password ¦ *]]
        [/USER:[domainname\]username]
        [[/DELETE] ¦ [/PERSISTENT:{YES ¦ NO}]]
NET USE [devicename ¦ *] [password ¦ *]] [/HOME]
NET USE [/PERSISTENT:{YES ¦ NO}]
```

Options

devicename — Specifies a name to assign to the connected resource or specifies the device to be disconnected. Device names can consist of the following:

- disk drives (D through Z)
- printers (LPT1 through LPT3)

Type an asterisk instead of a specific device name to assign the next available device name.

\\computername — Specifies the name of the computer controlling the shared resource. If the computer name contains blank characters, enclose the double backslash (\\) and the computer name in quotation marks. The computer name may be from 1 to 15 characters long.

\sharename — Specifies the network name of the shared resource.

\volume — Specifies the name of a volume on a NetWare server. You must have Client Services for NetWare (Windows NT Workstations) or Gateway Service for NetWare (Windows NT Server) installed and running to connect to NetWare servers.

password	Is the password needed to access the shared resource.
*	Produces a prompt for the password. The password is not displayed when you type it at the password prompt.
/USER	Specifies a different user name with which the connection is made.
domainname	Specifies another domain. If *domainname* is omitted, the current logged on domain is used.
username	Specifies the user name with which to log on.
/HOME	Connects a user to his or her home directory.
/DELETE	Cancels a network connection and removes the connection from the list of persistent connections.
/PERSISTENT{YES ¦ NO}	YES saves connections as they are made, and restores them at next logon. NO does not save the connection being made or subsequent connections; existing connections will be restored at next logon. The default is the setting used last. Use the /DELETE switch to remove persistent connections.

Examples

To connect drive M to a directory with the share name APPS on the server BLIVETS, which has the password LETMEIN, you would type the following:

```
NET USE M: \\BLIVETS\APPS LETMEIN
```

If you do not want the password displayed on the screen, include an * in the password position as follows, so that you will be prompted to enter one:

```
NET USE M: \\BLIVETS\APPS *
```

You can access a share that is secured to another user account if you have a valid password. To access the share using Mabel's account, enter this command:

```
NET USE M: \\BLIVETS\APPS * /USER:MABEL
```

NET USER

NET USER creates and modifies user accounts on computers. When used without switches, it lists the user accounts for the computer. The user account information is stored in the user accounts database.

Syntax

```
NET USER [username [password ¦ *] [options]] [/DOMAIN]
NET USER username {password ¦ *} /ADD [options] [/DOMAIN]
NET USER username [/DELETE] [/DOMAIN]
```

Options

username	Specifies the name of the user account to add, delete, modify, or view. The name of the user account can consist of up to 20 characters.
password	Assigns or changes a password for the user account. A password must meet the minimum length requirement set with the /MINPWLEN option of the NET ACCOUNTS command. The password can consist of up to 14 characters.
*	Displays a prompt for the password, which is not displayed when typed.
/DOMAIN	Specifies the action should be performed on the primary domain controller of the current domain.
	This parameter is effective only with Windows NT Workstation computers that are members of a Windows NT Server domain. By default, Windows NT Server computers perform operations on the primary domain controller.
/ADD	Adds a user account to the user accounts database.
/DELETE	Removes a user account from the user accounts database.
options	The available options are shown in table A.1:

Table A.1
Available Options

Option	Description
/ACTIVE:{YES ¦ NO}	Activates or deactivates the account. When the account is deactivated, the user cannot access the server. The default is YES.
/COMMENT:"*text*"	Adds a comment consisting of up to 48 characters, as specified by *text*. Enclose the text in quotation marks.
/COUNTRYCODE:*nnn*	*nnn* is the numeric operating system country code that specifies the language files to be used for a user's help and error messages. A value of 0 signifies the default country code.
/EXPIRES:{*date* ¦ NEVER}	Specifies a date when the account will expire in the form *mm,dd,yy* or *dd,mm,yy* as determined by the country code. NEVER sets no time limit on the account. The months can be a number, spelled out, or abbreviated with three letters. The year can be two or four numbers. Use commas or slashes(/) to separate parts of the date. No spaces may appear.
/FULLNAME:"*name*"	Specifies a user's full name (rather than a user name). Enclose the name in quotation marks.
/HOMEDIR:*pathname*	Specifies the path for the user's home directory. The path must have been previously created.
/HOMEDIRREQ:{YES ¦ NO}	Specifies whether a home directory is required. If a home directory is required, use the /HOMEDIR option to specify the directory.
/PASSWORDCHG:{YES ¦ NO}	Specifies whether users can change their own password. The default is YES.
/PASSWORDREQ:{YES ¦ NO}	Specifies whether a user account must have a password. The default is YES.
/PROFILEPATH[:*path*]	Specifies a *path* for the user's logon profile.
/SCRIPTPATH:*pathname*	*pathname* is the location of the user's logon script.
/TIMES:{*times* ¦ ALL}	*times* specifies the hours a user account may be logged on. *times* is expressed as `day[-day][,day[-day]],time[-time][,time [-time]]`, limited to 1-hour increments. Days can be spelled out or abbreviated. Hours can be specified using 12- or 24-hour

continues

Table A.1, Continued
Available Options

Option	Description
	notation. With 12-hour notation, include am, pm, a.m., or p.m. ALL means a user can always log on. A blank value means a user can never log on. Separate day and time entries with a comma, and separate multiple day and time entries with a semicolon.
/USERCOMMENT:"*text*"	Specifies a comment for the account.
/WORKSTATIONS: {*computername*[,...] ¦ *}	Lists as many as eight computers from which a user can log on to the network. If */WORKSTATIONS* has no list or if the list is *, the user can log on from any computer.

Examples

To display information about a user named Charles, type the following:

NET USER CHARLES

An example of a user display is shown in figure A.4

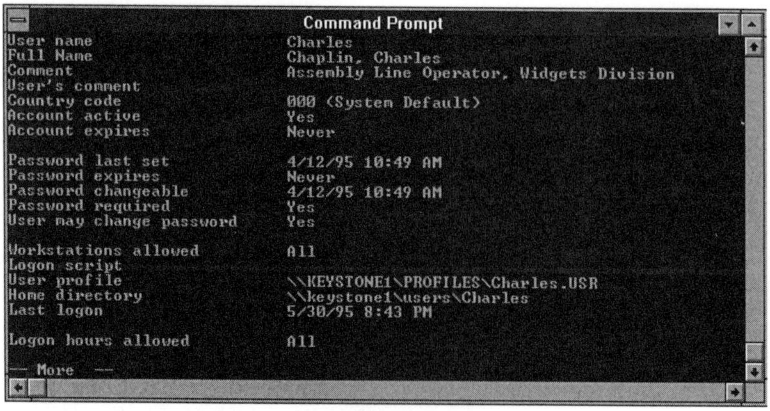
Command Prompt
User name Charles
Full Name Chaplin, Charles
Comment Assembly Line Operator, Widgets Division
User's comment
Country code 000 (System Default)
Account active Yes
Account expires Never
Password last set 4/12/95 10:49 AM
Password expires Never
Password changeable 4/12/95 10:49 AM
Password required Yes
User may change password Yes
Workstations allowed All
Logon script
User profile \\KEYSTONE1\PROFILES\Charles.USR
Home directory \\keystone1\users\Charles
Last logon 5/30/95 8:43 PM
Logon hours allowed All
-- More --

Figure A.4
Example of using the NET USER command to display information about a user account.

To create an account for a user named Harold, while prompting for a password to be assigned, enter the following command:

```
NET USER Harold * /ADD
```

Notes

This command works only on servers.

If you have large numbers of users to add, consider creating a batch file with the appropriate NET USER command. Following is a simple example of a file:

```
NET USER %1 NEWUSER /ADD /HOMEDIR:C:\USERS\%1 /PASSWORDREQ:YES
```

Of course, you would include other options as required. This file makes use of a batch file parameter %1 to pass a command argument to the batch file commands. %1 will pass a user name you specify to the NET USER command where it is used to name the user account and the user's home directory.

If the file is named ADDUSER.BAT, you could add the user Mabel by typing this:

```
ADDUSER Mabel
```

NET VIEW

The NET VIEW command lists resources being shared on a computer. NET VIEW without options displays a list of computers in the current domain or network.

Syntax

```
NET VIEW [\\computername ¦ /DOMAIN[:domainname]]
NET VIEW /NETWORK:NW [\\computername]
```

Options

`\\computername`	Specifies a computer with shared resources you want to view.
`/DOMAIN:domainname`	Specifies the domain with computers whose shared resources you want to view. If *domainname* is omitted, NET VIEW displays all domains in the local area network.
`/NETWORK:NW`	Displays all available servers on a NetWare network. If a computer name is specified, the resources available on that NetWare computer are displayed.

Examples

To list the resources shared by the computer Widgets1, enter the following command:

```
NET VIEW \\WIDGETS1
```

If Widgets1 is in another domain, include the domain name with the /DOMAIN option:

```
NET VIEW \\WIDGETS1 /DOMAIN:WIDGETS
```

To list all available domains, omit the *computername* parameter:

```
NET VIEW /DOMAIN
```

Index

Symbols

A

B

C

D

G

H

I

J-L

N

O

P

R

S

T

U

V

W

X-Z

Fold Here

NO POSTAGE
NECESSARY
IF MAILED
IN THE
UNITED STATES

BUSINESS REPLY MAIL

FIRST-CLASS MAIL PERMIT NO. 9918 INDIANAPOLIS IN

POSTAGE WILL BE PAID BY THE ADDRESSEE

NEW RIDERS PUBLISHING
201 W 103RD ST
INDIANAPOLIS IN 46290-9058

REGISTRATION CARD

Inside Windows NT Server

Name ______________________ Title ______________________

Company ______________________ Type of business ______________________

Address ______________________

City/State/ZIP ______________________

Have you used these types of books before? ☐ yes ☐ no

If yes, which ones? ______________________

How many computer books do you purchase each year? ☐ 1–5 ☐ 6 or more

How did you learn about this book? ______________________

Where did you purchase this book? ______________________

Which applications do you currently use? ______________________

Which computer magazines do you subscribe to? ______________________

What trade shows do you attend? ______________________

Comments: ______________________

Would you like to be placed on our preferred mailing list? ☐ yes ☐ no

☐ **I would like to see my name in print!** You may use my name and quote me in future New Riders products and promotions. My daytime phone number is: ______________________

New Riders Publishing 201 West 103rd Street ◆ Indianapolis, Indiana 46290 USA

Fax to **317-581-4670** Orders/Customer Service **1-800-653-6156** Source Code **NRP95**